MAPPING DEATH

For Eamon

In memory also of my grandfather, Pte Patrick Joseph Stafford, Royal Inniskilling Fusiliers, whose remains lie in an unidentified First World War trench in a field near Richebourg, France.

Mapping Death

Burial in Late Iron Age
&
Early Medieval Ireland

Elizabeth O'Brien

FOUR COURTS PRESS

Typeset in 10.5 pt on 12.5 pt Ehrhardt by
Carrigboy Typesetting Services for
FOUR COURTS PRESS LTD
7 Malpas Street, Dublin 8, Ireland
www.fourcourtspress.ie
and in North America for
FOUR COURTS PRESS
c/o IPG, 814 N Franklin St, Chicago, IL 60610.

© Elizabeth O'Brien and Four Courts Press 2020, 2025

First published 2020
Paperback edition 2025

A catalogue record for this title is available
from the British Library.

ISBN 978–1–80151–199–5

All rights reserved.
Without limiting the rights under copyright
reserved alone, no part of this publication may be
reproduced, stored in or introduced into a retrieval system,
or transmitted, in any form or by any means (electronic, mechanical,
photocopying, recording or otherwise), without the prior
written permission of both the copyright owner and
publisher of this book.

SPECIAL ACKNOWLEDGMENT

This publication has been greatly assisted by a financial grant from the
Marc Fitch Fund for Research and Publication (established by Marcus Felix
Brudenell Fitch, CBA DLitt HonFBA FSA, in 1956)

MARC FITCH FUND

Printed in England by
CPI Group (UK) Ltd, Croydon CR0 4TD.

Contents

ILLUSTRATIONS, PLATES, MAPS AND TABLES	vii
ACKNOWLEDGMENTS	xi
ABBREVIATIONS	xiii
INTRODUCTION	1
1 Iron Age cremation burial, c.400BC–AD400	7
2 Iron Age inhumation burial, c.200BC–AD200	34
3 Inhumation in the Early Medieval period, c.AD400–800	49
4 Grave, burial and secular cemetery types	58
5 Grave goods	103
6 Atypical or deviant burials	132
7 Mobility of peoples	171
8 Unusual or exceptional women: evidence from the grave	182
9 Cessation of burial of Christians among 'pagan' ancestors	196
10 Church cemeteries	201
CONCLUSION	226
GAZETTEERS	
1 Artefacts in cremation deposits	227
2 Early Medieval burial and cemetery types	228
3 Early Medieval burials with grave goods	233
4 Early Medieval atypical or deviant burials	236
5 Iron Age and Early Medieval burials selected for isotopic analysis	241
6 Early Medieval exceptional or unusual women's burial	243
7 Ecclesiastical sites	245
BIBLIOGRAPHY	246
INDEX	271

Illustrations

FIGURES

1.1	Iron Age cremation pit during excavation	
	(a) Pit partially excavated	8
	(b) Pit after excavation	8
1.2	Glass jar from Stoneyford, Co. Kilkenny	9
1.3	Sum of c14 dates for Iron Age cremations	9
1.4	Fibulae from Iron Age cremations	
	(a) Kiltierney, Mound 13, Co. Fermanagh	23
	(b) Grannagh, Co. Galway	23
	(c) Loughey, Co. Down	23
	(d) Kiltierney (1969), Co. Fermanagh	23
1.5	Decorated Iron Age bone dice, gaming pieces or auguries	
	(a) Ballyboy 1, Co. Galway	25
	(b) Navan Fort, Co. Armagh	25
	(c) Cush, Co. Limerick	25
	(d) Ballybronoge South, Co. Limerick	25
	(e) Ballybronoge South, suggested reconstruction	25
2.1	Sum of c14 dates for crouched inhumations	34
2.2	Distribution of Iron Age crouched burials, Knowth, Co. Meath	36
2.3	c14 date sequence for Knowth Iron Age burials	37
2.4	Burial B7, Knowth, Co. Meath	37
2.5	Burials (a) B4, (b) B10, Knowth, Co. Meath	38
2.6	Burial F238, Betaghstown (Anchorage), Co. Meath	39
2.7	Plan of infant crouched burials, Mullamast Hill, Moone, Co. Kildare	43
2.8	c14 date sequence for crouched infant burials, Mullamast Hill, Moone, Co. Kildare	43
3.1	Plan of all infant burials at Mullamast Hill, Moone, Co. Kildare	52
3.2	c14 date sequence for all infant burials at Mullamast Hill, Moone, Co. Kildare	53
3.3	Mullamast Stone, Co. Kildare	53
3.4	(a) Cross of the Scriptures, Clonmacnoise, Co. Offaly	55
	(b) Lower panel	55
4.1	Slab- and stone-lined graves.	
	(a) Slab-lined cist grave	59
	(b) Stone-lined grave	59
4.2	Unprotected and wood-lined graves	
	(a) Unprotected dug grave: B4 Ballymacaward, Donegal	60
	(b) Wood-lined grave: Collierstown, Co. Meath	60

4.3	c14 date sequence Prumplestown Lower, Co. Kildare	69
4.4	Distribution of Early Medieval burials at Knowth, Co. Meath	70
4.5	Sketch of mound at Farta, Co. Galway	73
4.6	Radiocarbon determinations for Farta female and horse	74
4.7	Overview of sites A, B, C, Carbury Hill, Co. Kildare	77
4.8	Connections to Carbury Hill, Co. Kildare	78
4.9	Holdenstown 1, Co. Kilkenny	80
4.10	Silver ring from Rossnaree, Co. Meath	83
4.11	Plan Site 6. The Curragh, Co. Kildare	85
4.12	Turoe Stone, Co. Galway	86
4.13	Site plan of Cross, Co. Galway	87
4.14	Sites with penannular enclosures	
	(a) Corbally sites 1, 2, 3, Co. Kildare	90
	(b) Greenhills, Co. Kildare	90
4.15	Plan of cemetery at Westreave, Co. Dublin, showing burials 29, 32	93
4.16	Plan of cemetery and cashel at Owenbristy, Co. Galway	97
5.1	Neck rings	
	(a) Ratoath, Co. Meath	105
	(b) Bergh Apton, Norfolk	105
5.2	Copper-alloy object (sceptre?) with B29, Ardsallagh 1, Co. Meath	107
5.3	Boxes and pin from burial at Dromiskin, Co. Louth	
	(a) Stone box	109
	(b) Wooden box	109
	(c) Ringed pin (key?)	109
5.4	Objects with B11, Betaghstown (Brookside), Co. Meath	111
5.5	Iron shears, Burial 1, Site B, Carbury, Co. Kildare	113
5.6	Method of modification of red deer antler into picks	114
5.7	Red deer antler picks associated with burials	
	(a) Holdenstown 1, Co. Kilkenny	115
	(b) Farta, Co. Galway	115
5.8	Deer antler objects in burials	
	(a) Ballygarraun West, Co. Galway	116
	(b) B39, Collierstown, Co. Meath	116
	(c) Grave 3, Lehinch, Co. Offaly	116
	(d) B420, Ranelagh, Co. Roscommon	116
5.9	Burials and post-hole beneath West Cross, Clonmacnoise	124
6.1	Site 4, The Curragh, Co. Kildare	
	(a) Overall plan of Site 4	134
	(b) Possible 'live' burial in Site 4	134
6.2	Paired burials displaying peri-mortem trauma	
	(a) Mount Gamble, Swords, Co. Dublin	146
	(b) Augherskea, Co. Meath	146
6.3	Paired burial, B78/B79, Site 3, Corbally, Co. Kildare	148
6.4	Crouched, and partially crouched burials	
	(a) Crouched burial, Mount Gamble, Swords, Co. Dublin	156
	(b) Partially crouched burial, Johnstown, Co. Meath	156

6.5	Flexed burial, Faughart, Co. Louth	157
6.6	Burial 181, Betaghstown (Anchorge), Co. Meath	158
6.7	Disarticulated 'boxed' burial 161, Colp West 1, Co. Meath with detail of corner brackets	165
6.8	Burial 7, Castlefarm, Co. Meath	166
10.1	Positions of North, West, and South crosses at Clonmacnoise, Co. Offaly	205
10.2	Rock-carved crosses on Dalkey Island, Dublin	221

PLATES
(between pages 146 and 147)

1. Bowl from Fore, Co. Westmeath, and possible parallels
   (a) Fore, Co. Westmeath, Ireland
   (b) Spetisbury Rings, Dorset, Britain
   (c) Lamberton Moor Hoard, Berwickshire, Scotland
   (d) The Glastonbury bowl, Somerset, Britain
2. Glass and amber beads from Iron Age cremations
   (a) Knockcommane, Co. Limerick
   (b) Donacarney Great, Co. Meath
   (c) Marlhill, Co. Tipperary
   (d) Claureen, Co. Clare
   (e) Ballyboy 1 & 2, Co. Galway
3. Cylindrical box from Chariot Burial 2, Wetwang Slack, Yorkshire
4. Burial B59, Holdenstown 2, Co. Kilkenny.
5. Cemetery settlement sites
   (a) Ninch 2, Co. Meath
   (b) Castlefarm 1, Co. Meath
6. Neck ring with SK 70, Owenbristy, Co. Galway
7. Quartered male SK 42, Owenbristy, Co. Galway
8. 'Splayed' burial SK 119, Carrowkeel, Co. Galway
9. Burials in enclosure entrances and termini
   (a) SK 72, Carrowkeel, Co. Galway
   (b) Skeleton in inner ditch, Loughbown 1, Co. Galway
10. Burial 3, Ballymacaward, Co. Donegal
11. Facial reconstruction of B4, Ballymacaward, Co. Donegal
12. Monastic enclosure at Durrow, Co. Offaly, and burials at Sheean Hill, based on geophysical survey
13. Plan showing post-holes in cemetery at Owenbristy, Co. Galway

MAPS

| 1 | Distribution of sites with Iron Age cremation deposits | 11 |
| 2 | Distribution of cremation deposits with artefacts | 21 |

3	Distribution of Iron Age crouched and extended inhumations	35
4	Distribution of Early Medieval *ferta*	67
5	Distribution of Early Medieval burials with grave goods	104
6	Distribution of Early Medieval cemeteries with atypical/deviant burials	133
7	Distribution of cemeteries demonstrating Early Medieval population mobility	175
8	Distribution of cemeteries included in chapter 10	203

TABLES

1.1	Iron Age cremation site types	12
1.2	Iron Age cremation deposit contents	20
2.1	Iron Age crouched inhumations	41
3.1	Numbers of burials in Early Medieval cemeteries	58

Acknowledgments

My thanks to Cormac Bourke, Professor Thomas Charles-Edwards, Professor John Blair and Raghnall O Floinn for reading early drafts of the text, and for offering critical comments and sound advice; to the anonymous reader for insightful observations and suggestions; to Dr Edel Bhreathnach for her encouragement during the long gestation of this book, and reading, discussing, and undertaking the task of editing the draft of the text, and to Susan O'Brien for reading the final draft, and for organising the bibliography, for all of which I am eternally grateful; to Martin Fanning of Four Courts Press for his guidance through the editorial process; to Christopher Catling and the Marc Fitch Fund for generous financial support of this publication.

The compilation of much data relative to burial in Early Medieval Ireland was facilitated by participation in the Heritage Council's INSTAR project (2008–10) 'Mapping death: people, boundaries and territories in Ireland, first to eighth centuries AD'.

Sourcing of, and permission to reproduce, images was facilitated by: Helena King of the Royal Irish Academy for permission to reproduce images of a bone plaque from Cush, Co. Limerick; sketch of the mound at Farta; image of plan of Site 6, The Curragh, Co. Kildare; image of plan of Site 4, The Curragh, image of skeleton in Site 4, The Curragh; composite image of the distribution of Iron Age crouched burials at Knowth, Co. Meath; composite image of the distribution of Early Medieval burials at Knowth, Co. Meath; image of burial 4, Knowth; image of crouched burial 7, Knowth, and image of burial 10, Knowth; Professor George Eogan for permission to reproduce various images from Knowth; Heather A. King for permission to reproduce image of burials beneath West Cross, Clonmacnoise, and permission to reference her unpublished material; Dr Paula Gentil, Hull and East Riding Museum, for providing image of the cylindrical box from Wetwang Chariot Burial and permission to use same; Dr Fraser Hunter and the National Museums Scotland, for permission to reproduce image of the bowl from the Lamberton Moor Hoard, Berwickshire; The Trustees of the British Museum, for providing image of the bowl from Spetisbury and permission to use same; Dr T. Hopkinson-Ball, Chairman, Glastonbury Antiquarian Society, for permission to reproduce image of the bowl from Glastonbury; Valerie J. Keeley, for permission to reproduce plan of Greenhills, Co. Kildare, and antler piece from Ballygarraun West, Co. Galway; Julian Richards & Jane Brayne, for permission to reproduce image of face reconstruction for B4, Ballymacaward, Co. Donegal; Jerry O'Sullivan, TII, for facilitating permission to reproduce images of: glass and amber beads from Ballyboy 2, Co. Galway, and bone die from Ballyboy 1, Co. Galway; Mrs Susan Mercer, for permission to reproduce drawing of antler pick published by the late Professor Roger Mercer; Royal Society of Antiquaries of Ireland, for providing drawing of shears from Site B, Carbury, Co. Kildare, and permission to use same; Edmund O'Donovan, for providing images of burials from Mount Gamble, Swords, Co. Dublin, and permission to use same; Christine Baker, for providing image of double burial at Augherskea, Co. Meath, and permission to use same; Kate Taylor and Graham Hull, for permission to use image of beads from Claureen, Co. Clare, and for providing information regarding an Iron Age ring-ditch at Coolnahorna 3, Co. Wexford; Chris Lynn and the National Monuments and Buildings Record (NI), for permission to use image of die from Navan Fort, Co. Armagh; James Eogan, for permission to reproduce drawings of die/gaming piece from Ballybronoge, and photos of B181 Bettystown, B258 Bettystown; Claire Foley and the National Monuments and Buildings Record (NI), for permission to reproduce images of fibulae from Kiltierney, Co. Fermanagh; Maeve Tobin, for her assistance in sourcing material from Holdenstown 1 & 2, Co. Kilkenny, Ranelagh, Roscommon, and Kill of the Grange, Co. Dublin; Shane Delaney, for permission to photograph SK 420 at Ranelagh, Roscommon; Eoin Halpin, for permission to reproduce site plan of Ninch, Co. Meath, and image of SK 1299A from Faughart Lower, Co. Louth; Angela Wallace, for permission to reproduce image of the neck-ring from Ratoath, Co. Meath; Linda Clarke, for permission to reproduce images from: Castlefarm, Co. Meath, Johnstown, Co. Meath, Collierstown 1, Co. Meath, and Ardsallagh 2, Co. Meath; Margaret Gowen (MGL), for permission to reproduce many images. Jenny Glazebrook, for supplying, and obtaining permission to reproduce image of necklet in grave 50, Bergh Apton, Norfolk, from Historic Environment Service, Norfolk County Council; Frank Coyne, for permission to reproduce image of paired burial at Corbally 3, Co. Meath, and for re-drawing combined plan of Corbally sites 1, 2, 3; Professor Michael Alexander and Penguin Books Ltd, for permission to quote a thirteen-line excerpt from the translation of the poem Beowulf (Penguin Books, 2003).

Numerous colleagues have been generous in providing information about burials and burial sites. These include: Heather A. King, Maeve Tobin, Jerry O'Sullivan TII, Margaret Gowen (MGL), Maria Fitzgerald, Jacinta Kiely, Tracy Collins, Maeve Sikora NMI, Mary Cahill NMI, Teresa Bolger, John Tierney, Margaret Keane, Matthew Seaver NMI, John Sheehan UCC, Stuart Elder, Michael Stanley TII, Sarah McCutcheon, Charles Doherty, Ronán Swan TII, Noel Dunne TII, Angela Wallace, Catherine McLoughlin, Malachy Conway, Laurence Dunne, Donald, Linda, and Deirdre Murphy, Dr John Dent, Dr Melanie Giles, Pamela Cross, Dr Ros Ó Maoldúin, Conor Newman, Niamh Carty, Dr Mario Novak, Dr Sharon Greene, John Curtin UCC, Dr Tomás Ó Carragáin UCC, Martin Timoney, Göran Burenholt. Dr Thomas F. Shaw offered insights into skeletal medical conditions. Dr Jacqueline Cahill Wilson provided information regarding isotopic analysis.

The production of distribution maps was facilitated in the Discovery Programme Ltd, by Gary Devlin, and especially Rob Shaw. Anthony Corns was responsible for the construction of the Mapping Death on-line database. Michael Ann Bevevino provided important assistance in the input of data to the database.

Finally, grateful thanks to my husband Eamon, my children Susan, Simon, Mark and Jennifer, and my extended family, for their unfailing patience, love and encouragement over many years, without which this book would not have seen the light of day.

Abbreviations

AClon	*The annals of Clonmacnoise (to AD 1408)*, ed. Denis Murphy SJ (RSAI, 1896; reprint, Llanerch Publishers, 1993)
ACSU	Archaeological Consultancy Services Unit
Adomnán	*Adomnán's Life of Columba*, ed. and trans. Alan Orr Anderson & Marjorie Ogilvie Anderson (Oxford, 1991); *Adomnán of Iona, Life of St Columba*, trans. Richard Sharpe (London, 1995)
ADS	Archaeological Development Services (now ADS (ROI))
AJ	*Archaeological Journal*
AL	Ancient Laws of Ireland
ASSAH	*Anglo-Saxon Studies in Archaeology and History*
AU	*The annals of Ulster (to AD 1131)*, ed. Seán Mac Airt & Gearóid Mac Niocaill (Dublin, 1983)
BAR	British Archaeological Reports
BM	British Museum
CELT	Corpus of Electronic Texts (UCC)
Chron. Ire.	*The chronicle of Ireland*, notes & trans. Thomas M. Charles-Edwards (Liverpool, 2006)
CIH	*Corpus iuris Hibernici*, ed. D.A. Binchy (Dublin, 1978)
DIL	*Contributions to a dictionary of the Irish language*, Royal Irish Academy (Dublin, 1913–76)
EAP	Eachtra Archaeological Projects
EOB	Elizabeth O'Brien
Fél.	*The martyrology of Oengus the Culdee: Félire Óengusso Céli Dé*, ed. and trans. Whitley Stokes (1905, reprint 1979) (London, Henry Bradshaw Society)
HE	Bede, *Historia ecclesiastica*, ed. Bertram Colgrave & R.A.B. Mynors (reprint, 1992) (Oxford)
HES	Historic Environment Service
Hib.	*Collectio canonum Hibernensis*, ed. Hermann Wasserschleben, Die Irische Kanonensammlung, 2nd edition (Leipzig, 1885)
IAC	Irish Archaeological Consultancy
IAI	Institute of Archaeologists of Ireland
IJO	International Journal of Osteoarchaeology
INSTAR	Irish National Strategic Archaeological Research Programme
JAS	*Journal of Archaeological Science*
JCLAHS	*Journal of the County Louth Archaeological and Historical Society*
JCLAS	*Journal of the County Louth Archaeological Society*
JCKASSD	*Journal of the County Kildare Archaeological Society and Surrounding Districts*

JGAHS	*Journal of the Galway Archaeological and Historical Society*
JIA	*The Journal of Irish Archaeology*
JKAS	*Journal of the County Kildare Archaeological Society and Surrounding Districts*
JRSAI	*Journal of the Royal Society of Antiquaries of Ireland*
KAHJ	*Kerry Archaeological and Historical Journal*
Med. Arch.	*Medieval Archaeology*
MGL	Margaret Gowen Ltd
Muirchú	Muirchú, *Vita S. Patricii*, in ed. and tr. Ludwig Bieler (with Fergus Kelly) *The Patrician texts in the Book of Armagh*. Scriptores Latini Hiberniae, 10 (Dublin, 1979)
NMAJ	*North Munster Antiquarian Journal*
NMI	National Museum of Ireland
NRA	National Roads Authority (now TII)
Peritia	*Peritia, Journal of the Medieval Academy of Ireland*
PPS	*Proceedings of the Prehistoric Society*
PSAS	*Proceedings of the Society of Antiquaries of Scotland*
PRIA	*Proceedings of the Royal Irish Academy*
RIA	Royal Irish Academy
RSAI	Royal Society of Antiquaries of Ireland
TII	Transport Infrastructure Ireland
Tírechán	Tírechán, *Collectanea*, in ed. and tr. Ludwig Bieler (with Fergus Kelly), *The Patrician texts in the Book of Armagh*. Scriptores Latini Hiberniae, 10 (Dublin, 1979)
TKAS	*Transactions of the Kilkenny Archaeological Society*
UJA	*Ulster Journal of Archaeology*
VJK	Valerie J. Keeley, Ltd
WARP	Wetland Archaeology Research Project

Introduction

Death represents the ultimate confrontation between the human and the supernatural worlds. The surviving burial remains and the associated funerary monuments thus provide us with the clearest and most tangible surviving evidence of religious beliefs and practices. (Raftery, 1994, 188)

CONTEXT AND METHODOLOGY OF VOLUME

Burial rites and associated phenomena can provide a unique insight into the attitudes and beliefs of diverse communities at any given moment in time. Hence the purpose of this book is to undertake an interdisciplinary approach to burial practices in Ireland, in order to attempt an interpretation, and to chart the development of burial rites as they appear in the archaeological repertoire of the Late Iron Age (*c*.200BC–AD300) and Early Medieval period (*c*.AD400–800). Interdisciplinary sources used include: archaeological excavation evidence (published and grey literature); c14 (radiocarbon) dating evidence for cremation and inhumation burials; strontium and oxygen isotope evidence for movement of peoples; and osteo-archaeology. Together with careful and discerning examination of references to death, burial and associated phenomena that appear in Irish hagiography, penitentials, laws and canons, written during the seventh and eighth centuries, which often provide invaluable insights into the rationale behind many burial practices and rites that prevailed during the period.

As the chosen temporal cut-off point is AD800, Viking burial in Ireland has been excluded, a topic that has recently been extensively covered (Harrison and Ó Floinn, 2014). It must also be stated at the outset that this publication concentrates solely on terrestrial burial, and does not include bog bodies, which are the subject of ongoing research (Ó Floinn, 1995, 137–45, 221–34; Turner and Scaife, 1995; Delaney, Ó Floinn and Heckett, 1999, 67–8; Kelly, 2006); or, aquatic skeletal depositions which are also the subject of ongoing research by the Discovery Programme (Fredengren, 2002).

* * *

The manner in which the emerging study of Irish Iron Age burial was perceived and interpreted in the early-to-mid-twentieth century can be observed in R.A.S. Macalister's *The archaeology of Ireland*, particularly chapter III, under the heading 'The disposal of the dead' (Macalister, 1928, 202–6). Much of the material depicted by Macalister was obtained by him from local people, and can often only be described as fabulous or fanciful. However, it is now possible to place two of the sites described by him into a known era. These are the site at Grannach (*sic*),[1] Co. Galway, which was re-excavated by Etienne Rynne, and is now known to be Iron Age in date; and the site at Lochrea (*sic*),[2] Co. Galway, which has now been dated by this writer, with the aid of the Discovery Programme, to the Early Medieval period. In 1941, Joseph Raftery published his paper 'Long stone cists of the Early Iron Age' (*PRIA* C, 46, 299–315), in which, having reviewed and described details of around eighty burials, he concluded that long stone cists in Ireland dated to the Iron Age. With hindsight, and the advent of c14 dating, these burials can now be firmly placed in the Early Medieval period. Professor Barry Raftery furthered the discussion in his 1981 paper 'Iron Age burials in Ireland' (1981, 173–204), in which he positively identified several Iron Age burial sites that contained cremation deposits. However, inhumation burials included in his paper as being Iron Age, with the exception of the Bray burials (see 2.2), can now be identified as Early Medieval, and in one instance, Carrowbeg North, Co. Galway, as High Medieval. This writer's effort at researching and identifying Iron Age and Early Medieval burials began in 1981 and has progressed over almost four decades. Ongoing research into the subject, and observations accumulated during participation in, and directing of, burial excavations, resulted in publications listed in the bibliography.[3]

Much data relating to Early Medieval burial in Ireland are now encapsulated in condensed form in the on-line Mapping Death database compiled as part of the Heritage Council's INSTAR (Irish National Strategic Archaeological Research) project (2008–2010) 'Mapping death: people, boundaries and territories in Ireland, first to eighth centuries AD', of which this writer was principal researcher, and curator of the database, tasks which the writer now undertakes in a voluntary capacity. Originally based in the UCD Mícheál Ó Cléirigh Institute, the on-line database, which is freely accessible at www.mappingdeathdb.ie, is now hosted by the Discovery Programme Ltd.

Modern publications which have been invaluable in augmenting the research for this book include: the volumes edited by Christiaan Corlett and Michael Potterton, *Death and burial in Early Medieval Ireland in the light of recent archaeological excavations* (2010); *Life and death in Iron Age Ireland in the light of recent archaeological excavations* (2012); and *The Church in Early Medieval Ireland in the light of recent archaeological excavations* (2014), each of which includes several papers with summary details of comparatively recent burial excavations; Mary Cahill and Maeve Sikora's excellent two-volume work, *Breaking ground, finding graves: reports on the excavations of burials by the National Museum of Ireland, 1927–2006* (2011), provides dating for all unpublished burials excavated by the NMI between 1927 and 2006, including accounts of burials now dated to the Early Medieval period (Cahill and Sikora, 2011). Publications by the NRA (National Roads Authority), now TII (Transport Infrastructure Ireland), in their SEANDA and Monograph series often contain articles relating to burial. Many TII excavation reports have recently become accessible via the Digital Repository of Ireland, www.dri.ie. Referenced and acknowledged throughout the text and the bibliography are the various excavators, who have been generous in supplying unpublished information regarding cemeteries

---

1 Grannagh, Co. Galway.   2 Farta, Loughrea, Co. Galway.   3 Late Prehistoric burial in Ireland has also been examined by Tiernan McGarry in his PhD thesis (McGarry, 2008).

and burials. While every effort has been made to examine all available relevant excavation reports, some items may have slipped through the net.

As the purpose in undertaking this publication is to concentrate on and exemplify diverse aspects of burial, burial rites, and directly associated phenomena, it has not been possible to include everyday living, industrial activity, and the wider landscape, associated with life in Early Medieval Ireland. A significant amount of this additional material is available in O'Sullivan et al., *Early Medieval Ireland AD400–1100: the evidence from archaeological excavations* (2013/14), published by the Royal Irish Academy. An excellent guide to the Irish historical background of the period has been published by Edel Bhreathnach, *Ireland in the Medieval world, AD400–1000* (2014).

KEY TERMS

c14 dating
c14, or radiocarbon dating, is the method used for determining the age of an organic object and is particularly suitable for determining the age of skeletal material. For reasons of clarity, and in order to present a level of uniformity, all c14 dates recorded in this work are cited in full and have been re-calibrated using the calibration curve IntCal 13; Version OxCal 4.2 (Bronk Ramsey, 2009, 337–60; Reimer et al., 2013). This re-calibration will sometimes result in a slight modification of c14 dates relating to sites, especially older sites, published elsewhere. Calibrated dates are indicated at 2σ, which represents 95.4% probability. Where the highest probability differs from 95.4% this is highlighted in the text.

Strontium and oxygen isotope analysis

> Tooth enamel is the most highly mineralised tissue in our body and while it is forming it records the chemical signatures of the geological and climatic environment in which people and their livestock lived. Unlike bone, which is completely remodelled within the body over approximately a ten-year cycle, once complete mineralisation of enamel has taken place in humans (usually around the age of twelve) it does not alter further in life. Measuring the ratios of the various isotopes present in the tooth enamel can therefore offer an indication of an individual's place of geographic origin and/or where they spent their early childhood years (Cahill Wilson, 2014, 131).

The use of strontium and oxygen isotope analysis in archaeological burial contexts is an emerging scientific discipline that is still evolving, but even at this stage of its progress it can be used to indicate whether or not an individual was born in the locality in which he/she was buried. If the individual was not born locally, it is sometimes possible to indicate a potential place of origin.

Osteo-archaeology
Osteo-archaeology is the scientific study of skeletal material excavated from archaeological sites. The analysis of human skeletal material can reveal details of

approximate age of a person at death; sometimes the cause of death; sex determination; health; lifestyle; and physique, including injuries or deformities. Studies undertaken in recent years by osteo-archaeologists in Ireland have made a significant contribution to our understanding of life and death in the Early Medieval period. These analyses and reports have been invaluable in the compilation of this publication.

LITERARY REFERENCES TO DEATH AND BURIAL

An important caveat must be made regarding the use of literary evidence. When using early written material it is essential to be cognisant of the contextual framework of the sources, for example the temporal and spatial milieu into which the material is set is that in which the work was written and with which the author and his audience were familiar, and does not necessarily reflect the contemporary milieu of the events being described. For example, if the life of a saint who lived in the sixth century was written in the eighth century, the environment portrayed in that life will likely be that with which the eighth-century author and his audience were familiar. It would not therefore be valid to use material written in the eighth century to explain or describe practices (burial or otherwise) of the sixth century. Consequently, it is necessary that the documentary material being alluded to should be dated to, or be seen to refer with reasonable accuracy to, the date of the archaeology under consideration. Bearing in mind these precautions, references extracted from datable early literature and included in the text of this book may be of interest to archaeologists and/or historians.

In Ireland, we are fortunate in having access to material that can help to build up an extensive image of life in Early Medieval Ireland. Works consulted by the author include: *Ammianus Marcellinus* for his comments on Ireland in the fourth century (Hamilton, 1986); *Epistola ad milites Corotici*, St Patrick's Letter and Confessio, written in the fifth century (Howlett, 1994; RIA website – www.ria.ie-research-projects-st-patricks-confessio-hypertext-stack); *Adomnán's Life of Columba*, written in the seventh century (Anderson and Anderson, 1991; Sharpe, 1995); *Adomnán's 'Law of the Innocents'*, written in the seventh century (Márkus, 1997; Ní Dhonnchadha, 2001, 53–68); *Córus bésgnai*, an Old Irish law tract, written in the seventh century (Breatnach, 2017); *A guide to Early Irish law* (Kelly, 1988); *Marriage disputes: a fragmentary Old Irish law-text*, written in the late seventh century, with twelfth-century comments (Kelly, 2014); *Muirchú: Vita Patricii*, written in the seventh century (Bieler, 1979); *Tírechán: Collectanea*, written in the seventh century (Bieler, 1979); *Vita prima Sanctae Brigitae*, written in the seventh century (Connolly, 1989); *Bethu Brigte*, written in the ninth century (Ó hAodha, 1978); *Collectio canonum Hibernensis*,[4] written in the late seventh–early eighth century (Wasserschleben, 1885). Various early Irish annals have been consulted including *The annals of Ulster* (Mac

---

[4] Compiled by Rubin of Dair-Inis (a monastery near Youghal, on the south coast of Ireland), who died AD 725, and Cú Chuimne of Iona, who died AD 747. Translation from the Latin of the relevant passages in Hibernensis was undertaken by this writer, some years ago, under the guidance of Professor Thomas Charles-Edwards. I, however, accept full responsibility for any errors or omissions in the translation.

Introduction

Airt and Mac Niocaill, 1983); *The chronicle of Ireland* (Charles-Edwards, 2006). For early Anglo-Saxon background material, the eighth-century works consulted include *Felix's Life of Saint Guthlac* (Colgrave, 1956); *Bedae Vita Sancti Cuthberti* (Colgrave, 1940) and *Bede: Ecclesiastical history of the English people* (Colgrave and Mynors, 1969).

* * *

The corpus of burial sites consulted during the compilation of this publication includes sixty-eight Iron Age sites that contain cremation burial deposits, 156 Early Medieval secular cemetery sites, containing a total of approximately 11,000 burials, and twenty-seven Early Medieval ecclesiastical cemetery sites. The text is accompanied by eight maps outlining site locations for differing categories of burial; four tables and six gazetteers outlining detailed information regarding site types, burial numbers, burial types, and artefacts; together with relevant images of burials, objects, and site plans.

Chapter 1 discusses the rite of cremation burial in Late Iron Age Ireland. This includes an examination of cremation deposits excavated before the emergence of c14 dating, which can now be placed in context by cross-comparison with more recently dated cremations; the veneration of ancestors as indicated by the re-use of pre-existing ancestral burial places and monuments, together with the construction of imitative monuments; grave goods in cremation deposits; the continuing use of the rite of cremation alongside the newly introduced rite of extended inhumation during the conversion period.

Chapter 2 includes examination and analysis of the rite of Iron Age crouched inhumation, probably introduced from Britain, for a relatively short time-period around the turn of the first millennium, into a confined geographical area in the east of Ireland. Analysis of these burials includes c14 dating; strontium and oxygen isotopic analysis (which indicates the possible origin of some of these people in north-east Britain); re-use of indigenous ancestral burial places; and the occurrence of grave goods. Some atypical or deviant burials are also examined.

Chapter 3 covers the historical background to the introduction into Ireland of extended inhumation in the late fourth–early fifth century; the transition from cremation to extended inhumation; the transition from crouched to extended inhumation; the acceptance of the burial rite of extended inhumation by the majority of the indigenous population in a comparatively short temporal period; and the difficulties this presents in attempting to identify Christian burial in secular cemeteries.

Chapter 4 includes a description and discussion of types of grave, burial, and cemetery; isolated burial; an explanation of the importance of ancestral burial places known as *ferta*; the re-use of established ancestral *ferta*; the construction of imitative *ferta*; the establishment of communal secular cemeteries, and settlement cemeteries; and the continuing usage (albeit on a small scale) of the rite of cremation.

Chapter 5 details, examines and considers grave goods, which are rare in Early Medieval burials in Ireland, therefore those that are present assume additional importance. Grave goods include such diverse artefacts as three neck collars; a possible sceptre; a spear; a box set; several pins; a toe ring; an earring; knives and buckles; two brooches; a shears; several antler pieces; beads; quartz pebbles; animal bone; and burnt grain/hearth rakings.

Chapter 6 incorporates details of 153 deviant or atypical Early Medieval burials, which represents a tiny minority (1.40%) of the total corpus of approximately 11,000. Included are a possible live female burial; skeletons that have been mutilated after death; decapitated skeletons; head only burials; skeletons with fatal weapon trauma; male paired burials with weapon trauma; male paired burials without weapon trauma; burials in kilns; prone burials; crouched burials; a disarticulated burial in a box; burials in ditch termini-entrances; and a possible sentinel burial. These are described and examined in detail, together with relevant literary references to, and the possible rationale behind, some of the burial practices involved.

In chapter 7, emerging evidence for mobility of people into and within Ireland, in the Iron Age and in the Early Medieval periods, is explored. This evidence is based mainly on the results obtained from strontium and oxygen isotope analysis of a small sample of the overall corpus, namely nine Iron Age burials, and fifty-four Early Medieval burials. The results indicate that a certain number came from various places overseas; others may have been born in Ireland, but could equally have been born in Britain; others were born in Ireland, but not in the locality in which they were buried; but a significant number were buried at the place of their birth.

Chapter 8 evolved from a personal interest in unusual female burials, in the Iron Age, but mainly in the Early Medieval period. This has led to the compilation and examination of the burial status of selected women, whose unusual burials may be a reflection of how they were perceived during life.

Chapter 9 outlines the cessation of the burial of Christians among their 'pagan' ancestors in secular cemeteries, which emerged in Ireland around the beginning of the eighth century. This observation is supported not only by the archaeological evidence, but also by seventh-century literary references, and by rules regarding acceptable burial practices for Christians, compiled by the Church authorities in the eighth century.

Chapter 10 contains material based around a limited number of early church cemeteries where excavation has been undertaken and burials recovered. These are examined under a variety of classifications, from major ecclesiastical cemeteries, to local community church cemeteries, to island cemeteries, and a hermitage (*díseart*) cemetery, in order to discover what can be learned about the usage of these sites. Doubtful church sites are also considered.

Conclusions includes personal observations on the importance of ongoing research into the archaeology of burial in Iron Age and Early Medieval Ireland; together with hopes and suggestions for future research.

I accept full responsibility for the interpretations, opinions and arguments presented in this book. Every effort has been made to cover as wide a range of burials, burial practices, and burial sites as possible, but, inevitably, some will have been inadvertently overlooked or omitted.

CHAPTER 1

Iron Age cremation burial, *c*.400BC–AD400

OVERVIEW OF CREMATION IN IRON AGE IRELAND

In Ireland, the indigenous Iron Age burial rite, albeit with a few notable exceptions, was a continuation of the later Bronze Age practice of cremation. This contrasts with Britain where the indigenous Iron Age population used differing burial rites, varying between crouched inhumation that emerged in the north-east and south-east around the fourth century BC (Whimster, 1981, 194; O'Brien, 1999, 1–9) and the introduction, *c*.100BC, of the rite of cremation into southern Britain, probably from north-west France (Whimster, 1981, 147, O'Brien, 1999, 9–11).

The great enigma for the Iron Age in Ireland is that despite evidence for the widespread use of ceramic containers for funerary and domestic purposes during the Neolithic and Bronze Age (Kavanagh, 1973, 507–617; 1976, 293–403; 1977, 61–95; Herity, 1982, 274–404; Waddell, 2000), at some point between 700BC and 400BC the use of pottery was abandoned leading to a complete absence of ceramic containers for domestic or for funerary purposes (Raftery, 1995, 152). The reason for this cultural change is currently unknown, but some interesting comments on the phenomenon have been made, especially in relation to the lack of linguistic references to pottery and potters in the Early Irish period (Mallory, 2009, 181–92). This absence of native pottery continued until the emergence of domestic coarse pottery, known as 'souterrain' ware, in the east Ulster region in the later eighth century AD (Ryan, 1973; McSparron, 2018, 68–73).

In order to identify Iron Age cremations that were deposited directly into small pits in the earth, probably wrapped in organic containers which left no residue (Figure 1.1), Irish archaeologists are dependent on the evidence of c14 dating, examination of the context of deposition, and investigation of comparative material for the limited range of grave goods (mainly items of personal adornment in the form of beads, fibulae and other small objects) which sometimes accompany cremation deposits of this period in Ireland.

Two sites have been identified, however, in which cremations were deposited in non-organic containers. The first of these, discovered in 1988 in an inland promontory fort at Fore, Co. Westmeath (Kelly, 2002, 137), contained the cremation deposit of an older adult male dated third–first century BC[1] (Lanting and Brindley, 1998, 6), in a distinctive type of bronze bowl (Plate 1), the closest comparisons for which are found in Britain. Examples include bowls from Spetisbury Rings, Dorset, dated by the British Museum to *c*.AD1–50 (James and Rigby, 1997); the Lamberton Moor Hoard, Berwickshire, Scotland, dated to between AD80–180[2] (MacGregor, 1976, nos. 292–6);

---

1 GrN–13391: 2110±40BP; calibrated at 2σ = 351–4 cal BC (at 88.5% probability 210–38 cal BC). Date has been re-calibrated using OxCal v 4.2.4 (© Bronk Ramsey et al.).   2 I am grateful to Dr Fraser Hunter for drawing my attention to this artefact.

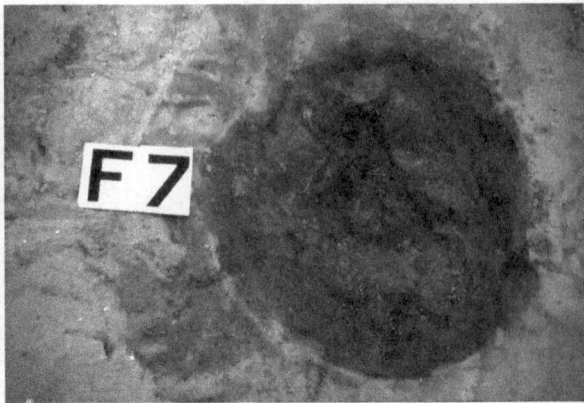

1.1 Iron Age cremation pit during excavation: (a) pit partially excavated; (b) pit after excavation.

and the slightly smaller Glastonbury bowl, Somerset, dated to the first century BC.[3] A tiny handle on the rim of the Fore bowl, in the form of a bird, may be compared to the 'drinking cup' recovered in a watercourse at Keshcarrigan, Co. Leitrim, and dated to around the first century AD (Kelly, 2002, 137). The bowl from Fore and the Keshcarrigan cup are regarded as imports from Britain. The Fore bowl is a prestigious object perhaps used in gift-exchange and undoubtedly a prized possession of the individual whose cremated remains were buried in it.

The second site is located near Stoneyford, Co. Kilkenny,[4] in the valley of the King's River, a tributary of the River Nore. Discovered in 1852, the find consisted of a green glass urn containing cremated bone and a small glass lachrymatory, covered by a bronze mirror, and described as having been found protected by stones within a rath (a circular enclosure) (Clibborn, 1852; Ireland, 2013, 8–27; 2015, 27–44). The glass urn has been identified as being of Isings 67A-type and datable to the first century AD (Figure 1.2). This type of burial was known in Roman Britain during this period (Bourke, 1989, 56–7; 1994, 163–209; O'Brien, 2009a, 136; Cahill Wilson, Standish, and O'Brien, 2014a, 129). The process of cremation was a public and communal rite which suggests the presence of Romanised people in the region of Stoneyford. The location is important in that it is within striking distance of the River Nore which flows south and joins the River Barrow before entering the sea at Waterford, a possible indication that this burial may represent trading activity from Roman Britain in the immediate vicinity. There is also some indication (so far unconfirmed) that cremations with Roman affiliations may have been deposited in metal bowls at Drumanagh promontory on the coast of north Co. Dublin (Cahill Wilson, Cooney, Dowling and Elliott, 2014b, 98), but this awaits further investigation.

Evidence suggests that when a body was cremated in Ireland, a portion of the cremated bone, occasionally accompanied by small objects (mainly personal adornments), was collected from the pyre, and then deposited in an organic container

---

[3] Note by Dr Peter Northover, dated 27 Nov. 2007, posted on www.glastonburyantiquarians.org. Accessed 26 Sept. 2015. [4] Full details available under 'Stoneyford' at www.mappingdeath.ie.

Iron Age cremation burial c.400BC–AD400

1.2 Glass jar from Stoneyford, Co. Kilkenny, © courtesy of the National Museum of Ireland and Edward Bourke.

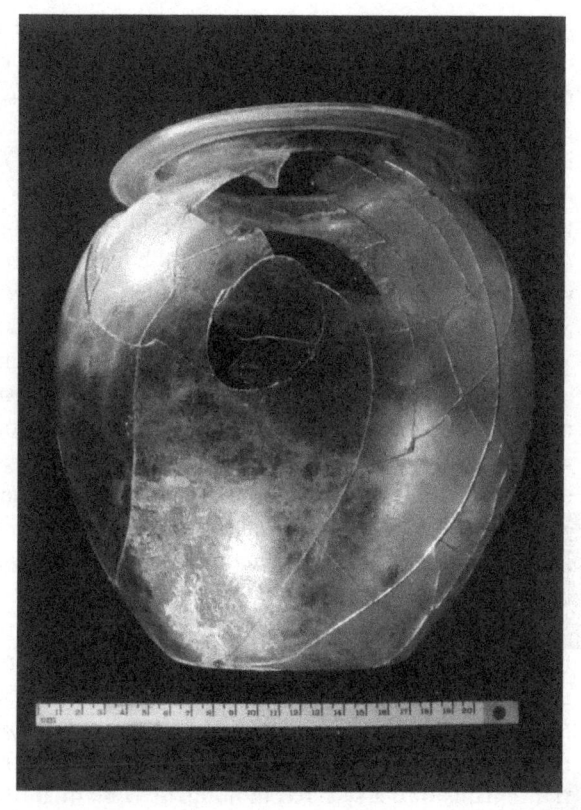

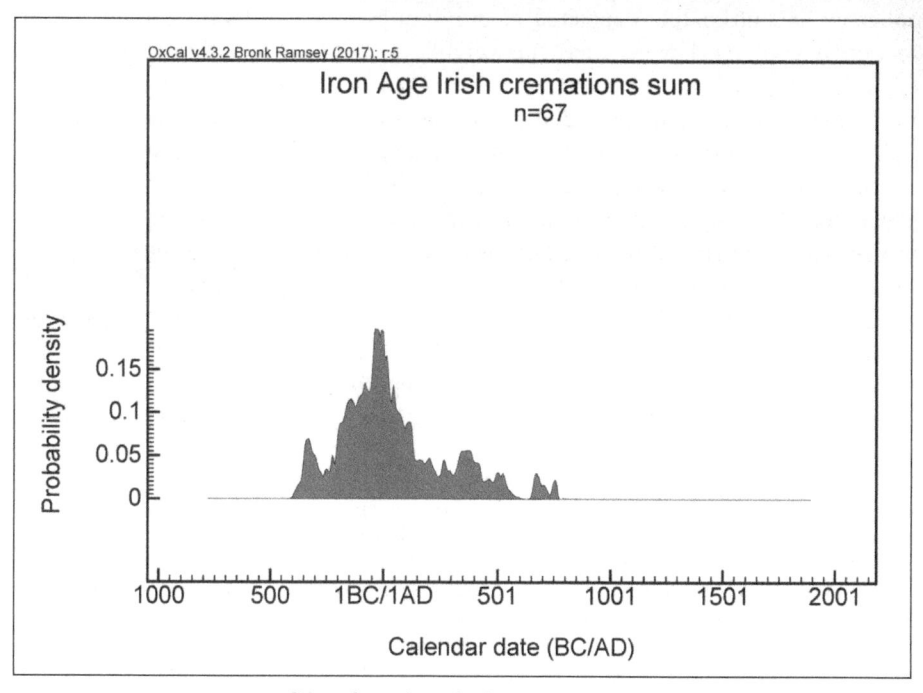

1.3 Sum of c14 dates for Iron Age cremations.

into the enclosed area, or the fosse, of a pre-existing Bronze Age ring-ditch, or burial mound. The deposit might also be inserted into the enclosed area, or the fosse, of a newly constructed Iron Age ring-ditch, burial mound, or flat cemetery.[5]

Sixty-eight sites that contain Iron Age cremation deposits have so far been identified, spread throughout the country (Map 1). The c14 dates, obtained for cremation deposits, range from the fourth century BC to the eighth century AD, with the optimum period of use being between 200BC and AD200 (Figure 1.4).[6] It has been established that the weight of cremated bone from archaeological contexts, provided that the full remains are present, for females is between 1001.5g and 1757.5g, with an average of 1271.9g; and for males, between 1384.6g and 2422.5g, with an average of 1861.9g (McKinley, 1993, 285). Since a typical cremation deposit usually consists of a small token portion of cremated bone, it has been postulated that many such deposits may not have been intended as formal burial but may represent disposal of pyre material (McKinley, 1997, 129–45; Becker, 2014, 13–15). However, in Ireland the deposition of these cremation deposits into established ancestral burial monuments, and the deliberate construction in the Iron Age of imitative burial monuments, must indicate a degree of intent, combined with respect for the deceased, which does not concur with mere disposal of pyre remains.

The burial of cremated bone represents the end-product of a protracted process that involved the sourcing, felling, and transportation of suitable wood to a pyre site, the construction of a pyre, the laying-out of the body on the pyre accompanied by the prescribed ritual, the cremation process, the collection of the cremated remains from the pyre (which could be time-consuming), and the transportation and deposition of the remains into a selected monument. The quantity of human cremated remains collected and ultimately deposited at burial sites in Ireland varies from tiny to moderate amounts. For instance, the weights for deposits recorded at Bruff, Co. Limerick, ranged from 1.8g to 293.7g; at Ferns Lower, Co. Wexford, from 9g to 456g. In the case of fourteen discrete deposits in the ditch of an Iron Age ring-barrow at Ballybronoge South, Co. Limerick, the deposits ranged from 3.3g to 128.9g of cremated bone (Eogan and Buckley, 2012). It is possible that the burial rite concentrated mainly on the cremation of the body and its accompaniments, which was seen as a releasing of the spirit of the dead person into the atmosphere, and the remains of the pyre were then left for dispersal by the elements. However, a small quantity of the cremated remains could be retrieved, possibly by relatives, and placed into recognisable burial places as a memorial to the deceased.

A breakdown of the placement of cremated deposits into varying monument types in the sixty-eight Iron Age sites identified and excavated (Map 1) is outlined in Table 1.1.

---

5 The term 'ring-ditch' is used in this publication as an overall term to describe a variety of enclosures including those generally defined as: ring-ditch (annular or penannular), embanked ring-ditch, ring-barrow, bowl-barrow with outer bank, and bowl-barrow, many of which, due to the passage of time and farming practices, now appear only as ditch features encircling a central area (O'Brien, 1992b, 130; Newman, 1997, 156–7).   6 I am aware of potential difficulties when using Summed Probability Functions (SPF); however, attention is drawn to the similarity of this SPF with the positive conclusions drawn in the case study on data from Later Prehistoric Ireland, undertaken by Armit, Swindles and Becker, 2013, 433–8. All dates in this SPF have been calibrated using OxCal 4.2.

Iron Age cremation burial c.400BC–AD400

Map 1 Distribution of sites with Iron Age cremation deposits, © The Discovery Programme and EOB.

Table 1.1 Iron Age cremation site types

Site type	No. of sites
Re-use of pre-existing monument	10
Iron Age mound	7
Iron Age penannular ring-ditch	14
Iron Age annular ring-ditch	21
Iron Age flat cemetery	11
Other (miscellaneous)	5
Total number of sites	**68**

When contemplating the difference between annular and penannular ring-ditches, one could interpret the opening in a penannular ring-ditch as a means of access perhaps to a special burial in the interior. However, analysis of the evidence suggests otherwise: of the fourteen Iron Age penannular ring-ditches recorded, only five contained a cremation deposit in the interior with deposits mainly found in the ditch. On the other hand, of the twenty-one Iron Age annular ring-ditches recorded, seven contained a cremation deposit in the interior, but again most deposits were contained in the ditch. It would appear, therefore, that the entrance feature in penannular enclosures had perhaps another purpose other than access to a burial deposit. It is also possible that cremated deposits were placed in the ditch area of these monuments to act as guardians of an enclosed sacred area.

The influence and veneration of ancestors is demonstrated by the insertion of cremation deposits into ancient burial monuments, and the erection of imitative burial monuments in locations that already contained Neolithic and Bronze Age burial monuments. The temporal gap which occurs between the original use of prehistoric burial monuments and their re-use in the Iron Age may be attributed to the result of climate deterioration and related economic changes, from the later Bronze Age, *c*.800BC, until the Early Iron Age, *c*.300BC, which contributed to a probable socio-economic collapse, now being recognised in the pollen record (Armit et al., 2014, 17045–9; Becker et al., 2017, 98–9).[7] These changes in turn may have led to depopulation in some areas. The revival of agricultural activity in the Early Iron Age could have caused populations to return to regions where they recognised or remembered the ancient burial places of their ancestors. Then, by placing the remains of selected persons from their community into existing monuments, or into newly constructed imitative burial monuments, they made a deliberate effort to create an impression of uninterrupted continuity. Or, it may be the case that new groups who colonised vacant lands placed remains of selected members of their own communities among the ancient indigenous ancestors, claiming these ancestors as their own, and thereby gaining their protection. They may have constructed imitative monuments

---

[7] Current research into this phenomenon, funded by the Heritage Council and Transport Infrastructure Ireland (TII), entitled 'Settlement and landscape in Later Prehistoric Ireland – seeing beyond the site', being undertaken by Dr Katharina Becker and her team at University College Cork, is confirming the contribution of climate-change to the downturn at this period.

into which they placed the remains of selected persons who would in future be regarded as ancestors (O'Brien, 2003, 67–8; 2009, 142–3; O'Brien and Bhreathnach, 2011, 53–64).

RE-USE OF PRE-EXISTING BURIAL MONUMENTS

The re-use of pre-existing burial monuments is evident at the following: Ballymacaward, Co. Donegal (O'Brien, 1999b; O'Brien and Bhreathnach, 2011), where a mound (originally a pseudo-cairn built over a rock outcrop), containing two Bronze Age cists, was re-used in the Iron Age[8] with the insertion of a small pit, F7, containing a cremation deposit identified as female (McKinley, 1998) and dated to between the third century BC and the first century AD.[9] In an annex, delimited by small upright slabs, at the north-eastern fringe of the mound, there was a spread of cremation and charcoal deposits dated to between the first and fourth century AD.[10] This site was subsequently re-used for inhumation burial in the Early Medieval period.

At Kiltierney, Co. Fermanagh, three pits that were inserted into a partially destroyed Neolithic passage tomb (Foley, 1988, 25–6; 2014, 862–4; McHugh and Scott, 2014, 130) contained cremation deposits, one of which, accompanied by a bronze fibula, and four glass beads, produced a c14 date placing it in the second century BC–first century AD[11] (Foley, 2014, 129–30, 863). Further cremation deposits were inserted into nineteen small mounds created around the main monument, one of which (no. 13), recently dated to between the second/first century BC[12] (Murphy and O'Donnabhain, forthcoming; Foley, 2014, 127–8, 863–4), contained a cremation deposit accompanied by an iron fibula, fragments of an enamelled mirror handle and other burnt fragments of iron and bronze.

At Cappydonnell Big, Co. Offaly (Coughlan, 2010, 14, 74; 2011, 77–8), the fosse of a Late Bronze Age double ring-ditch contained an Iron Age cremation deposit, B10 (C563), dated to the first century BC–first century AD,[13] accompanied by nineteen yellow glass beads, and burnt animal bone, mainly of dog. A token Iron Age cremation deposit was inserted into the upper capping of a Bronze Age ring-ditch (barrow) at Cherrywood, Co. Dublin (Site 4) (Ó Néill, 1999), with further probable Iron Age cremation deposits inserted into the surrounding ditch. An annular ring-ditch at Cappakeel, Site F, Co. Laois (Muldoon, 2011), contained cremation deposits dated eighth–fifth century BC[14] and fourth–second century BC[15] in the ditch fill. A Bronze Age cairn (D) at Cahermackirilla, Co. Clare, contained an Iron Age cremation deposit representing one adult, dated second–first century BC[16] (Grant, 1995, 31–3; 2006,

---

8 This monument is located on the northern bank of the River Erne, where the river enters Ballyshannon Harbour. It may be more than coincidence that Ballyshannon Harbour was the find-spot of the only La Tène III, anthropoid hilted sword (*c.*150BC–AD50) known in Ireland (O'Brien, 2009b, 193–8).   9 UB-4196: 2091±56BP; at 2σ (87.7% probability) = 212 cal BC–cal AD 26.   10 UB-4425; F28-29; 1804±51BP; at 2σ = cal AD 83–343.   11 UBA-20341 = cal 170 BC–AD 5 (date as published).   12 Thanks to Eileen Murphy for allowing access to this date prior to publication: UBA-13537; Mound 13; 2091±25BP; at 2σ = 181–45 cal BC.   13 UBA-10174: 2011±27BP; at 2σ (92.8% probability) = 58 cal BC–cal AD 60.   14 UBA-14890: 2433±27BP; at 2σ = 749–405 cal BC.   15 UBA-14888: 2197±22BP; at 2σ = 362–198 cal BC.   16 NZA-32716; 2098±35BP; at 2σ (94.3%) = 204–38 cal BC.

553; 2010; Power, 2003). At Tullyallen 1, Co. Louth (Chappel, 2002, 242–3), a ring-ditch (barrow) with a Bronze Age urn-burial at the centre had its ditch re-cut and re-used for the insertion of cremation deposits, possibly in the Iron Age.

Some tombs at the Neolithic megalithic necropolis at Carrowmore, Co. Sligo, appear to have been re-used for burial purposes in the Iron Age. c14 dates obtained from charcoal in pits and post-holes indicate that activity had taken place in tombs 26 and 27 during this period, and human teeth representing a number of individuals were recovered from the possible Iron Age context in tomb 27 (Burenult, 1980, 47, 67, 133).

BURIAL MONUMENTS CONSTRUCTED IN THE IRON AGE AMONG PRE-EXISTING MONUMENTS

Burial monuments, mounds and ring-ditches, constructed in the Iron Age, often occur in landscapes where evidence for funerary, ritual, or other forms of occupation had been established from as early as the Neolithic period. The practice of constructing new primary burial monuments imitative of those already present in the landscape was probably undertaken as a method of creating visible links with the established ancestors.

At Cush, Co. Limerick (Ó Ríordáin, 1940, 133–9, 155–6; Raftery, 1981, 181; O'Brien, 1992b, 130), Tumulus I contained a Bronze Age burial, but Tumulus II contained a cremation accompanied by a small decorated bone plaque which can now be paralleled at several dated Iron Age sites. At Carrowjames, Co. Mayo (Raftery, J., 1941a, 28–37; Raftery, B., 1981, 181; O'Brien, 1992b, 96–8), at least one, no. 8, among a complex of ten tumuli, and possibly nos. 5, 7, 9, date to the Iron Age, while the remaining tumuli date to the Bronze Age. At Rathdooney Beg, Co. Sligo (Mount, 1999, 337–71; 2012, 189–98), two burial monuments, a barrow-mound (Site 2) and a ring-ditch (Site 3), dated to the Iron Age, were erected beside a large Neolithic burial monument. Carbury Hill, Co. Kildare (Wilmot, 1938) which has three burial monuments, mound A, and enclosure C, contain only undated cremations and are probably Bronze Age, but enclosure B contains four cremation deposits in small pits located in the central area (all identified as juveniles), one of which, cremation II, contained artefacts in the form of two small iron rings and a pin-shaped fragment of iron. This enclosure was subsequently re-used for inhumation burial in the Early Medieval period. The site at Rath, Co. Meath (Schweitzer, 2005, 93–8), consisted of three ring-ditches, two of which are undated but may be Bronze Age. The third, which contained cremated bone in the northern ditch fill, is likely to be a primary Iron Age ring-ditch. The trivallate Rath of the Synods, located immediately north of the Neolithic passage tomb (known as the Mound of the Hostages) (O'Sullivan, 2005), on the Hill of Tara, Co. Meath, contains ten undated cremation deposits, which appear to be Iron Age, based on radiocarbon dates obtained from charcoal samples (Grogan, 2008, 37–40, 141–6). This site was subsequently re-used for inhumation burial. An Iron Age penannular ring-ditch with a cremation deposit in the southern terminal, at Ballydowney, Co. Kerry (Kiely and O'Callaghan, 2010), is located in an area showing activity from the Neolithic–Bronze Age periods.

Two Iron Age penannular ring-ditches at Ardsallagh II, Co. Meath (Clarke and Carlin, 2009, 1–20), are located in close proximity to an Early Bronze Age flat cemetery. At Busherstown 5, Co. Carlow, and at Ballybannon 5, Co. Carlow, Iron Age ring-ditches were in locations that contained Bronze Age burial material (Bolger, Moloney and Shiels, 2015, 36, 72–3). Similar multi-period uses occur at Glebe South, Co. Dublin (Carroll, Ruan, Wiggins, 2008, 107–58), Kerlogue, Co. Wexford (McLoughlin, 2012a, 161–74), Mullamast, Co. Kildare (Hackett and Twomey, 2009), and Ballynakelly, Co. Dublin (McCarthy, 2012, 157–9). At Ballydavis 1, Co. Laois (Stevens, 2011), penannular ring-ditch C125, and annular ring-ditch C105, both of which contained Late Iron Age cremations in the ditch fill,[17] were located in close proximity to Early Bronze Age and Late Bronze age cremations. At the small annular Iron Age ring-ditch, with a central cremation deposit, at Coolnahorna 3, Co. Wexford,[18] located in an area of Bronze Age cremation pits (Rajic and Hardy, 2013), cremated bone from deposit 71, 70, in the north-east segment of the ditch, have been dated to second century BC–first century AD.[19] At Ask, Co. Wexford (Stevens, 2007, 35–46; 2012, 49–60), in a location with evidence of a funerary ritual landscape dating back to the Neolithic period, cremation was still being practised within and without an enclosure in the seventh and eighth centuries AD.[20] Further evidence for the continued use of cremation into the conversion period has been discovered at Annaghilla (Site 4), Co. Tyrone (Kimber, 2010, 501; Dunlop and Barkley, 2016), where a small Iron Age annular ring-ditch containing a cremation deposit within a central pit, dated second–first century BC,[21] was located on a low hill that also produced evidence for Neolithic and Bronze Age occupation. This ring-ditch was subsequently enclosed within a larger ring-ditch (settlement cemetery), which contained cremation deposits of human bone dated up to the ninth century AD,[22] together with a small cemetery of Early Medieval extended inhumations.

The intention of the builders to merge these Iron Age burial monuments within groups of existing monuments was obviously realised, because, prior to their excavation, it was not possible to visually differentiate between pre-existing and Iron Age monuments, or burials, at these sites.

RING-DITCHES CONSTRUCTED IN THE IRON AGE

While the intention of some groups in the Iron Age was to assimilate their burial monuments with those of earlier ancestors, other groups constructed burial monuments in 'green field' locations, thus creating their own ancestors.

A ring-ditch constructed in the Iron Age in close proximity to a contemporary habitation site was discovered at Bruff, Co. Limerick (O'Connell, 2010, 1–14; Cosham

---

17 C125: UBA–11705: 1947±27BP: at 2σ = cal AD 0–124: C105: UBA–11707: 1991±24BP: at 2σ = 44 cal BC–cal AD 61. 18 Thanks are due to Kate Taylor of TVAS (Ireland) Ltd, for providing information about this site. 19 Fill 71 – UBA–21355: 2035±29BP; at 2σ = 160 cal BC–cal AD 50 (at 88.8% probability = 116 cal BC–cal AD 30). Fill 70 – UBA–21356: 2025±38BP; at 2σ = 173 cal BC–cal AD 25. 20 Cremation pit C545 located within enclosure E: SUERC–32851: 1330±30BP: at 2σ = cal AD 640–770. Cremation pit C350 located approx. 50m n-e of enclosure E: SUERC–31627: 1290±30BP: at 2σ = cal AD 660-780. 21 SUERC–21380: 2090±30BP: at 2σ = 195–46 cal BC. 22 Human cremated bone in post-hole. SUERC–21631: 1240±40BP; at 2σ = cal AD 680–881.

and MacLeod, 2009). Here an annular ring-ditch produced small token cremated burials, dated second century BC–first century AD,[23] and fourth–first century BC,[24] in two pits within the interior of the enclosure. There were four deposits in the ditch, three of which produced minute quantities of cremated bone, one of these is dated second century BC–first century AD.[25] The fourth deposit (1081), dated first century BC–second century AD,[26] was accompanied by an unburnt human femoral shaft.[27] This latter cremation deposit has been published as being a 'full body burial' (O'Connell, 2010, 4), which appears to be an incorrect description, even allowing for the presence of an unburnt bone, when it is recognised that the recorded weight of the deposit (293.7g) represents approximately one-quarter of the average weight expected for a full female cremation, and one-sixth of the average weight for a full male cremation.[28] The temporal spread of the c14 dates obtained for four of the cremated burial deposits at this site indicates that the ring-ditch was re-visited for the insertion of deposits of selected individuals at different periods during the Iron Age. The probable habitation evidence is provided by a concentration of fifteen pits located close to the ring-ditch. One of the pits contained minute fragments of cremated human bone but the remainder contained what is described as domestic waste which included animal bone, slag, corroded metal artefacts and residual prehistoric pottery. Based on radiocarbon dating of contents, this latter group of features has been interpreted as being contemporary with the funerary activity at the ring-ditch.

An example of the care, time and effort involved in the construction of a ring-ditch can be demonstrated at the, admittedly unusual, annular ring-ditch (external diameter 5.38m, internal diameter 4.5m) at Ferns Lower, Co. Wexford (Ryan and Buckley, 2012, 273–89), where almost the entire circumference of the ditch had been lined with charred planks held together with iron nails prior to the insertion of the cremation deposits. A further feature at this site was, of the four cremation deposits inserted on and into the plank lining, three were of adults each accompanied by a juvenile. Burial 1, a male, dated to the fourth–first century BC,[29] was accompanied by a juvenile, and the range of grave goods accompanying them included fragments of iron, copper alloy, flint, and more than ten beads. Burial 2, an adult, was accompanied by an infant, and fragments of iron, flint and a bone handle. Burial 3, an adult, dated fourth–first century BC,[30] was also accompanied by a juvenile, and fragments of iron, copper alloy and a selection of beads. Burial 4, an adult, had no grave goods. Allowing for the fact

23 SUERC–25829: 2065±50BP; at 2σ = 201 cal BC–cal AD 52.   **24** SUERC–25830: 2165±50BP; at 2σ = 366–58 cal BC (at 93.2% probability = 366–89 cal BC).   **25** SUERC–25832: 2045±50BP; at 2σ = 186 cal BC–cal AD 59.   **26** SUERC–25831: 1930±50BP; at 2σ = 42 cal BC–cal AD 213 (at 91.6% probability = 42 cal BC–cal AD 179).   **27** This inclusion warrants further investigation in view of the c14 results, sixth–seventh century AD, recently obtained for unburnt foot and lower leg bones which accompanied an Early Bronze Age cremation at Ballykilroe, Co. Westmeath (Lucas, 1973, 188–9) (Dr Kerri Cleary, pers. comm.).   **28** The conclusion that deposit 1081 represents a full body cremation appears to be based on a misinterpretation, i.e., that the amount of cremated bone which may be recovered from an undisturbed adult cremation burial would be between 57g and 2200g (McKinley, 1993, 139). McKinley's reference relates only to the amount of cremated bone collected from a pyre and deposited as a burial, which then remains undisturbed [until excavated]. McKinley continues: 'it is clear that widely different quantities of bone were included in burials at the time of depositing'.   **29** UCD-0011: Charcoal sample beneath cremation: 2190±65BP; at 2σ = 392–91 cal BC.   **30** UCD-0010: Charcoal from fill: 2090±65BP: at 2σ = 365 cal BC–cal AD 54.

that the c14 dates were obtained from charcoal, it would still seem that all the burials are roughly contemporary. A further example of a cremation deposit consisting of an adult and a child, dating to the first century BC–first century AD,[31] is noted at ring-ditch C105, Ballydavis 1, Co. Laois (Stevens, 2011, sect. 9.1.3. 81–2). At Ballydavis Townland[32] (Keeley, 1995; 1999, 27), the ditch surrounding ring-ditch 1 had brushwood laid down in the fill and burnt *in situ*, possibly as part of a purification ritual undertaken either before or after the insertion in the centre of the enclosed area of a cremation deposit with artefacts, dated to the third–first century BC,[33] and a pit with a cremation deposit unaccompanied by artefacts.

At Knockcommane, Site 4700.1a, Co. Limerick (Molloy, 2007; McQuade et al., 2009, 163–5), an Iron Age penannular ring-ditch with a central pit contained a token cremation deposit (F15) identified as female, dated to the third–first century BC,[34] with three further token cremation deposits in the enclosing ditch, one of which (F19), dated to the fourth–first century BC,[35] was accompanied by a blue glass bead (E2341.1).[36] A small annular ring-ditch (6m diameter), dated to the second century BC–first century AD,[37] at Claureen, Co. Clare, contained three cremation deposits in the ditch fill which also contained two unburnt yellow glass beads, and one unburnt blue glass bead (Hull, 2006, 4). A penannular ring-ditch at Marlhill, Co. Tipperary (Site 148.1), dated to the third–first century BC,[38] produced token cremations deposits in the enclosure ditch, together with seven blue glass beads, and miscellaneous fragments of metal (McQuade et al., 2009, 166–9, 366; McQuade and Molloy, 2012, 182–3).

Occasionally it may be possible to catch a glimpse of the possible visual appearance of a ring-ditch monument when it was in use. At Ballyboy 1, Co. Galway (McNamara, 2010a; Delaney and Tobin, 2010; McNamara and Delaney, 2012, 123–37), a post-hole was centrally located in the enclosed area of an annular ring-ditch. One metre to the west of the post-hole a small oval pit (C11) contained a deposit representing partial cremated remains of a female dated to the first century BC–first century AD.[39] It is possible that the post-hole may have held a pole with an emblem or marker that could identify the affiliation of the female and that of two further individuals whose cremated remains were deposited in the surrounding ditch. All the cremation deposits were contemporary.[40] Approximately 1 km to the south of Ballyboy 1, a small annular ring-ditch, Ballyboy 11, which contained several cremation deposits in the interior and in the ditch, contemporary with those at Ballyboy 1, had a stake-hole in the ditch which

---

31 UBA–11707: Cremated bone C576: 1991±24BP; at 2σ = 44 cal BC–cal AD 6.   32 The nomenclature 'Ballydavis Td' is used to differentiate between this site (excavated in 1995) and the nearby site excavated in 2003 which is referred to as 'Ballydavis 1'.   33 GrA–13494: 2140±50BP; at 2σ = 359–47 cal BC (at 71.1% probability = 261–47 cal BC).   34 UB–7515: 2104±33BP; at 2σ = 338–42 cal BC (at 94.6% probability = 204–42 cal BC).   35 UB–7514: 2133±39BP; at 2σ = 355–48 cal BC (at 78.1% probability = 232–48 cal BC).   36 The blue glass bead E2341.1 is recorded in the final excavation report (Molloy, 2007, 5) as accompanying cremation deposit F19; but in the published article (McQuade et al., 2009, 165) it is recorded as accompanying central cremation deposit F15.   37 Beta–207732: 2010±40BP; at 2σ (93.4%) = 114 cal BC–cal AD 75.   38 Beta–231089: 2130±40BP; at 2σ = 355–46 cal BC (at 79.5% probability = 232–46 cal BC). This date was derived from animal bone retrieved from the enclosure ditch.   39 UBA:13025; 2019±23 BP; at 2σ = 90 cal BC–cal AD 53.   40 C35: UBA–13026: 2026±19BP; at 2σ = 91 cal BC–cal AD 47: C4: UBA–13024: 2024±19BP; at 2σ = 90 cal BC–cal AD 47.

may have held a marker. A similar function might be ascribed to the stake-hole in the interior and the several stake-holes inserted throughout the eastern part of the ditch at Ferns Lower, Co. Wexford.[41]

A hint, or indication, of the ceremonies that undoubtedly took place during the construction of an Irish burial monument may be observed at the ring-ditch complex, close to the River Nore, at Holdenstown 1, Co. Kilkenny (Whitty and Tobin, 2009, 20; Whitty and Coughlan, 2012, 313–14) (Figure 4.9). Twelve red deer antler fragments, some of which are described as 'picks', were deposited into the shallow fill of the ditch of ring-ditch 1, and four similar objects were discovered in the ditch fill of ring-ditch 2 (Figure 5.7a). Ring-ditch 1, which did not contain any evidence for burial, was originally constructed in the second–first century BC,[42] and a recut has been dated to the fifth–sixth century AD.[43] However, a c14 date obtained for one of the antler picks places it in the third–fourth century AD.[44] The deposition of these antler 'picks' suggests that they were used to re-cut the ditch in a ritualistic manner at this period. While functioning antler picks have been identified in the Early Medieval period,[45] more efficient iron digging-implements would have been available to those who re-cut this ditch.

FLAT OR FIELD CREMATION CEMETERIES

Not all Iron Age burials were inserted into recognisable monuments. Several sites have been recognised where some sections of the Iron Age population chose to place their cremation deposits directly into the soil, thus rendering them invisible, prior to their discovery during excavation. This suggests that flat or field cremation cemeteries may be more numerous than is currently believed.

At an Iron Age flat cemetery at Bricketstown, Co. Wexford (Elder and Johnston, 2006), four of five pits in Area 2 produced small deposits of cremated human bone, together with burnt vegetation and burnt stone. Charcoal (oak) from pit C7 produced a c14 date between the first century BC and the first century AD.[46] The excavator concluded that the evidence suggested the presence of a flat cemetery. A similar site is at Knockgraffon, Co. Tipperary (Site 133.1) (McQuade, Molloy, and Moriarty, 2009, 173–4; McQuade and Molloy, 2012, 181), where a pit containing a small deposit of cremated bone, identified as that of an adult female, was dated to between the first and third century AD.[47] This pit was located among a cluster of pits which contained non-burial charcoal-rich deposits. The site at Cross, Co. Galway, located on a low ridge, produced evidence for several pit cremations, some of which were Bronze Age. However, one pit contained a token cremation deposit (F137) dated to between the

---

41 An interesting suggestion/observation has been made (Thomas Charles-Edwards, pers. comm.) that the area enclosed by a ring-ditch might symbolise the land held by a kin-group, with cremation-deposits in the ditch representing burials on the symbolic boundary. The central post-hole, where one existed, might be the remains of a marker representing the house, as involved in *tellach* (legal entry).   42 C14 date from sample of hazel: 2119±25BP; at 2σ = 203–53 cal BC.   43 C14 date from willow charcoal: 1567±23BP; at 2σ = cal AD 426–546.   44 UBA-20005: 1703±25BP; at 2σ = cal AD 256–408 (date obtained courtesy Mapping Death Project).   45 Pers. comm., Ian Riddler and Nicola Trzaska-Nartowski.   46 UB-6955: 1963±34BP: at 2σ (91.1% probability) 50 cal BC–cal AD 90.   47 Beta-220335; 1870±50BP = at 2σ (94.9% probability) cal AD 25–252.

second century BC and first century AD,[48] thus placing it in the Iron Age (Mullins, 2009, 11; Mullins and Birmingham, 2014, 101). This site was subsequently re-used for inhumation burial in the Early Medieval period. A multi-period site, with evidence for occupation from the Neolithic period, at Ballycuddy More, Site 1, Co. Tipperary (Taylor, 2011), included a flat cemetery of nine small pits containing small quantities of cremated human bone dated to the fourth–first century BC,[49] and first century BC–first century AD.[50] The temporal span of these dates suggests recurring use over a long time, and the fact that the pits did not intersect over time would suggest that the individual deposits were marked in some way (Taylor, 2011, 34).

GRAVE GOODS IN IRISH CREMATION DEPOSITS

Although artefacts from Irish non-burial contexts, dateable to the Iron Age, are well-known and have been researched (Raftery, 1984; Ó Floinn, 2009, 199–210; O'Brien, 2009b, 193–8), the range and quantity of artefacts found with cremation burial deposits is comparatively small (see Gazetteer 1). However, the absence of recognisable objects cannot be taken as an indication that the body on the pyre was not finely arrayed, and merely implies that such an array consisted of combustible organic material, which would have included fine textiles, wooden vessels or implements, leather goods and floral-plant embellishments. The inclusion of burnt animal bone in some cremation deposits suggests that parts of animals were placed with the body on the pyre as accompanying offerings for the dead individual. For instance, at Ferns Lower, cremation deposit 3 contained fragments of burnt animal bone. Alternatively, the presence of unburnt animal bone may represent the ritual deposit of animal parts accompanying the human cremation deposit. For example, at Mullamast, Co. Kildare (Hackett and Twomey, 2009), the fill of the northern part of a ring-ditch contained three deposits of cremated human bone, one of which has been dated to the fourth–first century BC,[51] while the fill of the southern part of the ditch contained the skeleton of a large dog, and the skulls of a horse and a cow. The presence of unburnt animal bone among cremation deposits could be an indication that feasting took place as part of the burial ritual, an example being Ballybronoge South, Co. Limerick, where cremation deposits 6 and 9 contained unburnt animal bone.

Of the sixty-eight sites recognised to date, thirty-six (53%) contained only cremation deposits with no artefacts; fourteen (21%) contained only cremation deposits with artefacts; and eighteen (26%) contained a mixture of deposits with artefacts and some without artefacts (Table 1.2 and Map 2). The application of c14 dating to some recently excavated Irish cremation deposits, including those with, and those devoid of, artefacts, has placed these firmly in an Iron Age context. These results have also facilitated cross-comparison with artefacts contained in older undated excavations, thus providing these with a likely date and context.

---

48 Beta–241006: 2080±40BP; at 2σ = 201 cal BC–cal AD 05.   49 Pit 101: Beta–244830: 2140±40BP; at 2σ = 356–51 cal BC.   50 Pit 112: UBA–13692: 2003±33BP; at 2σ = 91 cal BC–cal AD 73 (at 92.0% = 61 cal BC–cal AD 73).   51 SUERC–25467: 2145±50BP; at 2σ = 359–51 cal BC.

Table 1.2 Absence or presence of artefacts in Iron Age cremation deposits

Cremation deposit contents	No. of sites	Percentage
Absence of artefacts in all deposits	36	53%
Presence of artefacts in all deposits	14	21%
Combination: deposits with/without artefacts	18	26%
Total number of sites	**68**	**100%**

The types of artefacts recovered from Iron Age cremation deposits are listed in Gazetteer 1. The most frequently occurring artefacts are beads which can range from tiny blue glass, blue-green glass, or yellow glass beads (Plate 2), to more elaborate forms. Beads recovered at the now unidentifiable and undated site of Loughey, near Donaghadee, Co. Down, included sixty-five small plain blue glass beads and seventy-one small yellow glass type (Carruthers, 1856; Jope and Wilson, 1957, 84; Jope, 1960, 40). The undated ring-ditch at Oranbeg, Co. Galway,[52] produced five small plain blue glass beads and seventy-seven small yellow glass beads (O'Brien, 1984, 39, 81). These beads, and their context, can now be dated by comparison with glass bead types recovered from dated cremation contexts which include tiny blue glass beads recovered from cremation deposits in the ring-ditches dated to the first century BC–first century AD at Ballyboy 1 and 2, Co. Galway (McNamara, 2010a-b; Delaney, McKeon and McNamara, 2012, 99; McNamara and Delaney, 2012, 130; Carroll, 2010, 5). Ballyboy 1 produced three examples and Ballyboy 2 produced twenty-eight (Plate 2e). Knockcommane, Co. Limerick, dated to the fourth–first century BC,[53] has produced unburnt and burnt examples (Plate 2a); Marlhill, Co. Tipperary (Molloy, 2009, 166–9; McQuade and Molloy, 2012, 182–3), dated to the third–first century BC,[54] produced seven examples (Plate 2c); Glebe South, Co. Dublin, dated fourth–first century BC,[55] produced seventeen examples (Ryan, 2008, 118–19). A number of unburnt examples were retrieved from the central cremation in ring-ditch F1, Ballydavis Townland, Co. Laois (Keeley, 1995; 1996, 52; 1999, 27, 31). At Claureen, Co. Clare, one unburnt example was recovered among cremation deposits in the ditch fill of a 6m diameter ring-barrow dated to the second century BC–first century AD[56] (Hull, 2006, 4, 13). Two unburnt yellow glass beads were also recovered at Claureen (Plate 2d). Tiny yellow glass beads (burnt) have been recovered in contexts at Ferns Lower, Co. Wexford (Ryan, 2012, 280), dated to the fourth–first century BC. A yellow glass bead was recovered in the fill of a small ring-ditch, together with cremated bone, at Haynestown, Co. Louth (O'Sullivan, 1994), and at Ballydavis Townland, an unknown number of unburnt examples were recovered. Parallels and dating for the ten examples

---

[52] Excavated by the late Professor Etienne Rynne who kindly granted permission to the writer, in the early 1980s, to examine and comment on the material from Oranbeg, and Grannagh, Co. Galway. [53] UB–7514: 2133±39BP; at 2σ = 335–48 cal BC (at 78.1% probability = 232–48 cal BC). [54] Beta–231089: 2130±40BP; at 2σ = 355–46 cal BC (at 79.5% probability = 232–46 cal BC). This date was obtained from animal bone in the ditch. [55] Charcoal from C272 (ring-ditch 2) Beta–239118: 2160±40BP; at 2σ = 361–92 cal BC. [56] Charcoal (Fraxinus) Beta–207732: 2010±40BP; at 2σ (93.4%) = 114 cal BC–cal AD 75.

Iron Age cremation burial c.400BC–AD400

Map 2 Distribution of cremation deposits with artefacts, © The Discovery Programme and EOB.

of tiny beads of pale blue-green glass recovered at undated Tumulus 8 (ring-barrow) at Carrowjames, Co. Mayo (Raftery J, 1941a, 28–37; Raftery, B., 1981, 181; O'Brien, 1984, 96–8), can now be proposed by the twenty tiny beads of pale blue-green glass recovered at Donacarney Great, Co. Meath, dated to the second–first century BC[57] (Giacometti, 2010; Carroll 2010), twenty-eight recovered at Ballyboy 2, Co. Galway, five at Ballyboy 1, and approximately fifteen from burial 1, and approximately eighteen from burial 3, at Ferns Lower, Co. Wexford (Ryan, 2012, 280–1).

Nineteen small cylindrical yellow glass beads were recovered from the Iron Age cremation deposit in a Bronze Age ring-ditch at Cappydonnell Big, Co. Offaly (Coughlan, 2010, 14). The cremation recorded at Loughey also included eight beads of colourless glass with yellow spirals, similar to Guido's Meare-type, class 10 (Guido, 1978, 79).[58] These can be paralleled at the undated cremation deposits at Grannagh, Co. Galway[59] (O'Brien, 1984, 79–80; Hawkes, 1982, 60), and ring-ditch F3 at Ballydavis Townland, Co. Laois (Keeley, 1996, 52; 1999, 31). In the 1969 excavation at Kiltierney, Co. Fermanagh, now dated to the second century BC–first century AD[60] (Flanagan, 1969; O'Brien, 1984, 76; Raftery, 1984; McHugh and Scott, 2014, 130; Foley, 2014, 863), a round glass bead with herring-bone design was recovered, which can be equated to Guido's Meare variant type 'a' (Guido, 1978, 81), and is similar to three glass beads recovered at the undated Tumulus 8 at Carrowjames, Co. Mayo (Raftery, J., 1941a, 28–37; O'Brien, 1984, 96–8). The Kiltierney excavation also produced a knobbed blue glass bead with spirals around the knobs, similar to Guido's class 6 Oldbury-type (Guido, 1987, 53–7), which can be paralleled with the knobbed blue glass bead from Loughey (Jope, 1960, 40), and with a bead from ring-ditch F1 at Ballydavis Townland (Keeley, 1996, 52; 1999, 33). Also recovered from Kiltierney was a brown glass oculus bead with yellow-circled brown eyes, similar to Guido's class 1 Arras-type (Guido, 1978, 45–8), which can be paralleled at undated Grannagh (O'Brien, 1984, 80).

An elaborate bead type recovered from Donacarney Great, Co. Meath, dated to the second–first century BC, is of dark blue translucent glass decorated with six inlaid circular motifs, 13mm x 14mm (Plate 2b). This bead is somewhat similar to the Garrow Tor-type introduced into Britain in the fourth to third century BC (Guido, 1978, 61–2), but is very rare in Ireland (Carroll, 2010a, 3, 5). It can be compared however with the undated bead E82.9, from Grannagh, Co. Galway. Eight bone beads also recovered at Donacarney Great, Co. Meath, can offer a parallel for three similar undated beads from Grannagh, Co. Galway.

Twenty-eight amber beads were recovered at Ballyboy 2, Co. Galway (Plate 2e), also, one at Ballyboy 1, and four examples at Ferns Lower, Co. Wexford. A cremation deposit, dated first century BC–first century AD,[61] in a pit outside the ring-ditch at Coolnahorna 3, Co. Wexford, included two clear white glass cable beads.

---

57 UBA–26150: 2088±24BP; at 2σ = 175–45 cal BC (date provided by Mapping Death Project).
58 Recent research has identified problems with Guido's typology, and a new typology has now been proposed by Elizabeth Foulds (Foulds, 2017, 65–7). However, until a new typology becomes mainstream, Guido's typology is still relevant and is used in this publication.   59 Excavated by the late Professor Etienne Rynne.   60 UBA–20341 = 170 cal BC–cal AD 5 (information as published).
61 UBA–21351: 2011±29BP; at 2σ = 91 cal BC–cal AD 64 (at 91.5% probability = 61 cal BC–cal AD 64).

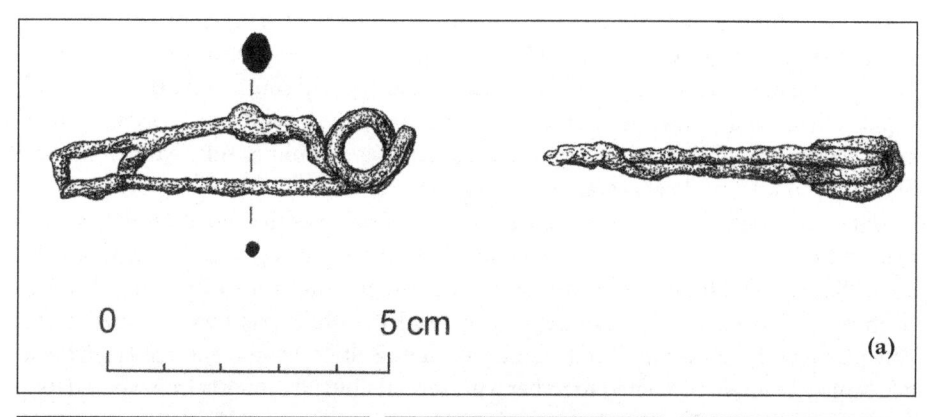

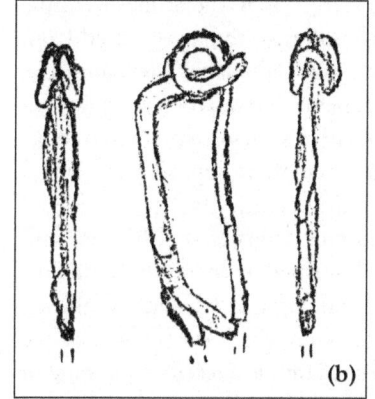

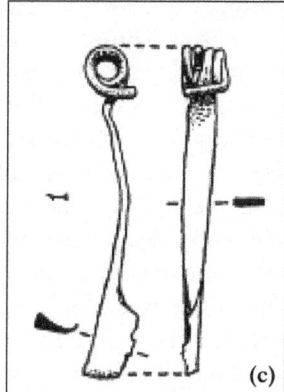

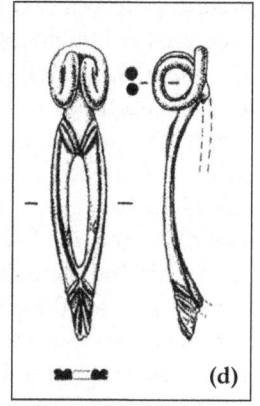

1.4 Fibulae from Iron Age cremations: (a) Kiltierney, Mound 13, Co. Fermanagh, © Crown DfC Historic Environment Division; (b) Grannagh, Co. Galway, after E. Rynne; (c) Loughey, Co. Down, from Jope and Wilson, 1957, fig. 1.1; (d) Kiltierney (1969), Co. Fermanagh, © Crown DfC.

The quantity of beads recovered from cremation deposits can vary widely. It can range from two tiny blue glass beads recovered at Knockgraffon, Co. Tipperary (McQuade and Molloy, 2012, 182), up to 127 glass beads, three amber beads, and one bone bead, recovered from Burial 1 at Ferns, Co. Wexford (Ryan, 2012, 280), and 150 beads from Loughey, Co. Down. While beads are often fused and vitrified from contact with fire, unburnt beads are occasionally recovered among cremation deposits, as at Ballydavis Townland, Co. Laois, Claureen, Co. Clare, and several other sites. These beads appear to have been placed with the cremated material after it had been gathered from the pyre site and subsequently deposited into the ground. Why this occurred is difficult to explain, but it is possible that the beads had a cultural significance and may have been regarded as a representation of the identity and/or status of the cremated person, or they may represent a tangible link between the living and the dead. Cross-comparison between dated and undated sites suggests that the floruit of the use of beads in Iron Age Ireland was between the second century BC and the first century AD.

In Ireland, to date, no centres have been discovered where glass beads were manufactured in the Iron Age. This introduces the question of whether their presence is the result of trading connections, or the movement of people. It is perhaps a combination of both. Carroll (2010b, iv) suggests that comparisons between most beads found in Irish Iron Age cremations and bead types of south-west Britain would suggest that Britain was the source of origin. Apart from south-west Britain, other known Iron Age glass bead-making centres such as Culbin Sands, Moray, in east Scotland, could have been a source of manufacture.

Safety pin-type fibulae were recovered in association with cremation deposits at five, and possibly seven, sites. Excavations at Kiltierney in 1983–4 (Foley, 1988, 26; 2014, 862–4; McHugh and Scott, 2014, 127–9) produced an iron fibula brooch (Figure 1.4a) from a cremation deposit (mound 13) which has now returned a c14 date placing it in the second–first century BC. The Kiltierney fibula is similar in form to a bronze example recovered together with several fibula fragments from an undated cremation deposit at Grannagh, Co. Galway (Figure 1.4b), and to the bronze example recovered at Loughey, Co. Down (Figure 1.4c). The unburnt fibula recovered from the important central cremation deposit ring-ditch F1 at Ballydavis Townland, Co. Laois, is described by the excavator as being of 'Nauheim derivative-type, 3.9cm in length, the bow, maximum width 6.5mm, decorated with a series of six small tubular pieces with ribbed surfaces' (Keeley, 1999, 30). The cremation deposit from which this fibula was recovered has been dated to the third–first century BC[62] (Lanting and Brindley, 1998, 6). The dates obtained for the cremation deposits at Kiltierney and Ballydavis Townland, which contained the fibulae described as being of Nauheim-type,[63] allow for the dating of the examples from Grannagh and Loughey, and by extension the beads from those sites. A further fibula, from which the pin is missing, recovered in a pit near ring-ditch F2 at Ballydavis Townland, is described as being of a plainer type. A bronze fibula recovered from the cremation deposit excavated at Kiltierney in 1969 (Figure 1.4d) is a Navan-type derivative[64] (Hawkes, 1982, 64), and the second century BC–first century AD date now available for this deposit (Foley, 2014, 863; McHugh and Scott, 2014, 130) provides an Irish context for this brooch type. At Glebe South, Co. Dublin (Carroll, et al., 2008, 110–12), a cremation deposit (C178) dated to the second century BC–first century AD,[65] in the fill of penannular ring-ditch 1 (C135), also produced three small copper-alloy fragments of a probable fibula of Navan-type. At Carbury Hill, B, Co. Kildare (Willmot, 1938, 136), cremation deposit II was accompanied by what is described as 'a pin-shaped' fragment of iron, which might represent a safety pin-type fibula. Included in this latter cremation deposit were two small iron rings. Two bronze rings were recovered, together with miscellaneous fragments of metal, among the cremation deposits in Tumulus 8, Carrowjames, Co. Mayo (Raftery, 1939, 157–67; 1940–1, 16–88). At Coolnahorna 3,

---

62 GrA–13594: 2140±50BP; at 2σ = 359–47 cal BC (at 71.1% probability = 261–47 cal BC). **63** 'Nauheim-type' brooches have a flat bow (but occasionally with a leaf or rod bow) and unperforated catch-plate (Jope and Wilson, 1957, 77). **64** The term 'Navan-type' derives from two brooches recovered at the site of Navan Fort, Co. Armagh, one of which may have been recovered with an unrecorded inhumation burial (Ó Floinn, 2009, 28–9). These brooches are described as a uniquely Irish development, characterised by open work bows bearing raised, finely-cast trumpet and lentoid-boss decoration (Raftery, 1984, 153). This observation suggests that this brooch type was copied and manufactured by Irish craftsmen. **65** Beta–229060: 2060±40; at 2σ = 187 cal BC–cal AD 25.

Iron Age cremation burial c.400BC–AD400

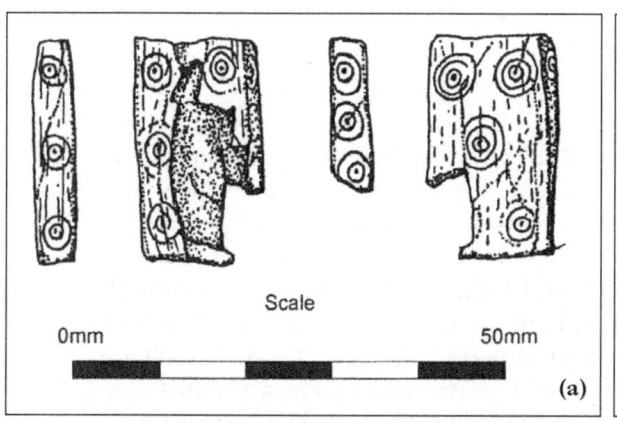

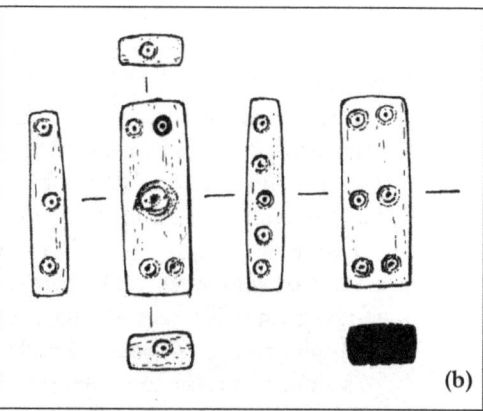

1.5 Decorated Iron Age bone dice, gaming pieces or auguries: (a) Ballyboy 1, Co. Galway, from McNamara, 2010, fig. 6; (b) Navan Fort, Co. Armagh, © Crown DfC Historic Environment Division; (c) Cush, Co. Limerick, © RIA; (d) Ballybronoge South. Co. Limerick, © J. Eogan; (e) Ballybronoge South, suggested reconstruction © C. McHale.

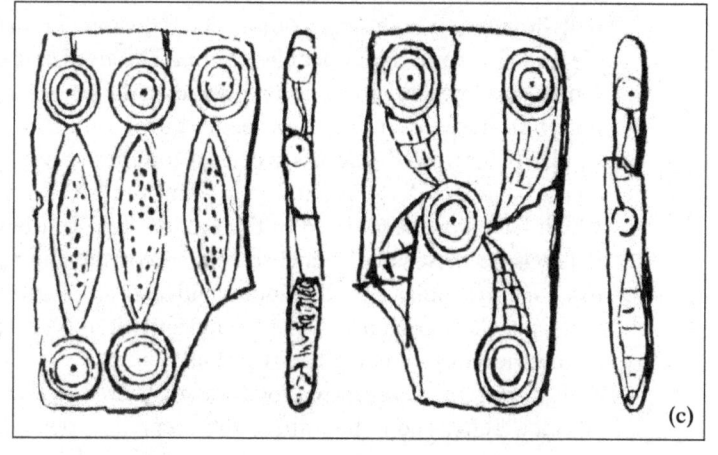

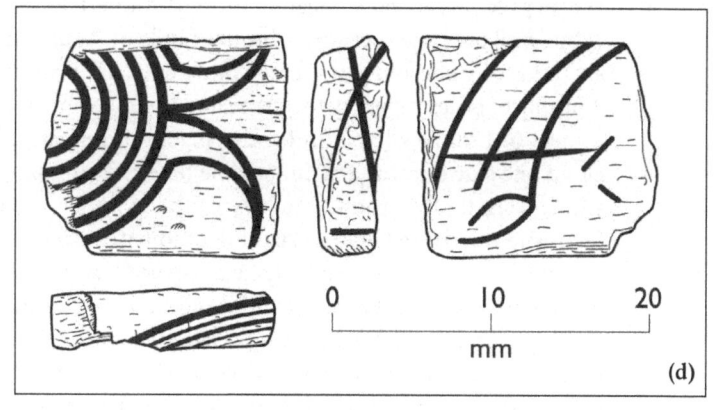

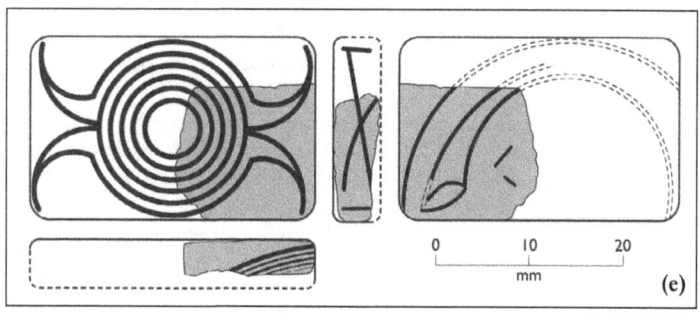

Co. Wexford (Rajic and Hardy, 2013), a cremation deposit in a small pit located outside the ring-ditch contained three fragmented copper-alloy pins which may represent the remains of fibulae.

Decorated bone or antler parallelepiped dice or gaming pieces were recovered from cremation deposits in ring-ditches at Ballyboy 1, Co. Galway (McNamara, 2010; Riddler and Trzaska-Nartouski, 2012, 132) (Figure 1.5a); Ballybronoge South, Co. Limerick (Eogan, J., 2012, 107) (Figures 1.5d, 1.5e), at T II, Cush, Co. Limerick (Ó Ríordáin, 1940, 154–6)[66] (Figure 1.5c). These dice or gaming pieces can be paralleled with an example from a non-burial context, at Navan Fort, Co. Armagh (Figure 1.5b) (Raftery, B., 1997, 94–5, Lynn, 1997, 87–8, 95), and with the three examples recovered from a double crouched burial at Knowth, Co. Meath. All are of a similar size, the example from Ballyboy 1 measures 26.3 x 15.1 x 5.4mm; Cush, 28 x 15 x 2mm; Navan Fort, 28.3 x 10.4 x 5.8mm; and the incomplete example from Ballybronoge, 13.4 x 12.1 x 3.6mm. The Ballyboy 1 cremation deposit, containing the die and six water-rolled pebbles, can be closely dated to the first century BC–first century AD,[67] which, by extension, helps date the other examples. All, except the Navan Fort non-burial example, were badly burned on the pyre. It is worth noting the similarity between the decorative motifs on these gaming pieces/dice and the motifs on the bone slips deposited at the Neolithic tomb, Cairn H, at Loughcrew, Co. Meath, which have now been dated to the second–first century BC (Vejby, 2013, 12–14).[68] Parallels for these have been observed in Scotland and England where they are dated to a roughly similar period (Riddler and Trzaska-Nartowski, 2010, xiv). While these items may have been used in a gaming context, it is also possible that they were used as auguries for foretelling future events.

A most remarkable grave good was recovered at Ballydavis Townland, Co. Laois (Keeley, 1995; 1999, 30), where the cremation deposit, dated to the fourth–first century BC,[69] centrally located in ring-ditch F1, contained a damaged bronze cylindrical box, together with a bronze fibula of Nauheim derivative-type, and eighty-six beads of stone and glass, all of which were unburnt (pers. comm., Valerie Keeley). The object is described by the excavator as consisting of a cylindrical box, comprising a sheet of bronze 38.7cm in length, 6.3cm in height, 0.8cm thick, riveted together along one side to form a cylinder. The base is a circular plate of bronze, the edges of which were folded around the base of the cylinder and crimped to hold it in place. Opposite the riveted edge, a small flat tab with two perforations was attached to the side of the box. The riveted edge was covered by a bronze mount 5.38cm in length, bearing three bosses decorated with concentric circles and containing paste or enamel. A circular iron mount, which would have been placed in a central position on the lid, measures 3.9cm diameter, and is decorated with four concentric circles of red enamel, separated by four iron ridges, surrounding a brambled central boss (Keeley, 1999, 30).[70] The description of this object is strikingly similar to the bronze box recovered from Chariot Burial 2 at Wetwang, Yorkshire (Dent, 1985, 88–90), an inhumation

---

66 Full details of these sites are available under their respective site names at www.mapping deathdb.ie. 67 UBA–13026 (cremated bone from deposit C34) 2026±19BP; at 2σ = 91cal BC–cal AD 47. 68 OxA–27956: 2078±26BP; at 2σ = 177–4 cal BC: OxA–27957: 2108±25BP; at 2σ = 197–53 cal BC. 69 GrA–13594: 2140±50BP; at 2σ = 359–47 cal BC (at 71.1% probability = 261–47 cal BC). 70 An image of this box is currently unavailable for publication.

burial of a young female (burial 454), dated to the fourth–third century BC[71] (Jay, Haselgrove, et al., 2012, 170, Table 1), within a square-ditched enclosure, accompanied by an elaborate cart, an iron pin, a mirror and a bronze box with a chain attached (Plate 3).[72] It is described by the excavator as 'a closed cylinder made from sheet bronze with the ends crimped into position around the rim. The centre of each end bears a roundel of red enamel and the whole surface of the ends and the circumference is treated with incised curvilinear ornament. A chain is attached to the circumference by a riveted loop, and a second loop exists in one face'. Plate XXI accompanying the Dent article gives a diameter for the object of 90mm, which is close to the diameter of 110mm (Keeley, 1995) for the Ballydavis object. These artefacts were recovered from what are obviously two very different burial types: the Ballydavis example was placed into a cremation deposit within a circular enclosure, located near the centre of Ireland, and the Wetwang example accompanied an inhumation burial in a cart, within a square enclosure, located in Yorkshire in the north-east of Britain. The only common denominator is the presence of the almost identical bronze cylindrical boxes. As the female at Wetwang is now known to have been born locally (Jay, Montgomery et al., 2013) it is possible that the box in her grave is of British manufacture. The place of origin for the person cremated at Ballydavis is unknown, raising the possibility that the accompanying box was an import from Britain, or that the cremated person was an immigrant from Britain. It is, of course, possible that both objects reflect trading connections with mainland Europe, and that both have a common European origin.

Part of a bronze mirror handle with traces of red enamel recovered from the cremation deposit, dated to the second–first century BC, in mound 13 at Kiltierney, Co. Fermanagh (Foley, 1988; 2014, 863; Murphy and Ó Donnabháin, forthcoming), has been compared to British examples of roughly the same period from Old Warden in Bedfordshire and Holcombe in Dorset (McHugh and Scott, 2014, 130–2). At Stoneyford, Co. Kilkenny, a bronze mirror covered the glass urn which contained a cremation.

Miscellaneous artefacts, including objects with no known parallels and metal scraps, have been recovered from among cremation deposits at several sites. In the fill of ring-ditch F3 at Ballydavis Townland were glass beads, decorated bone fragments and a possible bone hilt-guard from a small sword or dagger (Keeley, 1999, 29, 32).[73] At Ask, Co. Wexford (Stevens, 2007, 35–46; 2012, 49–60), an undated cremation deposit in a pit, within enclosure E, produced an insular gilded copper-alloy cross-shaped mount, possibly part of a harness, dateable to around the eighth century AD.

Finally, many of the cremation deposits that contained identifiable artefacts have also produced fragments of copper alloy and/or iron. Numerous iron nails recovered at Ferns Lower (Ryan, 2012) appear to be associated with the plank lining of the ditch. Bronze rivets and other fragments of iron and bronze were recovered from the cremation deposit in mound 13 at Kiltierney (Foley, 1988, 26; 2014, 863), and one tiny bronze knobbed rod or toggle, and three fragments of a striated bronze armlet

---

71 OxA–14113; 2227±30BP; at 2σ = 390–200 cal BC (at 75.5% probability = 329–204 cal BC).
72 This item is now lodged in the Hull and East Riding Museum: Hull Museums (Accession No. KINCM:2010.8.38), who have generously supplied the image.   73 Unfortunately, no illustrations of these objects are available.

were recovered in the cremation deposit in the fosse at Oranbeg, Co. Galway. Four possible corroded iron nails were recovered from a cremation deposit in a small pit outside the ring-ditch at Coolnahorna 3, Co. Wexford (Rajic and Hardy, 2013).

It is worth noting that several cremation deposits contained artefacts that were unburnt, including the beads, fibula and bronze box from Ballydavis Townland (pers. comm., V. Keeley). The reason for this ritual is unknown, but it might represent recognition of the importance and possible wealth of the individuals who were cremated by publicly including valuable personal items when burying the cremation deposit, or it could represent a symbol of identity or status.

The evidence indicates that many of the artefacts in Irish cremation deposits were imports. They confirm that in the Iron Age the Irish were not insular but continued their age-old practices of interacting and trading with the outside world. A further explanation for the appearance of these imported grave goods may relate to an influx of new settlers from Britain or perhaps further afield, who have become absorbed into, and have adopted the burial practices of, the indigenous population.

IRON AGE PYRE SITES

There are two methods of cremation: the first method, known as *ustrina*, is the familiar practice whereby the body is cremated on a pyre built directly on the ground surface, after which the remains may be collected and buried elsewhere, or left to be dispersed by the elements; the second method, known as *bustum*, is a less familiar practice whereby the pyre is built over a pit grave, and the cremated remains which fall into the pit are left *in situ* (Philpot, 1991, 48, n. 1;[74] O'Brien, 1996, 24; 1999, 11).

Despite extensive excavation in Ireland in recent years, evidence for pyre sites is rare. This is not unusual. For example, in Britain, where in excess of 10,000 cremation burials have been excavated over the past century, no more than 100 pyre sites are known, some of which are Bronze Age (McKinley, 1997, 132).

The currently recognised sparse evidence for Irish Iron Age pyre sites includes areas of burnt ground associated with charcoal and fragments of cremated bone located beneath the interior of ring-ditches Tumulus II and Tumulus III at Cush, Co. Limerick (Ó Riordán, 1940, 137, 139); two small areas of burnt ground, which may represent the remains of pyre sites beneath the Iron Age mound (Site 2) at Rathdooney Beg, Co. Sligo (Mount, 1999, 352); and a pyre site excavated at Rockfield, Co. Kerry, which contained charcoal and cremated bone, dated to 390–60 cal BC (at 2σ), placing it in the Early Iron Age (Collins and Lynch, 2001, 494; Connolly, 2000). Three linear shallow probable pyre pits, measuring on average 2.85m x 0.62m x 0.23m deep, with evidence for intense burning, containing charcoal and fragments of burnt bone, were excavated in 1999 at Ballyvelly, Co. Kerry (Dunne, 1998; 1999, 10–11). One of the pits (C63) has produced a date placing it in the third to fifth century AD.[75] These linear

---

[74] (Festus.29) '*bustum proprie dicitur, in quo mortuus est combustus et sepultus...ubi vero compustus quis tantummodo, alibi vero est speultus, is locus ab urendo ustrina vocatur ...*' my translation: ('that in which a dead person is cremated and buried is properly called a *bustum*; where, however, someone is only cremated, but is buried elsewhere, that place is called an *ustrina* from [the word for] burning (*urendum*)'). [75] UCD 9914: 1670±50BP; at 2σ = cal AD 244–535; at 84.4% probability = cal AD

pyre pits could belong to the category termed *bustum*, but in the Ballyvelly instance the pits appear to have been cleared of debris and re-used. Sixteen cremation deposits in small pits, not dated, were located within a 25m radius of these latter probable cremation pyre pits, in what appears to be a flat or field cemetery. As the Ballyvelly pyre-cremation features were located downslope from the hillfort of Knockanacuig which produced c14 dates ranging from the later Bronze Age to the Early Medieval period, it is possible that those involved in their use were part of the population which occupied the hillfort.[76] The paucity of evidence for pyre sites in Ireland suggests that in many cases the pyre was probably built directly on to the ground surface, which would come under the category of *ustrina*. Evidence obtained from experimental pyre cremations has shown that when the pyre had collapsed, and all subsequent ceremonial activity had been completed, a pyre constructed on a flat ground surface would leave only ephemeral traces of its existence, which were then easily eradicated by soil erosion, ploughing, or other disturbance (McKinley, 1997, 134). It is possible that pyre material may have been partially retrieved by the community or relatives, and the remainder simply consigned to the elements.

While we cannot know what preparation and ritual was involved in the construction of an Irish Iron Age pyre, we might get some impression by examining how English Christians understood the funerary rites of their pagan ancestors. An example is the fantastic and anachronistic view of Beowulf's pyre (lines 3137–49):

> The Geat race then reared up for him
> a funeral pyre. It was not a petty mound,
> but shining mail-coats and shields of war
> and helmets hung upon it, as he had desired.
> Then the heroes, lamenting, laid out in the middle
> their great chief, their cherished lord.
> On top of the mound the men then kindled
> the biggest of funeral-fires. Black wood-smoke
> arose from the blaze, and the roaring of flames
> mingled with weeping. The winds lay still
> as the heat at the fire's heart consumed
> the house of bone. And in heavy mood
> they uttered their sorrow at the slaughter of their lord.
> (Translation, © Michael Alexander, 1973, 2001, 150)

As the cremated burial deposits considered in the pages above represent a minute proportion of the general population and are probably representative of an elite, what then of the remainder of the population? One can only assume that, after cremation, their remains were either disposed of by being spread on the land, as was the case at Ballymacaward, Co. Donegal, where a cremation deposit, spread on the ground on the periphery of the mound, produced a date between the second and fourth century AD[77] (O'Brien, 2000, 56–61: O'Brien and Bhreathnach, 2011, 53–64). Similarly, at

244–435. Thanks to Laurence Dunne for providing dating information. **76** Laurence Dunne provided the dating information for the hillfort, for which the writer is grateful. **77** UB-4425:

Tara, a cremation deposit dated to the fourth–third century BC[78] appears to have been scattered onto the surface of a Bronze Age ring-ditch in close proximity to the Mound of the Hostages (O'Sullivan, 2005, 53). Otherwise cremation deposits were buried in a flat or field cemetery not associated with a burial monument, and therefore invisible in the landscape, or, left at the place of cremation to be dispersed by the elements, or deposited into water. In these circumstances, such remains, unless discovered accidently, are unlikely to be revealed by archaeological investigation.

CONTINUING USE OF CREMATION AFTER AD400

Archaeological and literary evidence exists which confirms that the practice of cremation did not cease completely with the introduction of inhumation in the fourth or fifth century AD. After the introduction of Christianity in the fifth century, cremation was viewed as a pagan rite.

An Irish cremation pyre is anachronistically referenced by Muirchú, who, when writing in the seventh century,[79] describes Patrick's intention, on his return to Ireland in the fifth century, to seek out his pagan slave master Miliucc in order to buy his freedom and convert Miliucc to Christianity. When, however, Miliucc heard of this he decided to act in order to avoid conversion, ... *et in domu in qua prius habitauerat rex congregato ad se omni instrumento substantiae suae incensus est...* ('He gathered all his wealth together in the house where until then he had lived as king and burnt himself along with it'). Patrick reputedly witnessed this, ... *Stans autem sanctus Patricius in praedicto loco a latere dextero montis Miss, ubi primum illam regionem in qua seruiuit cum tali gratia adeuniens uidit ... ilico sub oculis rogum regis incensum intuitus ...* ('Holy Patrick, standing in the said place on the right flank of Slíab Miss, from which, on his return full of grace, he had the first view of the district where he had lived as a slave ... he at once saw, right under his eyes, the pyre of the king') (*Muirchú*, I 12 (11), Bieler, 1979, 80–1). It is possible to infer from this passage that Miliucc's possessions were placed on his pyre, which appears to have been erected in his house, which at that time would have been constructed of wood and wattle thus making it ideal for burning. The possessions placed on the pyre would undoubtedly have consisted of jewellery, clothes fasteners, organic/vegetable material, perhaps exotic clothing, leather, wooden objects and even portions of animals.

That cremation in Ireland was regarded as a non-Christian rite is further confirmed when, according to Muirchú, Patrick is reputed to have commented ... *Nescio Deus scit, hic homo rex, qui se ipsum igni tradidit ne crederet in fine uitae suae et ne seruiret Deo aeterno ...* ('I know not, God knows, this man and king, who chose to burn himself in fire rather than believe at the end of his life and serve eternal God') (*Muirchú*, I 12 (11) (3), Bieler, 1979, 80–1). Another indication that cremation was regarded as a pagan rite is contained in a further anachronistic passage in Tírechán's *Collectanea*, written in the seventh century, describing a visit by Patrick to a well which was honoured by the druids, where he was told by the *increduli* (the pagans or infidels):

1804±51BP; at 2σ = cal AD 83–343. 78 GrA-17294: 2255±30BP; at 2σ = cal 396-208BP.
79 Archaeological evidence confirms that cremation continued to be practised as a minority rite in

... *quidam profeta mortuus fecit bibliothicam sibi in aqua sub petra, ut dealbaret ossa sua semper, quia timuit ignis exust (ion)em* ... ('a certain prophet [now] dead made a compartment for himself in the water under the stone, so that it should always bleach his bones, because he feared burning by fire')[80] (*Tírechán*, 39 (3); Bieler, 1979, 152–3). The 'wise man' in question appears to have been a pagan who feared cremation. A further reference to the use of cremation is contained in a note in the late seventh–early eighth-century *Collectio canonum Hibernensis* at XLIV, Cap. 20, *De nominee basilicae et ejus scissura* ('Concerning the name of a basilica and its splitting (or cutting)') which states ... 'Basilion is king in Greek, rex in Latin and hence basilica, royal, acquired its name, because in early days great kings used to be buried in it; for other men were disposed of either by fire or under a cairn of stones' (Wasserschleben, 1885, 179).

For a seventh- or eighth-century audience (whether readers or listeners) to understand references to cremation, it would have been necessary that they be familiar with the concept. This would not have presented a problem, because we are now aware that cremation continued to be practised in Ireland, admittedly by this time as a minority rite, into the Christian/Early Medieval period. For example, at Carrickmines Great, Co. Dublin, a clay-lined pit located close to a waterhole contained the cremated remains of a human femur, dated to the fourth to sixth century AD[81] (Ó Drisceoil, 2007, 23, 27: Ó Drisceoil and Devine, 2012, 249–66). At Furness, Co. Kildare, a token human cremation deposit at the base of a post-hole, centrally located within an annular ring-ditch, produced a date between the fifth–sixth century AD[82] (Grogan, 1984, 298–316). At Inchinclare, Co. Limerick, a pit containing a token amount of human cremated bone produced a date in the fourth–sixth century AD[83] (Grogan et al., 2007, 284–5). At Glebe South, Co. Dublin (Carroll, et al., 2008, 113), a pit (C143) inside ring-ditch 1 contained a small token human cremation deposit (C144), charcoal from which has been dated to between the third–fifth centuries AD.[84] And at Ask, Co. Wexford (Stevens, 2007, 35–46; 2012, 49–60), human cremated bone from two separate pits, one within and one outside enclosure E, have produced dates in the seventh–eighth centuries AD.[85] At the latter site a further undated pit with a cremation deposit, within enclosure E, contained a gilded copper-alloy cross-shaped mount, likely part of a harness, which could be described as broadly Insular eighth century AD.[86]

Evidence that the rite of cremation was practiced in parallel with the rite of extended inhumation is confirmed at two locations: Prumplestown, Co. Kildare (Clark and Long, 2010), where a cremation deposit (c1042), dated to the fourth–sixth centuries AD[87] was uncovered in a floodplain at the base of a ridge containing four extended inhumations. And at Annaghilla (Site 4), Co. Tyrone, where a small Iron Age annular ring-ditch with a central pit containing a cremation deposit of an adult female, dated second–first century BC,[88] together with four cremation deposits in pits

---

Ireland up to at least the eighth century.   80 Translation by Charles-Edwards, 2000, 47.   81 GrA–29944: 1625±35BP; at 2σ = cal AD 347–538.   82 GrA–10472: 1540±30BP; at 2σ = cal AD 426–588.   83 UB–6053: 1612±27BP; at 2σ = cal AD 393–536.   84 Beta–229059: 1690±50BP; at 2σ (92.0%) = cal AD 231–432 (re-calibrated using Ox Cal 4.2).   85 Pit C545, central within enclosure E: SUERC–32851: 1330±30BP; at 2σ = cal AD 649–767: and pit C350 (outside enclosure), SUERC–31627: 1290±30BP; at 2σ = cal AD 664–770.   86 Pers. comm., Susan Youngs.   87 SUERC–25396: 1600±50BP; at 2σ = cal AD 344–569.   88 SUERC–21308: 2090±30BP; at 2σ = 195–46 cal BC.

and gullies dating to roughly the same period, was later enclosed within an Early Medieval settlement cemetery with twenty-three (undated)[89] extended inhumations. Both the Iron Age and the Early Medieval enclosures at this site continued to be used for the insertion of at least twelve cremation deposits from the fifth–sixth century AD,[90] up until the seventh–ninth century.[91] These dates correspond with dates from occupation features within the settlement cemetery enclosure. For example, oak charcoal from a pit has been dated sixth–seventh century AD;[92] other dates for occupation material at the site range from the seventh to ninth century. These cremated human bones have been dated to the Early Medieval period, and is therefore not the result of the incorporation of residual Iron Age cremated bone being found in later post-holes and pits. The people who occupied this site continued to use the rite of cremation, in parallel with the rite of inhumation, well into the Early Medieval period.

As the ritual associated with cremation was communal and public, one can only assume that this ancient burial rite undertaken by those who still adhered to older traditions was tolerated by Church authorities until at least the seventh–eighth centuries.

* * *

The indigenous burial rite in Iron Age Ireland was that of cremation, but as a result of the adoption of an aceramic culture, cremation deposits (with two known exceptions) were placed not in ceramic containers, but directly into pits, in organic containers which perished over time. Consequently, it has, until recently, been difficult to recognise cremation deposits datable to the Iron Age. However, with the advent of c14 dating of cremated bone, combined with examination of context, and cross-comparison of the limited range of grave goods in some cremation deposits, this difficulty has eased, and the recognition of Irish Iron Age cremation deposits has become less problematic.

The continuing veneration and influence of ancestors is demonstrated by the re-use of ancient burial monuments, and by the construction of imitative burial monuments, often among already ancient monuments. The rarity of non-combustible grave goods in the majority of cremation deposits in Ireland does not imply lack of ceremonial regalia, or that the body on the pyre was not finely arrayed, albeit in perishable/combustible material. Where charred artefacts are present, they consist primarily of beads, in the form of tiny blue glass, blue-green glass, yellow glass, decorated glass, and occasionally amber beads. Other artefacts, some of which have not been burned, include several fibulae, dice/gaming pieces/or auguries, a bronze cylindrical box, and mirror fragments. The presence of unburnt objects in some cremation deposits indicates that after the collection of cremated remains had been

---

89 C14 dating was not possible due to the lack of skeletal remains. 90 Cremation (human bone) deposit in pit in ring-ditch: SUERC–21300: 1570±30BP; at 2σ = cal AD 416–557. 91 Cremation (human bone) deposit in post-hole in settlement cemetery enclosure: SUERC–21631: 1240±40BP; at 2σ = cal AD 680–881. 92 Oak charcoal from occupation pit: SUERC–21328: 1420±30BP; at 2σ = cal AD 582–661.

undertaken, these objects were interred along with the cremation deposit, perhaps in a ritualistic fashion. Many of the artefacts recovered were imported, and this provides evidence for interaction and trading by the inhabitants of Ireland with the outside world. The presence of imported objects might also be indicative of an influx of settlers who became absorbed into, and adopted, the burial practices of the indigenous population.

CHAPTER 2

Iron Age inhumation burial, *c*.200BC–AD200

The rite of crouched inhumation, together with cremation, was the burial rite practiced in Ireland throughout the Bronze Age, but inhumation declined during the Late Bronze Age (*c*.1000–600BC), and by the Early Iron Age (*c*.600BC) cremation had become the preferred burial option of the indigenous population.[1] The burial rite of crouched inhumation was re-introduced into Ireland in the Iron Age during a comparatively short interlude spanning the second century BC and the first century AD (Figure 2.1). This newly introduced rite was neither absorbed into, nor adopted by, the indigenous population who continued to use the burial rite of cremation (O'Brien, 2003, 65; 2009, 136–8; 2017a, 261).

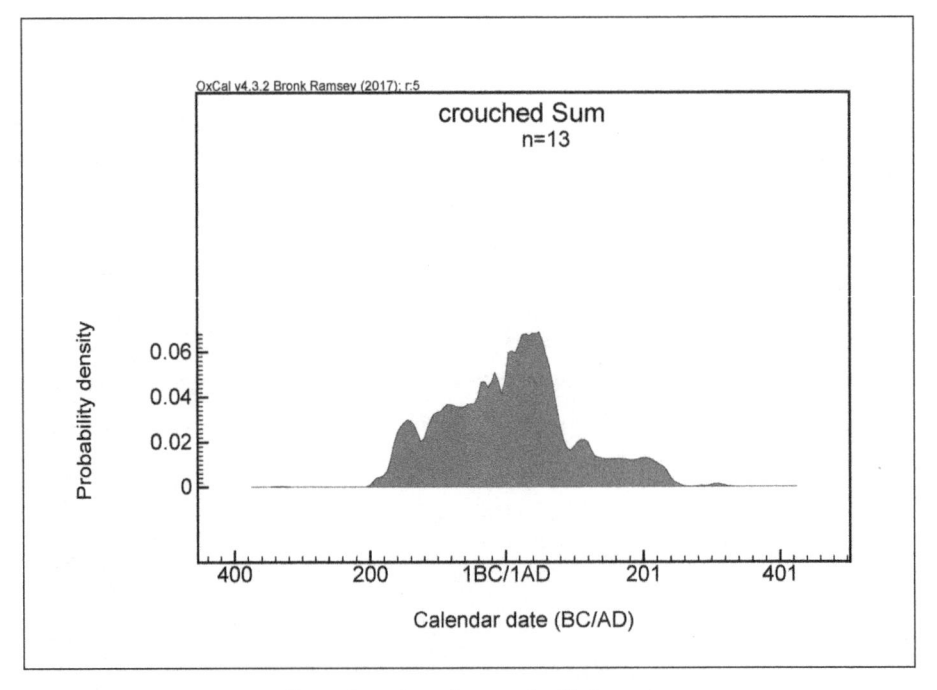

2.1 Sum of c14 dates for crouched inhumations.

---

[1] There are some examples of Late Bronze Age crouched inhumation, including that of an isolated male burial at Mullamast, Co. Kildare, dated to the eighth–fifth century BC (Hackett and Twomey, 2010), and a possible Late Bronze Age/Early Iron Age example is an adult crouched inhumation, with evidence of stab wounds to the chest, dated fifth–third (probably fifth–fourth) century BC, recently located and excavated outside a Bronze Age wedge tomb at Parknabinnia, Co. Clare (Ros Ó Maoldúin, pers. comm.).

Iron Age inhumation burial, c.200BC–AD200 35

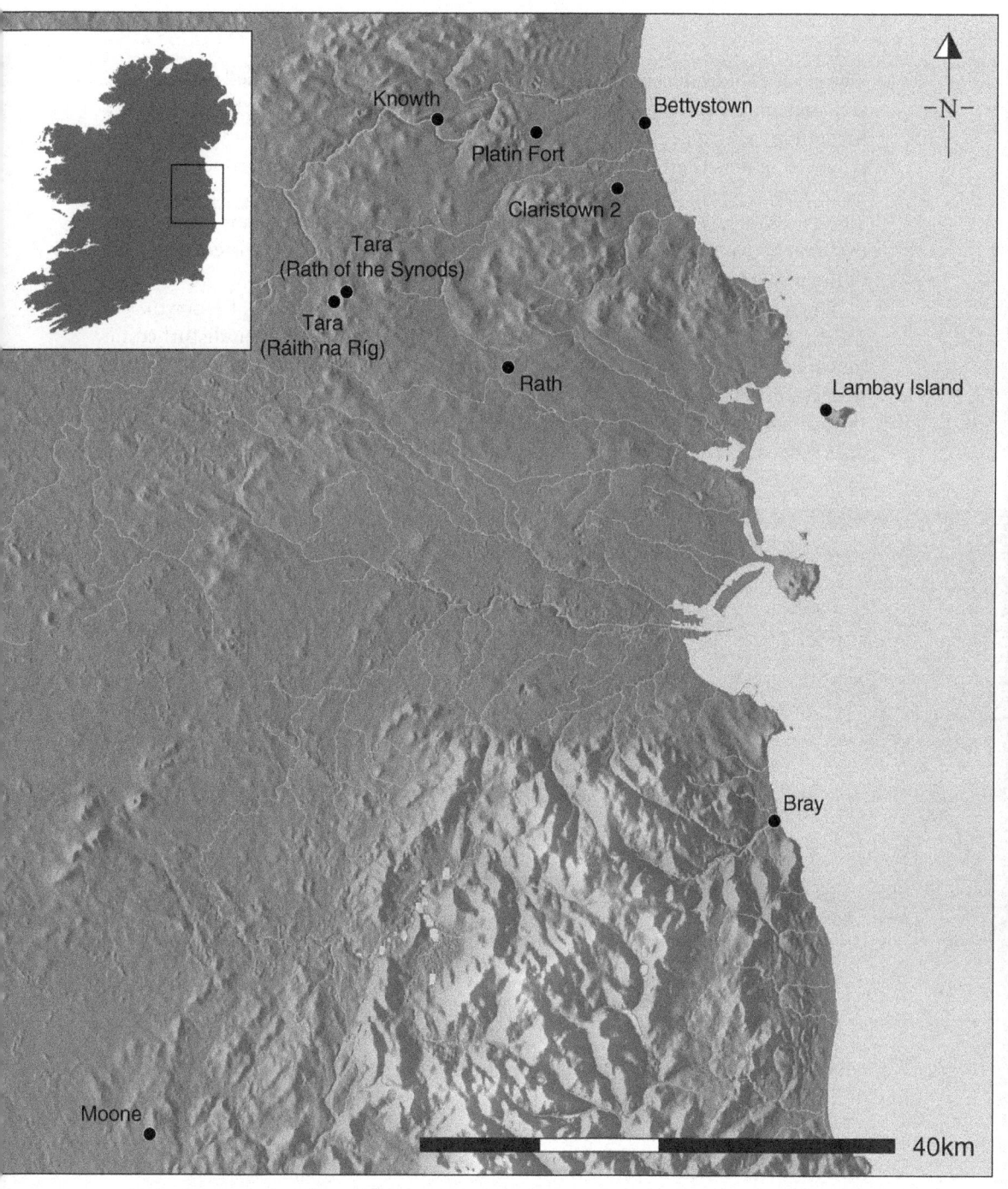

Map 3 Distribution of Iron Age crouched and extended inhumations, © The Discovery Programme and EOB.

CROUCHED INHUMATION

The newly re-introduced crouched burial rite was limited to a confined geographical area stretching from south of the River Liffey, northward to the River Boyne (Map 3). Strontium and oxygen isotope analysis undertaken on teeth from several of these crouched inhumations indicates that while some of the individuals concerned were local, many originated from north-eastern Britain (Cahill Wilson et al., 2014, 127–49). This conclusion is not unexpected, as burial in a crouched position was the common tradition in that region of Britain during this Iron Age period (Whimster, 1981, 194; O'Brien, 1999, 1).

When the primary use of the Neolithic passage grave complex at Knowth, Co. Meath, ceased at the start of the Bronze Age, the monument lay undisturbed for millennia. However, in the Iron Age it was re-used for burial with the insertion of fourteen crouched inhumations in and around the satellite tombs which surrounded the main monument (Figure 2.2) (Eogan, G., 2012; O'Brien, 2012, 61–71; McGarry, 2012, 689–94). This re-use of an indigenous burial monument, especially after such

2.2 Distribution of Iron Age crouched burials, Knowth, Co. Meath.
Composite image based on Google Earth and G. Eogan, 2012, fig. 2.1, © RIA.

Iron Age inhumation burial, c.200 BC–AD 200

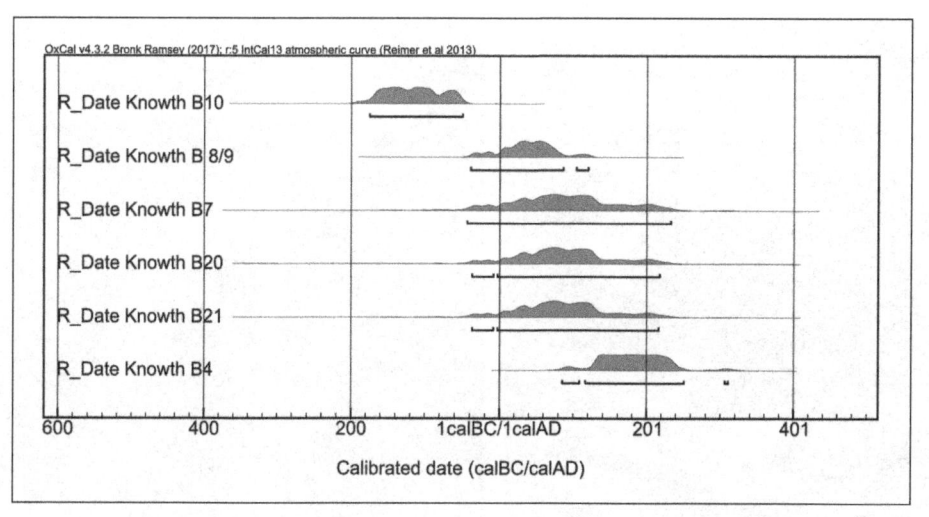

2.3 c14 date sequence for Knowth Iron Age burials.

a long temporal lapse, is indicative of a new group moving into the district and using this ancient necropolis as a portal to the otherworld, thereby making contact with the indigenous ancestors, probably as a means of claiming control of the region.

Unusually, the earliest dated burial in this Knowth group (B10), a crouched female (Figure 2.5b), with no grave goods, dated to the second–first century BC,[2] was born locally (Cahill Wilson, 2012, 782). This local woman had been buried by people who were familiar with a burial rite which was alien to the indigenous population. Perhaps she was buried here to create a link between a people newly arrived in the area and the indigenous ancestors, presenting a possible example of integration.

The dated burials in this group centre mainly during the first century AD (Figure 2.3) and include a double crouched burial of two decapitated males (B8–9), dated to between the first century BC and second century AD,[3] accompanied by three bone dice, twelve gaming pieces (pegs),

2.4 Burial B7, Knowth, Co. Meath, © RIA and G. Eogan.

---

2 GrN–15372: 2095±20BP; at 2σ = 175–50 cal BC. 3 GrN–15371: 1960±30BP; at 2σ = 40 cal BC–cal AD 121.

2.5 Burials (a) B4, (b) B10, Knowth, Co. Meath, © RIA and G. Eogan.

twenty-one small water-rolled pebbles, and two bronze rings (Eogan, 2012, 23–6).[4] These individuals have produced strontium and oxygen measurements establishing that they probably originated in the northern part of Britain (Cahill Wilson et al., 2012, 775–87). A crouched female child (B7) (Figure 2.4), aged about 7 years, with no grave goods, dated to between the first century BC–third century AD,[5] was not born in the local area, but probably in northern or south-eastern Britain. Crouched burial (B21), a young adult male, dated to the first century BC–third century AD,[6] who was buried with grave goods including six copper rings and 272 glass (mainly blue) beads, was not of local origin (Eogan, 2012, 33–5; Cahill Wilson and Standish, 2016, 237). A flexed and splayed, prone, female (B4), dated to the first–third century AD,[7] had a large stone placed over her head, and this unusual disposition, lying on the ground surface, suggests that her body had been hastily disposed of. The prone disposition, and lack of a grave-cut, together with being weighted down with a large stone, suggests

---

4 While artefacts of this nature could be associated with gambling, they could also be associated with divination, or occult practices. 5 GrN–15370: 1920±60BP; at 2σ = 43 cal BC–cal AD 232. 6 GrN–15395: 1921±50BP; at 2σ (91.0% probability) = 4 cal BC–cal AD 217. 7 GrN–15369: 1830±30BP; at 2σ = cal AD 86–253.

that she may have been feared as a revenant, and that her body was disposed of in this manner to prevent her returning to haunt the living (Figure 2.5a). She was likely to have been born locally, but she may have come from further afield (Cahill Wilson et al., 2014, 141–2). This woman was accompanied by forty-three blue glass beads, indicating a probable relationship within the local population.

Most of the remaining identified crouched burials at Knowth, which included three further juveniles aged around 6–7 years, were accompanied in some cases by hundreds of blue glass beads. One of these child burials (B20) has been dated to around the turn of the first century BC–second century AD.[8] The beads included in the burials at Knowth may have been suspended on string, or they may have been stitched to clothing in designs representing group identification.

It is probably coincidental, but the positioning of these Iron Age crouched burials around the main Neolithic tomb at Knowth, is reminiscent of the positioning of Iron Age cremation deposits in small mounds around the destroyed Neolithic tomb at Kiltierney, Co. Fermanagh.

2.6 Burial F238 Betaghstown (Anchorage) Co. Meath, © J. Eogan.

At Betaghstown (Bettystown), Co. Meath (Anchorage site) (Eogan, J., 2010, 106), a female crouched inhumation (F238), dated to the second–first century BC,[9] was interred in an unenclosed multi-period secular cemetery located on a ridge overlooking the Irish Sea. This woman had a large stone placed overlying her abdomen, the purpose of which may have been to 'contain' her within the grave, possibly to prevent her spirit returning to haunt the living (Figure 2.6). Strontium and oxygen isotopic analysis of a tooth indicates that this woman originated in south-eastern Scotland or Yorkshire (with a slight possibility of an origin in mainland Europe) (Cahill Wilson et al., 2014, 139). Nearby, a crouched inhumation of a juvenile (F155), undated, is presumed by the excavator to be contemporary with the female.

At Rath, Co. Meath (Schweitzer, 2005, 93–8), a crouched female burial was inserted through the fill in the southern section of the Iron Age ring-ditch referred to in the previous chapter as containing cremation deposits in the northern section

---

8 GrN–13595: 1920±50BP; at 2σ = 38 cal BC–cal AD 219 (at 91.3% probability = 4 cal BC–AD 219).
9 UBA–13072: 2057±25BP; at 2σ = 165 cal BC–cal AD 3 (c14 date obtained courtesy of the Mapping Death Project).

of the ditch. This woman is unique in an Irish context in that she had three copper-alloy rings on her toes. Two of the rings are spiral, one on each foot, and appear to be attachments for sandals, but the third ring, on the toe next to the little toe on the right foot, appears to be purely decorative, with a herring-bone motif (commonly associated with Roman contexts) similar to the decoration on a silver earring or finger ring (Figure 4.10) found with a flexed female burial at Rossnaree, Co. Meath, dated to the third–sixth century AD (probably fourth–fifth century) (Cahill and Sikora, 2011, 113–20).[10] Unfortunately, the skeletal material from Rath was too degraded to produce a c14 date, but the method of deposition, crouched in a ring-ditch which also contained cremation deposits, is indicative of an Iron Age date. Strontium isotope analysis of her teeth indicates that she is probably of local origin (Montgomery et al., 2006), and like B10 at Knowth is possibly an example of some integration between local and incoming people.

Female burials accompanied by a toe ring are rare. The closest parallel for the female burial at Rath, Co. Meath, appears to be a female burial with a toe ring on each foot recovered in an Iron Age ironworking milieu at Mine Howe in Orkney (Card et al., 2005, 322–7). There are, however, known instances of male burials accompanied by a single toe ring at this period. Examples include a flexed male burial (GS7) at Garton Station, Yorks (Stead, 1991, 33, 291); at Poundbury, Dorset, a contracted male burial (432), dated 50 BC–AD 50, had a copper-alloy spiral ring on one toe (Farwell and Molleson, 1993, 93, 267); and three male burials in the War Cemetery at Maiden Castle, Dorset, each had a single toe ring (Wheeler, 1943, Figure 92, 1–3). These single toe rings, which are attachments for a sandal, represent the wearing of a single sandal which is a motif of great antiquity, the earliest depictions of which one is aware appear on cylinder seals of the Neo-Babylonian period (c.1000–539BC) (Eisenberg, 1998, 15–16, Figures 33, 34, 35).[11] The motif has been described in an Irish context as follows: 'an international motif of kingship was the man of one sandal, the man who would be king' (Doherty, 1998, 296–7; O'Brien, 1999a, 21, 57). This could hardly be applied to the female from Rath. However, considering the similarity in the decoration of the third toe ring at Rath and the possible earring associated with the female burial at Rossnaree, together with the fact that both individuals are local to the area in which they are buried, these rings may represent a familial tribal affiliation or identity, or the status of a queen or prophetess.

Analysis of the thirty-six Iron Age crouched inhumations identified in Ireland has produced an unusual result indicating that infants make up 25%, and young juveniles 22%, i.e. 47% of the total number of burials (Table 2.1).

Excavation across a section of the rock-cut, 3m deep, ditch enclosing the monument known as Ráith na Ríg (the Enclosure of the Kings) at Tara, Co. Meath, revealed a burial of a crouched infant, about six months old (F103), accompanied by disarticulated dog bones and covered by clumps of clay (Roche, 2002, 45). Dates obtained for animal bone retrieved from layers above the burial produced a date in the first–second century AD.[12] A c14 date obtained from skeletal material from the

10 GrA–24354: 1660±40BP; at 2σ = cal AD 256–534 (at 76.2% probability = cal AD 317–434).
11 These seals formed part of an exhibition of Near Eastern cylinder seals arranged by Sidney Babcock, at the Pierpoint Morgan Library, New York, in 1998, of which I was privileged to have an individual viewing.   12 UB–4480: 1890±20BP; at 2σ (92.9%) = cal AD 62–170.

Table 2.1 Iron Age crouched inhumations

Identification	Number	Percentage
Male	6	17%
Female	9	25%
Adult (sex unknown)	4	11%
Infant	9	25%
Juvenile	8	22%
Total	36	100%

infant burial[13] confirmed that he/she was buried in the first century BC to first century AD.[14] Strontium and oxygen isotope analysis of a tooth indicates that the infant was born locally (Cahill Wilson and Standish, 2016, 233). It has been suggested (Dowling, 2006, 29–31) that the deep rock-cut ditch of Ráith na Ríg represents a sacred boundary, a liminal space into which the crouched infant was placed, perhaps as a sacrifice related to the fertility of the land and of the tribe. It could also be possible that it is a foundation sacrifice. The dog bones accompanying the burial could be interpreted as perhaps a dog guarding the infant, or alternatively as a special food or sacrificial offering (Bhreathnach, 2002, 117–22). Dates obtained from samples at various levels of the ditch fill indicate that the ditch of the enclosure at Ráith na Ríg was used and re-used from the second century BC[15] to the fifth century AD.[16]

During excavations at Tlachtga, The Hill of Ward, Co. Meath[17] (Moore, 2014:026), a trench opened across a rock-cut ditch surrounding a 30m circular enclosure, which had in turn been cut by the southern outer enclosure of the quadrivallate monument of Tlachtga,[18] contained the burial of a 3–5 month-old child, dated to the fifth century AD.[19] This burial, which was covered with several medium to large flat stones, was located at the base of the ditch. Cattle long-bones were also recorded at the base of the ditch. Although later than the infant burial in the ditch at Ráith na Ríg, this burial at Tlachtga may have been intended to perform a similar function.

A crouched burial of a juvenile aged 10–12 years (Burial B) was recovered in the eastern part of the Rath of the Synods, Tara (Grogan, 2008, 42). The burial has been dated to the fourth century AD.[20] However, this date ought to be treated with caution as it was not derived from skeletal material but from charcoal located close to the burial. It is, however, probable that the burial belongs in the later Iron Age. Strontium and oxygen isotope analysis indicated that this young person was born locally (Cahill Wilson, 2012, 23; Cahill Wilson and Standish, 2016, 233).

At Claristown 2, Co. Meath (Russell, 2004, 31; 2012, 268), a crouched infant burial (undated) accompanied by a pig jawbone, and covered by a large stone, was located in

---

[13] Date provided courtesy of the LIARI Project at the Discovery Programme. [14] UB–4476: 1973±28BP; at 2σ = 42cal BC–cal 78 AD. [15] UB–4479: 2105±21BP; at 2σ = 191–54 cal BC (sample from basal level-recalibrated). [16] UB–4476: 1689±16BP; calibrated at 91.7% = cal AD 330–400. [17] This excavation is part of a research project, headed by Dr Stephen Davis, Dept of Archaeology, University College Dublin. [18] Tlachtga is located, like Tara, in the ancient kingdom of Mide, and was regarded as an important assembly place. [19] Full details of radiocarbon date awaited. [20] UBA–8533: 1691±20BP; at 2σ = cal AD 260–405; at 87.3% probability = cal AD 325–405.

a sunken hearth within a demolished possible Iron Age hut structure. Located close to the structure, a burial of an adult male (B14), dated to the second–fifth century AD,[21] covered by a cairn, and centrally located within a ring-ditch, was considered by the excavator to be Iron Age, but ought to be assigned to the Early Medieval period on morphological grounds and date.

A single crouched burial of a juvenile aged around 3 years, in an unprotected dug grave, dated to the second–fourth century AD,[22] was recovered on the western side of the summit of an inland limestone outcrop known as Platin Fort, Duleek, Co. Meath (Conway, 2003, 316–17).[23] The fact that Platin Fort is located on a rocky promontory and has also produced charcoal dating to the Neolithic period might indicate that it was perceived as a liminal or sacred place.

On at least two, and perhaps three, occasions between the second century BC and the first century AD, five crouched infant burials were interred in small circular pits at an unusual field site on the lower slopes of Mullamast Hill, in the townland of Moone, Co. Kildare (Lenihan and Dennehy, 2010). The townland boundary between Mullamast and Moone runs along the northern perimeter of the field. The site is unusual in that it consisted mainly of a dense series of roasting-pits, dating from the Bronze Age through to the Iron Age, and post-holes, with some evidence for at least two flimsy circular structures (Figure 2.7). Large quantities of animal bone were recovered throughout the site, and evidence for iron smelting was revealed in the south-eastern quadrant. The earliest burials are SK 8 (129) and SK 5 (405) (Figure 2.8). SK 8, a crouched infant, aged less than one year, dated to the second–first century BC,[24] was located towards the centre of the site, and was accompanied by a copper-alloy ring and a single unburnt mammal shaft; no pathologies were noted on the infant. SK 5, a crouched infant, aged 0–6 months, also dated second–first century BC,[25] was located in the north-western section of the site as were the remainder of the infant burials. The next episode of burial comprised of SK 2 (290), a crouched infant aged 3–6 months, dated to the first century BC–first century AD.[26] This infant, who was accompanied by a copper-alloy ring, an iron ring, a small off-cut of antler, and thirteen fragments of animal bone, displayed evidence for systemic infection. SK 6 (411), a crouched neonate, dated to the first century BC–first century AD,[27] was protected by a large flat stone. Perhaps of a slightly later date, SK 4 (322), an infant aged 2–3 months, dated to the first century BC–first century AD,[28] displayed evidence for systemic infection (Tourunen and Pálsdóttir, 2010; Troy and Lalonde, 2010). These burials at Moone present a conundrum. All these infants were buried with care, for instance, the two burials which had grave goods, SK 8 and SK 2, were also accompanied by fragments of animal bone probably representing food offerings. The extraordinary feature of these burials is that despite a significant temporal gap between the earliest and the latest interments, four are in a confined area close to the northern

---

21 Beta–185352: 1720±80BP; at 2σ = cal AD 126–535; at 90.7% probability = cal AD 126–474 (it is noted that this date covers a wide time span).   22 Beta 159656: 1800±40BP; at 2σ (95.2%) = cal AD 125–338.   23 The outcrop had been subjected to quarrying activity in the Medieval period.   24 SUERC–25245: 2075±30BP; at 2σ = 181–1 cal BC.   25 SUERC–25242: 2085±30BP; at 2σ = 193–40 cal BC.   26 SUERC–24995: 2015±30BP; at 2σ = 95 cal BC–cal AD 61.   27 SUERC–25243: 2005±30BP; at 2σ = 89 cal BC–cal AD 68.   28 SUERC–25241: 1965±30BP; at 2σ = 42 cal BC–cal AD 115.

Iron Age inhumation burial, c.200BC–AD200	43

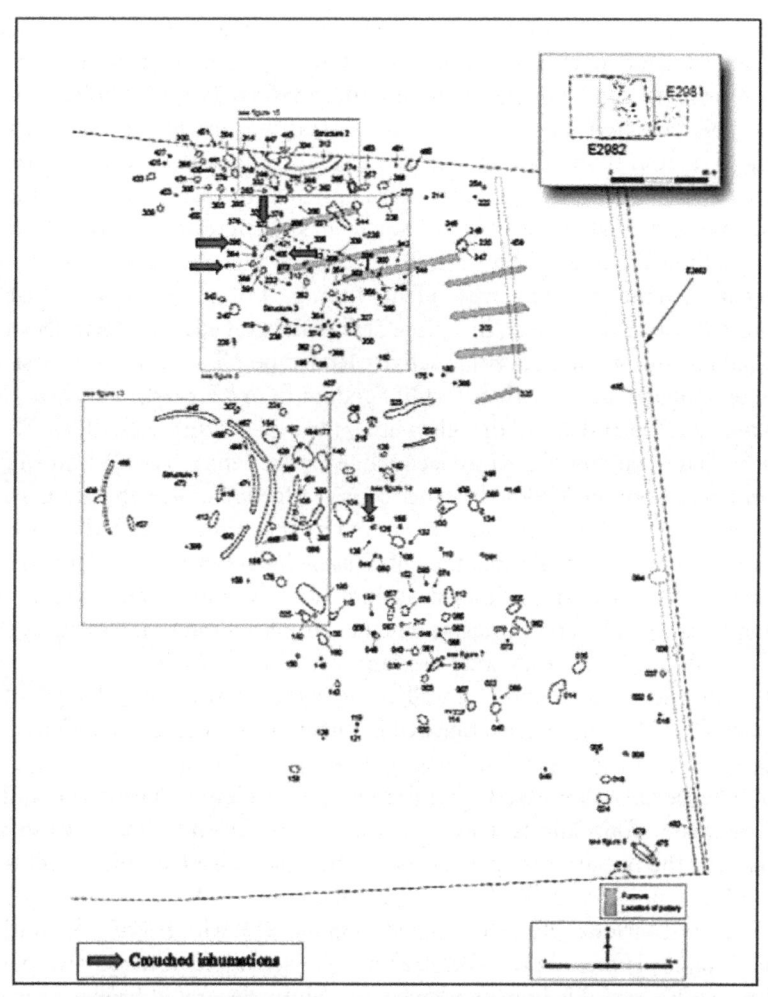

2.7 Plan of infant crouched burials, Mullamast Hill, Moone, Co. Kildare. Based on Lenihan and Dennehy, 2010, fig. 3, © Rubicon Heritage.

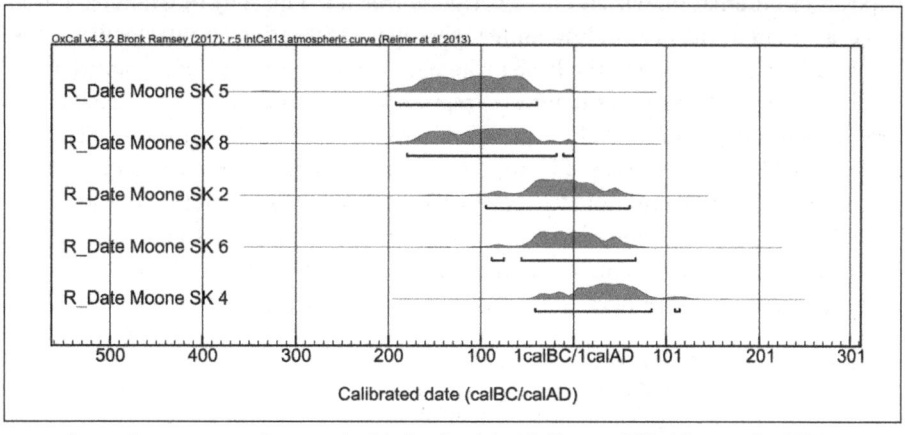

2.8 c14 date sequence for crouched infant burials, Mullamast Hill, Moone, Co. Kildare.

field boundary that also later functioned as the townland boundary between Moone and Mullamast. How does one explain this? This is a place with no evidence for permanent habitation, which appears to have been visited and utilised from time to time over millennia, perhaps for festivals and/or feasting, and for iron smelting.[29] In the event of infants dying during one of these visitations it is surely more than coincidence that generations apart they were buried at the same spot. The modern townland boundary might reflect the location of an ancient territorial boundary, or, it may reflect a liminal boundary between this world and the other world.

Taking an extreme view, did these infants form part of a fertility ritual that took place at specific times of the year, in a place deliberately set apart for festivals and/or feasting and for iron smelting (a ritual activity landscape)? The sacrifice of first-born children, or animals[30] to an earth or fertility god, in return for milk and corn-yields, anachronistically recorded in the eleventh-/twelfth-century Middle Irish text *dindshenchas* has been considered by Jacqueline Borsje (2007, 31–54) who suggests that information from the Middle Irish period is a reflection of how the pre-Christian past, based on biblical references, was viewed at that time, rather than a key to knowledge about the historical veneration of *Cenn* or *Crom Crúaich*, the deity to whom the text refers. At some future time, strontium and oxygen isotope examination of teeth from these burials might indicate whether they are local to the place in which they are buried, or whether they were brought from further afield.

In 1927, during construction of a wall at the harbour on Lambay Island, off the coast of north Co. Dublin, several crouched inhumations were uncovered (Macalister, 1929, 240–6; Rynne 1976, 231–44; Cooney, 2009, 9–22; Cahill Wilson et al., 2014b, 91–112). The burials comprised a minimum of one identifiable female and one identifiable male, four adults (sex unknown), one juvenile and one infant.[31] Accompanying the burials were grave goods including an iron sword, a shield-boss, three dolphin-type Roman fibulae, a Langton Down- and a rosette-type fibula, scabbard mounts, various rings, a decorated repoussé disc with triskele decoration, a triangular bronze plaque, a beaded bronze torc with separated beads and washers, an iron mirror with a possible bone/antler handle, and a decorated bronze bracelet.[32] These grave goods are imports and are unlike any others found either with cremation deposits or inhumation burials of the period in Ireland. This may be a familial burial place, associated within a trading milieu, perhaps representing an intermediate stop between Roman Britain and the Irish mainland, datable to the first or second century AD. Evidence that Ireland was familiar to mariners, and undoubtedly to traders, in the second century AD can be deduced from the map of Ireland produced by Claudius Ptolemaeus as part of his map of Europe *c*.AD 150, which includes place-names based on a British pronunciation of Primitive Irish names.[33] It is possible that the island named in that map as Limnos is the island now known as Lambay (Cooney, 2009, 21).

Integration between communities of newcomers who buried their dead as crouched inhumations and their indigenous contemporaries who cremated their dead is hinted

---

[29] For possible connections between burial and the role of the smith see Williams, 2012, 39–55. [30] It is perhaps worth noting that this site also contained the burial of a complete neonatal calf (Lenihan and Dennehy, 2010, 36). [31] The numbers for Lambay are based on recently located skeletal material not yet fully published. [32] The burials and associated artefacts are the subject of current research by Prof. Gabriel Cooney, UCD. [33] Professor Thomas Charles-Edwards, pers. comm.

at by the two female crouched burials, B10 from Knowth, and the burial from Rath, both of whom are local to their place of burial. Apart from B10 which can be placed in the first century BC (Figure 2.3) and may therefore indicate an initial contact with the indigenous population, the remaining burials at Knowth, who are not local to their place of burial, can be placed in the first century AD. The small number of burials involved, spaced over perhaps a century, would indicate that only a few, deemed to be of a status that enabled them to be regarded as ancestors,[34] were selected for burial in the manner of the ancestors from their homeland. The remainder, or descendants, of the group may have assimilated with the local population and were buried according to indigenous rites. It is noticeable that the only artefacts which the Knowth burials have in common with burials of the indigenous population are the ubiquitous tiny blue glass beads, which occur in very large numbers at Knowth, and are similar to blue glass beads which are also found in occasional cremation deposits. It is noticeable that the more exotic bead types associated with some cremations are absent at Knowth, as are fibulae which are present in some cremations, but are absent from crouched inhumations.[35] The evidence suggests that disparate communities adopted a distinctive form of clothing, perhaps indicating distinct social identities. This further suggests the probable presence in Ireland of two communities, who appear to have co-existed, during the period spanning the first century BC and the first century AD.

Two of the sites outlined, Knowth and Lambay Island, contain infants and juveniles in familial or communal settings, and in both cases the evidence points to non-indigenous adult occupants. Familial connections might also be applied to the juvenile buried close to the non-indigenous female at Bettystown (Anchorage), and to the juvenile at the Rath of the Synods. The remaining infants, unaccompanied by adults, present a puzzling phenomenon.

EXTENDED INHUMATION IN THE IRON AGE

The burial rite of extended inhumation has been recognised in Romano-British contexts from the second century AD onwards (Philpott, 1991, 210–16), but was, with the exception of one occurrence, unknown in Ireland at that time.

This one occurrence of extended inhumation in Iron Age Ireland is represented by a small group of inhumation burials discovered in 1835 by workmen who were erecting gateposts above the high waterline on the beach at Bray, Co. Wicklow (Map 3). This discovery is first recorded two years later, in 1837, when it is described as 'several skeletons laid side by side with a stone at the head and feet, and accompanied by coins of Trajan AD97–117 and Hadrian AD117–38 found in the thoracic region of the skeletons'[36] (Lewis, 1987, 223).[37] These individuals were buried by their peers who were familiar with the burial rite, accompanied by coins

---

[34] With the possible exception of B4 from Knowth, who may have met with a violent death.
[35] With the exception of burials at Lambay Island, which may represent a trading post. [36] It is usual that coins placed in the mouth will fall into the upper thoracic region with decomposition of the body. [37] These burials have been referred to many times in the interim (Drummond, 1844, 186–7; Scott, 1913, 41–5; Bateson, 1973, 21–79, esp. p. 35; O'Brien, 1990a, 37–42; 1992b, 132; 2009, 138; 2017b, 341–55; Warner, 1976; Raftery, B., 1981, 194–5; Cahill Wilson et al., 2014a, 129).

representing the Roman custom of including Charon's obol to enable the deceased to pay the ferryman to cross the River Styx, a custom otherwise unknown in an Ireland that did not operate a coin-based economy. These are the only known extended inhumation burials to be accompanied by coins in Ireland, an indication that the rite did not spread further at that time. As coastal erosion has been, and still is, a major problem in this part of the east coast up to the present time, it seems likely that when the Bray burials were interred, almost 2,000 years ago, the shoreline was very different to that of the nineteenth century, so that the burials could originally have been part of a dry-land cemetery, the greater part of which, has, over time, been eroded by the sea. Rather than these being shipwreck victims, as has previously been hypothesised, the evidence suggests that the persons buried at Bray perhaps represent the presence of a Romano-British trading post, or even an unofficial Roman settlement, on the coast, south of Dublin, during the early second century AD.

Several coins from the reign of Trajan and Hadrian have also been discovered at the probable Romano-British trading post located at the promontory of Drumanagh, on the coast north of Dublin (Cahill Wilson, 2014, 26); and it is recorded that a coin of either Trajan or Hadrian was recovered at Lambay Island (Cahill Wilson, Cooney et al., 2014b, 92).

DEVIANT OR ANOMALOUS IRON AGE INHUMATIONS

Deviant or anomalous burials occur in all cultures and in all eras, and the Iron Age in Ireland is no exception. Deviant burials include the two female burials already mentioned, namely the crouched female (F238) from Betaghstown (Anchorage), Co. Meath, and the prone and splayed female (B4) from Knowth, Co. Meath, both of whom had been weighted down with large stones. Both were probably feared as possible revenants.

A further deviant burial has recently been excavated in an area with evidence for prehistoric activity at Carroweighter 2, Co. Roscommon (Tobin, 2019; McIlreavy, 2018).[38] Male burial SK 1, aged 35–40 years, dated to the fourth–second century BC,[39] was buried prone, head east, in the ditch of a ring-ditch which contained a central cremation deposit dated eighth–fourth century BC,[40] and an undated spread cremated deposit. SK 1 was buried face down, with his arms outstretched above his head, a posture which did not occur naturally. His right foot had been amputated, either at death or shortly after, and placed, fully articulated, between his legs. This act was either a punishment for some misdeed, and/or as a method of preventing his becoming a revenant. This burial is unique in the Irish burial record, but is reminiscent of burial in Roman Britain where a decapitated head was often placed between the legs (O'Brien, 1999, 7). A further punitive measure inflicted on this person was that of being denied cremation, in an era where cremation was the norm, thus preventing the release of his spirit into the elements and the afterlife.

[38] Grateful thanks are due to Maeve Tobin of IAC, for providing information about, and permission to refer to, this as yet unpublished burial.   [39] UB-39768: 2169±33BP; at 2σ = cal BC361–113 (at 91.5% probability = cal BC 361–151).   [40] UB-39769: 2390±37BP; at 2σ = cal BC741–392 (at 83.6% probability = cal BC 550–392).

Anomalous burials which have been recovered at other sites include partial human remains, dated to the second century BC–first century AD,[41] recovered approximately 0.6m from the inner enclosing wall of the Late Bronze Age stone fort, Dún Aonghusa, located on a cliff edge overlooking the Atlantic on Inis Mór, Aran Islands, Co. Galway. This burial comprised the forearm, wrist and hand bones of an adult,[42] together with a fragment of scapula, and a fragment of jawbone and some teeth found nearby (Burial 2683-F240). The remains were discovered in a layer of disturbed material close to an abandoned Late Bronze Age structure (no. 6); there was no evidence for a grave-cut indicating formal burial, and no further traces of human remains were recovered (Cotter, 2012, i 339, 357; ii 191, 276–7). This presents a paradox: do these fragmentary remains, which appear to have been articulated when deposited, represent the deposition of a complete person? Are they the remains of a person who died alone? Or are they the remains of a body which had been deliberately exposed? This latter practice, which is known in Iron Age Britain, is otherwise unknown in the Irish Iron Age archaeological record. So, could these be the remains of a voyager or sailor, who perhaps died at sea, was placed by his peers into the imposing structure of Dún Aonghusa, and exposed to the elements and birds of prey? Unfortunately, there is no answer to this enigma, except to note that this body was deposited in Dún Aonghusa during a period of inactivity and non-occupation of the fort.

Unburnt human remains, comprising a fragment of skull with sharp-force injuries, and fragments of rib and scapula, were discovered beneath the imitative Iron Age barrow-mound (Site 2), at Rathdooney Beg, Co. Sligo, dated to the fourth–first century BC,[43] and appear to represent deliberately dismembered body parts scattered on the ground surface prior to the erection of the mound (Mount, 1999, 345, 367, 369; 2012, 192). Recently, two fragments of skeletal material dating to the Iron Age have been discovered in two different locations in the promontory at Drumanagh, Co. Dublin (Baker, 2018, 29, 32).[44] These comprise an adult femur, dated to the first century BC/first century AD,[45] and a cranium fragment from a probable female adult, dated to the second century BC/first century AD.[46] This material is currently undergoing further analysis. The discovering of human skeletal parts such as these is, so far, unique in Iron Age Ireland, but is reminiscent of rites of disposal of the dead practised in Iron Age Britain (Wait, 1985, chapter 4).

Another form of deviant or anomalous burial is of course that of bodies disposed of in bogs. Because this type of deposition is currently the subject of ongoing research (Ó Floinn, 1995, 137–45, 221–34; Turner and Scaife, 1995; Delaney, Ó Floinn and Heckett, 1999, 67–8; Kelly, 2006) these are not included here as this volume concentrates on terrestrial burial.

---

41 GrA–1360: 2035±45BP; at 2σ = 169 cal BC–cal AD 57. 42 There is some confusion in the report as to whether this is a left or a right arm (Cotter, 2012, i 341, ii 191). 43 GrA–9269: 2150±50BP; at 2σ = 360–53 cal BC. 44 My thanks to Christine Baker for supplying this as yet unpublished information. 45 UBA–38843: 1976±35BP; at 2σ = 50 cal BC–cal AD 120 (at 93.7% probability = 50 cal BC–cal AD 87). 46 UBA–38844: 2041±44BP; at 2σ = 171 cal BC–cal AD 53.

* * *

During a comparatively short temporal episode spanning the second century BC–first century AD, the rite of crouched inhumation burial was introduced into Ireland, probably from Britain, into a confined geographical area in the east of the country. This burial rite did not spread and was not adopted by the larger indigenous population who continued to use the rite of cremation. Isotopic analysis undertaken on six of the fourteen crouched burials inserted into the iconic ancestral burial monument at Knowth, Co. Meath, has indicated that four of these (three adults, one child) were probably immigrants from Britain; a further adult female was perhaps born locally, but may have come from further afield; and another adult female (c14 dated as the earliest in the group) was born locally. The majority of the burials at Knowth were accompanied by large numbers of small blue glass beads (the large numbers involved suggest that these beads were possibly sewn on to garments); finger-rings; and a double male burial (immigrants) was accompanied by gaming pieces (or auguring devices). The absence at Knowth of exotic bead types, and of fibulae of any type, is noticeable, and is possibly indicative of a distinct cultural group. The crouched burials at Lambay Island, Co. Dublin, which were accompanied by fibulae, probably represent a kin-group associated with an offshore trading post.

Of the thirty-six Iron Age crouched inhumations examined, infants and young juveniles make up 47% of the total. While several of these children can be assigned to possible kin-groups, others appear to have been deliberately segregated. This aspect warrants further research.

An anomalous group of extended inhumation burials, recovered in 1835 on the east coast shoreline at Bray, Co. Wicklow, which have been dated to the second century AD by the presence of coins of Trajan (AD 97–117) and Hadrian (AD 117–38), possibly represent the presence of a coastal trading post. This burial rite was otherwise unknown in Ireland at this period.

Fear of some of the dead returning to haunt the living is demonstrated by the placing of large stones over the bodies of at least two individuals, and also by a prone burial.

The deposition of disarticulated human remains has been recorded at three sites, representing an Iron Age burial ritual previously unrecognised in Ireland.

CHAPTER 3

Inhumation in the Early Medieval period, *c*.AD400–800

THE INTRODUCTION OF EXTENDED INHUMATION

In the Roman world, the rite of cremation was replaced by inhumation in the second century AD (Toynbee, 1971, 44; Philpott, 1991, 53), and as a direct result of the ritual laying-out and waking of the dead, the deceased remained in an extended supine position for burial. This new burial rite was introduced into Romanised Britain in the later second century, and spread to Ireland in the later fourth, or early fifth century, probably as a result of contacts with the western and northern fringes of Romanised Britain (Philpott, 1991, 111; O'Brien, 1999a, 26–7; 2003, 65–6; 2009, 143–5). Orientation of the body does not appear to have been an important factor in the earlier period, but by the fourth century when the rite had become predominant in the Romanised world, west–east orientation (head to the west) became the norm. Although this rite eventually became identified with Christianity in Britain and Ireland, it cannot automatically be seen as a sign of Christian burial during the fifth-century conversion period in Ireland (O'Brien 1992b, 131–2; 1999b, 5). In Ireland, the fact that this new burial rite did not include non-perishable grave goods, which are often useful in assessing the date of burials, has engendered the widespread use of radiocarbon dating, and latterly the use of strontium and oxygen isotope analysis which can provide an indication of the possible place of origin for a deceased person.

The strong cultural and physical contacts that existed between Ireland and western Britain in this period are well documented (Bateson, 1973, 21–92; 1976, 171–80; Thomas, 1981; Warner, 1976, 267–92; O'Brien, 2003, 66; 2009, 143–4; Cahill Wilson, 2014, 11–58). For instance, there is evidence to suggest that in the fourth century a treaty existed between the Irish (known to the Romans as *Scotti*) and the Roman authorities in Britain, which, according to the Roman historian Ammianus Marcellinus, was broken by the *Scotti* (and *Picti*) in AD360 when they raided the frontiers of Britain (Ammianus, book 20.1, Hamilton, 1986, 185; Charles-Edwards, 2000, 158–60; 2013, 33). In the year AD367 Ammianus Marcellinus also recorded incursions into Britain by the *Atacotti* and the *Scotti* (Ammianus, books 27–8). It has been proposed that the *Atacotti* and the *Scotti* represent two Irish confederations, the former comprising Ulstermen (*Ulaid*) in north-eastern Ireland, the latter comprising Leinstermen (*Laigin*) in eastern Ireland (Charles-Edwards, 2000, 159–60). There is also a suggestion that the *Atacotti* may have been active in the Roman military in the fourth century (Cahill Wilson, 2014, 35, 45). Later tradition, and especially the *Historia Brittonum* (*Nennius*, chapter 14), suggests that the *Déisi* and *Uí Liatháin* from south-east and southern Ireland established settlements on the Welsh coast, the former being responsible for founding the Welsh kingdom of Dyfed (Byrne, 1973, 72, 183; Richards, 1960, 133–62; Thomas, 1994, 41–9; Davies, 1989, 87–8). The evidence in *Nennius* is, however, late, and should be approached with caution. It has also been argued, based on place-name evidence, that the Leinstermen (*Laigin*) of eastern Ireland had connections with the Llŷn peninsula in north Wales, as the place-names Lleyn and Dinllaen contain respectively a declined form of Laigin (Charles-Edwards, 2000, 159; 2013, 176). Further important evidence for an Irish presence in Wales and south-western Britain (Devon and Cornwall) during the period in question is demonstrated by the presence in these regions of memorial stones with inscriptions containing Irish personal names in both Latin script and Irish ogam characters (McManus, 1991, 61–4; Davies, 1989, 87–9; Okasha, 1993, 37–9; Charles-Edwards, 2013, 174–6; Edwards, 2017, 383–91; O'Brien, 2017a, 261–3). The importance of the cultural links illustrated by this combined use on memorial stones of Irish ogam and Roman letterforms in Latin has been examined in detail by Charles-Edwards (2000, 163–72), and he concludes that in the sixth century both Latin and Irish were minority, but high-ranking, spoken languages in Wales, and were therefore used in stone inscriptions.

When the Roman authorities commenced their withdrawal from Britain in AD410, that country became vulnerable to increased raiding from Ireland and elsewhere. St Patrick was reputedly, when a boy, taken as a slave in an Irish raid on Britain in the first half of the fifth century. That this raiding was not a one-way phenomenon is demonstrated in Patrick's condemnation, in his letter to Coroticus, of a raid on Ireland from Britain[1] in the fifth century when newly baptised Irish Christians were taken as slaves (*Epistola ad milites Corotici* – Howlett, 1994, 26–39; and www.ria.ie). It is evident that during the Late Antique period, the Irish, living on the frontier of the Empire, exploited their position to the full (Johnston, 2017, 107–23). During this period, contact took place on many levels, settlers and traders moved in both directions, resulting in the introduction of novel customs and practices, among which was the new burial rite of extended inhumation, and the all-important new Christian religion.

TRANSITION FROM CREMATION TO EXTENDED INHUMATION

The burial rite of cremation, whereby the spirit of the deceased was released by fire into the elements, was replaced by the rite of extended inhumation, whereby the spirit of the deceased was either retained in the body or was released probably through a series of rituals, and represents a complete change of mindset, which may have paved the way for the reception of Christianity. There is, however, evidence of a transitional period lasting several centuries during which cremation was still practised in parts of the country.

Important examples of the contemporaneity of cremation and extended inhumation in this transitional period is represented at the site of Prumplestown Lower, Co. Kildare, where a cremation deposit (C.1042), dated to the fourth–sixth century AD,[2] was discovered in a layer of brush-wood (a possible trackway) in a flood

---

[1] It is, however, noted that Thompson (1999, 132–3) has argued that Coroticus and his henchmen were Britons resident in Ireland (pers. comm., Cormac Bourke).   [2] SUERC–25396: 1600±50BP; at 2σ = cal AD 344–569.

plain at the base of a low ridge on which four extended inhumations, also dated to the fourth–sixth century AD, were located (Clark and Long, 2010, 32–4, 67–8), and at Annaghilla (Site 4), Co. Tyrone (Kimber, 2010, 501; Dunlop and Barkley, 2016), where a small Iron Age annular ring-ditch, with cremation deposits dated second–first century BC, was later enclosed within an Early Medieval settlement cemetery enclosure with inhumation burials. Human cremated bone continued to be deposited in pits and post-holes, alongside inhumation burials, within the enclosures, from the fifth–sixth century AD, until the seventh–ninth century.[3]

TRANSITION FROM CROUCHED TO EXTENDED INHUMATION

At Mullamast Hill, Moone, Co. Kildare, the occasional burial of infants, referred to in chapter 2, continued in the same area of that site. The burial rite, however, changed from crouched inhumation in circular pits in the Iron Age, to the interment of three extended infant burials into rectangular graves, between the third and sixth century AD (Lenihan and Dennehy, 2010, 34–6) (Figure 3.1). SK 3 (288), a perinate, buried in a rectangular partially stone-lined grave-cut, oriented east–west, has been dated to the third–fourth century AD.[4] SK 7 (244), aged 3–4 months, buried in a rectangular grave-cut, oriented north-east–south-west, has been dated to the fourth–sixth century AD,[5] and SK 1 (238), aged between 1½ and 2 years, was buried extended in a rectangular grave-cut, partially stone-lined, oriented east–west (head west), and dated to the fifth–sixth century AD.[6] All three burials contained fragments of animal bone in the fill. The c14 dating indicates that the intermittent burial of infants at this site ceased in the sixth century AD (Figure 3.2).

These infant burials may represent a fertility ritual. They might also be seen as an Irish pre-Christian precursor to the subsequent Christian tithe-rule of the offering of (living) 'firstlings', including human first born, to the Church, outlined in Ó Corráin, Breatnach and Breen (1984, 410–12). At this site they represent but one facet of the ritual landscape in the district of Moone and Mullamast Hill, which also includes a prehistoric standing stone known as the Long Stone, and the sixth-century decorated Mullamast Stone with its sword-sharpening grooves (Newman, 2009, 428–9) (Figure 3.3). By the seventh century, Mullamast (*Maistiu*) had become a stronghold of the Uí Dúnlainge, who ruled Leinster from the eighth to the eleventh century (Charles-Edwards, 2000, 95), and who were arch enemies of the Uí Néill. This enmity is characterised by Tírechán, writing in the seventh century, when he refers to the burial of Loíguire, son of Níall, on the ridges of Tara, face to face with the sons of Dúnlang in Maistiu in Mag Liphi[7] in the manner of men at war, until the day of judgement (*Tírechán*, §12.2, Bieler, 1979, 132–3).

---

3 Cremation (human bone) deposit in pit in ring-barrow. SUERC–21300: 1570±30BP; at 2σ = cal AD 416–557. Cremation (human bone) deposit in post-hole in EM enclosure: SUERC–21631: 1240±40BP; at 2σ = cal AD 680–881.   4 SUERC–24996: 1710±30BP; at 2σ = cal AD 251–397.   5 SUERC–25244: 1605±30BP; at 2σ = cal AD 396–539.   6 SUERC–24994: 1595±30BP; at 2σ = cal AD 401–540.   7 Mag Liphi is the Liffey Plain, which stretches from Tara, Co. Meath to Maistiu, Co. Kildare.

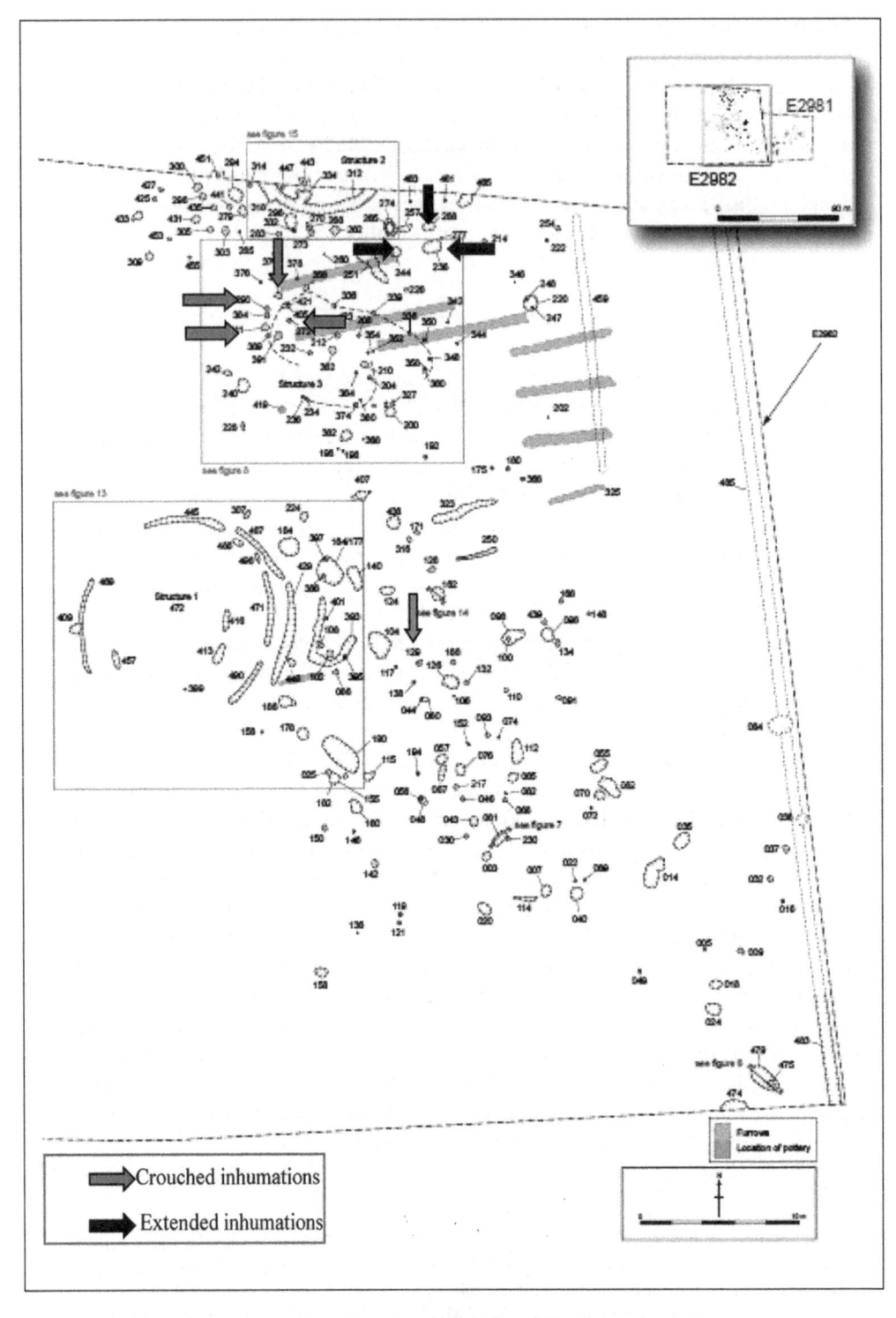

3.1 Plan of all infant burials at Mullamast Hill, Moone, Co. Kildare. Based on Lenihan and Dennehy, 2010, fig. 3, © Rubicon Heritage.

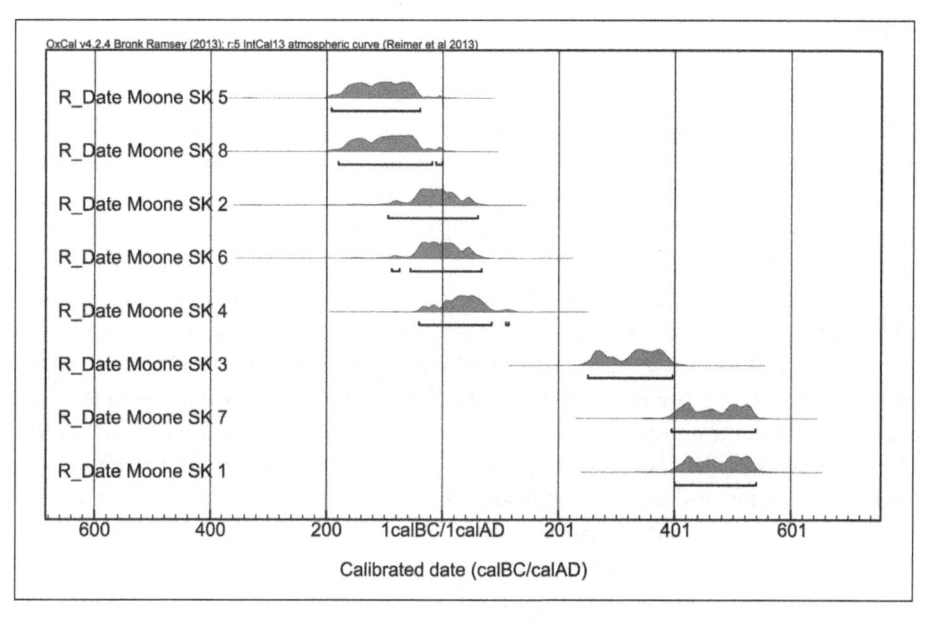

Inhumation in the Early Medieval period, c.AD400–800

3.2 C14 date sequence for all infant burials at Mullamast Hill, Moone, Co. Kildare.

3.3 Mullamast Stone, Co. Kildare, © courtesy of the National Museum of Ireland.

DIFFICULTIES IN IDENTIFYING CHRISTIAN BURIALS IN IRISH SECULAR CEMETERIES

When Irish secular cemeteries evolved, probably in the sixth century, they contained people of varying beliefs, interred in graves containing extended supine inhumations, unaccompanied by non-perishable grave goods, all being similar in outward appearance, making it almost impossible to differentiate between Christian and pagan graves. This difficulty is brought sharply into focus by both Muirchú and Tírechán who, writing in the late seventh century, refer, anachronistically, to an incident whereby Patrick, while travelling along a road, reputedly stopped at two identical new graves, one of which was marked by a cross. When questioned by Patrick, a voice from the grave marked by the cross admitted that he was a pagan and that the cross had been placed in error on his grave instead of that of his Christian neighbour (*Muirchú*, II.2, *Tírechán* §41, Bieler, 1979, 114–15, 154–7). The fact that both Tírechán and Muirchú mention the incident indicates that they, and their audience, were still familiar in the late seventh century with the concept of the burial of Christians and pagans adjacent to each other in secular cemeteries.

Those buried in monastic or church cemeteries are obviously Christian, but what guidelines can be used to archaeologically identify Christians buried in secular cemeteries? There are indications that from the introduction of extended inhumation, bodies may have been wrapped or covered with vegetation, as can be seen in the mound at Ninch 1, Co. Meath (Sweetman, 1983, 58–68) where burial B.1, dated to the fifth–seventh century,[8] was buried in an unprotected dug grave accompanied by the remains of bracken or fern that may have been used to cover or enclose the body. Animal skins may also have been used to wrap a body. For example, a poem accompanying the annalistic record in AD669 of the death of Mael Fothartaig contains the words '*o bretha Mael Fothartaigh ina geimnen do Dhairiu*' ('Since Mael Fothartaig was taken in his shroud to Daire') (*AU*, Mac Airt et al., 1983). The use of the word *geimnen* would suggest that the body was wrapped in an animal hide.[9] However, it would appear that being wrapped in a winding sheet soon became the preferred option for Irish Christians, who were then laid either directly into a dug grave, a plank- lined grave, or a slab- or stone-lined grave (never in a coffin). The winding sheet was secured in place either by tying or stitching. It was never secured with a metal shroud pin, as these do not appear in the Irish archaeological record until the Middle Ages. Physical evidence that the body had been wrapped in a winding sheet can be deduced when the arms are close to the body, the legs are close together and the feet appear fused (Figure 4.2a). However, it must be borne in mind that perhaps not all Christians, especially during the conversion period, followed this custom. This burial type is based on the description of the burial of Christ, as for instance in Luke 23:53,[10] where the body of Christ is described as having been wrapped in a linen winding sheet, and in Mark 15:45, where Jesus is described as having been wrapped in fine linen, before being laid in the tomb. A ninth–tenth century Irish interpretation of the buried Christ, wrapped in a winding sheet decorated with embroidered crosses, is depicted on the

---

8 GU-1453. Published date at 2σ = cal AD 420–650.   9 *DIL* 'G', 55, '*geimnén*' = a covering of hide used as a cere-cloth. A cere-cloth is a wrapping for corpses.   10 Vulgate Gospel.

3.4 (a) (*right*) Cross of the Scriptures, Clonmacnoise, Co. Offaly; (b) (*above*) Lower panel.

lower panel on the west face of the Cross of the Scriptures at Clonmacnoise, Co. Offaly. The interpretation of Christ's tomb is that of a dug grave covered with a graveslab (Figure 3.4). Similar depictions also appear on the High Cross at Durrow, Co. Offaly, on Muiredach's Cross at Monasterboice, Co. Louth, and on the lower panel of the east face of the Market Cross in Kells, Co. Meath.

There are several early literary indications that the wrapping of the body in a winding sheet was regarded as the appropriate mode of burial for Christians in Ireland and in parts of Britain. For instance, Adomnán, writing in the seventh century, describing the burial of Columba at Iona in AD597, states that after three days of funeral ceremonies, 'the venerable body of the holy and blessed patron was wrapped in clean fine linen cloths (*inuolutum sindonibus*), and laid in the appointed burial-place' (*Adomnán*, [iii. 23], Anderson and Anderson, 1991, 230–1). There is no mention of a coffin, so it must be assumed that the body, wrapped in a linen winding sheet, was laid directly into a dug grave and covered with earth, in the Irish manner.

Included in the seventh-century *Vita prima Sanctae Brigitae* at §58.7,8 is an instruction purported to have been given by Patrick to Brigit[11] which states 'Patrick told Brigit to make with her own hands a linen shroud to cover his body with after his death, as he desired to rise to eternal life with that shroud. Brigit accordingly made the shroud and it was in it that St Patrick's body was later wrapped' (Connolly, 1989, 30). Alongside this may be related the instructions of the Anglo-Saxon Guthlac (died AD714) to his sister Pega regarding his burial as described by Felix: 'Tell her to place my body in the coffin, and, wrap it in the linen cloth[12] which Ecgburh sent me. While I was alive, I was unwilling to cover my body with any linen vestment, but out of affection for the virgin beloved of Christ who sent me this gift, I have taken care to keep it to wrap my body in' (*Felix's Life of St Guthlac*, Colgrave, 1956, 154–7). Pega subsequently spent three days in commending the spirit of her brother to heaven with divine praises, and 'on the third day in accordance with his command she buried his blessed limbs in his oratory, covering them with earth' (ibid., 158–61). Bishop Cuthbert, who died AD687, had received a gift of a *sindon* from the Abbess Verca. He requested that his body was to be wrapped in this and buried in a stone coffin which he had received as a gift from Abbot Cudda (Bede's Life of St Cuthbert: Colgrave, 1940, 272–3). Cuthbert had envisaged a simple burial on the island of Farne where he died, but the monks of Lindisfarne persuaded him otherwise, and a year after his death they re-clothed him and removed him for burial in Lindisfarne (ibid., 286–9). His remains were re-clothed in more splendid apparel when in AD698 his body was placed in a new coffin on the floor of the sanctuary where it could be seen and venerated by the faithful (*HE* iv.30; Colgrave and Mynors, 1991, 442–5).

There are many secular cemeteries in Anglo-Saxon England which include possible Christian burials. Examples include the cemetery at Buttermarket, Ipswich, Suffolk (Wade, 1989, 209; O'Brien, 1999a, 116), where Anglo-Saxon burials of the earlier seventh century were accompanied by grave goods including weapons, while burials dated to the later seventh–eighth centuries had no grave goods and by the ninth century this cemetery had been abandoned and streets laid across it. Another example is the cemetery at Castledyke South, Barton-upon-Humber (Humberside) (Bryant, 1994, 48–51, 116; O'Brien, 1999a, 84), where Anglo-Saxon burials with grave goods commenced in the sixth century, but west–east supine inhumations, without grave goods, located in the south-eastern part of the cemetery, appear to indicate a continuation of burial into the Christian period. This cemetery was subsequently abandoned and superseded in the ninth century by the Christian cemetery at nearby St Peter's Church. Changes in the use of grave goods in the Anglo-Saxon conversion or 'final phase' period has been fully explored by Helen Geake (1997), who concludes that the near-complete abandonment of grave goods in the first decades of the eighth century occurs suddenly among almost all types of graves (ibid., 125).

---

11 This reference is apocryphal; Patrick is reputed to have died in AD 461 (AU), or in AD 492 (aged 102 years!); Brigit (Brigid) died between AD524–526 (AU) and her birth date is estimated at AD 454–6 based on an age at death of 70. If Patrick died *c*.AD 461, Brigit would have been about 7 years old at the time.   12 The same format, '*in sindone involvat*', is used.

* * *

In the Roman world the rite of cremation was replaced by that of extended inhumation in the second century AD, and was introduced into the Romanised regions of Britain in the later second century. By the later fourth–early fifth century this new burial rite (without accompanying grave goods) was introduced into Ireland, probably as a result of cultural and physical links with western and northern Britain, which are well recorded. Although this new burial rite replaced the indigenous rite of cremation, there are indications, in the archaeological and the literary record, of a transition period where cremation was still used sporadically, and occasionally in parallel with inhumation, until the seventh–eighth century.

Extended supine inhumation cannot automatically be assumed to represent Christian burial, because, although the rite eventually became identified with Christianity, in the earlier period it was universal and used by all, irrespective of religious affiliation. However, by the sixth century, the burial of Christians in secular cemeteries can possibly be recognised by the fact that the bodies of Christians were usually wrapped in a winding sheet, and laid either directly into a dug grave, or into a slab- or stone-lined grave. Coffins were never used in Early Medieval Ireland. The wrapping of a Christian in a winding sheet for burial is based on the description by the evangelists Mark and Luke of the burial of Christ, whose body is described as being wrapped in a linen winding sheet. A guide to recognising a body thus wrapped is that the arms remain close to the body, the legs close together, and the foot bones appear fused together in a lump. Shroud pins were not used. Bodies which were not wrapped for burial can often be recognised by the flat disposition and spread-pattern of the foot bones.

CHAPTER 4

Grave, burial and secular cemetery types

Subsequent to the introduction of the rite of extended inhumation into Ireland, the use of the following forms of burial and grave types became universal in both secular and ecclesiastical burial places. The corpus of Early Medieval secular burial sites consulted during the compilation of this publication includes approximately 11,000 burials, spread throughout 156 burial sites (Table 3.1). A breakdown of the numbers of burials in these sites range from single burial, 2–10 burials, 11–50 burials, 51–100 burials, 100+ burials, and at least three cemeteries which have a minimum of 1,000 burials. The latter are, Mount Offaly, Cabinteely, Co. Dublin (Conway, 1999), which was established in the fifth century, and continued in use until at least the eleventh century; Ardreigh, Co. Kildare (Opie, 2006; Moloney et al., 2016), where a cemetery appears to have been established around the seventh century and continued in use until about the sixteenth century; and Ballyhanna, Co. Donegal (McKenzie et al., 2015), where the cemetery was established in the eighth century and continued in use until the eighteenth century.

Table 3.1 Burial numbers in Early Medieval cemeteries

Burials per site	*No. of sites*	*Percentage*
1	33	21%
2–10	50	32%
11–50	39	25%
51–100	15	10%
100+	16	10%
1,000+	3	2%
Total number of sites	156	100%

GRAVE TYPES

Grave types for extended supine inhumation burials throughout Ireland include:

Slab-lined cists (Figure 4.1a), which are lined, roofed, and floored with stone slabs, and similar cist-like graves, usually referred to as lintel graves, which although lined with slabs are devoid of basal slabs, and are roofed with a series of narrow lintel-type slabs. The construction of slab-lined graves involved a degree of labour and probably ritual, including the sourcing of suitable slabs, digging the grave, and placing the slabs *in situ*.

Grave, burial and secular cemetery types

4.1 Slab- and stone-lined graves: (a) (*left*) Slab-lined cist grave; (b) (*right*) Stone-lined grave, © J. Eogan.

Stone-lined graves (Figure 4.1b), where the body is surrounded by stones (not slabs), probably specifically sourced, which supported a wooden grave cover. While several burials in slab-lined and stone-lined graves represent bodies that have been wrapped in a winding sheet, the flat spread-position of the skeletal foot bones in some graves suggests decomposition of a body in a void, perhaps covered with vegetation, or loosely wrapped, or clothed in a loose garment.

Unprotected dug graves (Figure 4.2a), where the body was usually wrapped in a winding sheet and placed directly into the grave-cut and covered with earth. The disposition of the feet in dug graves often suggests decomposition of the body while tightly bound within a winding sheet.

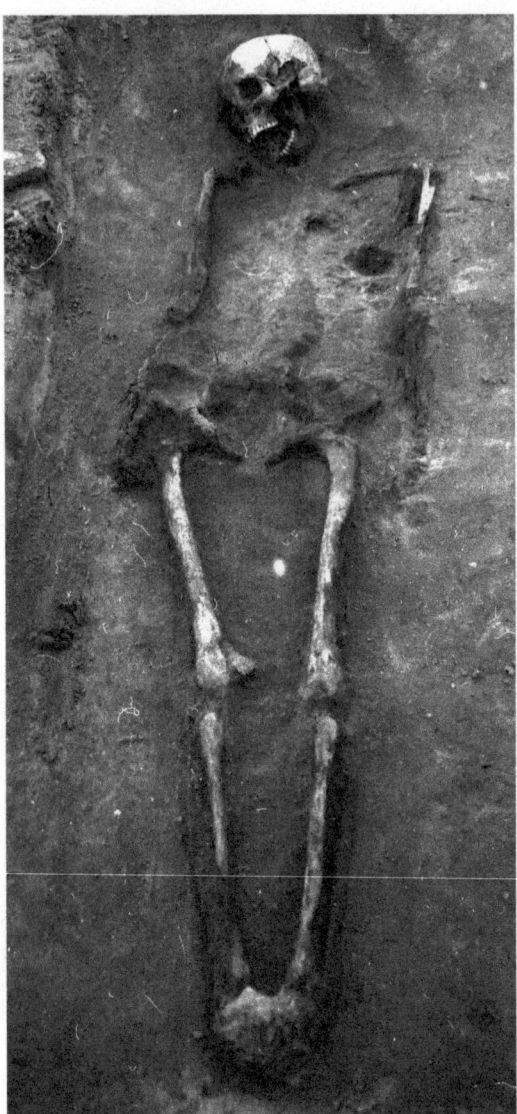

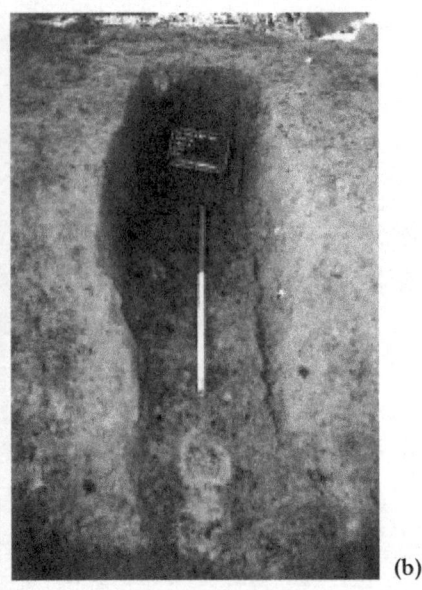

4.2 Unprotected and wood-lined graves: (a) unprotected dug grave, B4, Ballymacaward, Co. Donegal; (b) Wood-lined grave: Collierstown, Co. Meath © ACSU.

Plank-lined graves In Ireland, burials of this period were never placed in manufactured wooden or stone coffins but there is evidence that some graves may have been lined with planks (Figure 4.2b). For example, the grave of a male, B18, dated to the sixth–seventh century,[1] and the double-grave of two males, B54, B55, also dated sixth–seventh century,[2] at Collierstown 1, Co. Meath, together with two other graves in that cemetery, produced evidence for this practice (O'Hara, 2009a, 27; 2009b, 93). One grave, SK 52, among 152 graves at Camlin, Co. Tipperary, produced evidence for the presence of wooden planks along the inside of the stone lining (Flynn, 2011, 86). Two elm lined graves (undated) have been recorded in the earliest phase of the cemetery

---

[1] Beta–247003: 1460±40BP; at 2σ (95.1%) = cal AD 536–659. [2] Beta–247007: 1430±40BP, at 2σ = cal AD 559–663.

at Mount Offaly, Cabinteely, Dublin (Conway, 1999, 21–2), and several of the graves within the inner enclosure of the settlement cemetery at Carrigatogher (Harding), Co. Tipperary (Taylor, 2010, 288), had vertical sides and a flat base, which suggests that they were probably lined with wooden planks.

Log coffins An example of the use of a log coffin can be seen in Grave G at Scotch Street, Armagh (Lynn, 1988, 79–80), dated variously to the fifth–seventh, and sixth–seventh century AD.[3] A possible further example has recently been uncovered in a settlement cemetery at the site known as Newtown Rath, at Dublin Airport Logistics Park, Co. Dublin (pers. comm., Maeve Tobin, IAC).[4] A log coffin could have been used as a means of transporting a body over some distance to its place of burial. An interesting case of the survival, due to waterlogging, of plank-lined, and log-coffin graves, dating to around the seventh century, excavated by Mark Holmes of MOLA, at Great Ryburgh, Norfolk (Hilts, 2017, 18–23), provides a context for this type of grave.

Possible sources for the introduction to Ireland of slab-lined cists, stone-lined and dug graves include the following sites where parallels for these grave types are known: the Romano-British cemeteries of Bradley Hills, Somerset, where the majority of graves were lined and covered with lias slabs (Leech, 1981), and Poundbury, Dorset, where thirty-three burials were in stone-lined or cist graves (Farwell and Molleson, 1993, 62, 70; O'Brien, 1996b, 161; 1999a, 11). Early Medieval cemeteries in Wales, for example from the excavation at Caer, Bayvil, which produced simple dug graves, cist and lintel graves (James, 1992, 94–95). Arfryn, Bodedern, Anglesey (White, 1971–2), contained cist and dug graves, and the cemetery at Atlantic Trading Estate, Barry, contained slab-lined and dug graves (James, 1992, 96–7).[5] Early Medieval cemeteries in Scotland whose origins span the period fifth to seventh century, such as Whithorn, which contained slab-lined graves, dug graves, and log coffins (Hill, 1997, 37, 70–3, 552), the Catstane, Kirkliston, Midlothian, which contained mainly slab-lined graves, as did the cemeteries at Hallowhill, St Andrews, and Four Winds, Longniddrey, East Lothian (Dalland, 1992, 203–4).[6]

Among concessions included in Early Irish law outlining limited rights on private property is an allusion to 'cutting rods for a bier' (Kelly, 1988, 105–6). This suggests that a body may have been transported in procession to the grave, lying on a bier of wood or other organic material supported by wooden rods. Social inequality appears to be the basis for a reference to carrying the dead to the grave contained in a fragmentary Old Irish law text on marriage disputes, which declares *IM-fedhat daeir daeru* (Lowly persons carry lowly persons), which outlines penalties to be incurred if the dead person is carried by people of a differing social rank (Kelly, 2014, 50–1, 125 §39[a]).

---

3 UB–2437: (wood sample): 1510±50BP; at 2σ = cal AD 427–638. UB–2438: (wood sample): 1400±40BP; at 2σ = cal AD 571–679.   4 Post excavation analysis has not yet commenced.
5 Further cemeteries in Wales which have produced slab-lined, stone-lined, and dug graves, are listed in Longley, 2009, 106–12.   6 For an overview of Early Medieval burial in Scotland, especially in long cists, see Maldonado (2013, 33–4; 2016, 39–62).

BURIAL AND CEMETERY TYPES

During the period of the introduction of extended inhumation, formally organised cemeteries were unknown in Ireland. Consequently, the earliest inhumation burials are represented by:

- isolated burials.
- burials inserted into pre-existing burial monuments (*ferta*).
- burials in imitative monuments (*ferta*) constructed in the Early Medieval period.
- secular unenclosed cemeteries often located on gravel/sand ridges.
- foundation or focal burials around which secular familial or communal cemeteries and 'settlement cemeteries' evolved. These various types will be discussed below (and see Gazetter 2).

Isolated burials

Prior to the establishment of cemeteries for inhumation burial, isolated burial appears to have been common. Isolated graves are mentioned in seventh-century literature. For example, an anachronistic reference in Tírechán (*Tírechán* §38, Bieler, 1979, 152–3), regarding the death and burial of Patrick's charioteer, states 'And his charioteer died at Muiresc Aigli (Murrisk, Co. Mayo) that is, the plain between the sea and Mons Aigli,[7] and there Patrick buried his charioteer Totmáel, and gathered stones for his burial-place'. This would imply that in the fifth century Totmáel was buried, in isolation, in a slab- or stone-lined grave, which was then covered by a cairn of stones. Similarly, Adomnán (*Adomnán* [i.33], Anderson and Anderson, 1991, 62–3), referring to the death, after baptism by Columba, of an old man on the island of Skye, states 'he presently died in that place ... and there his companions buried him, building a cairn of stones. It can still be seen to-day upon the sea-coast'. A further isolated burial is referenced by Muirchú (*Muirchú* I 27 (26) = B II 1 (8), Bieler, 1979, 98–101) in relation to the baptism and death of Monesan, the daughter of a British king, 'she fell to the ground and gave up her spirit into the hands of the angels. She was buried on the spot where she died'.

In the Irish archaeological record, early isolated extended inhumation burials, detailed in Gazetteer 2, include: the burial at Ballygarraun West, Athenry, Co. Galway, of an elderly female dated to the fifth–seventh century AD,[8] interred in a dug grave, lying on a layer of domestic hearth residue containing burnt grain, and accompanied by a fragment of deer antler. The grave was originally covered by a small cairn (Randolph-Quinney, 2006b; 2007, 30–1; Lehane, 2008). This woman did not originate in the west of Ireland where she was buried as her strontium and oxygen isotope signatures indicate an origin in regions further east that overlie older or silicate-rich geology, perhaps in the east of Ireland, or in regions of Britain with similar geology (Cahill Wilson et al., 2014a, 137; Cahill Wilson and Standish, 2016, 233, 238). The fact that this is an isolated burial, there being no evidence for any other burial in the

---

[7] This is in the region of Croagh Patrick, Co. Mayo. [8] Radiocarbon date for human bone: UBA–7683: 1471±67BP; at 2σ = cal AD 428–661; Radiocarbon date from carbonised plant remains beneath skeleton: UBA–7863: 1530±33BP; at 2σ = cal AD 427–600.

vicinity, suggests that she was likely to have been part of a group in transit. Groups of this type were known as *immairche* or *immairge*, migrants who moved from one home to another (Charles-Edwards, 2012, 11). Evidence that such groups existed in the Early Medieval period is referenced in an episode in the eighth-century *Vita prima* (Connolly, 1989, 22–3, §38) and in the ninth-century *Bethu Brigte* (Ó hAodha, 1978, 13–14 §38, 30, §38), which record that when a group of people who were relocating to another place were travelling too slowly for Bishops Mel and Melchú, Brigid stayed behind with the slow-moving travellers, who were transporting their crippled brother and blind sister in carts. Perhaps the burial at Ballygarraun represents a similar travelling group, one of whose matriarch died, but was sufficiently respected to have been accorded a formal burial and not merely hurriedly buried on the spot. Her grave was carefully prepared and in this case the ashes from a domestic hearth were placed into the grave with whatever ritual accompanied this act, her body was then placed into the grave accompanied by a portion of deer antler, possibly as a symbol of regeneration, and the grave was covered with a small mound of stones. These stones would have acted as protection against disturbance by animals, and as a grave marker.

Other isolated burials include an isolated extended male, dated fifth–sixth century AD,[9] in a dug grave on the lower slopes of Athgoe Hill at Ballynakelly, Co. Dublin. Athgoe Hill, which overlooks the Liffey plain, is an archaeological landscape containing cremated burials from the Bronze Age and Iron Age. But this extended inhumation, which is isolated from these cremations, was discovered during excavation of a ringfort-farmstead, dated to the eighth–tenth century (McCarthy, 2011, 247–8; 2012, 159). It is probable that the builders of the ringfort-farmstead were unaware of the presence of the earlier burial. The fragmented skull of this individual was in the pelvic region of the skeleton, but it is unclear whether this is an original feature, or if it is the result of plough disturbance.

A somewhat similar circumstance occurred at Portmarnock Estuary in north Co. Dublin, where an older middle adult male, dated fifth–sixth century,[10] was interred, head to the west, in an isolated, deep and well cut grave (McLoughlin, 2017, 20).[11] This grave was later incorporated into the south-west quadrant of a large elliptical enclosure dated seventh–eighth century.[12] That the builders of this enclosure may have been aware of the presence of this burial is indicated by an undated recut which respected the outline of the original grave but did not expose the burial. There was evidence of *in situ* burning along the edge of the recut, and the back-fill included animal bone, charcoal, seashell, a flint scraper and a cetacean caudal vertebra fragment, which the excavator suggests could represent a votive deposit. If this recut was made by those responsible for constructing the enclosure (which contained kilns and pits) it might be their method of placating, or purifying, the burial.

At Ballykeel South, Co. Clare (Cahill and Sikora, 2011, 11–15), a single long-stone cist, located on the 60m contour, contained an extended supine, west–east, male, dated to the fourth–sixth centuries.[13] At Belladooan, Co. Mayo, in 1932, two slab-lined long

---

9 Lab code unavailable: 1595±33BP; at 2σ = cal AD 399–544.   10 UBA–35733: 1545±48BP; at 2σ = cal AD 410–608 (at 68.2% probability = cal AD 429–564).   11 Thanks are due to Gill McLoughlin and Maeve Tobin for providing details of this interesting burial prior to its publication.   12 UBA–32895: 1348±27BP; at 2σ = cal AD 641–764 (at 90.0% probability = cal AD 641–710). Date obtained from a wooden hoop recovered at the base of the deep enclosure ditch.   13 GrN–18567:

cists were recovered on a ridge surrounded by boggy land, one cist was empty but the other contained an extended supine skeleton, dated fourth–seventh century AD[14] (Morris, 1932, 191–200; Raftery, 1941, 299–315; O'Brien, 1984, 95–6; Hedges et al., 1993, 305–6). At Courtmacsherry, Co. Cork, an isolated, well-constructed slab-lined lintel grave contained a west–east oriented extended male burial dated to the sixth–seventh century[15] (Cahill and Sikora, 2011, 15–18).

An isolated long-stone cist at Aghalahard, Co. Mayo, contained an extended skeleton, accompanied by an iron knife and an ox metacarpal (Raftery and Moore, 1944, 171–2). Although the skeletal remains were not retained, the morphology of this grave and burial suggests it belongs in the Early Medieval period. The knife was lodged with the National Museum. At Tinnapark Demesne, Co. Wicklow (Raftery, 1994, 166–9), an undated isolated slab-lined and slab-covered cist grave, containing a male, supine, extended, west–east, could also, on morphological evidence, be placed in the Early Medieval period.

An isolated burial of an adult female, dated seventh–ninth century,[16] extended, west–east, in a slab-lined cist grave, was recovered beneath a low mound close to the River Boyne at Ferganstown and Ballymacon, Co. Meath (Kelly, 1976, 35; 1977, 65–7).

There are many other, undated, isolated graves, often in slab-lined cists, discovered mainly in the earlier part of the twentieth century throughout the country, the morphology of which suggests that they may belong in this earlier period, but as the skeletal remains were not retained the dates remain unknown (Raftery, 1941, 299–315; O'Brien, 1984, 33–4).

The reason for such isolated burials probably lies in the fact that although in this early period cemeteries for the interment of inhumation burials had not yet evolved in Ireland, the individuals concerned were respected, valued, cherished, or perhaps even distinguished, in their own right, and were afforded formal burial, possibly at the place of death, with all the accompanying ceremonial that this entailed. In the case of slab-lined graves this would have involved the acquisition of suitable stone slabs with which to line the grave, the laying-out, and possibly the displaying of the body in the grave, and ceremonies involved in the closing of the grave.

Burials inserted into pre-existing burial monuments (ferta)

The global phenomenon of veneration and influence of the ancestors is as old as time. This veneration, which can take many forms, is often demonstrated by the practice of inserting the bodies of deceased members of a community into the burial places/monuments of ancestors. In Ireland, this practice can be identified in the archaeological record, from prehistoric times up to the late seventh–eighth century AD (see Gazetteer 2). Ancestral burial places/monuments, known in Ireland as *ferta*, are known as *hláw* in Anglo-Saxon England where examples abound (O'Brien, 1999a; Semple, 1998, 109–26; Williams, 1998, 90–108; Williams, 2006; Reynolds, 2002; Reynolds, 2009).

The Old Irish term *fert* translates as burials within monuments or tombs (*DIL*, 1950, F, fasc. III, Joynt and Knott, 93–4). A statement in the seventh-century law

1625±35BP; at 2σ = cal AD 345–539. 14 OxA–3226: 1590±90BP; at 2σ (90.5%) = cal AD 316–640. 15 GrA–24500: 1445±45BP; at 2σ = cal AD 537–665. 16 OxA–3227: 1290±80BP; at 2σ

tract, *Coibnes uisci thairidne* §11 (Kinship of conducted water), includes the observation that one of the lands across which it is improper to conduct water is in the precinct of a grave or grave mound (*maigen feirt*), and later (§13) one of the ditches exempt from liability in the event of a drowning is the ditch of a burial site or grave mound (*clad feirt*) (Binchy, 1955, 70–1). The use of the words *maigen* and *clad* indicates that the grave(s) or grave mound was surrounded by open space, which was, in turn, enclosed by a ditch.

Ancestral *ferta* (singular *fert*) involve the episodic re-use of already existing burial places/monuments, and/or the deliberate construction of imitative *ferta*, either in the form of mounds or of ring-ditches, in the Iron Age and Early Medieval period. The association of *ferta* with ancestral burial is emphasised by Muirchú, when he refers to an episode where Patrick and his disciples arrive at Inber Colpdi (an inlet at the mouth of the River Boyne), and then journey across 'the great plain' until they came to *ferti virorum Feec* ('the burial place of the men of Fíacc') (*Muirchú*, I 14 (13), Bieler, 1979, 84–5). A further reference (*Tírechán*, 8 (1), Bieler, 1979, 130–1) describes the burial place of Fíacc's men as being in the region of Slane, where Patrick spent his first Easter, thus placing this ancient burial place close to the Neolithic passage-tomb complex at the Bend of the Boyne, which encompasses Newgrange, Knowth and Dowth and associated monuments.

That *ferta* were essentially pre- or non-Christian in character is demonstrated by a seventh-century reference in Tírechán to Patrick's meeting at Cruacháin, Co. Roscommon,[17] with the two daughters of King Loíguire (king of Tara) whom he (Patrick) converted, baptised, and having received the eucharist they fell asleep in death. Tírechán states that after due days of mourning the two maidens were buried in a *fert*, 'And they made a *fossam rotundam* ('a circular ring-ditch') after the manner of a *fert*, because this is what the heathen Irish used to do, but we call it *relic*'[18] (*Tírechán*, 26 (20), Bieler, 1979, 144–5). Although Tírechán was referring to an event that reputedly occurred in the fifth century, his seventh-century audience would have understood that the term *fert* was an older name for a grave or burial place associated with the burial of pagans, but it could also be used for a pre-seventh-century burial place of Christians, as instanced by the reference in Muirchú to the … *fertae martyrum iuxta Ardd Mache* … ('the burial place of the martyrs beside Armagh')[19] (*Muirchú*, I 24 = BII 6. Bieler, 1979, 108–9). However, by the seventh century the term '*relic*' was generally used to describe the burial place of Christians.

The inclusion of the term *fert* in early Irish law tracts written in the seventh or eighth century confirms that while these graves or burial monuments were recognised in Early Medieval Ireland as burial places of the ancestors, they could also, on many occasions, function as territorial boundary markers. Based on evidence contained in the law tract *Din techtugad* ('The legal process of taking possession of land'), outlining the legal procedure of *tellach* ('legal entry') (*CIH*, 1.205.22–213.37), the boundary to a territory could be marked by a *fert* (Charles-Edwards, 1976, 83–7; 1993, 259–61;

(93.8%) = cal AD 605–898.   **17** Cruacháin is, like Tara, a royal site which features many earthen barrows and ring-ditches, and Tírechán, who was very familiar with the region, was describing what he considered to be a suitable form of burial for the daughters of a king.   **18** *Reilic* = Latin *reliquiae*: 'a burial place', *DIL*, 'R', Joynt, 1944, 35.   **19** 'martyrs' being the term used to identify Christians.

O'Brien and Bhreathnach, 2011, 53–4). A very specific process was defined in order to make a claim to land, and an ancestral burial place located on the boundary was essential to this process. This involved a claimant entering the land by crossing the boundary *fert*, in the presence of a witness, taking with him two yoked horses. He did not unyoke his horses, and allowed them to graze on only half of the land. He then withdrew and waited for five days for a response from the occupant of the land regarding arbitration. In the absence of a response, ten days later the claimant again entered the land, this time with four horses and two witnesses. He then unyoked his horses and allowed them to graze freely. The occupant had a further three days to respond. In the absence of a response, the claimant entered the land after a further ten days, for the third and last time, when he brought eight horses and three witnesses. If the occupant did not respond immediately, the claimant went to the house, where he attended to his animals, kindled a fire and spent the night. The claimant had now established the right to occupy the land as the legal owner. The perception was that the ancestor, or ancestors, who were buried in the *fert* acted as guardians of the land, and it was therefore necessary to obtain the 'permission' of these guardians to legitimise a claim and to legally gain possession of the land in question.

It is argued here that burials were inserted into existing *ferta* either by the legitimate occupants of a territory to reinforce their valid title to their land, or, by intrusive groups who, by inserting their own 'guardians' into the *fert*, created a contrived form of continuity as part of the process of legitimising their claim to territory. In either case this can be interpreted as the deliberate incorporation of important individuals into the ancestral environment. The later literary convention of manipulating family genealogies by the insertion of additional ancestral names (Ó Corráin, 1998, 184) might be viewed as a perpetuation of this tradition.

Ferta, when used as territorial boundary markers, were usually located in prominent positions in the landscape overlooking, or close to, natural boundaries which could be represented by a special tree, rivers or streams, specific rocks, or standing stones (Kelly, 1997, 409). Boundaries also included the coastline, a bog, or as in at least one case in the Burren, Co. Clare, a ravine. One must be cognisant however of the fact that territorial boundaries that were familiar in the landscape in the past may no longer be identifiable today.

The topic of burial in pre-existing, and imitative monuments, located on boundaries in Anglo-Saxon England has been the subject of much recent research, indicating that such monuments were often feared as the home of dragons or demons (Semple, 1998, 109–26), and were utilised as 'execution' places and cemeteries (Williams, 1998, 90–108; 2006, 186–7; Reynolds, 2002, 171–94; 2009, 96–160). Irish Medieval literature and folklore often identifies ancient burial mounds as *sidh*, the dwelling places of fairies, mythological queens, gods and goddesses, about whom feelings were ambiguous (MacCana, 1970, 65–6, 85). Although the words 'gallows' and 'gibbet' are sometimes included in Irish place-names,[20] there is, to date, no demonstrable evidence that ancient burial monuments were used as execution places or execution cemeteries in Ireland in the Early Medieval period.

20 For example: Gallows Hill (Cnoc na Croiche), in Kilkenny, Lisnacroghy or Gallowstown, Ballintober, Co. Roscommon, Gibbet Hill (Cnoc na Croiche), a hill in Co. Wexford, Gibbet Hill (Cnoc na Croiche), a townland in the barony of Middlethird, Co. Waterford. www.logainm.ie.

Grave, burial and secular cemetery types

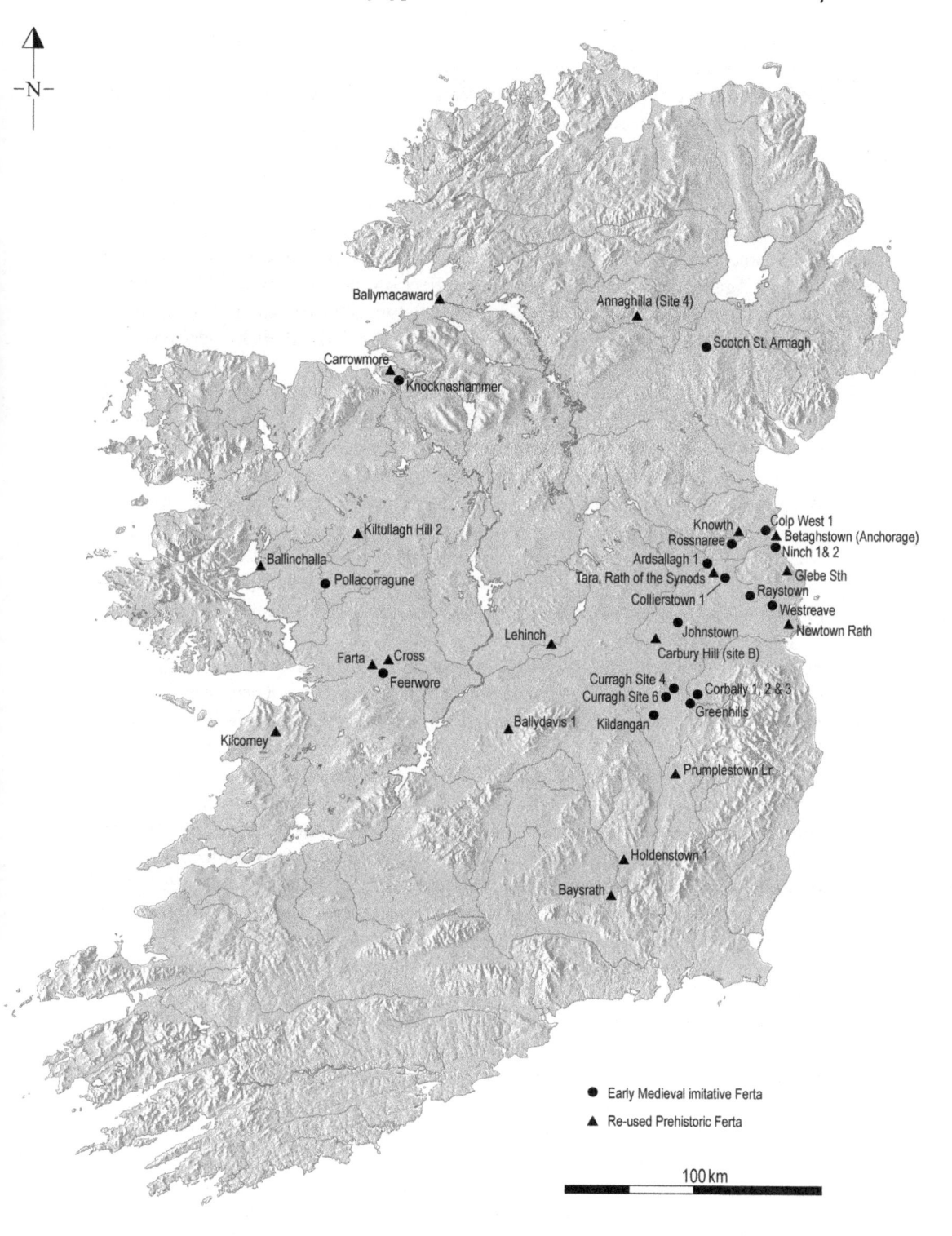

Map 4 Distribution of Early Medieval *ferta*, © The Discovery Programme and EOB.

It is fortunate, especially from an archaeological viewpoint, that the term *fert*, and the important function of *ferta* as boundary markers, had already been recorded in the late seventh-century Early Irish law tracts before the cessation of burial activity in these monuments around the eighth century AD.

In Ireland, the Iron Age practice of interring human remains into prehistoric ancestral burial places emerged between BC300–200, and ceased around AD200. Following a further interval, the practice was revived, or re-introduced, in the Early Medieval period, *c*.AD400, and continued until around AD700. While the temporal gap between the use of monuments for burial in the Bronze Age and their re-use in the Iron Age may be accounted for by the effect on the population of deteriorating climate, the temporal gap of several centuries between the cessation of re-use in the Iron Age and the re-introduction of the practice in the Early Medieval period is more difficult to evaluate.

To date, forty-three probable Early Medieval *ferta* sites have been identified, twenty-four of which contained secondary burials placed into pre-existing burial-places, and nineteen contained burials placed into imitative monuments constructed in the Early Medieval period, creating the impression of antiquity and continuity. When reviewing distribution, as seen on Map 4, imitative burial monuments constructed in the Early Medieval period tend to be grouped mainly in the east of the country, whereas re-used ancestral prehistoric burial places tend to be located mainly in the west of the country. There is not, at present, any explanation for this phenomenon, except that the grouping of imitative *ferta* in the eastern region might have been due the presence of newcomers.

Examples chosen to illustrate re-use of established burial monuments that were recognised by the people as ancestral burial places (outlined in Gazetteer 2) include Prumplestown Lower, Co. Kildare, located on a low gravel ridge bordering the marshy floodplain of the River Lerr, which encompasses elements that span the transition from cremation to inhumation burial. The ridge has produced evidence of activity from the Mesolithic until the High Medieval period, and the adjacent floodplain contains activity ranging from the Middle Bronze Age through to the Early Medieval period. On the ridge, a dual-entranced ring-ditch datable to the Late Iron Age[21] was re-used for the insertion of two extended inhumations. Male burial (SK 4), aged 35–45 years, extended, supine, west–east, was in a dug grave, dated to the fourth–sixth century,[22] and female burial (SK 2), aged 35–45 years, extended, supine, west–east, was in a grave lined with medium to large stones probably to support a wooden grave-cover, dated fifth–sixth century.[23] The grave fill of the latter contained several quartz pebbles, together with unidentified burnt bone dated first–second century AD,[24] which the excavator suggests represents perhaps the remains of a cremation associated with the ring-ditch (Clark and Long, 2010, 32). Male inhumation burial SK 1, dated fifth–seventh century,[25] also contained pieces of quartz. A cremation deposit dated fourth–sixth century AD[26] was located on marshy ground below the northern edge of the ridge,

---

21 Charcoal sample from fill of southern arc of ring-ditch: SUERC–27191: 1880±30BP; at 2σ = cal AD 66–222.   22 UBA–9403: 1643±40BP; at 2σ (93.8%) = cal AD 330–537.   23 UBA–9401: 1565±38BP; at 2σ = cal AD 408–574.   24 SUERC–27169: 1940±30BP; at 2σ (94.2%) = 1 cal BC– cal AD 130.   25 SUERC–25246: 1515±30BP; at 2σ = cal AD 428–615.   26 SUERC–25396:

Grave, burial and secular cemetery types 69

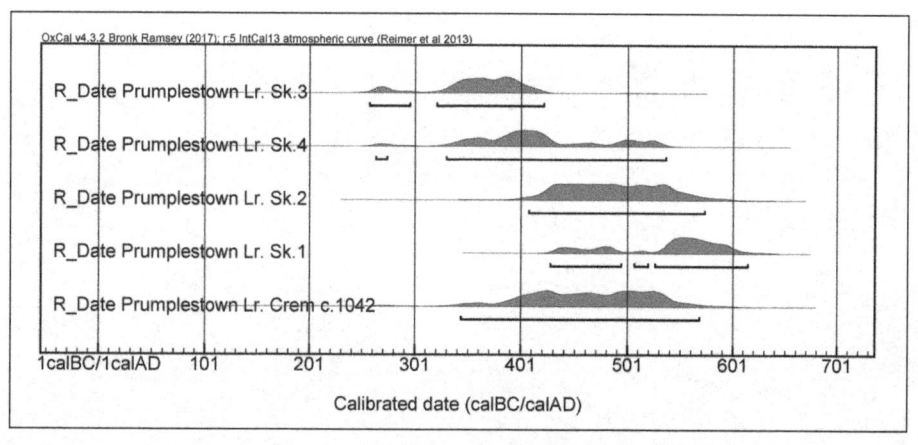

4.3 C14 date sequence, Prumplestown Lower, Co. Kildare.

lying on a concentration of roughly horizontal brushwood representing the remains of a *togher* (trackway) through the floodplain. This cremation deposit is contemporary with inhumation SK 4 within the ring-ditch, and post-dates inhumation SK 3[27] on the ridge north of the ring-ditch. The importance of this evidence cannot be overstated, as it reveals that peoples, or kin-groups, with two distinct burial traditions, were burying their dead in parallel at this ancestral, and probably sacred, site perhaps as late as the sixth century AD (Figure 4.3).

Another site that exhibits elements potentially spanning the transition between cremation and inhumation is that at Glebe South, Co. Dublin (Carroll, Ryan and Wiggins, 2008, 113–17, 127). This site, which contained Bronze Age and Iron Age ring-ditches, produced a cremation deposit in ring-ditch 1, dated to the third–sixth century AD,[28] and an undated inhumation grave (G6) which may have been wood-lined. Sixteen inhumation burials located immediately south of, and intercutting ring-ditch 1, probably represent a secular cemetery; one of the burials (G7) has been dated to the fifth–seventh century AD.[29] The dates obtained for the cremation deposit, and for inhumation G7, suggest an overlap between differing burial rites at this cemetery in the Early Medieval period.

Similarly, the site at Annaghilla (Site 4), Co. Tyrone (Kimber, 2010, 501; Dunlop and Barkley, 2016), which included Bronze Age and Iron Age cremation deposit activity, also contained a small Early Medieval cemetery of twenty-three inhumation graves, and the simultaneous insertion of cremation deposits up until at least the eighth–ninth century AD.

The re-use of an iconic *fert* is exemplified at the passage tomb complex at Knowth, Co. Meath (Eogan, G., 1974, 11–112; 2012). The insertion of the alien Iron Age burial rite of crouched inhumation at Knowth ceased during the second century AD, and the practice of inserting secondary burials was not revived there until the seventh century, when seventeen extended inhumation burials, oriented west–east, with no grave goods,

1600±50BP; at 2σ = cal AD 344–569. 27 SUERC–25247: 1680±30BP; at 2σ (85.2%) cal AD 321–422. 28 Beta–229059: 1690±50BP; at 2σ = cal AD 232–531. 29 Beta–243093: 1440±40BP:

4.4 Distribution of Early Medieval burials at Knowth, Co. Meath. Composite image based on Google Earth and G. Eogan, 2012, fig. 2.1, © RIA.

were placed primarily inside the smaller satellite tombs that surrounded the main passage tomb (Figure 4.4) (Eogan, 1974, 68–87; O'Brien and Weekes, 2012, 45–71). The insertion of burials into these peripheral ancestral burial monuments suggests that an emphatic and symbolic statement of continuity (whether real or contrived) with the indigenous ancestors was being made. Strontium and oxygen isotope analysis undertaken on teeth from several of these burials indicates the presence of individuals who did not have their origins in the Meath area (Cahill Wilson, 2012, 775–88; Cahill Wilson and Standish, 2016, 230–41). For example, a young adult (B27, KnH27), sex unknown, interred together with male burial (B28) and possible female (B29) into satellite passage tomb 15, produced results indicating that this person originated in the northern part of Ireland or in northern Britain. Possible male burial (B32, KnH32), aged about 17 years, dated to the eighth–ninth century,[30] in a slab-lined grave, had an origin either in the northern counties of Ireland, or Yorkshire, or eastern Scotland. The adjoining female burial (B33, KnH33) (undated), aged mid-20s, also in a slab-lined grave, produced results indicating that she was born locally in the district around Knowth. Male burial (B14, KnH6), dated to the seventh–ninth century,[31] discovered lying transversely across the base of the Early Medieval enclosing ditch on the main passage tomb, originated either in eastern Scotland or in Scandinavia, and a female burial (B18),[32] who appears to have been hastily interred

at 2σ = cal AD 551–659.   30 UBA–11697: 1210±28BP; at 2σ = cal AD 710–891.   31 GrN–13335: 1260±40BP; at 2σ = cal AD 666–875.   32 This burial has been identified as B16 in Cahill Wilson,

in a shallow dug grave, originated in either the northern part of Ireland or possibly in northern Britain. Isotope analysis was not obtained for the double burial (B11–12), possibly a male and a female, dated to the seventh century,[33] placed into the chamber of satellite passage tomb 6, nor for extended female (B30) placed into satellite passage tomb 16. Early Medieval burials at the Knowth necropolis ceased after the ninth century AD.

The population in the territory around Knowth in the seventh to ninth centuries was undoubtedly Christian, but it is evident that during this period some individuals were still being selected for burial among the (pagan) ancestors. The archaeological and scientific evidence indicates that some of these selected people were immigrants from other regions of Ireland or from abroad, while others were native to the region. This raises many questions, the answers to which may lie in the turbulent history of the various branches of the Uí Néill that vied for control of the territory of Northern Brega at that time (Byrne, 1973, 54; 1962–5, 383–400; Swift, 2008, 5–53). The remainder of the local community would probably have been buried at the chief church of Northern Brega in nearby Slane (Byrne and Francis, 1994, 14), or perhaps in the enclosed secular cemetery, located immediately north-east and downslope of the passage tomb complex, designated as Knowth Site M, which was in use between the sixth–tenth centuries AD (Stout and Stout, 2008).[34]

The further re-use of an iconic *ferta* site can be observed at the Neolithic megalithic necropolis of Carrowmore, Co. Sligo. The arm bone of a child, dated to the fifth–seventh century AD,[35] was recovered between two of the orthostats in the north-west part of the chamber of Tomb 51 (also known as *Listoghil*), which is located in the central part of the Carrowmore complex (Burenholt, 1998; and pers. comm.). This discovery is a strong indicator that the prehistoric Carrowmore complex was re-used for burial in the Early Medieval period.

Early Medieval and Medieval burials inserted into the ancestral monument known as the Rath of the Synods, Tara, Co. Meath (Grogan, 2008, 45–9), included: an adult, possibly male (E), partially crouched, head east, originally presumed to be Iron Age, but now dated to the eighth–ninth century AD,[36] who was accompanied by animal bones around the skull, a bone pin at the neck, and a bone object (now lost) on the chest. Strontium and oxygen isotope analysis indicates that this person, who was not native to the region around Tara, is likely to have originated in the northern region of Ireland (Cahill Wilson, 2012, 23–5). Partially crouched male burial (I), head east, undated, originated in the northern region of Ireland (ibid., 23–5). Extended male burial (H), oriented west–east, dated to the tenth–eleventh century AD,[37] had animal bones around the head and an animal jawbone on the chest, appears to have a local origin (ibid., 24–5). Extended inhumation (D), buried minus his hands (an indicator of punitive burial) (O'Brien, 2013, 244), dated to the thirteenth century AD,[38] originated in the southern/midland region of Ireland (Cahill Wilson, 2012, 23–5).

2012, Table A5:1, 780. 33 GrN–15384: 1355±20BP; at 2σ = cal AD 645–85. 34 As bone preservation at Knowth Site M was very poor, all c14 dates are based on samples of charcoal, seeds, shell and mineralised wood (Stout and Stout, 2008, 155–9). 35 UA–12733: 1500±60BP; at 2σ = cal AD 426–647. 36 UBA–11698: 1205±24BP; at 2σ = cal AD 721–890. Date obtained by J. Cahill Wilson with the aid of the RIA dating programme. 37 UBA–9030: 1055±26BP; at 2σ (87% probability) = cal AD 950–1024. 38 UBA–9029: 732±28BP; at 2σ = cal AD 1224–96.

This latter burial was located just outside the enclosing cemetery wall of the adjacent church[39] and may therefore have been debarred from that cemetery rather than having an association with the Rath of the Synods. A probable reason for the burial of individuals E and H at the royal site at Tara is examined under 'Dant mir: Meat-portions in graves'.

Re-use of the Bronze Age mound at Ballymacaward, Co. Donegal, for the insertion of cremation deposits in the Iron Age has been discussed above. However, in the Early Medieval period, after a temporal lapse of several centuries, four slab-lined long cists, oriented west–east, containing extended female inhumations, without grave goods, were inserted into the surface of the mound (O'Brien, 1999b, 56–61; Richards, 1999, 170–91; O'Brien and Bhreathnach, 2011, 55–6, 59–60). One of these (B3), a very elderly female, aged over 60 years, who suffered from post-menopausal osteoporosis of the spine, has been dated to the fifth–sixth century AD.[40] This woman's degenerative condition would have led to immobility and an inability to participate in everyday tasks, so, in her old age, she was respected and cared for by her community (Plate 10). Strontium and oxygen isotope analysis implies that she had been born and raised in the immediate locality.[41] While these four long cist burials conform to the newly introduced rite of extended inhumation, there is no evidence to indicate whether they represent burials of pagans or Christians.

The final period of use of the monument at Ballymacaward involved the introduction, in the sixth–seventh century AD, of nine extended inhumations, all female, laid supine, west–east and with no grave goods, in unprotected dug graves. One of these (B4),[42] aged 45–50 years, displayed evidence, by the disposition of the skeleton, that she had been wrapped in a winding sheet, an indication that she was probably a Christian (Figure 4.2a). Strontium and oxygen analysis reveal that this woman was not born locally, but originated in the north-east, or the south-east of Ireland (Cahill Wilson et al., 2014, 138–9; Cahill Wilson and Standish, 2016, 238). One piece of butchered bovine tibia, which could not be assigned to any specific burial, also produced a date in the sixth–seventh century,[43] but as there was no evidence for any domestic activity at, or in the vicinity of, the monument, this appears to indicate that at least one of the burials was accompanied by a food offering, a practice that was unusual in Ireland at that time. An important aspect of the burials in this ancient mound is that all were female.

Of further interest is the location, in close proximity to the Ballymacaward site, of a fresh-water lake known locally as Lough Namanfin, a modification of *Loch na mBan Finn* (the lake of the fair/bright women). The women who were buried here may represent a previously unknown female cult, or community, spanning the pre-Christian and Christian era, who controlled territory in the region.[44] The River Erne, on whose northern bank the monument is situated, has long been regarded as an

---

39 An Anglo-Norman church founded late twelfth century. 40 UB–4171: 1592±20BP; at 2σ = cal AD 420–540. 41 Analysis conducted by Dr Jacqueline Cahill Wilson for the Mapping Death Project. 42 UB–4172: 1448±21BP; at 2σ = cal AD 570–650. 43 OxA–8430: 1495±40BP; at 2σ = cal AD 430–645. 44 Perhaps the name of the lake is an indication of the survival of a memory of the female burial monument. It is of interest that there is another lake located further north in Donegal named Lough Namanfin, at Bogagh, approximately 6.6km north-east of Inver; and attention has been drawn by Prof. Elizabeth FitzPatrick, NUI Galway, to a similarly named lake at

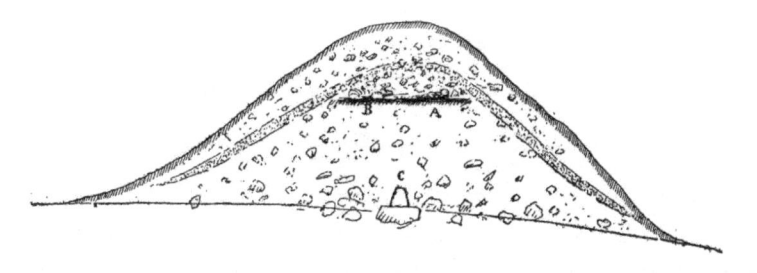

4.5 Sketch of mound at Farta, Co. Galway (after Coffey, 1904–5, fig. 1), © RIA.

important territorial boundary. Control of the territory north of the Erne was hotly contested in the late sixth–seventh centuries between the Uí Néill dynasties of Cenél Cairprí and Cenél Conaill. Cenél Conaill were ultimately successful and Cenél Cairprí lost most of their lands (Lacey, 2006, 61–5; O'Brien and Bhreathnach, 2011, 60). It has been suggested that in cases where a kin-group moved into territory not formerly held by their family, the new king frequently married the daughter of the old king. This ensured that the blood of both lines would run in the veins of their progeny. The old king's daughter would thus be seen as an ancestor of this fusion (Connon, 2005, 226; 2009). It is probable that specific females were selected for burial among the ancestors by whichever group occupied this territory at different periods. Burial at Ballymacaward ceased in the seventh century, but the monument undoubtedly continued to be recognised as a boundary feature in the landscape for a considerable period after this.

An important example of an early extended inhumation burial inserted into a prehistoric burial mound or *fert* is that at Farta (an anglicised version of *ferta*),[45] Co. Galway. This burial mound, excavated in 1903, was described by the excavator as measuring 45 feet in diameter and 9 feet in height. Close to the top of the mound, a female skeleton was uncovered, lying east–west, with the head to the west (the bones were poorly preserved), and by the south side of, and lying parallel to the human skeleton, were remains of a small horse. The horse lay on its left side, the head to the west, and the excavator noted that the number of bones found indicated that the horse was buried whole. A Bronze Age cremation in an inverted urn was uncovered at ground level within the mound. The female inhumation was originally published in 1904 as being 'The burial of a slave or concubine, perhaps as guardian of the grave … and a case of *sati*, as an accompaniment to the Bronze Age cremation' (Coffey, 1904, 14–20; Macalister, 1928, 204–5)[46] (Figure 4.5). The extended inhumation, now dated to the fourth–sixth century AD,[47] is that of a female aged between 20–5 years. This young woman suffered from a disability known as bilateral medial torsion, which is inward twisting of the knees, resulting in 'in toeing'. In children, this generally clears up by the age of 7, however, in the case of this woman the condition had not

Corbally, Moycullen, Co. Galway. This phenomenon merits further research. 45 www.logainm.ie (Irish place-names website). 46 The skeletal remains of the female and horse from Farta were misplaced for over a century, but were re-discovered in 2011, following investigation by this writer, with the assistance of Nigel Monaghan, Keeper, National History Museum, Dublin. 47 OxA-X-2488.42: 1625±26BP; at 2σ (94.6% probability) = cal AD 381–536. Date obtained courtesy of the

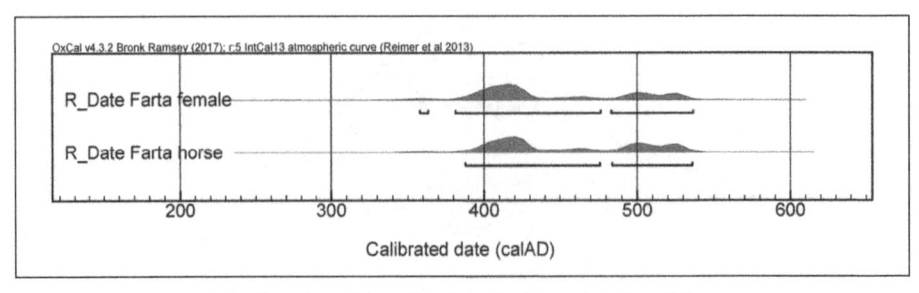

4.6 Radiocarbon determinations for Farta female and horse.

corrected itself and had persisted into adult life (Buckley, 2012), which would have resulted in a deformity, impairing her ability to walk with a normal gait. The horse has been identified as a small horse, estimated shoulder height 1.27 metre, aged about 7 years. It has not been possible to confirm the sex of the horse due to the absence of canine teeth (McCormick, 2013). The c14 dates illustrate the contemporaneity of the female's death and that of the horse[48] (Figure 4.6) (O'Brien in Cahill Wilson et al., 2014, 141–2; O'Brien, 2016, 11–14). As it was most unusual for a woman to own a horse in Early Medieval Ireland, this being a male prerogative (Kelly, 1997, 96), it would appear that this young woman was part of a family, or kin-group, of sufficient status and wealth, to be in a position to permit a horse to be killed and accompany her to the afterlife.

Strontium and oxygen isotope analyses of teeth from the woman and from the horse reveal that neither was of local origin (Cahill Wilson et al., 2014, 141–2; Cahill Wilson and Standish, 2016, 238). There is a possibility that both the woman and horse originated in the east of Ireland, a possibility which may be reflected at Lehinch, Co. Offaly, by the presence of horse portions and deer antler in a grave of an individual (G3), dated to the fifth–sixth century, who was born in the region of their burial. However, the isotope signatures for the Farta burials are also consistent with a possible origin in eastern Britain.

The prospect of a possible connection with East Anglia, where human and horse burial is known in the early Anglo-Saxon period, is attractive, but unfortunately appears unsustainable. A comparison has been proposed with the burial of a female and horse at Sedgeford, East Anglia (Cross, 2009; Faulkner et al., 2014, 96–7), however, that burial has been dated to the seventh–ninth century (cal AD 670–820), and the burial at Farta is dated to the fourth–sixth century. A further suggested comparison is the undated burial of a female (B55) and horse (H1) at Great Chesterton, Essex, but doubt surrounds the link between this human burial and the horse (Evison, 1994, 29). The majority of human and horse burials in East Anglia and other regions of eastern Britain comprise cremated burials, or inhumed male warriors whose horses were usually accompanied by harnesses (O'Brien, 1999a, 112–13; Fern, 2007, 92–108). The most recently researched of these burials is the inhumed warrior and horse burial in Mound 17, Sutton Hoo. The horse has been c14 dated to the sixth–

Mapping Death Project. 48 UBA–23699: 1618±26BP; at 2σ = cal AD 388–536. Date obtained by this writer with the assistance of a grant from the Royal Irish Academy.

seventh century,[49] but there are problems with the date obtained for the male burial, i.e., the fifth–sixth century.[50] Based on the grave assemblage accompanying the male burial, and the date obtained for the horse, a date in the sixth–seventh century has now been assigned to the burials in Mound 17 (Hines and Bayliss, 2017, 236–8, Table 6.1, 319, 326; Carter, 1993, 11, 18).

A fully equipped male warrior, buried with a horse wearing a bridle, discovered at Eriswell, Lakenheath, Suffolk (grave 323, skeleton 4222; horse 4206), previously dated by grave-good evidence to the second quarter of the sixth century, has now been c14 dated to the late fourth–early fifth century (at 95% – cal AD 395–535), the same period as the burial at Farta (Fern, 2007, 96; Hines et al., 2017, Table 6.1, 234). However, based on morphology and grave assemblages, it is unlikely that an origin for the Farta burial can be found in eastern Anglo-Saxon England.

Given the connection between women, horses, and sovereignty (Bhreathnach, 2014, 126), there is the possibility that this burial at Farta might be of someone connected with kingship. There is an intriguing reference contained in the late Middle Irish mythical story *Cath Boinde* (O'Neill, 1905, 178.20), which refers to a *ban echlach* (a female horse messenger). Perhaps the burial at Farta could be that of a *ban echlach* of the Early Medieval period. It is of interest to note the high value placed on a British horse in Ireland, referenced in the seventh–ninth-century *Heptad* XXVIII, where, under the heading 'seven stocks for which it is difficult to return full restitution and profit', among the stocks listed is *gaillite tacair* (foreign mares), which are usually understood to be British mares (*CIH* i, 126–7; Kelly, 1997, 91). As late as AD 1029 in *AU* (Mac Airt and Mac Niocaill, 1983, 466–7), the ransom for Amlaib son of Sitriuc included six score British-Welsh horses (*ech mBretnach*) and sixty ounces of gold. In *DIL* (reprint 1967, fasc. II, E. Joynt and Knott, 27, lines 11–14), under *ech* (horse), *ech bretnach* is defined as a British (Welsh) horse; there is also a reference that *in t-ech bretnach* was sufficient ransom for a life.

Whatever the origin of the Farta burials, isotope results denote the arrival of a new population group into the Galway region, who deliberately interred this female and a horse in an indigenous ancestral burial-mound or *fert*. A recent radiocarbon date obtained for one of two red deer antler objects recovered with, and assumed by the excavator to have accompanied, the burial at Farta indicates that the antler was placed into the mound in the sixth–seventh century AD,[51] sometime after the burial of the female and horse. Perhaps the burial mound had entered local folklore by this time, and the insertion of the antler acted as an offering or perhaps a sealing deposit. While there is currently no indication of a physical territorial boundary associated with this *ferta*, there may be a clue to the presence of an earlier boundary at a point adjacent to the monument, where the barony, townland, and parish boundaries all coincide. The townland name 'Farta' probably evolved from the existence of this, and other *ferta*, in the region.

At Lehinch, Co. Offaly, a sand/gravel hillock,[52] which contained a Bronze Age cremation and an Iron Age penannular ring-ditch, was re-used for the insertion of

---

49 UB–4423: 1420±28BP; at 2σ = cal AD 580–660 (date as published).   50 UB–4422: 1534±35BP; at 2σ = cal AD 426–599.   51 UB–27057: 1407±43BP; at 2σ = cal AD 564–677 (c14 date obtained by the writer, courtesy of the Mapping Death Project).   52 Discovered during gravel extraction.

six+[53] extended inhumation burials, heads to the west, in the Early Medieval period. These included a decapitated male (G5) in a dug grave, whose head was missing, dated to the fifth–sixth century,[54] an elderly male (G4), in a stone-lined dug grave, who had healed fractures to his skull, dated to the fifth–sixth century,[55] and adult (G3), sex undetermined, in a stone-lined dug grave, dated to the fifth–sixth century,[56] who had horse portions (tibia, pelvis and scapula), together with a set of deer antler inserted tine downwards placed beside his/her right side along the southern edge of the grave (Figure 5.9 (c)) (Ó Floinn in Cahill and Sikora, 2011, vol. ii, 139–66; O'Brien and Bhreathnach, 2011, 53–64). Strontium and oxygen isotope analysis indicates that this individual (G3) was of local origin (Cahill Wilson, 2014, 144). A combination of factors, including the possibility that this burial is that of a female (Buckley, 2011, 161), accompanied by the partial remains of a horse, and antler tine, raises the possibility that the people responsible for this burial at Lehinch, Co. Offaly, may have some connection with the people responsible for the burial of the woman and horse at Farta, Co. Galway.

At Ballydavis 1, Co. Laois (Stevens, 2011, 19), an adult male (C908), aged 18–34 years, dated to the fifth–sixth century,[57] was inserted extended, west–east, in a dug grave, into the enclosure of penannular ring-ditch (C125) which already contained Iron Age cremated deposits dated to the first–second century AD.[58]

In Baysrath, Co. Kilkenny (Channing, 2012), an Iron Age penannular ring-ditch (c2064)[59] contained in its north-west quadrant a small penannular Bronze Age ring-ditch with a central cremation pit (c2197) and in its south-east quadrant, a single sub-rectangular grave, partially lined with stones, containing an extended, possibly prone,[60] older adult inhumation (c2189), head east, undated because of the poor quality of the skeletal material. This burial had been set apart from an unenclosed, but organised, cemetery of forty-seven burials,[61] dated to the fifth–sixth, and sixth–seventh century,[62] situated immediately outside the north and east of the Iron Age ring-ditch. This prone individual, who was probably related to those buried in the nearby cemetery, had, for whatever reason, been accorded a different burial rite; he/she was interred in a pre-existing ring-ditch (probably regarded as a pagan burial place), laid prone, and orientated in a direction opposite to the norm. Rather than being accorded the distinction of 'ancestor', this burial is more likely to have been punitive. At this site, the burials and ring-ditches were superseded by the construction of a ringfort in the eighth–ninth century,[63] an occurrence for which there are at least three possible explanations: the siting of the ringfort was a deliberate act either incorporating or suppressing ancestral memory; local memory of the earlier ancestral association had

---

[53] Other disarticulated skeletal material, which had been disturbed by machinery, was also discovered.   [54] GrA–24350: 1550±40BP; at 2σ = cal AD 418–594.   [55] GrA–29065: 1550±40BP; at 2σ = cal AD 418–594.   [56] GrA–24445: 1625±40BP; at 2σ = cal AD 399–541.   [57] UBA–11708: 1608±22BP; at 2σ = cal AD 397–536.   [58] UBA–11705: 1947±27BP; at 2σ = cal AD 0–124.   [59] Date obtained from basal ditch fill: UBA–10704: 2065±24BP; at 2σ (90.5%) = 169–36 cal BC. Date obtained from upper ditch fill: UBA–10679: 2083±22BP; at 2σ = 171–46 cal BC.   [60] It is noted in the description of this very poorly preserved burial that 'both arms were found in an extended and prone position' (Channing, 2012, 181).   [61] The burials could not be sexed owing to the poor quality of the skeletal material.   [62] Grave c2399: UBA–10700: 1538±20BP; at 2σ = cal AD 427–579. Grave c2197: UBA–14016; 1556±27BP; at 2σ = cal AD 424–562. Grave c2332: UBA–11216; 1457±22BP; at 2σ = cal AD 566–646.   [63] Basal fill of ringfort ditch: UBA–10492: 1200±22BP; at 2σ (91.7%) =

receded before the construction of the ringfort; or, the ringfort was constructed and inhabited by people new to the district who were unaware of the pre-existing burials.

Quarrying on the Mayo side of the summit of Kiltullagh Hill, which straddles the Mayo–Roscommon county boundary, resulted in the discovery of the remains on the Mayo side of the hill of five individuals, mainly consisting of skull parts, which had been scattered by quarrying machinery (Cribbin et al., 1994, 61–5). One of these produced a date in the second–fifth century AD,[64] while another has been dated to the fourth–sixth century AD.[65] It is not possible to say whether the earlier burial was crouched or extended, but both were inserted into a small mound. The recognition of the summit of Kiltullagh Hill as an ancestral burial place or *fert* is further highlighted by the adjacent presence on the Roscommon side of the hill of an extended, west–east, slightly flexed, male inhumation, dated to the fifth–sixth century,[66] in a stone-lined grave, marked by a standing stone (McCormick et al., 1995, 89–98). The stone lining of this grave undoubtedly supported a plank grave cover, as the disposition of the skeleton indicates that the body had decomposed in a void. A ring-barrow of unknown date is located on the hill-summit, and an undated cremation deposit in a shallow pit was also discovered nearby.

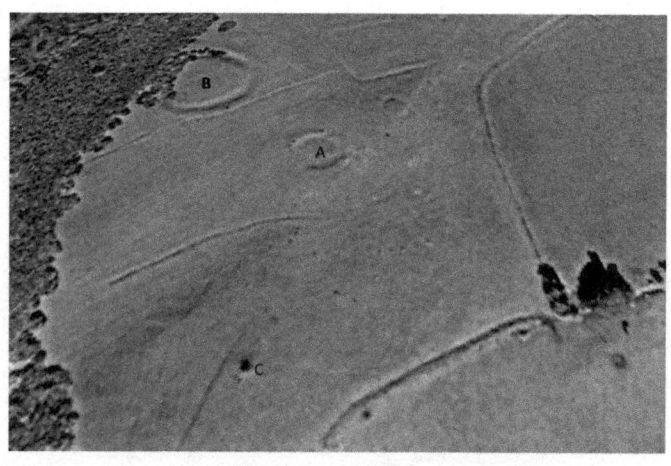

4.7 Overview of sites A, B, C, Carbury Hill, Co. Kildare. (Google Earth)

The insertion of extended inhumation burials into pre-existing ancestral burial places can also be demonstrated at Carbury Hill, Co. Kildare[67] (Figure 4.7). Excavated and re-instated in 1936 (Wilmot, 1938, 130–42), the site consists of two ring-ditches, sites A and B, and a small tumulus, Site C, at the summit of the hill. The following discussion concentrates on Site B, but it is worth mentioning that Site A, a large ring-ditch, contained cremated remains (undated), which produced worked flint artefacts of various types, an iron file, and a burnt blue glass bead, objects indicating probable use in the Neolithic, Bronze Age, and Iron Age. And, Site C, situated at the summit of the hill, had, near its centre, a small pit containing an undated cremation deposit with no grave goods.

Site B is a large circular ring-ditch with an outer bank, an inner rock-cut ditch, and a possible entrance in the north-east quadrant. Four cremation deposits in small pits were discovered in the central excavated area (all identified as juveniles), one of

cal AD 767–892. **64** OxA–3871: 1765±70BP; at 2σ (93.2%) = cal AD 118–411. **65** OxA–3872: 1590±60BP; at 2σ = cal AD 340–598. **66** UB–3847: 1602±19BP; at 2σ = cal AD 404–536. **67** Carbury Hill, located just north of the Bog of Allen, has uninterrupted views across to the Hill of Allen.

4.8 Connections to Carbury Hill, Co. Kildare.

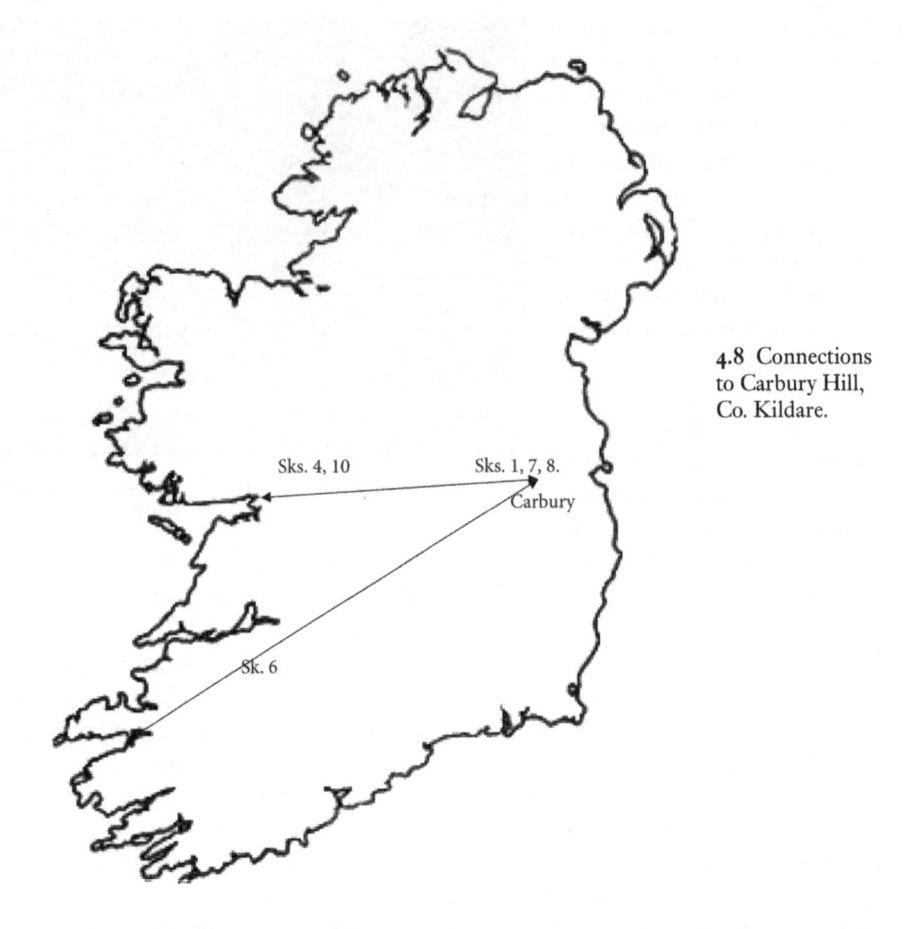

which, Cremation II, contained two small iron rings and a pin-shaped fragment of iron. The central area also contained fifteen extended inhumation burials, heads to the south-west, consisting of five males, three females, four children, two adults (sex undetermined) and one multiple burial comprising an adult, a 6-year-old child, and a neonate. Two post-holes, post-hole A located on the south-east periphery of the burial area, and B, located on the western side of the burials, were cut into the underlying bedrock, and would have contained relatively large posts, perhaps as markers, or, as the excavator pointed out, they might be the remnants of a post circle, the remaining posts of which did not penetrate the bedrock (Wilmot, 1938, 135–6).

Four of the inhumation burials have now been radiocarbon dated,[68] and six have been subjected to strontium and oxygen isotope analysis (Cahill Wilson and Standish, 2016, 237–8).[69] A male (SK 4) produced a date in the third–fourth century AD,[70] thus

---

[68] The date for SK 1 was obtained by Dr Jacqueline Cahill Wilson, and dates for SK 4, 6, 10, were obtained under the auspices of the Mapping Death Project. The cooperation of the National Museum of Ireland in allowing access to the skeletal material from Carbury Hill is gratefully acknowledged. [69] Strontium and oxygen isotope analysis undertaken by Dr Jacqueline Cahill Wilson, under the auspices of the Mapping Death Project. [70] UBA–20008: 1747±37BP; at 2σ (93.5% probability) = cal AD 211–394.

representing one of the earliest dated examples in Ireland of the newly introduced burial rite of extended inhumation. Isotope analysis indicates that this person originated in the west of Ireland. Female (SK 10) produced a date in the fourth–fifth century,[71] and isotope analysis indicates that she also came from the west of Ireland. Female (SK 6) has been dated to the fifth–sixth century,[72] and isotope analysis indicates her place of origin in the south-west of Ireland, around the Kerry coastline. Male (SK 1), who was accompanied by an iron shears, has been dated to the sixth–seventh century,[73] and isotope analysis indicates that he was of local origin. Extended male burials (SK 7 and SK 8) are undated, but isotope analysis indicates that they are both of local origin (Figure 4.8). This is a very interesting mix, with the earliest burials, two of whom are female, having their origins in the western and south-western extremities of Ireland, and the later male burials all being of local origin. Burial at the monument ceased after the seventh century.

While not located on an obvious physical boundary, Carbury Hill may have been regarded as a liminal boundary between the natural world and the otherworld. The hill is known as *Síd Nechtain*, the home of *Nechtan*, the deity consort of *Bóind*, goddess of the River Boyne, which rises at the well of *Segais* located at the base of Carbury Hill. The well of *Segais* is associated with the myth of magical hazelnuts that induced *imbas* ('poetic or prophetic inspiration') (Bhreathnach, 2014, 135; Doherty, 2015, 50–1, 53, 55–6). Burial at Carbury Hill would undoubtedly have been regarded as a great privilege, reserved for the few, which perhaps explains the presence in the fourth–sixth century of persons from far afield. Of interest is the fact that in cemeteries in south Wales three individuals have been identified with strontium and oxygen isotope signatures indicating that they originated possibly in the extreme western coastal region of Ireland (Hemer et al., 2013, 2356), suggesting that perhaps privileged people from that region were permitted to travel over long distances. By the sixth–seventh century, burial at Carbury Hill appears to have been reserved for males from the immediate locality. The inclusion of an iron shears with male burial SK 1, a custom otherwise unknown in Ireland, may have had a ritual significance or may be an indication of his profession.

At Holdenstown 1, Co. Kilkenny, existing Iron Age ring-ditched enclosures were re-used in the Early Medieval period for the insertion of eight extended inhumations (Figure 4.9) (Whitty and Tobin, 2009, 19–21; O'Brien and Bhreathnach, 2011, 53–64). Three extended burials were inserted into the area enclosed by the large penannular ditch which encompassed the complex of smaller ring-ditches. Male burial (B8) has produced a date in the fifth–sixth century,[74] and strontium isotope analysis of his teeth indicates that this person was of local origin (Montgomery and Milns, 2010). Five burials (two female, three male) were inserted into RD2, of which female (B2) has been dated to the sixth–seventh century.[75] Strontium isotope analysis indicates that this female did not originate at her place of burial, rather, she originated either in the south-east corner of Ireland, or in the north or west of Britain[76]

---

[71] UBA–20010: 1659±23BP; at 2σ = cal AD 335–425. [72] UBA–20009: 1535±24BP; at 2σ = cal AD 428–591. [73] UBA–11696: 1491±28BP; at 2σ (93.5% probability) = cal AD 535–643. [74] UBA–13659: 1556±23BP; at 2σ = cal AD 429–558. [75] UB–15562: 1464±30BP; at 2σ = cal AD 551–646. [76] The addition of oxygen isotope analysis might help pinpoint this individual's place of birth.

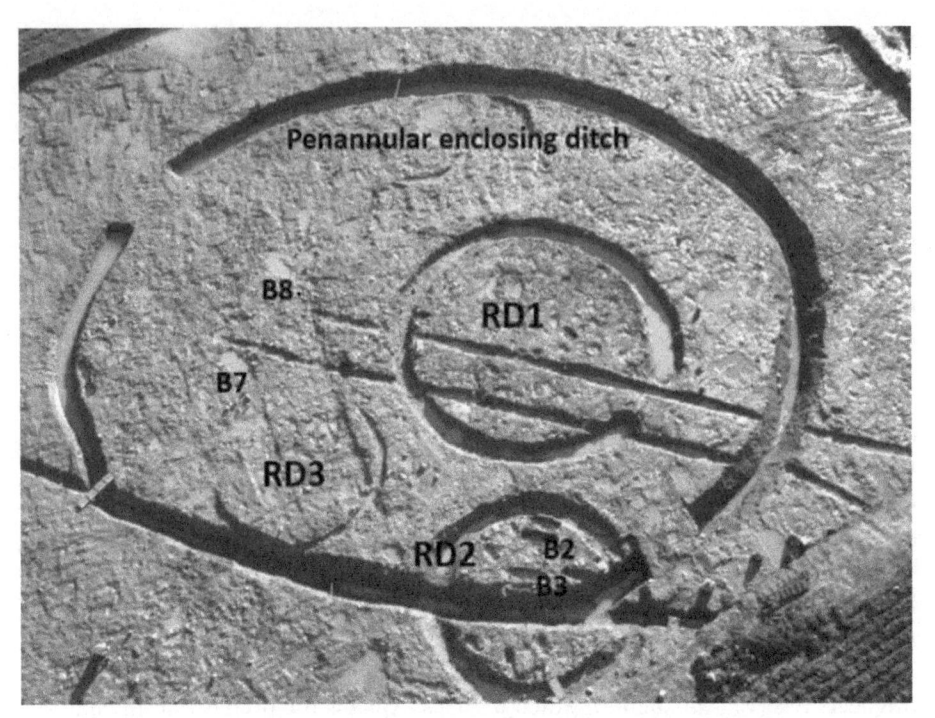

4.9 Holdenstown 1, Co. Kilkenny, based on G. Duffy, airshots, © IAC.

(Montgomery and Milns, 2010). This *ferta* site is closely associated with Holdenstown 2, an unenclosed secular cemetery situated approximately 550m to the north-west.

The Early Medieval unenclosed cemetery of over sixty burials at Betaghstown (Anchorage), Co. Meath, is located on a ridge that already contained prehistoric burials (Eogan, 2010, 101–16). Four of these burials have been dated, female (F44) has been dated to the fifth–sixth century AD,[77] male (F181), a crouched burial, has been dated to the fifth–sixth century AD,[78] female (F251) has been dated to the fifth–sixth century AD,[79] and female (F279) has been dated to the fifth–sixth century AD.[80]

Overlooking a ravine, at Kilcorney, in the Burren, Co. Clare, three slab-lined cist graves were observed in a prehistoric cairn (Grant, 1995, 31–3; 2006, 553; 2010). The central cist, unexcavated, is prehistoric in appearance, while two later insertions are Early Medieval long cists. One Early Medieval slab-lined cist was excavated, and it contained a young female, dated to the sixth–seventh century,[81] accompanied by the bones of an infant. It is probable that the adjoining ravine formed part of a territorial boundary.

At Cross, Co. Galway (Mullins, 2007, 101–10; 2009; Mullins and Birmingham, 2014, 102), located on a low ridge that already contained Late Bronze Age and Iron Age cremation deposits, a male burial (B5), dated to the third–fifth century,[82] in a

[77] UBA-13070: 1565±20BP; at 2σ = cal AD 425–545. [78] UBA-13071: 1612±22BP; at 2σ = cal AD 394–535. [79] UBA-13073: 1526±22BP; at 2σ = cal AD 430–599. [80] UBA-13074: 1583±27BP; at 2σ = cal AD 413–543. [81] UBA-14245: 1419±29BP; at 2σ = cal AD 584–661 (date obtained courtesy Mapping Death Project). [82] Wk21252: 1674±38BP; at 2σ (93.9%) = cal AD 252–429.

stone-lined grave, was partially destroyed by the construction of annular ring-ditch (RD1) in what may have been a deliberate act of 'slighting' what was possibly perceived as a pagan grave, or local memory of the burial had receded.

At Newtown Rath, Swords, Co. Dublin, a site that had previously been used for the burial of a Bronze Age crouched individual, in a partial stone cist, accompanied by two pottery vessels, and a possibly later cremation deposit, became the location for a settlement cemetery containing more than nine burials, surrounded by a wide and deep circular enclosure ditch (Maeve Tobin, IAC, pers. comm.).[83]

A slab-lined grave which contained an undated adult extended inhumation was unearthed in the 1930s at Ballinchalla, Co. Mayo, among a cemetery of several Bronze Age cremation cists (Cahill and Sikora, 2011, vol. 1, 290–303). The grave was 1.5m long and aligned east–west (ibid., 291), making it very likely that this was an Early Medieval grave that had been inserted into an ancestral burial place.

One must be aware that sometimes appearances can be deceptive, for example, at Carrowbeg North, Co. Galway, two Bronze Age tumuli were excavated in 1938 (Wilmott et al., 1939, 121–40). Tumulus 1, a low mound containing a central Bronze Age cremation, was surrounded by a fosse, into the north/north-west quadrant of which four inhumations, one crouched female (SK 1), and three extended burials, female (SK 2), male (SK 3), female (SK 4), had been inserted. The crouched female (SK 1) was accompanied by a small bronze locket at the shoulder and twelve oval bone beads at the left foot. A fragment of linen attached to the locket was identified as 'linen tabby being probably the most important type of cloth in areas under Roman influence' (Bender Jørgensen, 1983). Based on the typology, and morphological evidence, a logical conclusion was that these inhumation burials dated to the Later Iron Age (Raftery, 1981, 187) or to the Early Medieval period (O'Brien, 1984, 76–7). However, c14 dating now places two of the extended burials in the fifteenth–seventeenth century AD[84] (Lanting and Brindley, 1998, 6). Crouched burial (SK 1) was not dated and may be of an earlier era. Why these burials were inserted in the High Medieval period into a Bronze Age monument one will never know, but some hint might be gleaned from a recorded incidence of secondary burial in an Irish prehistoric monument, that is, an entry for AD1581 in the Annals of Loch Cé (Hennessey, 1871, 436), which reads: 'Brian Caech O'Coinnegain, an eminent cleric, and keeper of a general house of guests, died; and the place of sepulture which he selected for himself was, i.e. to be buried at the mound of Baile-an-tobair.[85] And we think that it was not through want of religion Brian Caech made this selection, but because he saw not the service of God practised in any church near him at that time'.

An Anglo-Saxon literary counterpart to the re-use of prehistoric monuments for burial might be the early eighth-century reference to the practice concerning Guthlac who lived in a hut built by him on an island, in the chamber of a prehistoric barrow that had previously been opened by grave-robbers (*Felix*, Colgrave, 1956, 92–5). This was the place in which Guthlac was eventually buried, hence he was buried in a prehistoric burial chamber.

---

83 Post-excavation analysis is ongoing. 84 SK 3: GrA–13603: 270±50BP; at 2σ (81.3% probability) = cal AD 1471–1681. SK 4: GrA–13620: 330±50BP; at 2σ = cal AD 1454–1649. 85 Near Ballintubber Abbey, Co. Mayo.

A further instance of mistaken classification is at the ringfort of Raheennamadra, Co. Limerick, where a male and a female had been buried side by side with knives beside their heads (concealed by hair?), and one had a buckle in the pelvic region. These burials had previously been dated, by this writer among others, to the seventh century AD, based on c14 dates obtained in 1964 from oak posts in an adjacent souterrain[86] (Stenberger, 1965, 37–54; Olsson and Kilicci, 1964, 304–5). A c14 date obtained from the recently discovered skull fragment from one of the burials now places the burials in the seventeenth–nineteenth century AD.[87] It is possible that these individuals were interred here by newcomers to the district during that later period, probably in the mistaken belief that the circular enclosure represented an old burial ground.

Burials in imitative monuments (ferta) constructed in the Early Medieval period
Early Medieval imitative *ferta* were often, but not always, constructed in areas which already contained burial monuments of previous eras. Twenty such *ferta*, constructed between the fourth and seventh centuries AD, have been recognised to date. These include imitative mounds, and ring-ditches which echo Tírechán's description of a *fossa rotunda* (Map 4).

Mounds

A large mound, 5m high, at Ninch 1, Co. Meath, which appears to have been erected in the Early Medieval period, situated on a high bluff on the north side of the River Nanny and overlooking the Irish Sea, was partially excavated and reinstated in 1979 (Sweetman, 1983, 58–68). It contained two extended inhumation burials at its base, one of which, B.1, was excavated. This burial, in an unprotected dug grave, dated fifth–seventh century,[88] contained the remains of bracken or fern that may have been used to cover or enclose the body. B.2, in a slab-lined grave, was not excavated. The location of the mound suggests that it functioned as a boundary *fert*, with the incumbents perhaps guarding against incursion from the Irish Sea.

At Knocknashammer, Co. Sligo (Timoney, 1977; 1984, 324; 1987/88, 77),[89] a burial mound was constructed in the fifth–sixth century, on top of a gravel ridge, close to, and within sight of, the megalithic cemetery complex at Carrowmore, and is imitative of at least some of the burial mounds associated with that ancestral burial complex. The mound was well-built, 1.4m high, 11m diameter, surrounded by a shallow fosse and slight outer bank. At the centre of the mound, in a layer of soil between layers of stones, were the remains of three extended burials, two male (SK 1, SK 2) and one female (SK 3) (Buckley, 2019), in unprotected dug graves. C14 dates indicate that the central male (SK 2), aged 25+, who died in the fifth–sixth century,[90] and the female

---

86 Dates as published Upsala, Radiocarbon vol. 6, 1964, 304. 1430±130BP = AD 520 (recent calibration at 2σ = cal AD 339–888); 1260±120BP = AD 690 (recent calibration at 2σ = cal AD 576–1016): 1280±120BP = AD 670 (recent calibration at 2σ = cal AD 548–996).   87 UB-14415: 174±31BP; at 75.4% probability = cal AD 1657–1878. Thanks are due to the National Museum of Ireland for releasing material to this writer for c14 dating, which was conducted under the auspices of the Mapping Death Project.   88 GU-1453: Uncalibrated date unavailable. Published date, at 2σ = cal AD 420–650.   89 Grateful thanks are due to Martin Timoney for providing details, including a recently obtained osteology report, and c14 dates, and permission to use these, for this significant *ferta*.   90 UBA-40297: 1548±43BP; at 2σ = cal AD 416–599.

Grave, burial and secular cemetery types 83

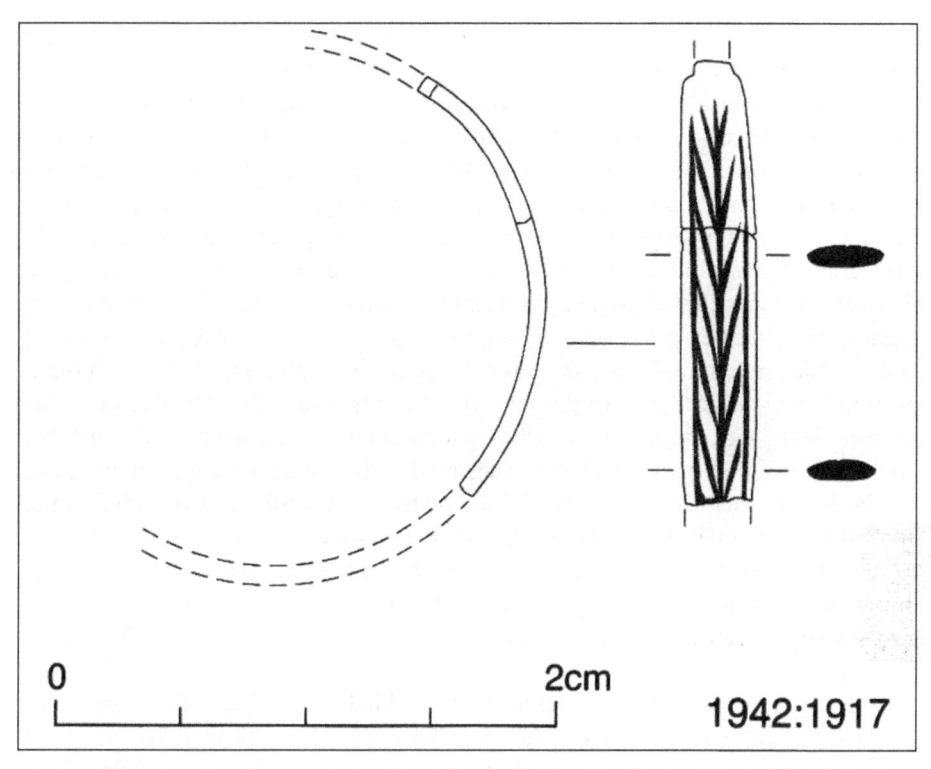

4.10 Silver ring from Rossnaree, Co. Meath, © courtesy of the National Museum of Ireland.

(SK 3), middle-aged, located approximately 1m north of SK 2, who also died in the fifth–sixth century,[91] were contemporaries, and probably represent members of a kin-group, who were, after their deaths, regarded as ancestors. The second male (SK 1), aged 45+, died in the sixth–seventh century,[92] but was interred in the same grave as male SK 2, thereby disturbing the original skeletal remains, a possible indicator that the earlier grave had been marked in some way.[93] This imitative mound was deliberately constructed within sight of an ancient ancestral burial complex in order to give an impression of continuity, by a kin-group who claimed control of territory in the fifth–sixth century. The later sixth–seventh century burial of an elderly male (SK 1) in the same grave as the original male burial (SK 2) marked the cessation of burial in the monument. This cessation of use is in line with the fate of other burial monuments of this period, but the mound may have continued to be recognised by subsequent generations of the kin-group as the burial place of their ancestors.

At Rossnaree, Co. Meath, on the south bank of the River Boyne, directly across the river from the Knowth burial complex, a small mound/cairn (known locally as King Cormac's mound), which covered an unprotected dug grave containing the

[91] UBA-40298: 1577±29BP; at 2σ = cal AD 413–547. [92] UBA-40295: 1458±27BP; at 2σ = cal AD 559–647. [93] The remains of SK 2 and SK 3 appear to have petrous bone remains which would enable DNA scrutiny to determine if there is a familial relationship between them; and SK 1 and SK 2 have teeth that would enable isotopic analysis to determine whether they are local to the area, or are incomers.

remains of a middle-aged female, dated fourth–fifth century,[94] accompanied by an infant (0–6 months), was excavated in 1942 (Cahill and Sikora, 2011, 113–19). The burial was supine with legs slightly flexed at the knees, but, was unusual in that the head was at the eastern end of the grave. Accompanying the skeleton were two fragments of a silver ring (possible earring) with herring-bone decoration (Figure 4.10) very similar in design to that used on Roman finger rings (ibid., 116). The design on the ring also resembles that on a toe ring from the Iron Age crouched burial at Rath, Co. Meath. Strontium and oxygen isotope analysis indicates that this woman from Rossnaree was possibly of local origin (Cahill Wilson et al., 2014a, 130). Osteological examination (Buckley, 2011, 117–18) suggests that she had performed hard physical labour, which might imply that she was not a person of importance in her own right, perhaps it was the accompanying infant who was important. The orientation of this woman's body, with the head to the east, could mean that she was not a Christian, but might also be a preventative measure to ensure that she did not return from the grave. Partial remains of two further female burials had previously been recorded in the general vicinity in slab-lined graves, but details are limited (Raftery, 1941, 302).[95]

At Kildangan, Co. Kildare, a hillock, which had the appearance of an ancestral burial mound, contained a dug grave, possibly lined with wood, with the remains of a young adult female dated fourth–sixth century,[96] who had borne children (Ó Floinn, 2011, 51–4).

A natural mound used for burial in the Early Medieval period at Pollacorragune, Co. Galway, was located on the same gravel ridge as Carnfanny Bronze Age cairn, and contained four extended, supine inhumations in unprotected dug graves (Riley, 1936, 44–54; Shea, 1936, 54–64; Raftery, B., 1981, 186; O'Brien, 1984, 82). The central burial (SK D), a male, has been dated to the fourth–sixth century[97] (Lanting and Brindley, 1998, 6). Located close to the back of his skull a circular fragment of iron, 5 inch in diameter, was identified by the excavator as the remains of a shield boss and a further small fragment of iron was located on his chest. Is it possible that this male had been placed into the grave with his head resting on a shield? If so, this is unique in Ireland. In the same mound, a female burial (SK B), dated to the sixth–seventh century,[98] had two small fragments of iron by her right elbow. The fill of both burials contained fragments of split animal bone. The temporal gap between the insertion of these two burials demonstrates that this mound was used for burial on at least two separate occasions during the Early Medieval period, reinforcing the possibility that this was regarded as an ancestral burial place.

Imitative ring-ditches[99]
Examples of ring-ditches imitative of Bronze Age and Iron Age types, but constructed in the Early Medieval period, indicated in Map 4, and in Gazetteer 2, include: two

[94] GrA–24354: 1660±40BP; at 2σ = cal AD 256–534, but with a high probability (76.2%) cal AD 317–435. [95] In Cahill and Sikora, 2011, these two burials have been combined in the text with the burial beneath the mound, although they were located nearby as noted by Raftery. [96] GrA–24336: 1610±45BP; at 2σ = cal AD 344–551. [97] GrA–13613: 1620±70BP; at 2σ (89.4% probability) = cal AD 315–588. [98] GrA–13612: 1450±50BP; at 2σ (92.0% probability) = cal AD 534–666. [99] The practice of placing individual burials within small penannular enclosures was adopted in several large early Anglo-Saxon cemeteries, notably Finglesham, and St Peter's, Broadstairs, Kent, possibly to distinguish the persons thus interred as being 'different' from the majority in the

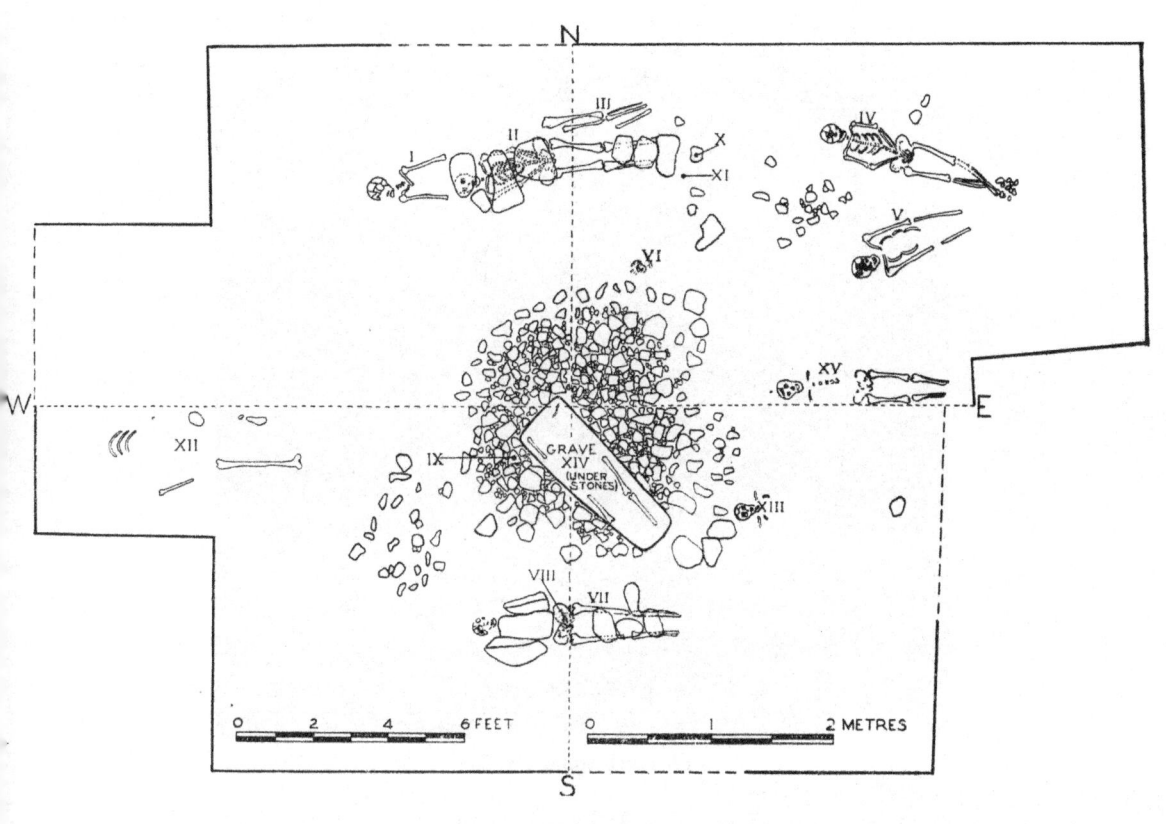

4.11 Plan Site 6. The Curragh, Co. Kildare (after Ó Riordáin, 1950, fig. 7), © RIA.

ring-ditches, sites 6 and 4, located on The Curragh, Co. Kildare.[100] The earliest phase of ring-ditch Site 6 (Ó Ríordáin, 1950, 200–69) consisted of a centrally placed dug-grave containing friable remains of an extended, west–east, supine, decapitated male (B XIV). His head was missing, and he was covered by a cairn surrounded by several small ditches (Figure 4.11). The monument was subsequently enlarged by the digging of the outer enclosing ditch with an external and an internal bank. Within this altered monument were placed approximately ten adult inhumations (four males, two females, four unidentified) together with one juvenile and one neonate.

The final burial in this monument (B II) has now been dated to the eleventh–twelfth century AD.[101] Unfortunately, the skeletal remains from the earliest burial (B XIV) were not suitable for c14 dating, but the disposition of the body suggests that it dates to the Early Medieval period. It would appear that this ring-barrow was recognised as an ancestral burial place throughout the Early Medieval period and was re-used for interment until the eleventh–twelfth century (for Site 4, see chapter 6).

cemetery (O'Brien, 1999, 135–9). **100** The Curragh is a 'ritual' landscape which consists of an ancient unenclosed grassland plain covering an area of 10km north-west/south-east, and 5km east-west (Clancy and Leigh, 2007, 3) incorporating many barrows, some of which have been excavated (Ó Ríordáin, 1950, 250–77). **101** UBA-21802: 934±37BP; at 2σ = cal AD 1022–1182. Date obtained by this writer, under the auspices of the Mapping Death Project.

4.12 Turoe Stone, Co. Galway.

At Castle Upton, Templepatrick, Co. Antrim (Gahan, 1998; O'Brien, 1999a, 183), a small penannular Early Medieval ring-ditch was uncovered in an area incorporating remains from the Neolithic to the Early Historic period. Centrally placed within the ring-ditch was a stone-lined grave, aligned west–east, together with a smaller parallel dug grave, probably for a child. Unfortunately, no skeletal material survived, but the morphology suggests that this is an imitative burial monument constructed in an ancestral landscape.

The Rath of Feerwore, a penannular ring-ditch, excavated in 1938 (Raftery, 1944a, 23–52), was constructed in close proximity to the original location of the iconic Turoe Stone (Figure 4.12), and approximately 500m south-east of Farta. The ring-ditch (now quarried) contained a centrally placed burial of an elderly female, extended west–east, supine, in a slab-lined cist grave. The lower part of the skeleton and the grave structure had been quarried away prior to excavation. A few disarticulated skeletal fragments were recovered beside the inner bank of the enclosure.[102] Feerwore and its associated central burial had previously been assumed to date to between 100BC and AD100 (Raftery, J., 1944a, 42; Raftery, B., 1981, 191) based on the presence within the enclosure of a cremation deposit (Knox, 1915) which has now been discounted (Waddell, 1975, 10) and prehistoric flint arrowheads, which were, in hindsight, residual. Radiocarbon determinations obtained in 2006[103] now place the central female

---

[102] Bone fragments are now untraceable, probably not retained after excavation. [103] Radiocarbon dates obtained by this writer with the aid of a grant from the Royal Irish Academy.

Grave, burial and secular cemetery types 87

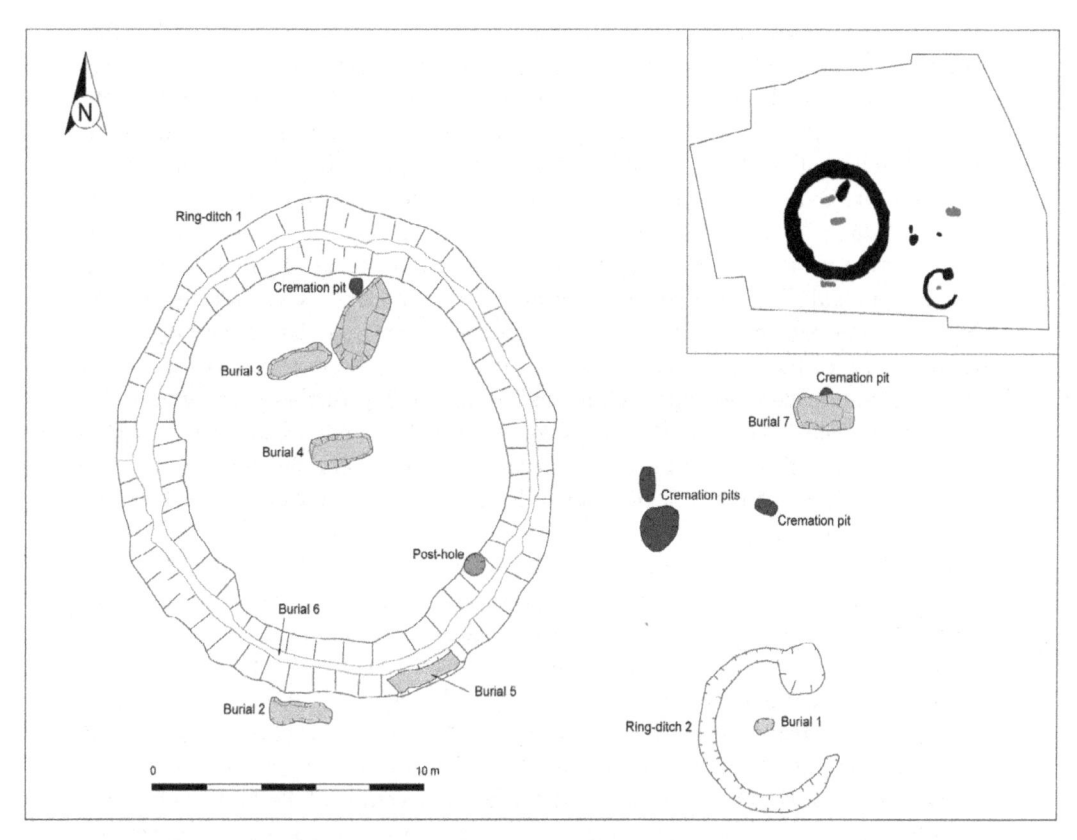

4.13 Site plan of Cross, Co. Galway, taken from Mullins & Birmingham, 2014, fig. 4.4.2.

burial in the fifth–sixth century AD.[104] Perhaps the proximity of the Iron Age Turoe Stone, which is currently dated to between the first century BC and the first century AD (Waddell, 2000, 356; O'Brien, 2006, 11), influenced the construction in the Early Medieval period of this ring-ditch with its central female burial. The finds from the enclosure (not associated with the burial), mainly iron fragments, and an iron bell,[105] suggest that limited industrial activity in the form of ironworking may have been undertaken inside the enclosure in the Early Medieval period.

At Cross, Co. Galway (Mullins, 2007, 101–10; 2009; Mullins and Birmingham, 2014, 102), located on a low ridge which already contained Late Bronze Age and Iron Age cremation deposits, a male burial (B5) dated to the third–fifth century[106] in a stone-lined grave was partially destroyed by the construction of annular ring-ditch (RD1) in what may have been a deliberate act of 'slighting' what may have been perceived as a pagan grave. Alternatively, local memory of the burial may have receded. RD1 surrounded a centrally placed stone-lined grave containing an extended female (B4), aged 25–35 years, dated to the fourth–sixth century[107] (Figure 4.13), the disposition of whose feet indicate that she was not shroud wrapped. An adolescent

---

[104] UB–7154: 1541±32BP; at 2σ = cal AD 429–591.   [105] The bell is of a type for use on animals; pers. comm., Cormac Bourke.   [106] Wk21252: 1674±38BP; at 2σ (93.9%) = cal AD 252–429.
[107] Wk21251: 1604±39BP; at 2σ = cal AD 342–538.

(B3), dated to the fifth–sixth century,[108] was interred in the north-west quadrant of the ring-ditch, an elderly female (B7), dated to the fourth–sixth century,[109] was interred in a stone-lined grave approximately 8.5m east of RD1, and a young female (B2), dated to the fifth–sixth century,[110] was subsequently interred in a dug grave immediately south of RD1. In the fifth–seventh century,[111] the body of a young male (B6) was interred across the fill of the ditch of RD1, perhaps indicating the cessation of use of that ring-ditch. The final use of this site for burial purposes involved the construction nearby of a small penannular ring-ditch (RD2) which contained the burial of a child (B1), aged about 2½ years, dated to the sixth–seventh century,[112] at its centre. The presence of white quartz pebbles in the graves of B1, B4 and B7 marks them out as 'different' and is a possible indicator that these represent Christians buried among pagan ancestors. The construction of ring-ditches surrounding the burial of female (B4) and child (B1) suggests that these individuals were possibly associated with a family or kin-group that set them apart from the norm.[113]

At Corbally, Co. Kildare, a complex of Early Medieval burials and cereal-drying kilns was uncovered on a gravel ridge (now demolished by industrial quarrying) in a ritual/sacred landscape with occupation from the Neolithic to the Medieval period. As quarrying progressed along the ridge several ring-ditches with internal and external burials were exposed, sites 1, 2, 3 (Figure 4.14a). Site 1 (Tobin, 2003, 32–7; Tobin and Sunderland, 2004) consisted of an Early Medieval ring-ditch (11.5m diameter) with entrances on the east and west, enclosing five extended, supine, west–east burials, two male, one female, two juveniles. The central male burial (B5), interred in a grave carefully lined with stones, has been dated to the fourth–sixth century,[114] and a young male (B1) has been dated to the fifth–sixth century.[115] Preliminary isotopic results (Daly, 2015) for central male burial (B5) suggest that he had spent his childhood locally, whereas young male (B1), while born locally, had moved away from the locality in childhood, but had been returned for burial, an indication that he may have been fostered by another family, in the Irish tradition (Kelly, 1988, 86–7; Charles-Edwards, 2000, 82–3, 115–17). Site 1 also produced the burial of an elderly female (B2) dated to the fourth–sixth century,[116] in a kiln situated 8m south-east of the ring-ditch.

The earliest feature at Site 2 (Coyne, 2003; Coyne and Lynch, 2010, 77–90) was an Early Medieval annular ring-ditch (phase 1), 12m diameter, with a central west–east grave containing two adult males (B59, B88), and one adult, sex unidentified (B89), none of which have been dated. However, a grave located immediately south of the head of the male grave, contained three adult females (B67, B90, B92), one of which (B92) has been dated to the fourth–sixth century.[117] A further burial (B27), an

---

108 Wk21250: 1581±38BP; at 2σ = cal AD 399–559.   109 Wk21254: 1604±38BP; at 2σ = cal AD 382–550.   110 Wk21249: 1587±38BP; at 2σ = cal AD 396–556.   111 Wk21253: 1538±39BP; at 2σ = cal AD 423–600.   112 Wk21248: 1489±38BP; at 2σ = cal AD 432–647; at 84.5% = cal AD 532–647.   113 Strontium and oxygen isotope analysis of teeth from B2, B4, B5, B7, is currently being undertaken by Niamh Daly UCC. The results may help provide answers to the origin of the persons interred at Cross.   114 UBA–31469: 1619±27BP; at 2σ = cal AD 385–537 (date obtained by Niamh Daly).   115 UBA–30392: 1539±30BP; at 2σ = cal AD 426–586 (date obtained by Mapping Death Project).   116 UBA–30393: 1636±41BP; at 2σ = cal AD 332–538 (date obtained by Mapping Death Project).   117 Beta–194919: 1630±50BP; at 2σ (93.1%) = cal AD 325–550.

elderly female, interred in a grave located in the entrance to phase 1 ring-ditch, has been dated to the fifth–seventh century.[118] It is possible that this latter grave represents a sealing of the entrance to the ring-ditch. A female burial (B125), recovered in a grave laid across the fill of the ring-ditch, had been subjected to sharp weapon trauma. This ring-ditch was subsequently enclosed by a phase 2 larger penannular ring-ditch (35m x 26m diameter), dated to between the late fifth to seventh century (Coyne and Lynch, 2010, 83), which enclosed burials representing over-spill from the phase 1 ring-ditch. The latest burial, an adolescent male (B140), dated to the eighth–eleventh century,[119] was one of seven juveniles all of whom were in the space between ring-ditch 1 and ring-ditch 2, indicating that perhaps certain families continued to return to this location for burial purposes into the Medieval period. Ring-ditches of phases 1 and 2 were finally enclosed in the sixth–eighth century within a larger penannular phase 3 enclosure (45m x 50m diameter) (Lynch and Coyne, 2010, 83). Preliminary strontium and oxygen isotope analysis of bone and teeth has been undertaken on six burials from Site 2 (Daly, 2015). Female burials (B90, B92), dated to the fourth–sixth century, female burial (B27), dated to the fifth–seventh century, B75 (undated), and male burial (B42) are all of local origin.

At Site 3 (Coyne, 2007; Coyne and Lynch, 2010, 79–80), three Early Medieval ring-ditches, two of which contained burials, and eight inhumations outside the ring-ditches, were excavated. None of the material from Site 3 has yet been dated. Six of the burials within annular ring-ditch (C53) at the northern part of the site were supine, west–east inhumations, but two of the burials were unusual in that they had been laid at right angles to each other (Figure 6.3). Penannular ring-ditch (C31), located approximately 5m south of ring-ditch (C53), contained one centrally positioned burial of an adult male (B180), supine, west–east, in a dug grave with stone lining along one side. An iron nail was found above the right shoulder of the skeleton, a possible indicator of the presence of a wooden grave cover. A third ring-ditch, located in the south-east quadrant of the area, contained no burials.

Aligned along a gravel ridge at Greenhills, Co. Kildare (Keeley, 1991a, 180–201) (Figure 4.14b), a small unenclosed cemetery containing sixteen burials had, at its southern end, a small penannular ring-ditch surrounding two parallel burials, an adult female (B15) in a wood-lined grave,[120] dated to the fourth–sixth century,[121] and a juvenile (B16), aged 6–9 years, undated, but apparently contemporary with the female. Unfortunately, the female (B15) had no surviving teeth, but strontium and oxygen isotope analysis obtained for the juvenile (B16) indicates that this child was born locally (Cahill Wilson et al., 2014, 142). One of the burials from the unenclosed portion of the cemetery, an elderly female (B6), is a contemporary of female B15 within the ring-ditch.[122] The female and juvenile were probably set apart in the ring-ditch because they were somehow different. They were either of a status which entitled them to such burial, or perhaps the remainder of the burials were Christian, and they were not.

118 Beta–194918: 1460±60BP; at 2σ = cal AD 429–665.   119 Beta–194920: 1130±60BP; at 2σ (95.0%) = cal AD 769–1019.   120 The presence of thin lines of 'charcoal' along the sides, and between the lower legs, lends itself to this hypothesis.   121 UBA–20007: 1622±23BP; at 2σ = cal AD 388–535 (date obtained by Mapping Death Project).   122 GrN–18242: 1610±35BP; at 2σ = cal AD 358–544.

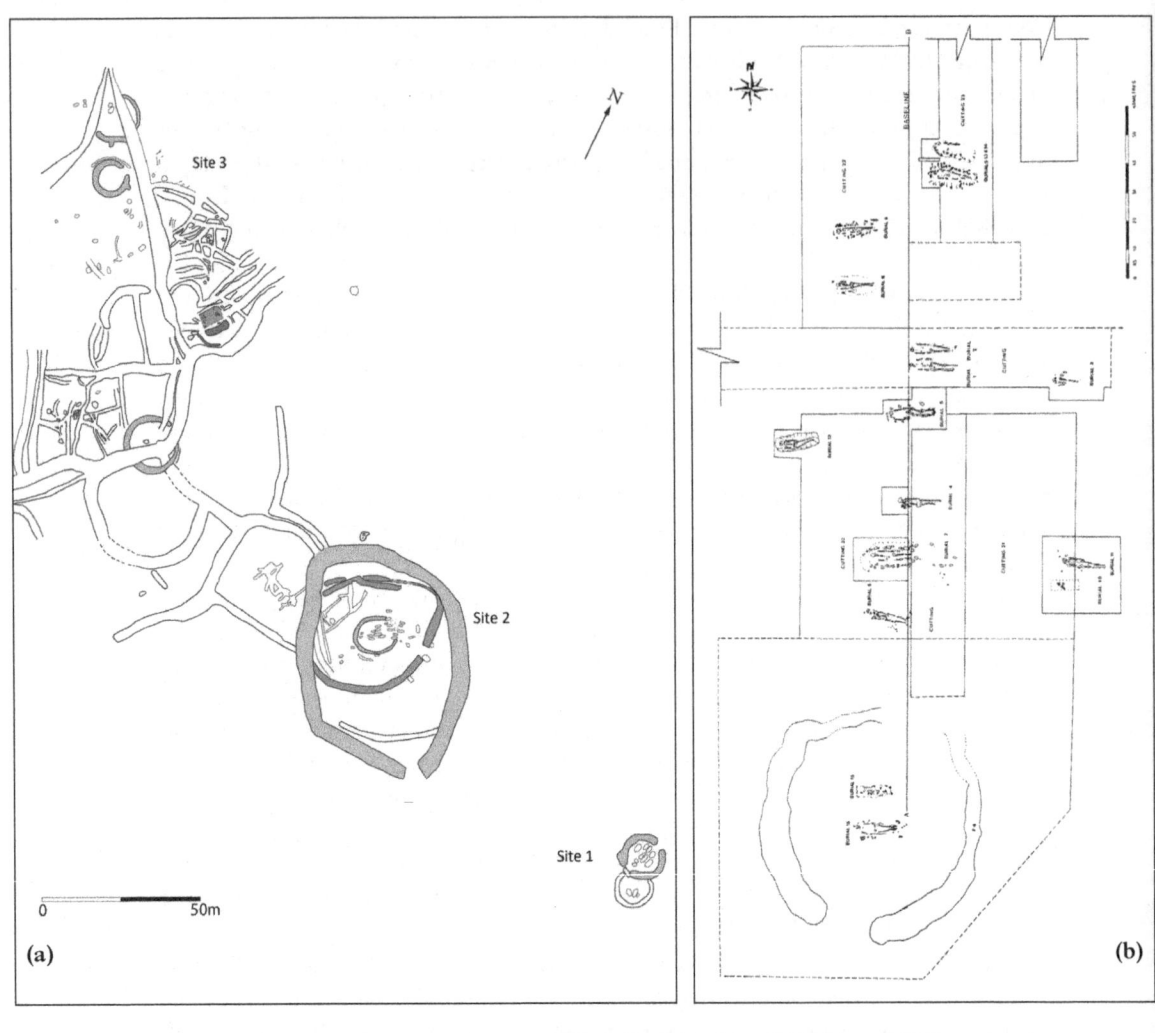

4.14 Sites with penannular enclosures: (a) Corbally sites 1, 2, 3, Co. Kildare © F. Coyne, Aegis Arch.; (b) Greenhills, Co. Kildare, ©VJK.

At Ardsallagh 1, Co. Meath (Randolph-Quinney, 2006a; Clarke and Carlin, 2009, 8–20), twenty-four of thirty inhumation burials in a secular cemetery, dating fifth–seventh century, were enclosed within an Early Medieval penannular ring-ditch, constructed in an area which has produced evidence for funerary activity from the Bronze Age and Iron Age. Male burial (B16), dated to the fifth–sixth century,[123] interred in a simple dug grave in the enclosure entrance, cannot be regarded as a 'closure' or 'sealing' burial, because his burial pre-dates four burials within the enclosure, B2, B11-B15 (double burial, adult male and juvenile),[124] and B29.[125] The

123 Beta–222016: 1560±40BP; at 2σ = cal AD 410–583.   124 B2: Beta–222041: 1470±40BP; at 2σ (92.3%) = cal AD 535–655: B11: Beta–237059: 1490±40BP; at 2σ =cal AD 450–640 (highest probability at 82.3% = cal AD 530–648).   125 B29: Beta–237060: 1460±40BP: at 2σ = cal AD 536–659. This burial is accompanied by an interesting grave good, a probable sceptre.

reason for placing burial B16 in the entrance is unknown, perhaps he was regarded as a 'guardian' of any burials subsequently placed within the enclosure. At this site the earliest dated burial, an adolescent (B4), dated to the fourth–sixth century,[126] sex unknown, is interred in a dug grave outside the enclosure.

In the cemetery at Collierstown 1, Co. Meath,[127] a young adult female (B48), dated to the fifth–sixth century,[128] was buried in a grave which was centrally placed within a penannular ring-ditch, 15m diameter, and covered by a small mound, around which a large cemetery subsequently grew (O'Brien, 2007; O'Hara, 2009a; 2009b, 83–100).

The site at Colp West 1, Co. Meath, represented a settlement cemetery with approximately 120 burials located within and surrounding a penannular ring-ditch (15m diameter). The central burial within the ring-ditch, a female (B102) and potentially the foundation burial, has been dated to the latter half of the sixth century.[129] A nearby male (B65), interred in the deepest grave within the ring-ditch, has been dated to the sixth–seventh century.[130]

The cemetery at Johnstown, Co. Meath (Fibiger, 2005, 99–110; Clarke and Carlin, 2008, 55–85; 2009, 1–20; Clarke 2010, 61–75), began with the construction of a small mound (F1187), beneath which were the foundation burials of an older adult female (B110) dated to the fourth–seventh century,[131] the disarticulated remains of three adults (B129) in an oval pit, which produced a date in the fourth–seventh century,[132] and an adult female (B33), supine, extended, within a dug grave, dated to the fifth–seventh century.[133]

Burial at the settlement cemetery at Raystown, Co. Meath (Seaver, 2016), commenced in the fourth–fifth century, with the establishment of a secular cemetery within a penannular ring-ditch (20m diameter). The earliest dated and the probable foundation burial is that of female (B853), aged 36–45 years, dated to the fourth–fifth century,[134] who was buried together with a juvenile, B852.

Located on a ridge overlooking the Irish Sea with evidence for activity dating back to the Neolithic, the unenclosed cemetery of thirty-two burials at Ninch 3, Co. Meath, included a penannular ring-ditch (11m diameter) (Powell, 2004; Park, 2008). The western part of the cemetery, with its contiguous burials, had been removed during the construction of the adjacent railway-line in the nineteenth century, but it seems that the ring-ditch originally formed a central focal feature in this cemetery and probably represents a foundation burial. A single stone-lined grave, central within the ring-ditch, contained four burials, who appear to represent a family group. These comprised an adult male (B25), aged 26–35 years, dated to the fourth–sixth century,[135] an adult female (B28), aged 26–35 years, dated to the fifth–sixth century,[136] two children, (B26) aged 1–5 years, and (B27) aged 6–12 years. However, excavation has

---

126 Beta–222015: 1620±40BP; at 2σ = cal AD 345–541. **127** This cemetery is located on the east bank of the Gabhra River, a sacred river (stream) which rises at nearby Tara and flows through the Gabhra Valley to the River Skane. **128** BA250161: 1550±40BP; at 2σ = cal AD 422–596. **129** UBA–15649: 1503±22BP; at 2σ (91.6%) = cal AD 535–619 (c14 dates for Colp West 1 were obtained courtesy of the Mapping Death Project). **130** UBA–15648: 1464±24BP; at 2σ = cal AD 556–645. **131** Beta–178195: 1560±70BP; at 2σ (93.8%) = cal AD 379–640. **132** Beta–178197: 1560±70BP; at 2σ (93.8%) = cal AD 379–640. **133** Beta–184610: 1460±70BP; at 2σ = cal AD 425–670. **134** Wk–16823: 1647±33BP; at 2σ = cal AD 263–535. At 78.6% = cal AD 330–435. **135** UBA–20057: 1620±24BP; at 2σ = cal AD 390–535. **136** UBA–20058: 1529±20BP; at 2σ = cal AD 435–547 (dates obtained by Mapping Death Project).

revealed that the female was the first to be interred in the grave, with the male inserted above and to the left of her. The younger child (B26) was placed directly above the female, while the older child (B27) was placed adjacent to B26. Strontium and oxygen isotope signatures (Cahill Wilson et al., 2014, 144–5) indicate that the male (B25) had his origin possibly in central or eastern Europe, and the female (B28) appears to have originated in north-eastern Ireland. The proximity of the site to the shore of the Irish Sea raises the option that one of these burials, male B25, represents an immigrant who was probably involved in the movement of peoples from post-Roman mainland Europe during the 'migration period', and who possibly established a family unit in this location, culminating in the development of the cemetery. It is also possible that the woman (B28) was part of an indigenous family or kin-group of status, albeit from another part of Ireland, and this ring-ditch was constructed as part of her burial ritual. A fifth burial (B22), located in the southern extremity of the ring-ditch, had been partially destroyed by the railway cutting.

An Early Medieval penannular ring-ditched enclosure (9.5m diameter) was a prominent feature in a secular cemetery of approximately fifty-seven burials in slab-lined and dug graves at Westreave, Co. Dublin (Gowen, 1989b, 18; O'Brien, 1992b, 133; 1993, 98; 1999, 181–2; 2003, 62–72; 2009, 149). The ring-ditch contained eleven burials, with a central, probable foundation burial (B32), sex unknown, dated to the fifth–sixth century,[137] in a larger than necessary dug grave,[138] directly aligned on the entrance feature. Seven further burials were dug across the enclosure ditch, and the remainder were interred, some in rows, outside the western side of the enclosure (Figure 4.15). That these outer burials were contemporary with those within the enclosure is indicated by B29, sex unknown, in a slab-lined cist grave, dated fifth–sixth century.[139]

At the Iron Age site at Ballydavis 1, Co. Laois (Stevens, 2011, 16), a probable Early Medieval imitative monument is represented by the annular ring-ditch (C140), undated, but which cut through, and therefore post-dated, the Iron Age ring-ditch (C105), dated to the first century BC–first century AD. Enclosed within C140 was a structure, defined by a slot trench and associated stake-holes, which formed a circular arrangement 6.3m diameter, which in turn enclosed a circular burial pit (C192) containing disarticulated human remains of a male and a female, dated to the third–fifth century AD,[140] together with animal bone. This structure, of a type otherwise unknown in Irish cemeteries of this period, was apparently deliberately constructed to surround the burial pit with its disarticulated burials, the deposition of which may represent the burial of ancestors whose remains had been previously curated elsewhere. Also interred within this ring-ditch were the undated remains of two full-term perinates (SK 101, SK 255).

Evidence for the curation of human remains has been discovered in the ceremonial site at Raffin, Co. Meath (Newman et al., 2007, 349–52), where a ritual pit, located within a triple ring-ditched enclosure, contained three distinct ritual levels of charcoal

---

137 UBA-13374: 1522±19BP; at 2σ = cal AD 431–600 (c14 dates for Westreave were obtained courtesy of the Mapping Death Project).   138 The large size of this grave-cut is an indication that perishable organic material was likely to have accompanied the burial.   139 UBA-13375: 1545±22BP; at 2σ = cal AD 427–567. This burial, B29, had a belt buckle at the waist.   140 SUERC-9014: 1690±35BP; at 2σ = cal AD 253–419 (at 75.5% probability = cal AD 312–419). As this date

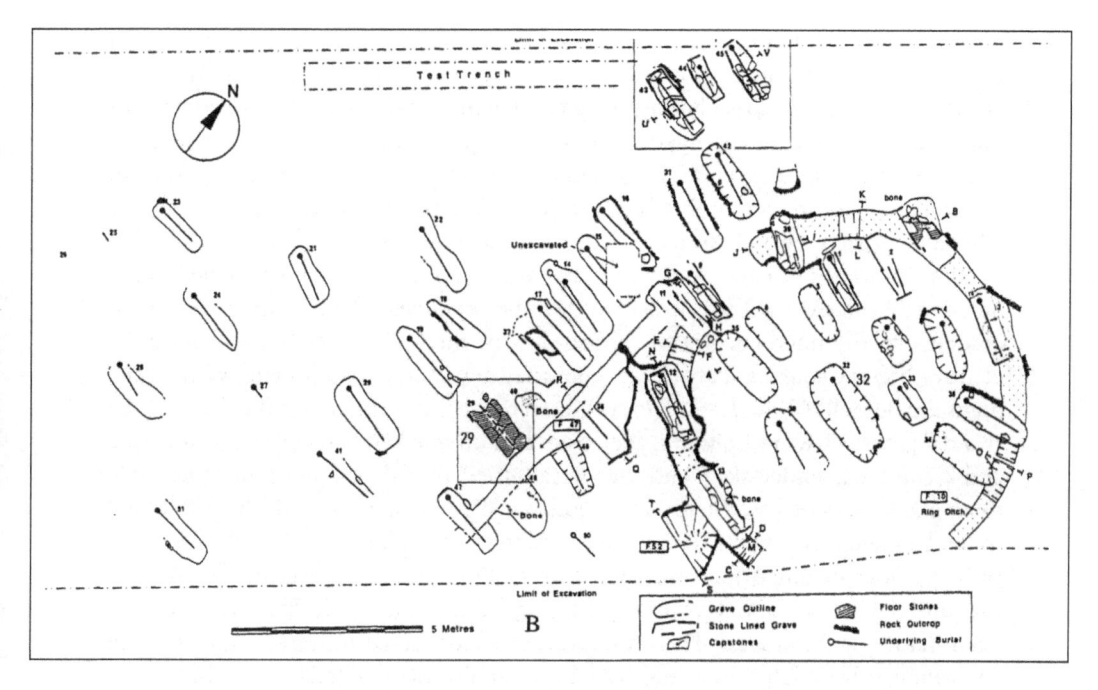

4.15 Plan of cemetery at Westreave, Co. Dublin, showing burials 29, 32 © MGL.

depositions, the latest level dating to the third–fifth century AD.[141] Placed above this level was a fragment of the frontal cranium of an adult human, possibly male, dated to between the second century BC–second century AD,[142] together with an animal rib and pelvic bone. The pit was then sealed by the erection of a standing stone. The excavator has observed that, as the skull fragment was at least a century old when deposited in the pit, and was worn smooth around the edges suggesting frequent handling, it represents a curated object.

Secular unenclosed cemeteries, often located on gravel/sand ridges
Ireland is traversed by many gravel/sand ridges deposited by retreating ice, representing areas of well-drained land surrounded by low-lying damp land. This well-drained land was eminently suitable for burial purposes. Numerous burials, disturbed during gravel and sand extraction throughout the country over many years, have been reported to the National Museum of Ireland, and are recorded in the NMI topographical files. In many cases, skeletal material has not been retained, but where it has been retained and deposited in the NMI, much of the material has now been dated and published by Cahill and Sikora (2011).

A limited number of the many examples have already been examined in this publication including the sites of Prumplestown, Greenhills, Ninch 3 and Corbally. Others include Kildimo, Co. Limerick, where quarrying over a period of years exposed

was obtained from oak wood in the pit-fill, it should be treated with caution in view of possible old-wood effect.   **141** GrA–25763: 1670±40BP; at 2σ (90.7% probability) = cal AD 252–431.   **142** AA–10281: 1975±50BP; at 2σ = cal 104 BC–AD 131.

human remains representing a possible small unenclosed secular cemetery, and in 2005 further skeletal material was uncovered and excavated (Lynch and Reilly, 2011, 65–76), which included two burials lying parallel in a single dug grave, an adolescent burial (B1), possible female, aged 12–14 years, supine, west–east, dated to the fifth–sixth century,[143] and a juvenile (B2), aged 6–9 years. These burials are exceptional in the archaeological record in that blue-bottle or blow-fly (*calliphera vicina-vomitoria*) adult and puparia remains were recovered, and examined, from the abdominal region of both burials.[144] The conclusion drawn by the excavators is that these two individuals may have been exposed for up to ten days before burial. Their conclusions lend credence to the phenomenon of 'laying-out' of the body, referenced in seventh-century literary sources. Patrick was mourned for twelve days (during which time night did not fall) (*Muirchú* §II 8 (7) (1); Bieler, 1979, 118–19). After the death of the two daughters of King Loíguire, they were laid on one bed and covered, lamenting and keening was undertaken, and they were buried after the days of mourning came to an end (*Tírechán*, §26; Bieler, 1979, 142–5). When Columba died, there followed three days and three nights of funeral ceremonies, followed by his burial (*Adomnán*, [iii 23]; Anderson and Anderson, 1991, 230–1). Pega buried her brother Guthlac 'on the third day' (*Felix* L. Colgrave, 1956, 154–5). The bodies at Kildimo had probably been 'laid out' for several days in a dwelling constructed of wattle and daub, an environment in which flies would have been omnipresent. Threads, or other textile material, embedded on the surface of the puparia is indicative of the presence of cloth around the bodies, perhaps a covering, a shroud, or a winding sheet, but, as there was no evidence that the flies could have infiltrated the cloth, these were already present on the bodies before they were covered.

On a sand ridge overlooking the Irish Sea, at Betaghstown (Bettystown), Co. Meath, a series of unenclosed burials ranging from the Bronze Age to the Iron Age included Early Medieval burials that were located at two adjacent sites – Brookside and Anchorage – during the construction of housing. At Brookside, a small unenclosed secular cemetery (Kelly, 1987–8, 75; O'Brien, 1984, 100–1; 1990, 40–1; 1993, 96–7) contained fourteen extended, west–east, inhumation burials, and two crouched inhumations in dug pits. Two of the extended burials were in slab-lined cist graves, the remainder were in stone-lined and dug graves. Crouched burial (B12), male, dated to the fourth–seventh century,[145] had spent his childhood years in the Mediterranean area of North Africa (Cahill Wilson and Standish, 2016, 237). Crouched burial (B11), female, dated to the late fourth–seventh century,[146] was accompanied by grave goods of personal adornment reminiscent of a British or Anglo-Saxon origin (O'Brien, 1990a, 40–1; 1993, 96–7). The males interred in the slab-lined cist graves (B2, B15), dated to the fifth–seventh century,[147] were locals (Cahill Wilson and Standish, 2016, 237). One of the slab-lined graves (unfortunately not identified) was placed immediately above, and disturbed, the crouched female (B11),[148] perhaps in a deliberate act of slighting the crouched burial, or perhaps unaware of its existence.

---

143 Beta–214238: 1580±40BP; at 2σ = cal AD 397–565.   **144** The excavator Linda Lynch and the osteo-archaeologist Eileen Reilly are to be congratulated on their expertise in handling this phenomenon.   **145** OxA–2652: 1565±60BP; at 2σ = cal AD 381–621.   **146** OxA–2651: 1550±60BP; at 2σ = cal AD 394–630.   **147** B2: OxA–2648: 1460±70BP; at 2σ = cal AD 425–670. B15: OxA–2655: 1560±60BP; at 2σ = cal AD 385–623.   **148** Unfortunately, the available reports do not identify

Excavations at the Anchorage site (Eogan, 2010, 103–16), located immediately north of Brookside, revealed sixty-one unenclosed inhumations. Two of the inhumations were crouched (F238, F181). Female (F238) was datable to the Iron Age. An elderly male (F181), crouched, interred in the centre of a full-length, stone-lined grave, dated to the fifth–sixth century,[149] (Figure 6.7) whose place of origin was probably in eastern Europe or Scandinavia (Cahill Wilson et al., 2014a, 139–40), was discovered on the periphery of the southern group of burials (Group 1). The remainder of the burials on the ridge, which may form two discrete, unenclosed, secular cemeteries, were interred west–east, in slab-lined, stone-lined and dug graves. The stone-lined graves of two elderly females (F251) dated to the fifth–sixth century,[150] and (F279) produced evidence for timber covers (Eogan, 2010, 109).

Two unenclosed cemeteries were discovered during sand quarrying in Co. Kilkenny. In the first cemetery, at Killaree, a row of six (perhaps more) supine extended skeletons was uncovered, one of whom had an iron knife beside the femur. An unidentified skeleton from this site has been dated to the sixth–seventh century[151] (Cahill and Sikora, 2011, vol. ii, 70–2). The second cemetery, at Sheastown, produced twelve skeletons, one of whom, an adult male, dated to the fifth–sixth century,[152] was accompanied by a knife placed beside his left hand and pointing towards his feet (ibid., 73–5).

The remains of a large unenclosed cemetery were discovered in 1997 during sand quarrying at Derryvilla, Portarlington, on the Laois-Offaly border (O'Brien, 1997a; Mullins, 2000, 175–6, no. 550). This secular cemetery, which included adults and children, buried supine, orientated heads to the west, in dug graves, is undated, but undoubtedly belongs in the Early Medieval period.

An interesting small unenclosed, but organised, cemetery of sixteen burials was located at the site of Cappogue Castle, Cappogue, north Co. Dublin (McQuade, 2009). A male adult burial (B9) in this cemetery has been dated to the fifth–sixth century.[153] When the cemetery, which was surrounded by field systems, ceased to be used, it became erased from local memory, and was superseded by settlement in the twelfth century.

A small collection of burials, an unorganised and scattered group, was uncovered a short distance from one of the Iron Age ring-ditches at Site D, Morett, Co. Laois (Cotter, 2011). Three females, extended, supine, west–east, and dated to the fifth–sixth century,[154] had been buried, apparently together, and at the same time, in a single dug grave. A fourth burial, located about 15m east of the multiple grave, contained an elderly female in a stone-lined grave, who was taller in stature than the others, but also dated to the fifth–sixth century.[155] Also, in Morett townland, approximately 400m south-west of the Site D burials (Morett 13, Dempsey, 2004), four further burials were recovered, three of which date to the eleventh–thirteenth century, but the fourth burial (C1302) was that of an adult of indeterminate sex, dated to the fifth–sixth century,[156] who had been buried extended, head to the west, but prone. This burial,

---

which grave. **149** UBA–13071: 1612±22BP; at 2σ = cal AD 394–535 (c14 dates for this site were obtained under the auspices of the Mapping Death Project). **150** UBA–13073: 1526±22BP; at 2σ = cal AD 430–599. **151** GrA–24440: 1445±40BP; at 2σ = cal AD 550–657. **152** GrA–24361: 1575±35BP; at 2σ = cal AD 406–560. **153** UBA–10060: 1572±31BP; at 2σ = cal AD 415–550. **154** Burial 2: SUERC–9164: 1540±35BP; at 2σ = cal AD 425–594. **155** Burial 4: SUERC–9168: 1535±35BP; at 2σ = cal AD 426–598. **156** AD 409–533 (full details awaited).

although dated to the same era as the four burials at Site D, had been set apart from them, an indication that the burial is probably punitive in nature. The people represented by these unorganised Early Medieval burials probably formed part of a kin-group who lived and worked in the area but who had not established an organised cemetery.

Cemeteries with foundation or focal burials, around which secular familial or communal cemeteries, and settlement cemeteries, evolved
The hypothesis that foundation burials in cemeteries are 'generally seen as a means by which families established their position via the public burial of ancestors' (Hamerow, 2016, 426) is particularly relevant in the Irish context. An excellent example of a foundation burial in a secular, possibly communal, cemetery is that of a young adult female (B48) dated to the fifth–sixth century[157] at Collierstown 1, Co. Meath (O'Brien, 2007; O'Hara, 2009a; 2009b, 83–100). Her grave, partially lined with stone slabs which probably acted as supports for a wooden cover, was centrally placed within a penannular ring-ditch, 15m diameter, and covered by a small mound. An offering of a deposit of domestic hearth material containing charcoal and burnt vegetation, including a tiny fragment of burnt pig bone, had been placed over the centre of her body. Strontium and oxygen isotope analysis of this woman's teeth indicate that she was born locally (Cahill Wilson et al., 2014a, 140–1). Subsequent burials in and around this central mound include male burial (B47), dated to the fifth–sixth century,[158] who had been placed in an oversized oak-lined grave, probably to accommodate perishable grave goods, and male burial (B39), undated, who was accompanied by a fragmented antler object. More than sixty-one burials were subsequently inserted within the penannular enclosure and when this was full, burials spread outwards and were contained within a further outer enclosure, until the eighth–ninth century. The importance and high status of the people buried in this cemetery is illustrated by the presence on the site (but not directly associated with any burial) of fragments of Phocaean Red Slip Ware bowls, and fragments of Bii (Late Roman 1) amphorae, from the eastern Mediterranean, datable to the fifth–sixth century, used for importing wine (Kelly, 2010, 49–52, 65), together with fragments of E ware jugs from western Gaul, datable to the sixth–seventh century (Doyle, 2009, 22; 2014, 81–94). Also recovered was a whale bone sword hilt datable to the fifth–sixth century. This centrally placed young woman (B48) was important enough to have been accorded a burial ceremony with its accompanying ritual, including burial beneath a mound within a circular enclosure. And, as possibly the first person to die in a newly formed kin-group, she was accorded foundational status in a new cemetery.

The cemetery at Holdenstown 2, Co. Kilkenny (Whitty and Tobin, 2009, 19–21; O'Brien and Bhreathnach, 2011, 57–8, 63–4), located 550m north-west of, and within sight of, the *ferta* site designated as Holdenstown 1, is an organised, unenclosed, secular cemetery, with slight evidence for industrial activity.[159] The cemetery contains ninety-four extended inhumation burials, comprising males, females and one child, laid out in five rows.[160] It has produced dates spanning the period fifth to seventh

---

[157] BA250161: 1550±40BP; at 2σ = cal AD 422–596. [158] BA247005: 1530±40BP; at 2σ = cal AD 427–609. [159] Five kilns were located outside the burial area. [160] It is noted that many

4.16 Plan of cemetery and cashel at Owenbristy, Co. Galway, © Eachtra Arch.

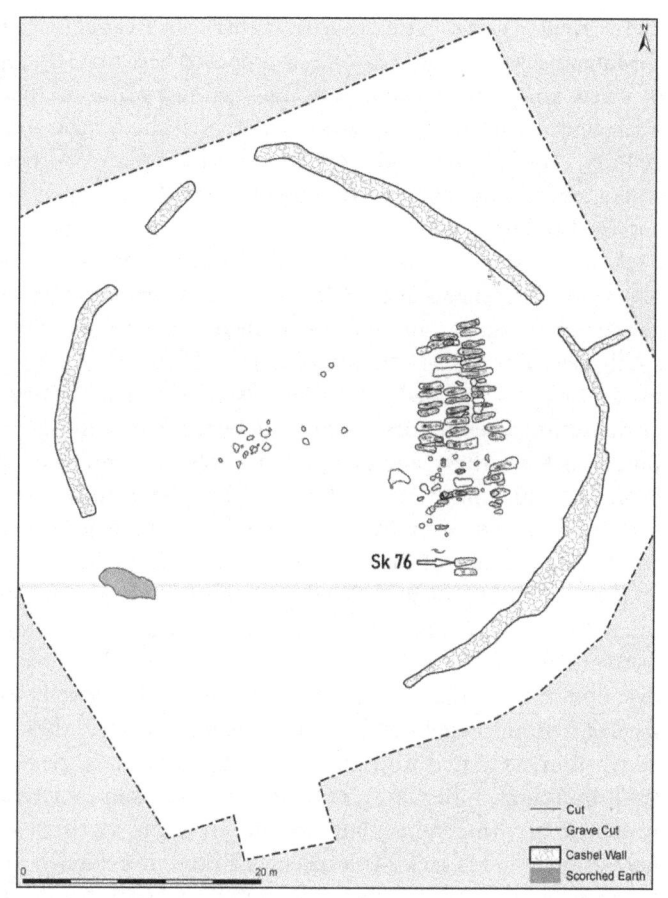

century.[161] The foundation burial at this cemetery appears to be a centrally placed young (possible) male, B59, dated to the fifth–sixth century.[162] The grave-cut for this burial is unusual in that it is deeper than the surrounding graves and lined with stones, probably to support a plank covering. The grave is wider than necessary at the eastern end, an anomaly that has been created to provide a space around the lower part of the body, into which perishable organic material could have been deposited (Plate 4). Fortunately, one object, placed beside the feet, survived. This was part of a red deer antler 'pick', dated third–fourth century,[163] which is considerably older than the date of the burial but matches the date of antler objects unearthed in the ditch surrounding RD1 at the nearby ancestral burial site of Holdenstown 1. It would appear that the antler object deposited with B59 was deliberately removed from the nearby *ferta* site and placed with this burial, thereby creating a symbiotic link with the indigenous ancestors. Strontium isotope analysis indicates that this person was not born locally,

---

cemeteries, including Holdenstown, are laid out in a regular fashion, with few intercutting graves. In the absence of identifiable grave markers this suggests that records of burial were kept, possibly by a designated person or family. 161 Full list of dates can be viewed under 'Holdenstown 2', at www.mappingdeathdb.ie. 162 UBA–13667: 1569±22BP; at 2σ = cal AD 427–544. 163 UBA–20006: 1698±24BP; at 2σ = cal AD 257–410. Date obtained under the auspices of the Mapping Death Project.

but originated either in the south-east corner of Ireland, or in north or west Britain[164] (Montgomery and Milns, 2010). It is proposed here that B59 represents the progenitor of a new kin-group moving into, and staking a claim in, this location, in the fifth–sixth century AD. It is of interest to note that the female (B2), dated sixth–seventh century,[165] in RD2 at the adjacent *ferta* site, has a place of origin similar to that of B59, a possible indication of a continuing link between the place of origin of these people, and the two burial sites.

A circular stone-walled cashel, with slight evidence for settlement, at Owenbristy,[166] Co. Galway (Lehane and Delaney, 2010; Delaney and Tierney, 2011, 71–109), contained, in the east and south-east quadrant, a cemetery regulated in three north–south rows of west–east orientated graves (Figure 4.16). An elderly female (SK 76), aged over 45 years, dated to the fourth–sixth century,[167] interred in a slab-lined grave at the southern extremity of the cemetery, roughly in line with the central row of burials, is the earliest, and therefore possibly the cemetery's foundation, burial. The cemetery, which in its Early Medieval phase dates to between the fourth and ninth centuries, contains sixty-five grave-cuts (thirty-nine dug graves, and twenty-six slab-lined graves). Some of the latter contained multiple burials.

'Cemetery-settlement' is the descriptive term formulated to describe a previously unknown Early Medieval Irish site type, where a secular cemetery is located within a 'settlement' complex (Ó Carragáin, 2009, 339).[168] I have chosen to reverse this description to 'settlement cemetery', because the cemetery element of these sites is located within an enclosed area of settlement. At such sites, 'settlement' consists of occupation associated with industrial activity such as, cereal drying (kilns), milling (mill buildings, mill races), craftworking, and some metalworking, as well as the presence of souterrains, but seldom, if ever, is there evidence for domestic habitation.[169] This lack of domestic habitation evidence need not be a cause for surprise, because the various activities undertaken, often involving the use of fire, are not conducive to being located among dwellings built of flammable material such as wood or straw. The cemetery is invariably located in a core position, or in the eastern sector of the settlement complex, and is not encroached upon by the activity taking place in the immediate vicinity (Plate 5). In Early Medieval Ireland, cereal drying and milling were activities often shared between communities, a fact which was important enough to be included in seventh-century laws on legal aspects of milling and mill construction (Kelly, 1997, 482–5). It is therefore probable that the secular cemeteries associated with this activity catered for several local kin-groups, and afforded contact with ancestors and deceased family members during everyday activity at the sites. The peoples involved in the activity at settlement cemeteries more than likely lived in nearby ringforts or raths which abound in the Irish countryside. The difference between a circular enclosure used for settlement activity, and a ringfort, can be

---

164 The addition of oxygen analysis might help pinpoint the individual's place of origin. 165 UB–15562: 1464±30BP; at 2σ = cal AD 551–646. 166 Owenbristy is the anglicised version of (a) *Abhainn Bhriste* (broken river), or (b) *Uamhain Bhriste* (broken cave). Both versions are apt, because the site is located beside a *turlough* (a dry lake) that overflows in winter, inundating the east, south and western sides of the cashel. 167 UB–11252: 1635±38BP; at 2σ = cal AD 337–537. 168 An alternative term 'Secular cemetery' has been suggested by Stout and Stout (2008). 169 The word 'habitation' is sometimes used in excavation reports relating to settlement cemetery sites, but on

explained by the fact that in order for a circular enclosure to be classified on excavation as a ringfort or rath, it should contain evidence for the presence of at least one domestic dwelling with a central hearth. These have not, to date, been shown to be present at settlement cemeteries.

There are, of course, exceptions to every rule, and one exception to the 'rule' that domestic habitation did not occur at settlement cemeteries may be that of Camlin, Co. Tipperary (Flynn, 2011). At this site, a secular cemetery of 152 burials occupied the eastern sector of an enclosure located in a region that had seen activity dating from the Neolithic, Bronze Age and Iron Age. Evidence for several putative buildings was excavated within the enclosure, some of which appear to have had possible domestic functions, especially a circular building, located east of the cemetery, and an ephemeral building in the cemetery area (Flynn, 2011, 46, 84). However, it should be noted that these buildings pre-date the establishment of the cemetery which functioned between the early eighth and tenth century. It would appear, therefore, that this cemetery was established in a location where industrial-type activity, and possible habitation, had begun prior to the commencement of burial. Although industrial-type activity continued in parallel with the use of the cemetery, it did not impinge upon the cemetery area.

A settlement cemetery at Ninch 2, Co. Meath (McConway, 2010, 157–72; Buckley et al., 2008), is located on a low ridge, close to the Ninch 3 cemetery, and consists of a series of concentric enclosures with evidence for industrial activity in the form of corn drying kilns, animal enclosures, cobbled surfaces and souterrains. Towards the centre of the site, a discrete area within the inner ring-ditch was reserved for an organised cemetery which contained ninety-two inhumation burials mainly in stone-lined graves (Plate 5(a)). Two burials from the earliest phase, male (B856) and female (B770), were selected for radiocarbon dating as it was felt that these might be foundation burials. The results indicate that male (B856), aged 36–45 years, died in the sixth–seventh century,[170] and female (B770), aged 17–25 years, died in the seventh century.[171] Strontium and oxygen isotope analysis of a tooth from male (B856) indicates that this person was not of Irish origin, and the possible suggested place of origin is in central or eastern Europe. Strontium and oxygen isotope analysis of a tooth from female (B770) indicates that while there is a slight possibility that she may have originated in Britain, she might have come from central or eastern Europe (Cahill Wilson et al., 2014, 144–5). Further analysis of these results is ongoing, but the implications are that these burials represent movement of individuals or groups from the post-Roman European mainland into Ireland, possibly via Britain. It may be more than coincidence that male burial (B25) from nearby Ninch 3 also had a possible origin in central or eastern Europe, albeit almost a century earlier. It is not known whether these people represent pagans or Christians, but it is noted that at least some burials at this cemetery appear not to have been shroud wrapped, perhaps suggesting that it contained burials of both pagans and Christians.

An unusual, partially excavated, settlement cemetery located on a slightly elevated ridge which had evidence for occupation from the Neolithic through to the Iron Age,

closer inspection this usually relates to isolated hearths and not to dwellings.   170 UBA–20055: 1404±19BP; at 2σ = cal AD 549–633 (c14 dates were obtained under the auspices of the Mapping Death Project).   171 UBA–20056: 1479±20BP; at 2σ = cal AD 607–59.

at Castlefarm 1, Co. Meath (O'Connell and Clark, 2009), included concentric enclosures dating to between the fifth and thirteenth centuries AD.[172] Twelve burials were recovered, eight of which formed a small cluster or unenclosed cemetery of unprotected dug graves, unusual in that it was located immediately outside the causewayed entrance to the inner enclosure (F96). The burial of a child (B3), aged 6–8 years, undated, was recovered in the fill of the outer enclosure ditch, in the same general area (Plate 5(b)). Among the group of eight burials was a double burial in a single grave, consisting of a female (B1), aged 25–35 years, dated to the fifth–sixth century,[173] accompanied by a child (B2), aged 6–8 years (Coughlan, 2009). This small cluster of burials possibly represents a familial cemetery dating to the fifth–sixth century, related to the establishment of the enclosure complex. A further two burials were later interred in the upper fill of the northern part of the inner and outer enclosure ditches. A female (B10), aged 25–30 years, interred supine, west–east, in the fill of the inner ditch, has been dated to the seventh–eighth century.[174] Male (B11), aged 20–4 years, interred supine, west–east, but with legs flexed at the knees, in the fill of the outer ditch, has not been dated, but appears to belong to the seventh–eighth century. Why these burials were inserted into the upper fill of the ditches, at least a century or more after burial within the smaller group had ceased, is unknown.

The settlement cemetery at Johnstown, Co. Meath (Fibiger, 2005, 99–110; Clarke and Carlin, 2008, 55–85; 2009, 1–20; Clarke 2010, 61–75), commenced with the construction of a small mound (F1187) on the summit of a low promontory overlooking the floodplain of the River Blackwater. Beneath the mound were the foundation burials of an elderly adult female (B110), dated to the fourth–seventh century,[175] lying supine, flexed, within a dug grave; the disarticulated remains of three adults (B129) in an oval pit, which produced a date identical to that of B110;[176] and an adult female (B33), dated to the fifth–seventh century,[177] supine, extended, within a dug grave. It is probable that the disarticulated skeletal material (B129) represents the remains of ancestors that had been curated elsewhere, and re-interred when the cemetery was established, as had probably occurred at Ballydavis 1, Co. Laois. The mound was subsequently enclosed within a large ditched enclosure encompassing a cemetery of c.400 burials, dating from the fifth to the sixteenth/seventeenth century. Industrial activity, in the form of smelting pits and smithing hearths, was undertaken in the area surrounding the cemetery.

Burial at the settlement cemetery site at Raystown, Co. Meath (Seaver, 2016), commenced in the fourth–fifth century, with the establishment of a secular cemetery within a penannular ring-ditch (20m diameter). The earliest dated, and the probable foundation, burial is that of a female (B853), dated to the fourth–fifth century,[178] aged

---

[172] The settlement evidence was that of semi-industrial activity, including metalworking in iron and copper, a series of eight wells, and craftworking including artefacts of copper, iron, bronze, glass, wood, antler, bone and stone recovered from the ditch fills. There was no evidence for habitation in the form of house structures, but some of the artifactual material recovered would at least suggest habitation nearby. [173] Beta 229298: 1580±40BP; at 2σ = cal AD 402–572. [174] Beta 229300: 1280±40BP; at 2σ = cal AD 657–864: (at 87.4% = cal AD 657–779). [175] Beta–178195: 1560±70BP; at 2σ (93.8%) = cal AD 379–640. [176] Beta–178197: 1560±70BP; at 2σ (93.8%) = cal AD 379–640. [177] Beta–184610: 1460±70BP; at 2σ = cal AD 425–670. [178] Wk–16823: 1647±33BP; at 2σ = cal AD 263–535. At 78.6% = cal AD 330–435.

36–45 years, who was buried together with a juvenile (B852). The cemetery, which was centrally placed within a complex of extensive agricultural and industrial activity, comprising field systems, water management gullies, eight water mills, grain drying kilns,[179] and two souterrains, was enlarged in the seventh century by the creation of an outer enclosing ring-ditch. Burial ceased in the tenth century.

Partial excavation, along a gas pipeline corridor, on high land above the southern side of the estuary of the River Boyne at Colp West 1, Co. Meath, revealed a settlement cemetery with approximately 120 burials, some of which were in graves which may have been plank-lined, located within and surrounding a penannular ring-ditch (15m diameter). The central burial within the ring-ditch (B102), female, potentially the foundation burial, has been dated to the latter half of the sixth, early seventh century.[180] A male burial (B65), in the deepest grave within the ring-ditch, has been dated to the sixth–seventh century.[181] When burial within the ring-ditch had reached capacity, graves spilled out into the surrounding area. A post-hole in the centre of the entrance to the ring-ditch may have marked its closure to burial in the interior. Finds from part of the ditch fill, including B and E ware, are indicative of overseas contacts (Gowen, 1989a, 32; O'Brien, 1993, 93–102; 1999, 181–2; 2003, 62–72; 2009, 135–54; Keating, 2001). A geophysical survey undertaken by ACS Ltd in 2009, after the partial excavation had been completed, showed that the cemetery was centrally located within a large trivallate enclosure, an indication that this represents a very prestigious site, possibly a trading emporium near the mouth of the River Boyne.

The site excavated in 1990–1 at Marlinstown, Co. Westmeath (Keeley, 1991b, no. 113; 1992, no. 126; 1990s TII report), originally described as a ringfort, now reclassified as a settlement cemetery, located on raised ground, consisted of an oval penannular enclosure (42m x 29m), which produced evidence for metalworking and possible butchering, but no evidence for a dwelling, and contained a small cemetery in the eastern sector. The remains of fourteen individuals, males, females and children (all undated), were recovered, but two of these were recovered from enclosure ditch contexts. A child (B9), aged 6–8 years, was recovered in the enclosure ditch, and an adult male (B7) was recovered in the ditch of a later enclosure which enveloped the penannular enclosure.

The site known as Newtown Rath, at Swords, Co. Dublin, previously identified as a ringfort with burials (Kiely and Tierney, 2018), has now been re-classified as a settlement cemetery. Two of the burials have been dated, female (SK 3), aged 45+ years, to the sixth–seventh century,[182] and male (SK 7), aged 35–9 years, to the ninth–eleventh century.[183] Recent excavation[184] has revealed a wide and deep enclosure ditch and further Early Medieval burials, all oriented west–east,[185] together with a small partial cist containing a Bronze Age crouched burial with two ceramic pots and a cremation deposit.

---

179 A burial discovered in one of the kilns, and two burials with weapon trauma, are discussed in chapter 6.   **180** UBA–15649: 1503±22BP; at 2σ (91.6%) = cal AD 535–619 (c14 dates for Colp West 1 were obtained courtesy of the Mapping Death Project).   **181** UBA–15648: 1464±24BP; at 2σ = cal AD 556–645.   **182** UB–37844: 1400±33BP; at 2σ = cal AD 432–641 (at 82.4% probability = cal AD 532–641).   **183** UB–37845: 1066±33BP; at 2σ = cal AD 895–1023.   **184** Grateful thanks to Maeve Tobin of IAC for enabling a visit to this important site during recent excavations.   **185** The burials excavated in 2017 were described as being oriented east-west possibly due to an error in recording.

A further settlement cemetery, where the large penannular enclosure enveloped a small Iron Age annular ring-ditch with cremation deposits, dating second to first century BC, has been excavated at Annaghilla (Site 4), Co. Tyrone (Kimber, 2010, 501; Dunlop & Barkley, 2016). The Early Medieval occupation of the site involved ironworking and grain processing and included a cemetery of twenty-three extended inhumation graves in the eastern sector, but no evidence for habitation. These burials could not be dated because the acid soil had dissolved skeletal material. However, dates obtained for occupation material in pits indicate occupation between the sixth and ninth century. A most unusual feature of this settlement cemetery is continuity of cremation throughout its use, evidenced by deposition of cremated human bone in pits and post-holes, dated to between the sixth and ninth centuries AD. The occupants of this site practiced the rite of cremation, alongside that of extended inhumation, throughout the Early Medieval period.

* * *

Grave types in Early Medieval Ireland varied from slab-lined cist graves, which were lined, roofed and floored with slabs; cist-like graves (lintel graves) lined with slabs, but devoid of basal slabs, and roofed with a series of lintel-type slabs; stone-lined graves where the body was surrounded by stones (not slabs), which may have supported a wooden grave cover; unprotected dug graves, where the body was placed directly into the grave-cut and then covered with earth. While coffins were not used in Early Medieval Ireland, there is sometimes evidence for wood-lining of a grave, and two examples of the use of a possible log coffin have been identified. It is possible that a log coffin could be used as a means of transporting a body from afar to its place of burial.

In fifth-century Ireland, formally organised inhumation cemeteries were unknown, therefore the earliest burials are represented by burial of individuals in single isolated graves scattered throughout the countryside; the insertion of burials into existing ancestral burial monuments (*ferta*) which is a continuation of the aspiration for burial with the ancestors; and the construction of imitative ancestral burial monuments, representing an attempt to create the impression of ancestral continuity. Burial in these ancestral *ferta* ceased after the seventh–eighth century, probably due to the influence of the Church which equated such monuments with non-Christian burial. However, *ferta* continued to be recognised in early Irish law as boundary markers, and continued to be remembered especially in place-names.

Unenclosed cemeteries on sand-gravel ridges represent secular communal cemeteries. More formal secular communal cemeteries which often included a settlement element evolved around single foundation or focal burials. Christians and non-Christians alike were buried in these cemeteries.

Archaeological evidence also suggests a limited continuation of the use of cremation between the fifth and eighth centuries, and in at least one instance cremation deposits occurred alongside extended inhumation between the seventh and ninth centuries.

CHAPTER 5

Grave goods

Burials accompanied by identifiable grave goods are a rarity in Early Medieval Ireland. However, as even seemingly minor articles may have had special significance, it is essential that when recovered, these objects must be subjected to close material examination, possible comparisons be considered, and attempts be undertaken to place the objects into a context.

This paucity of grave goods in Irish burial contexts is demonstrated in Gazetteer 3 where it can be seen that of a corpus of approximately 11,000 burials, dispersed over 156 burial sites, examined in this publication, only eighty-nine burials (0.81% of the corpus), dispersed over forty-five burial sites, contained objects. That the distribution of these sites does not conform to any pattern can be seen on Map 5. While the majority of burials examined contained only one object, a small number contained more than one.

NECK COLLARS

There are three instances[1] of burials that were recovered wearing neck collars, otherwise unknown in Irish Early Medieval burial contexts. It is important to emphasise that these do not appear to represent slave collars. The first example was recovered around the neck of a young adult female (B38), dated to the sixth–seventh century,[2] aged 18–25 years, supine, extended, west–east, in an unprotected dug grave in the settlement cemetery at Ratoath, Co. Meath (Wallace, 2010, 295–316). While isotope analysis of this young woman's teeth has indicated that she was born locally, there is a slight possibility that she could have originated in the eastern part of England (Montgomery and Vaughan, 2010, 312). The neck collar consists of a band of copper alloy that had been cast as a single piece, decorated with a simple ring and dot motif.[3] One terminal is folded back on itself, the other terminal is broken, but the indications are that the terminals represent a simple interlocking clasp (Figure 5.1a) (Wallace, 2010, 306). There are at present no known parallels for this neck collar in Ireland, but a possible comparison could be made with an English copper-alloy necklet, which has a similar fastening device and similar ring and dot decoration, recovered among the grave goods of a male Anglo-Saxon warrior burial (Grave 50) at Bergh Apton,

---

[1] Some publications mention a fourth, a string of bone discs, found with a female burial, from Killeany, Co. Laois. This has been discounted as a neck collar; it has now been identified as a 'paternoster', dating to the ninth–eleventh century (Wiggins, 2014, 277), and is included in chapter 10. [2] Beta-196361: 1410±40BP: at 2σ = cal AD 569–671. [3] It is noted that this simple ring and dot motif has been recognised in Wales, not on a neck ring but on the terminal of a comparatively rare penannular brooch type dateable to the late sixth or early seventh century, for which a native (Welsh) origin is suggested (Redknap, 2009, 287–8).

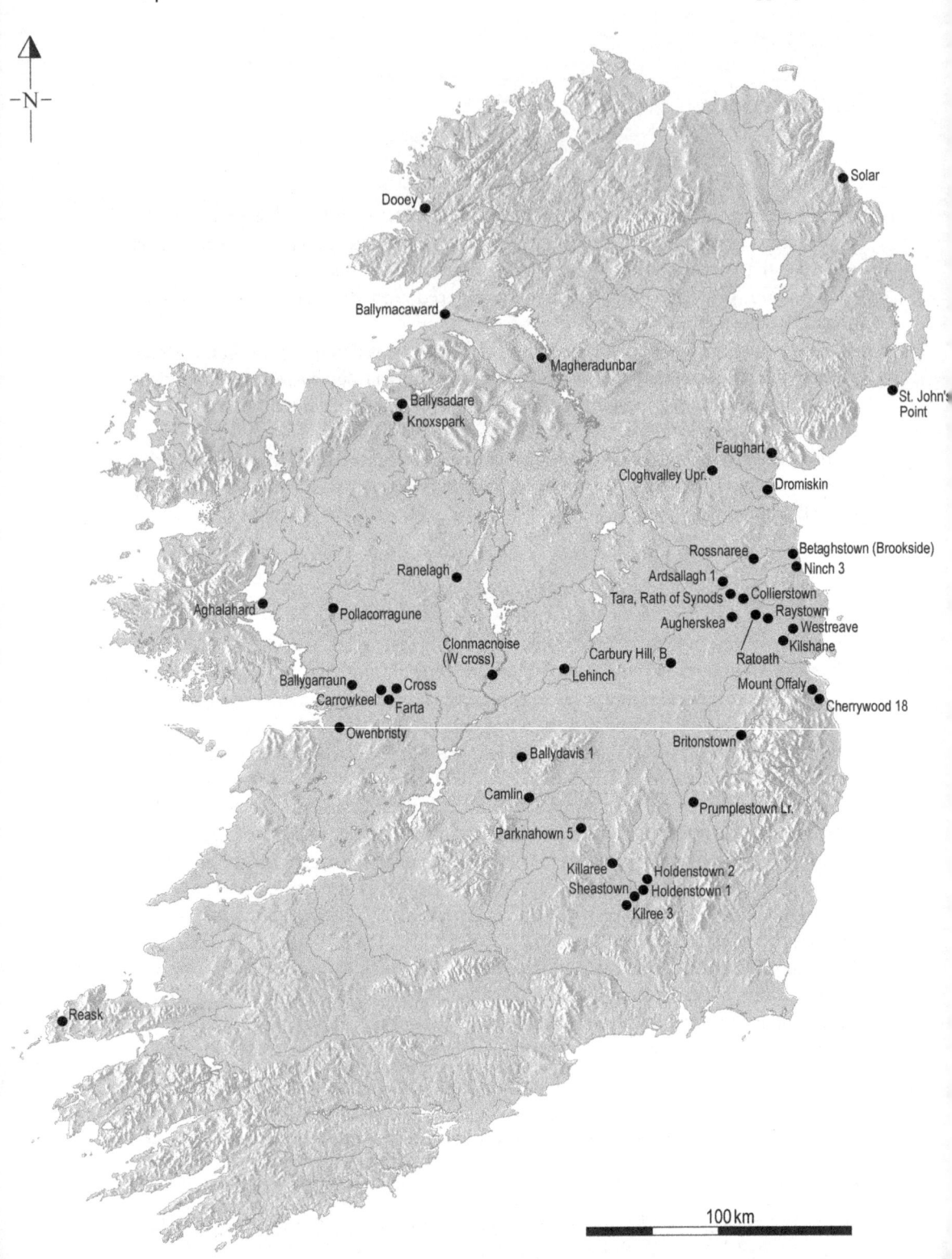

Map 5 Distribution of Early Medieval burials with grave goods, © The Discovery Programme and EOB.

Grave goods 105

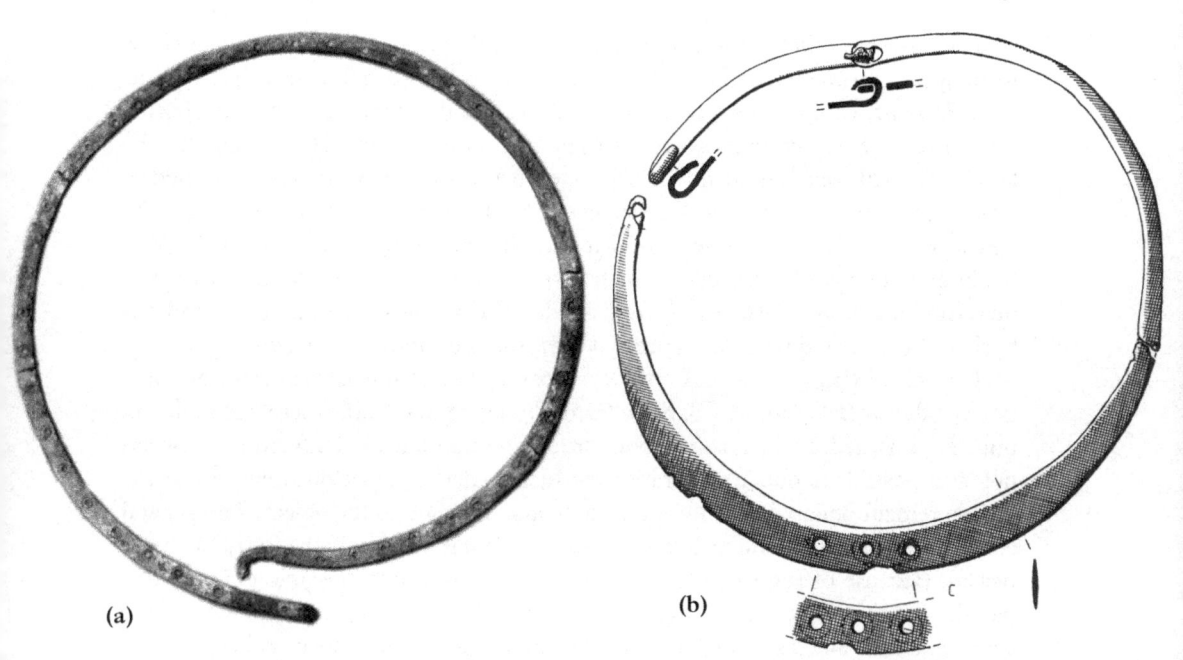

5.1 Neck rings: (a) Ratoath, Co. Meath (after Wallace, 2010, fig. 21.12), © A. Wallace/Arch. Tech. Ltd; (b) Bergh Apton, Norfolk (after Green & Rogerson, 1978, grave 50, fig. 91), © Historic Environment Service, Norfolk County Council.

Norfolk (Green and Rogerson, 1978, 35, 76) (Figure 5.1b). As the young woman from Ratoath was probably born locally (with a slight possibility that she may have been born in eastern England), it is worth noting that Ratoath is in Brega, a region that had a known Anglo-Saxon presence throughout the seventh century (Moisl, 1983; Ireland, 1991, 64–78; O'Brien, 1993, 93–6; 1999a, 45–8). This woman buried at Ratoath, or her kin-group, may have had an Anglo-Saxon connection, and the neck collar may be an heirloom, or even a form of group identification. At any rate, the object was considered to be of such personal value that it accompanied her to the grave.

The second example is from the cemetery at Owenbristy, Co. Galway (Lehane and Delaney, 2010; Delaney, Tierney et al., 2011), where a male burial (SK 70), dated to the sixth–seventh century,[4] had an iron tubular neck ring or torc around his neck. The neck ring is finely constructed of thin hollow sheet iron, with a clasp or fastener visible as a corroded partial break in the front of the ring (Plate 6). As there is no apparent evidence for a hinge, once this ring or torc had been placed around the neck of this man it was intended to remain *in situ*. His burial differed from the remainder of the burials in this cemetery in that it was crouched, laid on the right side, head to the west, in an unprotected dug grave. Strontium and oxygen isotope analysis indicates that the individual was not born locally, but probably came from further east in Ireland (Evans and Chenery, 2010, 384), with a slight possibility that he came from Britain. There are no known Early Medieval comparisons for this neck ring either in Ireland or in Britain. However, an explanation for the wearing of the neck ring might

4 UB–11248: 1457±36BP; at 2σ = cal AD 547–652.

lie in an interpretation of the Old Irish word *nasc*, that is, *nasc niad* ('a chain or collar worn by an approved champion'), or, *nasc druad* ('a collar worn by a druid') (*DIL* fasc. N-O-P, Joynt, 15, lines 58–73). This could indicate that this man may have been a warrior (unlikely, as no injuries recorded) or king, or even a druid (assuming that the latter were still recognised in the sixth–seventh century). Why was he buried at Owenbristy? His crouched posture suggests that he may have been an outsider who was buried by his peers who were familiar with this non-indigenous burial rite, or that his body may have been trussed for transport over a distance. Perhaps he was a powerful king or druid who was feared, or who died as a hostage in captivity, and was buried in a crouched position to prevent him from becoming a revenant.

The third example of a neck ring was recovered in an unenclosed cemetery on a gravel ridge at Ballysadare, Co. Sligo (Opie, 1996, 77, no. 144), where one skeleton, undated, unsexed, had an iron ribbon torque around its neck. Unfortunately, it has not been possible to obtain illustrations or further details about this item, and as the burials remain undated, it is not possible to assign a date to the object. The general layout of the cemetery and its burial rite suggest that it belongs in the Early Medieval period. Because of the lack of information, it has not been possible to locate any parallel for this neck ring. However, if the burial was that of a male, some of the comments mentioned above concerning the burial from Owenbristy might be relevant.

If these collars were insignia of identity, it is unlikely that they were concealed beneath a shroud, making it probable that these individuals were clothed, rather than shroud wrapped, at burial.

POSSIBLE SHIELD

In Mound 11 at Pollacorragune, Co. Galway, excavated in 1936, the central burial (SK D), male, dated to the fourth–sixth century,[5] aged 35–40 years, extended, supine, west–east, in a dug grave, was accompanied by a piece of iron, roughly circular in shape and about 5 inches in diameter, found approximately 8 inches from the skull to one side. The excavator noted that it was 'possibly the remains of a shield boss' (Riley, 1936, 47). If this was a shield boss, that is the remains of a shield on which the head of the deceased rested, or was covered by, then this burial is unique in the Irish archaeological record, and merits further study. A small fragment of iron was also found near the middle of the chest, but no further description is available.

SPEAR

There are two known instances of spears having been recovered from Early Medieval graves in Ireland. The first spear, at Lusk, Co. Dublin (O'Connell, 2014, 181), which was found embedded in the upper torso of a decapitated male (B9), dated to the fifth–sixth century, obviously cannot be regarded as a deliberately deposited grave good, but was the implement that caused the death of this individual.

5 GrA–13613: 1620±70BP; at 89.4% probability = cal AD 315–588.

5.2 Copper-alloy object (sceptre?) with B29, Ardsallagh 1, Co. Meath, © ACSU.

The second spear, found in the cemetery at Knoxspark, Co. Sligo (Mount, 2010, 192, 209), beside a decapitated male (B4) dated to the eighth–ninth century[6] (one of a paired male burial), consisted of a 'straight-sided, angular, socketed spearhead', which the excavator suggests may have been the remains of a spear held in the hand of the buried individual. The deliberate deposition of a spear to accompany a burial is unique in Early Medieval Ireland, and, bearing in mind the possibility that this latter site may have become a Viking longphort (Kelly, 2009, 485–97), this may not be the burial of an indigenous person, but that of a Viking. It is possible that this spear was also instrumental in the death of this individual.

POSSIBLE SCEPTRE

Included in a secular cemetery within a penannular ring-ditch at Ardsallagh 1, Co. Meath, was the burial of a young adult (B29), dated sixth–seventh century,[7] sex indeterminate, supine, extended, west–east, in an unprotected dug grave, who was accompanied by a copper-alloy object lying on the left shoulder (Figure 5.2) together with fragments of oak which might represent a rod or staff (Clarke and Carlin, 2009, 11). The object, which has been interpreted as a possible sceptre, is unique in an Irish context, and the closest comparison, which may well be coincidental, would appear to be British Iron Age terret-rings. This does not explain the object's use as a sceptre. One can only assume that it represents the insignia of a young person who was of some importance in the local community. This individual was either clothed on burial with the accompanying object being part of the ensemble, or, was shroud wrapped, with the object being placed above the shroud. The former is more likely.

6 UB–3836: 1184±31BP; at 87.5% probability = cal AD 767–901.

BOX SET OF STONE AND WOOD, WITH RINGED PIN

These unique objects were recovered in a long cist grave[8] located in a field outside the modern confines of the early monastic site at Dromiskin, Co. Louth, in 1862 (Reade, 1862, 199–206; Macalister, 1928, 206), together with a few much decayed skeletal bones and part of a skull (identified as male), which was positioned at the eastern end of the grave. Beside the skull was a small stone box, crafted from fine-grained sandstone, measuring 11.2cm x 9.8cm x 6.2cm, with a sliding lid (Figure 5.3a). Inside the stone box was a further box crafted from a single piece of yew, with a sliding lid (Figure 5.3b); two bronze straps and rivets kept this box fastened, and it was covered with a thin layer of leather. This inner wooden box contained a small bronze possible ringed pin[9] (Figure 5.3c), and fragments of possible charcoal[10] (Raftery and Tempest, 1942, 133–7). These boxes may originally have been intended to contain relics for placement in the cavity of an altar, and while they are unique in Ireland, they could be compared with Byzantine reliquary boxes of the fourth and fifth centuries (Ó Floinn, 2013, 221–2).[11] It has been suggested that the burial might be that of an early immigrant missionary to Ireland (ibid). The position of the body with the head at the eastern end of the grave would, however, be very unusual for a Christian, and the context would seem to dictate to the contrary. The ringed pin, if it is a dress pin, is of a type dating to the sixth–ninth centuries (Kelly, 1986, 196), and while this cannot provide an absolute date for the burial, the grave type is compatible with a date in that period.[12] These beautifully crafted boxes and content probably represent a cherished possession deemed necessary to accompany this individual in the grave. The burial appears to have formed part of a now destroyed cemetery, because a further long cist containing a female, supine, extended, with head to the west, was recorded approximately 10 feet from this grave, and the presence of further burials in the immediate vicinity is indicated by the unearthing of loose bones during ploughing, over many years, in the surrounding area.

SINGLE TOE RING

An unusual item, a single toe ring, representing the wearing of a single sandal, has been noted in burials in Iron Age cemeteries in Britain, and in one Iron Age burial in Ireland. An example dating to the Early Medieval period was uncovered in the early Anglo-Saxon cemetery at Burgh Castle, Norfolk, where male burial (93) was accompanied by a spiral toe ring (Johnson, 1983, 64; O'Brien, 1999a, 117; 2008, 293–4). An Early Medieval Irish example has recently been identified on an extended burial (SK 176), an elderly adult male, during excavation of a large secular cemetery of over 700 burials, located within a settlement cemetery, at Ranelagh, Co.

---

7 Beta–237060: 1460±40BP; at 2σ = cal AD 539–655.   8 It is possible that this grave included a wooden bier as several small pieces of wood (described as wood-charcoal) were observed on the basal flags (Reade, 1862, 200).   9 The ring of the pin, which was intact when found, was missing when the find was deposited in the National Museum in 1901.   10 Probably residue from decayed organic material.   11 Thanks to Raghnall Ó Floinn for providing a translation of this entry.   12 It is possible that the pin represents a locking device, and the resemblance to ringed pins is accidental

5.3 Boxes and pin from burial at Dromiskin, Co. Louth, © courtesy of the National Museum of Ireland: (a) stone box; (b) wooden box; (c) ringed pin (key?).

Roscommon[13] (Delaney, 2017, 13–14). This man's burial has been dated to the seventh–ninth century,[14] and several skeletons which appear to be deliberately clustered around his burial have all been dated to roughly the same period.[15] While no great importance has previously been attached by archaeologists to this small object, which represents the remains of a single sandal, it is potentially of immense significance. In Medieval Irish tradition the *topos* of the single sandal was associated with both kingship and the 'otherworld' (MacCana, 1973, 160–6) and it is probably not without significance that a tenth-century king of Dublin was named Amlaib Cúarán, which translates as Olaf the Sandal (Doherty, 1998, 296–7). The presence, therefore, of the toe ring of a sandal on one foot of a male burial may be a manifestation in the archaeological record of a social ranking that heretofore has only been recognised in the literary tradition (as in Fitzpatrick, 2004).

EARRING

Two fragments of a silver ring, with herring-bone decoration, identified as an earring (Figure 4.10), were recovered with the remains of an adult female, dated to the fourth–fifth century,[16] accompanied by an infant, in a dug grave beneath a small mound, on the south bank of the River Boyne, at Rossnaree, Co. Meath (Cahill and Sikora, 2011, 113–19). Unusually, the body was oriented with the head at the eastern end of the grave. The design on the ring is similar to that on the toe ring from the Iron Age crouched burial at Rath, Co. Meath, and corresponds to a design used on Roman finger rings. However, as this woman was born locally (Cahill Wilson et al., 2014a, 130), the ring is likely to have been an heirloom, or an indicator of group identity.

(Cormac Bourke, and Raghnall Ó Floinn, pers. comm.). **13** This excavation was conducted in 2016 by Shane Delaney, for IAC Ltd, and TII. The burial with a toe ring was identified by this writer during a visit to the excavation in August 2016. Post-excavation analysis is still ongoing. **14** UB–36186: 1231±33BP; at 2σ = cal AD 688–883. **15** Thanks to Maeve Tobin of IAC for providing the c14 date, and information regarding the burial, prior to publication. **16** GrA–24354:

POSSIBLE CLOTHED BURIALS

The normal/usual burial rite in Early Medieval Ireland was that of a body deposited into the grave, either wrapped in a shroud/winding sheet, covered by a sheet, or wrapped in an animal skin or vegetative material. There are, however, a few exceptions where burials show indications that the body may have been clothed on burial. These indications are represented by the presence of objects such as a knife, and/or buckle, and objects of personal dress ornament. Those responsible for the burial of clothed individuals in Ireland were making a public statement of identity, as with the neck rings and possible sceptre. The knife would usually be suspended in a sheath from a belt encircling a garment at the waist. The belt could be secured with a buckle or a knot. That a knife was an essential part of everyday life is brought into focus in an episode recounted by Adomnán (*Adomnán* [i.47], Anderson and Anderson, 1991, 84–5) when Columba prophesied to a layman named Góre that his death would be caused by a companion of his [life's] journey. Some years later, while working on a spear-shaft, in a sudden movement Góre struck his knee on his knife and was severely wounded. He then recognised that his knife was the companion who would cause his death.

While it is possible that clothed burial was a non-Christian practice based on an understanding that one needed to be clothed in the afterlife, it is also possible that some were Christian immigrants who had not yet adopted the practice of shroud-wrapping. It is noted that in the 'conversion period' in Anglo-Saxon England (*c.*600–850) people were still clothed on burial, with the most common form of grave good, numerically, being a knife, followed by a simple buckle (Geake, 1997, 102–3). As an Anglo-Saxon presence is historically well attested in Ireland in the seventh century (O'Brien, 1999a, 45–8), it is possible that occasional burials accompanied by a knife/buckle might be representative of such a presence.

A burial with personal dress ornament, indicating that the body was clothed on burial, is characterised by crouched female burial (BII) at Betaghstown (Brookside), Co. Meath, dated late fourth to mid-seventh century.[17] This burial was accompanied, in the region of her head, by a small oval bronze plaque with perforations at each end, and with traces of net attached; in the region of her shoulders were two iron penannular omega-type brooches, Fowler Type B (Fowler, 1960, 152), with textile fragments attached; at her neck was a small stone amulet with an hour-glass perforation at one end; and at her waist was a simple, oval, belt buckle (Figure 5.4) (Kelly, 1979, 4, 75; O'Brien, 1993, 96–7; 1999, 179). This woman was undoubtedly fully clothed on burial. The oval bronze plaque represents a hair ornament, the brooches appear to have held a peplos-type garment in place, with the amulet suspended between the brooches, and the buckle represents the remains of a belt around her waist. It was not possible to conduct isotopic analysis to ascertain this woman's place of origin, but her clothing suggests she was an immigrant.[18] While

---

1660±40 BP; at 2σ = cal AD 256–534 (highest probability 76.2% = cal AD 317–435).   17 OxA–2651: 1550±60BP; at 2σ = cal AD 394–630.   18 One Fowler Type B penannular brooch (and possibly others), dating to the fourth/fifth century, has been recovered in a settlement site in Fohrde and Hohenferschesar, northern Germany (Fowler, 1963, 149).

Grave goods

5.4 Objects with Bii, Betaghstown, (Brookside), Co. Meath (drawn by EOB), © courtesy of the National Museum of. Ireland.

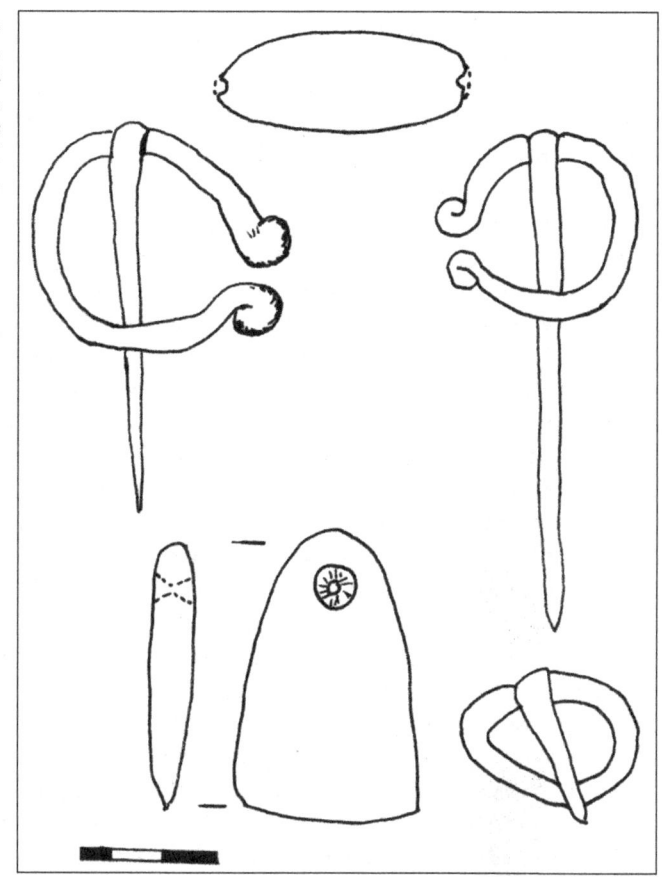

brooches certainly formed part of Irish dress at this period, they were worn singly by females on the breast, and by males on the shoulder. This woman's pair of brooches are worn in an Anglo-Saxon fashion (White, 1988, 24), indicating that she was likely to be British.

In the settlement cemetery at Raystown, Co. Meath (Seaver, 2016, 81), adult burial (B814), unsexed, undated, was probably displayed wrapped in a cloak for burial, indicated by the presence of the shaft of a ringed pin at the right shoulder. The position of the pin, on the shoulder, is an indication that this burial was that of an indigenous male.

The presence of a buckle at the waist of a body is a strong indication that the individual was clothed on burial. The small number of individuals with buckles include: at Knoxspark, Co. Sligo, a burial (B32) was accompanied by a probable bronze belt buckle (Mount, 2010, 199). An adult extended burial (B1) described as being dated to the sixth–seventh century, in the cemetery at Cherrywood, Site 18, Co. Dublin, had a D-shaped buckle on the top of the right femur; and a disturbed burial (Bxvi) in the same cemetery had a buckle fragment in the pelvic region. This latter grave also contained a socketed iron spade-shoe (Ó Néill and Coughlin, 2010, 243). In the secular cemetery at Ninch 3, Co. Meath, an extended adult (B8), undated, had a small belt buckle at the waist (Powell, 2004). At Westreave, Co. Dublin, extended adult (B29), dated to the fifth–sixth century,[19] sex unknown, interred in the only slab-lined and floored long cist grave in the cemetery, located outside the penannular enclosure (Figure 4.15), had a belt buckle at the waist (Gowen, 1989, 18; O'Brien, 1993, 93–102; 1999, 181–2). And at Ratoath, Co. Meath, extended adult burial (B35) had a belt strap-end at the waist (Wallace, 2010, 304–5).

There are a small number of burials accompanied by knives positioned in a manner which may indicate that they were suspended from a belt, suggesting that the individuals concerned were probably clothed at burial. Among these were an older adult male (SK 8), undated, extended, in a dug grave, in an unenclosed secular cemetery of fourteen graves at Cloghvalley Upper 1, Co. Monaghan, who had a single-edged knife with a spike-tang beside his left hand. The cemetery appears to have been used between the sixth and eighth centuries (Walsh, 2007). One skeleton in a row of six (perhaps more) supine extended skeletons, one of whom has been dated sixth–seventh century,[20] discovered during quarrying on a ridge at Killaree, Co. Kilkenny, had an iron knife beside the femur (Cahill and Sikora, 2011, vol. ii, 70–2). An adult male (SK 1), dated fifth–sixth century,[21] discovered during sand quarrying at Sheastown, Co. Kilkenny, had a small iron knife beside his left hand, with the point towards his feet (ibid., 73–5). At Camlin, Co. Tipperary (Flynn, 2011, 86), several skeletons were accompanied by knives: a young adult (SK 18), sex indeterminate, was accompanied by a whittle-tanged blade; a middle-aged adult (SK 32), sex indeterminate, had an iron whittle-tanged knife at the pelvis; and a middle-aged adult (SK 27), possible male, had a fragment of a composite iron knife with a bone handle on the right-side pelvis (Flynn, 2011, 97). These latter burials are undated.

Not all burials accompanied by knives represent the possibility of clothed burial. They sometimes represent a weapon that had caused the death of the individual, as in the case of adult (B32), undated, in an unenclosed secular cemetery at Kilshane, Co. Dublin, who was accompanied by a tanged iron knife recovered among the back bones of his ribcage (Gowen, 1989, 17; O'Brien, 1993, 93–102; 1997b; 1999a, 181–2). Similarly, the extended female burial (B988), dated fifth–seventh century,[22] at Raystown, Co. Meath, had a knife at her left side beside her ribs (Seaver, 2016, 81).

A further possibility is that a knife may have been deliberately placed into a grave as a display item, as in the case of the large knife that accompanied an undated, isolated burial in a slab-lined cist at Aghalahard, Co. Mayo. The position of the knife is unknown (Raftery and Moore, 1944, 171–2; O'Brien, 1993, 97; 1999a, 180, 182). In the settlement cemetery at Dooey, Co. Donegal (Ó Ríordáin and Rynne, 1961, 58–64), the broken blade of a large knife (described as a scramasax) rested on the chest, with the point towards the chin of a mature adult (SK 30), aged over 45 years.

SHEARS

There is only one positively recorded instance of a burial accompanied by a shears in the Early Medieval period in Ireland,[23] that is, a male of local origin (B1), dated sixth–

---

19 UBA–13375; 1545±22BP; at 2σ = cal AD 427–567 (date obtained courtesy Mapping Death Project).   20 GrA–24440: 1445±40BP; at 2σ = cal AD 550–657.   21 GrA–24361: 1575±35BP; at 2σ = cal AD 406–560.   22 WK–16828: 1496±36BP; at 2σ = cal AD 430–650.   23 The record of a

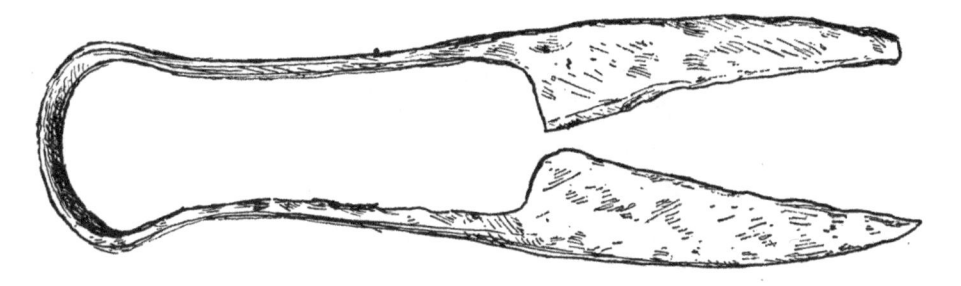

5.5 Iron shears, Burial 1, Site B, Carbury, Co. Kildare, © RSAI.

seventh century,[24] at Site B, Carbury Hill, Co. Kildare (Willmot, 1938, 137). This iron shears, which measures approximately 17.5cm in overall length, was discovered on the man's pelvis, perhaps suggesting that it had been held in his hand (Figure 5.5). The closest comparative material for this item is in Anglo-Saxon England, where shears usually occur in female graves, and are generally associated with cloth manufacturing (Geake, 1997, 96–7). However, it is probable that the shears present with B1 had a ritual function, possibly associated with the ritual cutting of hair, such as tonsuring and fashioning a king's hair as a crown-like tonsure.[25]

DEER ANTLER

Humans have been interacting with deer (*Cervidae*) from earliest recorded time. For example, archaeological evidence for a ritualistic deer cult is present in the Mesolithic era at Star Carr, Yorkshire, in the form of red deer stag skull frontlets with antlers, which were worn on the heads of those performing rituals, probably involved with hunting (Clarke, 1954). It has been suggested that with the decline of the Mesolithic hunter-gatherer economy, and the emergence in the Neolithic of a more stable farming and herding economy, the main function of deer antler changed, and it became a symbol of fertility and prosperity, with perhaps the regeneration properties of young deer antlers being a reason for their transformation into a symbol of fertility and life (Mikhailova, 2006, 195, 197). A further change in the use of red deer *(Cervus elaphus)* antler in the Neolithic is their adaptation into tools, as can be observed for example at the flint mines at Grimes Graves, Norfolk, where hundreds of pick implements manufactured from red deer antler have been recovered[26] (Mercer, 1981, 100–3) (Figure 5.6). Similar implements were used as tools during the construction of the iconic monuments of Stonehenge, Windmill Hill, Durrington Walls and Silbury Hill (Worley and Serjeanston, 2015, 120–1). Alongside their use as utilitarian objects these antler picks often had a dual purpose, whereby they were used as ceremonial objects deliberately deposited in a ritualistic manner (perhaps as a means of ensuring

---

shears recovered at Seskin, Co. Kilkenny (Graves, 1850, 32; Macalister, 1928, 203–4; Raftery, B., 1981, 183, 186), has now been discounted because there is no evidence for burial, and the find is undated.   **24** UBA–11696: 1491±28BP; at 2σ (93.5% probability) = cal AD 535–643.   **25** I thank Edel Bhreathnach for suggesting this function.   **26** The method of manufacture did not change

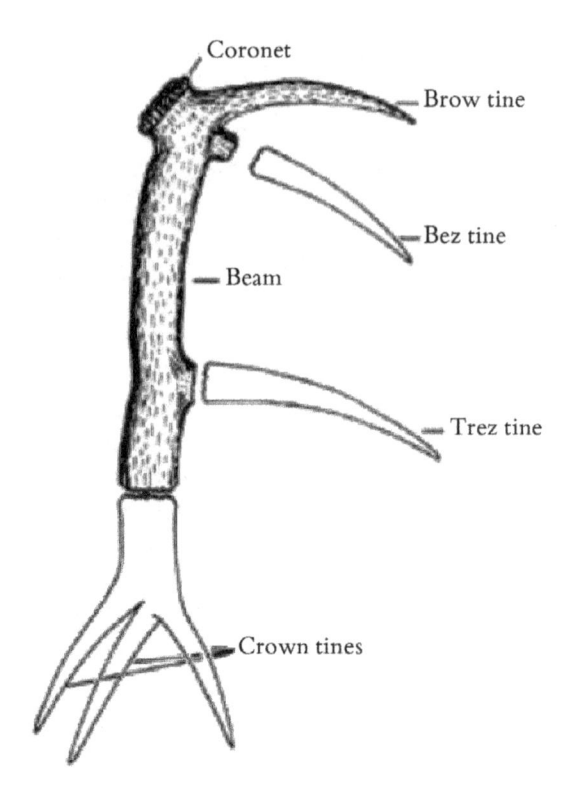

5.6 Method of modification of red deer antler into picks, © R.J. Mercer.

continuity or regeneration of the flint supply) in locations where they had previously been utilised as tools during mining. Examples include deposits at the base of shafts in Grimes Graves, and in the base of a pond-barrow at Barrow Hills, Radley, Oxfordshire (Worley and Serjeanston, 2015, 127). In all cases the antler used was shed by red deer stag.

In Ireland, seven sites, dating to the later Iron Age, and Early Medieval period, have now been identified where red deer antler has been deliberately deposited. Six of these are burial contexts, and one is a ring-ditch complex. In the ancestral ring-ditch complex at Holdenstown 1, Co. Kilkenny (Figures 4.9; 5.7(a)), the ditch of ring-ditch 1 contained twelve red deer antler picks, with four similar objects deposited in the ditch of ring-ditch 2. Ring-ditch 1 was constructed in the second–first century BC, but a c14 date obtained for one of the antler picks places the object in the third–fourth century AD.[27] This implies that the ditches of ring-ditch 1, and ring-ditch 2, were re-cut in the third–fourth century AD, possibly using antler picks, which were then deliberately deposited at the base of the ditches. Because of the ready availability

during subsequent eras.   27 UBA–20005: 1703±25BP; at 2σ = cal AD 255–400.

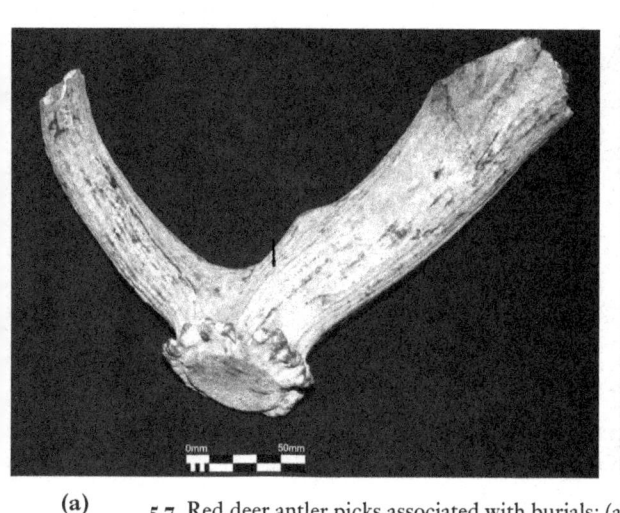

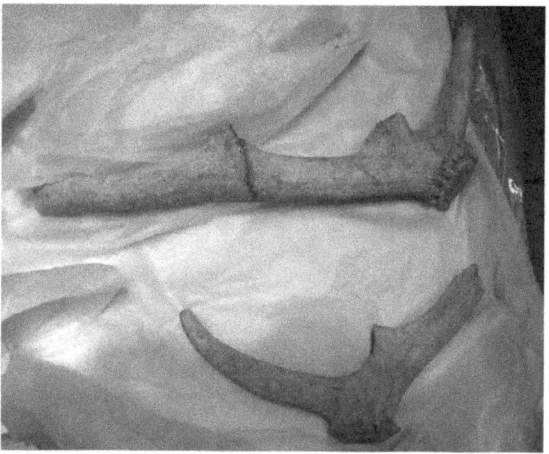

5.7 Red deer antler picks associated with burials: (a) Holdenstown 1, Co. Kilkenny, © IAC; (b) Farta, Co. Galway, © courtesy of the National Museum of Ireland.

of more efficient iron digging-tools at that time, the assumption must be that these antler picks are ritual objects and not utilitarian tools.

A further twist to this narrative is that at the nearby organised, unenclosed, secular cemetery at Holdenstown 2, the centrally placed foundation burial (B59), dated to the fifth–sixth century AD,[28] was accompanied by part of an antler pick identical in date[29] to the picks in the ring-ditches at Holdenstown 1. This object was apparently deliberately sourced in the ring-ditch at Holdenstown 1 and placed into the foundation grave at Holdenstown 2, probably in order to create a symbiotic link between the perceived indigenous ancestral *fert* and the newly established communal cemetery. This individual (B59) was not native to the locality in which he was buried, and probably represents the progenitor of a new kin-group moving into this area in the fifth–sixth century, in which case the antler could also be a symbol of fertility ensuring a link with the existing local population and the continued growth of the new family unit.

Two red deer antler picks, which conform to the classic type in use since the Neolithic, comprising coronet, beam and brow tine (Figure 5.7b), were inserted into the upper level of the ancestral burial mound at Farta, Co. Galway. When this site was excavated in 1903 (Figure 4.5), it was assumed that the burial in the mound was Bronze Age, and that the antler had accompanied the burial of a female and her horse (Coffey, 1904, 14–20). However, the female and horse have now been dated to the fourth–sixth century AD,[30] and the antler picks have been dated to the sixth–seventh century.[31] As these antler picks were inserted into the mound sometime after the burial of the female and horse, the question arises as to what they symbolise? Were they inserted as ritual objects into what was regarded as a venerated ancestral burial mound

---

28 UBA–13667: 1569±22BP; at 2σ = cal AD 423–544.   29 UBA–20006: 1698±24BP; at 2σ = cal AD 256–403.   30 Female: OxA-X–2488.42: 1625±26BP; at 2σ = cal AD 383–536. Horse: UBA–23699: 1618±26BP; at 2σ = cal AD 388–536 (dates obtained courtesy Mapping Death Project).
31 Antler: UB–27057: 1407±43BP; at 2σ = cal AD 564–677.

5.8 Deer antler objects in burials: (a) Ballygarraun West, Co. Galway, © VJK; (b) B39, Collierstown, Co. Meath, © ACSU; (c) Grave 3, Lehinch, Co. Offaly, © courtesy of the National Museum of Ireland; (d) B420, Ranelagh, Co. Roscommon, photo EOB, © IAC.

to ensure the continuation of the community? Or, perhaps the deposition of the antler picks was a deliberate 'sealing' of this ancestral burial monument in the seventh century.

A red deer antler object, comprising the coronet and part of the beam truncated above the trez tine, with the brow and bez tines removed (Figure 5.8a), was recovered in the pelvic girdle of the isolated elderly female burial, dated to the fifth–seventh century,[32] at Ballygarraun West, Co. Galway. Cut and chop marks, which occurred during manufacture, were visible on the object (Randolph-Quinney, 2006; Lehane, 2008). The shape of the object and the place of deposition on the body indicates that it probably represents a phallic symbol of reproduction and fertility. This elderly woman, who was not local to this region, was possibly the matriarch of a transient migrant family, and the deposition of the antler object, together with domestic hearth residue, might be seen as a method of keeping her content in her isolated grave.

A somewhat similar object was discovered in a recently excavated settlement cemetery at Ranelagh, Co. Roscommon, where a female adolescent (B420), dated eleventh–twelfth century,[33] had a worked antler object deposited in the pubic region (Figure 5.8d). This object does not appear to be a functional implement. It appears instead to be a phallic symbol related to regeneration and/or fertility. The date of this burial is an indication that the acceptance of the association between deer antler and fertility/reproduction was still being observed in the Medieval period.

In the cemetery at Collierstown 1, Co. Meath (O'Hara, 2009a), male burial (B39), undated but included in sixth–seventh century phase 3, had a fragmented antler object (Figure 5.8b) placed in his left hand. The object comprises a segment of beam and a junction with the trez tine. This object is not regarded as an implement by the excavator; reference is made in the excavation report to an early Christian poem in the *Lithica* (Meaney, 1981, 142) that recommends 'that a bridegroom take a stag's antler to his nuptial bed, then there will be an indissoluble affection between husband and wife all their lives' (Riddler and Trzaska-Nartowski, 2009a, 3). This antler object could, using this analogy, be regarded as a symbol of regeneration and fertility.

At Lehinch, Co. Offaly, the earliest burial (G3), sex undetermined, born locally, dated to the fifth–sixth century,[34] had antler tines inserted points downward (Figure 5.8c), on the southern side of the grave, together with three portions of horse meat. The tines, which appear to represent crown tines,[35] are not part of an antler tool, so one must conclude that they, together with the horse portions, were inserted into the grave as offerings or ritual objects.

The multi-symbolism of antler objects is apparent. They are variously used as tools/implements in mining, as implements used in the construction of ritual places, as a link between indigenous ancestors and newcomers, and as symbols of regeneration and fertility.

BEADS

The placing of a single bead, especially with a child's burial, is a pan-European tradition, and is usually interpreted as an amulet guarding against the evil eye (Gilchrist, 2008, 141). Beads occasionally found with adult females probably served a similar purpose. It has been suggested that anything desirable can come under the spell of the evil eye, but blooming life, as represented in babies and young cattle, is

---

32 UBA–7683: 1471±67BP; at 2σ = cal AD 428–661.   33 UB–36199: 903±27BP; at 2σ = cal AD 1039–1206. Thanks to Maeve Tobin, of IAC, for supplying this date prior to publication.   34 GrA–24445: 1625±40BP; at 2σ = cal AD 399–541.   35 Unfortunately, it has not been possible to examine

thought to be especially vulnerable to its harmful glance. Amulets and beads were worn as protection, 'sometimes conspicuously attached on the clothes to draw the attention of the evil eye to the amulet instead of to the person wearing it' (Borsje and Kelly, 2003, 3, 4).

Although belief in 'the evil eye' is well known in Irish texts and in folklore, Borsje concludes that in Ireland there is no archaeological evidence for evil eye amulets (ibid., 33). However, examples have been excavated in Ireland. In the settlement cemetery at Parknahown 5, Co. Laois (O'Neill, 2009, vols. 1, 11), four infants, one juvenile and two adult burials were accompanied by beads. Infant burial (585), dated to the seventh–ninth century,[36] was accompanied by a decorated bone bead, a perforated horse tooth, and a quartz pebble; infant burial (870), dated to the ninth–tenth century,[37] had a bone bead; infant burial (508), undated, had one blue glass bead located above the left pelvic bone; infant burial (149), undated, had a blue glass bead under the chin; juvenile burial (1007), undated, had two glass beads beside the head; adult burial (873) (sex undetermined), undated, had an incomplete gaming piece close to the left hand, which might have been used as a bead (Riddler and Trzaska-Nartowski, 2009b, 290–1); and, adult female (293), dated to the seventh–eighth century,[38] had three glass beads (rope, melon, segmented, with copper tops) and a copper rivet in the thorax region. It is possible in this latter instance that the beads may have been decorative.

At Raystown, Co. Meath, a 1-year-old child, dated eighth–tenth century,[39] had a blue glass bead at its neck (Seaver, 2016, 81).

In the cemetery at Faughart, Co. Louth, which has produced dates ranging from the fifth to tenth century, infant burial (1244A), undated, had a blue glass bead at its neck; juvenile burial (1436A), undated, had a blue glass bead at the neck; adolescent burial (1078A), undated, had two blue glass beads at the neck; adult female burial (1486A), undated, had a blue glass bead at her neck, and adult burial (1016A) sex undetermined, undated, had a stone bead near the fingers, perhaps indicating that it was held in the persons hand (Bowen and Dawkes, 2011, 73).

In the large cemetery, dating from the fifth to the twelfth century, at Mount Offaly, Cabinteely, Co. Dublin, three infant burials were each accompanied by a bone bead (Conway, 1999, 33; 2000, 36, 37, no. 124).

In the pre-oratory cemetery at Reask, Co. Kerry, where unfortunately there was no bone survival, a small-size slab-lined grave (g.23) contained a small green glass bead at the base of the fill (Fanning, 1981, 82, 121). The size of the grave suggests it was that of a child.

An empty grave (0318) at Camlin, Co. Tipperary, contained four blue glass beads and one bone bead, found close together (Flynn, 2011, 86), which perhaps were inserted as a memento or as a token burial.

A semi-crouched adult female in the cemetery at Solar, Co. Antrim (545), oriented south–north (head to the south), undated, was accompanied by a bone cylindrical object with incised decoration, which was possibly a bead (Hurl, 2002, 56).

the objects as they cannot be located. 36 SUERC–17324: 1230±35BP; at 2σ = cal AD 687–884. 37 SUERC–17304: 1120±35BP; at 2σ (87.8% probability) = cal AD 860–995. 38 SUERC–16998: 1270±35BP; at 2σ (86.8% probability) = cal AD 662–779. 39 WK–16309: 1130±35BP: at 2σ = cal

Grave goods

All the beads mentioned appear to be amulets whose purpose was probably to ward off the evil eye in life, and after death, with the possible exception of the three exotic beads accompanying female burial 293 at Parknahown 5, which may have been purely decorative.

QUARTZ PEBBLES AND WHITE STONES

Because of its whiteness,[40] and the glowing effect produced in the dark when two pieces are rubbed together, quartz is seen as having a symbolic value in many societies. The special association of quartz with the dead and the spirit world, and its use in commemorative deposits, has been recognised since Neolithic times (Cooney, 2000, 176–8; Thompson, 2005, 111, 113, 119). Evidence that the symbolism of quartz and of white stones was absorbed into, and adopted by, Christianity, from its earliest phase, is demonstrated in John's letter to the church at Pergamum, in modern Turkey (one of the seven churches of Asia), in which he states 'to everyone who conquers [evil] I will give some of the hidden manna, and I will give a white stone, and on the white stone is written a new name that no one knows except the one who receives it' (Revelation 2:17). Adomnán refers to an episode when Columba took 'a white stone from the river, and blessed it, so that it should effect some cure … contrary to nature, that stone, when immersed in water, floated like an apple' (*Adomnán* [i.1], Anderson and Anderson, 1991, 12–13). He repeats the reference (*Adomnán* [ii.33], ibid., 140–5) when describing Columba's visit to the district of the Picts, when Columba took a white stone from the River Ness and said 'Mark this white stone. Through it the Lord will work many cures of the sick among this heathen people'. When Broichan, reputedly the foster-father of the Pictish King Brude, was dying, Columba instructed that when he (Broichan) released a slave girl, the stone should be dipped in water, and where it floated, Broichan drank the water, and fully recovered his health. The stone became one of King Brude's treasures and reputedly cured many diseases but, unfortunately, when the king himself was dying it could not be found.

As white stones were associated with water and regeneration, which in a Christian context represented baptism and resurrection, it is not surprising that they were also included in burials in the conversion period, possibly as a method of identifying a Christian among the pagan ancestors. This does not, however, exclude the possibility that quartz pebbles still represented non-Christian magical or protective charms, and continued to be used as such, especially in an era of conversion to an alternative religious belief system, and beyond.

In view of the symbolism associated with such pebbles, one would expect to find multiple instances of inclusion in burials, but surprisingly, in the overall Early Medieval secular burial record, such occurrences are relatively rare.

Examples[41] include two of the four extended burials at the transitional burial site of Prumplestown Lower, Co. Kildare, which were accompanied by quartz. Female (SK 2), dated to the fifth–sixth century,[42] in a stone-lined grave, within a small re-used

---

AD 781–990.   **40** Quartz presents as white pebbles when water-rolled, hence the Irish name *clocha geala*.   **41** Examples are summarised in Gazetteer 3.   **42** UBA–9401: 1565±38BP; at 2σ = cal AD

ring-ditch, had eight 'chunks' (*sic*) of quartz in the grave fill; male (SK 1), dated to the fifth–seventh century,[43] buried outside the ring-ditch, had five 'chunks' (*sic*) of quartz located by the right arm and the right leg (Clark and Long, 2010, 32, 33). It is noted that the two remaining extended burials at this site did not contain quartz.

At Cross, Co. Galway (Figure 4.13), three of the seven extended inhumation burials contained quartz inclusions. Female (B4), dated to the fourth–sixth century,[44] centrally located, in a stone-lined grave, within ring-ditch 1, had small white quartz inclusions; female (B7), dated to the fourth–sixth century,[45] in a stone-lined grave outside ring-ditch 1, also had quartz inclusions; and child burial (B1), dated to the sixth–seventh century,[46] centrally located, in a dug grave, within ring-ditch 2, also produced white quartz inclusions, which the excavator felt had been deliberately placed in the grave (Mullins, 2007, 108; 2009, 17, 19, 21). The remaining burials at this ancestral site did not contain any quartz inclusions. The quartz inclusions may have identified Christians buried among pagans.

Two burials at the *ferta* site of Holdenstown 1, Co. Kilkenny, were accompanied by quartz pebbles. Adult male (B3), undated, located together with four other burials within ring-ditch 2, had one piece of quartz underneath the right pelvis, and the grave of an older adult (B7), sex undetermined, located within the outer penannular enclosure, contained water-rolled quartz pebbles (Whitty, 2009, 31, 34).

In the partially excavated, organised secular cemetery at Britonstown extension, Co. Wicklow (Tobin and Faith, 2015, 168), datable to the sixth–seventh century, a young adult of indeterminate sex (SK 4) had a quartz pebble, described as a manuport, placed beside the head.

In the cemetery at Parknahown 5, Co. Laois (O'Neill, 2009, vol. 1), several burials were accompanied by quartz pebbles. Infant burial (585), dated to the seventh–ninth century, was accompanied by a quartz pebble, an antler bead and a horse tooth; infant burial (670), undated, was accompanied by two quartz pebbles; juvenile burial (1096), undated, was accompanied by one quartz pebble; juvenile burial (549), undated, was accompanied by a quartz pebble and an iron nail; and adult female burial (362), dated to the eleventh–twelfth century,[47] was accompanied by three quartz pebbles. Although many of these burials are undated, it is interesting to note that the sporadic inclusion of quartz pebbles appears to have a wide temporal span.

In the partially excavated secular cemetery at Magheradunbar, Co. Fermanagh, an infant burial (B1), dated to the seventh–eighth century,[48] contained a piece of quartz in each hand, and a copper-alloy pin in its neck area, an indication that the infant may have been swaddled (Dunlop, 2003).

The settlement cemetery at Carrowkeel, Co. Galway, has been divided into three phases by the excavator. Phase 1 (AD 650–850) contained thirty-seven burials, of which three adults and three children were accompanied by quartz. The three adults and one child have been dated as follows: adult (B114) to the seventh–eighth century,[49]

408–574. **43** SUERC–25246: 1515±30BP; at 2σ = cal AD 428–615. **44** Wk21251: 1628±39BP; at 2σ = cal AD 342–538. **45** Wk21254: 1604±38BP; at 2σ = cal AD 382–550. **46** Wk21248: 1489±38BP; at 84.5% probability = cal AD 532–645. **47** SUERC–16991:930±35BP; at 2σ = cal AD 1023–1184. **48** Beta–186556: 1280±40BP; at 2σ (87.4% probability) = cal AD 657–779. **49** UB–7440: 1301±31BP; at 2σ = cal AD 659–770.

adult (B57) to the seventh–eighth century,[50] adult (B22) to the eighth–tenth century,[51] and child (B113) to the eighth–tenth century.[52] Phase 2 (AD850–1050) contained seventy-five burials, only two of which were adults. Eight of the children were accompanied by quartz (five children, two infants and one foetus). One of the older children (B33), dated to the ninth–tenth century, had five pieces of quartz.[53] Phase 3 (AD1050–1250) has not been included in Gazetteer 3, and is included here for information only. This phase contained eighteen burials, adults and children, four of which were each accompanied by one piece of quartz, a foetus, an infant, a younger child and an adult (Wilkins and Lalonde, 2009, 104–9, 141).

In the partially excavated cemetery inside the north wall of the ruined Medieval church at St John's Point, Co. Down (Brannon, 1980, 59–64), a young male (B7) was accompanied by two quartz pebbles, one underneath and behind the skull, and the other between the legs near the pelvis. None of the burials at this site have been dated, and while they may pre-date the ruined Medieval church, they might also be Medieval in date.

The following have been excluded from Gazetteer 3, but are included here for information: twelve+ burials excavated beneath a ruined Medieval church, at Collierstown 2, Co. Meath, each accompanied by a small rounded quartz pebble or a piece of rock-crystal (Ó hÉanaigh, 1934), have not been dated and it is possible that these are Medieval. The cemetery at Ballyhanna, Co. Donegal (McKenzie et al., 2015), which contained over 1,200 burials ranging in date from the eighth to the eighteenth century, contained at least eighteen burials with quartz pebbles in their hands, all dating to the Medieval and later Medieval periods (Macdonald and Carver, 2015, 81–4).

There are several explanations, relating to different eras, for the inclusion of quartz with burials. All the individuals buried in the conversion-period transitional burial sites of Prumplestown Lower, Co. Kildare, Cross, Co. Galway, and Holdenstown 1, Co. Kilkenny, were probably of a social status which set them apart from the norm. Selected individuals, two of four burials at Prumplestown Lower, three of seven burials at Cross, and two of eight burials at Holdenstown 1, were accompanied by quartz. Could this have been a means of distinguishing, in the perceived afterlife, those who were Christians buried alongside their pagan contemporaries? This might be particularly relevant in the case of the latest of these burials, the child (BI), dated to the sixth–seventh century, buried in ring-ditch 2 at Cross, Co. Galway.

Between the seventh and tenth century, it is noticeable that the proportion of burials with quartz appears to decrease. For example, quartz was associated with one burial in the sixth–seventh-century cemetery at Britonstown, Co. Wicklow; one burial in the partially excavated seventh–eighth-century cemetery at Magheradunbar, Co. Fermanagh; and one burial in the pre-church cemetery at St John's Point, Co. Down. However, the frequency increases again in the Medieval period when one of five burials containing quartz at Parknahown 5, Co. Laois, is dated to the seventh–ninth century, and a further four appear to belong in the eleventh–twelfth century. In the cemetery at Carrowkeel, six burials in the seventh–ninth century phase 1 contained

---

50 UB-7420: 1246±31BP; at 2σ (87% probability) = cal AD 666–779.   51 UB-7412: 1186±32BP: at 2σ (86.7% probability) = cal AD 766–901.   52 UB-7439: 1168±32BP; at 2σ = cal AD 771–968.   53 UB-7482: 1127±32BP; at 2σ (86.5% probability) = cal AD 860–990.

quartz, while eight in ninth–eleventh century phase 2 contained quartz. As it is unlikely that after the seventh century only a handful of burials in any cemetery were Christian, perhaps an explanation might be that the presence of quartz was used to identify a newly baptised person, especially in the case of children.

It would appear that the tradition was revived in the Medieval period, as all twelve undated burials excavated at the ruined Medieval church at Collierstown 2, Co. Meath, were accompanied by quartz, and the eighteen burials accompanied by quartz at Ballyhanna, Co. Donegal, date to between the Medieval and Late Medieval period. A possible comparison for this might be seen at the cemetery that pre-dates the phase 1 church at Capel Maelog, Powys, Wales, where the grave of 'focal' burial (G.241) was covered by a setting of stones within which was a spread of twenty-four white quartz pebbles. A further grave (G.271) was similarly covered. It is postulated that this cemetery was established between the ninth and eleventh centuries, prior to the construction of the twelfth–thirteenth century phase 1 church (Britnell, 1990, 36, 83).

FUNERAL FEASTS

The use of funeral feasts by Christians was condemned in the sixth-century Canons of the Greek Synods by Martin bishop of Braga, Portugal, who died AD 580: *non oportet, non liceat Christianis prandia ad defunctorum sepulchra deferre et sacrificari mortuis* (Rolleston, 1870, 424–5, note a) ('It is not right, and Christians may not be permitted to bring meals to the tombs of the dead for them to be sacrificed for the dead'), but this did not prevent references in seventh-century documents to the practice still being observed by Christians in the West.

Adomnán, in a reference to a funeral feast, relates an incident in which Columba purportedly arranged for food gifts to be sent to a former thief, who died before he received the gifts, and this food was then used at his funeral (*Adomnán* [i.41], Anderson and Anderson, 1991, 74–7). In the early Irish law text *Di dligiud raith 7 somaine* ('On the law relating to the fief and profit of a lord'), one of the seven duties which must be carried out by a client in the event of the lord's death is attendance at the commemorative feast (Kelly, 1988, 30, 271). A further reference to funeral feasting is contained in *Bretha comaithchesa* (Judgements of neighbourhood) when, after the burial, the clients took part in the *comaithmet anma* (the commemoration of the soul) which involved communal eating and drinking, the food and drink having been provided by the clients (*CIH* i. 204.18).[54] An Old Irish law text on marriage disputes contains a reference to a death feast, §35 *Cuna beith deithbir na fleidhe crolighi sin o cach grad uili* ('With there being the due of that feast of death-lying from every grade') (Kelly, 2014, 48–9). In the notes glossing this passage, it is suggested that the feast of death-lying took place after a month (ibid., 119). This raises the possibility that a month's mind feast may have been undertaken at the place of burial (the grave) in a cemetery. This practice was later replaced by Christian rites for the dead such as *immain anmae* ('hymns for the soul'), part of the entitlement of the laity in relation to the church, mentioned in the law tract *Córus bésgnai* §38 (Breatnach, 2017, 156–7).

---

54 I am indebted to Thomas Charles-Edwards for this reference.

In an Early Medieval archaeological context, remnants of a funeral feast held in a cemetery can often be recognised by the presence of animal bone, and/or shards of imported pottery or glass fragments (indicative of wine drinking and of the use of ceramic utensils), either in the back-fill of graves or in the general cemetery area. This context is especially relevant at sites which otherwise produce no evidence for settlement or industry.

The deliberate placing of portions of meat alongside a body in the grave during the Early Medieval period in Ireland is rare. But when it does occur it may be related to the Irish tradition known as *dant mir*, the 'hero's or warrior's portion' awarded to a dead person. If awarded to a living person this tradition was the *curad mir* (*DIL*, 1968, fasc. I, C, Ní Chatháin et al., 93, line 55), but when awarded to a dead person it was named *dant mir* (*dant*, 'a tooth', and *mir*, 'a morsel or portion') (*DIL*, 1913, fasc. I, D-*degóir*, Marstrander, 97). The latter signifies a piece of food, which, 'according to old custom', was put between the teeth of the dead, but it could be placed elsewhere on the body. The *DIL* entry also states that the Brehon Law punished the removal of *dant mir* with *athgabáil treise* ('seizure or reprisal by force'). The funeral feast associated with *dant mir* probably occurred in a dwelling, or at the place in which the deceased was 'laid out' prior to burial. During the feast, the deceased, as an honoured guest, was presented with a choice piece of meat, placed close to the mouth or close to a hand, and which then accompanied the body to the grave.

This phenomenon can be recognised at a limited number of burial sites in Ireland. In the Rath of the Synods, Tara, Co. Meath, a probable male burial (E), semi-crouched, with his head to the east, dated to the eighth–ninth century,[55] had an unidentified animal bone over his face, a bone pin at his neck (possibly a cloak fastener), and a worked-bone object on his chest (now lost) (Grogan, 2008, 44–7; O'Brien, 2013, 244). This individual was born in the northern region of Ireland (Cahill Wilson, 2012, 23–5; Cahill Wilson and Standish, 2016, 234, Table 1). A further male burial (H), extended (not shroud wrapped), dated to the tenth–eleventh century,[56] had animal bone (unidentified) placed around his head, and an animal jawbone on his chest. This man appears to have been of local origin (Cahill Wilson, 2012, 23–5). The presence of animal bone in the head region of these two burials marks them out as probable recipients of *dant mir*, indicating that they were of a status deemed special enough by their peers to be brought to, and accorded burial at, probably with much accompanying ceremony, the royal site of Tara. Burial E is unusual in that his head was to the east – perhaps he was not regarded as Christian. That these burials took place possibly two centuries apart, in an era after formal burial at Tara had long ceased, testifies that the tradition was still known and practised as late as the eleventh century.

Limited excavation conducted beneath the West Cross (Cross of the Scriptures) at the monastic site of Clonmacnoise, Co. Offaly (King, 1995, 74–5),[57] after the removal of the cross to the Interpretative Centre, and prior to the erection of a replica,

---

[55] UBA-11698: 1205±24BP; at 2σ (91.1% probability) = cal AD 767–889. [56] UBA-9030: 1055±26BP; at 2σ (87.0% probability) = cal AD 950–1024. [57] Grateful thanks to Heather A. King, the excavator of this site, for providing information relating to the burials at Clonmacnoise, and for granting permission to refer to the material prior to final publication by her. I, however, accept full responsibility for the interpretation of this material. The human skeletal material was examined by Laureen Buckley, and the animal bone by John Soderberg. Thanks are also due to Dr Paul Byrne

5.9 Burials and post-hole beneath West Cross, Clonmacnoise, © H.A. King.

revealed, at the lowest levels, six burials, dated to between the seventh and tenth centuries, carefully placed in simple dug graves around a square post-hole (Figure 5.9). Each burial was accompanied by a portion of meat. As none of these graves encroached on each other over an extended temporal period, this would suggest that either grave markers were used (for which no evidence survives), that the grave plot was managed probably by a designated family, or that a plan was available. The burials involved were: an older male (B15), dated to the seventh–eighth century,[58] who had a cattle rib located close to his right hand in the pelvic region; an older male (B24), dated to the seventh–eighth century,[59] who had a cattle rib located below the fingers of his right hand; an older male (B22), dated to the seventh–eighth century,[60] who had part of a horse femur located beside the top of his skull, and a cattle rib beside his chin (the inclusion of horse meat in this burial indicates that a horse had been slaughtered and may have formed part of the funeral feast); an older male (B25), dated to the eighth–ninth century,[61] who had an animal rib bone beside his head, and a piece of possible antler located beside his right elbow; an older male (B23), dated to the

for his observations regarding possible *dant mir* at this site. **58** UB–10330: 1288±18BP; at 2σ = cal AD 670–769. **59** UB–4634: 1271±20BP; at 2σ = cal AD 679–770. **60** UBA–10331: 1261±20BP; at 2σ = cal AD 678–774. **61** UBA–10333: 1201±18BP; at 2σ = cal AD 771–885.

eighth–ninth century,[62] the splayed position of whose feet indicates that he was not shroud wrapped, who had a cattle scapula beside the tibia of his left leg, and an animal rib was recovered from the grave back-fill; a younger male (B26), dated to the ninth–tenth century,[63] who had a cattle rib bone on his chin. Some of the animal bones in the graves appear to show signs that the meat may have been cooked (pers. comm., Heather King), which could indicate that the meat had formed part of a funeral feast.

The evidence suggests that those who participated in the relevant funeral feasts at Clonmacnoise, although Christians, may have been of a status that allowed them to be involved in a burial rite that crossed the line between Christian and non-Christian practice. The slaughter of a valuable horse was a display of disposable wealth, and if the horse meat was consumed, an act which is prohibited in the penitentials (McNeill and Gamer, 1938/1990, 120, 157), it is a further indication that those concerned considered themselves entitled to follow this rite. This then raises fundamental questions about the inter-action between Christian and non-Christian practices and beliefs at this quintessentially monastic establishment. These are not the burials of warriors. Burial 23 is the only one who displayed evidence for trauma, a healed rib fracture, and a non-healed fracture of the right clavicle, both of which could have occurred accidentally. Who were these men? It is possible that they were lay abbots, who as 'rulers' of the monastery (Kehnel, 1997, 30) were entitled to burial in a special burial plot, and who might have been accorded a burial rite which transcended the divide between the old religion and Christianity. The excavator has identified the post-hole beneath the West Cross as the remains of a wooden cross which preceded the erection of the stone cross which possibly dates to the late ninth century (Harbison, 2018, 138–9). However, in view of the fact that the burials in this plot differ markedly from the norm for burial during the same era in other parts of the cemetery at Clonmacnoise, is it possible that the post-hole might have held a wooden pillar marking out this special burial plot, or sector, for persons, such as lay abbots, whose status merited their being awarded *dant mir*? The erection of the elaborate West Cross in the late ninth century may have been intended to continue to honour this burial place. It is of course also possible that those buried in this plot were members of royal families, as the cemetery at Clonmacnoise has been described as a 'royal necropolis' (Bhreathnach, 2003, 100), and has produced approximately 700 cross-decorated and inscribed Early Medieval grave slabs recording the burials of kings, bishops, patrons and monks (Swift, 2003, 105–23).

Another possible example of *dant mir* is represented by an adult (B90), unsexed, undated, in phase 2 of the cemetery of Carrowkeel, Co. Galway, who had cattle ribs, a cattle molar and a horse molar placed around the head (Wilkins and Lalonde, 2009, 141).

One of the earliest burials (G3) at Lehinch, Co. Offaly, dated to the fourth–sixth century,[64] sex undetermined, supine, extended in a stone-lined grave (to support a wooden cover?), was accompanied by three portions of horse meat (tibia, pelvis and scapula), laid together with antler tine, along the right side of the skeleton, which may represent an example of *dant mir*. In this instance, a horse had been slaughtered

---

62 UB–4633: 1200±20BP: at 2σ = cal AD 770–887.   63 UBA–10332: 1139±17BP; at 2σ (93.1% probability) = cal AD 868–975.   64 GrA–24445: 1625±40BP; at 2σ = cal AD 339–541.

and probably eaten at a burial feast, suggesting that this was a display of disposable wealth.

A possible female recipient of *dant mir* is represented by B3, in the seventh–ninth century-settlement enclosure at Kilree 3, Co. Kilkenny.[65] This settlement contained five burials, three females, one unidentified individual, and one adolescent who was flexed and oriented north–south, randomly placed throughout the settlement. The burial of interest, an old-/middle-aged female (B3), extended supine in a dug grave located outside the southern part of the settlement, had a large animal bone (unidentified) which had penetrated her decomposed skull. As no other animal bone was found in the surrounding area, one must assume that this bone represents a portion of meat which had originally been placed over her face. In the osteological report it is noted that despite the advanced age of this woman, degeneration of the intervertebral disc was the only evidence for degenerative changes, suggesting that she had been subjected to little functional stress during life (Coughlan, 2010, 18–19). In other words, she did not participate in everyday labour, an indication that she was of high status in her community. The location of her grave is unusual, but this may merely indicate that she was buried close to her dwelling place. That this settlement was of high status in the sixth century is indicated by the discovery elsewhere on the site of a rim and flange of African Red Slip Ware (Kelly, 2009).

As none of the skeletons of the various individuals identified as having been accompanied by *dant mir* displayed any evidence for violent trauma, either during life, or at death, it is unlikely that they had participated in warfare. It is more likely that they occupied a high status in their kin-group. This is particularly notable when a valuable horse has been slaughtered and possibly used for feasting.

The deliberate inclusion of animal remains, but not as *dant mir*, can be observed at a burial at Augherskea, Co. Meath (Baker, 2010, 5–6). A young man (SK 87), who had suffered severe weapon trauma during and after his death, was buried in a secular communal cemetery, but part of a pig's head had been placed on his pelvic region, in what was probably an overt gesture of disrespect. A deposit of boar mandibles adjacent to male prone burial (B2) at the church site of Kill of the Grange, Co. Dublin (Tobin, 2018; Duffy, 2019, 5), could possibly be seen in a similar light.

The remains of random meat deposits discovered in a small number of graves probably represent the remnants of a funeral feast placed with the body to provide nourishment for the dead person in the afterlife. For example, the individual buried in an isolated long cist grave at Aghalahard, Co. Mayo, was accompanied by an ox metacarpal and an iron knife (Raftery and Moore, 1944, 172). It is not known where the meat portion was placed in the grave, as the skeletal material had been disturbed before being recorded. Male (SK D), dated to the fourth–sixth century,[66] in the ancestral burial monument at Pollacorragune, Co. Galway, was accompanied by split, and burnt, animal bone, and female (SK B), dated sixth–seventh century,[67] was also accompanied by split animal bone (Riley, 1936, 44–54; Shea, 1936, 555–64). These two burials were separated temporally by about two centuries, but both were

---

[65] The author is indebted to Maeve Tobin, IAC Ltd, for providing this information prior to completion of the final report. [66] GrA-13613: 1620±70BP; at 2σ (89.4% probability) = cal AD 315–588. [67] GrA-13612: 1450±50BP; at 2σ (92.0% probability) = cal AD 534–666.

accompanied by animal bone which had been split, probably to facilitate the removal of marrow during a burial feast.

The ancestral burial monument at Ballymacaward, Co. Donegal, in which all the burials were female, produced, in a disturbed context, a butchered bovine tibia, dated to the fifth–seventh century,[68] contemporary with the Early Medieval burials in the monument. This bovine tibia, which was the only animal bone present at the site, undoubtedly accompanied one of the disturbed burials.

At Ballydavis 1, Co. Laois, the disarticulated remains of a male and a female, dated to the third–fifth century,[69] placed in a pit in the foundation levels of the cemetery, were accompanied by animal bone (Stevens, 2011, 16). If, as seems probable, these remains had been curated elsewhere before being re-buried in this cemetery, the animal bone probably formed part of a possible feast associated with the original place of burial.

In the ancestral burial place at Site B, Carbury Hill, Co. Kildare, the multiple burial of an adult, a child, and a neonate (B III), undated, contained fragments of animal bone in the grave fill (Willmot, 1938, 141). As none of the other burials excavated at this site contained animal bone in the fill, this might be evidence that a meal took place at this graveside, with residue being incorporated into the grave fill.

Further evidence for feasting in cemeteries is indicated by, for example, the recovery in the cemetery at Collierstown 1, Co. Meath, of shards of prestige vessels, including a shard of a sixth-century Phocaean Red Slip Ware (PRSW) bowl from the Aegean area, shards of sixth-century Bii amphora from the eastern Mediterranean world, and shards of sixth–seventh-century E ware jugs from western Gaul, together with fragments of animal bone (some of which were burnt), suggesting episodes of high-status feasting and wine drinking in phase 2 of the cemetery (O'Hara, 2009a).

The large, partially excavated, cemetery at Mount Offaly, Cabinteely, Co. Dublin (Conway, 1999), where burial commenced in the fifth–sixth century and continued until about the twelfth century, produced in phase 2 ditch contexts shards of sixth-century Phocaean Red Slip Ware, Bi amphorae, sixth–seventh-century D ware and E ware, together with quantities of animal bone. The final report for this site has not yet been produced, but these finds suggest high-status feasting in an early phase of the cemetery.

The earliest phase of the cemetery at Raystown, Co. Meath, has produced animal bone fragments, a fragment of a glass cone beaker, and shards of E ware, which the excavator suggests are residue from funeral feasting (Seaver, 2016, 20, 22, 149).

The possible emporium site at Colp West 1, Co. Meath (Gowen, 1989, 31–2), produced quantities of animal bone, and shards of B and E ware, in the ditch surrounding the burials. The B and E ware is an indication of the importance of this site located close to the mouth of the River Boyne.

The burial site at Pelletstown, Co. Dublin (Frazer, 2005), produced several small fragments of animal bone with Burial 1, and the grave of Burial 2 (the child at the feet of Burial 1) contained burnt animal bone fragments. Burial 3 also contained

---

[68] OxA–8430: 1495±40BP; at 2σ = cal AD 430–645. [69] SUERC–9014: 1690±35BP; at 2σ = cal AD 253–419 (at 75.5% probability = cal AD 312–419). As this date was obtained from oak-wood in the pit fill it should be treated with caution.

fragments of animal bone in the grave fill. As there was no evidence for settlement in the immediate locality, it is possible that these bone fragments are part of the residue from meals eaten close to the graves.

At Knoxspark, Co. Sligo, thirteen of the burials contained animal bone fragments in the grave fill (Mount, 2010, 199), which the excavator suggests may indicate deliberate inclusion, and of course this is possible; however, it is probable that it represents residue from meals undertaken close to the graves.

The Irish were undoubtedly accustomed to funeral feasting in the pre-Christian Iron Age, and deeply rooted customs transcend religious belief, especially in an era of religious conversion. It is therefore not surprising that this custom would continue to be used by the population in general during the Early Medieval period.

DEPOSITION IN GRAVES OF BURNT GRAIN, AND OF DOMESTIC HEARTH RESIDUE

The association of burnt grain with death is a ritual which was so deeply rooted that it spanned and survived the pagan-Christian transition. It is likely that the burning of grain in the domestic hearth in a dwelling where a deceased individual was laid-out prior to burial initially had a practical use, as burning grain gives off a strong, but not unpleasant odour, which could mask the smell of bodily decomposition. Over time, this seemingly practical act appears to have become ritualised, whereby grain was now burnt to purify the house and the inhabitants. Archaeological evidence indicates that some of this burnt grain was occasionally gathered and deposited into the grave, possibly as part of a purification ritual. The rarity of this rite suggests that it was only performed in very special cases.

The Church regarded the ritual of burning grain as a pagan act, and continuously condemned it with the imposition of harsh penalties. In the literary evidence, the earliest Church condemnation of the ritual is to be found in the 'Penitential of Theodore', written *c.*668–90 in Anglo-Saxon England, where in Book 1, XV.3 it is stated: 'He who causes grains to be burned where a man has died, for the health of the living and of the house, shall do penance for five years' (McNeill and Gamer, 1938/1990, 179, 198). A further condemnation appears in the 'Penitential of Silos' written *c.*800 in Spain, where section XI includes: 'If for the health of the living, a woman burns grains where a man has died, she shall do penance for one year' (ibid., 285, 289). It next appears in the 'Penitential Canons from Regino's Ecclesiastical Discipline' written *c.*906 in France, where the question 'Has thou burnt grains where there was a dead man?' receives the answer 'Thou shouldst do penance for five years' (ibid., 314, 318). Finally, in the so-called 'Confessional of Egbert' written *c.*950–1000 in England, canon 32 includes, 'Anyone who burns corn in the place where a dead man lay, for the health of living men and of his house, shall fast for five years'. It is notable that this 'Confessional', which appears to have obtained much of its content directly from 'Theodore', was written not in Latin but in Anglo-Saxon (ibid., 243, 246). Curiously, the early Irish Canons or Penitentials do not include any penalties in relation to the burning of grain as a death ritual, but the fact that grain occasionally appears as a deposit in burials in the Irish archaeological record is an indication that the rite was known and practised in Ireland in the Early Medieval period, and based on the date obtained for burial (B20) at Kilshane, Co. Dublin, the rite continued until the early tenth century.

Burnt grain is known to have been associated with burials in early Anglo-Saxon cemeteries, and while it is probable that most of the burials concerned are likely to be those of pagan Anglo-Saxons, the possibility that some may have been Christians undoubtedly gave rise to the condemnation of the practice in the Penitential of Theodore (O'Brien, 1999a, 55; 2008a, 294–5; 2010, 49). The transition from paganism to Christianity in Anglo-Saxon England, and its effect on established customs, including the use of burnt grain, has been covered in detail by John Blair (2005, 166–81). Anglo-Saxon cemeteries associated with burnt grain include Spong Hill, Norfolk, where an old find made in 1844 included a cinerary urn filled with charred wheat (Meaney, 1964, 175); Balcombe Pit, Glynde, Sussex, where a wooden box containing grain was found near the skull of a skeleton (ibid., 249); Marston St Lawrence, Northamptonshire, where a trail of burnt corn was observed across the surface of the subsoil in the cemetery (ibid., 453); Andover, Hampshire, where burnt grain was found in two female graves of the sixth century, one of which (G9) had a spread of carbonised grain on the grave floor beneath the pelvic region (Cook and Dacre, 1985, 25–6); Burghfield, Berkshire, where carbonized seed and grain was found in burial G145 (Butterworth and Lobb, 1992, 65); a find of 'three-quarters of charred wheat' is reported from the cemetery at Sandy, Bedfordshire (Meaney, 1964, 40; Kennett, 1970, 29); and ash and burnt grain has been observed in at least four graves (Gr. 6, Gr. 57, Gr. 127, Gr. 369) at the late and post-Roman cemetery at Cannington, Somerset, with some charcoal in the fill of a further fifty-two graves. The excavator of this latter cemetery suggests that the practice is Germanic rather than indigenous in origin (Rahtz, Hirst and Wright, 2000, 84).

In an Irish context, an unenclosed secular cemetery of 123 burials at Kilshane, Co. Dublin, included two adults, (B20) dated to the eighth–tenth century,[70] and (B26), and child (B52), who had burnt grain deposited around their skulls (Gowen, 1989, 17; O'Brien, 1999, 182; 2008a, 295). A further instance is a sample of burnt grain preserved in the National Museum of Ireland (NMI 1943.222) recorded as having been discovered in 1943 in a grave at Levitstown, Co. Kildare. Unfortunately, no record of the burial was retained.

The following curious late manifestation of the ritual in Ireland (not included in Gazetteer 3) was recorded in Co. Cork, where a deposit of charred wheat (context 13), recovered from the chamber of the Bronze Age wedge tomb at Toormore, on the Mizen peninsula, during excavation in 1989–90 (O'Brien, B., 1991, 20–1. O'Brien, W., 1999, 181–3), surprisingly produced a date between the fifteenth and seventeenth century AD.[71] This phenomenon may be attributable to the fact that in the later sixteenth and the early seventeenth centuries this region was effectively depopulated of its indigenous inhabitants, and subsequently repopulated largely by English settlers as part of the Munster plantations of the period (Breen, 2007). Although the excavator

70 UBA–13373: 1159±19BP; at 2σ = cal AD 776–962 (at 73.2% probability = cal AD 776–902). Date obtained courtesy of INSTAR Mapping Death Project.   71 OxA–3996: 390±65BP; at 2σ = cal AD 1428–1643.

was of the opinion that this deposit represented the dumping of domestic food waste, a further possible explanation is that some of these English newcomers may have performed the ritual of depositing burnt grain in an ancient burial place to purify, placate, or appease, the spirits of the ancestors of the displaced indigenous population. Whatever the reason, the deposition indicates that this ancient ritual was known and practised in Cork in the later Middle Ages, possibly by newcomers to the district.

Another form of deposit in graves is that of domestic hearth-rakings. This has been described as representing a method of preventing the dead from returning home to seek the warmth of the hearth, or alternatively, as a gesture of home and comfort offered to a loved one (Gilchrist, 2008, 146–7, 150).

Some examples of this practice can be observed in Early Medieval burials in Ireland. The young adult female burial (B48), dated to the fifth–sixth century,[72] centrally located in enclosure 1, in the secular cemetery at Collierstown, Co. Meath, had a deposit of hearth debris containing a mixture of burnt clay, charcoal (including hazel, cherry and oak) and a tiny piece of burnt pig bone, placed in the pelvic region (O'Hara, 2009). This was the foundation burial at this cemetery, therefore the deliberate deposition of material from the domestic hearth into her grave may have been a method of creating a link between her and her household or family unit, and probably represents a symbol of her high status within her kin-group, or local *túath*.

A similar status could probably be accorded to the isolated single burial of a mature female, dated fifth–seventh century,[73] whose body had been laid on a deposit of domestic hearth debris, containing burnt vegetation and cereal grains, at Ballygarraun West, Co. Galway. This burial was also accompanied by a piece of worked red deer antler.

In England, there appears to have been a revival of a Christianised version of the rite between the thirteenth and fifteenth centuries, demonstrated by the lining of coffins with ash or hearth rakings before placement of the corpse (Gilchrist, 2008, 145). Burials of this type have been recovered from church associated cemeteries. Gilchrist suggests that this date range is an indication that the rite became prevalent in England during the Black Death, and may also have been used for plague victims.

Charcoal burial is a specifically Christian practice which became a popular type of high-class burial in England between the ninth and twelfth centuries, whereby a layer of charcoal was packed into the grave, below, around and occasionally above the coffin (Gilchrist, 2008, 145). The charcoal used was derived from mature oak branches, and it is thought that oak was used because it 'symbolizes strength of faith and virtue and is one of the trees from which belief would have it that the Cross was made' (Kjølbye-Biddle, 1992, 229). It is of interest that no charcoal burials of this type have been recognised in the Irish archaeological record, to date.

---

[72] BA250161: 1550±40BP; at 2σ = cal AD 422–596.   [73] UBA–7683: 1471±67BP; at 2σ = cal AD 428–661.

Grave goods

* * *

The rarity of burials accompanied by grave goods in the archaeological record for Early Medieval Ireland, with only eighty-nine burials (0.81% of the total burial corpus), spread throughout forty-five burial sites, having been identified to date, necessitated investigation of even seemingly minor artefacts. The items investigated comprise, three neck rings or collars (unlikely to be slave collars) which may be decorative or are a symbol of status; a possible shield, a grave good unique in Early Medieval Ireland; two spears, one of which may have been deliberately deposited with a burial, an act unique in Early Medieval Ireland, the second spear was one of the causes of death of an individual; a possible sceptre, which may have acted as a symbol of status; a unique set of inter-locking wooden boxes; dress pins including two omega-type brooches; a toe ring, which is a symbol of status; an earring; several knives and buckles which may indicate individuals who were clothed on burial; a set of shears; several deposits of deer antler, possibly representing fertility or regeneration; a stone amulet; several beads, which were probably used as amulets to ward off the evil eye; quartz pebbles; portions of animal bone some of which appear to represent food offerings known as *dant mir* and associated with status, while other animal bones may represent the remains of funeral feasts; and several instances of the presence in the grave of burnt grain and/or hearth rakings, a custom forbidden by the Christian Church.

CHAPTER 6

Atypical or deviant burials

Burials which are atypical in that they deviate from the norm are present, usually as a minority rite, in all cultures and societies in the Early Medieval period, and Ireland is no exception. The reasons for deviancy in burial rites are varied, but in an environment where the spirits of the dead were considered to be omnipresent among the living, the majority were associated with those who were respected in life and regarded as benevolent in death, but others were, for whatever reason, feared in life, and regarded as malevolent in death. It was the latter whose bodies were usually buried in a manner which was designed to prevent their spirit returning to harm the living. Other atypical or deviant burials were often the result of punitive actions and/or interpersonal conflict. The fact that atypical or deviant burial is a minority rite in Early Medieval Ireland is demonstrated by the following selection of 153 burials, which represent only 1.45% of the 11,000 burials in the corpus. The burials described in the various categories therefore represent but a minority of overall burial in Early Medieval Ireland, and ought not to be over-emphasised.

A small number of deviant burials, assigned to the post ninth-century period, but interred in cemeteries established in the fifth–sixth centuries, have been included for information only, and these are indicated where appropriate in the general text. This selection of Irish examples of atypical/deviant burial has been greatly facilitated by osteo-archaeological reports which have become increasingly available as an important component of published and unpublished excavation reports.[1] Map 6 records the distribution pattern of Irish cemetery sites which contain atypical or deviant Early Medieval burials. While some such burials were discovered during comparatively recent infrastructural excavations, a sizeable minority were discovered in older excavations; Map 6 gives a reasonable representation of the actual distribution. A general breakdown of categories of atypical or deviant burials is outlined in Gazetteer 4.

PROBABLE LIVE BURIAL

One of the most extreme instances of Early Medieval deviant burial is a probable live burial in Site 4, The Curragh, Co. Kildare (Ó Ríordáin, 1950, 249–77). Site 4 was a very elaborate, well-constructed ring-ditch consisting of a circular level area surrounded by a ditch and bank (32m diameter) (Figure 6.1a). There were two opposing entrances across the ditch and bank on the east and west sides. The eastern entrance contained two post-holes which may have accommodated posts for swing-gates. In the centre was an oval dug grave, 1.15m deep, containing a west–east

---

[1] Unpublished reports, which have generously been provided by TII and various excavators, are referenced in the text and Bibliography.

Atypical or deviant burials

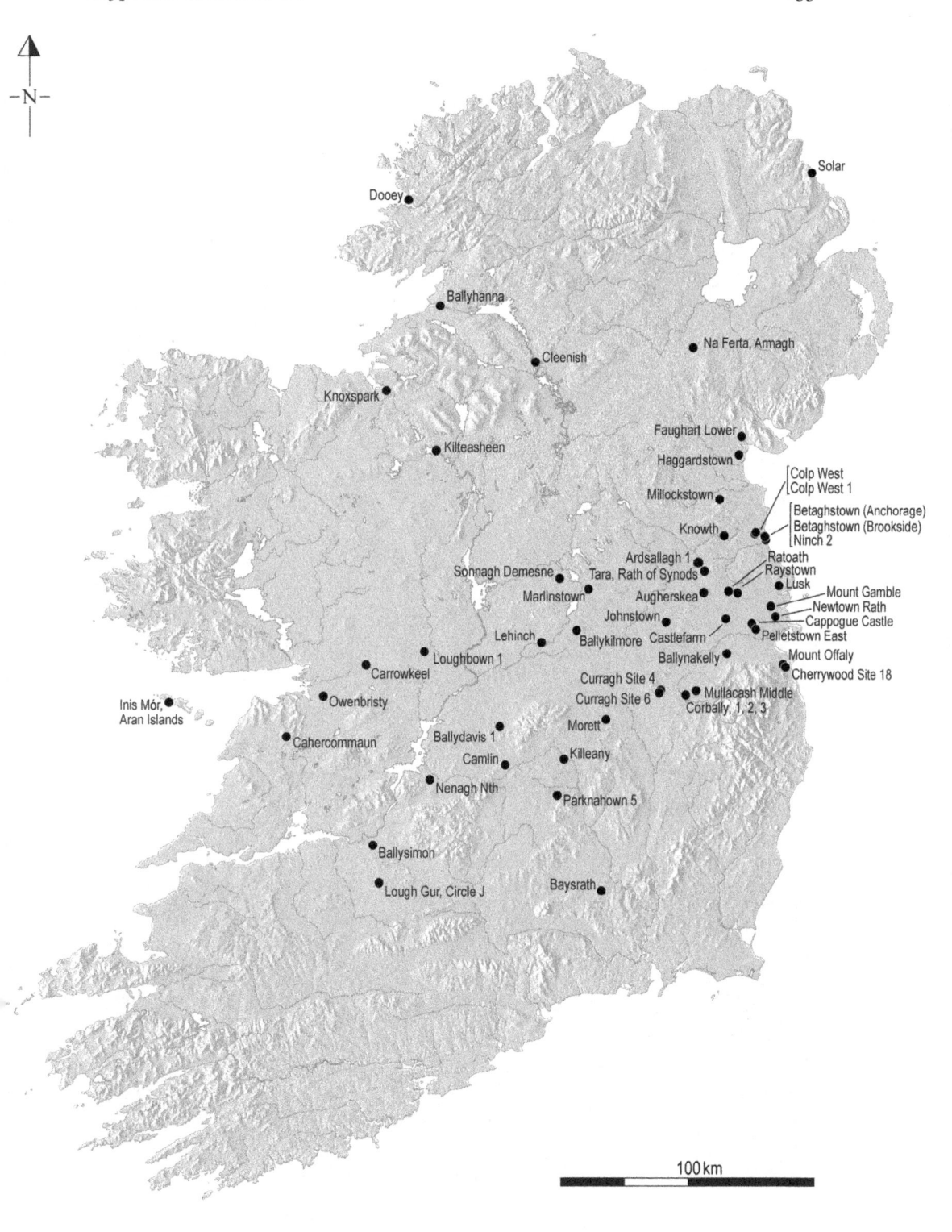

Map 6 Distribution of Early Medieval cemeteries with atypical/deviant burials, © The Discovery Programme and EOB.

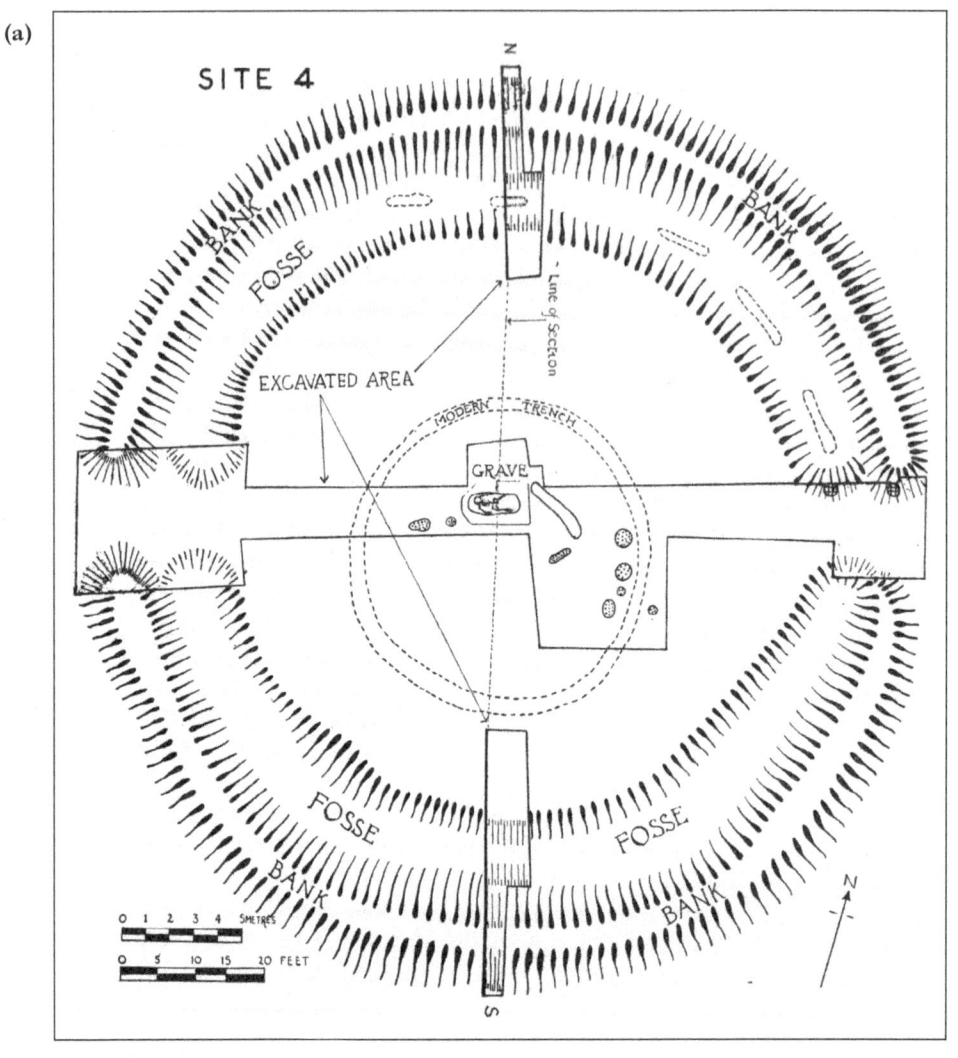

6.1 Site 4, The Curragh, Co. Kildare: (a) overall plan of Site 4 (after Ó Riordáin, 1950, fig. 5), © RIA; (b) possible 'live' burial in Site 4 (after Ó Riordáin, 1950, Plate XXII, 2), © RIA.

Atypical or deviant burials

orientated female skeleton lying in a very unusual position. The body was supine, twisted slightly to the left side, the arms were braced against the sides of the grave, and the legs were wide apart and similarly braced, the head was flexed forward on to the chest (Figure 6.1b). The remains were identified in the 1950 publication as those of a 20- to 35-year-old female, but recent osteological re-examination (Carty and Daly, 2013) shows that this was an elderly post-menopausal female with severe degenerative joint disease. The burial, originally regarded as Iron Age in date (Ó Ríordáin, 1950, 272–3; Raftery, B., 1981, 187), is now known to date to between the fifth and seventh century AD, with the highest probability being sixth–seventh century.[2] All who have examined this burial have arrived at the same conclusion – this was the burial of a live person. The excavator reluctantly arrived at this conclusion: 'one thinks in this connection of a voluntary ritual sacrifice in which the victim lay unbound in the grave which was then filled in' (Ó Ríordáin, 1950, 257).

This woman was not someone who was hastily disposed of; she was buried in a supine position, and was not weighted down. Prior to her burial, a significant amount of time and effort had been invested in the construction of the ring-ditch mortuary enclosure, and undoubtedly her death and burial were accompanied by specific and elaborate rituals. Probable gateposts in one of the entrances would indicate that this grave was re-visited possibly over an extended period, suggesting that the grave of this woman was of importance to the community. To the modern mind, the possibility that the death of this woman might represent a voluntary ritual sacrifice, possibly acting as an intermediary between the living and the ancestors, may well appear implausible, abhorrent, or even grotesque, but we, who do not know the full circumstances, must accept the visible evidence, and acknowledge our ignorance of whatever logic lay behind this act. Arrangements are in hand to undertake strontium and oxygen analysis of the teeth of this woman, which will indicate whether she was born locally or was an incomer to the area (pers. comm., Niamh Daly).

The fact that this burial does not appear to have been a forced burial is in stark contrast to other published possible 'live' burials. For example, the Iron Age female burial (B4) at Knowth, Co. Meath, buried prone, splayed, and with a large stone on her back, may have been a forced live burial. Also, at Knowth, is female burial (B18)[3] (KnH5), undated, but possibly Early Medieval, who was hastily interred in a shallow dug grave, apparently before she had attained *rigor mortis*. Her right arm was extended above her head and her legs were slightly flexed (O'Brien and Weekes, 2012, 53–5). While this may not be an actual 'live' burial, the disposition of her body suggests that she may have died violently and was quickly disposed of surreptitiously. As an isotope result indicates that she originated in the northern region of Ireland or possibly in northern Britain (Cahill Wilson, 2012, 780–5), she may have been regarded as an 'outsider' or even as an 'intruder'.

A possible parallel is the probable live burial of female (B41) at an early Anglo-Saxon cemetery in Sewerby, East Yorkshire, dating to approximately the same period as the Curragh burial, who was buried prone, above a supine extended burial, and

---

2 UBA–21801: 1503±32BP; at 2σ = cal AD 430–639; (at 80.1% = cal SD530–639). This date was obtained by the writer under the auspices of the Mapping Death Project.   3 This burial has been identified as B16 in Cahill Wilson, 2012, Table A5:1, 780.

who had a large stone on her back (Hirst, 1985, 38–9). Some bog bodies found in Ireland may also represent live burial (Delaney et al., 1999, 67–8; Kelly, 2006).

MUTILATION

Mutilation of a body after death is an ancient practice, the earliest recorded literary reference being when Aeschylus, writing in the fifth century BC, commenting on the death of Agamemnon, alludes to the custom by which the extremities of the murdered man were cut off and hung about the body, the object of which was to disable the spirit of the dead from taking vengeance on the murderer (*Aeschylus*, trans. Weir Smyth, 1926, 201 f.n.).

Mutilation of a body after burial transcends religious belief and cannot be regarded as a specifically pagan or Christian act (Bartlett, 1999, 623–4; O'Brien, 1999a, 54–5). This is brought to the fore in an episode reputed to have taken place in the twelfth century AD in the villages of Stapenhill and Drakelow, England (Geoffrey of Burton, ed. and trans. Bartlett, 2002, chapter 47; O'Brien, 1999a, 54–5; Blair, 2009, 539–40, 556–9), when 'two runaway peasants who had been suddenly struck down dead, returned from the grave to haunt the villagers. The villagers received permission from the bishop to go to the graves and dig them up. They cut off their heads and placed them in the graves between their legs, tore out the hearts and covered the bodies with earth again. After this, the haunting ceased!'

Further recorded instances of this phenomenon include the Icelandic Saga of Grettir the Strong, written in the fourteenth century, but purporting to relate to events that had taken place between 1030 and 1040 (Hight and Foote, 1972, v, 99). When Grettir was attacked by a thrall, who was the ghost of Glam, 'he drew his short sword, cut off Glam's head and laid it between his thighs'. A further reference, this time to an execution on Gotland in the nineteenth century (Ström, 1942, 164–5, n.284), reads, 'after that we dug a pit near the edge of the wood, dragged the dead man there and shovelled earth over him, after the turnkey had carefully seen to it that the dead man had his head between his legs'.

A modern archaeological excavation of an old graveyard that contained burials of the eighteenth and nineteenth century uncovered evidence for mutilation of a body. This was in the Walton family cemetery, Grimswold, Connecticut, US, and the burial in question was that of a male (Burial 4), aged 50–5 years, who had been interred in a stone- and brick-lined grave, in a well-made wooden coffin, identified on the coffin as JB55. It is estimated that ten or fifteen years after his death, the grave was re-opened, and JB's head and lower limbs were removed and placed on his chest, in a skull and crossbones position (Bellantoni et al., 1997, 146). This act of desecration is attributed to the fact that in mid-nineteenth-century New England there existed a strong folk belief in 'vampires', who, it was believed, returned to 'drain' the life from living persons. Apparently because JB had died from 'the wasting disease' (tuberculosis), the survivors thought that by disabling his spirit, they could stop him from returning from the dead and draining the life from the living, thus preventing the disease from spreading to other members of the community.[4]

---

[4] Further evidence for the practice of this custom worldwide has been examined in detail by John Blair (2009, 539–59).

The rationale behind the practice of desecration or mutilation of the dead, in whatever era, seems primarily to be to prevent the spirit of the deceased person from returning to haunt the living, whether because the deceased had been powerful in life and was therefore feared after death (Blair, 2010, 16–20), or was murdered, executed, considered to be evil, or might bring disease on the living.

The custom of preventing the dead from returning to haunt the living practised in Iron Age Ireland has been demonstrated at Betaghstown (Anchorage), Co. Meath, where a crouched female (F238) was pinned down by a large rock. At Knowth, Co. Meath, a prone female (B4) was also pinned down by a large rock, and at Carroweighter 2, Co. Roscommon, an adult male had been buried prone in a ditch, with his right foot amputated and placed between his legs.

Early Medieval examples

An unusual cemetery, where burial commenced in the Early Medieval period, but continued into the Medieval period, located at a bend of the Boyle River as it enters/or exits Lough Cé at Kilteasheen, Knockvicar, Co. Roscommon (Read, 2010, 41–66), contained a juvenile (BR25), aged 10–12 years, undated, who had, after death, been buried in the usual orthodox fashion, but after some time, while the body was still partially fleshed, the grave was re-opened, and the lower limbs were displaced, i.e. the right leg was removed from the hip-socket, flexed at the knee, and laid across the upper trunk, with the femoral head placed on the left side of the body. The left leg had also been disturbed and bent tightly at the knee so that the lower leg was parallel with the femur. This re-alignment gave the impression that the body had been wrapped around the large slab that was part of the base of the original grave. The child exhibited periostitis on a rib, which may indicate the presence of TB, pleurisy, or pneumonic plague (pers. comm., Chris Read). That this child appears to have suffered from TB (the wasting disease) may provide a reason for disturbing the grave, namely, to prevent the child from returning and further spreading the disease in the community. Two further burials in the Kilteasheen cemetery, young adults, (BR56) dated to the eighth–ninth century,[5] and (BR102) dated to the seventh–eighth century,[6] supine, west–east posture, had fist-sized stones inserted into their mouths (burial BR102 is illustrated in Read, 2010, 50, Figure 2.6). This action is attributed to the belief that it prevented the dead from returning to haunt the living, but perhaps in this case the rationale was one of preventing the dead from cursing the living.

At Parknahown 5, Co. Laois, mutilated burials included infant (B1035), undated, who was buried prone, head to the south, hands and feet missing, and a further juvenile (B549), aged 6–7 years, who was buried crouched, minus its right hand, and both feet (O'Neill, 2009, vol. 1, 230, 248). Perhaps the burial dispositions and mutilation of these bodies was because the children were illegitimate, ill with a contagious disease, or maybe they were regard as 'changelings',[7] or perhaps the mutilation was due to whatever family history was attached to their births. In all cases the mutilation was obviously deemed necessary to prevent them from returning to haunt the living.

---

5 AD 720–890 – full radiocarbon dating awaited.   6 AD 660–780 – full radiocarbon dating awaited.
7 Discussed further below at p. 154.

At Ballykilmore 6, Co. Westmeath (Channing, 2009, 49; 2014, 23–38), a middle-aged female was buried flexed on the left side, upper body prone, oriented south-west/north-east, undated, but her cranium and two cervical vertebrae were missing and had been replaced by a head-sized rounded stone. Because the mandible was present in its correct anatomical position, the excavator suggests that the skull may have been removed after decomposition had occurred. It may be that the semi-prone disposition of the body, and the later removal of her head, was a double deterrent to prevent this woman from returning to haunt the living.

An unusual case of mutilation of a body was discovered during excavation for the relocation of a badger sett to facilitate roadworks, at Ballysimon, Co. Limerick (Collins, 2012, 53–7; Birmingham et al., 2013, 69). Inserted into a small natural mound was a setting of twelve stones which surrounded the partial remains of a pair of adult leg bones, dated to the fourth–sixth century.[8] These remains, which were articulated when interred, consisted of tibiae and fibulae, oriented north–south with the proximal ends to the north. The excavator noted that the legs appear to have been bound together prior to burial, with the distal halves of the bones and the feet having been removed in antiquity (Collins, 2012, 55). This was a deliberate interment of articulated parts of a body. The binding of the legs could indicate that the person concerned may have been executed by hanging upside-down, an explanation which has been offered for such hangings in Anglo-Saxon contexts (Reynolds, 2009, 165). As there was no other skeletal material in the vicinity, obviously the remaining body parts of this person were buried elsewhere. The burial of these legs away from the remainder of the body could have been perceived as a method of preventing the deceased from returning from the dead, and 'walking' among the living.

The removal of internal organs, including the heart, after death, a form of mutilation also undertaken to prevent the dead individual returning to haunt the living, is demonstrated in a secular cemetery of long cist graves at Mullacash Middle, Co. Kildare (Cahill and Sikora, 2011, 55–70), where male burial (G3), aged 25–34 years, dating to the sixth–seventh century,[9] displayed extreme weapon trauma (Buckley, 2011, 57–70). He had been decapitated, his head was not in the grave, and he displayed numerous cut marks to his ribs, clavicles, scapulae, femur, tibia and pelvis. The number of wounds appears to indicate that the individual was tortured before death, and the cuts to the ribs have been interpreted as having been made to remove internal organs after death. Although this individual was buried in a long cist in a communal cemetery, action had been taken to prevent his possible 'return' to haunt the living perpetrators of his violent death.

Female burial (B125), aged 40–4 years, undated, buried in a dug grave laid across the ditch fill of phase 1 ring-ditch at Corbally 2, Co. Kildare,[10] had sharp-force trauma to the sixth and seventh ribs on the left side, caused by an upward single action with a double-edged sharp blade, which would have pierced her heart. The osteo-archaeologist who examined the skeleton has described this as a deliberate and purposeful injury, inflicted by an assailant who knew exactly where to aim. As there were no defence wounds visible, the conclusion is drawn that 'she may have been a

---

8 Beta–192433: 1620±60BP; at 2σ (92.4%) = cal AD 322–573.   9 GrA–24503: 1420±45BP; at 2σ = cal AD 553–670.   10 Phase 1 ring-ditch at Corbally 2 was in use from fifth to seventh century.

Atypical or deviant burials

victim of a deliberate and orchestrated assault, possibly for the benefit of the community' (Lynch 2005, 33–4). It is possible that this injury was inflicted when the woman was already dead, to remove her heart. This woman, who had been born in the region in which she was buried (Daly, 2015), was placed supine in a dug grave in a recognised burial area, but her left arm was bent from the elbow at an angle which resulted in her hand resting on the region of the wound in her chest.

In the settlement cemetery at Ratoath, Co. Meath (Fibiger, 2010, 119; Wallace, 2010, 305), a crouched possible female (B12), aged 36–45 years, dated to the fifth–sixth century,[11] was interred without her head, hands and feet. This is a curious case. Either it is an extreme form of mutilation of a body during and after death, with the removal of the head, hands and feet, and the trussing of the body; or, it is a case of a body being tightly bound for transport from a different place of death to Ratoath for burial. The former is the more likely, the intent being the absolute prevention of this person's spirit returning to haunt the living. Also, in this cemetery, an adult (B46), who had what are termed as 'ante-mortem' injuries to the skull, was accompanied by a metal knife-blade located between the left humerus and ribcage, and a small sub-spherical metal fragment retrieved from the left ribcage close to the sternum (Fibiger, 2010, 119; Wallace, 2010, 305). This person, who was killed by a blow to the skull, may also have been stabbed in the heart.

A further incident involving the removal of hands and feet is displayed in a double burial of two adolescents (B12, B13) among the small northern group of Early Medieval burials at Claristown 2, Co. Meath (Map 3) (Russell, 2004, 31; 2010, 270; Buckley, 2004, 119–22). These adolescents had been buried simultaneously in a dug grave, they were lying on their sides and facing each other. B12, undated, aged 12–15 years, had no hand or foot bones, though the radii and ulnae, and the tibiae and fibulae shafts were present; B13, undated, aged 10–13 years, also had no hand or foot bones present, though the shafts of the left and right radii, and tibiae and fibulae were present. While there is no evidence for weapon trauma, the evidence suggests that the hands and feet of both these young people were removed before burial. As some of the remainder of the burials in this small group have been dated to between the fifth and seventh century, it is reasonable to assume that these young people date to the same period.

Evidence that mutilation of a body, probably for misdeeds during life, continued well into the Medieval period is provided by extended male inhumation (D) at the Rath of the Synods, Tara, Co. Meath, dated thirteenth century,[12] who was buried with his head to the north, and without his hands (Grogan, 2008, 49; O'Brien, 2013, 244). This person, who originated probably in the southern-midland region of Ireland (Cahill Wilson, 2012, 23–5), had been buried immediately outside the enclosing wall of the adjacent Medieval church cemetery and may therefore have been deliberately excluded from that cemetery and buried at the Rath of the Synods in what may have been perceived as a pagan burial place, thus preventing him being buried among Christians.

---

11 Beta–198505: 1570±40BP; at 2σ = cal AD 402–572.   12 UBA–9029: 732±28BP; at 2σ = cal AD 1224–96.

DECAPITATION

The most common form of mutilation is decapitation.[13] The phenomenon of positioning a severed head in a non-anatomical position in a grave, usually between the legs, is relatively well represented in Roman Britain, and in Early Anglo-Saxon England (O'Brien, 1999a, 7, 173; Reynolds, 2009), but is unknown, apart from two tenuous exceptions, in Early Medieval Ireland. The first possible example is at the site of *Na Ferta* in Scotch Street, Armagh (Lynn, 1988, 80) where grave A, 1.3m in length (too short to contain an extended inhumation), contained at its eastern end the fragmentary friable remains of two parallel leg bones, and a human skull, with no evidence for the presence of any other skeletal material. The western end of the grave-cut contained two square post-holes which may have held grave markers. The skeletal material was too fragmentary to provide a radiocarbon date, but nearby grave G, with its log coffin, has been dated to the fifth–seventh century. The excavator concluded that grave A may have contained disarticulated remains (Lynn, 1988, 80), but an alternative explanation might be that the presence of a skull beside articulated lower limbs implies a deliberate act of deposition. The second possible example is that of the isolated burial at Ballynakelly, Co. Dublin (Athgoe Hill), where the fragmented skull was discovered in the pelvic region of the skeleton. However, whether this was a result of plough disturbance, or a deliberate deposition, is not clear.

Often, in cases of decapitation, the head is not present in the grave. This absence of the head will usually be attributed to it having been taken elsewhere, probably as a trophy, but an alternative justification for the removal of a severed head, in a limited number of cases, especially in a Christian context, is contained in the early eighth-century Canon, *Hib.* XLIX, *De martyribus* ('Concerning martyrs'),[14] Cap. 10, 'Concerning the resurrection of translated relics', 'Origen says: Some believe, they will arise in the place of death, others in the place where the bones are situated. Where for instance the head will have been, there all of the members will be assembled. Ezechiel saw bones approaching bones, each single one to its own joint ... their muscles and flesh grew up and after that the skin extended' (Wasserschleben, 1885, 206–7), implying that the place of resurrection on Judgement Day would be where the head had been buried. This belief could account for the claim contained in the Middle Irish text *Aided Dhiarmada* ('The Death Tale of Diarmait') that, after his murder in Ráith Becc (near Antrim) in AD 565, the head of Diarmait Mac Cerbaill, king of Tara, was taken for burial to Clonmacnoise, the burial place already chosen by him (Koch and Carey, 1995, §82, 202–4), and according to a later addition to the annals, his body was buried at the church at Connor close to where he died (*Chron. Ire.* AD 565.5).[15] This belief that resurrection would occur where the head was buried could also be the motivation behind the fact that Oswiu buried the head of King Oswald at Lindisfarne (the monastery founded by him) and his hands and arms were buried in the royal city of Bamburgh (*HE* iii.12, Colgrave and Mynors, 252–3). A

---

13 For a general overview of the osteological evidence for decapitation in Ireland see Carty, 2015, 1–20. 14 In an Irish context, the use of the term 'martyrs' is indicative of one who was Christian at death. 15 This information may have been added to the *Chron. Ire.* in the tenth century, and may not have an annalistic source, in which case it is possibly of little historical value (Charles-Edwards, 2006, 17). But it does confirm that the belief still existed that the burial place of the head

Atypical or deviant burials

further Irish example is recorded in 1067 when Murchadh Ua Briain (grandson of Brian Borumha) was killed by the men of Teathba. His head was taken to the monastery at Clonmacnoise and his body to the monastery at Durrow (*AClon*, Murphy, 1896, 179–80).

The burial of a human head separately from a body is difficult to identify archaeologically as the presence of detached skulls in cemeteries may often be attributed to the activity of grave diggers over a period of time, because, while grave diggers will often discard general skeletal material in charnel pits, they are likely to be more careful when handling skulls. A probable instance where this can be demonstrated was uncovered in 1934 at Collierstown 2, Co. Meath (Ó hÉanaigh, 1934), in a cemetery that predated the ruined Medieval church, and where small box-shaped slab cists, each containing a skull, were arranged in a circle.[16] The excavator concluded that these were skulls which had been disturbed and re-buried. But there is always the possibility that these were heads which had been deliberately buried separately from the body.

There are, however, a small number of cases where one can be reasonably sure that a severed head had been deliberately buried separately from a body. For example, included in the cemetery of over 100 burials, dating from the sixth to eighth century,[17] at Dooey, Co. Donegal[18] (Ó Ríordáin and Rynne, 1961, 58–64), was an unaccompanied skull (SK 49) of a young male, aged 17–25 years, who had been decapitated and his head deliberately buried separately (Carty, 2012).[19] At Nenagh North, Co. Tipperary, isolated human remains consisting of the complete skeleton of an adult male (SK 1), dated to the seventh–ninth century,[20] together with a further male skull (SK 2) were uncovered (Collins and Lynch, 2006, 7–14). It has been suggested by the excavator that SK 2 could represent the deliberate burial of a severed head. A similar possible deliberate burial of a severed head in a 'head cist' was uncovered in a small church cemetery in the south-east quadrant of a trivallate enclosure at Ballygarran, Co. Waterford (Power, 1941; Curtin, 2015). And at the inland promontory fort of Cahercommaun, Co. Clare (O'Neill Henken, 1938, 23), the skull of an adult male, discovered in souterrain B, surrounded by carefully laid small flat stones and accompanied by an iron hook with suspension ring, represents a severed head, probably dated to around the ninth century, which, according to the excavator, may have been publicly displayed prior to its deposition in the souterrain.

Decapitated persons, whose heads were missing from their graves, include the earliest burial at Site 6, The Curragh, Co. Kildare, which was that of a decapitated male (B xiv), head missing, who had been buried in a dug grave, supine, west–east, covered by a small cairn, and surrounded by at least two ring-ditches. As this appears to have been a formal burial, accompanied by the usual burial rituals of the period, and unlikely to be punitive, or an execution, why therefore is the head missing? It is possible that if this individual had been defeated in battle, the head may have been

---

was regarded as the place of resurrection. **16** One of the skulls, that of a 13-year-old, had been trephined. **17** Dates obtained by and supplied by Niamh Carty. Male (SK 65B): UB–3652: 1428±41BP; at 2σ = cal AD 556–664: Male (SK 50); UB3654: 1359±43BP; at 85.6% probability = cal AD 605–721: Male (SK 65A); UB3653: 1331±34BP; at 2σ = cal AD 646–768. **18** This would now be classified as a settlement cemetery. **19** Niamh Carty supplied this important unpublished information. **20** Beta–192432: 1240±60BP; at 2σ (93.2%) = cal AD 660–898.

taken by the victor, but the body retained and interred by his own people. Or, the head could have been taken to a cemetery attached to a church where the deceased wished to be present on Judgement Day.

Two decapitated males (B6, B7) were interred without their heads, at Castlefarm, Co. Meath. Male (B6), undated, aged 20–4 years (Coughlan, 2009), discovered in the small unenclosed cemetery outside the causewayed entrance to the inner enclosure (Plate 5b), was decapitated, interred extended, supine, west–east, in an unprotected dug grave similar to the remainder of the burials in the group, but his head and cervical vertebrae were missing, and male (B7), aged 28–34 years, dated to the fifth–sixth century,[21] was interred in the fill of the northern terminal of the inner enclosure ditch, in a supine position, but was oriented east–west (as opposed to the norm of west–east), without his head and vertebrae C1–C6. In addition, this person had two compression fractures of vertebrae T8 and T9, consistent with trauma caused by sudden impact on his back (Coughlan, 2009). This combination of factors, evidence for trauma to his back, decapitation, head missing, reversal of burial orientation, and burial in the fill of the enclosure entrance terminal, all point to exceptional circumstances. This has the appearance of perhaps being an execution and a punitive burial. In this case it is possible that the head may have been displayed.

At Sonnagh Demesne, Co. Westmeath, excavated in 1954 (Ó Ríordáin, in Cahill and Sikora, 2011, 204–7), two decapitated burials (G1, G3) had been placed on either side of a Bronze Age cist.[22] Elderly male (G1), aged about 60 years, supine, oriented with head to the north, in a stone-lined grave, has been dated to the fifth–sixth century.[23] The skull and upper three cervical vertebrae were missing, and the individual had suffered weapon wounds to the clavicle and femur (Buckley, 2011, 207–9). Male (G3), aged about 35 years, placed supine but in a crouched position with his knees tightly drawn up to his chest, in an unprotected dug grave, accompanied by a dog tibia that had been pared to a point, has also been dated to about the fifth–sixth century.[24] This individual had suffered numerous weapon wounds, some of which were defensive in nature, his skull and the upper three cervical vertebrae were missing (Buckley, 2011, 209–11). These two decapitated individuals are probable contemporaries who appear to have died in battle, but they were not accorded 'normal' burial. G1, although in a grave lined with stones suggesting that it may have had a wooden cover, was oriented north–south, and G3 was tightly crouched, which was not normal practice in Ireland at that time. Were these individuals outsiders buried by their peers who practised a different burial rite, or alternatively, were they accorded a punitive burial. In both cases their heads were taken elsewhere.

At the *ferta* site of Lehinch, Co. Offaly, a male burial (G5), dated to the fifth–sixth century,[25] oriented west–east, in a dug grave, had been decapitated and his head taken elsewhere (Cahill and Sikora, 2011, 146; Buckley, 2011, 164–5). In the settlement cemetery of Johnstown, Co. Meath, a secondary insertion into the foundation burial-mound (F1187) was that of a male (B25), aged 18–25 years, dated sixth–eighth

---

21 Beta-229299: 1530±40BP; at 2σ = cal AD 424–606. 22 Other burials in unprotected graves were discovered by workmen during earlier quarrying in the general area, but were not recorded. 23 GrA-24310: 1545±40BP; at 2σ = cal AD 420–597. 24 GrA-24313: 1520±40BP; at 2σ = cal AD 426–618. 25 GrA-24350: 1550±40BP; at 2σ = cal AD 418–594.

century,[26] who had been decapitated, his skull was not present in the grave (Clarke, 2004, 112, 292). Male burial (G3) at Mullacash Middle, Co. Kildare (Cahill and Sikora, 2011, 55–70), aged 25–34 years, and dating to the sixth–seventh century,[27] displayed extreme weapon trauma and decapitation; his head was missing from the grave (Buckley, 2011, 57–70). This individual was buried in a long cist grave in a communal cemetery.

A possible female decapitation is represented at the settlement cemetery of Marlinstown, Co. Westmeath (Keeley, 1991b, no. 113; 1992, no. 126; unpublished TII report). This was an adult female (Burial 8), undated, buried prone in a dug grave, whose head was missing. This is a punitive burial type, but as an osteological report is not available, it is not possible to provide more detail.

A most extreme case, in the cemetery at Owenbristy, Co. Galway, is that of male burial (SK 42), aged 24–9 years, dated to the seventh–eighth century,[28] on whom at least 127 cut marks were identified, including in the groin, which would suggest genital mutilation. The skeleton was quartered and decapitated, and the head taken elsewhere (Lehane and Delaney, 2010, 95). Remarkably, some person or persons cared enough about this individual to gather up his mutilated body parts, then transport these to the communal cemetery, and there, carefully place them in a small dug grave (Plate 7), which already contained the remains of a child.

Male burial (C23) at the ecclesiastical site of Cleenish, Upper Lough Erne, Co. Fermanagh, dated to the sixth/seventh century,[29] had been subjected to multiple stab wounds, and had possibly been decapitated as his head was missing[30] (Ó Maoldúin, 2014; Newman et al., forthcoming).

Decapitated persons whose heads were present in the correct anatomical position in their graves include a further six burials from the cemetery at Owenbristy, Co. Galway (Geber, 2010, 170–9; 2011, 92–3). Male (SK 9), aged 29–35 years, dated to the sixth–seventh century,[31] buried supine, in a slab-lined grave which was subsequently used for two further inhumations, displayed blade and stab wounds all consistent with several attempts at beheading. The head was present in the correct anatomical position in the grave. Strontium and oxygen isotope analysis indicates that this individual did not originate in this locality but hailed from elsewhere in Ireland (Evans and Chenery, 2010, 384). Male (SK 82), aged 27–35 years, dated to the seventh century,[32] disarticulated, in a slab-lined grave which also contained the remains of two other individuals, displayed a deep blade wound to the top of his skull, and at least fifteen stab wounds to the remainder of his body. He had been decapitated, but his head was present in the grave. Roughly contemporary with the latter was male (SK 93), aged 25–9 years, dated to the seventh century,[33] disarticulated (disturbed by the insertion of a later burial) in a simple dug grave, who displayed thirteen stab wounds to the chest and one to the back. He had been decapitated, but his head was present in the grave (Geber, 2010, 174–9). The remaining three decapitated burials,

26 Beta–178194: 1390±50BP; at 2σ (92.4%) = cal AD 560–711.   27 GrA–24503: 1420±45BP; at 2σ = cal AD 553–670.   28 UB–12369: 1351±22BP; at 2σ = cal AD 644–757.   29 Beta 408874: 1420±30BP; at 2σ = cal AD 582–661.   30 The excavator has noted the shallow nature of the grave, and the removal of soil overburden may have contributed to the loss of the head.   31 UB–11223: 1407±30BP; at 2σ = cal AD 594–666.   32 UB–11247: 1373±22BP; at 2σ = cal AD 619–63.   33 UB–12368: 1398±22BP; at 2σ = cal AD 610–63.

females (SK 75, SK 73) and juvenile (SK 49), are examined below, under 'females and juveniles'.

Male (B848), buried within the central penannular ring-ditch at the settlement cemetery of Raystown, Co. Meath (Seaver, 2016), aged 18–25 years, dated to the sixth–seventh century,[34] had suffered four peri-mortem blade injuries to the mandibular ramus and first and second cervical vertebra, suggesting decapitation (Fibiger, 2009, 74, 76). The head was present in the grave.

The secular settlement cemetery with 771 burials, at Faughart Lower, Co. Louth (Buckley et al., 2010; Buckley and McConway, 2010, 49–59; Bowen and Dawkes, 2011), contained three decapitated males whose heads were present in their graves. Male (SK 1739A), aged 17–25 years, dated to the fourth–sixth century,[35] had been subjected to extreme peri-mortem sharp-weapon trauma, resulting in injuries to his arms, right and left ribs, pelvis, buttocks and genital region, mandible, his left ear appears to have been severed, and he was decapitated. Male (SK 1659A), aged 35–44 years, undated, had three large cuts to his skull, cuts to his ribs, his right ear was apparently removed, and he was decapitated. Male (SK 1690A), aged 24–34 years, undated, displayed multiple locations of peri-mortem sharp-force trauma, including right pelvis, left leg, skull, his left ear was apparently removed, and he was decapitated (Buckley et al., 2010, 90–5). Despite the extreme violence associated with their deaths, these individuals had been accorded formal burial in a communal cemetery, presumably among family.

A male skeleton, undated, from phase 3 of the large Early Medieval secular cemetery at Mount Offaly, Co. Dublin (Conway, 1999, 33, 36–7; 2000, 37), had been decapitated, and while the head was in the correct anatomical position at the west end of the grave, it had been turned around so that it faced the top of the grave. This individual also displayed evidence for cut marks which appear to be defensive.

Among the Early Medieval burials at Knowth, Co. Meath, male burial (B14, KnH6), dated to the seventh–ninth century,[36] had been placed lying transversely across the base of the outer ditch of the double-ditched enclosing fosse dug around the circumference of the main passage tomb mound. The fosse was built inside the decorated stone kerb when the mound was fortified and became the stronghold of the kings of Knowth (local Uí Néill kings of Northern Brega) in the eighth century (Byrne, 1973, 54; Swift, 2008, 5–53; Eogan, G., 2012, 71–81). The skull of this man was detached from the body, but as there was no osteological evidence to indicate decapitation, and the excavator has suggested that the skull may have moved because of disturbance either after death, or during excavation, it is not possible to decide whether this is a deliberate decapitation. Strontium and oxygen isotope analysis indicates that this person possibly originated in eastern Scotland (or in Scandinavia) (Cahill Wilson, 2012, 780–5). His possible origin in eastern Scotland raises the option that he originated in Pictland and would therefore have been regarded as a *cú glas* ('grey wolf'), in other words, an outsider. A Pictish personal name carved (graffiti) in ogam script on orthostat 56 in the eastern tomb of the main mound (Byrne, 2008, 99–102, 114–15) indicates that there was a known Pictish presence at Knowth at that

---

[34] Wk–16826b: 1482±35BP; at 91.6% = cal AD 534–649.   [35] Beta–219263: 1600±40BP; at 2σ = cal AD 383–557.   [36] GrN–13335: 1260±40BP; at 2σ = cal AD 666–875.

period. It is possible that this man was killed, perhaps decapitated, and that his burial in the ditch was undertaken surreptitiously.

PAIRED MALE BURIALS DISPLAYING (FATAL) WEAPON TRAUMA

There are several instances of pairs of male individuals buried simultaneously in a single grave, who had suffered extreme weapon trauma, including decapitation. The reason for the pairing of these men is not clear. One possible explanation might be that some of these individuals may have been sibling victims of a succession dispute, with the unsuccessful candidates to kingship being subjected to a violent and perhaps ritual death ('kin-slaying' or *fingal*) (Bhreathnach, 2014, 98–9), but were then accorded formal burial in their familial or communal cemeteries. It is also possible that these men were perhaps comrades in arms who had died together in battle. Another possibility is that they were homosexual. However, it is unlikely that they were put to death for this reason, because while homosexual activity is referred to in early Penitentials, and Laws, the punishment for this activity is never death. For example, the Penitential of Cummean (seventh century), §14–15, prescribes penance of up to seven years (penance to be decided by a priest) (McNeill and Gamer, 1938 (1990) 113). In Early Irish law (Kelly, 1988, 74), the practice of homosexuality is referenced as a reason for divorce. It is always possible that these men were involved in relationships, either as siblings, as warriors fostered together,[37] or as comrades, and having died together (possibly in battle), their status was recognised, and they were accorded burial together.[38]

The examples examined include: a partially stone-lined grave containing the double burial of two decapitated males (B9 and B10) dated to the fifth–sixth century,[39] in the small unenclosed secular cemetery of fifteen burials, located outside the outer enclosure ditch of the Early Medieval ecclesiastical site at Lusk, Co. Dublin.[40] Both men, laid side by side with hands entwined, showed evidence of having suffered severe weapon trauma, and B9 had a spearhead embedded in his right shoulder; their heads had been taken elsewhere as they were not in the grave (O'Connell, 2009, 51–63; 2014, 173–86; O'Brien, 2015, 245–6). These men may have been killed in combat, and their heads taken as trophies. A further instance of two males with severe wounds being buried in the same grave occurs at the unenclosed cemetery of 281 burials, dating from the sixth to the twelfth century, at Mount Gamble, Swords, Co. Dublin (O'Donovan and Geber, 2009, 64–74; 2010, 227–38). Male burial (CCLXXXI), aged 25–35 years, undated, had suffered blade and stab wounds and had been decapitated, his head had been placed in the correct anatomical position in the grave (Figure 6.2a). His companion, male (CCLXXX), also aged 25–35 years, dated to the seventh–eighth century,[41] who had suffered a single fatal stab wound to the back, was not decapitated.

---

37 As in the Táin story of Cú Chulainn and Fer Diad.   38 Since writing this section on paired male burials, I have become aware of an article by Eileen Murphy and Colm Donnelly (Murphy and Donnelly, 2018, 119–42) in which they include some of the paired male burials referred to by me. Their conclusions, arrived at independently, are, in general, similar to mine.   39 B9: SUERC-16990: 1575±35BP; at 2σ = cal AD 406–560.   40 The basal fill of the outer enclosure ditch is dated: SUERC-17878: 1540±35BP; at 2σ = cal AD 425–594.   41 Lab. ref unknown: 1318±25BP; at 2σ =

6.2 Paired burials displaying peri-mortem trauma: (a) Mount Gamble, Swords, Co. Dublin, © E. O'Donovan and MGL; (b) Augherskea, Co. Meath, © C. Baker and MGL.

PLATES

(a)

Plate 1 Bowl from Fore, Co. Westmeath, and possible parallels: (a) Fore, Co. Westmeath, Ireland © courtesy of the National Museum of Ireland; (b) Spetisbury Rings, Dorset, Britain © Trustees of the British Museum; (c) Lamberton Moor Hoard, Berwickshire, Scotland © National Museum Scotland; (d) Glastonbury bowl, Somerset, Britain © Glastonbury Antiquarian Society.

(b)

(c)

(d)

(a)

(c)

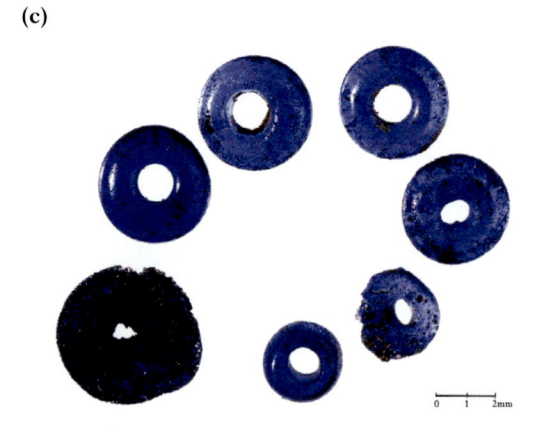

(b)

(e)
a) Glass bead fragment E3718:8:6
b) Glass bead E3718:14:9
c) Decorated glass bead E3718:16:2

(d)

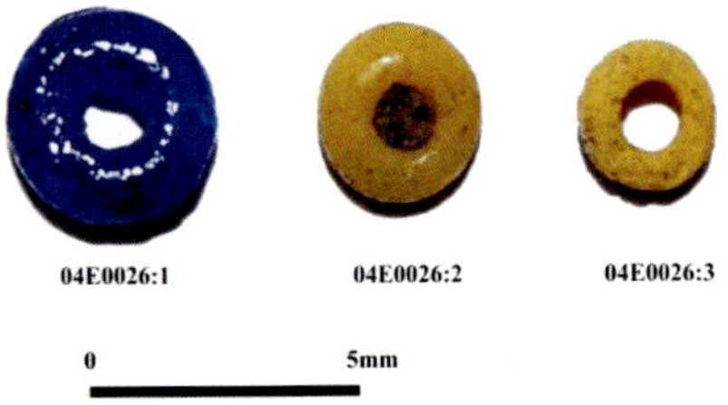

04E0026:1   04E0026:2   04E0026:3

0   5mm

d) Glass toggle bead E3718:23:2
e) Glass bead fragment E3718:17:21
f) Large clear glass bead E3719:4:3

g) Amber bead E3718:33:33
h) Amber toggle bead E3719:4:10

Plate 2 Glass and amber beads from Iron Age cremations: (a) Knockcommane, Co. Limerick, from McQuade & Molloy, 2012, fig. 13.13; (b) Donacarney Great, Co. Meath © A. Giocometti; (c) Marlhill, Co. Tipperary, from McQuade & Molloy, 2012, fig. 13.14; (d) Claureen, Co. Clare © TVAS (Ireland) Ltd; (e) Ballyboy 1 & 2, Co. Galway (from Delaney et al., 2012, fig. 5.4).

Plate 3 Cylindrical box from Chariot Burial 2, Wetwang Slack, Yorkshire, © Hull and East Riding Museum.

Plate 4 Burial B59, Holdenstown 2, Co. Kilkenny, © IAC.

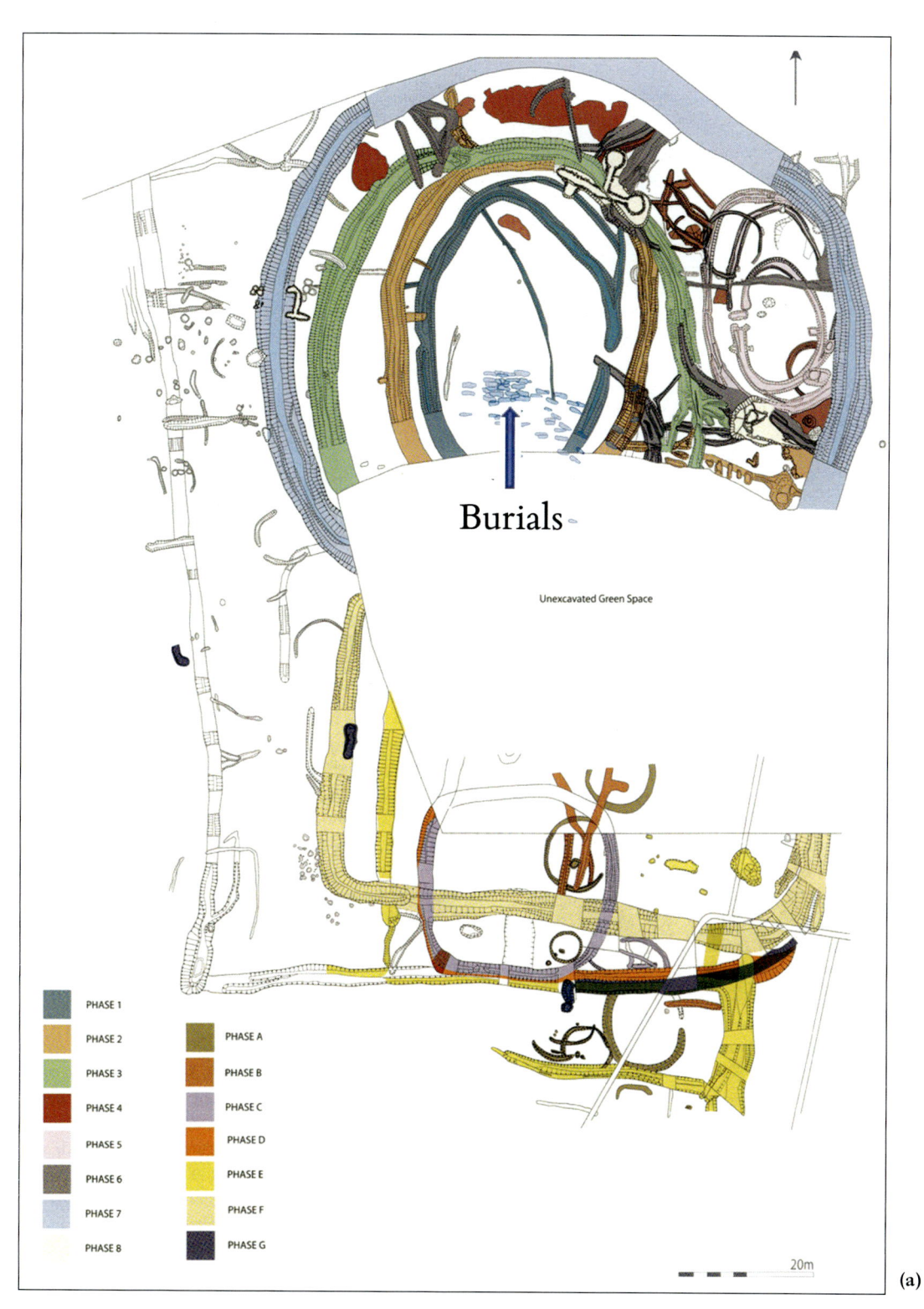

Plate 5 Cemetery settlement sites: (a) Ninch 2, Co. Meath (after McConway, 2010, fig. 12.4), © ADS (ROI); (b) Castlefarm 1, Co. Meath (after O'Connell et al., 2009, fig. 63), © ACSU.

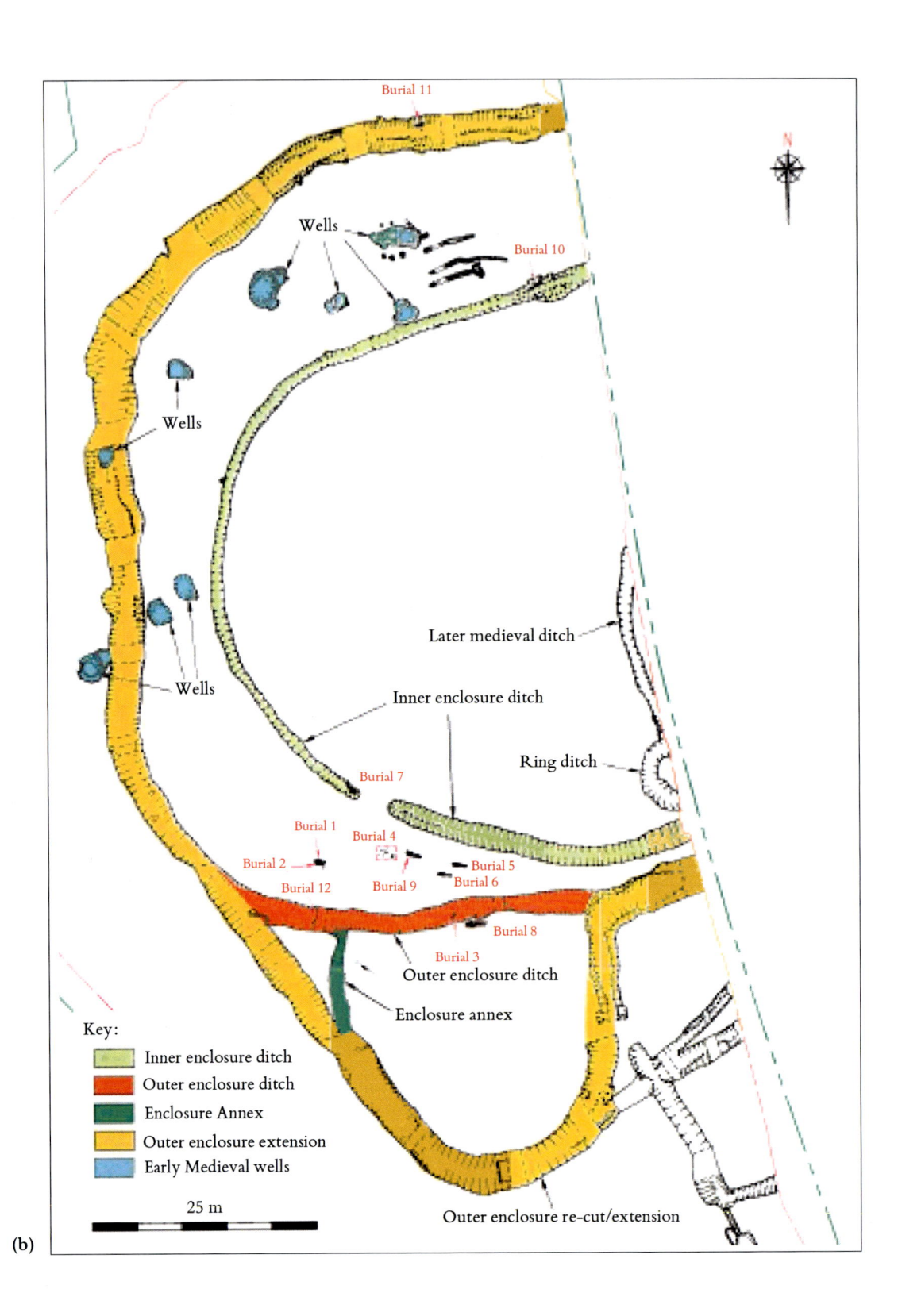

(b)

Plate 6 Neck ring with SK 70, Owenbristy, Co. Galway, © J. Sunderland/Eachtra Archaeology.

Plate 7 Quartered male SK 42, Owenbristy, Co. Galway, © Eachtra Archaeology.

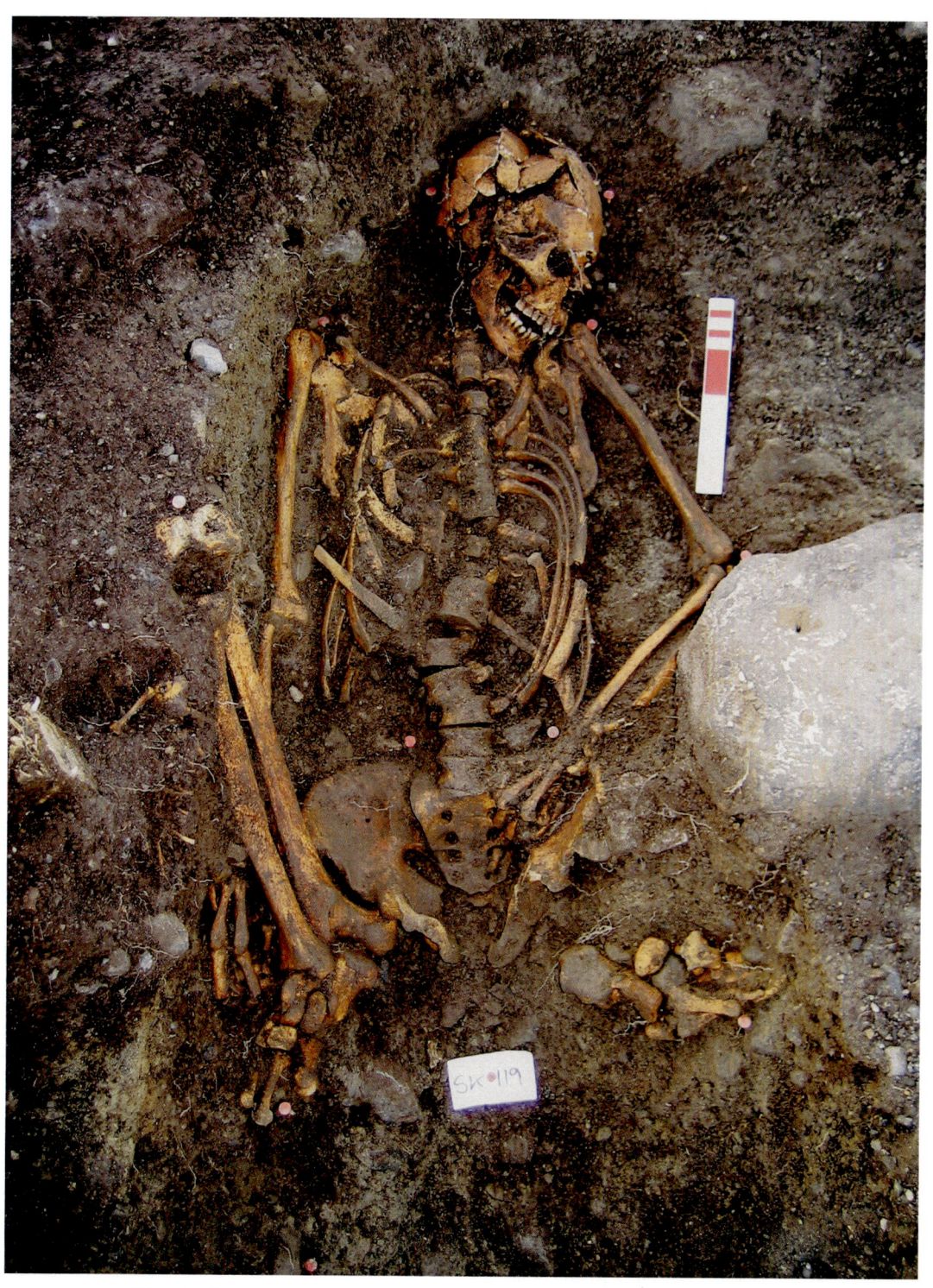

Plate 8 'Splayed' burial SK 119, Carrowkeel, Co. Galway, © Rubicon Heritage.

(a)

(b)

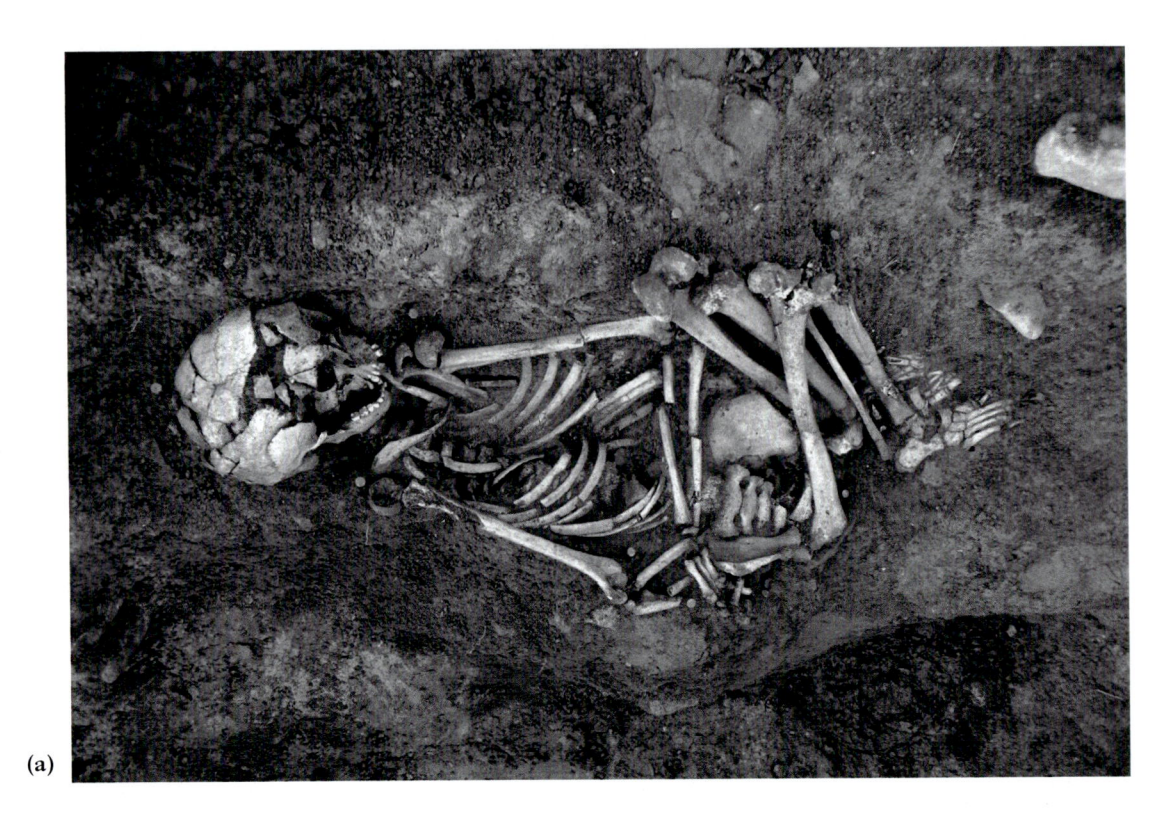

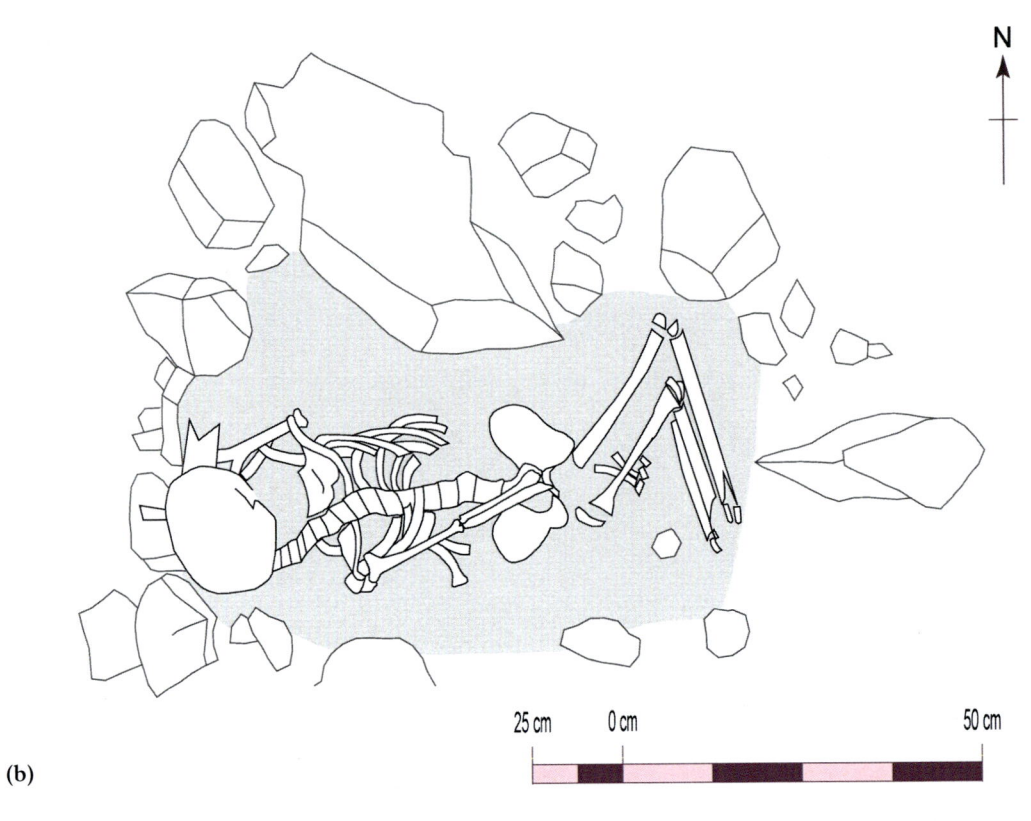

Plate 9 Burials in enclosure entrances and termini: (a) SK 72, Carrowkeel, Co. Galway, © Rubicon Heritage; (b) Skeleton in inner ditch, Loughbown 1, Co. Galway, © Eachtra Archaeology.

Plate 10 Burial 3, Ballymacaward, Co. Donegal, © EOB.

Plate 11 Facial reconstruction of B4, Ballymacaward, Co. Donegal, © J. Brayne.

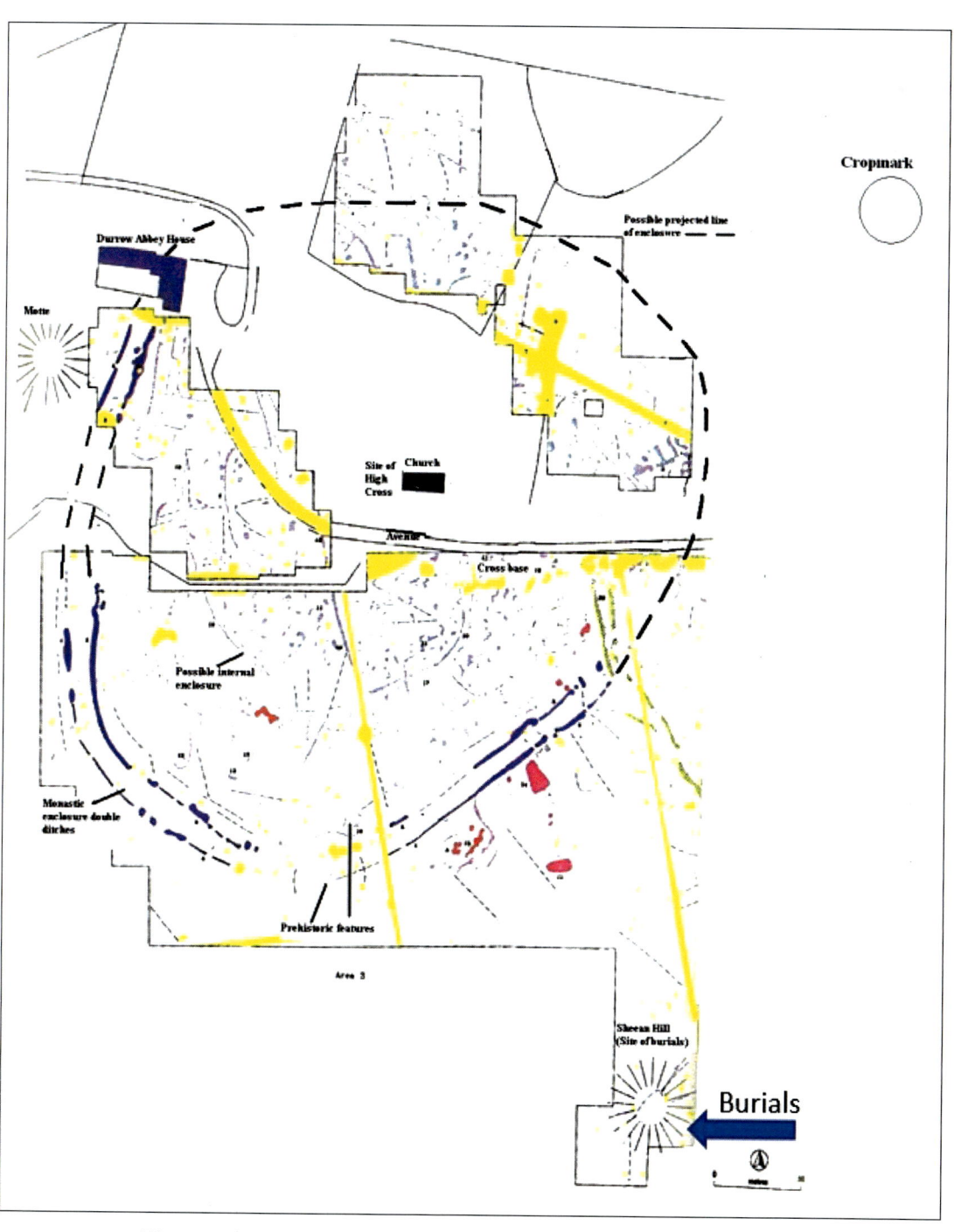

Plate 12 Monastic enclosure at Durrow, Co. Offaly, and burials at Sheean Hill, based on geophysical survey, © MGL and EOB.

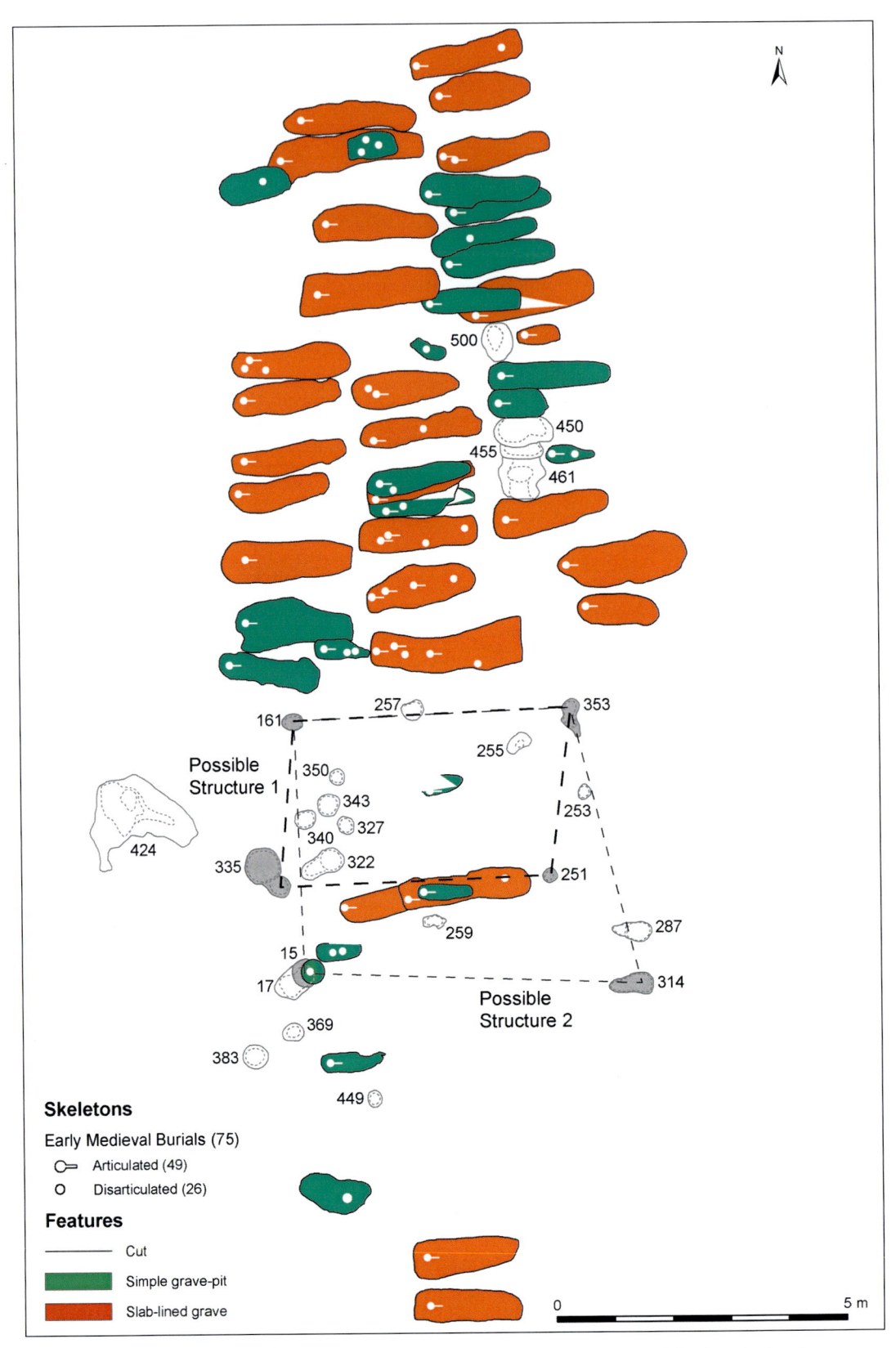

Plate 13 Plan showing post-holes in cemetery at Owenbristy, Co. Galway, © Eachtra Archaeology.

In the cemetery at Augherskea, Co. Meath (Baker, 2010, 5), two males, (SK 2) dated to the seventh–eighth century,[42] and (SK 165), aged 36–45 years, undated, were buried together in the same grave (Figure 6.2b). Both had been subjected to severe peri-mortem trauma. Osteological evidence for SK 2 showed that he was probably in a kneeling position when decapitated, which might indicate that he had been subjected to a formal execution. His head was placed in the correct anatomical position in the grave. The accompanying male (SK 165) had also been decapitated, but his head had been taken elsewhere, probably as a trophy. These men had been accorded formal burial in a communal cemetery.

The inland promontory on a bend of the Ballasadare River at Knoxspark, Co. Sligo (Mount, 2010, 187–216), contained a secular cemetery that included paired male burials (B4, B75); both had been decapitated, and interred with linked arms, in a single grave. Male (B4), dated to the eighth–ninth century,[43] had a socketed spearhead laid by his side (the deliberate deposition of weapons as grave goods is otherwise unknown in Early Medieval Ireland), and the head of male (B75), although included at the west end of the grave, was not in its correct anatomical position. Taking into consideration the possible Viking association with this cemetery[44] it is possible that these persons represent intruders.

In the settlement cemetery of Ballykilmore, Co. Westmeath (Channing, 2009, 50; 2014, 33, 35), an adult male (c399), aged about 30 years, dated to the twelfth–thirteenth century,[45] and a male juvenile (c415), aged between 13 and 14 years, were buried together in a dug grave. Both had suffered peri-mortem trauma. The adult male (c399) exhibited a series of fine blade cuts, one of which appeared to be defensive, and the remainder suggestive of dismemberment or execution, and the juvenile (c415) suffered a similar fate. The cemetery of 1,200+ burials, at Ballyhanna, Co. Donegal, dating from the eighth to the eighteenth century, which may have acquired a church building in the eleventh–twelfth century (McKenzie et al., 2015), included two adults, one male (SK 290) and a probable male (SK 289), buried together in one grave. SK 289 had two sharp-force peri-mortem injuries to the right femur and right patella, inflicted with a sword (Macdonald and Carver, 2015, 78–9). The burials are undated, but are located among burials dating from the fourteenth to the sixteenth century.

All the persons described had met with violent deaths, but the fact that they had been buried together, and with care, in communal cemeteries, suggests that they were not regarded as outcasts, or as criminals. The burials at Ballykilmore and Ballyhanna indicate that the phenomenon continued well into the Medieval period.

A possibly punitive paired male burial was uncovered at Corbally 3, Co. Kildare, where two adults, sex undetermined but probably male, undated, located within ring-ditch C53 (Figures 4.14a; 6.3), were laid at right angles to each other. Adult (B78),

---

cal AD 655–767.   42 UBA–28177: 1254±28BP; at 2σ (highest probability 82.1%) = cal AD 673–779 (thanks to Dr Mario Novak, University of Zagreb, Croatia, who provided this date).   43 UB–3836: 1184±31BP; at 87.5% probability = cal AD 767–901.   44 One must be wary when using material from this cemetery as it may represent an indigenous familial cemetery which has been re-used and disturbed by intruders, probably Vikings who first appeared on the west coast of Ireland in AD 795. It has been suggested (Kelly, 2009, 485–97) that Knoxspark became a Viking stronghold from the ninth century. For re-use of indigenous cemeteries by Vikings see O'Brien, 1992a, 170–3; 1998a, 219–21; 1998b, 40–1.   45 UBA–8681:840±26BP; at 2σ = cal AD 1160–1258. This originally secular

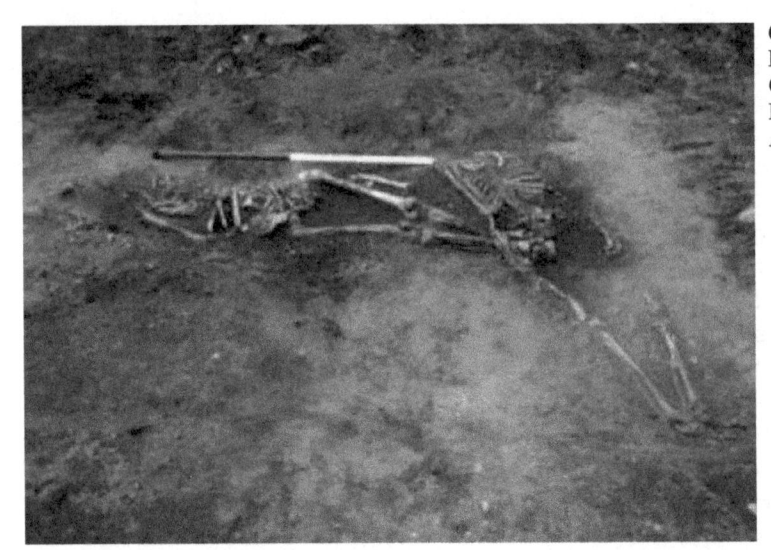

6.3 Paired burial, B78/B79, Site 3, Corbally, Co. Kildare, © Aegis Arch. Ltd.

whose head was missing, was buried supine, west–east, and adult (B79) was buried supine, south–north. The feet of B79 had been placed between the pelvis and right arm of B78, indicating that both had been interred simultaneously. The strange disposition of the bodies, the decapitation of B78, and burial within a ring-ditch is probably indicative of punitive burial for both parties.

A small number of paired male burials, which exhibit no evidence for weapon trauma, have also been recorded. While these persons could have died from natural causes, it is also possible that they were killed in a manner that left no visible marks on their skeletons. Their deaths could have been caused by poisoning, strangulation, smothering, or hanging. Hanging seems to have been the commonest form of execution in Early Medieval Ireland (Kelly, 1988, 217).

At Faughart Lower, Co. Louth (Bowen and Dawkes, 2011), two undated skeletons, an adult male (SK 1395A) and an unsexed adult (possibly male) (SK 1385A), were interred, flexed on their sides, one behind the other, in a single grave. In the northern group of burials at Claristown 2, Co. Meath (Map 3) (Russell, 2004, 30–1; 2012, 270; Buckley, 2004, 108–13), two males, (B5) aged 25–44 years, and (B6) aged probably less than 18 years, dated to the fifth–seventh century,[46] were buried simultaneously, supine, side by side, in a single grave. The cemetery at Collierstown 1, Co. Meath (O'Hara, 2009a, 27; 2009b, 93), contained a double burial of two extended males (B54 and B55), in a dug grave which had evidence for wood lining. B54 was an adolescent, dated to the sixth–seventh century,[47] and B55 was an adult, aged 30–40 years. The cemetery at Ardsallagh 1, Co. Meath (Randolf-Quinney, 2006a), contained two graves with double burials, both of which contained an adult male and a juvenile. In the first grave, an adult male (B11), dated to the sixth–seventh century,[48] was accompanied by a juvenile (B15) aged 10–11 years (sex unknown). The second grave, contained a young

---

cemetery acquired a probable church building in the tenth century, which had collapsed by the eleventh–thirteenth century.   46 Beta–185351: 1540±60BP; at 2σ = cal AD 403–634.   47 Beta–247007: 1430±40BP; at 2σ = cal AD 559–663.   48 Beta–237059: 1490±40BP; at 2σ = cal AD 430–648 (at 82.3% probability = cal AD 530–648).

adult male (B24) (undated), who was accompanied by (B26), a juvenile aged 7–10 years (sex unknown).

It is possible that these five paired burials may be representative of 'kin slaying'; some may represent the burial of a father and child, or siblings; or others may represent males who had a recognised relationship. They do not appear to represent comrades who had died in battle.

FEMALES AND JUVENILES WITH FATAL WEAPON TRAUMA

There are several instances of females and juveniles who were killed violently in Ireland in the Early Medieval period. It was this type of violent trauma which led to the enactment of the *Cáin Adomnán* (also known as *Lex Innocentium*, 'Law of the Innocents'), proclaimed by Adomnán, abbot of Iona, at the Synod of Birr, in the year AD697, the provisions of which were to ensure the protection of non-combatants, mainly clerics, but including women and children, in times of conflict. The document was signed and guaranteed by ninety-one eminent persons, comprising kings (including a Pictish king), bishops and abbots (Ní Dhonnchadha, 1982, 178–215). The penalties for inflicting injury on a woman were harsh. Item §33 includes 'Whoever kills a woman is condemned to a double punishment, i.e. his right hand and his left foot are cut off before death, and then he shall die, and his relations pay seven full *ancillae* ("female slaves") and a seventh of the penance. If a fine is imposed instead of life and amputation, the payment is fourteen years of penance and fourteen *ancillae*' (*Cáin Adomnán*, Márkus, 1997, 17–18; Ní Dhonnchadha, 2001, 61–2).

It is noticeable that, where it can be determined, the females and one of the juveniles who suffered fatal weapon trauma died before the proclamation of this law. However, one adolescent, Owenbristy SK 53, died after the enactment of the law, and it is probable that he may have been regarded as an adult by his attackers, as *Cáin* item §34 includes penalties for the killing of 'innocent youths until they are capable of killing a man, till they have a place in the *túath* and until their drove be known' (Ní Dhonnchadha, 2001, 62).

Two decapitated females at Owenbristy (SK 73, SK 75) were interred in the same slab-lined and slab-covered grave. Female (SK 75), aged 35–45 years, undated, had been decapitated by a single cut through her neck (Geber, 2010, 174; 2011, 91). Her skull was in the correct anatomical position in the grave. Female (SK 73), aged 25–35 years, dated to the first half of the seventh century,[49] had been subjected to severe stab wounds to her face, a sword or axe blow through the stomach, and had been decapitated. Her skull was placed in the correct anatomical position in the grave. Although both these women were interred in the same grave (Lehane and Delaney, 2010, 88), they did not die simultaneously. The skeleton of the older woman (SK 75) had been partially disturbed by the insertion of the younger woman (SK 73) suggesting that decomposition of the older woman's body had already commenced. As the younger woman has been dated to the first half of the seventh century, it is reasonable to assign a late sixth- or early seventh-century date to the death of the older person. These women may have been siblings, or perhaps a mother and daughter, who

[49] UB–12370: 1402±27BP; at 2σ = cal AD 602–65.

died during separate violent episodes. The fact that they were both buried in the same grave indicates that this was possibly a known family grave. There were also two instances at Owenbristy of violence causing the death of juveniles or adolescents. The first (SK 49), aged 13–15 years, dated to the sixth–seventh century,[50] extended, supine, in a dug grave,[51] had been subjected to three blade wounds, nine stab wounds, and was decapitated. The skull was in the correct anatomical position in the grave. The second, an adolescent (SK 53) dated to the seventh–eighth century,[52] extended, supine, in a slab-lined grave that also contained disarticulated (disturbed) remains of a female, had been subjected to a blunt-force blow to the top of the cranium, and sharp-force trauma to the parietal bone, causing death (Geber, 2010,172–4; 2011, 90–1). Strontium and oxygen isotope analysis has indicated that he was born locally (Evans and Chenery, 2010, 382–4). This young man was killed after the proclamation of the *Cáin*, and it is possible that he may have been regarded as an adult.

Females in other cemeteries who had suffered violent deaths include: a young adult female (SK 484), undated, in the settlement cemetery at Parknahown 5, Co. Laois, who had been subjected to thirteen sharp-force fatal injuries to her cervical vertebrae that indicates an attempted, or a successful, decapitation. An elderly female (SK 661) at Parknahown 5 showed evidence for a healed sharp-force lesion to her skull (Keating, 2009, 118–20). At Killeany, Co. Laois, a female (B39), aged 17–25 years, dated to the sixth–seventh century,[53] who was buried prone, head to the west, displayed a total of thirty-nine peri-mortem cut marks, inflicted with a sharp-bladed implement to the upper part of her torso (Keating in Wiggins and Kane, 2009, 335–7). The 'crime' she had committed, which resulted in her death, must have been extreme, as she was excluded from burial within the communal cemetery, and humiliated by being buried prone in the entrance passage to the cemetery enclosure, at a spot where it would be necessary that any person entering the enclosure would have to walk over her grave. The splayed position of this woman's feet also suggests that she was not shroud wrapped.

In the settlement cemetery at Marlinstown, Co. Westmeath (Keeley, 1991b, no. 113; 1992, 126; TII unpublished report), an adult female (Burial 8), undated, was buried prone, and her head was missing. Another female (B38?), who had been decapitated and her head was missing, was included in the cemetery at Knoxspark, Co. Sligo. She was accompanied in a simple dug grave by the remains of three children (B34, B39, B49), one of whom was also missing its head (Mount, 2010, 193). In the settlement cemetery at Ratoath, Co. Meath (Fibiger, 2010, 119; Wallace, 2010, 305), a crouched possible female (B12) aged 36–45 years, dated to the fifth–sixth century,[54] was interred without her head, hands and feet. Female burial (B125), undated, placed across the ditch fill of phase 1 ring-ditch at Corbally 2, Co. Kildare, had sharp-force trauma to the ribs caused by a double-edged sharp blade (Lynch, 2005, 25; Coyne and Lynch, 2010, 86).

The proclamation of the *Cáin* appears to have been, on the whole, successful, because instances of weapon trauma on women and children do not appear in the dated archaeological record after the eighth century.

---

50 UB-12371: 1351±22BP; at 2σ = cal AD 596–656.   51 This grave had a stone at each corner to support a plank cover.   52 UB-11238: 1263±17BP; at 2σ = cal AD 683–776.   53 SUERC-17622: 1445±35BP: at 2σ = cal AD 555–655.   54 Beta-198505: 1570±40BP; at 2σ = cal AD 402–572.

FATAL WEAPON TRAUMA WITHOUT DECAPITATION

Cases of fatal weapon trauma but without decapitation include: a male (B841), aged 26–35 years, dated to the fifth–sixth century,[55] buried within the central penannular ring-ditch at Raystown, Co. Meath, who had suffered 110 peri-mortem blade injuries, mainly to his upper body, which are described by the osteo-archaeologist as 'over-kill' (Seaver, 2016, 80; Fibiger, 2009, 76–80). Two male individuals (SK 367, SK 649), who had died from sharp-force trauma, but were not decapitated, were included in the settlement cemetery at Parknahown 5, Co. Laois. These were an elderly male (SK 367) dated to the eighth–ninth century,[56] who exhibited sharp peri-mortem stab wounds to his ribs, inflicted from the rear, and possible male (SK 649), undated, who had peri-mortem cut marks to the left humerus, left radius, and ribs (O'Neill, 2009; 2010, 251–60; Keating, 2009, 118–19). A female victim of peri-mortem trauma (SK 484) from this cemetery has been examined above. The small unenclosed, but organised, cemetery at Cappogue Castle, Co. Dublin (McQuade, 2009), included an adult male burial (B7) who had cut marks on his arms, caused by sharp weapon trauma, and which may be defensive peri-mortem injuries.

In the enclosed secular cemetery of thirty-nine burials, at Cherrywood (Site 18), Co. Dublin (Ó Néill and Coughlan, 2010, 247–8), a male (XXI), aged 25–9 years, undated, exhibited evidence for severe peri-mortem weapon trauma. He had sustained blunt-force trauma on the cranium, two blade wounds to the skull, and weapon trauma to the ribcage, pelvis and right femur, all inflicted at time of death. At Augherskea, Co. Meath, male burial (SK 87), aged 26–35 years, undated, had met a violent death, and showed evidence of extreme peri- and post-mortem weapon trauma (Baker, 2010, 5). His corpse was accompanied by part of a pig's head (mandible) on the pelvis. Despite his violent death this person had been buried in a normal dug grave in this communal cemetery, but perhaps during the burial ceremony part of a pig's head was overtly placed on the corpse as a sign of disapproval.

NON-FATAL WEAPON TRAUMA

Three individuals in the Owenbristy cemetery displayed evidence of violent trauma, which at the time of their deaths had either healed or was in the process of healing. Male burial (SK 38), aged 40–9 years, supine, extended, in a simple dug grave, undated, had been subjected to blade injury which caused severe facial injuries. He did not die immediately, but there was evidence that the wound had become infected, and this was the probable eventual cause of death. Male (SK 50), aged over 45 years, dated to the sixth–seventh century,[57] supine, extended, in a slab-lined grave, displayed a well-healed lesion caused by sharp blade force trauma which had penetrated his skull. He had survived the attack but may have suffered brain injury. Finally, male (SK 74), undated, aged 35–45 years, supine, extended, in a simple dug grave, displayed

---

[55] Wk-16825: 1537±34BP; at 2σ = cal AD 426–596. [56] A general date of 760–900 AD is listed in the Table, p. 55, of O'Neill, 2009, vol. 11, but details are not included in the information on pp 56–7.
[57] UB-11493: 1475±21BP; at 2σ = cal AD 554–639.

evidence for two parallel, healed, sharp-force cuts to the head. Neither of the cuts had penetrated the skull vault, but are likely to have caused excessive bleeding when they were inflicted (Geber, 2010, 171–2; 2011, 94).

At Parknahown 5, Co. Laois, three individuals displayed healed blunt-force trauma to their skulls. An older male (SK 200), undated; an adult (SK 359), unsexed, undated; and a possible male (SK 363), undated. An elderly male (SK 673), dated to the eleventh–twelfth century,[58] displayed healed sharp-force trauma to his skull (Keating, 2009, 118–19). In the cemetery at Faughart Lower, Co. Louth, a male (SK 1080), aged 40–4 years, undated, had a healed sharp-force trauma to the right frontal bone on his skull (Buckley et al., 2010, 90). At Lehinch, Co. Offaly, the earliest burial (G3), dated to the fifth–sixth century,[59] sex undetermined, oriented head west, in a stone-lined dug grave, showed evidence of physical trauma including a non-fatal skull fracture, and a healed serious injury to the left elbow. This person had fragments of horse (tibia, pelvis and scapula) placed along the inner (southern) edge of the grave together with a set of deer antlers inserted tine downwards. Strontium and oxygen isotope analysis indicates that this individual was of local origin (Cahill Wilson, 2014, 144). Also at this site, an elderly male (B4), dated to the fifth–sixth century,[60] oriented head west, in a stone-lined dug grave, had two depressed fractures to his skull that had completely healed (Buckley, 2011, 163–4).

Two male burials in the lintel grave cemetery[61] at Millockstown, Co. Louth (Manning, 1986, 135–81), displayed evidence of healed weapon trauma. Male (B XV), undated, aged over 40 years, had an oval depression on the forehead caused by a blow with a blunt object. Although this injury had healed, his death was caused by a later sword injury to the back of his head. Male (B XXXVIIIb), aged 18–28 years, undated, had also suffered a blow to the forehead from a blunt object, but this did not cause death (Ó Donnabháin, in Manning, 1986, 173). In the settlement cemetery at Ratoath, Co. Meath (Wallace, 2010, 305), an extended, supine, adult burial (B46) displayed evidence of ante-mortem injuries to the skull, but was accompanied by a metal knife blade located between the left humerus and ribcage, which may have been the cause of death.

BURIAL IN KILNS

Burial in a kiln is highly unusual, and is suggestive of surreptitious disposal of a body. There are four known examples of burial in corn-drying kilns in the Irish archaeological record. At Colp West, Co. Meath, a large multi-phase settlement site that had no other evidence for burial, the headless skeleton of an adult male was discovered in the base of a corn-drying kiln (Murphy, 2002, 254). This individual had been placed on a charcoal layer at the base of the kiln and then covered by large stones. The skeleton has not been dated but it post-dates the underlying charcoal, which has been dated to the second to fourth century[62] (Murphy, 2011, 255). This is a surreptitious burial, and it is probable that the act of removing the head, and the

---

58 SUERC–16987: 970±35BP; at 2σ = cal AD 1013–1158. This is one of the latest dated burials in the cemetery.   59 GrA–24445: 1625±40BP; at 2σ = cal AD 399–541.   60 GrA–29065: 1550±40BP; at 2σ = cal AD 418–594.   61 Originally designated as an ecclesiastical site (Manning, 1986, 163), this site is now recognised as a settlement cemetery.   62 UB–4664: 1781±35BP; at 2σ = cal AD 134–337.

weighting down of the body with very large stones, was undertaken to prevent the deceased from returning, either because he had been feared during his life, or to prevent him exacting revenge upon the perpetrators of his death.

At Corbally 1, Co. Kildare, a kiln, located approximately 8m south-east of the ring-ditch (Figure 4.14 (a)), contained the skeleton of an elderly female (B2), dated fourth–sixth century,[63] making her a contemporary of the male (B5) who had been buried centrally within the ring-ditch. She was lying on her side with knees bent, one arm was raised beside her head and the other lay across her abdomen, suggestive of a hasty informal or surreptitious burial. Her body had been covered with large stones, and kiln material was found below and above the body. She suffered from Paget's disease of her skull (Keating, 2004, 35–8) which may have resulted in distortion of her head, a drooping of her facial muscles, and impaired mental function, perhaps providing a reason for this woman's irregular burial. Preliminary results from strontium and oxygen isotope analysis (Daly, 2015) suggest that she had not been born locally but had moved to the area some years prior to her death. It is possible that she had been the spouse of the nearby male (B5).

A further example, at Baysrath, Co. Kilkenny (Channing, 2012, 185–6, 387–90), was that of an adult male (c320) deposited in a dumbbell-shaped kiln (c316), supine, extended, oriented north–south (head north). There was no skeletal evidence for physical trauma. It was not possible to obtain c14 dates as the skeleton was very poorly preserved. However, the north–south orientation of the body, together with its deposition in a kiln, suggest either a non-Christian, a punitive, or a surreptitious burial, probably in the Early Medieval period. Another kiln (c105) at this site contained the skeleton of a perinate (c1794) and several disarticulated human bones some of which had animal gnaw marks. It is suggested by the excavator that this later material may consist of casual deposits made when that kiln had ceased to be used. No c14 dates are available.

The final example is from the settlement cemetery at Raystown, Co. Meath (Seaver, 2016, 20–1, 80), where a male (B2398), dated to the fifth–sixth century,[64] aged over 25 years, oriented south–north (head south), was deposited in a flexed position into a disused corn-drying kiln. The kiln was located away from the main cemetery at this site. The c14 date suggests, however, that this person was a contemporary of those buried in the earliest phase in that cemetery. It is probable, therefore, that this burial may be surreptitious and hidden in a kiln so as not to be discovered, or deliberately buried in a kiln as a punitive measure, rather than in a normal grave.

PRONE BURIALS

Individuals buried in a prone position, that is, placed face down in the grave, are comparatively rare in the Early Medieval archaeological record in Ireland. The motivation for burying a person in a prone position is usually punitive. It can be viewed in a Christian context as a method of preventing the deceased person from rising on the Day of Judgement, or it can be a method of preventing the deceased person from re-emerging from the grave as a revenant to disturb the living.

---

63 UBA–30393: 1636±41BP; at 2σ = cal AD 332–539.   64 Wk.–16819: 1574±35BP; at 2σ = cal

This latter assumption is graphically illustrated in the Early Modern Irish text *Betha Cellaig*, a fabulous life of St Cellach (Byrne, 1973, 244). The relevant part of the 'life' concerns the saint's father Éogan Bél, a king of Connacht, who is recorded in the annals as having died in AD 543 or 547 (*Chron. Ire.*) defending Connacht against the Northern Uí Néill, and who gave instructions that he was to be buried upright on Knocknarea, facing north with his red spear in his hand. As long as he remained thus, the northerners could never defeat Connacht. However, the Uí Néill subsequently dug up his body and buried it face down at Lough Gill, thereby preventing his 'return', and leaving the Connacht territory undefended.

In the Irish archaeological record prone burials include children, individuals with physical deformity, and, occasionally, individuals who had suffered severe weapon trauma. The burial of children in a prone position might be accounted for by the fact that, from at least the Medieval period and until the Early Modern era, there existed a commonly held belief, not unique to Ireland, whereby a previously healthy child who became ill was spirited away and replaced by a fairy child, who was then regarded as a 'changeling'. When such children died, prone burial may have been seen as a method of preventing these 'otherworldly' children from returning to haunt the living. Another possibility is that some may have been unbaptised children who were buried prone perhaps because they were not regarded as being Christian.

Individuals with a physical deformity that marked them out as 'different' during life may have been buried prone because they were feared during life, and as possible revenants when dead. Individuals with severe weapon trauma, which may have been inflicted as punishment for a crime, could have been buried prone as an extension of that punishment.

Examples include two prone burials recovered in the cemetery at Faughart Lower, Co. Louth (Bowen and Dawkes, 2011, 70, 72): a young child (SK 1498), undated, aged 1–5 years, and an elderly female (SK 1542), undated, who had a rare congenital anomaly of the left femur (Buckley et al., 2010a, 6–7). This deformity would have marked her out as being 'different'. In the cemetery at Johnstown, Co. Meath (Clarke, 2010, 61–75), one prone male (B128) aged over 45 years, dated to the seventh–ninth century,[65] and one partially prone female (B204), undated, aged 36–45 years, who displayed a deformity in the form of thick cranial vault bones (Fibiger, 2004, 73, 82–3), were recorded. At Killeany, Co. Laois, a female (B39) aged 17–25 years, dated to the sixth–seventh century,[66] who had been subjected to severe weapon trauma, was then buried prone. A prone burial of a juvenile, oriented with head north, undated, is recorded in the cemetery at Ninch 2, Co. Meath (Buckley, 2010, 44). Among the burials in circle J, at Lough Gur, Co. Limerick, was the prone burial of an adult male (B40), oriented west–east, in a dug grave, who had a physical distortion of his upper spine (Grogan and Eogan, 1987, 330, 334). The prone burial of an infant (B50), undated, was recorded at the partially excavated cemetery at Carrowkeel, Co. Galway (Wilkins, in Lehane, Muñiz et al., 2010, 139–56). Four prone burials have been identified at Parknahown 5, Co. Laois (O'Neill, 2009): an adult female (B614), undated, had her head to the east; adult male (B988), undated; infant (B1035),

---

AD 407–560. [65] Beta–184704: 1240±40BP; at 2σ = cal AD 680–881. [66] SUERC–17622: 1445±35BP; at 2σ = cal AD 555–655.

undated, head to the south, had hands and feet missing; and juvenile (B572), 13 to 17 years old, buried prone and crouched, has been dated tenth–twelfth century[67] (O'Neill, 2009, 170, 274–5).

Two prone burials were recorded in the cemetery at Ardreigh, Co. Kildare; no further details have been published (Opie, 2006, 228–9). Two individuals were recorded as prone in the cemetery at Ballykilmore 6, Co. Westmeath (Channing, 2009, 49; 2014, 23–38).[68] One of these was a middle-aged female, oriented west–east, undated, whose head had been replaced after death by a head-sized stone. Details of the second prone burial have not been published (ibid., 2009, 49; 2014, 33). At Mount Offaly, Cabinteely, Co. Dublin (Conway, 1999, 33; 2000, 36), several prone burials were located among a group of burials, many of which were aligned with their heads either to the north or the east. Unfortunately, it has not been possible to obtain more details about these burials, but it raises the possibility that a specific sector in this large cemetery may have been reserved for punitive burial. One of the five dispersed Early Medieval burials at Morett, Co. Laois (Cotter, 2011; Dempsey, 2004), an adult of indeterminate sex (C1302) dated to the fifth–sixth century,[69] was buried oriented head west, but prone. In the settlement cemetery at Marlinstown, Co. Westmeath, female (Burial 8), whose head was missing, was buried prone. There is a possible prone adult (c2189) at Baysrath, Co. Kilkenny, found in the interior of a Bronze Age ring-ditch, oriented head to the east, undated, but in an Early Medieval milieu.

Finally, a prone burial of an adult male, aged 40–5 years, was recovered during a recent small excavation on the northern side of the early ecclesiastic site at Kill of the Grange, Dublin (Tobin, 2018; Duffy, 2019, 5). The burial had been deposited into a partially filled ditch dated to the fifth–seventh century.[70] As the skeletal material was not suitable for c14 dating this date was obtained from charcoal from the lower fill of the ditch, and as such it should be treated with caution, but it would appear that the burial is early. The skull and upper thorax of this body were missing. These may have been truncated in the past, but it is also possible that this man had been decapitated. A concentration of boar mandibles was found adjacent to the burial, and this is reminiscent of the pig's head placed on the pelvic region of SK 87 at Augherskea, Co. Meath. The deposition of the body, prone, into ditch fill, is indicative of either a punitive, or a surreptitious burial, deliberately placed on the northern enclosure perimeter, thereby excluding the burial from the main cemetery area.[71]

CROUCHED BURIALS

Excavators often differ in their description of crouched and/or flexed burials (see Gazetteer 4).[72] In this publication an attempt is made to clarify this anomaly by using the following descriptive terms:

---

[67] SUERC–17311: 975±35BP; at 2σ = cal AD 990–1160. [68] This settlement cemetery, originally secular, acquired what appears to be a church building in the cemetery, in the tenth century. The building had collapsed between the eleventh and thirteenth century, but burial continued up until the late eighteenth century. [69] AD 409–533 (full details unavailable). [70] UBA–38057: 1507±29BP; at 2σ = cal AD 431–632 (at 79.5% probability = cal AD 530–632). [71] From the Medieval period, until comparatively recently, burial in the area to the north of a church was accorded to outcasts, criminals, suicides, and occasionally those who had died violently. [72] In

6.4 Crouched, and partially crouched burials: (a) crouched burial, Mount Gamble, Swords, Co. Dublin, © E. O'Donovan and MGL; (b) partially crouched burial, Johnstown, Co. Meath © ACSU.

Atypical or deviant burials

6.5 Flexed burial, Faughart, Co. Louth, © ADS (ROI).

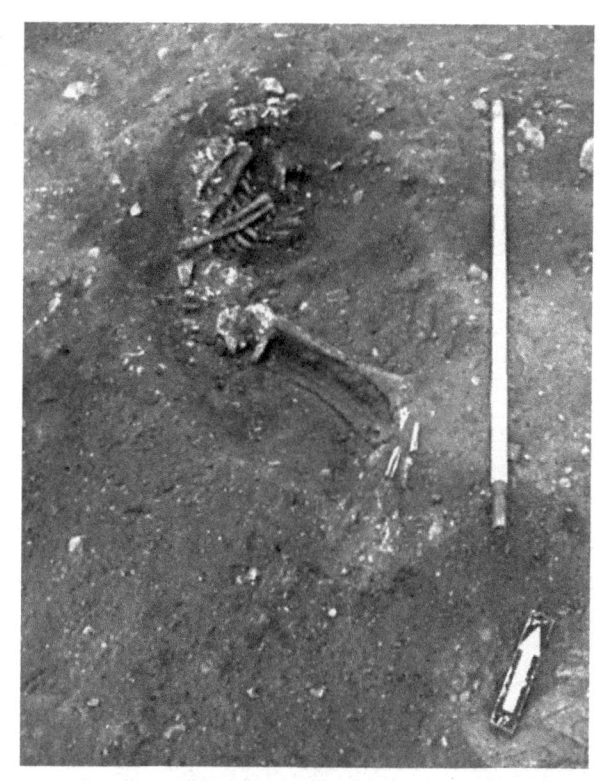

Crouched, when the individual's legs are drawn up so that the knees contact the chest, as in a foetal position (Figure 6.4a). For an individual to be buried in a crouched position, action must be taken to create this posture, either immediately after death before the onset of rigor mortis, or several days after death when the body again becomes pliable. It would also be necessary that a body be bound in order to maintain the crouched position. An anthropological explanation for this ancient custom is recorded in Hawaii, where the custom was still being practised in the nineteenth century. It was observed that when a body was being prepared for burial, 'a rope was attached to the joints of the legs and then being passed about the neck was drawn taut until the knees touched the chest. The body was then done-up in a rounded shape and at once closely wrapped in *tapa*,[73] and made ready for burial' (Malo, 1903, 97).

Partially crouched, when the legs are flexed at an angle of 45° to the upper body (Figure 6.4b). A partially crouched position could occur if the binding on a crouched individual became undone, or it might be a deliberate posture choice.

Flexed, when the legs are partially bent at the knees, so that the individual appears to be in a sleeping position, often laid on their side (Figure 6.5). Burials in a flexed position were probably intended to portray the deceased in a sleeping posture.

Gazetteer 4, for convenience, the item 'crouched' includes all positions from fully crouched to flexed. 73 *Tapa* (or *Kapa*) was a traditional cloth made from the inner bark of a plant or tree (Malo, 1903, 48).

6.6 Burial 181, Betaghstown (Anchorge), Co. Meath, © J. Eogan.

During the Iron Age, the rite of crouched burial had been practised in a confined geographical area in the east of the country for a comparatively short period spanning the final century BC and the first century AD. The subsequent occasional appearance of crouched burial in the Early Medieval period probably indicates that the individual concerned belonged to a non-indigenous cultural group within which burial in a foetal posture was a traditional rite; an individual had been 'trussed' for transport from a distant place of death, for burial in a familial or communal cemetery; or, burial in a crouched position was a method of preventing the deceased person from returning to haunt the living.

In the Irish archaeological record there are, so far, three instances where the rite of crouched inhumation may be associated with membership of a non-indigenous cultural group. All three burials were in unenclosed indigenous cemeteries located on the ridge at Betaghstown, Co. Meath, overlooking the Irish Sea coast. The first example is that of an older adult male (F181) buried on the outer edge of the unenclosed cemetery at Betaghstown (Anchorage), Co. Meath. This man, who has been dated to the fourth–sixth century,[74] was interred in a crouched posture in the centre of a full-length stone-lined grave (Figure 6.6). Strontium and oxygen isotopic analysis has indicated that he was not Irish, but, probably, had his origin in Eastern Europe or Scandinavia (Cahill Wilson et al., 2014, 139–40). Perhaps this burial represents an immigrant, or trader, who had become assimilated into a local kin-group, who, although prepared for burial by those familiar with an alien burial rite, was interred in an indigenous grave type, which, when back-filled, would appear identical to the remainder of the graves in the cemetery.

The second example are two crouched burials in the adjacent unenclosed cemetery at Betaghstown (Brookside), Co. Meath: male burial (B12), crouched, in a dug pit-grave, dated to the fourth–seventh century,[75] and female (B11), crouched, in a dug pit-grave, also dated to the fourth–seventh century.[76] Strontium and oxygen isotope analysis indicates that the male (B12) was not Irish, but originated in much hotter climes, probably North Africa (Cahill Wilson and Standish, 2016, 237). The movement of people from North Africa in the Early Medieval period is not unique to Ireland. Isotopic evidence is now available confirming that migration from North Africa to south Wales also occurred during this period (Hemer et al., 2013). Bearing in mind the evidence for links in the Early Medieval period between Ireland and Wales, and between the eastern Mediterranean and the east coast of Ireland, evidenced by the importation of Phocaean Red Slip Ware, and Bii ware (Doyle, 2009; Kelly, 2010, 37), it is likely that this burial may be that of a trader operating in the Irish Sea region. The female burial (B11) was accompanied by grave goods consisting of objects of personal adornment, which included an oval bronze disc with traces of fine network adhering, in the region of her skull, two iron omega-type penannular brooches on her shoulders, one small stone amulet at her neck, and an oval belt buckle at her waist (Figure 5.4) (O'Brien, 1993, 96–7; 1999a, 179). This woman was clothed on burial. The wearing of brooches in pairs is not an Irish custom, and the brooches (Fowler Type B), which are probably late Roman, were worn by this woman in an Anglo-Saxon fashion. The bulk of Anglo-Saxon burials using this type of brooch fall in the AD 450–550 period (White, 1988, 23). The stone amulet was probably suspended between the brooches in the manner of the more usual string of beads. Although isotopic analysis is not available for this woman, her burial attire makes it probable that she hailed from Britain. Both these individuals were buried by their peers who were familiar with the burial rite involved, and it is possible that the choice of burial place,

---

[74] UBA–13071: 1612±22BP at 2σ = cal AD 394–535. [75] OxA–2652: 1565±60BP; at 2σ = cal AD 381–621. [76] OxA–2651: 1550±60BP; at 2σ =cal AD 394–630.

close to the sea coast, is non-fortuitous. A slab-lined cist grave containing an extended, local male, dated to the fifth–seventh century, which cut into part of the grave pit of B11, is perhaps an indication that those responsible for the cist burial were not aware of, or chose to ignore, the presence of the woman's burial, even though both burials are roughly contemporary.

An interesting coincidence is the inclusion of one crouched burial in the nearby cemetery at Ninch 2, Co. Meath (Map 6). This adult, sex unknown, undated, had been buried in an oval grave-cut, crouched with knees drawn up to the chest (Buckley, 2010, 44). The place of origin of this person is unknown, but the possibility that he/she may be an immigrant is heightened by the presence of three supine, extended, burials in the cemeteries at Ninch 2 (B856, B770), and Ninch 3 (B25), whose origins were possibly in Central or Eastern Europe.

At Ballydavis 1, Co. Laois (Stevens, 2011, 18–19), a crouched burial (SK 103) possible male, aged about 20 years, was interred in a full-length dug grave, located outside and to the east of the ring-ditches at that site. This crouched burial within a full-length grave is similar to that of the immigrant male burial (F181) at Betaghstown (Anchorage), dated to the fifth–sixth century, and raises the possibility that this man was also an immigrant.

There was one crouched burial, female (B13), aged 25–35 years, dated to the eighth–ninth century,[77] among approximately sixty-seven burials in the cemetery enclosure at Killeany, Co. Laois. This woman appears to have been bound, as her knees were tightly drawn up, her arms were flexed at the elbow and her hands rested on each side of her face (Wiggins and Kane, 2009, 144, 356).

An exceptional burial in the cemetery at Owenbristy, Co. Galway, is crouched burial (B70), a late middle-aged adult, possibly male, dated to the sixth–seventh century.[78] This individual, who is not of local origin, but may be from another part of Ireland (Evans and Chenery, 2010, 382–4), is exceptional in that he had an iron torc or neck ring around his neck. The cemetery at Carrowkeel, Co. Galway, contained several crouched burials, and one unusual burial described as being 'akimbo' (Wilkins and Lalonde, 2014, CD-ROM vol. 1; 14, 139, 142, 152). The first burial is that of a female adult (SK 51), published as flexed but is crouched, dated to the seventh–ninth century;[79] the second, an adolescent (SK 72) aged 12–14 years, partially crouched, dated to the seventh–ninth century,[80] was interred in the terminus of a curvilinear ditch which surrounded the cemetery; the third was a juvenile (SK 82), aged 6–10 years, dated to the ninth–eleventh century,[81] crouched with hands wrapped around the knees. The 'akimbo' burial, a young female adult (SK 119), dated to the seventh–eighth century,[82] was supine with her legs tightly drawn up, but each leg was splayed outwards (Plate 8). Perhaps this posture was intentional, but it is also possible that this young woman had been tightly bound with her legs drawn up to her chest but laid on her back, and the binding had become undone causing her legs to fall to either side. This might occur if the grave had been covered by a wooden cover leaving the body to decompose in a void.

[77] SUERC–17625: 1205±35BP; at 2σ = cal AD 692–941: (highest probability 81.0% = cal AD 762–895). [78] UB–11248: 1457±36BP; at 2σ = cal AD 547–652. [79] UB–7417: 1228±31BP; at 2σ = cal AD 689–884. [80] UB–7423: 1244±32BP; at 2σ = cal AD 680–876. [81] UB–7429: 1104±31BP; at 2σ = cal AD 884–1015. [82] UB–7443: 1305±34BP; at 2σ = cal AD 656–770.

At Faughart Lower, Co. Louth, a crouched burial of an elderly female (SK 177A), undated, showed evidence that the ball of the thigh bone was out of the socket of the hip joint (Buckley and McConway, 2010, 54; Bowen and Dawkes, 2011, 70). This probably occurred when the body was being manipulated into a crouched posture, perhaps in preparation for transport to the cemetery. A further crouched burial at this cemetery (SK 1006A) was unsexed and undated. In the settlement cemetery at Ratoath, Co. Meath (Fibiger, 2010, 118–19; Wallace, 2010, 305), a crouched burial of an adult (B12), possible female, dated to the fifth–sixth century,[83] was unusual in that her skull, hands, and feet were missing. If this woman had died elsewhere her skull might have been buried at the place of death, but this does not explain the absence of her hands and feet. Perhaps the head and extremities were lost in transport, or it could be that the burial was punitive in nature. Another crouched burial at this site (B34) was that of an adolescent, dated to the seventh–ninth century,[84] who had been laid on his back with legs drawn up to his chest. A piece of slag recovered from the sacrum had probably been used as a plug to prevent the discharge of bodily fluids.

At Mount Gamble, Swords, Co. Dublin (O'Donovan and Geber, 2010, 253), a crouched female (CCLXXVI), aged 30–45 years, dated to the sixth–seventh century,[85] showed evidence for severe spinal degeneration. It is suggested by the excavator that this spinal condition might be the reason why this individual was buried in a crouched posture. Also included at Mount Gamble was a partially crouched burial of a child, c.9 years old, dated eighth–ninth century[86] (O'Donovan and Geber, 2010, 229–30). At Marlinstown, Co. Westmeath (Keeley, 1991b, no. 113; 1992, no. 126; unpublished TII report), the crouched burial of a child, aged 6–8 years, undated, lying on its back with knees drawn up to the chest, was found in the ditch of a settlement cemetery.

There are several crouched, partially crouched, and flexed burials, in the cemetery at Camlin 3, Co. Tipperary (Flynn, 2011). An adult, possible male (SK 85), dated to the ninth–tenth century,[87] was crouched, laid on his back with knees drawn up to his chest, suggesting that he had been bound. A further adult, possibly male (SK 152), aged 40–4 years, dated to the tenth–eleventh century,[88] was crouched and his head was missing. This burial was accompanied by a flint object. Both these burials are outside the temporal parameters of this publication, but it is worth noting that the practice was still being observed up to this time. In this cemetery two further undated crouched burials were of children: (SK 60), a child of between 1–3 years, and (SK 129), a child aged between 5–9 years. Two undated partially crouched burials, published as crouched, are an adult (SK 58), aged 26–35 years, and a possible male (SK 71), aged over 46 years. Several burials in this cemetery were flexed, a possible female (SK 127), aged over 30 years, dated to the eighth–tenth century[89] (published as crouched), was lying on her side in a sleeping posture in the terminal of the L-shaped enclosure ditch, with her head at the south-west. Also in a flexed posture were a child (SK 68) aged 6–9 years, a child (SK 79) aged 2–5 years, a male (SK 101)

---

83 Beta–198504: 1540±40BP; at 2σ = cal AD 426–601. 84 Beta–196360: 1260±40BP; at 2σ = cal AD 666–875. 85 Lab reference unknown: 1484±25BP; at 2σ = cal AD 542–637. 86 Lab reference unknown: 1191±28BP; at 2σ (91.2% probability) cal AD 767–895. 87 UBA–11439: 1133±21BP: at 2σ (93.7%) = cal AD 869–984. 88 SUERC–31483: uncalibrated date unknown: at 2σ (as published) cal AD 960–1050. 89 SUERC:31482: uncalibrated date unknown: at 2σ (as published)

aged 35 to 45 years, an adult (SK 126), indeterminate sex, an adult (SK 129), indeterminate sex, aged 17–25 years, and an adult (SK 148), slightly flexed. These latter burials have not been dated, and as it is likely that they fall outside the temporal parameters of this work they have not been included in Gazetteer 4, but have been included here for information purposes.

The cemetery at Ardnagross, Co. Westmeath (Eogan, 1996, 5–6), included the crouched burial of an older male (F1018), undated, laid on his left side, no further details available. There was one crouched burial in the large cemetery at Mount Offaly, Co. Dublin (CCCCLXII), undated, was crouched on its back with knees drawn up to the chest (Conway, 1999, 31, 33). At Ballykilmore, Co. Westmeath, there are several crouched burials dateable to the eleventh century and later. One of these, a young adult (c489), aged 16–19 years, undated, is published as being flexed, but is crouched (Channing 2009, 52; 2014, 33, 35). This demonstrates that in this cemetery crouched burial continued sporadically into the Medieval period. At Cherrywood, Site 18, Co. Dublin, two skeletons are described as having their legs drawn up towards their body (Ó Néill and Coughlin, 2010, 244), but no further details are available. In the site at Knoxspark, Co. Sligo, there are two crouched burials. An adult (Burial 31), undated, and a sub-adult (Burial 34), undated, who had been decapitated; no further information is available (Mount, 2010, 197, 200, Table 14–1).

Excavation at the Late Bronze Age cliff-edge stone fort of Dún Aonghasa, Inis Mór, Aran Islands, Co. Galway, revealed the crouched inhumation (B2680-B1) of a juvenile, aged 12–14 years, dated to the eighth–tenth century[90] (Cotter, 2012, i 257–9; ii 194, 290–3). This young person had been interred, in a supine position but with the legs drawn tightly up to the chest, into the back-fill at threshold 3 on the inner side of a passage through the inner fort wall. The burial was sealed by a large slab which did not cover the head. The skull was missing, but this may have been an accidental removal over a period, as loose teeth and a portion of the right temporal bone were found in the region of the neck and chest. The disposition of this skeleton suggests that it was likely to have been bound and transported to this place. Also associated with this burial were three leg bones from another juvenile (2684–B2), dated to the eighth–tenth century.[91] The posture of this latter burial is unknown, but in view of its proximity to B1, and the similarity in date, it has been concluded by the excavator that it also may have been crouched.

The cemetery at Parknahown 5, Co. Laois, included two crouched, and three partially crouched burials. These were, crouched infant (B384), dated to the seventh–ninth century;[92] an adolescent (B572) aged 13–17 years, who was crouched and prone, dated to the eleventh–twelfth century;[93] a partially crouched adult male (B168) aged 17–25 years, dated to the ninth–eleventh century;[94] a partially crouched juvenile (B549) undated, but right hand and both feet missing; and a partially crouched adolescent (B034) aged 13–17 years, undated (O'Neill, 2009, vol. 5, text; c14 dates vol. II, Appendix 3). Although some of these burials fall outside the temporal

cal AD 770–980. **90** Two dates were obtained for this burial, which when combined (Cotter, 2012, ii 291) calibrated at 2σ = cal AD 770–970. The closest date obtained was UB-4411: 1179±26BP; at 2σ = cal AD 770–946. **91** GrA-1275: 1205±45BP; at 2σ = cal AD 685–950. **92** SUERC-17338: 1225±35BP; at 2σ = cal AD 688–887. **93** SUERC-17311: 975±35BP: at 2σ (93.4%) = cal AD 1011–1155. **94** SUERC-16995: 1040±35BP; at 2σ = cal AD 890–1020.

Atypical or deviant burials

parameters under consideration, they have been included here because of the continuity of burial at the site of Parknahown 5.

A crouched burial (G3) decapitated with head missing, dated to the fifth–seventh century, was buried beside a Bronze Age cist, at Sonnagh Demesne, Co. Westmeath (Cahill and Sikora, 2011, 204–7). In the Rath of the Synods, Tara, Co. Meath, the crouched burial of a juvenile (B) aged 10–12 years, has been dated to the fourth century AD.[95] The date obtained for this burial ought to be treated with caution as it was derived not from skeletal material but from charcoal located close to the burial (Grogan, 2008, 42). It is probable that the burial is Iron Age in date. Strontium and oxygen isotope analysis indicated that this young person was born locally (Cahill Wilson, 2012, 23; Cahill Wilson and Standish, 2016, 233 – Table 1). Other burials in this monument include, a male burial (I) undated, partially crouched, head to the east, who had his origins in the northern part of Ireland (Cahill Wilson, 2012, 23–25), an adult burial (E) probable male, dated to the eighth–ninth century,[96] partially crouched, orientated with his head to the north-east, and accompanied by two small flat stones and an animal bone over the face, a bone pin in the neck region, and a perforated bone object on the chest (Grogan, 2008, 44–7). Strontium and oxygen isotope analysis indicates that this individual also originated in the northern region of Ireland (Cahill Wilson, 2012, 23–5; Cahill Wilson and Standish, 2016, 234, Table 1). A possible explanation for the burial of this latter individual in this posture, at the Rath of the Synods, long after burial at this site had ceased, is examined at p. 123. It would appear that those who carried out these burials at Tara felt that the individuals involved were entitled to burial at this ancient and venerable site.

Two partially crouched burials were included in the cemetery at Johnstown, Co. Meath (Clarke and Carlin, 2008, CD-ROM, Text, 46): an older male (B6) undated, in a dug grave, and an older female (B8) undated, in a dug grave. Finally, in the cemetery at Solar, Co. Antrim, a partially crouched adult female (545) undated, orientated with her head to the south, was accompanied by a cylindrical bone object, possibly a large bead (Hurl, 2002, 56). The orientation of the body suggests that this burial might be punitive.

Flexed burials, which occur in many cemeteries, albeit in small numbers, appear often to represent a sleeping posture. This might occur if an individual died in their sleep and was buried while still in rigor mortis, or it could be a deliberate decision to bury an individual as if asleep in the grave. A good example of flexed burial is represented by SK 1299A (Figure 6.5), at Faughart Lower, Co. Louth (Bowen and Dawkes, 2001).

As the above data represent the known list of crouched, partially crouched, and flexed burials of Early Medieval date in Ireland, it becomes apparent that this is a rare occurrence. The majority of cemeteries contain no such burials, and where they are present they represent a minute proportion of overall burial numbers. The possible reasons for the use of this burial rite in Early Medieval Ireland are, use of the rite by immigrants; preparation of a body for transport over some distance; use of the rite by the indigenous population as a punitive measure; to prevent revenant activity; or

---

95 UBA–8533: 1691±20BP; at 2σ = cal AD 260–405; at 87.3% probability = cal AD 325–405 (unfortunately, the calibrated date published in Cahill Wilson, 2012, 22, is incorrect).   96 UBA–

in the case of flexed burial, to possibly represent a sleeping position. What is evident is that while this burial rite was marginal throughout the period, it was occasionally still being used up to at least the tenth–eleventh century.

DISARTICULATED BURIAL IN BOX

The disarticulated remains of an adult male (B161) who had died in the fifth–sixth century,[97] contained within the remnants of a wooden box, measuring approximately 50cm x 20cm, with metal corner-brackets and nails[98] (Figure 6.7), were recovered at Colp West 1, Co. Meath, during excavation of the cemetery which was founded in the late sixth century (see Map 6).[99] It is noticeable that the box and its contents were inserted into the outer edge of the penannular ring-ditch enclosure, and not inside the enclosure (Figure 6.7), an indication that the remains were probably interred at a time when burial within the enclosure had ceased.

It has been suggested that the box could be a 'shrine' (Cormac Bourke, pers. comm.), and this is possible, because the remains of saints were often preserved in portable containers (Ó Floinn, 2012, 204).[100] If this was a shrine containing the corporeal relics of a holy man, perhaps the positioning of the box into the outer bank of the burial enclosure may have been due to the box and its contents being hastily concealed for safety during a time of turmoil. However, this would have had to occur after the seventh century when the cult of corporeal relics had become acceptable practice in Ireland (Doherty, 1984, 70–9; O'Brien, 1999a, 57–8). It is also possible that this burial could have been undertaken for other reasons. Perhaps the individual was a local man who had died abroad and his bones were repatriated to his ancestral place, or he may have been the revered ancestor of a non-indigenous immigrant group who had carried his bones with them on their travels, and who, eventually settling in the region of Colp, buried their ancestor in the perceived burial place of the ancestors of the indigenous people. The latter is a possibility when one bears in mind the presence in the nearby cemeteries at Ninch and Betaghstown (Map 6) of individuals who possibly hailed from Central, Eastern, and Northern Europe, Britain, and North Africa. Unfortunately, it was not possible to obtain isotopic analysis to determine the place of origin for this individual, as his teeth became lost during post-excavation storage.

BURIALS IN DITCH TERMINI AND IN ENCLOSURE ENTRANCES

There are ten (perhaps eleven) recorded instances of burial in the termini of ditched enclosures or in the entrance to an enclosure. Seven of these burials are associated

---

11698:1205±24BP; at 2σ (91.1% probability) = cal AD 767–889.   **97** UBA–15650: 1533±24BP; at 2σ = cal AD 428–595 (c14 date obtained courtesy of the INSTAR Mapping Death Project). **98** These corner brackets and nails are remarkably similar to the iron angle-brackets on some wooden coffins in the Late Roman section of the cemetery at Poundbury, Dorset (Farwell and Molleson, 1993, 119–29). This similarity suggests that the Colp box may have been constructed in Britain, and that this individual possibly died there.   **99** Probable foundation burial B102: UBA–15649: 1503±22BP: at 2σ (91.6%) = cal AD 535–619 (c14 date obtained courtesy of the INSTAR Mapping Death Project).   **100** Thanks to Raghnall Ó Floinn for providing a translation of his paper.

Atypical or deviant burials 165

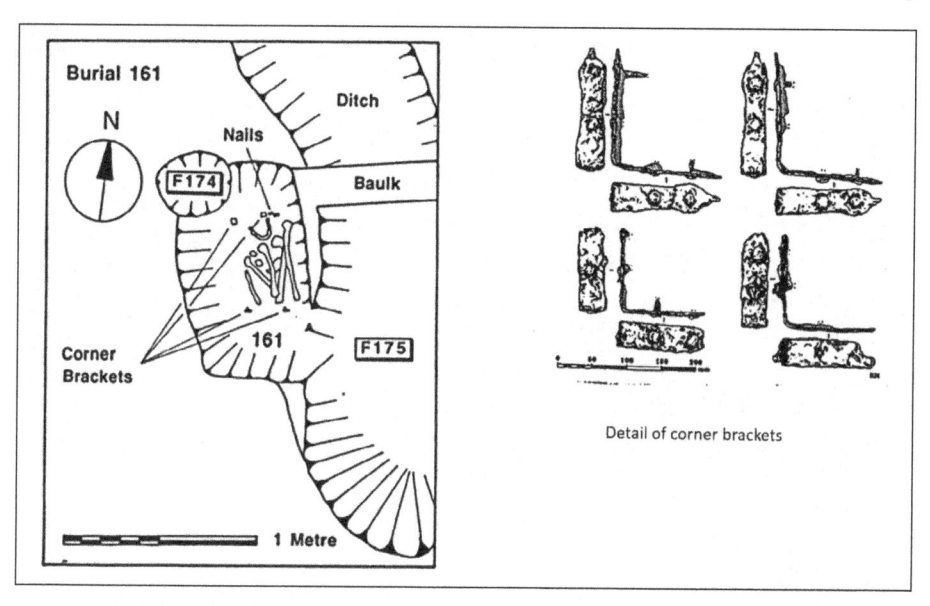

6.7 Disarticulated 'boxed' burial 161, Colp West 1, Co. Meath, with detail of corner brackets, © MGL.

with ditched enclosures that contain further burials, two are associated with ditched enclosures that contain no other burials, and one (possibly two) in the entrance to a walled enclosure that has no further burials. Six of the burials are of adolescents, two are adult female, two are male (one of whom is decapitated). While the reason for the deliberate placing of the burials of young persons in the termini of enclosing ditches, and in the entrance to an enclosure, is unknown, it does call to mind the Medieval Irish legend of Cú Chulainn, who, as a boy, guarded the entrance to the royal enclosure at Emhain Macha (Navan Fort) in Armagh. Perhaps these young people were acting as guardians of the entrance to the enclosed space.[101]

Examples include, the partially-crouched burial of an adolescent (SK 72) (Plate 9a) dated to the seventh–ninth century[102] interred in the north-facing terminus of the inner ditch (1260), which surrounded the eastern side of the cemetery at Carrowkeel, Co. Galway (Wilkins and Lalonde, 2014, 14, 106). The flexed skeleton of a juvenile (C251) aged 8–10 years, in a sleeping posture (Plate 9b), dated to the ninth–tenth century,[103] recovered from the southern terminus of the entrance to the ringfort at Loughbown 1, Co. Galway, was the only burial at this site (Bower, 2009, 16–17, 252); and a crouched juvenile (B68) aged 11–12 years, dated to the seventh–ninth century,[104] who was discovered in the northern terminus of the entrance to the outer enclosure

---

101 One must, of course, also make note of the presence of two adult female extended inhumations, one in a nailed coffin, at either side of the entrance to Site A, an Iron Age ring-barrow, re-used for occupation in the Early Medieval period, at Navan Fort, Co. Armagh (Lynn, 1997, 144–5). Controversy surrounds the dating of these burials. While there is a possibility that they may have Romano-British connections, Lynn places them in the Late Medieval period and regards their location at the entrance to Site A as fortuitous. Because of deterioration of the skeletal material it was not possible to obtain c14 dates from the remains. 102 UB–7425: 1250±34BP; at 2σ = cal AD 647–874. 103 UBA–8096: 1138±29BP; at 2σ = cal AD 777–983, at 81.2% probability = cal AD 856–983. 104 SUERC–17623: 1255±35BP; at 2σ = cal AD 671–872.

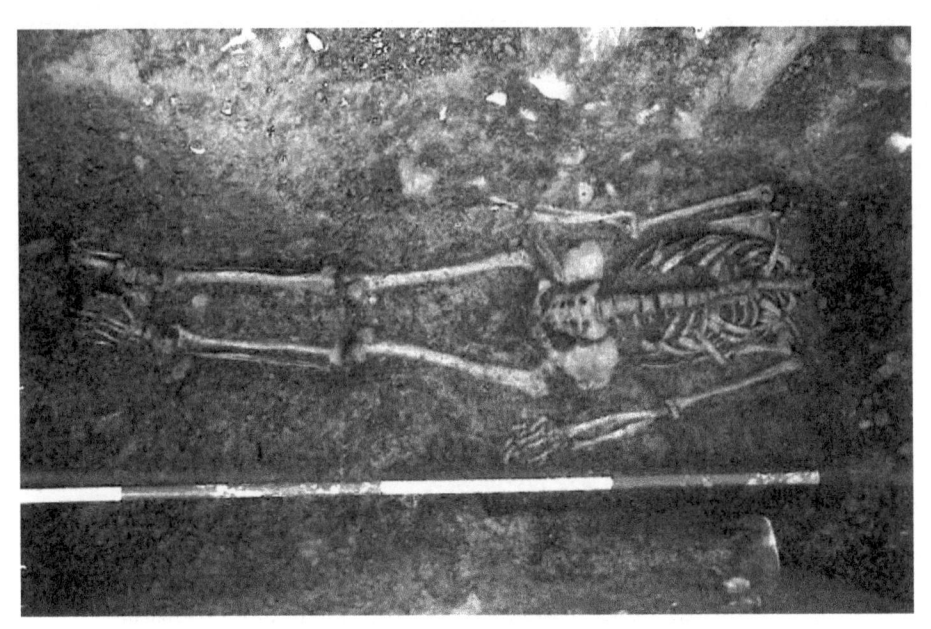

6.8 Burial 7, Castlefarm, Co. Meath, © ACSU.

that surrounded the inner cemetery enclosure at Killeany, Co. Laois. This burial is described consistently throughout the final report as being a 'casual' burial (Wiggins and Kane, 2009, 92, 198, 214; Wiggins, 2014, 277), but it is more likely to represent a deliberate deposition. A further child burial in a ditch is recorded at the settlement cemetery at Marlinstown, Co. Westmeath, but the exact location within the ditch is unknown. At the unusual site of Haggardstown, Co. Louth, the only burial was that of an adolescent aged 15–18 years, in a partially crouched posture, orientated south–north, dated to the eighth–ninth century,[105] interred in the eastern terminus of the northern arc (F26). This site consisted of a large irregular enclosed area formed by two opposing crescent-shaped arcs, creating the appearance of east and west enclosure entrances, and contained a souterrain (McLoughlin, 2012b, 528, and pers. com.). At Castlefarm, Co. Meath (O'Connell and Clark, 2009, 8), a male burial (7) was interred in the northern ditch terminal of the inner enclosure feature (Plate 5b). This was a young adult male, dated to the fifth–sixth century,[106] who had been decapitated and his head buried elsewhere. Although he had been buried in a supine position, his body was oriented east–west (head to the east), and the position of his hands and feet suggest that he was not shroud wrapped (Figure 6.8). This burial is probably punitive and may have been intended as a warning to others. A burial in the ditch terminal at Camlin 3, Co. Tipperary, is unusual in that it is of a possible female (SK 127) aged over 30 years, dated to the eighth–tenth century.[107] This person was buried flexed in a sleeping posture and orientated with her head to the south, in the northern terminal of the L-shaped ditch that enclosed the western and southern sides of the cemetery (Flynn, 2011, 89, 116).

[105] Lab ref unknown: 1200±36BP; at 2σ = cal AD 693–944, at 81.9% probability = cal AD 763–898.
[106] Beta–229299: 1530±40BP; at 2σ = cal AD 424–606.   [107] SUERC–31482: at 2σ = cal AD 770–980.

Burial in an entrance passage is demonstrated at Ardsallagh I, where a male (B16) dated to the fifth–sixth century[108] was interred in a simple dug grave in the enclosure entrance (Randolph-Quinney, 2006a; Clarke and Carlin, 2009, 8–20). This is not a 'sealing' or 'closure' burial because it pre-dates four of the burials within the enclosure, in which case it is possible that this person was regarded as a 'guardian' of the enclosure. A further, but very different, burial in an entrance feature is demonstrated at Killeany, Co. Laois, where in the passage-like entrance to the inner cemetery enclosure was the burial of a female (B39) aged 17–25 years, dated to the sixth–seventh century.[109] This young woman had been subjected to extreme violence, evidenced by thirty-nine cut marks to her upper torso, and was buried prone in the entrance passage to the cemetery. However, her grave was later (post-seventh century) disturbed by the insertion of the burial of an elderly person (B60), sex undetermined, undated, who was buried supine, head to the west. It is possible that by the time this latter burial was inserted, the earlier burial had receded from local memory, and the later burial, while it also may have been punitive, might, on the other hand, have been regarded as a 'guardian'.

Burial in the entrance passage to a stone-built enclosure is represented by the tightly crouched juvenile (2680-B1) aged 12–14 years, dated to the eighth–tenth century, located against the inner threshold of an entrance passage through the enclosure wall of the inner enclosure at Dún Aonghusa, Inis Mór, Aran Islands, Co. Galway. A further possible example, also from Dún Aonghusa, is represented by three leg bones of a juvenile (2684-B2) found in association with, and datable to the same era as, B1 (Cotter, 2012, i 257–9; ii 194–5, 290–3). These are the only Early Medieval burials at this site.

If the young people were acting as guardians, then adult SK 127, possible female, at Camlin, may also have been a guardian. She was deposited in a sleeping posture, with her feet towards the entrance to the cemetery. Similarly, male (B16), in the entrance to the ring-ditch at Ardsallagh I, and possibly burial (B60) at Killeany. However, the decapitated male (Burial 7) at Castlefarm is unlikely to have been a guardian of the enclosure, but, as his burial was probably punitive, and as there is a possibility that his head may have been displayed nearby, he may have been deliberately placed at the entrance as a warning to would-be intruders. The death of the young woman (B39) at Killeany, who had been violently killed and buried prone in the entrance passageway to the cemetery, was also punitive, and was obviously intended as a warning, because every person visiting this cemetery would have had to walk over her grave, pushing her face deeper into the ground.

A POSSIBLE SENTINEL BURIAL

Sentinel burial is represented by an individual, usually a warrior, buried close to a territorial boundary, facing into adjoining territory, in order to defend his home territory in the event of intrusion by enemies from the adjoining territory (O'Brien, 2008b, 323–30).

Full details of the c14 calculations are not included in the final report. **108** Beta–222016: 1560±40BP; at 2σ = cal AD 410–583. **109** SUERC–17622: 1445±35BP; at 2σ = cal AD 555–655.

The Irish were familiar with this practice, the earliest reference being in the seventh century, when Tírechán describes how he envisaged a fifth-century sentinel warrior burial. He describes how Loíguire, son of Níall, refused to accept the faith from Patrick because 'My father Níall did not allow me to accept the faith, but bade me to be buried on the ridges of Tara, I son of Níall, and the sons of Dúnlang in Maistiu in Mag Liphi, face to face in the manner of men at war ... because of such fierceness of our (mutual) hatred'[110] (*Tírechán* §12, Bieler, 1979, 132–3). The setting of this purported burial on Tara is important, because Tara commands an extensive view in all directions, especially across the Liffey plain towards Maistiu, where undoubtedly the sons of Dúnlang were envisaged as being similarly buried. A further reference to the practice is contained in the seventh–eighth-century text 'Conall Corc and the Corco Luigde' (Charles-Edwards, 2000, 522–3) and concerns Óengus mac Nad Froích (died AD 490), who was reputed to have been buried facing north, in a standing position, 'under the couch of the kings at Cashel, because of the hostility between Munster and Leth Cuinn' (Byrne, 1973, 194). Again, the location is significant, as the Rock of Cashel dominates the surrounding countryside, especially to the north. The story of Éogan Bél, who was to be buried upright on Knocknarea, facing north with his red spear in his hand, has already been referred to. The practice was also familiar to the British. The earliest British literary reference is in the Kentish Chronicle (possibly sixth century), included in Nennius's ninth-century *Historia Brittonum*, when Vortimer, son of Vortigern, is depicted dying after the rout of the invading German barbarians, instructing his followers to set his tomb beside the coast at the port from which the invaders had departed, so that they could never again settle in the land. His followers ignored his command and buried him at Lincoln, with the result that 'the barbarians returned in force' (Morris, 1980, 32, 72; Brooks, 2000, 82). A further British example occurs at the end of the Second Branch of the Mabinogi written in the eleventh–twelfth century, when the dying Bendigeidfran instructed his men that they should cut off his head and take it to the White Hill in London and bury it with its face to France, so that, while the head remained buried and undisturbed, no foreign oppression might come across the sea (Charles-Edwards, 1976, 86). Upright burials are unknown in the Irish archaeological record. Therefore, the depiction of a sentinel burial must be that of a warrior laid out in a supine position, in a border region, in such a manner that if raised upright he would be facing towards enemy territory.

While several burials that meet the required criteria in Early Anglo-Saxon England have been suggested (O'Brien, 1999a, 91, 163, 122; 2008b, 326–9), only one probable archaeological example has to date been identified in Ireland. This example is at Pelletstown East, north Co. Dublin (Frazer, 2005; 2006, 111–12), situated at 35m OD, on the northern spur of a hill overlooking the River Tolka (*An Tulcha*),[111] where three graves were excavated. The principal burial (disturbed) was that of an adult (B1) sex undetermined, aged 36–45 years, 1.62–1.65m tall, supine extended, dated to the sixth–seventh century.[112] The body was oriented south–north, with the head to the south,

---

110 This reference is anachronistic in that it reflects the political reality of the seventh century, and not that of the fifth century when the event was reputed to have taken place. 111 The River Tolka rises in Co. Meath and flows into the Irish Sea in Dublin Bay, immediately north of the estuary of the River Liffey. 112 UB–6226: 1489±29BP: at 2σ (93.4%) = cal AD 535–644.

whereby the deceased, on rising, would be facing north. This individual was interred in a carefully constructed grave, floored with slabs, and outlined with boulders. Unfortunately, the grave had been much disturbed before excavation, but it undoubtedly had originally been covered either with wooden planks, or stone slabs. At the northern end of this grave adjacent to the feet of B1, a shallow dug grave contained the remains of a juvenile (B2) aged 6–12 years, lying on its left side, with the head to the south, also dated to the sixth–seventh century,[113] and containing burnt animal bone fragments (species unidentifiable). The c14 dates indicate that the adult and child had died simultaneously, or that the child had died shortly after the adult. The burials are positioned on a protruding spur on the northern edge of an east–west tract of land roughly 4km wide, bordered on the north by the River Tolka and on the south by the River Liffey, which suggests that the individual (B1) may be protecting the tract of land behind him (between the Tolka and the Liffey) from those who occupied the land north of the River Tolka. The reason behind the inclusion of a juvenile at the foot of the grave is a matter for speculation – could this be an accompanying family member, a page, or even a foster-child? One of the criteria for identifying a warrior is the inclusion of at least one weapon in the grave. There were none recovered at Pelletstown, but this could be the result of illegal metal detecting which, according to the excavator, had taken place in the area for several years, and which would also account for the disturbance to the grave and the skeletons. One further burial (B3) was revealed approximately 40cm north of B1 and B2. This was also a juvenile, aged 6–15 years, laid supine, west–east, in a slab-lined grave (the burial and grave had also been greatly disturbed). This burial had been inserted, closer to the northern edge of the spur, some time after B1 and B2, and was dated to the seventh–eighth century.[114] The reason for the insertion of this third burial remains a mystery, but perhaps by the seventh century the site had attained the status of an ancestral burial place.

* * *

A limited number of burials recorded in Early Medieval Ireland deviate from the norm for various reasons including a fear of revenants, a result of punitive action, or as a result of interpersonal violence. Atypical or deviant burials considered in this publication include: a possible live burial; cases of decapitation where the head is either present in, or absent from, the grave; bodies which have been mutilated after death; individuals who died as a result of interpersonal weapon violence; individuals buried in a prone position; paired male burials exhibiting weapon trauma; paired male burials with no evidence of weapon trauma; individuals buried in a crouched position; bodies disposed of in kilns; a disarticulated burial in a box; and individuals buried in ditch termini and entrances. Included among the individuals who exhibited fatal weapon trauma were several females and juveniles. The infliction of trauma of this type was one reason that led to the enactment of the *Cáin Adomnán*, also known as

---

113 UB–6227: 1455±30BP; at 2σ = cal AD 555–650.   114 UB–6228: 1343±32BP; at 2σ = cal AD 640–767 (at 83.7% probability = cal AD 640–719).

Lex Innocentium ('Law of the Innocents'), by Adomnán, abbot of Iona, in 697. One of the provisions of this Law was to ensure the protection of non-combatants (women, clerics, and children) in times of conflict. Deviant burials of persons who had been subjected to extreme trauma represent a tiny minority of the overall burial corpus. While some of these may have been the result of punitive measures, the majority represent the remains of persons who perhaps having fallen in battle were retrieved by their followers or kin, and buried in the appropriate communal/familial cemetery. We cannot, of course, know the numbers of those whose bodies were not located and retrieved, and were left where they fell. Some deviant or unusual burials, usually prone, crouched, or buried in kilns, were regarded by those responsible for the burials as a means of preventing the dead from becoming revenant and returning to haunt the living. Other burials were probably punitive.

It is also worth noting that, to date, burials of persons who had suffered extreme weapon trauma as described in this publication, or other forms of unusual or deviant burial, have not usually been recorded in cemeteries associated with churches. There are two possible exceptions: male burial (B2) at Kill of the Grange, Dublin, who had been buried in a prone position, and the male burial who had suffered a violent death and may have been decapitated at Cleenish, Co. Fermanagh. It is noted that both these burials were located on the perimeter, in the northern sector of the church enclosure, separate from the general cemetery area, which suggests that they had been deliberately excluded from the main church cemetery.

CHAPTER 7

Mobility of peoples

During the Late Iron Age/Early Medieval period, displacement of populations occurred throughout Europe as a result of the rise and spread of the Roman Empire; the collapse of the Empire during the fourth–fifth century AD, resulting in what is now referred to as the 'migration period' throughout the continent of Europe; and the influx into Britain of Angles and Saxons from mainland Europe in the fifth–sixth century. Although there is no evidence for organised migration into Ireland during these episodes, inevitably some individuals, or groups, arrived and settled in the country, either as traders or immigrants, during the Iron Age and Early Medieval periods.

IRON AGE

Recognition of external contacts, resulting from trading or immigration, among the indigenous population who cremated their dead in the Iron Age is dependent on radiocarbon dating, or on recognition of comparisons for the modest assemblage of Irish grave goods available for this period; it can also be seen in the presence of an unmistakable Roman cremation at Stoneyford, Co. Kilkenny.

However, the recognition of external contacts among the minority population in the Iron Age who inhumed their dead has improved due to the emerging discipline of strontium and oxygen isotope analysis on teeth. It is now possible to recognise those who were born in the region in which they were buried, and to identify immigrants. The following sample of ten Iron Age burials that have been subjected to strontium and oxygen isotopic analyses are included in Gazetteer 5. Three males, one female, and one child are immigrants who were not born at their place of burial; three females and two children are of local origin. The latter two children may represent the first-generation offspring of immigrants.

Six of the burials in the largest cluster of crouched inhumations, inserted as secondary deposits in the ancient necropolis of Knowth, Co. Meath, during the Iron Age, have been subjected to strontium and oxygen isotope analysis. (Map 3; Figure 2.2). Two decapitated crouched males (B8–9) a double burial, dated to the first century BC–second century AD,[1] accompanied by gaming or possibly divination or occult related pieces, are now identified as having probably originated in the northern part of Britain (Cahill Wilson et al., 2012, 775–87). Crouched female child (B7) aged about 7 years, with no grave goods (Figure 2.4), dated to the first century BC–third century AD,[2] was probably born in northern or south-eastern Britain, and may have

---

1 GrN–15371: 1960±30BP; at 2σ = cal 40 BC–AD 121.   2 GrN–15370: 1920±60BP; at 2σ = cal 43 BC–AD 232.

been brought into Ireland as part of a family group. Young adult male (B21), crouched, dated to the first century BC–third century AD,[3] is not of local origin, and was accompanied by grave goods, which included six copper rings and 272 glass (mainly blue) beads, an indication that he was probably lavishly clothed at burial (Eogan, 2012, 33–5; Cahill Wilson and Standish, 2016, 237). Female (B4), flexed and splayed, buried prone and weighted down with a large stone (Figure 2.5a), dated to the first–third century AD,[4] may have been born locally but there is a possibility that she came from further afield (Eogan, 2012, 18–21; Cahill Wilson et al., 2014, 141–2). The earliest dated burial in the group, a crouched female (B10) (Figure 2.5b), with no grave goods, dated to the second–first century BC,[5] was born locally. This woman was buried by those familiar with an alien burial rite. Perhaps she was from a locally important kin-group and had been 'married' into an immigrant kin-group in order to create a link with the indigenous population.

The female crouched inhumation (F238), dated to the second–first century BC,[6] in the cemetery at Anchorage, Betaghstown, Co. Meath, buried with a large stone on her abdomen (Figure 2.6), had her probable origins in south-eastern Scotland or Yorkshire, with a slight possibility of an origin in mainland Europe (Cahill Wilson et al., 2014, 139). A crouched female burial inserted through the ditch fill in the southern section of the Iron Age ring-ditch at Rath, Co. Meath (Schweitzer, 2005, 93–8), was probably clothed on burial as she had three copper-alloy rings on her toes, two of which appear to be attachments for sandals. The third ring appears to be decorative, with a herring-bone motif of a type associated with Roman contexts. The skeletal material was too degraded to produce a c14 date, but strontium isotope analysis of her teeth indicates that she is probably of local origin (Montgomery et al., 2006). This burial combines the indigenous rite of (cremated) burial in the ditch fill of a ring-ditch, with the alien rite of crouched inhumation, which, together with the presence of a Roman-type ring, may also indicate the merging of indigenous and immigrant groups. A crouched infant burial (F103) dated to the first century BC–first century AD,[7] in the deep enclosure ditch of Ráith na Ríg, Tara, Co. Meath (Roche, 2002, 45), was born locally (Cahill Wilson and Standish, 2016, 233). This burial also combines indigenous and alien burial rites, and may be that of a locally born child with perhaps a combination of indigenous and immigrant parents. Similarly, the crouched burial of a juvenile (Burial B) recovered in the Rath of the Synods, Tara (Grogan, 2008, 42), dated to the fourth century AD,[8] was born locally (Cahill Wilson, 2012, 23; Cahill Wilson and Standish, 2016, 233, Table 1).

While this picture may change with future isotope analysis on further burials, the results so far support the thesis that in the Iron Age, the burial rite of crouched inhumation was introduced into the eastern region of Ireland by immigrants, probably from north-eastern Britain.

---

3 GrN–15395: 1921±50BP; at 2σ (91.0% probability) = cal 4 BC–AD 217. 4 GrN–15369: 1830±30BP; at 2σ = cal AD 86–253. 5 GrN–15372: 2095±20BP; at 2σ = cal 175–50 BC. 6 UBA–13072: 2057±25BP; at 2σ = cal 165 BC–AD 3. 7 UB–4476: 1973±28BP; at 2σ = cal 42 BC–78 AD. 8 Date obtained from charcoal located close to the burial, therefore needs to be treated with caution. UBA–8533: 1691±20BP; at 2σ = cal AD 260–405; at 87.3% probability = cal AD 325–405.

EARLY MEDIEVAL

Records exist for extensive travel, mainly by clerics, between Ireland, Britain and continental Europe, in the Early Medieval period.[9] In the fifth century, the kingdom of Dál Ríada was extended from north-eastern Ireland to the west coast of Scotland (Byrne, 1973, 9, 108, 110–13), and in AD 563 Columba left Ireland and founded his monastery in the island of Iona, in the kingdom of Dál Ríada. Adomnán in his Life of Columba (*Adomnán* [i.22] [i.30] [ii.14] [ii.15] [ii.45], Anderson and Anderson, 1991, 48–9, 56–7, 112–13, 114–15, 174–9) records voyages between Ireland and Iona as a common occurrence. In AD 590, Columbanus left the monastery at Bangor in Ireland, to start his famous journeys through Europe. Bede records (*HE* iii.3, Colgrave and Mynors, 1969, 218–19) that Oswald had received his Christian education among the Irish, and that the first bishop of Lindisfarne, Aidan, was an Irishman from Iona. Bede also refers (*HE* iii.27, Colgrave and Mynors, 312–13) to English 'nobles and commons' who went to Ireland either for religious studies or to live a more ascetic life. He also mentions the presence of English monks at the monastery of *Rath Melsigi*, identified as possibly Clonmelsh (*Cluain Melsigi*) in Co. Carlow,[10] the site of which has unfortunately been largely quarried away (Ó Cróinín, 1984, 23; Fanning, 1984, 43–9). The Irish monk, Fursa, travelled to East Anglia *c.*AD 636 where he founded a monastery at *Cnobheresburg* (Burgh Castle, Suffolk). When, in AD 640–1, Fursa travelled onwards to the Continent where he founded a monastery at Lagney on the Marne, he left his brother Foillán behind in *Cnobheresburg* as abbot (*HE* iii.19). Towards the end of the seventh century, Aldhelm, in correspondence with Heahfrith and Wihtfrith, was scathing in his remarks about the numbers of Englishmen travelling to Ireland to further their education 'whither assemble the thronging students by the fleet-load' (Lapidge and Herren, 1979, 139, 143, 154–5, 160–4).

Within Ireland, the laws laid down that 'Except when on military service or pilgrimage or when attending an *óenach* outside the territory, the ordinary freeman stays within his own *túath*. Beyond its borders he normally does not have rights: only the learned classes appear to be entitled to travel freely' (Kelly, 1988, 4). However, recent strontium and oxygen analysis undertaken on a selection of burials now indicates that while some persons, male and female, were born, spent their formative years, and were buried at their place of birth, or were returned to that place for burial, others travelled widely within the country and were buried at some remove from their place of birth. Locals and non-locals were often buried in ancestral *ferta*, which were already ancient monuments in the landscape when these burials took place. But what about those who arrived from overseas? A male immigrant, known in the Early Medieval period as *cú glas* ('grey hound/wolf'), would have had no legal status or honour price in his own right. If a male immigrant married an Irish woman, he attained half his wife's honour price (Kelly, 1988, 6). Yet, surprisingly, some of these male immigrants appear to be the foundation burials in newly established secular communal cemeteries, hence they were the possible progenitors of a family line as in Ninch 2 and 3, and Holdenstown 1.

---

9 For more detail on these records see O'Brien, 1999a, 45–51.   10 Located south of the modern town of Carlow, and approximately 2km east of the navigable River Barrow.

The following analysis, detailed in Gazetteer 5, is based on the results of strontium and oxygen isotope analysis undertaken on a selection of fifty-four burials, from twenty sites (Map 7), dateable to the Early Medieval period.[11] While this selection represents only a fraction of excavated burials, it nevertheless gives a glimpse into the movement of individuals and groups during the period. Ongoing research will inevitably broaden this picture.

A review of the fifty-four burials listed in Gazetteer 5 reveals the following: ten individuals (seven male and three female) are probable immigrants from overseas, nine individuals (one male, six female, one adult unsexed, and one juvenile) may have been born in Ireland but equally may have been born in Britain, eleven individuals (five male, six female) are Irish, but were not born in the locality in which they were buried, and, unsurprisingly, twenty-four individuals (eleven male, nine female, two adult unsexed, and two juvenile) were buried in the locality of their birth.

Immigrants who probably had their origin overseas include, an elderly male (F181) dated to the fourth–sixth century,[12] at Betaghstown (Anchorage), Co. Meath, buried tightly crouched but inserted into a full-length stone-lined grave (Figure 6.6), who had his probable origin in eastern Europe or Scandinavia (Cahill Wilson et al., 2014, 139–40). This burial combines the alien rite of crouched inhumation with a full-length indigenous-type grave, which, when back-filled, would appear similar to surrounding graves in the cemetery. This might be a possible indication that he had been accepted by the indigenous inhabitants of the district, or it may be an attempt by those responsible for the crouched burial to blend in with the surrounding graves. Crouched male (B12), dated to the fourth–seventh century,[13] buried in a dug pit grave at nearby Betaghstown (Brookside), Co. Meath, was probably born in the Mediterranean region of North Africa or southern Spain (Cahill Wilson and Standish, 2016, 237). This individual appears to have been buried by his peers, overtly using their alien burial rite, but in an indigenous burial zone. He was probably a trader, as Mediterranean-type pottery has been recovered throughout this geographical area (Kelly, 2010, 49–52). This hypothesis is reinforced by recent isotope research that has identified five individuals in cemeteries in south-western Wales, and an individual in the cemetery at Balladoole, Isle of Man, whose origins also appear to have been in the North African region of the Mediterranean (Hemer et al., 2013, 2356; 2014, 246). Further burials of immigrants at the Brookside cemetery include, female extended burial (B14), dated to the fourth–sixth century,[14] who had her origin in either Britain, continental Europe, or Scandinavia (Cahill Wilson and Standish, 2016, 238), extended male burials (B13), undated, and (B13A), dated to the fifth–seventh century,[15] who both originated in south-eastern Scotland/Greater Yorkshire, or continental Europe (Cahill Wilson, 2010); and female crouched burial (B11), dated to the fifth–seventh century,[16] has not been subjected to isotopic analysis, but her clothing accessories (Figure 5.4) suggest that her background is either British or Anglo-Saxon.

---

[11] This analysis does not include known Viking burials, as these are outside the scope of this publication.   [12] UBA–13071: 1612±22BP; at 2σ = cal AD 394–535.   [13] OxA–2652: 1565±60BP; at 2σ = cal AD 381–621.   [14] OxA–2654: 1620±65BP; at 2σ (90.5% probability) = cal AD 318–580.   [15] OxA–2653: 1530±60BP; at 2σ = cal AD 405–642.   [16] OxA–2651: 1550±60BP; at 2σ = cal AD 394–630.

Mobility of peoples

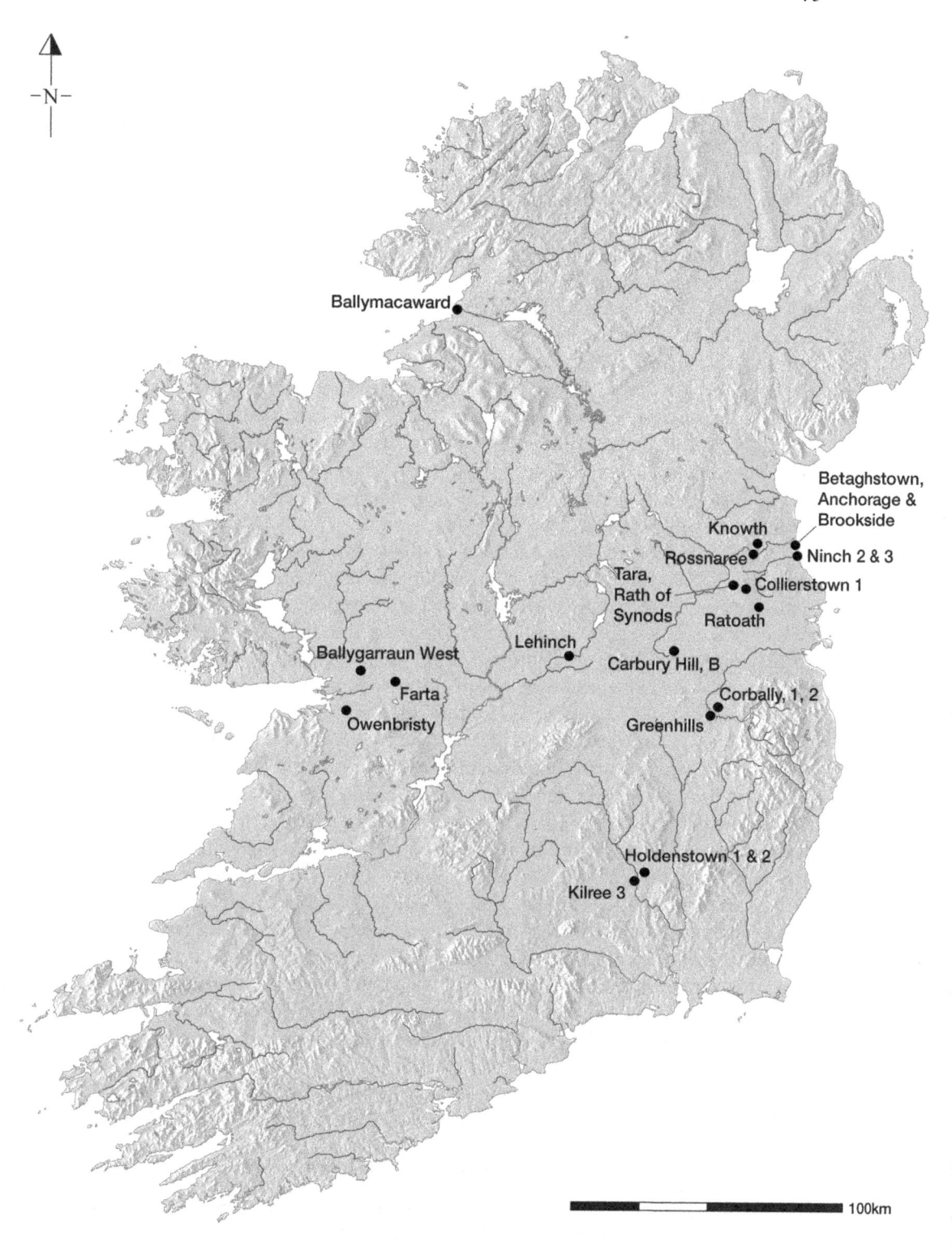

Map 7 Distribution of cemeteries demonstrating Early Medieval population mobility,
© The Discovery Programme and EOB.

An immigrant included among the Early Medieval burials at the passage grave complex at Knowth, Co. Meath (Eogan, 1974, 68–7; O'Brien and Weekes, 2012, 45–71), is male burial (B14), dated to the seventh–ninth century.[17] This individual, who may have been decapitated and was buried at the base of the defensive ditch which had been dug around the main passage-grave mound in the Early Medieval period, had his origin probably in eastern Scotland, or perhaps in Scandinavia (Cahill Wilson, 2012, 230–41). As there was a known Pictish presence in Ireland in the seventh century as related by Adomnán when he mentions a priest Iógenán who was a Pict located in Leinster (*Adomnán* [ii.9], Anderson and Anderson, 1991, 106–7), and at Knowth in the eighth century (Byrne, 2008, 99–102, 114–15), it is possible that this person may have been a Pict from eastern Scotland.

Centrally placed in the unenclosed cemetery at Ninch 3, Co. Meath (Powell, 2004), a small penannular ring-ditch surrounded a single family grave containing two adults and two juveniles. The adult male (B25), dated to the fourth–sixth century,[18] appears to have originated in central or eastern Europe (Cahill Wilson et al., 2014, 144–5). The accompanying female (B28), who was Irish, allowed him to integrate. By being buried in a grave surrounded by a ring-ditch this family was marked out as being special or different, perhaps because the female was of an elite status, or perhaps because the family were regarded as pagan.

Two of the earliest burials in the nearby settlement cemetery, Ninch 2, Co. Louth (Plate 5a) (McConway, 2010, 157–72), were immigrants. Male (B856), dated to the sixth–seventh century,[19] probably originated in central or eastern Europe (Cahill Wilson et al., 2014, 144–5), and female (B770), dated to the seventh century,[20] also possibly originated in eastern Europe, but could have originated in Britain (ibid.). These burials and their graves were indistinguishable from the remainder of the graves in the cemetery. Is this an indication that they were accepted by the local community? Or, could they be the founders of a new community and cemetery?

Individuals who returned ambivalent results indicating that while there was a possibility that their origins were in Ireland, it was also likely that they originated in Britain, include the unique burial of a female and horse dated to the fourth–sixth century[21] inserted into the Bronze Age mound at Farta, Co. Galway; this burial has produced isotope results which show that neither the woman nor the horse was of local origin (Cahill Wilson et al., 2014, 141–2; Cahill Wilson and Standish, 2016, 238). While both may have originated in the eastern region of Ireland, their signature is also consistent with a possible origin in eastern Britain. There is a burial of a female associated with a horse at the cemetery of Sedgeford, Norfolk (Cross, 2009, 25–7; Faulkner, et al., 2014, 96–7), but direct comparison with the Farta woman's burial is unlikely as the horse at Sedgeford has been dated to the seventh–ninth century,[22] which is considerably later than the Farta burial.

The elderly female, dated to the fifth–seventh century,[23] buried in an isolated grave at Ballygarraun West, Co. Galway, accompanied by a fragment of deer antler

---

17 GrN–1335: 1260±40BP; at 2σ = cal AD 666–875.   18 UBA–20057: 1620±24BP; at 2σ = cal AD 390–535.   19 UBA–20055: 1404±19BP; at 2σ = cal AD 549–633.   20 UBA–20056: 1479±20BP; at 2σ = cal AD 607–59.   21 Female: OxA-X–2488.42: 1625±26BP; at 2σ = cal AD 383–536. Horse: UBA–23699: 1618±26BP; at 2σ = cal AD 388–536.   22 At 2σ = cal AD 670–820 (full reference awaited).   23 UBA–7683: 1471±67BP; at 2σ = cal AD 428–661.

(Figure 5.8a), and domestic hearth residue, did not spend her formative years in the place where she was buried; she had her origins either in the eastern part of Ireland, or in Britain (Cahill Wilson et al., 2014, 137; Cahill Wilson and Standish, 2016, 233, 238).

The probable foundation burial, male (B59), dated to the fifth–sixth century,[24] in the cemetery of Holdenstown 2, Co. Kilkenny (Whitty and Tobin, 2009, 19–21; O'Brien and Bhreathnach, 2011, 53–64), was not born locally but originated either in the south-eastern corner of Ireland, or probably in northern or western Britain (Montgomery and Milns, 2010, 10, 14). Coincidentally, a female burial (B2), dated to the sixth–seventh century,[25] in the nearby *ferta* cemetery at Holdenstown 1, Co. Kilkenny, may also have originated in the far south-eastern corner of Ireland, but could also have originated in northern or western Britain (ibid.). Although this burial took place some time after the burial at Holdenstown 2, it might be an indication of a continuing link between a kin-group in the south-east of Ireland or northern-western Britain, and the kin-group in the region of Holdenstown, Co. Kilkenny.

At the unusual site of Kilree 3, Co. Kilkenny, located on the opposite side of the River Nore from Holdenstown (Maeve Tobin, pers. comm.; Kelly, 2009), female burial (B4), dated to the seventh–ninth century,[26] is not from the locality. She, also, may have originated either in the south-eastern corner of Ireland, or in northern or western Britain (Montgomery and Milns, 2010, 10, 14).

At Knowth, Co. Meath (Eogan, 1974, 68–87; O'Brien and Weekes, 2012, 45–71), female burial (B18), undated, who appears to have been hastily interred, was not from the locality. She originated either in the northern part of Ireland, or in northern Britain (Cahill Wilson, 2012, 780–5).[27] Also at Knowth, a young adult of unknown sex (B27) undated, and an adolescent (B32) dated to the eighth–ninth century,[28] who was buried in a slab-lined grave, came from either the north-eastern region of Ireland, or northern Britain (Cahill Wilson, 2012, 775–8; Cahill Wilson and Standish, 2016, 230–41).

There are several individuals who did not have their origins at their place of burial, but whose origins were elsewhere in Ireland. Female (B28), dated to the fifth–sixth century,[29] who formed part of the probable family group of two adults and two children buried within a small penannular ring-ditch at Ninch 3, Co. Meath, was not born locally but had her origin in north-eastern Ireland (Cahill Wilson et al., 2014, 144–5). The excavation report (Powell, 2004) indicates that the female was interred in the grave before the accompanying male, who was an immigrant possibly from central or eastern Europe, and before the two children. It is therefore probable that she was the person of importance in this group, with a rank that entitled her to burial in a ring-ditch. The accompanying male, as an immigrant, would have been regarded as being of an inferior rank, but possibly claimed a higher rank due to his association with the woman. It would be an interesting exercise if DNA samples from this group could be sequenced to identify whether this is in fact a family group, and further compared to other burials from the cemetery to establish whether or not they represent the progenitors of a kin-group.

---

[24] UBA–13669: 1569±22BP; at 2σ = cal AD 427–544.   [25] UB–15562: 1464±30BP; at 2σ = cal AD 551–646.   [26] UBA–13670: 1229±26BP; at 2σ = cal AD 690–882.   [27] Incorrectly published as B16.   [28] UBA–11697: 1210±28BP; at 2σ = cal AD 710–891.   [29] UBA–20058: 1529±20BP; at 2σ = cal

Female (B4) (Figure 4.2a, Plate 11), dated to the sixth–seventh century,[30] interred in a dug grave in the female ancestral burial monument at Ballymacaward, Co. Donegal, was not born locally, but had her origin in the north-eastern region of Ireland, with a slight possibility of the south-eastern region (Cahill Wilson et al., 2014, 138–9; Cahill Wilson and Standish, 2016, 238); therefore, her burial took place on the opposite side of the country to her place of birth.

Several of the burials at the important ancestral burial place on Carbury Hill, Site B, Co. Kildare, were born in Ireland, but not in the locality in which they were buried (Figures 4.7, 4.8). Male (SK 4), dated to the third–fourth century,[31] one of the earliest dated Early Medieval extended inhumation burials in the country, had his probable origin in the west of Ireland; female (SK 10), dated to the fourth–fifth century,[32] also had her origin in the west of Ireland; and female (SK 6), dated to the fifth–sixth century,[33] had her probable origin in the Kerry coastal region, in the far south-west of Ireland (Cahill Wilson and Standish, 2016, 237–8). Another individual who appears to have started her life on the Kerry coastline was female (B16), undated, in the cemetery located along the eastern coastline at Betaghstown (Brookside), Co. Meath (Cahill Wilson, 2010).

It is of interest that recent research on Early Medieval burials in cemeteries in south Wales has identified at least four individuals who had been born, and spent their early years, near the extreme western coast of Ireland or possibly Britain (Hemer et al., 2013, 2356), indicating a possible degree of outward mobility from Ireland during the period. This is not surprising, as an Irish presence in Wales is known from memorial stones of the period which incorporate inscriptions of Irish personal names in ogam characters and Latin script.[34]

The elderly female (B2), dated to the fourth–sixth century,[35] who was buried in a kiln at Corbally 1, Co. Kildare, was born in Ireland, but not locally. She had moved to the area sometime before her death (Daly, 2015). This elderly woman, who had Paget's disease of her skull (Keating, 2004, 35–8) and whose body had been covered with large stones, may have been buried in this way because she was feared due to her deformity. Two individuals at Owenbristy, Co. Galway (Lehane and Delaney, 2010; Delaney and Tierney, 2011, 71–109), were born in Ireland, but not in the locality of their place of burial. Male (SK 70), dated to the sixth–seventh century,[36] who was buried crouched and wearing a neck ring (Plate 6), had his origin further to the east in Ireland (Evans and Chenery, 2010, 348), and extended male (SK 31), dated to the sixth–seventh century,[37] also had his origin further to the east in Ireland (ibid.). The crouched disposition of SK 70 suggests that his body may have been trussed to enable transport to his place of burial.

Three burials (E, I, D) at the Rath of the Synods, Tara, Co. Meath (Grogan, 2008, 45–9), were born in Ireland, but are not local to their place of burial. Male burial (E), semi-crouched, head to the east, dated to the eighth–ninth century,[38] and male burial (I), semi-crouched, head to the east, undated, both had their origins in the northern

AD 435–547.   30 UB–4172: 1448±40BP; at 2σ = cal AD 570–650.   31 UBA–20008: 1747±37BP; at 2σ (93.5% probability) = cal AD 211–394.   32 UBA–20010: 1659±23BP; at 2σ = cal AD 335–425.   33 UBA–20009: 1535±24BP; at 2σ = cal AD 428–591.   34 See p. 50.   35 UBA–30393: 1636±41BP; at 2σ = cal AD 332–539.   36 UB–11248: 1457±36BP; at 2σ = cal AD 547–652.   37 UB–11233: 1402±33BP; at 2σ = cal AD 590–671.   38 UBA–11698: 1205±24BP; at 2σ = cal AD

regions of Ireland (Cahill Wilson, 2012, 23–5). Male burial (D), extended, head to the north, both hands missing, dated to the thirteenth century,[39] had his origin in the southern midlands of Ireland (ibid.). I have suggested that burials E and I were deliberately brought to this royal site and buried in a non-conformist fashion because of a belief that they were entitled to burial at this royal place. Burial D, who was located on the edge of the site, just outside the boundary wall of the burial ground attached to the nearby Medieval church, may be a punitive burial, deliberately buried outside the church boundary, and therefore may not be directly associated with burial at the Rath of the Synods.

Unsurprisingly, individuals born in or close to the cemetery in which they were buried form the largest segment of the burials sampled. The elderly female (B3) (Plate 10) at the female ancestral burial monument at Ballymacaward, Co. Donegal, dated to the fifth–sixth century,[40] in a slab-lined grave, was born locally. Three burials at Betaghstown (Brookside), Co. Meath, were born locally. These are, an extended adult (B2) dated to the fifth–seventh century,[41] a male (B15) dated to the fourth–seventh century,[42] both in slab-lined graves, and an undated extended adult (B10) (Cahill Wilson, 2010; Cahill Wilson and Standish, 2016, 237). The young adult female (B48) dated to the fifth–sixth century,[43] who was the foundation burial at Collierstown 1, Co. Meath (O'Brien, 2007; O'Hara, 2009a; 2009b, 83–100), a high-status secular communal cemetery, located on the bank of the sacred River Gabhra, which rises at nearby Tara, was born locally (Cahill Wilson et al., 2014, 140–1). At Carbury Hill, Site B, Co. Kildare, three male burials were individuals who were born locally (Cahill Wilson and Standish, 2016, 237–8). One of these, male (SK 1), dated to the sixth–seventh century,[44] was unique in that he was accompanied by an iron shears (Figure 5.5).

At Corbally 1, Co. Kildare (Tobin, 2003, 32–7; Tobin and Sunderland, 2004), male (B5), dated to the fourth–sixth century,[45] buried centrally within a ring-ditch, and young male (B1), dated to the fifth–sixth century,[46] were both born locally. The latter moved from the region at about age 9 years but was returned to the region for burial with his kin (Daly, 2015). The only outsider at this burial place was the woman (B2) who had been buried in a kiln. Five of the burials at Corbally 2, Co. Kildare (Coyne, 2003; Coyne and Lynch, 2010, 77–90), were all born locally (Daly 2015). These consisted of female burials (B90, B92), located within a ring-ditch, and dated to the fourth–sixth century,[47] female burial (B27), dated to the fifth–seventh century,[48] interred in the entrance to a ring-ditch, female burial (B75), undated, and male burial (B42), undated.

In the *ferta* site Holdenstown 1, Co. Kilkenny, male (B8), dated to the fifth–sixth century,[49] was born locally (Montgomery and Milns, 2010, 10). In view of the presence at this and at the adjoining cemetery, Holdenstown 2, of possible immigrants, this

721–890.   **39** UBA–9092: 732±28BP; at 2σ = cal AD 1224–1296.   **40** UB–4171: 1592±20BP; at 2σ = cal AD 420–540.   **41** OxA–2648: 1460±70BP; at 2σ = cal AD 425–670.   **42** OxA–2655: 1560±60BP; at 2σ (95.1% probability) = cal AD 381–638.   **43** BA–250161: 1550±40BP; at 2σ = cal AD 422–596.   **44** UBA–11696: 1491±28BP; at 2σ (93.5% probability) = cal AD 535–643.   **45** UBA–31469: 1619±27BP; at 2σ = cal AD 383–537.   **46** UBA–30392: 1539±30BP; at 2σ = cal AD 426–586.   **47** B92. Beta–194919: 1630±50BP; at 2σ (93.1% probability) = cal AD 325–550.   **48** Beta–194918: 1460±60BP; at 2σ = cal AD 429–665.   **49** UBA–13659: 1556±23BP; at 2σ = cal AD 429–558.

man may represent the amalgamation of an indigenous community with a newly arrived people.

At Knowth, Co. Meath, female (B33), dated to the seventh century,[50] in a slab-lined grave, was born locally (Cahill Wilson, 2012, 775–8; Cahill Wilson and Standish, 2016, 230–41). This burial was situated beside the slab-lined grave of adolescent (B32), who was born either in the northern part of Ireland or northern Britain. Burial (G3) at Lehinch, Co. Offaly (Ó Floinn, 2011, 143–5), sex undetermined, dated to the fifth–sixth century,[51] who was accompanied by deer antler and portions of horse meat, was born locally (Cahill Wilson, 2014, 144). The presence of the horse portions may indicate a possible, but tenuous, link, illustrated by the use of a roughly similar ritual, between this burial and the burial of the woman and horse at Farta, Co. Galway, who has a possible origin in the eastern part of Ireland.

Three of the individuals in the cemetery at Owenbristy, Co. Galway, had their origins in the local area (Evans and Chenery, 2010, 384). These were, adult male (SK 9), dated to the sixth–seventh century,[52] who had been decapitated, adolescent (SK 53), dated to the seventh–eighth century,[53] who had been subjected to peri-mortem head trauma, and young adult female (SK 25), undated. The adult male and the adolescent, who died as a result of conflict, were nevertheless accorded burial in their communal cemetery. In the cemetery at Ratoath, Co. Meath (Wallace, 2010, 295–316), a young adult female (B38) dated to the sixth–seventh century,[54] wearing a neck collar (Figure 5.1 (a)), has been identified as local, but with a very slight possibility of an origin in the east of England (Montgomery and Grimes, 2010, 309–11). The closest parallel to the neck collar is in the Anglo-Saxon cemetery at Bergh Apton, Norfolk (Figure 5.1 (b)) (Green and Rogerson, 1978, 35, 76), which may reflect familial connections between the occupants of this cemetery and Anglo-Saxon England.

At Greenhills, Co. Kildare (Keeley, 1991a, 180–201), a juvenile (B16) aged 6–9 years, one of two burials in a small penannular ring-ditch, was born locally (Cahill Wilson et al., 2014, 142). The second burial, a female (B15) who has been dated to the fourth–sixth century,[55] unfortunately had no teeth which could be used for isotopic analysis. These individuals were set apart from the remainder of the cemetery by being enclosed within a ring-ditch (Figure 4.14b).

The female buried at Rossnaree, Co. Meath (Cahill and Sikora, 2011, 113–20), dated fourth–fifth century,[56] accompanied by an infant, and with fragments of a silver ring with herring-bone decoration (Figure 4.10) similar to a design used on Roman finger rings, was born locally (Cahill Wilson et al., 2014a, 130). The fourth burial (H) at the Rath of the Synods, Tara, Co. Meath, an extended male, dated to the tenth–eleventh century,[57] has been identified as having been born locally (Cahill Wilson, 2012, 23–5). As with burials E and I, it is probable that either he, or his peers, considered that he was entitled to burial at this royal site.

If in future research, laser ablation could be undertaken on teeth from individuals identified as having been interred at a distance from their birthplace, it could provide

[50] GrN–15384: 1355±20BP; at 2σ = cal AD 645–83. [51] GrA–24445: 1625±40BP; at 2σ = cal AD 399–541. [52] UB–11223: 1407±30BP; at 2σ = cal AD 594–666. [53] UB–11238: 1263±17BP; at 2σ = cal AD 683–776. [54] Beta–196361: 1410±40BP; at 2σ = cal AD 569–671. [55] UBA–20007: 1622±23BP; at 2σ = cal AD 388–535. [56] GrA–24354: 1660±40BP; at 2σ (76.2% probability) = cal AD 317–435. [57] UBA–9030: 1055±26BP; at 2σ (87% probability) = cal AD 950–1024.

evidence as to the age at which they left their place of birth, and the route taken on their journey to their place of interment.

* * *

While historical records exist for frequent travel, mainly by clerics, between Ireland, Britain and continental Europe in the Early Medieval period, the concept has persisted that, except in exceptional circumstances, individuals in Ireland did not travel outside their own territory. However, emerging research in the use of strontium and isotope analysis on teeth, which can help indicate the possible place of an individual's birth, is challenging this concept. This small selection is only the start of ongoing research that will inevitably identify further trends in the mobility of individuals and groups into and within Ireland in the Iron Age and in the Early Medieval period. It is already possible to advance the thesis that in the Iron Age the rite of crouched inhumation was introduced into the eastern region of Ireland by immigrants from Britain. For the Early Medieval period, evidence is emerging that while some of the indigenous population travelled throughout the country, others remained at their place of birth, and immigrants have also been identified. Analysis undertaken on fifty-five burials, from twenty cemetery sites, dating to the Early Medieval period, has revealed ten individuals who appear to be immigrants from overseas, nine individuals who may or may not be immigrants, eleven individuals who were born in Ireland, but not at their place of burial, and twenty-four individuals who were buried in the locality in which they were born. The majority of those designated as immigrants were buried in local communal cemeteries, an indication that these individuals had apparently become integrated into local society. While a number of individuals did not move outside their local home territory, others, some of whom might represent marriage alliances, travelled throughout the country. Current ongoing isotopic research in Britain is adding to our knowledge of the presence of people of probable Irish origin in Wales and in the Isle of Man during the Early Medieval period.

CHAPTER 8

Unusual or exceptional women: evidence from the grave

> Exaggerated claims have sometimes been made about the degree of power and freedom enjoyed by women in early Irish society. It is certainly true that women feature prominently in Old and Middle Irish literature ... But in real life, the power of women was undoubtedly much more restricted.
>
> (Kelly, 1988, 68–9)

Early Irish laws, canons, rules and regulations, were drawn up by lawmakers and clergy for an ideal society, but everyday reality was undoubtedly quite different. Laws do not always take human emotion into account, and the following examples of how some women were selected for special treatment in death is probably reflective of how they were perceived in life.

IRON AGE

Before considering Early Medieval women's burials, it is worth taking a brief look at some Iron Age burials of probably important, and unusual, women. A cremation deposit dated third century BC–first century AD,[1] inserted into the ancestral burial mound at Ballymacaward, Co. Donegal (O'Brien, 1999b, 56–61), has been identified as female (McKinley, 1998). As this is the first of a succession of females interred in this ancestral monument she had probably been accorded the status of an ancestor. At Knockcommane, Co. Limerick (Molloy, 2007; McQuade et al., 2009, 163–5), a cremation deposit that has been identified as female was recovered in a small pit centrally placed within an Iron Age penannular enclosure. At Ballyboy 1, Co. Galway (McNamara, 2010a; Delaney and Tobin, 2010; McNamara and Delaney, 2013, 123–37), a cremation deposit (C11) identified as female, dated first century BC–first century AD,[2] was recovered beside a post-hole at the centre of the enclosure. The cremation deposit, centrally placed in a pit in a small Iron Age annular ring-ditch at Annaghilla (Site 4), Co. Tyrone, has been identified as an adult female (Dunlop and Barkley, 2016, 105) dated second–first century BC.[3] The central placement within ring-ditches of the cremation deposits of these females demonstrates that they were regarded as important, and of high status, within their communities.

The earliest dated crouched Iron Age inhumation burial at Knowth, Co. Meath, is a female (B10) (Figure 2.5b), dated second–first century BC,[4] who was born locally (Eogan, G., 2012; O'Brien, 2010, 61–71; McGarry, 2012, 689–94; Cahill Wilson, 2012, 782). Although she was born locally, this woman was buried by those who were familiar

---

1 UB-4196: 2091±56BP; at 2σ (87.7% probability) = 212 cal BC–cal AD 26. 2 UBA-13025: 2019±23BP; at 2σ = 90 cal BC–cal AD 53 (at 91.9% probability = 59 cal BC–cal AD 53). 3 SUERC-21380: 2090±30BP; at 2σ = 195–46 cal BC. 4 GrN-15372: 2095±20BP; at 2σ = 175–50 cal BC.

with an alien burial rite. Perhaps this was seen as a means of establishing a link between the indigenous population and newly arrived immigrants. Another female, whose burial could reflect a similar role, was the female, undated, who was inserted in a crouched posture into the fill of the Iron Age ring-ditch at Rath, Co. Meath (Schweitzer, 2005, 93–8). She had three copper-alloy rings on her toes, two were spiral rings, which appear to be sandal attachments, and the third ring, on her right foot, is purely decorative, with a herring-bone design commonly associated with Roman contexts. This woman was of local origin (Montgomery et al., 2006), but was buried crouched, and probably clothed in a non-Irish fashion, thereby making a statement that would have been visible to those who attended and observed her funeral.

Two burials which represent women who were probably rejected or feared by their community, both in life and in death, are female (B4), at Knowth, Co. Meath (Figure 2.5a), dated first–third century AD,[5] whose burial posture was prone and splayed, an indication of possible punitive burial. The fact that she was weighted down with a large stone on her back suggests that this was to prevent her returning to haunt the living. She was probably born locally, but there is a slight possibility that she came from further afield (Cahill Wilson et al., 2014, 141–2). Crouched female (F238) (Figure 2.6), dated second–first century BC,[6] at Betaghstown (Anchorage), Co. Meath (Eogan, J., 2010, 106), also had a large stone placed over her body. This woman was not born in Ireland, but had her origins either in south-eastern Scotland or Yorkshire (with a slight possibility that she originated in mainland Europe) (Cahill Wilson et al., 2014, 139). She may have been feared in life, perhaps because she was an outsider, hence the presence of the large stone to prevent her from returning to haunt the living.

EARLY MEDIEVAL

In Early Medieval Ireland important women are recorded as wives, mothers, sisters, or daughters, of kings, and while they were obviously regarded as important in their various roles, we have little personal information about them.[7] There are, of course, exceptions. For example, the death of an abbess, Condal, daughter of Murchad, abbess of the elders' house at Kildare, is recorded at AD797 (*Chron. Ire.*). Sources also indicate that during the Early Medieval period, high-ranking British and Pictish women were believed to have married into Irish ruling families. These were the mothers or wives of the mythical ancestors of various dynasties, and at least two of these are believed to have been married to known historic figures: Erc, daughter of Loarn (Cenél Loarn of the Dál Ríada), was the reputed wife of Muiredach, and mother of Muirchertach, king of Tara (d. AD434–6), and Caintigern, daughter of Conndach (Alba), was wife of Faichnae Lurgan, king of the Ulaid, and mother of Mongán (d. AD625).[8]

Between the seventh and ninth centuries, the deaths of eleven queens are recorded in the annals:[9]

---

[5] GrN–15369: 1830±30BP; at 2σ = cal AD 86–253. [6] UBA–13072: 2057±25BP; at 2σ = 165 cal BC–cal AD 3. [7] For information on the legal capacity of women see Kelly, 1988, 75–8. [8] Thanks to Dr Edel Bhreathnach and Anne Connon for discussions on this material. [9] All are referenced to *Chron. Ire.*

AD 643: Uasal, daughter of Suibne, queen (wife) of Fáelán, king of the Laigin.
AD 732: Cellach, daughter of Dúnchad of the Uí Liatháin, an excellent and kindly queen.
AD 748: Muireann, daughter of Cellach of Cualu, Írgalach's queen.
AD 754: Thaithlaithe, daughter of Cathal, queen of the Leinstermen.
AD 768: Eithne, daughter of Bresal of Brega, the queen of the kings of Tara.
AD 795: Bran Arddchenn, king of the Leinstermen, was killed and also his queen Eithne, daughter of Domnall of Mide.
AD 801: Bé Fáil, daughter of Cathal, Donnchad's queen.
AD 802: Éuginis, daughter of Donnchad, queen of the king of Tara.
AD 854: Muirgel, queen of the Leinstermen.
AD 861: Gormlaith, daughter of Donnchad, the most delightful queen of the Irish.
AD 890: Flann, daughter of Dúngal, queen of the king of Tara.

There are no references in the annals to a place of burial for any of these women.

Further references to named women of importance are included in texts such as the *Banshenchas* ('Lore of Women'), compiled in the eleventh–twelfth century, which provides lists of famous Irish women who had lived prior to that time (Connon, 2000, 98–108; 2005, 225–327); the Middle Irish *Metrical dindshenchas* ('Topographical lore of Ireland') has a list of 'buried women', which associates the names of various burial mounds or *ferta* with women who were purported to have been buried in these monuments (Gwynn, 1903, 35), and 'A list of the Mothers of the Saints' (Ó Riain, 1985, 169–81) provides names of putative mothers of Irish saints.

The two seventh-century Lives of Brigit, the leading Irish female saint, *Vita prima* (Connolly, 1989, 5–49) and *Cogitosus: Life of Saint Brigit* (Connolly and Picard, 1987, 11–27), have little to say about her death, recorded as AD 524–6. At §129.2 in *Vita prima* it is simply recorded that 'Brigit departed this life ... amid the ranks of angels and archangels'. Some possible information regarding her final resting place is provided at *Cogitosus*, §32, which states that the 'glorious bodies of Archbishop Conleth (Brigit's Bishop) and the virgin Brigit are laid on the right and left of the ornate altar and rest in tombs adorned with a refined profusion of gold, silver, gems and precious stones'. In an Irish context this is a unique record, but the description does not appear to be apocryphal, because Cogitosus, when writing his description of the church (a building that is also a unique record for that time), gives the impression that he is describing something with which he is personally familiar. It must be borne in mind that Cogitosus was writing about this church in the latter half of the seventh century, over a century after Brigit's death. An in-depth examination of Cogitosus's intent and inspiration has been published by Lisa Bitel (Bitel, 2004, 605–27). There are no further references in subsequent early literature to these tombs, nor to the layout of the church at Kildare.

The deaths of a further three important early Irish female saints are also recorded, and we assume that they were buried in the ecclesiastic establishments to which they were attached: Dar Ercae (also known as Mo Ninne), of Killevy, Co. Armagh, died AD 517; Íde (Íta) of Cluain Credail (Killeedy), Co. Cork, died AD 570; and Samhtann of Cluain Brónaig (Clonbroney), Co. Longford, died AD 739 (*Chron. Ire.*).[10]

10 For the Life of Dar Ercae (Esposito, 1910, 202–51; Ó Riain, 2011, 495–7). Life of Íde (Ó Riain,

There is ambivalence in the seventh–eighth-century literature about where, and with whom, women ought to be buried. Rules contained in *Hib.* XVIII, *De jure Sepulturae* ('Concerning the Law of Burial') (Wasserschleben, 1885, 55), reveal conflicting views on this subject. On the one hand, Cap. I, *De viris et uxoribus in uno sepulcro sepeliendis* ('Concerning [the rule that] husband and wife [should be] buried in one grave'), contains five rules. The first two relate to Old Testament burials, but the following three are more specific: (c) 'Jerome: Those whom one marriage joins together, let one tomb join together, because there is one body, and that which God has joined together, man may not separate'; (d) 'Augustine: Each woman should follow her man, whether in life or in death'; and (e) 'In the Acts of the Apostles: Arising they buried the man and returning they found his wife dead and carried [her] to her husband'. However, on the other hand, Cap. II, *De eo, quod in paterno sepulcro sepeliendum est* ('Concerning the rule that someone should be buried in the paternal grave'),[11] contains two rules, the first of which contradicts those in Cap. I: (a) 'A Roman Synod[12] says: Whether it be a man or woman, let them be buried in his-her paternal tomb'. Also, Cap. IV, *De eo, quod mulier post mortem viri libera sit sicut in vita, ita in morte* ('Concerning the fact that just as in life a woman may be free after the death of her husband, so also in death'), contains two rules, the second of which states (b) 'Paul: a woman is bound by the law of her husband during the life of her husband, however after the death of her husband she has been released from the law of the husband; because if she is permitted to marry, how much more freedom will she have for being buried'.

In a seventh-century fragmentary Old Irish law dealing with marriage disputes, ruling §38, '*Ní hadnaghar og lighiu fir l mna* ('One is not buried at the grave of husband or wife'), details the fines due if one spouse has been buried illegally in those places (Kelly, 2014, 48–9). This indicates that it was illegal, in the case of a divorce, for one spouse to be buried in the grave (or perhaps even in the cemetery) of the other.

In the archaeological record it is almost impossible to detect the burial of a husband and wife unless they were buried together in the same grave and were roughly contemporary, and even then, these might be the burial of siblings. Isotopic analysis, and DNA, could determine if the woman is an incomer, in which case she might be a spouse. On the other hand, a woman who is buried in a separate grave, but perhaps in close proximity to a contemporary male grave, might also be a spouse, and here again the use of isotopic analysis could be used to determine whether or not she is an incomer to the region.

While multiple burials in one grave are occasionally recovered archaeologically, it is often difficult without c14 dating to ascertain whether this is due to successive use of a grave in a crowded cemetery or is the deliberate act of inserting a subsequent burial into a known grave.

There are several instances where the deliberate inclusion of more than one burial in a grave can be demonstrated. For example, at the cemetery at Owenbristy, Co. Galway (Lehane and Delaney, 2010, 86–101), inter-generational re-use was facilitated

---

2011, 275–8). Life of Samhtann (Ó Riain, 2011, 545–6). 11 In an Irish context this could be taken to refer to the familial cemetery, or perhaps the ancestral burial place. 12 *Sinodus Romana* – this references is to a Synod involving those clerics and their churches, located in the southern part of Ireland, who had conformed to the Roman rite, between AD 630–3.

by ease of access to graves which had been lined and covered with stone slabs, but none of these graves contained male and female interred together. The graves contained only: male burials, or adult males accompanied by young children/ adolescents, or adult females accompanied by young children/adolescents, and one grave contained two exceptional females. This suggests that this cemetery was managed in such a manner that a record of burials was available, perhaps based in one family and handed down in oral tradition. Similar multiple burials can be observed at Site D, Morett, Co. Laois, where three females were buried in a single grave, and at Ardsallagh I, Co. Meath, where one grave contained a female adult (B10) and a child (B7) (Randolph Quinney, 2006a). Examples have also been recorded from other cemeteries.

The one exceptional instance where we can be reasonably certain that we are witnessing the deliberate insertion of a male, a female and two children, into a single, family grave is at Ninch 3, Co. Meath (Powell, 2004; Park, 2008). This grave, partially lined with stones which probably supported a removable wooden grave cover, was centrally placed within a penannular ring-ditch, specifically constructed to receive the first interment, that of an adult woman (B28) aged 26–35 years, dated fifth–sixth century.[13] A child (B26), aged 1–5 years, was placed directly above the woman, and child (B27), aged 6–12 years, was placed beside the younger child. An adult man (B25), aged 26–35 years, dated fourth–sixth century,[14] was interred above and slightly to the left of the woman. While this woman did not originate in the locality of her burial, she was born in Ireland, and had her origin in the north-eastern region of the country. The fact that she had been interred within a specifically constructed ring-ditch is an indication that she was regarded as 'different' and was possibly associated with a kin-group of some importance. The accompanying man had his origins probably in central or eastern Europe, and as such would have been regarded legally as a stranger or a *cú glas* ('grey hound/wolf'). Provided that he was recognised as her spouse, this man's status in Irish society depended on that of the woman since his honour price would be half of that of his spouse (Kelly, 1988, 6). The perception that burial in a ring-ditch was possibly reserved for persons of high social status is validated by Tírechán's anachronistic reference to the fifth-century burial of the two daughters of King Loíguire in such a monument (*Tírechán* §26 (20), Bieler, 1979, 144–5).

For the purpose of this chapter a sample of forty-five women, who represent unusual or exceptional individuals dateable to the Early Medieval period, has been chosen. It can be seen from Gazetteer 6 that, where age can be ascertained, these women come from all age groups. Nine are young adults (18–25 years), twenty are middle adults (25–45 years), and thirteen are older adults (45–60+ years).

The archaeological record has revealed that a number of these selected anonymous women were considered by their peers to be of a status that warranted burial either beneath a mound, within an ancestral burial monument, or in a ring-ditch. As several of these burial places were located close to territorial boundaries, the associated women were possibly regarded as guardians of a dynastic territory, and some also became foundation burials, around whose graves communal cemeteries evolved.

13 UBA–20058: 1529±20BP; at 2σ = cal AD 435–547.   14 UBA–20057: 1620±24BP; at 2σ = cal AD 390–535.

An important burial place that appears to have been reserved specifically for the interment of women is the ancestral mound (*ferta*) at Ballymacaward, Co. Donegal, located behind the sand dunes on the northern shore of Ballyshannon Harbour at the mouth of the River Erne, a river which at various times formed a physical boundary between western and northern kingdoms (O'Brien, 1999b, 56–61; Richards, 1999, 170–91; O'Brien and Bhreathnach, 2011, 55–6, 59–60). This monument originated as a Bronze Age cairn. It was re-used in the Iron Age for the insertion of at least two cremation deposits between the third century BC and the first century AD, one of which has been identified as female. Between the first and third century AD a cremation deposit was spread on the ground beside the monument. After a lapse of several centuries, four carefully constructed slab-lined long cists, oriented west–east, containing extended female inhumations, without grave goods, were inserted into the surface of the mound. One of these (B3), an elderly female aged over 60 years (which would have been extreme old age for a woman in that era), who suffered from post-menopausal osteoporosis of the spine, resulting in severe spinal-curvature, has been dated to the fifth–sixth century (Plate 10).[15] The fact that this woman had survived with this degenerative and disabling condition well into old age, by which time she would have been unable to undertake everyday tasks, indicates that she had been cared for by her community for some time. Strontium and oxygen isotope analysis indicates that she had been born and raised in the immediate locality.[16] Her obvious high-standing in her community is further indicated by the fact that she was buried in a well-constructed slab-lined cist, the construction of which would have involved the procuring and transporting of suitable flat slabs to the site, placing these slabs at the base and sides of the grave (one could speculate that the base of the grave may have been lined with furs or vegetation), followed by the careful placing of her body into that grave with whatever ceremonial accompanied the burial, and the sealing of the grave with a stone slab. The final period of use of this burial mound saw the introduction in the sixth–seventh century of nine extended inhumations, all female, laid supine, west–east, in unprotected dug graves. One of these women (B4), dated to the sixth–seventh century,[17] displayed evidence, by the disposition of the skeleton, that she had been wrapped in a winding sheet, an indication that she was probably Christian (Figure 4.2a, Plate 11).[18] Strontium and oxygen analysis reveal that she had not been born locally, but originated in the north-east, or the south-east of Ireland (Cahill Wilson et al., 2014, 138–9; Cahill Wilson and Standish, 2016, 238). Thus, she was an outsider who had moved to this region. A further feature of interest associated with this woman is that she had a groove worn between two of her upper front teeth, which was the result of years of drawing flax fibre through her teeth, an action which was necessary in order to keep the fibre moist when producing flax-thread on a hand-held spindle.[19] A small fresh-water lake known locally as Lough Namanfin, a

---

[15] UB-4171: 1592±20BP; at 2σ = cal AD 420–540.   [16] Analysis conducted by Dr Jacqueline Cahill Wilson for the Mapping Death Project.   [17] UB-4172: 1448±21BP; at 2σ = cal AD 570–650. [18] The reconstruction of the skull of this woman was undertaken by Richard Neave's team, and was then drawn by Jane Brayne, in conjunction with a BBC programme 'Meet the Ancestors' (Richards, 1999, 183–90).   [19] This action would not have been necessary when spinning wool, as wool contains natural oil and a thread could be drawn-out by hand without the need for extra moisture.

modification of *Loch na mBan Finn* ('the lake of the fair (or bright) women'),[20] is located behind the sand dunes, in close proximity to this site. This lake, according to locals, never dries out, and is regarded as a valuable asset, as it is the only source of fresh water adjacent to the seashore. The women who were buried in this ancestral monument may represent an unrecorded female cult or community, which spanned the pre-Christian and Christian eras. Although the final burials at this site appear to be those of Christians, there is no evidence that this possible cult evolved into, or was associated with, a Christian religious community. Burial at the monument ceased in the seventh century, giving rise to the probability that any cult function attached to the *fert* was supressed. An alternative explanation for the inclusion of Early Medieval women in this monument might be provided by the suggestion that in cases when a kin-group moved into territory not formerly held by them, the new king frequently married the daughter of the old king, thus ensuring that the blood of both lines would run in the veins of their progeny. The old king's daughter would thus be seen as an ancestor of this fusion (Connon, 2005, 226; 2009). It may be that the women buried in this monument were regarded as important ancestors of whichever kin-group held the territory at different times.

At Kilcorney, in the Burren, Co. Clare, a slab-lined cist containing the remains of a young woman, dated to the sixth–seventh century,[21] accompanied by infant bones, had been inserted into a prehistoric cairn (Grant, 1995, 31–3; 2006, 553; 2010). This burial undoubtedly represents the burial of a woman, important to her community, who was accorded the status of an ancestor by being buried in a prehistoric cairn (*ferta*) which was located beside a ravine which probably represents a territorial boundary.

The isolated grave of an elderly woman dated to the fifth–seventh century[22] beneath a small cairn at Ballygarraun, Co. Galway, was probably the burial of a family matriarch. This woman, who was not born locally, but was either from the eastern part of Ireland, or possibly Britain, was buried in an isolated grave, not associated with a *ferta*, nor with a cemetery;[23] she was regarded as being sufficiently important, or revered, to be accorded formal burial beneath a specially constructed cairn, possibly by a group who were in transit through the territory. She had been accorded a ritual that involved the digging of her grave, the spreading at the base of the grave of ashes from a domestic hearth, either as an offering, or perhaps as a method of 'warming' her cold grave, the interring of her body, the deposition of a portion of red deer antler over her pelvic girdle (a possible 'phallic' symbol of regeneration), the back-filling of the grave, and the erection of a small cairn, either to prevent the grave being despoiled by animals, or to mark the spot, enabling others who passed that way to acknowledge her grave. A similar deposition of a piece of worked antler in the pelvic area was discovered with a female adolescent at the settlement cemetery at Ranelagh, Co.

---

20 There is another lake named Lough Namanfin, located at Bogagh, further north in Donegal, approximately 6.6km north-east of Inver; and attention has been drawn by Prof. Liz Fitzpatrick, NUI Galway, to a similarly named lake at Corbally, Moycullen, Co. Galway. **21** UBA-14245: 1419±29BP; at 2σ = cal AD 584–661 (date obtained courtesy Mapping Death Project). **22** UBA-7683: 1471±67BP; at 2σ = cal AD 428–661. **23** This burial took place at a time when organised cemeteries were unknown in Ireland.

Roscommon, but this burial has been dated to the eleventh–twelfth century,[24] an indication that this symbol of regeneration was still recognised at this later period.

Another isolated burial of an adult female, dated to the seventh–ninth century,[25] was recovered close to the River Boyne at Ferganstown and Ballymacon, Co. Meath (Kelly, 1976, 35; 1977, 65–7). This woman who was laid in an extended position, west–east, in a slab-lined cist grave, beneath a low mound, close to the River Boyne, may have been regarded as a guardian for her territory.

The imitative mound erected at Knocknashammer, Co. Sligo, within sight of the cemetery complex at Carrowmore, contained three burials, one of whom was a middle-aged woman who died in the fifth–sixth century.[26] This woman, who was probably related, either as a mother, or a spouse, to the contemporaneous nearby burial of a young male, was undoubtedly highly esteemed, and was regarded as an ancestor by the kin-group who erected the monument (Timoney, 1977; 1984, 324; 1987/8, 77).

Other women, whose burials in mounds imply that they were held in high esteem by their respective communities, include: the young woman and her horse, both dated to the fourth–sixth century, who was inserted into the upper levels of a Bronze Age burial mound, located beside a possible territorial boundary, at Farta, Co. Galway. This young woman, who suffered from a disability known as bilateral medial torsion (inward twisting of the knees, resulting in in-toeing), which would have impaired her ability to walk with a normal gait, was, together with her horse, an immigrant into the district. Both had originated either in the eastern part of Ireland or possibly in eastern Britain. She was part of a kin-group of a rank or status which ensued, despite her deformity, her being accorded burial in an indigenous ancestral burial mound or *ferta*, accompanied by a valuable horse, unique in the Irish archaeological record. Her burial may have given rise to a local folk tradition, or myth, because, after a time-lapse following her death, two antler picks dated sixth–seventh century[27] were inserted, possibly as a sealing deposit, into the top of the mound above her burial. The possibility that memory of a myth persisted until the modern era is increased by the fact that the burial mound, after which the townland of Farta is named, survived intact until its excavation in 1904.

At Kildangan, Co. Kildare (Ó Floinn, 2011, 51–4), a young adult female, dated to the fourth–sixth century,[28] who had borne children, was inserted, in a dug grave lined with wood, into a natural hillock, which had probably been mistaken by those responsible for her burial as an ancestral burial mound. Also buried beneath a mound was the elderly woman (B110), dated to the fourth–seventh century,[29] in the settlement cemetery of Johnstown, Co. Meath (Fibiger, 2005, 99–110; Clarke and Carlin, 2008, 55–85; 2009, 1–20; Clarke, 2010, 61–75). This woman, who was buried flexed, in a dug grave, beneath a small mound that also covered a pit containing disarticulated remains of three adults that have produced a date identical to that of the woman, represents one of the foundation burials for the large enclosed cemetery that subsequently developed around the mound. One can only imagine the amount of

---

24 UB-36199: 903±27BP; at 2σ = cal AD 1039–1206. 25 OxA-3227: 1290±80BP; at 2σ (93.8%) = cal AD 605–898. 26 UBA-40298: 1577±29BP; at 2σ = cal AD 413–547. 27 UB-27057: 1407±43BP; at 2σ = cal AD 564–677. 28 GrA-24336: 1610±45BP; at 2σ = cal AD 344–551. 29 Beta-178195: 1560±70BP; at 2σ (93.8% probability) = cal AD 379–640.

ritual and ceremony that accompanied the burial of this woman, together with the deposition of probable ancestral skeletal remains in the pit; both interments were then covered by a mound.

Finally, there was the burial of a female aged 25–45 years, dated to the third–sixth (probably fourth–sixth) century,[30] at Rossnaree, Co. Meath, on the southern bank of the River Boyne (Cahill and Sikora, 2011, 113–20). This woman, buried with knees flexed, oriented head to the east, in a dug grave, beneath a small mound known as King Cormac's mound, was born locally (Cahill Wilson et al., 2014a, 130). She was accompanied by an infant, aged 0–6 months. Located close to her shoulder was portion of a silver ring (? earring) with decoration in the form of a herring-bone motif similar to a toe ring on the Iron Age crouched burial at Rath, Co. Meath, but also similar to a motif familiar on Roman finger rings. This burial is puzzling since her posture and body orientation make it unlikely that the woman was a Christian, also she is unlikely to have been of high birth as her skeleton displayed evidence that she had undertaken hard work and much walking during her life. Perhaps she was a favourite *cumal* who had borne a child to a noble or king, or perhaps it was the child who was the significant person in this burial.

Instances of women who were distinguished from the norm by being buried in ring-ditches, and who in some cases may have been regarded as ancestors, include: the female (B28) who formed part of a family group in a single grave surrounded by a ring-ditch, in the cemetery at Ninch 3, Co. Meath, and the young adult female (B48) at Collierstown 1, Co. Meath (O'Brien, 2007; O'Hara, 2009a; 2009b, 83–100), dated to the fifth–sixth century,[31] who was interred supine, west–east, in a grave partially lined with stone slabs which could have supported a wooden cover. Her burial was accompanied by an offering of domestic hearth debris comprising charcoal and burnt vegetation including a tiny fragment of burnt pig bone. This deposit could have been made to establish a link between a family dwelling and the grave but could also be seen as a means of 'warming' a cold grave before inserting the body. The grave of this young woman, who was of local origin, was centrally placed within a specifically constructed penannular ring-ditch, and covered by a small mound, all of which undoubtedly formed part of an elaborate burial ritual. It is possible that she was related, either as a sibling, a daughter, or a spouse, to a possibly newly established king of this region close to Tara, a status that resulted in her grave becoming the focus of a newly established secular cemetery.

At Raystown, Co. Meath, female (B853), aged 36–45 years, dated to the fourth–fifth century[32] (Seaver, 2016), was the earliest and probable foundation burial interred within a penannular ring-ditch, around which this secular cemetery evolved. The grave of this woman also contained a juvenile (B852). The multi-period site at Cross, Co. Galway (Mullins, 2007, 106–7; 2009; Mullins and Birmingham, 2014, 102), contained female (B4), aged 25–35 years, dated to the fourth–sixth century,[33] who was centrally placed within ring-ditch 1, in a grave lined with stones which probably supported a wooden grave cover. This woman does not appear to have been shroud wrapped.

---

30 GrA-24354: 1660±40BP; at 2σ = cal AD 256–534 (at 76.2% probability = cal AD 317–435). 31 BA-250161: 1550±40BP; at 2σ = cal AD 422–596. 32 Wk-16823: 1647±33BP; at 2σ = cal AD 263–535 (at 78.6% probability = cal AD 330–435). 33 Wk-21251: 1601±39BP; at 2σ = cal AD 342–538.

At Feerwore, Co. Galway (Raftery, 1944a, 23–52), a middle-aged female, dated to the fifth–sixth century,[34] was interred in a single, centrally placed slab-lined grave within a penannular ring-ditch that had an inner bank and outer rock-cut ditch, located in close proximity to the original location of the iconic Iron Age Turoe Stone, and was probably a person of importance in her community.

The unenclosed cemetery at Greenhills, Co. Kildare (Keeley, 1991a, 180–201), contained an adult female (B15) dated to the fourth–sixth century[35] interred in a probable wood-lined grave, at the centre of a penannular ring-ditch, at the southern end of the small linear unenclosed cemetery of sixteen burials (Figure 4.14 (b)). This woman was accompanied, in a parallel grave, by a juvenile (B16) aged 6–9 years. Isotopic analysis indicates that the child was born locally (Cahill Wilson et al., 2014, 142). As no teeth were recovered from the woman, it was not possible to ascertain her place of birth. Perhaps the child was her offspring, and they were both of a status that entitled them to burial, without an accompanying male, in this ring-ditch, or alternatively they were set apart from the remainder of the cemetery because they were somehow different.

One of five burials located within the ring-ditch with east and west entrances at Corbally 1, Co. Kildare (Tobin, 2003, 32–7; Tobin and Sunderland, 2004), was a female (B6). The grave of this middle-aged woman, undated, who had been born locally, was situated immediately beside and parallel to the central burial, which was that of a middle-aged male (B5) dated to the fourth–sixth century[36] who had also been born locally (Daly, 2015). One could speculate that this woman was the spouse of the central male, but she might also be his sibling, or perhaps his mother. Whatever her relationship to this man, she was obviously entitled to burial beside him in this ring-ditch. The other three burials in this ring-ditch were a young male and two infants.

Further along the same ridge, at Corbally 2 (Coyne, 2003; Coyne and Lynch 2010, 77–90), another ring-ditch surrounded a grave containing three females (B67, B90, B92). This grave adjoined a central grave which contained two males and another adult of indeterminate sex, undated. One of the women (B92) has been dated fourth–sixth century,[37] and she and one of the accompanying women (B90) were both born locally (Daly, 2015). These women were of a status that was on a par with that of the males. Were these women the spouses of those in the central grave? A further elderly female (B27) dated fifth–seventh century,[38] born locally, was interred in the entrance to the ring-ditch, perhaps as a sealing burial.

At Owenbristy, Co. Galway, an elderly female (SK 76) aged over 45 years, dated fourth–sixth century,[39] was the earliest and probably the foundation burial for this cemetery. This woman, who was buried in a slab-lined grave at the southern extremity of three parallel rows of burials which extended northwards across the cemetery, may have been the matriarch of a kin-group who established this cemetery (Figure 4.16).

Other categories of burial that indicate the graves of women who were special in some way include: an elderly post-menopausal female with severe degenerative joint

---

34 UB–7154: 1541±32BP; at 2σ = cal AD 429–591.   35 UBA–20007: 1622±23BP; at 2σ = cal AD 388–535.   36 UBA–31469: 1619±27BP; at 2σ = cal AD 385–537.   37 Beta–194919: 1630±50BP; at 2σ (93.1% probability) = cal AD 325–550.   38 Beta–194918: 1460±60BP; at 2σ = cal AD 429–667.   39 UB–11252: 1635±38BP; at 2σ = cal AD 337–537.

disease (Carty and Daly, 2013) at Site 4, The Curragh, Co. Kildare (see Figure 6.1), who appears to have been a live burial, was centrally placed in a dug grave, in a very elaborate well-constructed ring-ditch consisting of a circular level area surrounded by a ditch and bank, overall diameter 32m, with two opposing entrances across the ditch and bank on the east and west sides, one of which contained two post-holes for possible swing-gates. This woman was lying in a very unusual posture, her body was supine, twisted slightly to the left side, her arms were braced against the sides of the grave, her legs were wide apart and braced against the sides of the grave, her head was flexed forward on to her chest. This burial is now known to date to between the fifth–seventh century AD, with the highest probability being sixth–seventh century.[40] This was the burial of a living woman,[41] who had not been hastily disposed of. She was buried in a supine position, and was not weighted down. Prior to her burial, a significant investment of time and effort had been afforded to the construction of the mortuary enclosure, and undoubtedly her death and burial were accompanied by specific and elaborate rituals. The probable gateposts in one of the entrances suggest that the grave was re-visited over an extended period, indicating that the burial was that of a person of importance to the community. She may have been regarded as an intermediary between the living and the dead.

The young adult female (B38) aged 18–25 years, dated sixth–seventh century,[42] in the settlement cemetery at Ratoath, Co. Meath, who had a copper-alloy collar or necklet around her neck (Figure 5.1 (a)) (Wallace, 2010, 295–316), had probably been born locally, but there is a possibility that she could have originated in the eastern part of England (Montgomery and Vaughan, 2010, 312). There are at present no known parallels for her neck collar in Ireland, but a possible English parallel is a copper-alloy necklet (Figure 5.1 (b)) recovered among the grave goods of a male Anglo-Saxon warrior burial (Grave 50) at Bergh Apton, Norfolk (Green and Rogerson, 1978, 35, 76). The probability that this young woman was born locally in Brega, a region that had a known Anglo-Saxon presence throughout the seventh century (Moisl, 1983, 123; Ireland, 1991, 64–78; O'Brien, 1993, 93–6; 1999a, 45–8), raises the possibility that she, or her kin-group, may have had an Anglo-Saxon connection, with the neck ring being an heirloom, or even a form of group identification.

A possible female recipient of *dant mir* ('hero's portion') is represented by Burial 3, an isolated burial in the seventh- to ninth-century settlement enclosure at Kilree 3, Co. Kilkenny.[43] This middle-aged/old female had a large animal bone at her head. As no other animal bone was found in the vicinity, one must assume that this bone represents a portion of meat which had deliberately been placed over her face, probably in recognition of the fact that she was of high status in her community. A further indication of the high status of this woman is that despite her advanced age she had not participated in everyday labour as there was little evidence for degenerative changes in her skeleton (Coughlan, 2010, 18–19).

Women who were born elsewhere, but were accorded burial in ancestral indigenous burial places, may have moved to the locality in which they died and were buried

---

40 UBA–21801: 1503±32BP; at 2σ = cal AD 430–639; (at 80.1% = cal AD 530–639). This date was obtained by the writer under the auspices of the Mapping Death Project. 41 To the modern mind this burial type appears implausible, but we must accept and acknowledge our ignorance of whatever logic lay behind this act. 42 Beta–196361: 1410±40BP; at 2σ = cal AD 569–671. 43 *Dant mir*

possibly because of important marriage alliances: two women (SK 10, SK 6), buried at the ancestral burial place at Site B, Carbury Hill, Co. Kildare – one of whom (SK 10), dated to the fourth–fifth century,[44] was born in the west of Ireland, and the other (SK 6), dated to the fifth–sixth century,[45] was born possibly around the Kerry coastline, in the south-west of Ireland. Three women (B11, B14, and B16) in the unenclosed cemetery at Betaghstown (Brookside), Co. Meath, one of whom (B11) dated to the fifth–seventh century,[46] who was buried in a crouched position and clothed on burial, is unlikely to be Irish, but probably originated in Britain; the second, extended (B14), dated to the fourth–sixth century,[47] originated in either Britain, continental Europe, or Scandinavia; and the third, extended (B16), undated, originated probably along the Kerry coastline in south-west Ireland.

There are women, sometimes with physical disabilities, which marked them out as 'different', who may have been powerful during their life, perhaps as 'wise women', and therefore feared by their peers as being powerful enough to return and haunt the living after death, or possibly feared because of their disability, and were accorded unusual and restrictive burials. An elderly female (B2), dated to the fourth–sixth century,[48] was discovered in a disused kiln, approximately 8m south-east of the ring-ditch at Corbally 1, Co. Kildare. Her posture is suggestive of an informal or surreptitious burial, and her body had been covered with large stones. This woman, who had developed Paget's disease of her skull (Keating, 2004, 35–8), had been born elsewhere in Ireland, and had moved to the area sometime before her death (Daly, 2015). She was a contemporary of the locally born male (B5), who was buried in the nearby ring-ditch. Perhaps she was his spouse who had been rejected and was possibly feared as her Paget's disease became more pronounced with age. An elderly female (SK 1542), undated, buried in a prone position, in the large cemetery at Faughart Lower, Co. Louth (Bowen and Dawkes, 2011, 70, 72), had a rare congenital anomaly of the left femur (Buckley et al., 2010a, 6–7), which would have affected her ability to walk normally and may have marked her as 'different' during her life. Prone burial would have been seen as a method of preventing her from re-emerging from the grave. Female (B204), undated, aged 36–45 years, who was buried in a partially prone position at the settlement cemetery of Johnstown, Co. Meath (Clarke, 2010, 61–75), had thick cranial vault bones (Fibiger, 2004, 73, 82–3), which would have caused disfigurement of her head, and may also have marked her as 'different'. Here again prone burial was used as a method of preventing her becoming a revenant.

An adult female (B614), undated, in the settlement cemetery at Parknahown 5, Co. Laois, had been buried prone and orientated with her head to the east (O'Neill, 2009, 170), thus providing a double deterrent against her possible re-appearance. A middle-aged female at Ballykilmore 6, Co. Westmeath (Channing, 2009, 2014, 23–38), was buried flexed and partially prone; her cranium and two cervical vertebrae were missing and had been replaced by a head-sized rounded stone. Because the mandible was present in its correct anatomical position, the excavator suggests that the skull may

---

translates literally as 'tooth portion'.   44 UBA-20010: 1659±23BP; at 2σ = cal AD 335–425.   45 UBA-20009: 1535±24BP; at 2σ = cal AD 428–591.   46 OxA-2651: 1550±60BP; at 2σ = cal AD 394–630.   47 OxA-2654: 1620±65BP; at 2σ (90.5% probability) = cal AD 318–580.   48 UBA-30393: 1636±41BP; at 2σ = cal AD 332–539.

have been removed after decomposition had already occurred. Perhaps this was also a double deterrent to prevent her becoming a revenant.

Women who were violently killed, but who were still recognised as part of their community and afforded normal burial in their communal cemetery include: a young adult female (SK 484), undated, in the settlement cemetery at Parknahown 5, Co. Laois, who had been subjected to thirteen sharp-force fatal injuries to her cervical vertebrae as the result of an attempted, or a successful, decapitation (Keating, 2009, 118–20). She was buried supine, west–east, in a communal cemetery. Female burial (B125) at Corbally Site 2, born in the region (Daly, 2015), undated, but placed across the ditch-fill of phase 1 ring-ditch,[49] had died from sharp-force trauma to the ribs caused by a double-edged sharp blade, which appears to have deliberately pierced her heart (Lynch, 2005, 25; Coyne and Lynch, 2010, 86). She was buried supine in a dug grave with her left arm bent from the elbow at an angle which resulted in her hand resting on the site of the wound in her chest. Two females (SK 73, SK 75) in the cemetery at Owenbristy, Co. Galway, were interred in the same slab-lined and slab-covered grave (but not simultaneously). Female (SK 75), aged 35–45 years, undated, had been decapitated by a single cut through the neck. Her burial was partially disturbed by the later insertion of female (SK 73), aged 25–35 years, dated to the first half of the seventh century,[50] who had been subjected to severe stab wounds to her face and a blow through the stomach with a sword or an axe, and had been decapitated (Geber, 2010, 174; 2011, 91). These women may have been siblings, or perhaps a mother and daughter, who died during separate violent episodes, but were afforded normal burial, probably in a family grave, in this communal cemetery.

At Knoxspark, Co. Sligo, a female burial (B38?), undated, whose head was missing, was accompanied in a simple dug grave by the remains of three children (B34, B39, B49), one of whom was also missing its head (Mount, 2010, 193). This possibly represents an undated violent episode,[51] but the victims (perhaps a mother and her children) were buried in a communal cemetery. A crouched (possible) female (B12) aged 36–45 years, dated to the fifth–sixth century,[52] in the settlement cemetery at Ratoath, Co. Meath (Fibiger, 2010, 119; Wallace, 2010, 305), was interred minus her head, hands and feet. While this posture may have been a device to prevent her from 'walking', she was still accorded burial in a familial or communal cemetery. This could, however, be a case where a body had been trussed for transportation from another place, and the bodily extremities became lost on the way. This might also be the reason behind the crouched burial of female (B13), dated to the eighth–ninth century,[53] at Killeany, Co. Laois, whose body appears to have been trussed or bound (Wiggins and Kane, 2009, 144, 356), or perhaps it was a method of preventing her becoming a revenant. Among the burials in the small cemetery at the settlement cemetery at Marlinstown, Co. Westmeath (Keeley, 1991b, no. 113; 1992, no. 126; unpublished TII report), an adult female, undated, had been buried prone, and her head was missing. Despite the lack of an osteological report, this woman appears to have been

---

[49] Phase 1 ring-ditch at Corbally 2 was in use from the fifth to the seventh century. [50] UB–12370: 1402±27BP; at 2σ = cal AD 602–65. [51] This cemetery may have a Viking input (Kelly, 2009, 485–97). [52] Beta–198505: 1570±40BP; at 2σ = cal AD 402–572. [53] SUERC–17625: 1205±35BP; at 2σ = cal AD 692–941 (highest probability 81.0% = cal AD 762–895).

decapitated. Even though the removal of her head and prone burial indicate that she may have been regarded as a possible revenant, she was still accorded burial among her community.

Denied burial among her community was female (B39), aged 17–25 years, dated to the sixth–seventh century,[54] at Killeany, Co. Laois, who had been subjected to extreme weapon trauma. She was buried prone in the entrance passage to the cemetery enclosure. This was a punitive death and burial, with the further ignominy that any person entering the enclosure would have to walk over her grave.

* * *

Little is known of the legal status of women in the Iron Age in Ireland, however, the location and positioning of several cremation deposits, identified as female, would suggest that some, at least, were accorded high-status burial. The legal status of a woman in early Irish law, drawn up by lawyers and clerics, was defined by the status of, and her relationship to, the men in her kin-group. She was recognised as a mother, sister or wife. However, laws that were drawn up for an ideal society did not allow for everyday reality and human emotions. A sample of forty-five women, spanning the age-spectrum from late teens to old age, whose treatment at death may be regarded as unusual or exceptional, have been examined. Several of these women were obviously considered by their peers to be of a status that warranted burial either within ancestral monuments or in ring-ditches, while others became foundation burials, around whose graves cemeteries evolved. These women were recognised as ancestors. In one instance, a prehistoric burial mound received, between the fifth and seventh century, the burial of thirteen women. In another instance, a young woman and her horse were interred in a Bronze Age burial mound. There is also the strange case of a possible live (voluntary?) burial of an elderly woman within a specially constructed ring-ditched enclosure. Several women were buried far from their place of birth. The burials of females seemingly regarded as possible revenants, include: the burial in a kiln of a woman who had Paget's disease; six women who were buried in a prone position, two of whom had a physical deformity, but were nevertheless buried in communal cemeteries; a further woman who had suffered fatal violent weapon trauma, was also buried prone, but in the entrance-passage to a cemetery; two women were buried in a crouched position, one of whom was minus her head, hands and feet.

These women represent a cross-section of early Irish society. Several were obviously much-loved and revered, in spite of physical defects in two cases, and were apparently of high standing in their communities. Others, who had physical deformities or disabilities which marked them out as 'different', may have been powerful during life, perhaps as 'wise women', but were apparently feared after death and were accorded unusual or restrictive burial. Others, who had been subjected to violent deaths, were, except in one instance, accorded formal burial in communal cemeteries.

54 SUERC–17622: 1445±35BP; at 2σ = cal AD 555–655.

CHAPTER 9

Cessation of burial of Christians among 'pagan' ancestors

Although Christianity had been introduced into Ireland in the fifth century, it was only from the early eighth century onwards that the Church authorities in Ireland began to compile rules regulating the lives of Christians, including rules regarding acceptable burial practices for Christians. This emerging trend becomes evident in the seventh-century anachronistic reference to an incident where Patrick came across two similar graves, which pointed out to the faithful the danger that those Christians whose graves were located *inter malos homines* ('among wicked men'), that is their pagan ancestors, risked not being recognized.

The *Collectio canonum Hibernensis* (Wasserschleben, 1885) includes the earliest rules, that we are aware of, urging the faithful to abandon burial among their ancestors in favour of burial in church cemeteries. The compilers of these rules or canons are sympathetic to a desire to be buried among one's ancestors; for example, *Hib.* XVIII, *De jure sepulturae* ('The law of burial') includes at Cap 2 (Wasserschleben, 1885, 56) *De eo, quod in paterno sepulcro sepeliendum est* ('Concerning the rule that a person should be buried in the paternal grave'), which seeks to justify burial among the ancestors, by stating that a man or woman may be buried in his/her paternal tomb, and that every man is accursed who is not buried in the tomb of his fathers. The example given is Jacob and Joseph's request that their bones be carried back from Egypt to the land of Canaan so that they might be buried at the tomb of their ancestors. However, on the other hand, monks and ecclesiastical tenants were encouraged to seek burial at the cemetery of the church to which they were affiliated: *Hib.* XVIII, Cap. 3 (idem, 57), *De eo, quod debet homo sepeliri in ecclesia cui monachus est* ('Concerning the fact that a person ought to be buried in the church of which he is a monk'). Also, *Si quis in ecclesia coniunctus fuerit, in ea sepelietur* ('If anyone should have been joined to a church, he will be buried there').

Ancestral cemeteries were not to be totally abandoned as is evidenced by *Hib.* XVIII, Cap. 5 (idem, 57): *De eo, quod sors mittenda est inter ecclesiam et sepulcrum paternum* ('That lots should be cast [to decide] between the church and the ancestral tomb'); it stated that: *Si unusquisque secularis voluerit, dividat sors inter ecclesiam et sepulcrum paternum, sed dona sua plurima ecclesiae suae conferre debet, pauca autem in sepulcro paterno in honorem patrum* ('if any secular person has so wished, let lots make the division between the church and the ancestral tomb, but he ought to contribute the greater gift to his church, a few [items] however to the ancestral cemetery in honour of the ancestors').

Some of the rules laid down in *Hib.* are echoed in *Córus bésgnai*, an Old Irish law tract concerned mainly with Church governance. For example, §46 *Cach n-adnacal cona airthéchtu imnai do eclais cháich íarna míad* ('Every burial with its appropriate prior bequest to every person's church in accordance with his rank') is followed by

§47, which sets out what is appropriate for every burial from the laity, from every grade in accordance with his rank, as a fee to the church (Breatnach, 2017, 36–9).

Hib. demonstrates, however, that the Church was always conscious of the importance of ancestral graves and had to find ways to accommodate the change, hence the inclusion of rules referring specifically to traditional burial practices. A further rule (LI, Cap. 2, Wasserschleben, 209), *De mortuis in somno uisis* ('Concerning the dead seen in dreams'), emphasises this point by including the statement '*siue admonendo humano generi, ut sepulturae prebeatur humanitas, quae licet defunctis non opituletur, tamen culpatur, si in religiositate neglegitur*' ('to remind mankind that respect should be given to a burial, though it may perhaps not be given to the dead, yet it is a matter for blame if it is neglected by those in the religious state'). In other words, Christians were still being held responsible for the upkeep of their ancestors' graves.

The rule which was crucial to the argument that Christians should be buried among Christians is (L, Cap. 3, idem, 208–9), *De eo, quod magis visitantur martyres in deserto humati, quam inter malos homines* ('Concerning the fact that martyrs who are buried in desert places are more visited [by angels] than [those buried] among evil men'), and includes *Martyres inter malos sepultos ab angelis visitari, sed tamen tristes reversos angelos* ('Martyrs buried among evil persons are visited by angels; however, the angels return sorrowful') and *Post resurrectionem multi audisse voces testantur dicentium angelorum: transeamus ex his sedibus* ('After the resurrection many testify that they have heard voices of angels saying: let us depart from these places'). This illustrates the point that, although Christians were still being buried in ancestral cemeteries, they were now being earnestly encouraged to consider being buried in *díseart* places, which in this context meant monastic or ecclesiastic cemeteries, rather than *inter malos homines* (evidently meaning pagan ancestors), because they would then be more likely to be visited by angels whose purpose was to escort the souls of Christians to heaven.

There are numerous references in the early literature that reinforce the belief that the accompaniment of angels was a necessary part of the journey of a soul to heaven. These include Adomnán's reflection that Columba, shortly before his death, spoke of an angel who had been sent to recover a deposit (his soul), and after Columba's death, a holy man in Ireland was reputed to have seen angels bearing aloft his holy soul (*Adomnán* [iii.23], Anderson and Anderson, 1991, 218–19, 226–7). There are many other references in Adomnán to the souls of holy men being accompanied to heaven by angels, but there are also instances where the company of angels was also given to the souls of lay people. For instance (*Adomnán* [iii.9], idem, 194–7), the soul of an iron-smith was carried by angels to heaven; (*Adomnán* [iii.10], idem, 196–7), the soul of a woman, and later that of her husband, were carried by angels to paradise; (*Adomnán* [iii.13], idem, 200–1) when a boat carrying monks sank and they drowned, the souls of the monks were recovered by angels, but the angels had to fight with demons for the soul of a lay guest in the boat who also drowned. They were ultimately successful and carried his soul to heaven; (*Adomnán* [iii.14], idem, 200–3) angels arrive to receive the soul of a pagan, whom the saint had baptized on the point of death. In the seventh-century *Vita prima Sanctae Brigitae* (Life of Brigit) (who lived AD 425–524 (or) 526, 528), it is stated at §129.2 'Brigit departed this life … amid the ranks of angels and archangels' (Connolly, 1989, 49).

The Venerable Bede makes several references to souls being accompanied by angels on their journey to heaven. At *HE* iii.8 (Colgrave and Mynors, 1969, 238–9), when Eorcengota, daughter of King Eorcenbhert of Kent, died, choirs of angels were heard singing and her soul was borne away on a great light; at *HE* iv.3 (idem, 342–3), when Bishop Chad died, 'his holy soul was released from the prison-house of the body and in the company of angels, as one may rightly believe, sought the joys of heaven'; and at *HE* iv.3 (idem, 344–5), it is recorded that Egbert, speaking in Ireland about the death of Chad, states that 'he knew a man (in this island) who saw the soul of Chad's brother Cedd, descend from the sky with a host of angels and return to the heavenly kingdom, taking Chad's soul with him'. At *HE* iv.23 (idem, 412–13), a nun named Begu, describing her vision of the death of Abbess Hild, stated that she saw 'the soul of the handmaiden of the Lord being borne to Heaven in the midst of that light, attended and guided by angels'. In Cuthbert's letter on the death of Bede (idem, 584–5), he states that 'his (Bede's) soul was carried by angels to the joys of heaven, which he longed for'. Further references to angels being present at the journey of souls to heaven are to be found in other saints' lives, including that of Cuthbert.

The message contained in *Hib.* was clear, the lack of the company of angels, which was essential if a soul was to make its way to heaven, became a serious drawback if the angels did not visit, or returned sorrowful from, the graves of Christians who had been buried among the (pagan) ancestors.

While literary indications imply that there may have been resistance to the abandonment of ancestral burial places, even after almost three centuries of Christianity, the Church was obviously successful in its endeavours because, based on the archaeological evidence, by the eighth or ninth century, the sporadic use of the rite of cremation, and deliberate burial in ancestral burial places or *ferta*, had more or less ceased. Radiocarbon determinations also indicate that while burial in the majority of secular communal cemeteries ceased during the same period, some secular cemeteries continued to be used for burial until the Church reforms of the late eleventh and first half of the twelfth centuries, and very occasionally even later than that. These include: Raystown, Co. Meath, fifth–twelfth century; Castlefarm, Co. Meath, fifth–thirteenth century; Faughart Lower, Co. Louth, fifth–tenth century; Mount Offaly, Cabinteely, Co. Dublin, fifth–twelfth century; Parknahown 5, Co. Laois, fifth–twelfth century; Johnstown, Co. Meath, fifth–sixteenth century, and Newtown Rath, Co. Dublin, sixth–eleventh century.

One possible explanation for this continued use is because 'industrial/settlement' activity continued to take place at some of these sites for some time after the ninth century, and certain communities or kin-groups may have been able to reach a form of compromise with the Church authorities whereby some members were buried in the local church cemetery, while others continued to be permitted burial in the ancestral secular cemetery. This appears to have changed with the Church reforms of the twelfth century.

Another possible reason for the continued use of secular cemeteries until at least the twelfth century could lie in the fact that for the laity in general, burial in important ecclesiastical cemeteries might not have been an option, as burial in these cemeteries appears to have been a closely guarded privilege for those of high status. For example, evidence for the continued exclusion of the laity from within a major ecclesiastical cemetery is evident at the Columban foundation at Durrow, Co. Offaly, where in 1985, approximately 200 metres outside the south-eastern part of the monastic outer boundary enclosure, in slightly raised ground known as Sheean Hill, a circular enclosure surrounding burials which included males, females, and juveniles was discovered and excavated (Plate 12) (Ó Floinn and O'Brien, in Cahill and Sikora, 2011, 120–39; O'Brien, 2012, 118, 122). C14 dating places the use of this external familial or communal cemetery to between the eighth and thirteenth century AD. There is evidence for a possible further similar cemetery outside the north-eastern part of the Durrow monastic enclosure boundary with the discovery in 2006 of a circular cropmark with human bone exposed in the ploughed surface (King, 2012, 125–32).

This type of exclusion may also account for the fact that a small number of cemeteries, which started out as secular and communal, appear at a later period to have become consecrated and acquired a church. For example, the secular settlement cemetery at Ballykilmore, Co. Westmeath, where burial began in the fifth–sixth century, acquired a probable church building in the eighth–tenth century, which subsequently collapsed and disappeared between the eleventh and thirteenth century (Channing, 2009, 171; 2014, 28–30). Burial continued in the cemetery until the eighteenth century, but the cemetery was erased from local memory when a roadway was built through it in the early nineteenth century. Similarly, the cemetery at Ballyhanna, Co. Donegal, where burial began in the eighth century, acquired a church probably in the twelfth century, and burial continued until the eighteenth century. By the mid-nineteenth century this church and cemetery had disappeared from local memory, until its re-discovery during roadbuilding in 2003 (McKenzie et al., 2015).

Ultimately, however, the increasing power of the Church in Ireland, from the late seventh century onwards, influenced the abandonment of the burial of Christians, who had been, for political or familial reasons, buried among the pagan ancestors, and instead burial close to the saints gradually became an acceptable substitute.

The recognition of ancestral *ferta* as boundary markers in the early law tracts helped to prolong the memory of their role and ensured that they were still recognized as the burial places of ancestral guardians. After the ninth, and up until about the sixteenth century, many *ferta* became places of assembly and a focus for displays of ancestral attachment among Gaelic ruling dynasties (Fitzpatrick, 2015, 52–68). Further evidence that these burial places continued to be remembered as important features in the landscape is evident from modern place-name evidence (www.logainm.ie). There are many recorded instances of place-names throughout the country that include elements of the word *fert*; Ardfert, Co. Kerry, Clonfert, Co. Galway, and 'Fertagh' place-names in Cos. Kilkenny, Leitrim, Cork and Meath, and of course there is the Galway site of Farta with its female and horse burial.

* * *

Although the Christian religion had been introduced into Ireland by the fifth century, it was not until almost three centuries later, in the early eighth century, that the Church began to circulate rules regulating the lives of Christians, including rules outlining acceptable burial practices. Despite some indications that there may initially have been resistance to the new rules, archaeological evidence confirms that by the eighth–ninth century the Church was ultimately successful in persuading Christians to abandon the sporadic use of the rite of cremation, and burial in ancestral monuments (*ferta*), to be replaced with burial among Christians. Burial in the majority of secular communal cemeteries ceased around that time, but some of these cemeteries continued to be used until the Church reforms of the eleventh–twelfth centuries, and even later. One possible reason for the latter could be the fact that for the laity, burial in important ecclesiastical cemeteries might not have been an option, as burial in these cemeteries appears to have been a closely guarded privilege. To overcome this, some cemeteries, which were originally founded as secular, appear to have been consecrated and acquired church buildings later in their lifespan.

CHAPTER 10

Church cemeteries

In this chapter I concentrate on an examination of a selection of twenty-seven church cemeteries that have been at least partially excavated and have produced burials, as well as three sites which have been assigned as early church sites, but which do not on closer examination appear to be so (Map 8). Some burials have been c14 dated, and when combined with on-site religious paraphernalia, and in some cases literary references, can help to determine the date of the church site, and/or the date of its use (Gazetteer 7).[1]

Extended supine inhumation, introduced into Ireland, probably from the western fringes of Romanised Britain, in the late fourth–early fifth century, soon became the norm. The Christian religion was also introduced, probably from Romanised Britain, and mainland Europe, in the early fifth century. The presence at several church cemetery sites, especially in south-western Ireland, of late fifth-/mid-sixth-century Bii imported ware that originated in the eastern Mediterranean region (Doyle, 2010, 19–20), containing wine or oil, raises the possibility that Christianity may have been introduced into that region through trading contacts, either from south-western Britain, which had connections with the south of Ireland, or from the eastern Mediterranean region via mainland Europe and the Irish Sea.

Many church cemeteries undoubtedly coexisted alongside emerging secular familial or communal cemeteries. Research into the origins, background, familial, and/or communal connections to early local churches is ongoing (O'Brien, 1980; 1988, 504–25; Charles-Edwards, 1992, 63–80; Sharpe, 1992, 81–109; Hamlin, 2008; Ó Carragáin, 2009, 239–61; 2017, 67–79; Corlett and Potterton, 2014; Ó Carragáin and Turner, 2016). Hundreds of abandoned churches and their cemeteries still survive throughout the Irish countryside, but few have been excavated.

It is important to note that in Ireland, early church buildings were usually constructed with wood, and can only be archaeologically identified by the presence of post-holes, or were constructed with turves, which usually leave no remains but occasionally leave slight identifiable remains. The latter form of construction is referred to in the seventh century by Tírechán when describing the burial of the kings daughters in a round ditch, after which 'he [Patrick] made an earthen church in that place' (*Tírechán*, §26. 21, Bieler, 1979, 144–5). The earliest reference to a church built of stone in Ireland is the record at AD725 to the death of Aldchú of Dom Liacc (*Chron. Ire.*) (Duleek, Co. Meath).[2] The next known reference is in AD789 (*Chron. Ire.*) when a man was killed in the doorway of the stone church in Armagh. In general, stone churches in Ireland appear to have replaced churches built of organic material in the ninth–tenth century. These stone churches are sometimes built over the remains of earlier wooden churches thus preserving post-hole evidence. Occasionally, the

---

[1] The three suspect sites are not included in Gazetteer 7. [2] Dom or Dam = Domus, and Lia = stone ('a church of stone') (www.logainm.ie).

presence of an earlier organic structure may be indicated by graves which are on a different orientation to that of a stone church and its associated graves.

While it is difficult to separate church cemetery sites into discrete categories, for the purpose of this publication a general classification has been devised, although the parameters between classifications is flexible:

- monastic cemeteries
- early community church cemeteries
- community church cemeteries with wide temporal span
- other possible community church cemeteries
- church cemeteries associated with conversion-period saints
- island church cemeteries
- hermitage, or *díseart*, cemeteries
- quartz pebbles
- doubtful church cemeteries.

MONASTIC CEMETERIES

The classic model for the layout of a monastery as it was envisaged in the early eighth century is set out in *Hib.* XLIV, *De locis consecratis* ('Concerning consecrated places'). Cap. 5, *De numero terminorum sancti loci* ('The number of boundaries in a sacred place') (Wasserschleben, 1885, 175, and note 'e'), defines the boundaries as: the first division,[3] which is called holy, into which laymen and women enter; the second division, which is holier, into which clergy only go; and the third division which is very holy. This third or inner sanctum contained the church and cemetery. These divisions are further emphasised by note 'e', which declares that only saints and clerics may enter the central sanctum, but not men who are not clerics, nor women; the second division may be entered by laymen (rustics); and the third may be entered by murderers and adulterers. In other words, anyone could enter the outer division.

Included in this category are three cemeteries that fit the model: first, is the monastery at Clonmacnoise said to have been founded in AD548 (*Chron. Ire.*), at a strategic crossing-point on the River Shannon, by Ciarán, who died, aged 35 years, in AD549 (ibid.), a few months after the foundation of the monastery.[4] The early outer enclosure surrounding this monastic site was identified as a large ditch, 5–6.20m wide and *c.*3.75m deep, together with a possible internal bank (Murphy, 2003, 19, ill. 27). Despite the early death of its founder, the monastery continued and thrived, as is evidenced by the list of abbatial succession (Ryan, 1940, 490–507; Kehnel, 1997, 29–34, 246–57). The cemetery at Clonmacnoise, with its iconic high crosses, has been described as a 'royal necropolis' (Bhreathnach, 2003, 100), and has produced approximately 700 cross-decorated and inscribed Early Medieval grave slabs recording the burials of kings, abbots, bishops, patrons and monks (Swift, 2003, 105–23). The removal in the early 1990s of the West Cross, the South Cross and the

---

[3] The first division here refers to the outer enclosure.   [4] See Bhreathnach, 2014, 183–92, for a concise history of the monastery at Clonmacnoise.

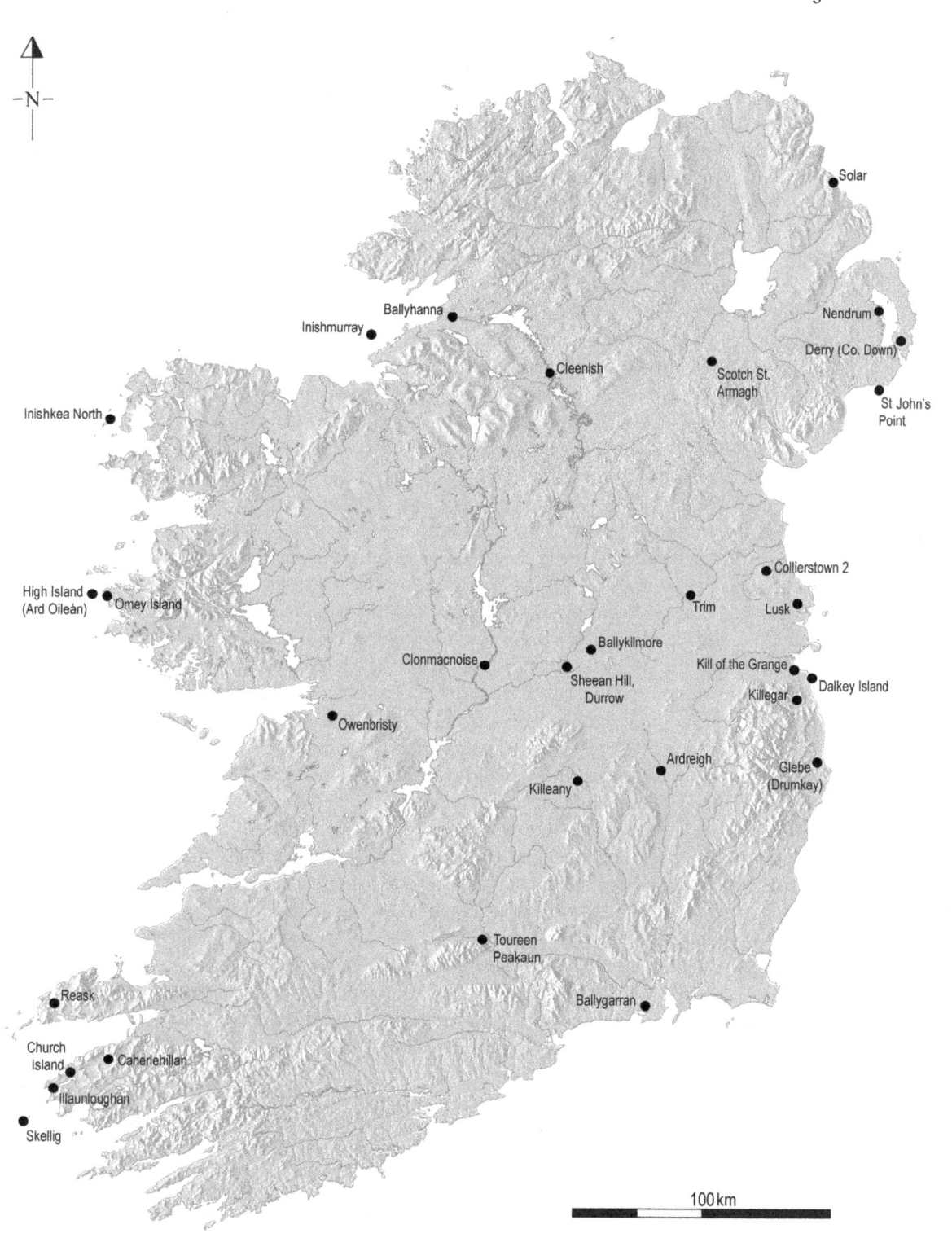

Map 8 Distribution of cemeteries included in chapter 10, © The Discovery Programme and EOB.

shaft of the North Cross, into the Interpretative Centre for conservation purposes, and prior to their subsequent replacement by replicas, provided a window of opportunity to examine the area beneath each cross (for location of crosses see Figure 10.1). This task was undertaken by Heather A. King of the National Monument Service. The levels immediately beneath and around the crosses revealed burials, male and female, dating from the later Medieval and Early Modern periods. Burials at the lowest levels were Early Medieval in date, and were exclusively male. The unusual male burials, dated to between the seventh and tenth centuries, recovered beneath the West Cross (Cross of the Scriptures) have been examined in detail in chapter 5.

A problem is presented by one of the three male burials recovered at the lowest levels beneath the North Cross (King, 1994, 66), where the badly damaged skeleton (B14) of an older adult male, extended, in a dug grave in the natural gravel, with no grave goods, has produced a date in the fifth–sixth century.[5] As this man apparently died before, or possibly in the very early stages of, the foundation of the monastery, could it be possible that there was already a group of men living and dying at Clonmacnoise before the formal establishment of the monastic foundation? Or could this be a 'foundation' burial, similar to the apocryphal story of the sacrificial death and burial of Odrán (Orán) during the foundation of the monastery at Iona, contained in the fifteenth-century 'Irish Life of Colum Cille'? (Herbert, 1996, §52, 237, 261). Two further male burials were recovered beneath the North Cross; (B9), who was lying immediately above (B14), has been dated to the sixth–seventh century,[6] and a further partially excavated burial (B15), dug into the natural gravel, is dated to the seventh–eighth century.[7] These burials indicate possible continuity of exclusively male burial beneath the North Cross[8] from the fifth to eighth century.

The area around and beneath the South Cross was excavated in 1994 (King, 1995, 74–5). A circular pit, 0.6m diameter and 0.85m deep, was located beneath the cross, which may represent the location of an earlier wooden cross, or a marker, perhaps similar to that beneath the West Cross. In the lower levels around the South Cross, there were eleven burials dating from the seventh to the eleventh century, one of which (B26) was located beneath the circular pit, an indication that this possible wooden cross or marker had been erected after burial had already commenced in this area in the seventh century. Some of the burials had been disturbed in antiquity and others were partially excavated. All were male, extended, in dug graves, without grave goods, and, where observable, appear to have been shroud wrapped. The following is a summary of the burials in chronological order based on c14 dates: B26, dated to the seventh century;[9] B7,[10] B2,[11] B22,[12] B25,[13] B1,[14] all dated to the seventh–eighth century; B3, dated to the seventh–ninth century;[15] B23, dated to the eighth–ninth

---

[5] GrN–20667: 1570±25BP; at 2σ = cal AD 420–547.   [6] UBA–10329: 1440±29BP; at 2σ = cal AD 568–654.   [7] UBA–10328: 1280±43BP; at 2σ = cal AD 657–867 (at 84.7%, highest probability, = cal AD 657–779).   [8] See Manning, 1992, 8–9, for details of the North Cross.   [9] GrN–21778: 1390±30BP; at 2σ = cal AD 602–674.   [10] GrN–21775: 1290±30BP; at 2σ = cal AD 664–770.   [11] UBA–10292:1291±25BP; at 2σ = cal AD 665–770.   [12] UBA–10303:1252±22BP; at 2σ = cal AD 678–860 (at 83.6%, highest probability, AD 673–779).   [13] UBA–10305:1270±20BP; at 2σ = cal AD 680–770.   [14] UBA–10291:1246±21BP; at 2σ = cal AD 684–863 (at 81.9%, highest probability, AD 682–779).   [15] GrN–21774: 1220±30BP; at 2σ = cal AD 692–887.

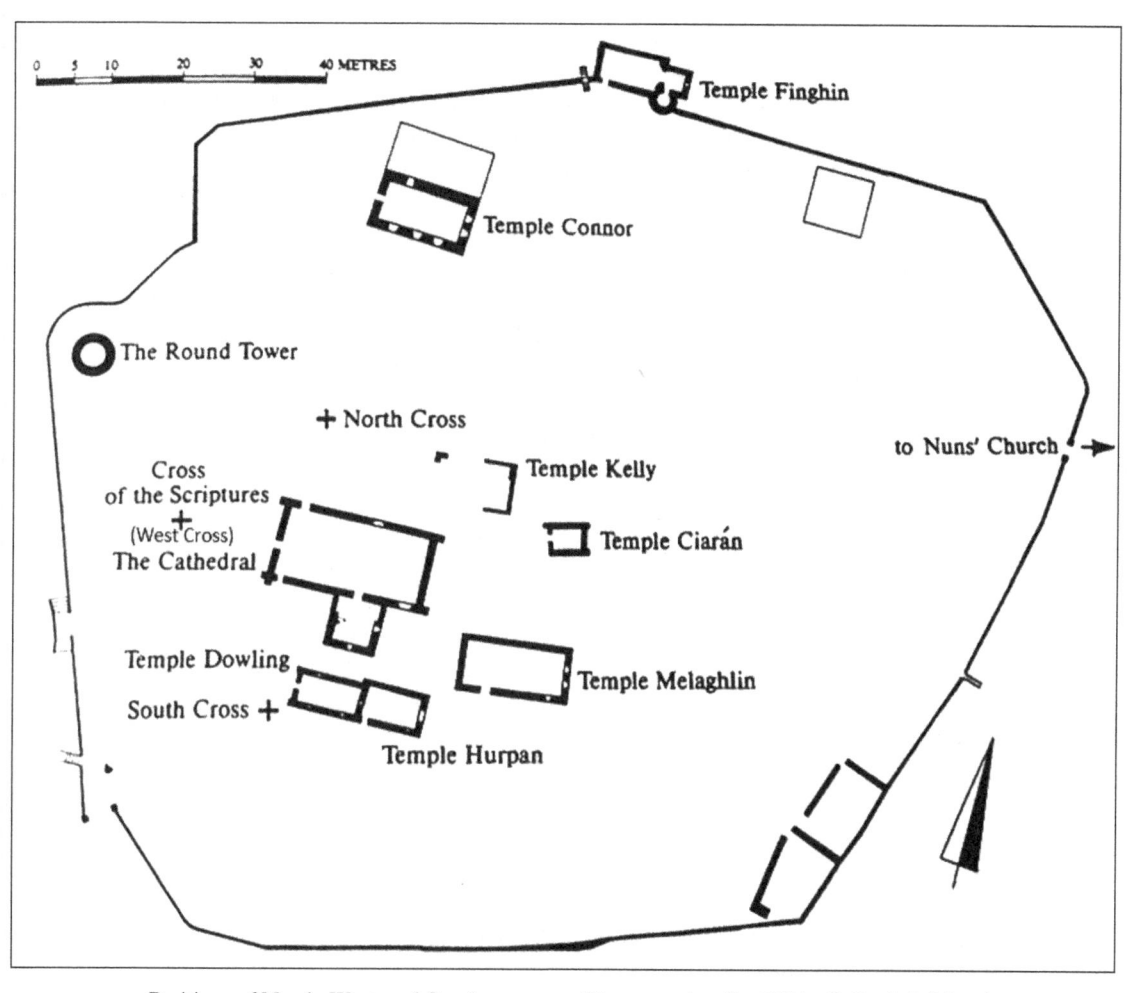

10.1 Positions of North, West, and South crosses at Clonmacnoise, Co. Offaly, © Conleth Manning.

century;[16] B24, dated to the eighth–ninth century;[17] B18, dated to the ninth–tenth century;[18] it is noted that the skull of this latter burial was propped on either side by rounded stones (ear-muffs) and that a piece of corroded iron at the waist may be the remains of a belt; B21, dated to the ninth–eleventh century.[19] These dates suggest continuity of exclusively male burial in this location from the seventh century when the monastery was growing in importance, until perhaps the eleventh century.

All the burials recovered beneath the North and South crosses conform to the burial rite considered to be the norm for Christians in the Early Medieval period, supine, extended, heads west, shroud wrapped, and with no grave goods. This is in stark contrast to the burials, dated to the same period, recovered beneath the West

---

[16] GrN–21778: 1215±25BP; at 2σ = cal AD 711–889 (at 83.5%, highest probability, AD 764–889).
[17] UBA–10304:1205±26BP; at 2σ = cal AD 720–890 (at 89.8%, highest probability, AD 766–890).
[18] GrN–21776: 1120±20BP; at 2σ = cal AD 887–981.   [19] GrN–21777: 1070±30BP; at 2σ = cal AD 895–1021.

Cross, which, although buried extended, heads to the west, were, where observable, not shroud wrapped, and contained grave goods in the form of strategically placed meat portions. Burials around all three crosses are located within the central monastic core, but it would appear that a discrete sector in the region of the West Cross was set aside for the burial of specific persons, who were entitled to a form of burial that traversed the boundary between Christian and non-Christian practice, but which took place in parallel with, and during the same temporal period, as the remaining burials in this monastic cemetery.

The second monastery is Nendrum, located on the tidal Mahee Island,[20] in Strangford Lough, Co. Down, dedicated to Mo-Choí (original name Cáelán), who reputedly died AD 497 (*Chron. Ire.*), but which was (probably) founded in the seventh century by a cleric named Crídán, who died AD639 (ibid.) (McErlean, 2007, 306–8). This monastic site, with its three enclosures (Hamlin, 2008, 310–17),[21] is included because of its obvious importance, even though the archaeological evidence relating to burials recovered during excavation (Lawlor, 1925) is less than satisfactory. Burials were mainly confined, as would be expected, to the central monastic enclosure, and included slab-lined lintel graves, stone-lined graves, and unlined dug graves. The lack of information regarding skeletal material and dating evidence makes classification difficult, but the grave types suggest that burial commenced at the foundation of the monastery in the seventh century, and continued until the seventeenth century (McErlean, 2007, 345–50). The importance of some of the people buried in the Early Medieval period is demonstrated by the recovery of sixteen cross-carved grave slabs. These include part of a decorated slab with an inscription, previously described as 'runic', but now identified as an inscription in Latin geometric display capitals, probably dating to around the eighth century (G. Charles-Edwards, 2007, 396–404). An iron handbell, dateable to the seventh–tenth centuries (Bourke, 2007, 412–13), was also recovered at the site.

Third, is a group of burials located outside the perimeter of the monastery founded by St Columba at Durrow, Co. Offaly, during a visit to Ireland from Iona sometime between AD585 and his death in AD595, which became the burial place for kings, abbots, patrons and monks (O'Brien, 2012). A geophysical survey,[22] together with a recent trial excavation at Durrow monastic site, has revealed that the outer enclosing element of the ecclesiastical site consists of a fosse 6.8m wide (Collins, 2018, 27). The depth was not excavated, but is undoubtedly comparable to the outer fosse at Clonmacnoise, width 6.2m, depth 3.8m. Elements of two inner enclosures are also visible on the survey (O'Brien, 2012, 120, Figure 2). Approximately 200 metres outside the south-eastern area of the outer monastery boundary enclosure (Plate 12), in slightly raised ground known as Sheean Hill,[23] a circular enclosure was exposed which surrounded a cemetery of extended, supine, west–east, burials of males, females and juveniles, in dug graves, with no grave goods (Ó Floinn and O'Brien, 2011, 120–39; O'Brien, 2012, 118, 122). Three of these burials have been dated; adult female

---

20 Island Mahee = *Inis Mo-Choí*. 21 This publication, based on the 1970s PhD thesis of the late Ann Hamlin, contains a good synopsis of the monastery at Nendrum. 22 Undertaken by Margaret Gowen. 23 Also known as the Relic Fort (a possible reference to the burial enclosure), and as Fairy Hill.

(GW2), to the eighth–eleventh century,[24] adult male (GW1), to the eleventh–twelfth century,[25] older female (GW5), to the eleventh–thirteenth century.[26] This group of burials provides evidence for the continued exclusion of the laity from burial within the central ecclesiastical cemetery even after the eighth-century Church legislation encouraging the Christian laity to seek burial in church cemeteries, and probably represents the closest the laity could get to burial at the monastery. That the barriers to entry were not just cultural, but were also physical, is demonstrated by the formidable outer boundary. The further discovery in 2006 of a circular cropmark outside the north-eastern section of the outer ecclesiastical boundary enclosure, with human bone exposed in the ploughed surface, points to the possible site of a further outer cemetery (King, 2012, 125–32). Burial of high-ranking individuals continued within the monastic cemetery at Durrow up to at least the fifteenth century (O'Brien, 2012, 117). After the Reformation, the church at Durrow Demesne (Durrow Monastery) became a parish church, with the monastic cemetery thereafter becoming available for burial to all.

This type of exclusion from burial within established ecclesiastical or monastic cemeteries may also account for the fact that some cemeteries, which started as secular, appear to have become consecrated and acquired a church at a later period.

EARLY COMMUNITY CHURCH CEMETERIES

An interesting cemetery, with ecclesiastical and familial or communal aspects, in a circular enclosed site, is that at Caherlehillan, Co. Kerry (Sheehan, 2009, 191–206; 2014, 247–58), where the primary feature in the 'ritual' area in the eastern half of the enclosure was a cemetery of eighteen graves, a small church represented by postholes, and a 'special' grave which was later covered by a stone shrine. Due to lack of preservation of skeletal material it was not possible to obtain c14 dates, or to identify the sex of the burials. However, the recovery of spindle whorls among deposits of waste material in the domestic area (Sheehan, 2014, 254) points to the presence of females, suggesting to this writer that the cemetery is probably familial, possibly representing the kin-group of a *monachus* ('a lay tenant of the church'), or perhaps the descendants of an *érlam* ('a founding saint'), rather than being strictly monastic. While it was not possible to obtain radiocarbon dates for the burials, material from the fill of the primary foundation trench produced a date between the fifth and seventh centuries (probably sixth–seventh century).[27] Present in the 'ritual' section of the site were decorated stone slabs, one of which displayed an engraved Maltese cross with a handle, reminiscent of a *flabellum*, above which is the profile of a peacock. The excavator indicates a parallel for the design in Mediterranean Christian culture. Further evidence for contact with the Mediterranean region and mainland Europe, either directly, or indirectly via south-western Britain, was the recovery from the shrine feature, and from among waste material, of shards from ceramic containers of

---

24 GrA–24319: 1115±40BP; at 2σ = cal AD 778–1016 (at 87.4% probability = cal AD 861–1016).
25 GrA–24318: 940±40BP; at 2σ = cal AD 1019–1185.   26 GrA–24320: 895±40BP; at 2σ = cal AD 1035–1217.   27 GrA–24462; 1490±40BP; at 2σ = cal AD 430–648 (at 82.3% = cal AD 536–648).

north-eastern Mediterranean Bii-type, datable to the late fifth/mid-sixth century, used for the importation of wine (Kelly, 2010, 57, 65), and E ware from western Gaul, dateable to the late sixth/mid-seventh century (Doyle, 2009, 23), probably originally used for the importation of wine or oil, but also used for cooking. The presence in the domestic sector, outside the 'ritual' area, of the remains of two conjoined circular buildings, and a 9-post-hole structure, interpreted as an elevated granary (Sheehan, 2014, 254–5), together with remnants of ironworking, spindle whorls and burnt animal bone, indicates that the occupants were self-supporting. Burial appears to have ceased at this cemetery after the eighth century, after which the site was abandoned.

The cemetery and settlement site at Reask, Co. Kerry, bears some resemblance to the site at Caherlehillan, in that the circular walled enclosure at Reask, excavated between 1972 and 1979 by Tom Fanning on behalf of the Office of Public Works (Fanning, 1981, 67–172), was also divided into a domestic and a cemetery/ecclesiastical area. The cemetery, located in the south-eastern quadrant of the enclosure and separated from the domestic area by a wall, contained forty-two graves, mainly of lintel-type, but some dug graves, all aligned west–east, in rows extending from north to south. Due to lack of surviving skeletal material c14 dating of the burials was not possible, but several of the graves underlay the foundation levels of a stone 'oratory', the building of which the excavator places between the eighth and tenth centuries (ibid., 151). A small 'shrine' feature was located immediately outside the 'oratory' at the same level as the lintel graves, and phosphate analysis suggests that this feature had contained bone. A possible date for the shrine feature is provided by a fragment of Bii ware found within the fill, which would suggest a date in the fifth–sixth century (Kelly, 2010). It has, however, been suggested (Doyle, 2009, 33–4) that the placing of shards of Mediterranean pottery into this, and the shrine at Caherlehillan, were votive offerings creating a symbolic connection to Rome. Reask also contains fourteen decorated stone slabs, including the highly decorated Reask pillar-stone (Fanning, 1981, Plate IX). The earliest occupation level, at the centre of the enclosure, has produced charcoal dating to the fourth–seventh century.[28] As this date was derived from wood-charcoal, it must be treated with caution. Finds from the site include evidence for iron smelting, many shards of undatable handmade coarse pottery, six shards of Bii ware, and one shard of Biii ware. Finds of stone spindle whorls and possible loom weights, which are indicative of the presence of women at the site, points to this possibly being the church of a kin-group, with its own cemetery. The final use of the site was as a *ceallúnach*.[29]

The 'ecclesiastical' site at Ballygarran, Co. Waterford, excavated in 1940 by Michael Bowman (Power, 1941), was recently reassessed (Curtin, 2015),[30] and indications are that it represents a habitation site, with a possible early church and cemetery. A recent geophysical survey (Bonsall and Gimson, 2007) shows that the excavated penannular cemetery enclosure was actually located in the south-eastern quadrant of a heretofore unknown trivallate enclosure (a *dún* or *lios*), and thereby

28 UB-2167: 1565±90BP; at 2σ = cal AD 260–651 (at 93.7%, highest probability, = cal AD 325–651). This date, which has been re-calibrated by me, using OxCal 4.3, is at odds with the published date of AD 385 (Fanning, 1981, 104).   29 *Ceallúnach* = Killeen (or cilleen); a burial place for unbaptised children.   30 Thanks to John Curtin for making his unpublished MA thesis available, and for permission to refer to it.

represents an internal division between a possible domestic sector and cemetery/ church area. The 1940s excavation of the penannular enclosure revealed post-hole evidence for a possible wooden church measuring 8m east–west, by 4.7m north–south; eight possible burials; an upright stone, *c.*1m high, inscribed with a Greek cross; six shards of fifth–sixth century Bii ware (Weadick, 2013); and seven shards of sixth–seventh century E ware (Curtin, 2015, 46–51). The burials (ibid., 34–7) comprised a 'head cist' (F22) which contained a skull, a fragment of which is in the NMI (1940-824). This skull burial could represent a 'trophy', but is likely to represent the head of a person of importance in the community, who had died elsewhere, the body being buried at the place of death, but the head being buried among his/her own people at the place of 'resurrection'; a slab-lined cist (F26) contained fragments of bone and a tooth; a slab-lined cist (F27) had no bone survival; two stone-lined graves (F23, F25) contained no surviving bone; dug grave (F29) contained bone fragments suggesting that the grave had contained an adult and a child (ibid., 68–9); dug graves (F24, F28) had no surviving bone.

The evidence suggests that this cemetery served a kin-group of high status. The trivallate enclosure consisted of three concentric, closely spaced ditches, with possible (now eroded) banks. This is a comparatively rare monument in Early Medieval Ireland, and implies that the person or persons responsible for building it wished to make a visible display of wealth, and had access to a large labour force to facilitate this. The presence of Bii and E ware indicates the consumption of wine, perhaps for religious ritual, and that the occupants were in a position to trade for luxury goods. There is some indication that the enclosure was abandoned around the eighth–ninth century, but the presence of Leinster cooking ware indicates re-occupation in the thirteenth–fourteenth century (Curtin, 2015, 51–2). Modern analysis of the iron slag recovered in the excavation indicates that ironworking occurred between the fifteenth and eighteenth centuries (ibid., 85–6, 88). A stone-lined well shaft (F36) was located outside the northern perimeter of the cemetery enclosure (ibid., 32–4). The final use of the enclosure as a *ceallúnach* is indicated by the local name for the site, anglicised as Killeenagh. This important and interesting cemetery and settlement in a trivallate enclosure would undoubtedly benefit from c14 dating of the skull fragment, and excavation of the remaining two-thirds of the site.

COMMUNITY CHURCH CEMETERIES WITH A WIDE TEMPORAL SPAN

Kill of the Grange, Co. Dublin, originally named *Cluain Caoin*, was dedicated to St Fintan (of *Cluana Eidneach* (Clonenagh), Co. Laois, and Clonkeen, Dublin) who reputedly died AD 603 (*Chron. Ire.*) (O'Brien, 1980, 94; 1988, 520). An early date for the foundation of this church, which possibly represents the spread of the saint's cult from one foundation to another, appears to be confirmed by a recent small excavation north-north-east of the Early Modern boundary wall of the cemetery, but within the bounds of a possible inner enclosure ditch (Tobin, 2018; Duffy, 2019, 5), in which a burial (SK 1), adult, sex unidentified, dated to the sixth–seventh century,[31] had been interred in a grave lined with thin slabs of red coloured mica-schist. Nearby, a further

---

[31] UBA-37311: 1466±34BP; at 2σ = cal AD 543–649.

burial (SK 2), possibly contemporary with (SK 1), had been buried prone, in the fill of the possible inner boundary ditch. The location of these burials north of the Medieval stone church may however be problematic, as burial would normally take place west, south, or east of a church building. The implication is that these burials were deliberately excluded from the main cemetery and were interred in a place usually reserved for the burial of outcasts, criminals, suicides, or those who had died violently.

The stone church at the site is pre-Norman, with a flat-lintelled west doorway and antae, and was later extended by the addition of a chancel, probably in the thirteenth century. The church fell into disuse in the seventeenth century, but the cemetery continued to be used until the nineteenth century. The layout of this church site is highlighted by the presence of the inner enclosure ditch recently partially excavated; the presence of a possible outer enclosure represented by a laneway that existed at this site prior to 1960; two stone high crosses (now broken), each with a cube shaped base; a probable holy well, known as the Roman or the Briton's well (now covered); a large boulder with two deep bullauns and an inscription that translates as DOM (now buried below ground level); a cross-inscribed stone; and a Medieval stone font, now in the nearby Church of Ireland churchyard (O'Brien, 1980, 88–91; 1988, 506, 510–14). In 1179, this ecclesiastical establishment was confirmed by Pope Alexander III as part of the possessions of the Canons of Christ Church, Dublin (O'Brien, 1980, 92).

Cemeteries that originated as early secular cemeteries, which appear to have become consecrated after the eighth century, acquired a church possibly because of the Church rules regarding the burial of Christians, and continued to be used for burial until after the Reformation, have now been recognised in the archaeological record. A good example is the site at Ballykilmore, Co. Westmeath (Channing, 2009, vols 1 and 2; 2014, 23–38). This partially excavated cemetery, located in the south-eastern quadrant of a penannular enclosure that produced evidence for industrial activity, contained over 900 burials of men, women and children. The earliest dated burial, an older male, is fifth–sixth century.[32] A rectangular stone building, oriented west–east, was erected in the ninth–tenth century. This was probably a church. The structure, which overlay burials, one of which has been dated to the eighth–ninth century,[33] appears to have collapsed, or was demolished, by the eleventh century, and a burial that cut through the collapsed rubble has been dated to the eleventh–thirteenth century.[34] Although the 'church' was never rebuilt, burial continued at the cemetery until the sixteenth–seventeenth century,[35] by which time the enclosing ditch had become filled and the site had become a *ceallúnach*. All local memory of the cemetery seems to have been erased by the nineteenth century when the site was bisected by the Tyrellspass-Croghan road.

A similarly forgotten, but long-lived cemetery was re-discovered during roadworks in 2003 at Ballyhanna, Co. Donegal, located close to a crossing-point on the southern bank of the River Erne (see McKenzie et al., 2015, for an in-depth analysis of the cemetery). Over 1,200 burials of men, women and children, in simple dug graves, were uncovered. This cemetery, which may originally have been secular, commenced

---

[32] UBA–8352: 1578±44BP; at 2σ = cal AD 393–575. [33] UBA–8364: 1197±32BP; at 2σ = cal AD 713–945 (at 86.6%, highest probability, = cal AD 765–898. [34] UBA–8340: 892±50BP; at 2σ = (93.5%) cal AD 1027–1225. [35] Infant burial; UBA:8359: 280±31BP; at 2σ (92%) = cal AD 1513–1666.

use in the seventh–eighth century based on the date of burial (SK 1242).[36] Six other burials dispersed throughout the cemetery have been dated to the eighth–tenth century.[37] A stone church was built in the thirteenth or early fourteenth century, dated by burial (SK 787),[38] that underlay the church wall foundation. It is not possible to say whether there was an earlier church built of wood or turves at the site, as the interior of the stone church has not been excavated. There is, however, evidence for a small stone 'reliquary shrine' located immediately outside the southern wall of the stone church. Although no dates were obtained for this 'shrine', similar shrines in Ireland are usually dated to the eighth century and later. The area around the Ballyhanna shrine was avoided by burials. The cemetery fell out of use in the seventeenth century, the latest dated burial (SK 530) is sixteenth–seventeenth century.[39] It is also possible that the church was deliberately demolished in the seventeenth century (McKenzie et al., 2015, 44). The location of this church and cemetery was then erased from local memory until its re-discovery in the twenty-first century.

Another forgotten church/cemetery was uncovered during road works at Glebe, Co. Wicklow (O'Donovan 2007; 2014, 187–223). The excavator has suggested that this may be the church of Drumkay, associated with St Berchán, an early saint of the Leinster sept, the Dál Messin Corb (O'Donovan, 2014, 188), but it is also possible that this may originally have been a secular cemetery. A total of 191 burials were recovered during a partial excavation, including adults and children, in lintel-type graves and simple dug graves. The earliest skeletons were not suitable for c14 dating, but the excavator suggests that burial commenced c.AD600. The early burials pre-date the remains of a stone church which is estimated to have been in use from AD1000 to 1500. Later burials produced dates from the eleventh to the seventeenth century. There is no positive evidence for an earlier church at the site, but the excavator suggests that trenches excavated close to the stone church may indicate the presence of an earlier building (ibid., 189–90). After the cemetery ceased to be used, it was erased from local memory.

The cemetery at Ardreigh, Co. Kildare (Opie, 2006, 228–9; Moloney et al., 2016), poses a problem. Approximately 1,259 burials were recovered, of which approximately 155 were estimated to be Early Medieval in date. The early burials, which comprise men, women and children, appear to have been enclosed by a small circular ditch dated to the eighth–ninth century.[40] The earliest dated burial (B1550) is seventh–eighth century.[41] The excavators believe that the burials were associated with an early church (Moloney et al., 2016) but there is no archaeological evidence to support this. There is, however, evidence for kilns within the outer enclosure, suggesting that this cemetery may have started as a secular settlement cemetery. The town of Ardreigh was subsequently established, and it is probable that a church, which is recorded as

---

36 UBA–11453: 1286±22BP; at 2σ = cal AD 668–770 (the dates from Ballyhanna have been recalibrated using Ox-cal 4.3).   37 Sample SK 885: UBA–1449: 1168±35; at 2σ = cal AD 771–970.   38 UBA–14972: 708±25BP; at 2σ = cal AD 1262–1381 (at 89.5% probability = cal AD 1262–1300).   39 UBA–1444: 278±24BP; at 2σ = cal AD 1520–1665.   40 Ditch, north section, D5661, at 2σ = cal AD 766–895; south section, D1277; at 2σ = cal AD 765–892. Personal communication Colm Moloney. No further information available at time of writing.   41 At 2σ = cal AD 661–773. Personal communication Colm Moloney. No further information available at time of writing.

'location of' on the 1837 OS map, was also established in the cemetery area at this time. The lands at Ardreigh and its appurtenances were granted between 1181 and 1199 to the archbishop of Dublin, and a church is mentioned between 1219 and 1220 (McNeill, 1949, 24, 42). Burial continued in the cemetery until at least the Reformation.

At Omey Island, Co. Galway, a cemetery being eroded by the sea was excavated over several seasons (O'Keeffe, 1993, 31; 1994a, 39; 1994b, 14–17). The island, which is linked to the mainland at low tide, is regarded as the site of a monastery reputed to have been founded by St Féichín, of Fore, who died AD665 (*Chron. Ire.*). Over 250 burials of adults and children were recovered, mainly from beneath and within a large rectangular stone enclosure, 14m x 8m. The burials, which overlay a Bronze Age shell midden, were very disturbed, but one (SK 235) has been dated to the seventh–eighth century.[42] Unfortunately, the stratigraphic location of this burial is unknown to this writer. One burial in the cemetery appears to have been of an important individual, perhaps a local holy person, in that it was covered by a stone *leacht*, which was refurbished over time. Although there is a Medieval stone church elsewhere on the island, there was no excavated evidence for a church at this cemetery. The presence of a coffin (O'Keeffe, 1994a) indicates that burial continued well into the Early Modern period. While this cemetery is referred to in the literature as 'monastic', it is possible that it is a secular cemetery which was in use from the seventh until the eighteenth century, the monastery being located elsewhere on the island. This cemetery was erased from local memory when several houses were built on the site at about the year 1800 (O'Keeffe, 1993, 31). Another cemetery on the island is still used for burial by people from the adjoining mainland up to the present day.

OTHER POSSIBLE EARLY COMMUNITY CHURCH CEMETERIES

Further probable community churches/cemeteries that appear to have been founded in the Early Medieval period and continued to operate until as late as the fourteenth century, and even later, which often then became *ceallúnaigh*, include an early cemetery at Solar, Co. Antrim, where there is evidence for a Medieval stone church. Partial excavation in 1993 (Hurl et al., 2002, 37–82) revealed, at the earliest levels, eight male burials in slab-lined cist graves, one of which (B628) has been dated to the seventh–eighth century.[43] The remaining 115 burials comprised males, females and children, all in unprotected dug graves, one of which (B602) has been dated to the tenth–twelfth century.[44] A Class 1 iron handbell, of a type dateable to the seventh–tenth century (Bourke, 1980, 59, 65), had previously been recovered from the site (Hamlin, 2008, 218; Hurl et al., 2002, 87). Burial at this cemetery appears to have ceased after the thirteenth century.

A trial excavation undertaken in 1977 at St John's Point, Co. Down (Brannon, 1980, 59–64), revealed a slab-lined cist burial beneath, thereby pre-dating, the north wall

---

42 UBA-27807: 1281±30BP; at 2σ = cal AD 664–773 (I am indebted to Dr Mario Novak, University of Zagreb, Croatia, for providing this date).   **43** GrA-6971: 1340±50BP; at 2σ = cal AD 608–772.   **44** GrA-6970: 960±50BP; at 2σ = cal AD 990–1185.

of the Medieval stone church.[45] The burial was not excavated, but a further two slab-lined cists (undated) were uncovered at a similar level outside the wall, one of which contained a male burial (B23) and the fragmentary remains of another burial (Brannon, 1980, 61–2). A further nineteen burials, plus disarticulated remains, were of males, females and children, and appear to post-date a pit containing souterrain ware, indicating that these burials were post eighth century in date. One of these burials was accompanied by deliberately placed pieces of quartz. The final use of the cemetery was as a *ceallúnach*.

In the townland of Derry, Co. Down, an early cemetery, with evidence for possible early habitation, was uncovered during restoration work on two ruined Medieval stone churches, referred to as the north and south churches (Waterman, 1967, 53–69; Hamlin, 2008, 289–91). A total of thirty-six burials, mainly male, but with some females and children, were recovered beneath the foundations, thereby pre-dating, both churches. Burials beneath the south church, which was a small building with antae and with possible evidence for an earlier structure, were in slab-lined lintel graves, while the burials beneath the foundations of the larger north church were mainly in dug graves. Several cross-inscribed stones are recorded from this site (Hamlin, 2008, 290–1). These stone churches at Derry were abandoned for ecclesiastical purposes and replaced by secular occupation and ironworking, probably in the thirteenth or fourteenth century (Waterman, 1967, 62). The site was used as a *ceallúnach* in the later Medieval or Early Modern period.

Burials recovered beneath, and thereby pre-dating, the wall foundations of a ruined Medieval church at Collierstown 2, Co. Meath (Ó hÉanaigh, 1934), included males, females and children. Two were in slab-lined graves, and about twelve were in dug graves, and all were accompanied by quartz pebbles. An unusual feature was the presence of small box-shaped cists, arranged in a circle, each containing a skull, one of which was that of a juvenile aged about 13 years, whose skull had been trephined. The reason for these box-like features is unknown, but it may be that they were constructed by grave diggers when disposing of charnel, especially skulls, over a period. Also recovered was a Class 1 bronzed iron handbell, dateable to the seventh–tenth century (Bourke, 1980, 61, 65).

Over forty burials in slab-lined graves were discovered in 1929 during sand quarrying close to the ruined Medieval stone church of Killegar (Cell Adhgair?), Co. Wicklow. The site was not formally excavated but was visited by Liam Gogan of the National Museum (Gogan, NMI 1929; Gogan, 1929, ns 15–16). Finds from the site include, two Class 1 iron handbells, dateable to the seventh–tenth century (Bourke, 1980, 59, 66), recovered in the vicinity of the graves, and four highly decorated grave slabs (one now missing), of the type known as Rathdown slabs,[46] dateable to the pre-Norman period, possibly ninth to eleventh centuries (Ó hÉailidhe, 1957, 75–88; 1973, 51–64; O'Brien, 1988, 508–12). The finding of souterrain ware at the site would suggest that burial continued into the Medieval period. It has been suggested that the cemetery ceased to operate in the sixteenth century (Gogan,

---

45 The stone church at this site had antae and a west doorway (Hamlin, 2008, 324). 46 This grave slab type is confined to the region of the half barony of Rathdown, in south Dublin and north Wicklow.

1929, 16), but this does not appear to be the case, because some local families still retain, and use, burial rights in the surviving part of the cemetery up to the present time.

CHURCH CEMETERIES ASSOCIATED WITH CONVERSION-PERIOD SAINTS

At Loman Street, Trim, Co. Meath, six burials discovered during trenching for services beside the Medieval church and Early Modern cathedral (Seaver, 2014, 241–5) may indicate the position of the early church founded by Lommán at Trim. After the excavation the burials were left *in situ*, but one (B1), dated to the fifth–seventh century,[47] is indicative of the presence of an early cemetery. Lommán [Lommanus] is included by Tírechán in his seventh-century list of priests accompanying Patrick (*Tírechán* 6 (4), Bieler, 1979, 128–9), and he is further referred to in another list by Tírechán as 'Lommán, his brother', presumably relating to Brocidius, the preceding name in that list (*Tírechán* 30 (3), Bieler, 1979, 146–9). The *Additamenta* in the ninth-century Book of Armagh (Bieler, 1979, 166–71) contains a legend that includes: a description of Lommán accompanying Patrick when he first arrived in Ireland; the foundation of the church at Trim; Lommán's meeting with the British mother of Fedelmid (the grandson of King Loíguire), to whom he describes himself as 'Lommán, a Briton'; and an assertion that the church at Trim was built twenty-five years before the church of Armagh was founded. This latter assertion is interesting, because the church at Armagh is reputed to have been founded in AD 444 (*Chron. Ire.*), making a possible date for the Trim foundation around AD 419, thus prior to the reputed arrival of Patrick in Ireland in AD 432. It is possible that Lommán was a pre-Patrician British missionary active in Ireland, who founded the church at Trim, and who, together with his church, was later assimilated into Patrick's narrative by scribes in seventh-century Armagh.

Legend has it that before Patrick obtained the hilltop site where Armagh is located, he was granted, and lived, at a place lower down, where 'is now the burial-ground of the martyrs [*fertae martyrum*]' (*Muirchú*, 1.24 = BII 6(2), Bieler, 1979, 108–9). Excavation in 1979/1980 at 46–8 Scotch Street, Armagh (Lynn, 1988, 69–84), in an area generally believed to be the location of *Na Ferta* ('the graves'), revealed evidence for pre-burial occupation in the form of a fire pit, dated by charcoal to the fourth–fifth century.[48] Fourteen graves were exposed, and as these did not intercut each other the excavator has suggested that they were in use for a short time. Poor bone survival ruled out c14 dating. Two graves are of interest. Grave A, which measured 1.3m in length, was too short to have contained an extended adult, but at the east-end were remains of two parallel long bones (tibia?), and beside these was a human skull. A pit (F6) across the west-end of the grave contained two post-holes that may represent the remains of a grave marker (Lynn, 1988, 80). This grave could represent the previously curated remains of an important person, but if associated with Christians,

---

47 Wk–24840: BP date unpublished; at 2σ = cal AD 430–640.   48 UB–2439: 1685±30BP; at 2σ = cal AD 257–419 (at 82.0%, high probability, = cal AD 320–419). As this date was obtained from charcoal it must be treated with caution.

translation and re-burial would not have occurred until after the seventh century when the cult of corporeal relics became acceptable in Ireland (Doherty, 1984, 70–9; O'Brien, 1999a, 57–8). Or, it might represent a punitive form of burial whereby a decapitated head was placed at the foot-end of the grave, a rite which was known in Britain in the Late Roman and Early Anglo-Saxon period (Philpott, 1991, 77–89; O'Brien, 1999a, 7), in which case it would not represent Christian practice. Grave G, a full-length, west–east grave, contained the remains of a single piece of oak, probably representing an oak log coffin (Lynn, 1988, 80), samples from which have been dated to the fifth–seventh century and sixth–seventh century,[49] indicating that possible Christian burial took place at this cemetery from about the fifth–sixth century. Until recently, this was the only example of a log coffin known in Ireland.[50] It is possible, in view of the presence of Grave A at Armagh, that the term *ferta* was originally associated with a non-Christian burial place which may have been appropriated for burial by Christians who were possibly associated with Patrick. The name would then have been altered, from *ferta* to *fertae martyrum*, to commemorate the burial place of conversion-period Christians.

ISLAND CHURCH CEMETERIES

Islands (Map 8) would usually have been regarded as liminal or *díseart* (desert) places, isolated from conventional living, often difficult to access as in the case of Skellig, High Island, Inishmurray and Inishkea North, each of which, located in the Atlantic, were probably regarded as being on the edge of the known world and therefore ideal places for the establishment of penitential monastic life. While being easier to access, especially at low tide, others such as Illaunloughan, Church Island, Omey Island, Nendrum, and Cleenish, on upper Lough Erne, Co. Fermanagh, would also have been regarded as suitably liminal places, especially for pilgrimage. Dalkey Island on the east coast, while it might also be regarded in the same light, was probably more likely to have been an off-shore stopping-off point for travellers using the Irish Sea, either arriving into, or leaving, the mainland.

Church Island, Valencia Harbour, Co. Kerry, is a small island joined by a sandbar at low tide to the nearby larger island of Beginish. The 'sacred' area is located on the highest point in the west and south of the island, with the domestic or secular area located in the centre and north-eastern quadrant. This arrangement, which differs from the norm in which a sacred area is usually located in the south-eastern quadrant, is probably due to the topography of the island (Hayden, 2013, 79). Excavations conducted in the 1950s (O'Kelly, 1958, 57–136) and between 2003 and 2006 (Hayden, 2013, 67–138) in advance of conservation works necessitated by sea erosion revealed over 100 burials that, where identifiable, were of males, with perhaps a few children; a small number were in slab-lined graves, but the majority were in dug graves. Some of the burials are associated with a turf or wooden church which underlay the stone

---

49 (a) UB–2437: 1510±50BP; at 2σ = cal AD 427–638: (b) UB–2438: 1400±40BP; at 2σ = cal AD 571–679. **50** A possible second example has now been excavated at Newtown Rath, Co. Dublin.

'oratory' on the island. One of the burials (F3), in a slab-lined grave that underlay the wall of the stone oratory, has been dated to the tenth–eleventh century,[51] an indication that the oratory was built perhaps shortly after this date (Hayden, 2013, 78). An important discovery at the highest point of the island, in the more recent excavations, was a probable gable shrine, within which several undated but apparently translated burials were recovered. Several c14 dates have been obtained indicating that two individuals (Burials 18 and 44), who were buried to the east of the shrine, died in the seventh–eighth century,[52] and a further individual (Burial 1), who appears to have been interred directly into the shrine, died in the eighth–tenth century.[53] The excavator suggests that the earlier part of the shrine was constructed by at least the late eighth century. A shrine was also uncovered lower down the terraced area and a date of between the ninth and eleventh centuries has been suggested for its construction. A corner-post subsidiary shrine that overlay a grave with minimal skeletal survival was located on a lower terrace (Hayden, 2013, 85, 87, 90–2, 116–17). Other finds from the sacred area include, fragments of a Class 1 handbell, dateable to the seventh–ninth centuries; a stone slab, with a well-carved Maltese cross or flabellum and superimposed ogam inscription dated to the seventh century (McManus, 1991, 69–70, 100); an unstratified shard of E ware, dateable to the sixth–seventh century; several fragments of slate crosses that are undatable; and hundreds of quartz pebbles, mainly associated with the shrines, which suggests that the island and its shrines may have become a place of pilgrimage during the Medieval period. The presence of domestic houses in the secular area of the site suggests that this was a familial or communal rather than a monastic foundation. The island may have been abandoned for a time from the ninth century and reoccupied about the eleventh century (Hayden, 2013, 128–9). The final occupation and subsequent abandonment of the island appears to have occurred around the fifteenth century.

Also excavated in Co. Kerry, a small low-lying island known as Illaunloughan (Loughan's Island), in the Portmagee channel, has produced evidence for early church activity and burial (White Marshall and Walsh, 2005). The eastern side of the island consisted of a 'sacred' area with evidence for an early oratory built of turves, which was succeeded by a dry-stone structure; north of the oratory was a gable shrine. Both the oratory and the shrine provided focal points for Early Medieval burial. Five burials in dug graves, but with no bone survival, were associated with the eastern end of the turve-built oratory. However, two graves on the north-western and western sides contained bone. One grave (SK 103) was undated, the second grave contained two burials, one of which (SK 119) is undated, but the other (SK 120), which was laid on top of (SK 119), has been dated to the eighth–ninth century.[54] These graves partially underlay the wall of the stone oratory, an indication that the structure was probably built to replace the turve-built church in the later eighth or in the ninth century. The second focal point for burial was a reliquary shrine consisting of large slates laid in the fashion of a gable shrine. This reliquary shrine, built on a rock outcrop enlarged

---

51 UB–7622: 1047±31BP; at 2σ = cal AD 899–1029 (at 87.0% probability = cal AD 947–1029). 52 B18: UB–7631: 1277±34BP; at 2σ = cal AD 659–860 (at 91.9% probability = cal AD 659–778. B44: UB–7634: 1289±33BP; at 2σ = cal AD 661–773. 53 B1: UB–7624: 1142±32BP; at 2σ = cal AD 776–980 (at 89.0% probability = cal AD 800–980). 54 UB–4103: 1191±22; at 2σ = cal AD 771–892. 55 UB–4104: 1248±18BP; at 2σ = cal AD 681–861 (at 89.6% probability = cal AD 681–779).

by an artificial mound, had two miniature cist graves containing translated bones (White Marshall and Walsh, 2005, 60–2). Cist F174 had skeletal remains of a male (SK 176) who had died in the seventh–eighth century,[55] together with the remains of an infant, dated to the seventh–eighth century;[56] cist 187 had skeletal remains of a male (SK 188) who had also died in the seventh–eighth century.[57] The translation of these individuals from their original burial place must have occurred after the eighth century, thereby placing the construction of the shrine in this period. Seven burials were in the eastern section of the mound, two of which were juveniles. One grave contained two burials, the lower of which (SK 192), oriented east–west (head east), has been dated to the seventh–eighth century;[58] overlying this individual was SK 180, oriented west–east, dated to the seventh–ninth century[59] (White Marshall and Walsh, 2005, 66, 229 endnote 57). The presence of juveniles among male burials in what is regarded as a monastic cemetery may seem odd, but we must remember Bede's declaration that when he was 7 years of age he was put, first into the charge of Abbot Benedict, and then of Ceolfrith, to be educated, and he spent all his life in the monastery (*HE* v.24, Colgrave and Mynors, 1969, 566–7). The presence of an infant is slightly more problematic, but it is possible that infants, especially first-born male infants, may have been presented to a monastery as oblates fostered to the Church. White quartz pebbles were scattered over some graves, and two cist graves (F104, F24) with no bone survival, therefore undated, situated south-west of the stone oratory, were lined with white quartz pebbles. This, and the presence of scallop shells in the reliquary shrine and in some graves, is discussed in detail by the excavators (White Marshall and Walsh, 2005, 87–102). The domestic, or secular, western part of the island was occupied originally by two turve-built circular huts, one of which (hut B) has been dated to the seventh–eighth century.[60] These huts were succeeded, on the same spot, by a circular dry-stone building (hut D) which has been dated by cattle bones under its base to the eighth–tenth century,[61] suggesting a possibility that it is associated with the stone-built oratory. The island appears to have been vacated for religious purposes sometime in the ninth century but continued to be used for secular purposes during the Middle Ages, although it is possible that the shrine continued to be used as a place of pilgrimage. The graveyard continued to be used during the Medieval period and up the nineteenth and twentieth centuries, during which time it was also used as a *ceallúnach*.

The iconic island of Skellig Michael, located 11.6km off the westernmost tip of the Iveragh peninsula, Co. Kerry, is a UNESCO World Heritage site.[62] This rock in the Atlantic represents the ultimate *díseart* retreat.[63] Access is gained via a sea journey and then by climbing a long flight of stone steps that cling to the steep rock-face. Briefly, the main monastery consists of two dry-stone oratories, a mortared church

56 OxA–10132: 1308±33BP; at 2σ = cal AD 656–770.   57 UB–4107: 1290±22BP; at 2σ = cal AD 666–770.   58 UB–4108: 1283±22BP; at 2σ = cal AD 670–770.   59 UB–4106: unfortunately, the date published, 1508±45BP, appears to be incorrect.   60 UB:4357: 1346±32BP; at 2σ = cal AD 639–766 (at 85.3% probability = cal AD 639–716).   61 UB–3860: 1172±34BP; at 2σ = cal AD 770–968 (at 79.7% probability = cal AD 770–907).   62 A full account, by Bourke, Hayden and Lynch, 2011, of archaeological works undertaken within the main monastery and the South Peak, is available in pdf format at www.worldheritageireland.ie.   63 During a recent TV documentary (RTÉ, Oct. 2018) Richard Foran, the last keeper of the lighthouse on Skellig before it became automated,

(St Michael's Church), seven beehive cells, a small cemetery, two *leachta* (stone-built platforms or altars) with quartz pebbles, two large plain stone crosses, and cross slabs. The upper South Peak contains an oratory, crosses and cross slabs. During excavations at the main monastery, three articulated skeletons and a quantity of disarticulated remains were recovered, resulting in a minimum number of nine individuals, five adults and four juveniles[64] (Bourke et al., 2011, 375–6). The three articulated skeletons, two adults and one juvenile, recovered east of St Michael's Church, were dated.[65] Juvenile (SK 1), aged 9–11 years, oriented west–east, dates to the tenth–twelfth century;[66] adult male (SK 2), aged 25–35 years, oriented west–east, dates to the twelfth–thirteenth century;[67] adult male (SK 3), aged 50–60, oriented south–north, against the east wall of the church, dates to the tenth–twelfth century.[68] However, earlier dates in the seventh–ninth centuries have been obtained from sheep and cattle bones recovered from the region of the entrance to the monastery (Bourke et al., 2011, 371). Possible evidence that individuals SK 1, SK 2 and SK 3 did not reside permanently on the island is provided by stable isotope analysis undertaken by Dr Peter Ditchfield[69] which indicates that all appear to have had a mainly terrestrial diet. Sheep from the island, dated to the seventh–ninth centuries, also had a terrestrial diet, indicating that they had been imported from the mainland. The date at which the monastic settlement on Skellig Michael was founded is unknown. The earliest recorded reference is to a raid by Vikings in AD 824 when 'Étgal of Scelec was seized by the *gentes* ('heathens') and soon afterwards died of hunger and thirst' (*Chron. Ire.*). It is unknown to whom the original monastery was dedicated, although a dedication to a St Fionán is postulated but cannot be proven. The dedication to St Michael was in place by the eleventh century. The island probably became a place of religious pilgrimage in the Medieval period. The lighthouse was built in the early nineteenth century, and the island was taken into care by the Office of Public Works in 1880.

High Island (*Ard Oileán*) (Scally, 2014), located approximately 4km from the Galway coast, has high cliffs around its perimeter, and landing is hazardous. Traditionally the monastic foundation is attributed to St Féichín, who died in AD 665, and who is also reputed to have founded the monastery on Omey Island. However, the only known ecclesiastic associated with the island is Gormgal, who died in AD 1018 (AU). The ecclesiastic site is located within a circular enclosing wall (or cashel), in a sheltered valley, close to a fresh-water lake, in the south-west of the island. At the centre of the walled enclosure, a further squared enclosure surrounds a small stone church. During excavation, evidence for pre-church activity, perhaps the presence of an earlier (organic) church, was uncovered beneath the stone church, and c14 dates from sheep bone and charcoal indicate that whatever existed in this location had been destroyed between the eighth and eleventh century.[70] The first phase of construction of the stone church has been suggested as mid-to-late eleventh century (Scally, 2014, 53–9). Eleven graves were uncovered, of which six contained burials and five were pseudo or imitation graves that had never contained burials. Graves 1–8 were aligned

---

commented that he regarded it as one of the most peaceful places he had experienced. **64** The presence of juveniles may be accounted for by the reference to Bede quoted regarding Illaunloughan. **65** Edward Bourke provided details of c14 dates. **66** UB-4710: 955±44BP; at 2σ = cal AD 995–1170. **67** UB-4711: 826±54BP; at 2σ = cal AD 1045–1280 (at 85.4% probability = cal AD 1120–1280). **68** UB-4712: 968±44BP; at 2σ = cal AD 991–1163. **69** Thanks to Dr Ditchfield for

side by side, oriented west–east, immediately outside the eastern wall of the stone church. Graves 1, 3, 4, 5 contained burials, and graves 2, 6, 7, 8 were pseudo or imitation graves. Grave 1 contained an older male (F42) dated to the eleventh–twelfth century[71] who had originally been buried in a simple dug grave that had become covered by some quartz pebbles and lumps of mortar. Grave 3 contained a male (F70) aged over 55 years, dated to the tenth–eleventh century[72] whose original burial was in a slab-lined cist grave, and who had a quartz pebble laid beside his right elbow and several more located around his feet. Grave 4 contained an adult male (F40) dated to the tenth–eleventh century.[73] Initially buried in a slab-lined grave, he had quartz pebbles placed beneath the pelvis, between the legs and around the feet. He also had a fragment of porphyry near his skull. Grave 5 contained a possible male (F37) aged over 55 years, dated to the ninth–tenth century,[74] initially buried in a simple dug grave, the head of which underlay, and therefore pre-dated, the stone church. At some time between the mid-eleventh and early thirteenth century the eight graves in this row were restructured, slightly re-aligned, and marked by elaborately decorated stone grave slabs. The heads of the graves, and the headstones, were incorporated into the east wall of the stone church (Scally, 2014, 78–85). A further burial (F8026), dated to the eleventh–twelfth century,[75] was discovered outside the north-east entrance to the church enclosure, and this grave had also been reconstructed, with a slab-lined cist and decorated slabs being placed above the original grave. Inside the north-east corner of the stone church was an unmarked grave containing an adult male (F208) aged 20–30 years, dated to the twelfth–thirteenth century.[76] This burial was accompanied by a bone pin below the pelvis, a stone hone placed on his right shoulder, and a stone line-sinker on his left shoulder. Isotopic analysis undertaken on a tooth indicates that the place of origin for this individual was not in the west of Ireland, but probably elsewhere in Ireland, or in Britain (Cahill Wilson et al., in Scally, 2014, 236–7). It is possible that the church had ceased to function by the time of this burial. Also located within the church was a small, undated, pseudo grave. High Island was, possibly after the death of Gormgal, deliberately established as a place of pilgrimage. The presence of several *leachta* or altar tables on the island lend credence to this possibility.

The island of Inishkea North is located off the coast of the Mullet peninsula, which encloses Blacksod Bay, Co. Mayo. Partial excavations were undertaken by Françoise Henry in 1938 (Henry, 1945, 127–55) and in 1946 (unpublished). Dr Henry's excavation notes have been re-assessed as part of a PhD thesis by Sharon Greene (Greene, 2009).[77] Excavation in 1938 at Bailey Mór, a large sand mound on the eastern shore of the island, revealed six burials together with disarticulated human bone, and beehive-shaped habitation structures. Excavation in 1946 revealed an unusual area floored with quartz cobbles, located beneath beehive house C. This sub-rectangular

---

granting permission to refer to his unpublished data. 70 Sheep bone: OxA–8946: 1182±36BP; at 2σ = cal AD 721–967 (at 81.6% probability = cal AD 766–905). Charcoal: OxA–8918: 1110±40BP; at 2σ = cal AD 778–1018 (at 89.5% probability = cal AD 862–1018). 71 UB–4156: 913±19BP; at 2σ = cal AD 1038–1165. 72 UB–4266: 1023±23BP; at 2σ = cal AD 981–1033. 73 UB–4155: 1027±19BP; at 2σ = cal AD 986–1027. 74 UB–3999: 1126±22BP; at 2σ = cal AD 879–985. 75 OxA–13665: 956±22BP; at 2σ = cal AD 1022–1155. 76 UB–4000: 849±16BP; at 2σ = cal AD 1160–1225. 77 Thanks to Dr Sharon Greene for providing the relevant extract from her unpublished PhD thesis, and for granting permission to refer to same.

area, 10m x 4.5m approximately, had been divided with edging slabs into at least seven compartments. Compartments 1 and 2 had a large Latin cross inlaid in black stones into the white quartz floor. It is probable that this feature represents an early ecclesiastical element at Bailey Mór (Greene, 2009, 144–6). The presence on the island of slabs decorated with various types of crosses, including a crucifixion scene, and some flabella, also suggests an early ecclesiastical establishment on the island (Henry, 1937, 273–4; 1945). One of the decorated slabs was re-used as a lintel in house B. Unfortunately, the six burials are undated, and the skeletal remains were not retained. Skeletons 1 and 2, sealed below the floor of house C, and skeleton 3, recovered outside the wall of the house, were extended and orientated in a west–east direction. Skeleton 1 had a large heart-shaped white quartz pebble on the breast. It seems probable that these three burials were associated with the quartz cobbled area. Skeleton 4 was found lying on the cobbled surface but the grave had been dug through accumulated habitation debris, a sample from which has been dated to the ninth–tenth century,[78] indicating that the burial probably post-dates the tenth century. Skeleton 5 was found in front of house C, and skeleton 6, oriented north–south, was located outside the enclosing wall of the settlement. It is probable, bearing in mind the presence of early decorated cross slabs on the island, that the compartments in the quartz cobbled area with crosses outlined in the floors represent some form of pre-ninth-century pilgrimage shrine, which was later abandoned and covered by habitation in the form of beehive huts.

The foundation on the island of Inishmurray, located approximately 7km from the Sligo coast, is reputed to have been established in the sixth century by Molaise, possibly associated with Devinish, Co. Fermanagh, but it appears more likely that the foundation is simply associated with the cult of Molaise (Ó Carragáin, 2009b, 208). A large dry-stone cashel contains the remains of two churches, beehive huts and a cemetery. The island also contains several *leachta* and cross-inscribed slabs. Excavations undertaken by Jerry O'Sullivan on behalf of Dúchas, between 1997 and 2000 in areas subject to sea erosion, revealed two main phases of burial at Relickoran, one of the main cemeteries on the island (ibid., 209). The earliest phase of burials pre-dated a *leacht*, one of which burials produced a date in the eighth–tenth century,[79] while the second phase of burials, which post-date the *leacht*, have produced dates ranging from the eleventh–twelfth centuries,[80] and as late as the fifteenth–seventeenth centuries.[81] A bell, and part of a crozier (Molaise's bell and crozier), dating to the eighth–tenth century (Bourke, 1985, 145–68), have previously been recovered at Inishmurray. The evidence suggests that the foundation at Inishmurray was probably established after the eighth century, and the island subsequently became a place of pilgrimage.[82]

Situated on an island (now connected to the mainland by a bridge) in Upper Lough Erne, Co. Fermanagh, is the ecclesiastical establishment of Cleenish, reputed to have been founded in the seventh century by Sinell. Recent small-scale excavations (Ó Maoldúin, 2014) and geophysical survey have revealed the presence of two

---

78 UBA–10239: 1127±20BP; at 2σ = cal AD 882–982.   79 UB–4636: at 2σ = cal AD 711–982 (dates as published in Ó Carragáin, 2009b, 222).   80 UB–6443: at 2σ = cal AD 1044–1158.   81 UB–6449: at 2σ = cal AD 1495–1663.   82 For further details of pilgrimage to Inishmurray see Ó Carragáin, 2009b.

10.2 Rock-carved crosses on Dalkey Island, Dublin.

concentric boundary enclosures, and a possible indication of an early church (Newman et al., forthcoming). In cutting 2, in the northern section of the enclosure, the remains of an adult male (C23) in a shallow grave were uncovered. This male, dated to the sixth–seventh century,[83] had suffered multiple stab wounds, and was possibly decapitated as his head was not present in the grave (ibid). The body had been oriented west–east (head west), a small sandstone disc had been placed between his knees, and the evidence suggests that he had been shroud wrapped. The location of this burial in the northern sector suggests that this man had been excluded from the general cemetery area, possibly because of his violent death.

Dalkey Island (*Delg Inis* 'Thorn Island') in the Irish Sea is located approximately 400 metres from the mainland in south Co. Dublin (Map 8). The island can be clearly seen from the mainland, and conversely the coastline around Dublin can be clearly seen from the island. This island has been occupied periodically since the Mesolithic period, and four prehistoric crouched burials, one of which (burial II) has been dated to the fourth–third century BC,[84] were found in midden material during excavation of

---

[83] Beta 408874: 1420±30BP; at 2σ = cal AD 582–611 (date given in report re-calibrated).
[84] BM–78: 4340±75BP; at 2σ = cal 3333–2760 BC.

sites II and V on the promontory (fortified in the Early Medieval period by the digging of a deep ditch across the neck portion) at the north-western section of the island (Liversage, 1968, 63, 103–4, 176–8; Leon, 2005, 3, 6–8). These fortifications have been dated by the presence of fifth–sixth century shards of B ware from the eastern Mediterranean, and sixth–seventh century E ware from western Gaul (Doyle, 1998, 91–3). Fragments of imported glass vessels, datable to the fifth–seventh and seventh–ninth century, were also recovered elsewhere on the island (Bourke, 1994, 167–8, 170–3). During the excavation, a trench was opened along the north wall of the tenth–eleventh century stone church, on the western side of the island (Site IV), from which eleven burials were recovered. Four of these, in graves cut into boulder clay at a depth of 65cm from the surface, were extended, oriented west–east, in a well-ordered row. One burial (B XII) had a fragment of glass datable to the fifth–seventh century in the grave fill (Bourke, 1994, 167). These burials appear to pre-date the stone church. The upper layer of seven burials were more haphazardly placed, in very shallow graves, one of which (BXI) contained an eleventh-century silver coin struck by the Counts of Normandy (Liversage, 1968, Appendix 4, 179–81). An Early Medieval feature associated with the church/cemetery site is the presence of two early crosses engraved on the vertical face of a rock outcrop (Figure 10.2) facing towards the church, which may represent grave markers, or perhaps form part of an early cemetery boundary (O'Brien, 1988, 510). The church on Dalkey Island, and the church in Dalkey town on the mainland, are dedicated to St Begnat, a female saint who is associated with the early Leinster sept of the Dál Messin Corb (O'Brien, 1988, 518, 521; Ó Riain, 2011, 94), adding credence to the possibility that this is an early ecclesiastical establishment. There is no evidence for the island having been used as a place of pilgrimage in the Medieval period, and the church appears to have been abandoned by the fourteenth century. The island is recorded in AD 1326 as grazing land valued at 12*d*. (O'Brien, 1980, 42). The church structure was adapted for habitation purposes by the builders of the nearby Martello tower in the nineteenth century.

HERMITAGE OR *DÍSEART* CEMETERIES

While sites on islands represented the ultimate *díseart* place, terrestrial sites in remote locations were also utilised. One example, where partial excavation has been undertaken and burials recovered, is at Toureen Peakaun, Co. Tipperary (Ó Carragáin, 2017, 67–79).[85] (Map 8) Originally known as Cluain Aird, the establishment was founded in the seventh century by Beccán, who was regarded as an ascetic (*Fél.*, 126, 136), and who died AD 690 (*Chron. Ire.*). The site contains the remains of a ruined stone church with Romanesque features, several stone crosses, a corner-post shrine, a sundial, and many small stones, some of which display crosses and inscriptions. A possible Anglo-Saxon connection with Toureen is indicated by the inclusion of the female name *Osgyð* at the end of the inscription dedicated to Beccán on the east cross, suggesting that she was the possible instigator of the construction of the cross (G. Charles-Edwards, 2002, 114–18; Ó Carragáin, 2017, 70). The inclusion of an

---

[85] Contains a review of the history, and excavation of the site.

Anglo-Saxon name need not be a cause for surprise, as Toureen is in a region where there was a known Anglo-Saxon presence in the seventh–eighth centuries (O'Brien, 1999, 47–8). The excavated burials include eight that pre-date the stone church, comprising one male, six unidentified adults, and one child, whose burial orientation suggests that they were aligned on an earlier, possibly wooden, church (Ó Carragáin, 2017, 71). Although the ecclesiastical establishment had royal associations, it appears to have begun to decline from about the ninth century. It was used in the later Medieval period as a burial ground for men, women and children, and in recent centuries was used as a burial ground for infants (*ceallúnach*).

QUARTZ PEBBLES

The symbolism associated with quartz pebbles and the possible motivation for their inclusion with individual burials has been examined in chapter 5, pp 119–22. When quartz is included directly with a body in the grave, usually only one or two pieces are used. However, at several church cemeteries – Ballyhanna, Co. Donegal, Church Island, Co. Kerry, Valencia, Co. Kerry, Illaunloughan, Co. Kerry and Skellig, Co. Kerry – large quantities of quartz pebbles have been found. In all cases these are associated with shrines or *leachta*, datable to after the eighth century. It would appear that these pebbles were deposited by pilgrims on to the surface of the shrines as part of a penitential pilgrimage ritual which resulted, over a period of time, in large accumulations of quartz on what were envisaged as the graves of the saints. Pilgrimage and the accompanying ritual continued long after the associated churches had ceased to function.[86]

DOUBTFUL CHURCH CEMETERIES

There are at least three cemeteries designated as church cemeteries, but which are more likely to be secular. These have not been included in Gazetteer 7, but have been included in Map 8 for reference purposes. The sites in question include, a small group of burials (men, women, children) recovered external to the western side of the outer of three concentric enclosures surrounding the early ecclesiastical site founded by Mac Cuilinn, died in AD496 (*Chron. Ire.*), at Lusk, Co. Dublin (O'Connell, 2009, 51–63; 2014, 173–86). Burial B9, one of a decapitated duo who had suffered extreme weapon trauma, has been dated to the fifth–sixth century,[87] and the nearby outer ecclesiastical enclosure ditch has been dated to perhaps slightly later in the fifth–sixth century.[88] It is suggested elsewhere (O'Brien, 2015, 245–6) that had these burials been associated with the nearby ecclesiastical establishment they would have been interred within the central enclosure close to a church. It is more likely that they formed part of a small secular cemetery which may have been in existence either before the establishment of the ecclesiastical site, or may have been contemporaneous with it,

---

[86] For a recent article which presents an unusual and novel perspective on this practice see Lash, 2018, 83–104. [87] SUERC–16990: 1575±35BP; at 2σ = cal AD 406–560. [88] SUERC–17878: 1540±35BP; at 2σ = cal AD 425–594.

but was never intended to be part of the ecclesiastic establishment. These burials cannot be compared with the external burials dated to the eighth–thirteenth century, at Durrow, Co. Offaly, which were deliberately excluded from that monastic cemetery.

At the partially excavated site at Killeany 1, Co. Laois (Wiggins and Kane, 2009; Wiggins, 2014, 273–86), a cemetery with sixty-seven individuals, men, women and children, was located in a penannular enclosure which had unusual overlapping terminals, surrounded by a larger penannular enclosure which contained kilns and pits. The earliest dated burial in the cemetery is male (B36), dated to the fifth–sixth century,[89] and the latest dated burial is that of a young female (B1) dated to the ninth–tenth century,[90] who was interred with a paternoster of forty-four perforated discoidal bone beads (Wiggins, 2014, 277), indicating that she was a Christian. This cemetery contains several deviant burials, including: female (B39), who died from extreme weapon trauma, and was buried prone in the entrance to the cemetery enclosure; a tightly crouched female (B13); and a crouched juvenile (B68) who was interred in one of the terminals of the outer enclosure while the inner cemetery was still in use. Though not impossible, it is unlikely that these burials would have occurred in a church cemetery. During this, admittedly partial, excavation, no evidence for a church building, or any ecclesiastical paraphernalia, was uncovered. Considering the presence of kilns and pits in the larger outer enclosure, this site probably represents a settlement cemetery, which ceased to function by the tenth century, and subsequently faded from local memory.

The evidence for an early church structure at Owenbristy, Co. Galway (Lehane, 2011, 78–9; Delaney and Silke, in Lehane, 2011, 107), is questionable, and is based on the presence in the Early Medieval cemetery area of five post-holes surrounding a void, designated by the excavators as Structure 1 (Plate 13). Charcoal recovered from two of the post-holes has been dated; north-west corner post-hole (161) dated to the mid-seventh century,[91] and post-hole (257) dated to the late sixth to mid-seventh century.[92] If the postulated south wall was substantial enough to have been part of a building it would have cut through, or at least overlain, the grave containing burial (B93), which has been dated to the first half of the seventh century.[93] The short-term nature of this possible structure is demonstrated by the presence within it of a grave containing a juvenile (B69) dated mid-seventh to mid-eighth century.[94] Burial within a functioning church is unknown in Early Medieval Ireland. Also, the majority of the burials in this cemetery are located north of this structure, and burial to the north of a church was usually reserved for suicides, outsiders and those who had died by extreme trauma. Admittedly, some of those buried at Owenbristy had died from extreme trauma, but the majority of burials in the cemetery consisted of 'normal' burials. It is noticeable that no objects of religious significance were recovered either from within Structure 1, or from the cemetery area. It is probable, bearing in mind the individuals buried in the cemetery who had died by extreme weapon trauma, that this 'void' represents a zone that was cordoned off, perhaps on a temporary basis, to accommodate the preparation for burial of those individuals who, because of their

---

89 SUERC–17613: 1555±35BP; at 2σ = cal AD 418–579.   90 SUERC–17631: 1125±35BP; at 2σ = cal AD 777–993 (at 84.8% probability = cal AD 856–993).   91 UB–12366: 1385±19BP; at 2σ = cal AD 621–68.   92 UB–12367: 1442±20BP; at 2σ = cal AD 579–650.   93 UB–12368: 1398±22BP; at 2σ = cal AD 609–64.   94 UB–11245: 1306±30BP; at 2σ = cal AD 657–769.

traumatic injuries, could probably not be laid out in the usual manner in a domestic dwelling prior to burial. The 'void' zone may subsequently have been regarded as having some special significance whereby burial within it was generally avoided.[95] The outline of the area designated as Structure 2 (Plate 13) also does not appear to represent a viable structure. Early Medieval burial ceased in the cemetery after the eighth–ninth century, but burial was revived in or about the thirteenth–fourteenth century, possibly by new settlers moving into the locality. These people were probably unaware of the perceived importance of the 'void', as several of their burials were inserted into that space.

* * *

Cemeteries associated with churches emerged in Ireland from the sixth century, and it is probable that many of these co-existed in close proximity to emerging secular cemeteries. Twenty-seven of these church cemeteries, which have produced archaeological evidence for burial, were examined. Some church cemeteries present difficulties to the archaeologist in that the earliest churches in Ireland were constructed with either wood, which can only be identified by the presence of post-holes, or they were built with turves, which leave little in the way of identifying features. These early wooden/turf churches were later replaced by stone constructions, the earliest recorded example of which, dated to AD725, is at Duleek (*Dom Liacc*), Co. Meath. Where skeletal survival is present church cemeteries have been dated by c14 dating. This is augmented by possible literary references to the foundation and on-site paraphernalia of a religious nature. Many church cemeteries encompass a wide temporal span, with burial commencing in the Early Medieval period, and despite the ruination of church buildings and their abandonment for religious use, these cemeteries continued to be used for burial, in some cases until comparatively recently as *ceallúnach* (the burial places of unbaptised children), and in other cases continue to be used as regular cemeteries up to the present time. Unusual burial groups, for example, in the monastery of Clonmacnoise, and outside the monastery at Durrow, raise questions that warrant further investigation. The presence at church cemeteries, especially in the southern region of Ireland, of shards from ceramic containers (Bii ware, and E ware) used for the importation of wine and oil from the north-eastern Mediterranean region, and from western Gaul, suggests either direct contact with those regions, or indirect contact via the south-western region of Britain which had known trading contacts with Mediterranean regions. Island church cemeteries represent *díseart* hermitage places and places of pilgrimage. The designation of at least three sites as church cemeteries is doubtful; in these cases, the excavated evidence suggests a probable alternative designation as secular cemeteries.

---

95 There is also the possibility that the postulated structures at Owenbristy might be equated with an open-ended structure (8), described as a possible sanctuary, excavated in an area which already contained much pre-historic occupational evidence at Kilmainham, Co. Meath (Walsh, 2011, 9–12). Structure 8 was not associated with a cemetery, although two isolated disturbed burials, one dated to the fifth–sixth century, were recovered outside its open-ended western boundary.

Conclusion

In an Irish context, the adage 'The more things change, the more they stay the same' is apt. Petrie,[1] commenting in the nineteenth century on prevailing burial customs, wrote;

> ... (Old Irish families) however humble in station, preserve with a jealous tenacity, not unmingled with pride, their hereditary right to the posthumous honour of interment in the sepulchre of their lordly ancestors ...
> (Doherty, 2004, 175)

The substance of this observation is evident in the veneration of ancestors demonstrated from the earliest period by those who chose to bury their selected dead in ancient burial monuments (*ferta*), and in secular cemeteries close to the ancestors. When this activity was discouraged by the Christian Church in the eighth century, the preferred burial place, especially for the elite, changed from burial among the ancestors, to burial among the saints. This eventually resulted in the cemeteries attached to major monastic sites, for example, Clonmacnoise and Durrow, becoming the preferred burial place for kings and nobles. Burials are still undertaken in a modern extension to the cemetery at Clonmacnoise up to the present day.

The interest currently being expressed in Iron Age and Early Medieval burial archaeology by emerging scholars is very encouraging. Radiocarbon (c14) dating, not only of inhumed skeletal material, but also of cremated remains, is now becoming the norm in all excavations. Scientific advances in speciality subjects are showing interesting results. DNA analysis of skeletal material, based on the petrous bone, is currently being undertaken at various centres, and results are eagerly awaited; advances in strontium and oxygen isotope analysis of dental material, which can help identify an individual's probable place of birth, and when combined with laser ablation can track the movements of an individual during their early life, will be greatly improved by the ongoing production of improved detailed geological and biosphere maps for Ireland and Britain. The combined use of scientific methods on dated cremated and skeletal material will ultimately result in the prospect of plotting inter-relationships within cemetery populations, within the country generally, and with communities beyond our shores.

Results obtained in scientific research on burial in the Early Medieval period would benefit from being combined with further translations of dated early Irish source material. This could be a two-way process with the archaeological results contributing to a greater understanding of the literary source material and vice versa. My hope is that this publication will make some contribution to the knowledge of burial practices in Iron Age and Early Medieval Ireland and provide a platform for potential future research.

[1] George Petrie (1780–1866).

GAZETTEER 1

Artefacts in cremation deposits

County	Site name	Glass vessel	Metal vessel	Blue beads	Yellow beads	Decorated beads	Amber beads	Bone beads	Fibulae	Dice	Cylindrical box	Mirror & frags	Rings	Misc. metal objects	Misc. fragments
Clare	Claureen			√	√										
Down	Loughey			√	√	√			√						
Dublin	Cherrywood, Site 4				√										
	Glebe Sth	√							√						
Fermanagh	Kiltierney			√	√				√			√		√	
Galway	Ballyboy 1			√			√		√						
	Ballyboy 2			√			√								
	Grannagh				√		√	√							
	Oranbeg			√	√									√	
Kerry	Ballydribeen														√
Kildare	Ballyvass														√
	Carbury Hill B								√?			√			
Kilkenny	Stoneyford	√										√			
Laois	Ballydavis Td			√	√	√			√			√	√	√	√
Limerick	Ballybronoge Sth										√				
	Bruff				√										
	Cush										√				
	Knockcommane			√											
Louth	Haynestown				√										√
Mayo	Carrowjames			√		√								√	√
Meath	Donacarney Gt			√		√	√								
Offaly	Cappydonnell Big				√										
Sligo	Rathdooney Beg													√	
Tipperary	Knockgraffon			√											√
	Marlhill			√											√
Westmeath	Fore		√												
Wexford	Ask													√	
	Coolnahorna 2				√		√?								√
	Ferns Lwr			√	√		√							√	√

227

GAZETTEER 2

Early Medieval burial and cemetery types

County	Site name	Total graves excavated	Skeleton ID	Male	Female	Adult sex unidentified	Juvenile/child	Date	Isolated burial	Pre-existing burial area	Imitative burial monument	Unenclosed cemetery	Settlement cemetery	Foundation/focal burial	Early Med. cremation
Armagh	Scotch Street	9+	Gr.G		√			5th/7th c	?						
Clare	Ballykeel Sth	1	B1	√				4th/6th c	√						
	Kilcorney	1	B1		√		√	6th/7th c		√					
Cork	Courtmacsherry	1	B1	√				6th/7th c	√						
Donegal	Ballymacaward	13	B3		√			5th/6th c		√					
	"		B4		√			6th/7th c		√					
Dublin	Ballynakelly	1	B1	√				5th/6th c	√						
	Cappogue Castle	16	B9	√				5th/6th c				√			
	Glebe Sth	17	G7					5th/7th c		√					
	Kilshane	123	B20			√		8th/10th c				√			
	Newtown Rath	9+	SK 3	√				6th/7th c		√			√		
	"		SK 7	√				9th/11th c		√			√		
	Portmarnock	1	B1	√				5th/6th c	√						
	Westreave	57	B32		√			5th/6th c				√			
	"		B29		√			5th/6th c				√			
Galway	Ballygarraun West	1	B1	√				5th/6th c	√						
	Cross	7	B5	√				3rd/5th c	√						
	"		B4		√			4th/6th c				√			
	"		B3				√	5th/6th c				√			
	"		B7	√				4th/6th c				√			
	"		B2	√				5th/6th c				√			
	"		B6	√				5th/7th c				√			
	"		B1				√	6th/7th c				√			

228

GAZETTEER 2 Early Medieval burial and cemetery types (continued)

County	Site name	Total graves excavated	Skeleton ID	Male	Female	Adult sex unidentified	Juvenile/child	Date	Isolated burial	Pre-existing burial area	Initiative burial monument	Unenclosed cemetery	Settlement cemetery	Foundation/focal burial	Early Med. cremation
	Farta	1	B1		√			4th/6th c	√						
	Feerwore	1	B1		√			5th/6th c		√					
	Owenbristy	79	SK 76		√			4th/6th c					?	√	
	Pollacorragune	4	SK D	√				4th/6th c	√						
	"		SK B		√			5th/6th c	√						
Kildare	Carbury Hill, Site B	15	SK 4	√				3rd/4th c	√						
	"		SK 10		√			4th/5th c	√						
	"		SK 6		√			5th/6th c	√						
	"		SK 1	√				6th/7th c	√						
	Corbally Site 1	6	B5	√				4th/6th c				√			
	"		B1	√				5th/6th c				√			
	Corbally Site 2	31	B92		√			4th/6th c				√			
	"		B27		√			5th/7th c				√			
	"		B140	√				8th/11th c				√			
	Curragh Site 4	1	B1		√			6th/7th c				√			
	Curragh Site 6	11	B11	√				11th/12th				√			
	Greenhills	16	B15		√			4th/6th c				√			
	"		B6		√			4th/6th c					√		
	Kildangan	1	SK 1		√			4th/6th c	√						
	Prumplestown Lwr	4	SK 4	√				4th/6th c	√		√				
	"		SK 2		√			5th/6th c	√		√				
	"		SK 1	√				5th/6th c	√		√				
	"		C1042				√	4th/6th c	√		√				√

GAZETTEER 2 *Early Medieval burial and cemetery types (continued)*

County	Site name	Total graves excavated	Skeleton ID	Male	Female	Adult sex unidentified	Juvenile/child	Date	Isolated burial	Pre-existing burial area	Initiative burial monument	Unenclosed cemetery	Settlement cemetery	Foundation/focal burial	Early Med. cremation
Kilkenny	Baysrath	47	c2189			√		undated		√					
	"		c2399			√		5th/6th c		√					
	"		c2197			√		5th/6th c		√					
	"		c2332			√		6th/7th c		√					
	Holdenstown 1	8	B8	√				5th/6th c		√					
	"		B2		√			6th/7th c		√					
	Holdenstown 2	94	B59	?				5th/6th c				√		√	
	Killaree	6+	?				√	6th/7th c				√			
	Sheastown	12	?	√				5th/6th c				√			
Laois	Ballydavis 1	7	C908	√				5th/6th c	√						
	"		C192	√	√			3rd/5th c			√			√	
	Morett Site D	4	B2		√			5th/6th c				√			
	"		B4		√			5th/6th c				√			
	Morett 13		c1302				√	5th/6th c				√			
Limerick	Kildimo	6+	B1	√				5th/6th c				√			
Louth	Faughart	772+						5th/10th c					√		
Mayo	Aghalahard	1	B1		√			undated	√						
	Ballinchalla	1	?		√			undated		√					
	Belladooan	1	B1		√			4th/7th c	√						
	Kiltullagh Hill 1	5	?		√			2nd/4th c		√					
	"		?		√			4th/6th c		√					
Meath	Ardsallagh 1	30	B16	√				5th/6th c			√				
	"		B2		√			4th/7th c			√				
	"		B11	√				6th/7th c			√				
	"		B29		√			6th/7th c			√				
	"		B4				√	4th/6th c				√			

GAZETTEER 2 *Early Medieval burial and cemetery types (continued)*

County	Site name	Total graves excavated	Skeleton ID	Male	Female	Adult sex unidentified	Juvenile/child	Date	Isolated burial	Pre-existing burial area	Imitative burial monument	Unenclosed cemetery	Settlement cemetery	Foundation/focal burial	Early Med. cremation
	Betaghstown (Anchorage)	61	F44		√			5th/6th c		√	√				
	"		F181	√				5th/6th c		√	√				
	"		F251		√			5th/6th c		√	√				
	"		F279		√			5th/6th c		√	√				
	Betaghstown (Brookside)	16	B12	√				4th/7th c			√				
	"		B11		√			4th/7th c			√				
	"		B2	√				5th/7th c			√				
	"		B15	√				5th/7th c			√				
	Castlefarm	12	B1		√			5th/6th c				√			
	"		B10		√			7th/8th c				√			
	Collierstown 1	61+	B48		√			5th/6th c		√			√		
	"		B47	√				5th/6th c		√					
	Colp West 1	120+	B102		√			6th c		√		√	√		
	"		B65	√				6th/7th c		√		√	?		
	Ferganstown/ Ballymacon	1	B1		√			7th/9th c	√						
	Johnstown	398	B110	√				4th/7th c			√	√	√		
	"		B129			√		4th/7th c			√	√	√		
	"		B33	√				5th/7th c			√	√	√		
	Knowth	17	B11/12	√	√			7th c	√						
	"		B14	√				7th/9th c	√						
	"		B12	√				8th/9th c	√						
	Ninch 1	1	B1				√	5th/7th c		√					
	Ninch 2	92	B856	√				6th/7th c				√	√	?	
	"		B770		√			7th c				√	√		
	Ninch 3	37	B25	√				4th/6th c			√				
	"		B28		√			5th/6th c			√				
	Raystown	133	B853	√				4th/5th c			√		√	√	
	Rossnaree	2	SK F		√			4th/6th c			√				
	Tara (Rath of Synods)	8	BE	√				8th/9th c	√						
	"		BH	√				10/11th c	√						
	"		BD	√				13th c	√						

GAZETTEER 2 Early Medieval burial and cemetery types (continued)

County	Site name	Total graves excavated	Skeleton ID	Male	Female	Adult sex unidentified	Juvenile/child	Date	Isolated burial	Pre-existing burial area	Imitative burial monument	Unenclosed cemetery	Settlement cemetery	Foundation/focal burial	Early Med. cremation
Monaghan	Cloghvalley Upr.	14	C52				√	6th/7th c				√			
	"		SK 4				√	6th/7th c				√			
	"		SK 11				√	7th/8th c				√			
Offaly	Lehinch	6+	G3				√	5th/6th c		√					
	"		G4	√				5th/6th c		√					
	"		G5	√				5th/6th c		√					
Roscommon	Kiltullagh Hill 2	1	B1	√				5th/6th c		√					
	Ranelagh	700+	SK 176	√				7th/9th c					√		
	"		SK 420		√			11th/12th					√		
Sligo	Carrowmore Tomb 51	1	ID-60168			√		5th/7th c		√					
	Knocknashammer	3	SK 1	√				6th/7th c			√				
	"		SK 2	√				5th/6th c			√				
	"		SK 3		√			5th/6th c			√				
Tipperary	Camlin	152	?					8th/10th c					√		
Tyrone	Annaghilla (Site 4)	23	?			√	√	undated		√			√		
	"		crem				√	5th/6th c		√			√		√
	"		crem				√	7th/9th c		√			√		√
Westmeath	Marlinstown	14		√	√		√	undated					√		
Wexford	Ask	2	crem				√	7th/8th c		√					√
	"		crem				√	7th/8th c		√					√
Wicklow	Tinnapark Demesne	1	B1	√				undated	√						

GAZETTEER 3

Early Medieval burials with grave goods

County	Site name	Total burials excavated	Skeleton ID	Male	Female	Adult, sex unknown	Child/juvenile	Neck collar	Shield ?	Spear	Sceptre ?	Box set	Pin	Toe ring	Earring	Knife	Buckle	Amulet	Brooch	Shears	Antler	Beads	Quartz	Animal bone	Burnt grain/hearth rakings	Miscellaneous
Antrim	Solar	123	B545	√														√								
Donegal	Ballymacaward	13	?																						√	
	Dooey	100	SK30			√								√													√
Down	St John's Point	23	B7	√																	√						
Dublin	Cherrywood 18	39	B1		√											√											
	"		Bxvi		√											√											√
	Kilshane	123	B32		√								√														
	"		B20		√																					√	
	"		B26		√																					√	
	"		B52			√																				√	
	Mount Offaly	1553	?			√3																	√				
	Westreave	57	B29		√										√												
Fermanagh	Magheradunbar	8	B1			√				√														√			
Galway	Ballygarraun	1	B1	√																	√			√			
	Carrowkeel	132	B22		√																			√			
	"		B57		√																			√			
	"		B114		√																			√			
	"		B113			√																		√			
	"		B33			√																		√			
	"		B90		√																					√	
	Cross	7	B4	√																			√			
	"		B7	√																			√			
	"		B1			√																	√				
	Farta	1	B1	√																	√		√			
	Owenbristy	79	SK70	√			√																				
	Pollacorragune	4	SKD	√			√																	√			
	"		SKB	√																				√			
Kerry	Reask	42	G23			√																√					
Kildare	Carbury Hill, Site B	19	B1	√												√										
	"		B111	√	√																			√		
	Prumplestown Lwr	4	SK2	√																				√		
	"		SK1	√																					√		

County	Site name	Total burials excavated	Skeleton ID	Male	Female	Adult, sex unknown	Child/juvenile	Neck collar	Shield ?	Spear	Sceptre ?	Box set	Pin	Toe ring	Earring	Knife	Buckle	Amulet	Brooch	Shears	Antler	Beads	Quartz	Animal bone	Burnt grain/hearth rakings	Miscellaneous
Kilkenny	Holdenstown 1	8	B3	√																				√		
	"		B7		√																			√		
	Holdenstown 2	94	B59	√?																		√				
	Killaree	6	?		√												√										
	Kilree 3	5	B3	√																					√		
	Sheastown	12	SK 1	√													√										
Laois	Ballydavis 1	7	C192	√	√																				√		
	Parknahown 5	425	B585				√																	√	√	√	
	"		B870				√																	√			
	"		B508				√																	√			
	"		B149				√																	√			
	"		B1007				√																	√			
	"		B293	√																				√			√
	"		B873		√																			√			
	Parknahown 5		B670				√																		√		
	"		B1096				√																		√		
	"		B594				√																		√		√
	"		B362	√																					√		
Louth	Dromiskin	2	?		√							√	√														
	Faughart	772	1244A			√																	√				
	"		1436A			√																	√				
	"		1078A		√																		√				
	"		1486A	√																			√				
	"		1016A			√																	√				
Mayo	Aghalahard	1	B1		√											√								√			
Meath	Ardsallagh	30	B29		√					√														√			
	Augherskea	187	SK 87	√																				√			
	Betaghstown (Brookside)	16	B11	√									√	√	√										√		
	Collierstown	61	B39	√																	√						
	"		B48	√																					√		

GAZETTEER 3 *Early Medieval burials with grave goods (continued)* 235

County	Site name	Total burials excavated	Skeleton ID	Male	Female	Adult, sex unknown	Child/juvenile	Neck collar	Shield?	Spear	Sceptre?	Box set	Pin	Toe ring	Earring	Knife	Buckle	Amulet	Brooch	Shears	Antler	Beads	Quartz	Animal bone	Burnt grain/hearth rakings	Miscellaneous
Meath (*ctd.*)	Ninch 3	37	B8		√											√										
	Ratoath	56	B38	√			√																			
	"		B35		√																					√
	Raystown	133	B84	√?						√																
	"		B988	√												√										
	"		?			√																√				
	Rossnaree	1	1	√						√																
	Tara, Rath of the Synods	4	BE	√																					√	√
	"		BH	√																					√	
Monaghan	Cloghvalley Upr	15	SK 8	√												√										
Offaly	Clonmacnoise (W Cross)	6	B5	√																					√	
	"		B22	√																					√	
	"		B23	√																					√	
	"		B24	√																					√	
	"		B25	√																				√?	√	
	"		B26	√																					√	
	Lehinch	6	B3	√												√									√	
Roscommon	Ranelagh	800	B176	√							√															
	"		B420		√																√					
Sligo	Ballysadare	37	?		√		√																			
	Knoxspark	185	B4	√						√																
	"		B32		√												√									
Tipperary	Camlin	153	SK 18		√									√												
	"		SK 32		√									√												
	"		SK 27	√										√												
	"		?		√																	√				
Wicklow	Britonstown	32	SK 4		√																			√		

GAZETTEER 4

Early Medieval atypical or deviant burials

County	Site name	Total burials excavated	Skeleton ID	Male	Female	Adult, sex unknown	Child/juvenile	Live burial?	Mutilation after death	Decapitated	Head only burial	Head missing	Head present	Fatal weapon trauma	Paired burial/trauma	Paired burial/non trauma	Non-fatal weapon trauma	Kiln burial	Prone	Crouched (all forms)	Box burial	Termini/entrance	Hands/feet amputation	Head west	Head east	Head south	Head north
Antrim	Solar	123	B545	√																√						√	
Armagh	Na Ferta, Scotch St.	9	A		√								√															
Clare	Cahercommaun	1	B1	√					√	√																		
Donegal	Ballyhanna	1200	SK 290	√									√							√							
"	"		SK 289		√							√	√							√							
	Dooey	100	SK 49	√					√	√															√		
Dublin	Ballynakelly	1	B1	√					√		√									√							
	Cappogue Castle	16	B7	√									√							√							
	Cherrywood, Site 18	39	XXI	√									√							√							
	"		?		√														√								
	"		?		√														√								
	Kill of the Grange	2	SK 2	√					?		√					√											
	Lusk	15	B9	√					√		√		√	√						√							
	"		B10	√					√		√		√	√						√							
	Mount Gamble	281	CCLXXXI	√					√				√	√	√					√							
	"		CCLXXX	√										√	√					√							
	"		CCLXXVI		√														√		√						
	"		?			√													√		√						
	Mount Offaly	1553	Phase 3	√					√		√	√								√							
	"		?		√													√			√			√	√
	"		CCCCLXII		√															√		√					
	Pelletstown East	3	B12		√																			√			

236

GAZETTEER 4 *Early Medieval atypical or deviant burials (continued)* 237

County	Site name	Total burials excavated	Skeleton ID	Male	Female	Adult, sex unknown	Child/juvenile	Live burial?	Mutilation after death	Decapitated	Head only burial	Head missing	Head present	Fatal weapon trauma	Paired burial/trauma	Non-fatal weapon trauma	Paired burial/non trauma	Kiln burial	Prone	Crouched (all forms)	Box burial	Termini/entrance	Hands/feet amputation	Head west	Head east	Head south	Head north
Fermanagh	Cleenish	1	C23	√					?	√	√													√		
Galway	Carrowkeel	132	SK 50			√													√					√			
	"		SK 51	√																	√			√			
	"		SK 72			√																√	√					
	"		SK 82			√																√			√			
	"		SK 119	√																		√						
	Inis Mór, Aran Islands	2	B2680/B1			√																√	√					
	"		B6484/B2			√																√?	√					
	Loughbown 1	1	C251			√																√						
	Owenbristy	79	SK 42	√					√	√	√																	
	"		SK 9	√					√			√	√												√			
	"		SK 82	√					√			√	√															
	"		SK 93	√					√			√	√												√			
	"		SK 75		√				√	√															√			
	"		SK 73		√				√			√	√												√			
	"		SK 49			√			√			√	√												√			
	"		SK 53			√						√													√			
	"		SK 38	√											√										√			
	"		SK 50	√											√										√			
	"		SK 74	√											√										√			
	"		SK 70	√																√					√			
Kildare	Corbally 1	6	B2		√													√										
	Corbally 2	31	B125		√			√				√													√			
	Corbally 3	19	B78			√			√	√		√													√			
	"		B79			√							√													√		
	Curragh, Site 4	1	B1		√		√																		√			
	Curragh, Site 6	11	XIV	√					√	√															√			
	Mullacash Middle	3	G3	√				√	√	√	√														√			
Kilkenny	Baysrath	47	C320	√													√											√
	"		C2189		√													√					√					

GAZETTEER 4 Early Medieval atypical or deviant burials (continued)

County	Site name	Total burials excavated	Skeleton ID	Male	Female	Adult, sex unknown	Child/juvenile	Live burial?	Mutilation after death	Decapitated	Head only burial	Head missing	Head present	Fatal weapon trauma	Paired burial/trauma	Paired burial/non trauma	Non-fatal weapon trauma	Kiln burial	Prone	Crouched (all forms)	Box burial	Termini/entrance	Hands/feet amputation	Head west	Head east	Head south	Head north
Laois	Ballydavis 1	7	SK 103	√																	√			√				
	Killeany	68	B68		√																√	√						
	"		B39	√										√						√			√	√				
	"		B13	√																	√			√				
	"		B60			√																		√	√				
	Morett	5	C1302			√															√			√				
	Parknahown 5	425	SK 367	√										√										√				
	"		SK 649	√										√										√				
	"		SK 484		√				√		√	√												√				
	"		SK 661		√									√										√				
	"		SK 200	√										√										√				
	"		SK 359		√									√										√				
	"		SK 673	√										√										√				
	"		SK 363	√										√										√				
	"		B614		√													√						√	√			
	"		B988	√														√						√				
	"		B1035			√	√											√			√			√		√		
	"		B572		√													√	√									
	"		B284		√													√						√				
	"		B168	√														√						√				
	"		B549		√	√												√			√	√						
	"		B034		√													√						√				
Limerick	Ballysimon	1	B1		√		√														√							
	Lough Gur, Circle J	95	B40	√														√						√				
Louth	Faughart Lower	771	SK 1739A	√			√			√	√												√				
	"		SK 1659A	√			√			√	√												√				
	"		SK 1690A	√			√			√	√												√				
	"		SK 1089	√						√														√				
	"		SK 1080	√											√									√				
	"		SK 1498A			√											√							√				
	"		SK 1542A	√													√							√				
	"		SK 1777A	√															√					√				
	"		SK 1006A			√													√					√				
	"		SK 1395A	√							√					√								√				
	"		SK 1385A		√						√					√								√				

GAZETTEER 4 *Early Medieval atypical or deviant burials (continued)*

County	Site name	Total burials excavated	Skeleton ID	Male	Female	Adult, sex unknown	Child/juvenile	Live burial?	Mutilation after death	Decapitated	Head only burial	Head missing	Head present	Fatal weapon trauma	Paired burial / trauma	Paired burial / non trauma	Non-fatal weapon trauma	Kiln burial	Prone	Crouched (all forms)	Box burial	Termini / entrance	Hands/feet amputation	Head west	Head east	Head south	Head north
Louth	Haggardstown	1	?				√													√							√
	Millockstown	23	BXV	√								√		√						√							
	"		BXXXVIIIb	√											√					√							
Meath	Ardsallagh 1	30	B16	√																√	√						
	"		B11	√									√								√							
	"		B15				√						√								√							
	"		B24	√									√								√							
	"		B26				√						√								√							
	Augherskea	187	SK 87	√							√										√							
	"		SK 2	√				√			√	√	√								√							
	"		SK 165	√				√		√		√									√							
	Betaghstown (Anchorage)	61	F181	√													√				?							
	Betaghstown (Brookside)	16	B12	√													√				√							
	"		B11		√												√											
	Castlefarm	12	B6	√				√	√												√							
	"		B7	√				√	√	√							√					√						
	Claristown 2	15	B12			√	√			√										√	√							
	"		B13			√	√			√										√	√							
	"		B5	√							√										√							
	"		B6	√							√										√							
	Collierstown 1	61	B54	√							√										√							
	"		B55	√							√										√							
	Colp West	1	B1	√				√	√					√														
	Colp West 1	120	B161	√														√										
	Johnstown	398	B25	√				√	√												√							
	"		B128	√														√		√								
	"		B204		√													√		√								
	"		B6	√														√		√								
	"		B8		√													√		√								
	Knowth	8	B14	√				√?		√										√								
	"		B18		√																	√						
	Ninch 2	92	?			√											√											√
	"		?				√											√										

GAZETTEER 4 *Early Medieval atypical or deviant burials (continued)*

County	Site name	Total burials excavated	Skeleton ID	Male	Female	Adult, sex unknown	Child/juvenile	Live burial?	Mutilation after death	Decapitated	Head only burial	Head missing	Head present	Fatal weapon trauma	Paired burial/trauma	Paired burial/non trauma	Non-fatal weapon trauma	Kiln burial	Prone	Crouched (all forms)	Box burial	Termini/entrance	Hands/feet amputation	Head west	Head east	Head south	Head north
Meath	Ratoath	56	B12		√			√	√		√									√			√	√				
	"		B46	√				√					√?							√								
	"		B34			√														√			√					
	Raystown	133	B841	√								√											√					
	"		B848	√				√		√													√					
	"		B2389	√												√									√			
	Tara, Rath of Synods	8	BI	√																√					√			
	"		BE	√																√					√			
	"		BD	√				√														√						√
Offaly	Lehinch	6+	B3		√											√				√								
	"		B4	√												√				√								
	"		B5	√						√	√									√								
Roscommon	Kilteasheen		BR25			√	√													√								
Sligo	Knoxspark	185	B4	√					√		√									√								
	"		B75	√					√		√									√								
	"		B49		√				√	√																		
	"		B31			√														√								
	"		B34?			√			√	√	√									√								
Tipperary	Camlin	152	SK 85	√																√			√					
	"		SK 152	√					√	√										√			√					
	"		SK 60		√															√			√					
	"		SK 129			√														√			√					
	"		SK 58		√															√			√					
	"		SK 71	√																√			√					
	"		SK 127		√																	√		√				
	Nenagh Nth	2	SK 2	√					√	√																		
Westmeath	Ballykilmore	817+	?		√			√		√													√					
	"		?		√													√										
	"		c399	√				√?					√	√	√								√					
	"		c415		√								√	√	√								√					
	"		c489	√																	√		√					
	Marlinstown	14	B8	√				√?	√									√					√					
	"		B9		√															√							√?	
	Sonnagh Demesne	2	G1	√					√	√	√																	√
	"		G3	√					√	√	√									√								√

GAZETTEER 5

Iron Age and Early Medieval burials selected for isotopic analysis

County	Site name	Total burials excavated	Number selected	Skeleton ID	Male	Female	Adult sex unidentified	Child/juvenile	Origin outside Ireland	Ireland non-local	Ireland or Britain	Ireland local
	IRON AGE											
Meath	Betaghstown (Anchorage)		1	B28	√				√			
	Knowth		6	B8/9	√				√			
	"			B7					√	√		
	"			B21	√				√			
	"			B4	√							?
	"			B10	√							√
	Rath	1	1	B1	√							√
	Tara, Ráith na Ríg	1	1	F103		√						√
	Tara, Rath of Synods		1	B.B		√						√
	EARLY MEDIEVAL											
Donegal	Ballymacaward	13	2	B4	√				√			
Galway	Ballygarraun West	1	1	B1	√						√	
	Farta	1	1	B1	√						√	
	Owenbristy	79	5	SK 70	√				√			
	"			SK 31	√				√			
	"			SK 9	√							√
	"			SK 53		√						√
	"			SK 25	√							√
Kildare	Carbury Hill B	19	6	SK 4	√				√			
	"			SK 10		√			√			
	"			SK 6	√				√			
	"			SK 1	√							√
	"			SK 7	√							√
	"			SK 8	√							√
	Corbally 1	6	3	B2	√				√			
	"			B5	√							√
	"			B1	√							√

GAZETTEER 5 *Iron Age and Early Medieval burials (continued)*

County	Site name	Total burials excavated	Number selected	Skeleton ID	Male	Female	Adult sex unidentified	Child/juvenile	Origin outside Ireland	Ireland non-local	Ireland or Britain	Ireland local
	EARLY MEDIEVAL (*ctd.*)											
Kildare (*ctd.*)	Corbally 2	31	5	B90	√							√
	"			B92	√							√
	"			B27	√							√
	"			B75	√							√
	"			B42	√							√
	Greenhills	16	1	B16				√				√
Kilkenny	Holdenstown 1	8	2	B2		√					√	
	"			B8	√							√
	Holdenstown 2	94	1	B59	√						√	
	Kilree 3	5	1	B4	√						√	
Meath	Betaghstown (Anchorage)	59	1	F181	√				√			
	Betaghstown (Brookside)	16	9	B12	√				√			
	"			B14		√			√			
	"			B13	√				√			
	"			B13A	√				√			
	"			B11	√				√			
	"			B16	√					√		
	"			B2		√						√
	"			B15	√							√
	"			B10			√					√
	Collierstown 1	61	1	B48	√							√
	Knowth	8	5	B14	√				√			
	"			B18	√						√	
	"			B27		√					√	
	"			B32			√				√	
	"			B33	√							√
	Ninch 2	92	2	B856	√				√			
	"			B770		√			√			
	Ninch 3	32	2	B25	√				√			
	"			B28	√					√		
	Ratoath	56	1	B38	√						√	
	Rossnaree	1	1	B1	√							√
	Tara, Rath of the Synods	5	5	B E	√					√		
	"			B I	√					√		
	"			B D	√					√		
	"			B H	√							√
Offaly	Lehinch	6	1	B3	√?							√

GAZETTEER 6

Early Medieval exceptional or unusual women's burial

County	Site name	Skeleton ID	Young Adult 18–25 yrs	Mid. Adult 25–45 yrs	Older Adult 45–60+ yrs	Live burial	Mound	Ring-ditch	Foundation burial	Isolated burial	Kiln burial	Neck ring	Clothed burial	Physical deformity	Violent trauma	Prone burial	Outsider	Antler	Miscellaneous
Clare	Kilcorney	SK 1	?		√														
Donegal	Ballymacaward	B3		√	√														
"	"	B4		√	√											√			
Galway	Ballygarraun	B1		√	√			√								√	√		
	Cross	B4	√				√												
	Farta	B1	√			√		√				√		√					
	Feerwore	B1		√		√	√												
	Owenbristy	SK 76		√				√											
	"	SK 75	√											√					
	"	SK 73	√											√					
Kildare	Carbury Hill, Site B	SK 10		√			√									√			
	"	SK 6		√			√									√			
	Corbally 1	B6	√				√												
	"	B2		√							√		√		√				
	Corbally 2	B67	√				√												
	"	B90	√				√												
	"	B92	√				√												
	"	B27		√			√												
	"	B125	√										√						
	Curragh, Site 4	B1		√	√		√												
	Greenhills	B15	√				√												
	Kildangan	B1	√			√		√											
Kilkenny	Kilree 3	B3		√															√
Laois	Killeany	B39	√											√	√				
	"	B13	√																√
	Parknahown 5	B614	√											√			√		√
	"	SK 484	√											√					

243

GAZETTEER 6 Early Medieval exceptional or unusual women (continued)

County	Site name	Skeleton ID	Young Adult 18–25 yrs	Mid. Adult 25–45 yrs	Older Adult 45–60+ yrs	Live burial	Mound	Ring-ditch	Foundation burial	Isolated burial	Kiln burial	Neck ring	Clothed burial	Physical deformity	Violent trauma	Prone burial	Outsider	Antler	Miscellaneous
Laois	Killeany	B39	√												√	√			
	"	B13		√															√
	Parknahown 5	B614		√												√			√
	"	SK 484	√													√			
Louth	Faughart	SK 1542		√										√		√			
Meath	Betaghstown (Brookside)	B11		?									√				√		
	"	B14		?													√		
	"	B16		?													√		
	Collierstown 1	B48	√					√	√										
	Ferganstown & Ballymacon	B1	√				√		√										
	Johnstown	B110		√					√										
	"	B204	√										√		√				
	Ninch 3	B28	√				√	√											
	Ratoath	B38	√								√								√
	"	B12	√											?					
	Raystown	B853	√				√	√											
	Rossnaree	B1	√			√		√											
Roscommon	Ranelagh	B420	√																√
Sligo	Knocknashammer	SK 3	√			√		?											
	Knoxspark	SK 38?	√											√					
Westmeath	Ballykilmore	?	√													√			√
	Marlinstown	B8	√												√?	√			

GAZETTEER 7

Ecclesiastical sites

County	Site name	Graves excavated	Male	Female	Unidentified adult	Child/juvenile	Mainland	Island	Founder saint	Wooden/sod church	Stone church	Shrine	Stone cross	Cross-inscribed slabs	Bii, E ware, glass	Quartz	Handbell
Antrim	Solar	123	√	√	√	√					√						√
Armagh	Na Ferta, Scotch St.	9		√		√			?								
Donegal	Ballyhanna	1000+	√	√	√	√	√				√	?				√	
Down	Derry	36	√	√	√	√	√				√		√				
	Nendrum	?		√			√	√			√	?	√				√
	St John's Point	23	√	√	√	√	√				√			√			
Dublin	Dalkey Island	11	√	√		√		√	√		√		√	√			
	Kill of the Grange	2	√		√		√			√	√		√				
Fermanagh	Cleenish	1	√						√	√	?						
Galway	High Island	6	√						√		√		√	√		√	
	Omey Island	250+	√	√	√	√			√	√	?	√					
Kerry	Caherlehillan	18		√		√				√		√	√	√			
	Church Island	100+		√	√		√			√	√		√	√	√	√	
	Illaunloughan	25	√		√		√			√	√	√	√		√		
	Skellig	3+	√					√	?		√	√	√				
	Reask	42		√	√	√				√	√	√	√	√			
Mayo	Inishkea North	6+	√	√			√			√	?	√		√			
Meath	Collierstown 2	12+	√	√	√	√	√				√		√		√	√	
	Trim	6		√		√	√										
Offaly	Sheean Hill, Durrow	9+	√	√	√	√	√	√									
	Clonmacnoise	EM 21	√			√			√		√		√	√			
Sligo	Inishmurray	?	√	√	√	√		√	√		√	√	√				√
Tipperary	Toureen Peakaun	8	√		√	√	√		√	√	√	√	√	√			
Waterford	Ballygarran	5		√		√			√					√	√		
Westmeath	Ballykilmore	817	√	√	√	√	√				√						
Wicklow	Glebe	191	√	√	√	√	√		√	?	√						
	Killegar	40+		√		√			√	√			√				√

Bibliography

PRINTED PRIMARY SOURCES

Additamenta in *The Patrician texts in the Book of Armagh*, ed. and trans. Ludwig Bieler (Dublin, 1979), pp 166–79.
Adomnán's Life of Columba, ed. and trans. Alan Orr Anderson & Marjorie Ogilvie Anderson (2nd ed. Oxford, 1991).
Adomnán of Iona: Life of St Columba, trans. Richard Sharpe (London, 1995).
Adomnán's 'Law of the Innocents', trans. Gilbert Márkus (Glasgow, 1997).
Aeschylus 'Libation-bearers', trans. Herbert Weir Smyth, Loeb Classical Library (London & Cambridge, MA, 1926; repr. 1992).
Ammianus Marcellinus. The Later Roman Empire (AD354–378), ed. and trans. Walter Hamilton (London, 1986).
Annals of Clonmacnoise, ed. Denis Murphy (Dublin, 1896; repr. Llanerch, 1993).
Annals of Loch Cé, ed. and trans. W.M. Hennessey (London, 1871).
Annals of Ulster (to AD 1131), ed. and trans. Seán Mac Airt & Gearóid Mac Niocaill (Dublin, 1983).
Bedae Vita Sancti Cuthberti [Two Lives of Saint Cuthbert: A Life by an anonymous monk of Lindisfarne, and Bede's Prose Life], ed. and trans. Bertram Colgrave (Cambridge, 1940).
Bede: Ecclesiastical history of the English people, ed. and trans. Bertram Colgrave & R.A.B. Mynors, Oxford Medieval Texts (Oxford, 1969).
Bethu Brigte [The Life of Brigit], ed. and trans. Donncha Ó hAodha (Dublin, 1978).
Coibnes uisci thairidne, ed. and trans. Daniel A. Binchy, 'Irish law tracts re-edited', *Ériu*, 17 (1955), 52–85.
Collectio canonum Hibernensis, ed. Hermann Wasserschleben, *Die Irische Kanonensammlung* (2nd ed., Leipzig, 1885).
Cogitosus: Life of Saint Brigit, trans. Seán Connolly & Jean-Michel Picard, *JRSAI*, 117 (1987), 5–27.
Contributions to a dictionary of the Irish language (DIL) (Dublin: Royal Irish Academy).
Corpus iuris Hibernici, ed. Daniel A. Binchy, 6 vols (Dublin, 1978).
Córus bésgnai. An Old Irish law tract on the Church and society, ed. and trans. Liam Breatnach (Dublin, 2017).
Epistola ad milites Corotici in *The book of letters of Saint Patrick the Bishop*, ed. and trans. David R. Howlett (Dublin, 1994), pp 25–39.
Geoffrey of Burton: Life and miracles of St Modwenna, ed. and trans. Robert Bartlett (Oxford, 2002).
Marriage disputes: a fragmentary Old Irish law-text, ed. and trans. Fergus Kelly (Dublin, 2014).
Metrical dindshenchas, Edward John Gwynn, Todd Lecture Series, 5 vols (Dublin, 1903–35; repr. Dublin 1991).
Muirchú: Vita Patricii in *The Patrician texts in the Book of Armagh*, ed. and trans. Ludwig Bieler (Dublin, 1979) pp 61–123.
Nennius: British history and the Welsh annals, ed. and trans. John Morris (London, 1980).
The chronicle of Ireland, trans. Thomas M. Charles-Edwards, Translated Texts for Historians 44 (Liverpool, 2006).
The Law of Adomnán: a translation, Máirín Ní Dhonnchada (2001) in Thomas O'Loughlin (ed.), *Adomnán at Birr, AD 697: essays in commemoration of the Law of the Innocents* (Dublin, 2001), pp 53–68.
The martyrology of Oengus the Culdee: [Félire Óengusso Céli Dé], ed. and trans. Whitley Stokes (London, 1905; repr. 1984).
Tírechán: Collectanea, in Ludwig Bieler (ed. and trans.), *The Patrician texts in the Book of Armagh* (Dublin, 1979), pp 123–67.

Vita prima Sanctae Brigitae, trans. Seán Connolly, *JRSAI*, 119 (1989), 5–49.
Vita Sancti Guthlaci auctore Felice: Felix's Life of Saint Guthlac, trans. Bertram Colgrave (Cambridge, 1956).

PRINTED SECONDARY SOURCES

Alexander, Michael, trans., *Beowulf* (London, 1973, 2001).
Armit, Ian, Graeme T. Swindles & Katharina Becker, 'From dates to demography in Later Prehistoric Ireland? Experimental approaches to the meta-analysis of large 14C data-sets', *JAS*, 40 (2013), 433–8.
Armit, Ian, Graeme T. Swindles, Katharina Becker & Maarten Blaauw, 'Rapid climate change did not cause population collapse at the end of the European Bronze Age', *Proceedings of the National Academy of Science USA*, 3:48 (2014), 17045–9.
Baker, Christine (ed.), *Axes, warriors and windmills: recent archaeological discoveries in North Fingal* (Dublin, 2009).
— 'Occam's duck: three Early Medieval settlement cemeteries or ecclesiastical sites?' in Christiaan Corlett & Michael Potterton (eds), *Death and burial in Early Medieval Ireland* (Bray, Co. Wicklow, 2010), pp 1–21.
— 'Unpublished preliminary report: Drumanagh Promontory Fort, Loughshinny, Co. Dublin' (Dublin, 2018: Fingal County Council). http://fingal.ie/planning-and-buildings/heritage-in-fingal/communityarchaeology/.
Bartlett, Robert, *England under the Norman and Angevin kings, 1075–1225* (Oxford, 1999).
Bateson, J. Donal, 'Further finds of Roman material from Ireland', *PRIA*, 76C (1976), 171–80.
— 'Roman material from Ireland: a re-consideration', *PRIA*, 73C (1973), 21–97.
Baxter, Stephen, Catherine Karkov, Janet L. Nelson & David Pelteret (eds), *Early Medieval studies in memory of Patrick Wormald*, Studies in Early Medieval Britain and Ireland (Abingdon, 2009).
Becker, Katharina, 'Token explanations: Rathgall and the interpretation of cremation deposits in Prehistoric Ireland', *Archaeology Ireland*, 28:1 (2014), 13–15.
Becker, Katharina, Ian Armit & Graeme T. Swindles, 'New perspectives on the Irish Iron Age: the impact of NRA development of our understanding of later prehistory' in Michael Stanley, Rónán Swan & Aidan O'Sullivan (eds), *Stories of Ireland's past*, TII Heritage 5 (Dublin, 2017), pp 85–100.
Bellantoni, Nicholas F., Paul S. Sledzik & David A. Poirier, 'Rescue, research, and reburial: Walton family cemetery, Griswold, Connecticut' in David A. Poirier & Nicholas F. Bellantoni (eds), *In remembrance: archaeology and death* (Westport, CT, 1997), pp 131–54.
Bender Jørgensen, Lise, 'Unpublished report on textile remains analysed at National Museum of Ireland' (Dublin, 1983).
Bennett, Isabel (ed.), *Excavations Bulletin: summary accounts of archaeological excavations in Ireland* (Dublin, 1986–).
Bhreathnach, Edel, 'Observations on the occurrence of dog and horse bones at Tara', *Discovery Programme Reports*, 6 (2002), 117–22.
— 'Learning and literature in Early Medieval Clonmacnoise' in Heather A. King (ed.), *Clonmacnoise studies: vol. 2. Seminar papers 1998* (Dublin, 2003), pp 97–104.
— *Ireland in the Medieval world, AD 400–1000: landscape, kingship and religion* (Dublin, 2014).
Bhreathnach, Edel (ed.), *The kingship and landscape of Tara* (Dublin, 2005).
Birmingham, Nora, Frank Coyne, Graham Hull, Fiona Reilly & Kate Taylor, *River Road: the archaeology of the Limerick Southern Ring Road*, NRA Scheme Monographs 14 (Dublin, 2013).
Bitel, Lisa M., 'Ekphrasis at Kildare: the imaginative architecture of a seventh-century hagiographer', *Speculum*, 79:3 (July 2004), 605–27.
Blair, John, *The Church in Anglo-Saxon society* (Oxford, 2005).
— 'The dangerous dead in Early Medieval England' in Baxter & Karkov et al. (eds), *Early Medieval studies in memory of Patrick Wormald* (2009), pp 539–59.

— *Bede and the culture of the laity*, Jarrow Lecture 2010 (Jarrow, Tyne and Wear, 2010).
Blair, John & Richard Sharpe (eds), *Pastoral care before the parish* (Leicester, 1992).
Bolger, Teresa, Colm Moloney & Damian Shiels (eds), *A journey along the Carlow corridor: the archaeology of the M9 Carlow bypas*, NRA Scheme Monographs 16 (Dublin, 2015).
Bonsall, James & Heather Gimson, 'Unpublished report R708 Airport Road realignment, phase 3, Co. Waterford. Archaeological geophysical survey. Detection licence No. 07R0003' (Co. Waterford, 2007), Earthsound.
Borsje, Jacqueline, 'Human sacrifice in Medieval Irish literature' in Jan N. Bremmer (ed.), *The strange world of human sacrifice* (Leuven, 2007), pp 31–54.
Borsje, Jacqueline & Fergus Kelly, 'The Evil Eye in early Irish literature and law', *Celtica*, 24 (2003), 1–39.
Bourke, Cormac, 'Early Irish handbells', *JRSAI*, 110 (1980), 52–66.
— 'A crozier and bell from Inishmurray and their place in ninth-century Irish archaeology', *PRIA*, 85C (1985), 145–68.
— 'The monastery of Saint Mo-Choí of Nendrum: the Early Medieval finds' in Thomas McErlean & Norman Crothers (eds), *Harnessing the tides* (Norwich, 2007), pp 406–21.
Bourke, Edward, 'A first century Roman burial from Ireland', *Archaeology Ireland*, 3:2 (1989), 56–7.
— 'Glass vessels of the first nine centuries AD in Ireland', *JRSAI*, 124 (1994), 163–209.
Bourke, Edward, Alan R. Hayden & Ann Lynch, *Skellig Michael, Co. Kerry: the monastery and South Peak (Archaeological stratigraphic report: excavations 1986–2010)* (Dublin, 2011).
Bowen, Peter & Giles Dawkes, 'Unpublished final excavation report of Phase 2 excavations, A1–N1 Newry–Dundalk Link Road, Area 15, Site 116, Faughart Lower, Co. Louth', vol. 1 (Dublin, 2011) NRA & Transport 21.
Bower, Nik, 'Archaeological excavation report, Loughbown 1, Co. Galway. Ringfort with souterrain and metalwork', *Eachtra Journal*, 2 (Cork, 2009).
Brannon, Nick F., 'A trial excavation at St John's Point church, County Down', *UJA*, 43 (1980), 59–64.
Breatnach, Liam (ed.), *Córus bésgnai. An Old Irish law tract on the Church and society* (Dublin, 2017).
Breen, Colin, *An archaeology of southwest Ireland, 1570–1670* (Dublin, 2007).
Britnell, William J., 'Capel Maelog, Llandrindod Wells, Powys: excavations 1984–87', *Med. Arch.*, 34 (1990), 27–96.
Bronk Ramsey, Christopher, 'Bayesian analysis of radiocarbon dates', *Radiocarbon*, 51:1 (2009), 337–60.
Brooks, Nicholas, 'The English origin myths' in Nicholas Brooks (ed.), *Anglo-Saxon myths: State and Church, 400–1066* (London, 2000), pp 79–89.
Bryant, Geoffrey F., *The early history of Barton-upon-Humber* (Barton-upon-Humber, 1994).
Buckley, Laureen, 'Skeletal Report, Claristown 2, Co. Meath' in Ian Russell (ed.), 'Unpublished final report on the archaeological excavation at Claristown 2, Co. Meath' (2004), appendix 3. Unpublished Report for NRA. Accessed via TII Digital Heritage Collections at www.dri.ie.
— 'Farta skeletal report' (Dublin, 2012), Unpublished osteo-archaeological report prepared for Mapping Death Project.
— 'Knocknashammer, Co. Sligo. Skeletal report' (2019), Unpublished report prepared for Martin Timoney.
Buckley, Laureen, Mara Tesorieri & Victoria Park, 'Ninch, Co. Meath, skeletal report, final. 98E0501 ext' (2008, Archaeological Development Services). Unpublished report for Woodgreen Builders.
Buckley, Laureen et al., 'Skeletal report, Site 116, Faughart Lower, Co. Louth', vol. 11 (2010), Unpublished, prepared for NRA & Department for Regional Development for N.I.
Buckley, Laureen & Cia McConway, 'Early Medieval settlement and burial ground at Faughart Lower, Co. Louth' in Corlett & Potterton (eds), *Death and burial in Early Medieval Ireland* (2010), pp 49–59.
Burenhult, Göran, *The archaeological excavation at Carrowmore, Co. Sligo, Ireland, excavation season 1977–79* (Stockholm, 1980).

Butterworth, Chris A. & Sue J. Lobb, *Excavations in the Burghfield Area, Berkshire* (Old Sarum, 1992: Wessex Archaeology Report).

Byrne, Francis John, 'Historical notes on Cnogba [Knowth]' in G. Eogan, 'Excavations at Knowth, Co. Meath, 1962–65', *PRIA*, 66C (1968), 383–400.

— *Irish kings and high kings* (London, 1973).

— 'The inscriptions in the main passage tomb at Knowth' in F.J. Byrne et al. (eds), *Historical Knowth and its hinterland*, Excavations at Knowth 4 (Dublin, 2008), pp 88–132.

Byrne, Francis John & Pádraig Francis, 'Two Lives of Saint Patrick', *JRSAI*, 124 (1994), 5–16.

Cahill, Mary & Maeve Sikora, *Breaking ground, finding graves: reports on the excavations of burials by the National Museum of Ireland, 1927–2006*, 2 vols (Dublin, 2011).

Cahill Wilson, Jacqueline, 'Becoming Irish, the materiality of transcultural identities in the later Irish Iron Age' (PhD, University of Bristol, 2010).

— 'Lost in transcription: rethinking our approach to the archaeology of the later Iron Age' in Corlett & Potterton (eds), *Life and death in Iron Age Ireland* (2012), pp 15–33.

— 'Romans and Roman material in Ireland: a wider social perspective' in *Late Iron Age and Roman Ireland*, Discovery Programme Reports 8 (Dublin, 2014), pp 11–58.

— 'Et tu, Hibernia? Frontier zones and culture contact: Ireland in a Roman World' in Sergio Gonzales Sanchez & Alexandra Guglielmi (eds), *Romans and Barbarians beyond the frontiers: archaeology, ideology and identities in the North*, TRAC Themes in Roman Archaeology (Oxford, 2017), pp 48–69.

Cahill Wilson, Jacqueline, Hege Usborne, Carolyn Taylor, Peter Ditchfield & Alaister Pike, 'Strontium and oxygen isotope analysis on Iron Age and Early Historic burials around the great mound at Knowth' in George Eogan et al., *The archaeology of Knowth in the first and second millennia AD*, Excavations at Knowth 5 (Dublin, 2012), pp 775–88.

Cahill Wilson, Jacqueline, Christopher Standish & Elizabeth O'Brien, 'Investigating mobility and migration in the Later Irish Iron Age' in *Late Iron Age and 'Roman' Ireland*, Discovery Programme Reports 8 (Dublin, 2014), pp 127–49.

Cahill Wilson, Jacqueline, Gabriel Cooney, Ger Dowling & Ian Elliott, 'Investigations on Lambay, Co. Dublin' in *Late Iron Age and 'Roman' Ireland*, Discovery Programme Reports 8 (Dublin, 2014), pp 91–112.

Cahill Wilson, Jacqueline & Christopher D. Standish, 'Mobility and migration in Late Iron Age and Early Medieval Ireland' *JAS: Reports*, 6 (2016), pp 230–41.

Card, Nick, Jane Downes, Julie Gibson & Paul Sharman, 'Mine Howe, Orkney – religion and metal working', *Current Archaeology*, 199 (2005), 322–7.

Carlin, Neil, Linda Clarke & Fintan Walsh (eds), *The archaeology of life and death in the Boyne floodplain: the linear landscape of the M4*, NRA Monograph 2, including CD with final excavation and specialist reports (Dublin, 2008).

Carney, James (ed.), 'Three Old Irish accentual poems', *Ériu*, 22 (1971), 23–80.

Carroll, Judith, Frank Ryan & Ken Wiggins, *Archaeological excavations at Glebe South and Darcystown, Balrothery, Co. Dublin*, Balrothery Excavations, vol. 2 (Dublin, 2008).

Carroll, Judith, 'Glass & bone beads from a ring-ditch at Donacarney Great, Co. Meath' in Antoine Giacometti, 'Preliminary archaeological excavation report – proposed development site, Donacarney Great townland, Bettystown, Co. Meath', Appendix 5 (2010, Arch-Tech), Unpublished report for Relative Developments.

— 'Glass and amber beads from Ballyboy 1, E3719' in Shane Delaney & Maeve Tobin (eds), 'N18 Gort to Crusheen road scheme. Site name: Ballyboy 1. Ringditch, final report' (2010: Irish Archaeological Consultancy), Unpublished report prepared for Galway County Council.

Carruthers, James, 'Communication on Roman remains found in Ireland', *Proceedings and Papers of the Kilkenny and South-East of Ireland Archaeological Society*, 1:1 (Dublin, 1856), 164.

Carty, Niamh, 'Demographic data for Dooey, Co. Donegal', unpublished (Dept of Archaeology, UCC, 2012).

— '"The halved heads": osteological evidence for decapitation in Medieval Ireland', *Papers from the Institute of Archaeology*, 25:1 (2015), 1–20. Access via http:-dx.doi.org-10.5334-pia.477.

Carty, Niamh & Niamh Daly, 'Osteological report for The Curragh, Co. Kildare' (Cork, 2013), Unpublished.

Carver, Martin O.H. (ed.), 'Research reports 1990–92. Bulletin no. 8, 1993' in *Sutton Hoo Research Committee Bulletins 1983–1993* (Woodbridge, 1993).

Channing, John, *Final report: vols 1–3; Site reg. no. E2798; Ballykilmore 6, Ballykilmore Townland, Co. Westmeath* (Kilkenny, 2009: VJK).

— 'Final report, vols 1–3, Site AR053–54, Baysrath Townland, Co. Kilkenny. N9–N10 Kilcullen to Waterford Scheme: Phase 2: Waterford to Knocktopher' (2012: VJK), Unpublished.

— 'Ballykilmore, Co. Westmeath: continuity of an Early Medieval graveyard' in Corlett & Potterton (eds), *The Church in Early Medieval Ireland* (Dublin, 2014), pp 23–38.

Chapple, Robert M. 'Tullyallen 1: ringbarrow' in Isabel Bennett (ed.), *Excavations 2000* (Dublin, 2002), pp 242–3.

Charles-Edwards, Gifford, 'The East Cross inscription from Toureen Peacaun: some concrete evidence', *JRSAI*, 132 (2002), 114–26.

— 'Reading the Nendrum "runestone"' in Thomas McErlean & Norman Crothers, *Harnessing the tides: the Early Medieval tide mills at Nendrum Monastery, Strangford Lough*, Northern Ireland Archaeological Monographs 7 (Norwich, 2007), pp 396–404.

Charles-Edwards, Thomas M., 'Boundaries in Irish Law' in Peter Sawyer (ed.), *Medieval settlement: continuity and change* (London, 1976), pp 83–7.

— 'The pastoral role of the Church in the early Irish laws' in Blair & Sharp (eds), *Pastoral care before the parish* (1992), pp 63–80.

— *Early Irish and Welsh kinship* (Oxford, 1993).

— *Early Christian Ireland* (Cambridge, 2000).

— *St Patrick and the landscape of Early Christian Ireland*, Kathleen Hughes Memorial Lectures 10 (Cambridge, 2012).

— *Wales and the Britons, 350–1064* (Oxford. 2013).

Clancy, Pádraig & Joanna Leigh, 'The Curragh Research Project; Geophysical Survey' (2007), Unpublished report prepared for the Heritage Council, Kilkenny, Ireland.

Clark, John Grahame D., *Excavations at Star Carr: an early Mesolithic site at Seamer, near Scarborough* (Cambridge, 1954).

Clarke, Linda, 'Archaeological excavation of a multi-period settlement and burial site (2004)', Unpublished excavation report M4 Kinnegad Enfield Kilcock Motorway Scheme. Johnstown, Co. Meath. Prepared by ACS Ltd for Westmeath County Council.

—, 'Johnstown 1, Co. Meath: a multi-period burial, settlement, and industrial site' in Corlett & Potterton (eds), *Death and burial in Early Medieval Ireland* (2010), pp 61–75.

Clarke, Linda & Neil Carlin, 'Living with the dead at Johnstown 1: an enclosed burial, settlement and industrial site' in Carlin, Clarke & Walsh (eds), *The archaeology of life and death in the Boyne floodplain: the linear landscape of the M4* (2008), pp 55–85.

Clarke, Linda & Neil Carlin, 'From focus to locus: a window upon the development of a funerary landscape' in Deevy & Murphy (eds), *Places along the way: first findings on the M3* (2009), pp 1–20.

Clark, Lyndsey & Patricia Long, 'N9–N10 Kilcullen to Waterford Scheme: Phase 3, Kilcullen to Carlow. Archaeological Services Contract No. 6 – Resolution, Moone to Prumplestown. Final report on archaeological investigations at Site E2967, in the townland of Prumplestown Lower, Co. Kildare' (2010), Unpublished report prepared by Headland Archaeology (Ireland) for NRA.

Clibborn, Edward, 'Relating to articles exhibited to him by a Mr Perry of Stoneyford, Co. Kilkenny' (1852: Royal Irish Academy MSS 24–E-34).

Coffey, George, 'On the excavation of a Tumulus near Loughrea, Co. Galway', *PRIA*, 25C (1904–5), 14–20.

Coles, Bryony, John Coles & Mogens Schou Jørgensen (eds), *Bog bodies, sacred sites and wetland archaeology*, WARP Occasional Paper 12 (Exeter, 1999).

Collins, Tracy, 'Week at the knees: the discovery of partial human remains in a badger sett, Ballysimon, Limerick' in Corlett & Potterton (eds), *Life and death in Iron Age Ireland* (2012), pp 53–7.

— 'Preliminary archaeological excavation at Durrow Demesne, Co. Offaly in advance of a walking route at Durrow Abbey' (2018). Unpublished final preliminary report prepared by Aegis Archaeology for Offaly County Council.
Collins, Tracy & Linda Lynch, 'Prehistoric burial and ritual in southwest Ireland', *Antiquity*, 75:289 (2001), 493–4.
Collins, Tracy & Linda Lynch, 'Excavation of human remains at Nenagh North, St Conlan's Road, Nenagh, Co. Tipperary', *North Tipperary Historical Journal* (2006), 7–14.
Connolly, Michael, www.excavations.ie, Rockfield, Co. Kerry; no. 2000:044, Licence no. 00E0863 (2000).
Connon, Anne, 'The *Banshenchas* and the Uí Néill queens of Tara' in Smyth (ed.), *Seanchas: studies in Early and Medieval Irish archaeology, history and literature in honour of Francis J. Byrne* (2000), pp 98–108.
— 'A prosopography of the early queens of Tara' in Bhreathnach (ed.), *The kingship and landscape of Tara* (2005), pp 225–327.
— 'Women as dynastic ancestors in Early Irish society', Unpublished paper read at Instar Mapping Death Conference, 27–28th November 2009 (Dublin, 2009: School of History and Archives, UCD).
Conway, Malachy, *Director's first findings from excavations in Cabinteely*, Transactions, vol. 1 (Dublin, 1999: Margaret Gowen).
— 'Mount Offaly, Cabinteely, Dublin' in Isabel Bennett (ed.), *Excavations 1998* (Dublin, 2000), pp 36–7.
— 'Platin Fort: inland promontory fort and environs' in Isabel Bennett (ed.), *Excavations 2001* (Dublin, 2003), pp 316–17.
Cook, Alison M. & Maxwell W. Dacre, *Excavations at Portway, Andover, 1973–1975*, Oxford University Committee for Archaeology Monograph no. 4 (Oxford, 1985).
Cooney, Gabriel, *Landscapes of Neolithic Ireland* (London, 2000).
— 'The Prehistory of Lambay, a long view' in Christine Baker (ed.), *Axes, warriors and windmills: recent archaeological discoveries in North Fingal* (Dublin, 2009), pp 9–22.
Cooney, Gabriel, Katharina Becker, John Coles, Michael Ryan & Susanne Sievers (eds), *Relics of old decency: archaeological studies in Later Prehistory, festschrift for Barry Raftery* (Dublin, 2009).
Corlett, Christiaan & Michael Potterton (eds), *Death and burial in Early Medieval Ireland in the light of recent archaeological excavations* (Dublin, 2010).
— *Settlement in Early Medieval Ireland in the light of recent archaeological excavations* (Dublin, 2011).
— *Life and death in Iron Age Ireland in the light of recent archaeological excavations* (Dublin, 2012).
— *The Church in Early Medieval Ireland in the light of recent archaeological excavations* (Dublin, 2014).
Cosham, B. & R. MacLeod, 'Preliminary report on the archaeological excavation of a ring-barrow and other features in the townland of Bruff, Co. Limerick' (2009), Unpublished report for Limerick County Council by Headland Archaeology (Ireland) Ltd.
Cotter, Claire, *The Western Stone Forts Project: excavations at Dún Aonghasa and Dún Eoghanachta*, Discovery Programme Monograph, 2 vols (Dublin, 2012).
Cotter, Eamon, *Final report, excavation no. 03E0461; Site D, Morett Townland, Co. Laois* (Kilkenny, 2011: Valerie J. Keely).
Coughlan, Jennie, 'The human skeletal remains from Castlefarm 1' in Aidan O'Connell & Allister Clark, 'Final report on the archaeological excavation of Castlefarm 1, Co. Meath' (2009: ACS Ltd), Appendix 7a, Unpublished report for Meath County Council.
Coughlan, Jennie, 'Osteological analysis of the human skeletal remains from Kilree 3, Co. Kilkenny' (2010), Unpublished report prepared for Irish Archaeological Consultancy Ltd.
Coughlan, Tim, 'The continuing enigma of Cappydonnell Big', *Seanda NRA Archaeology Magazine*, 4 (Dublin, 2009), 42–4.
—, 'N6 Kinnegad–Athlone Scheme Phase 2: Kilbeggan to Athlone Dual Carriageway: Cappydonnell Big 1' (2010: Irish Archaeological Consultancy), Unpublished final report for Westmeath County Council and NRA.

— 'The occupation of earlier prehistoric monuments in the Early Medieval period: the evidence from Cappydonnell Big, Co. Offaly' in Corlett & Potterton (eds), *Settlement in Early Medieval Ireland* (2011), pp 73–92.

Coyne, Frank, 'Archaeological excavations at Corbally, Kilcullen, Co. Kildare' (2003: Aegis Archaeology), Unpublished report prepared for Kilsaran Concrete, Dunboyne, Co. Meath.

— 'Preliminary stratigraphic report on archaeological excavations at Brownstown Quarry, Corbally, Kilcullen, County Kildare' (2007: Aegis Archaeology), Unpublished report prepared for Kilsaran Concrete, Dunboyne, Co. Meath.

Coyne, Frank & Linda Lynch, 'Corbally, Co. Kildare: the results of the 2003–4 excavations of a secular cemetery' in Corlett & Potterton (eds), *Death and burial in Early Medieval Ireland* (2010), pp 77–90.

Cribbin, Gerry, Finbar McCormick, Michael E. Robinson & David Shimwell, 'A destroyed Late Iron-Age burial from Kiltullagh, Ballyglass Middle td., Co. Mayo' *Emania: Bulletin of the Navan Research Group*, 12 (1994) 61–5.

Cross, Pamela J., 'Horses among the Christians: a biocultural interpretation of the human-horse burial and other horse burials in the 7th–9th-century cemetery at Sedgeford, Norfolk, UK' (MSc, University of Bradford, 2009).

Curtin, John, 'A reassessment of Michael J. Bowman's excavation of Killeenagh Burial Ground, Ballygarran, Co. Waterford, 1940' (MA, UCC, 2015).

Dalland, Magnar, 'Long cist burials at Four Winds, Longniddry, East Lothian', *PSAS*, 122 (1992), 197–206.

Daly, Niamh, 'Ties that bind: isotopic results from the human skeletal remains at Corbally 1 and 2, Co. Kildare', *JCKASSD*, 20:4 (2014–15), 40–55.

Davies, Wendy, *Wales in the Early Middle Ages*, Studies in the Early History of Britain (Leicester, 1982).

Deevy, Mary & Donald Murphy (eds), *Places along the way: first findings on the M3*, NRA Scheme Monograph 5 (Dublin, 2009).

Delaney, Finn & John Tierney (eds), *In the lowlands of south Galway: archaeological excavation on the N18 Oranmore to Gort national road scheme*. NRA Scheme Monographs 7 (Dublin, 2011).

Delaney, Máire, Raghnall Ó Floinn & Elizabeth Heckett, 'Bog body from Clongownagh, Baronstown West, County Kildare, Ireland' in Bryony Coles, John Coles & Mogens Schou Jørgensen (eds), *Bog bodies, sacred sites and wetland archaeology*, WARP Occasional Paper 12 (Exeter, 1999), pp 67–8.

Delaney, Shane, 'M18 Gort to Crusheen road scheme – summary of the final archaeological results', *The Other Clare, Journal of the Shannon Archaeological and Historical Society*, 35 (2011), 56–65.

— 'Ranelagh, County Roscommon: preliminary observations', *IAI News*, 2:17 (Summer 2017), 13–14.

Delaney, Shane & Maeve Tobin (eds), 'N18 Gort to Crusheen road scheme, Site name: Ballyboy 1 Ringditch' (2010, IAC), Unpublished final report prepared for Galway County Council.

Delaney, Shane, Jim McKeon & Siobhán McNamara, 'Two Iron Age ring-ditches in Ballyboy, Co. Galway' in Corlett & Potterton (eds), *Life and death in Iron Age Ireland* (2012), pp 93–104.

Delaney, Shane, David Bayley, Ed Lyne, Siobhán McNamara, Joe Nunan & Karen Molloy (eds), *Borderlands: archaeological investigations on the route of the M18 Gort to Crusheen road scheme*, NRA Scheme Monographs 9 (Dublin, 2012).

Delaney, Tom (ed.), *Excavations 1975–76: summary accounts of archaeological work in Ireland* (Belfast, 1976).

Dempsey, Jonathan, 'Excavation report: Site: Morett 15, County Laois, Excavation no. 03E1624' (2004: Archaeological Consultancy Services), Accessible via TII database on Digital Repository Ireland, www.dri.ie.

— 'Excavation report for sites: Morett 2, 5, 6, 12, 13, 14, Co. Laois. Excavation no. 03E1367' (2004: Archaeological Consultancy Services), Accessible via TII database on Digital Repository Ireland, www.dri.ie.

Dent, John, 'Three cart burials from Wetwang, Yorkshire', *Antiquity*, 59 (1985), 85–92; Plates XVIII–XXI.

Discovery Programme Reports 8, *Late Iron Age and 'Roman' Ireland* (Dublin, 2014).
Doherty, Charles, 'The use of relics in Early Ireland' in Proinseas Ní Chatháin & Michael Richter (eds), *Ireland and Europe: the Early Church* (Stuttgart, 1984), pp 70–9.
— 'The Vikings in Ireland: a review' in Howard Clarke, Máire Ní Mhaonaigh & Raghnall Ó Floinn (eds), *Ireland and Scandinavia in the Early Viking Age* (Dublin, 1998), pp 288–330.
— 'Lough Ree and mythic landscapes' in Bernadette Cunningham & Harman Murtagh (eds), *Lough Ree: historic lakeland settlement* (Dublin, 2015), pp 48–69.
Doherty, Gillian M., *The Irish Ordnance Survey: history, culture and memory* (Dublin, 2004).
Dowling, Gerard, 'The liminal boundary: an analysis of the sacral potency of the ditch at Ráith na Ríg, Tara, Co. Meath', *JIA*, 15 (Dublin, 2006), 15–37.
Doyle, Ian W., 'The Early Medieval activity at Dalkey Island, Co. Dublin: a re-assessment', *JIA*, 9 (1998), 89–103.
— 'Excavation of a prehistoric ring-barrow at Kilmahuddrick, Clondalkin, Dublin 22', *JIA*, 14 (2005), 43–75.
— 'Mediterranean and Frankish pottery imports in Early Medieval Ireland', *JIA*, 18 (2009), 17–62.
— 'Early Medieval E ware pottery; an unassuming but enigmatic kitchen ware?' in Kelly, Roycroft & Stanley (eds), *Fragments of lives past: archaeological objects from Irish road schemes* (2014), pp 81–94.
Drummond, William Hamilton, 'On Roman coins found in Ireland', *PRIA*, 2 (1840–4), 185–90.
Duffy, Paul, 'Final report on excavation at Saint Fintan's Park, Kill of the Grange, Co. Dublin, Ministerial consent: C00845; Excavation reg. no. E004940' (2019: IAC), Unpublished final report for Dún Laoghaire Rathdown County Council.
Dunlop, Colin, 'Proposed development at Magheradunbar Quarry, Enniskillen, Co. Fermanagh: results of test trenching, Northern Ireland Sites and Monuments Record. No. FER211-011' (2003: Northern Archaeological Consultancy). Unpublished report.
Dunlop, Colin & Barkley, Jonathan, *Road to the West: the archaeology of the A4/A5 Road Improvements Scheme from Dungannon to Ballygawley, A road to the past*, vol. 2 (Belfast, 2016).
Dunne, Laurence, 'Ballyvelly, Tralee, Kerry. No. 1998:825: licence no. 98E0240' (1998), www.excavations.ie.
— 'Late Iron Age crematoria at Ballyvelly, Tralee', *Archaeology Ireland*, 13:2 (Summer 1999), 10–11.
Edwards, Nancy (ed.), *The archaeology of the Early Medieval Celtic churches*, The Society for Medieval Archaeology Monograph 29; The Society for Church Archaeology Monograph 1 (Leeds, 2009).
— 'Chi-Rhos, crosses, and Pictish symbols: inscribed stones and stone sculpture in Early Medieval Wales and Scotland' in Edwards, Ní Mhaonaigh & Flechner (eds), *Transforming landscapes of belief in the Early Medieval Insular world and beyond* (2017), pp 381–407.
Edwards, Nancy & Alan Lane (eds), *The Early Church in Wales and the West*, Oxbow Monograph 16 (Oxford, 1992).
Edwards, Nancy, Máire Ní Mhaonaigh & Roy Flechner (eds), *Transforming landscapes of belief in the Early Medieval Insular world and beyond*, Converting the Isles 2, CELEMA 23 (Turnhout, 2017).
Eisenberg, Jerome M., '"A seal upon thine heart": glyptic art of the Ancient Near East Pt II', *Minerva: The International Review of Ancient Art and Archaeology* (1998, July–August), 8–17.
Elder, Stuart & Penny Johnston, *Archaeological excavation report, Bricketstown, N25 Harristown to Rathsillagh, Co. Wexford. Cremation Cemetery* (2006: Eachtra Archaeological Projects).
Eogan, George, 'Excavations at Knowth, Co. Meath', *PRIA*, 66 (1968), 299–400.
— 'Report on the excavations of some passage graves, unprotected inhumation burials, and a settlement site at Knowth, Co. Meath', *PRIA*, 74C (1974), 11–112.
Eogan, George et al., *The archaeology of Knowth in the first and second millennia AD: Excavations at Knowth 5* (Dublin, 2012).
Eogan, James, 'Excavation of an unenclosed Early Medieval cemetery at Bettystown, Co. Meath' in Corlett & Potterton (eds), *Death and burial in Early Medieval Ireland* (2012), pp 103–16.
Eogan, James & Laureen Buckley, 'An Iron Age penannular ring-ditch at Ballybronoge South, Co. Limerick' in Corlett & Potterton (eds), *Life and death in Iron Age Ireland* (2012), pp 105–120.

Esposito, M. (ed.), 'Conchubrani Vita Sanctae Monennae', *PRIA*, 12C (1910), 202–57.
Evans, Jane A. & Carolyn A. Chenery, 'Unpublished: report on strontium and oxygen isotope analysis of tooth enamel from five individuals from the Owenbristy site, Ireland' in John Lehan & Finn Delaney, *Final archaeological excavation report, Owenbristy, Co. Galway. Cashel and burial ground* (2010: Eachtra Archaeological Projects), Appendix 13, pp 382–4.
Evison, Vera I., *An Anglo-Saxon cemetery at Great Chesterford, Essex*, CBA Research Report 91 (York, 1994).
Fanning, Thomas, 'Excavation of an Early Christian cemetery and settlement at Reask, County Kerry', *PRIA*, 81C (1981), 67–172.
— 'Some field monuments in the townlands of Clonmelsh and Garryhundon, Co. Carlow', *Peritia*, 3 (1984), 43–9.
Farwell, D.E. & Theya Molleson, *Excavations at Poundbury 1966–80, vol. II: The cemeteries*, Dorset Natural History and Archaeological Society Monograph Series 11 (Dorchester, 1993).
Faulkner, Neil, Keith Robinson & Gary Rossin (eds), *Digging Sedgeford: a people's archaeology* (Cromer, 2014: Poppyland Publishing, The SHARP Team).
Fern, Chris, 'Early Anglo-Saxon horse burial of the fifth to seventh centuries AD', *ASSAH*, 14 (2007), 93–109.
Fibiger, Linda, 'Report on the human skeletal remains, Church Road, Lusk', Unpublished, Prepared for ACS Ltd (2008).
— 'Report on human skeletal remains from Raystown, Co. Meath' in *Final excavation report on excavation of Site 21, Raystown, Co. Meath*, vol. 4 (2009: CRDS). Included on DVD accompanying Matthew Seaver (2016) *Meitheal: the archaeology of lives, labours and beliefs at Raystown, Co. Meath*, TII Heritage 4 (Dublin, 2016).
— 'The human skeletal remains from Ratoath, Co. Meath' in Corlett & Potterton (eds), *Death and burial in Early Medieval Ireland* (2010), pp 117–37.
FitzPatrick, Elizabeth, 'Rite of the single shoe' in Elizabeth FitzPatrick (ed.), *Royal inauguration in Gaelic Ireland, c.1100 to c.1600* (Woodbridge, 2004).
— 'Assembly places and elite collective identities in Medieval Ireland', *Journal of the North Atlantic*, special vol. 8 (2015), 52–68.
Flanagan, Laurence N.W., '1969:002 – Kiltierney – Archdall Deerpark, Fermanagh' (1969), accessed via www.excavations.ie.
Flynn, Colm, 'Final report – vol 1. CAMLIN 3, Excavation no. E3580' in 'N7 Castletown to Nenagh (Derrinsallagh to Ballintotty) road improvement scheme' (2011: Valerie J. Keeley), Unpublished report for Laois County Council and NRA.
Foley, Claire, 'An enigma solved' in Hamlin & Lynn (eds), *Pieces of the past* (1988), pp 24–6.
— 'Kiltierney Deerpark – Prehistoric, Medieval, 18th-century and defence heritage landscape' in Foley & McHugh (eds), *An archaeological survey of County Fermanagh, vol. 1, part 2* (2014), pp 857–70.
Foley, Claire & Ronan McHugh, *An archaeological survey of County Fermanagh, vol. 1, part 2: the Early Christian and Medieval periods* (Belfast, 2014).
Foulds, Elizabeth M., *Dress and identity in Iron Age Britain: a study of glass beads and other objects of personal adornment* (Oxford, 2017).
Fowler, Elizabeth, 'The origins and development of the penannular brooch in Europe', *PPS*, 26 (1960), 149–77.
— 'Celtic metalwork of the fifth and sixth centuries AD: a re-appraisal', *AJ*, 120:1 (1963), 98–160.
Frazer, William O., 'Final report, archaeological excavation, Pelletstown (East), Castleknock, Dublin 15' (2005: Margaret Gowen), Unpublished report for Ballymore Properties.
— 'Pelletstown and Cabragh, Castleknock – Three unenclosed burials' in Isabel Bennett (ed.), *Excavations 2003* (Dublin, 2006), pp 111–12, no. 467.
Fredengren, Christina, *Crannógs: a study of people's interaction with lakes, with particular reference to Lough Gara in the north-west of Ireland* (Dublin, 2002).
Gahan, Audrey, 'Castle Upton, Templepatrick' in Isabel Bennett (ed.), *Excavations 1997* (Dublin, 1998), no. 3.

Geake, Helen, *The use of grave goods in conversion-period England, c.600–c.850*, BAR 261 (Oxford, 1997).
Geber, Jonny, 'Osteological report' in John Lehane & Finn Delaney, 'Final archaeological excavation report, Owenbristy, Co. Galway. Cashel & burial ground' (2010: Eachtra Archaeological Projects), Appendix 6, pp 131–85. Unpublished report for Galway County Council and NRA.
— 'Human remains from Owenbristy' in Delaney & Tierney (eds), *In the lowlands of south Galway* (2011), pp 86–94.
Giacometti, Antoine, 'Preliminary archaeological excavation report re proposed development site, Donacarney Great Townland, Bettystown, Co. Meath' (2010: Arch Tech). Unpublished report prepared for Relative Developments.
Gilchrist, Roberta, '"Magic for the dead?": The archaeology of magic in Later Medieval burials', *Med. Arch.*, 52 (2008), 119–19.
Gogan, Liam S., 'Killegar and its memorials', *Irish Travel* (September 1929), 15–16.
Gowen, Margaret, 'Colp West: Early Christian enclosure, cemetery' in Isabel Bennett (ed.), *Excavations 1988* (Dublin, 1989), p. 32.
— 'Westreave: Christian cemetery' in Isabel Bennett (ed.), *Excavations 1988* (Dublin, 1989), p. 18.
— 'Kilshane, Co. Dublin' in Isabel Bennett (ed.), *Excavations 1988* (Dublin, 1989), p. 17.
Graham-Campbell, James & Michael Ryan (eds), *Anglo-Saxon/Irish relations before the Vikings* (Oxford, 2009).
Grant, Christine, 'Mapping a Bronze Age Burren landscape', *Archaeology Ireland*, 9:1, Issue 31 (Spring 1995), 31–3.
— 'Kilcorney' in Isabel Bennett (ed.), *Excavations 2003* (Dublin, 2006), pp 553–4.
— 'The Burren in prehistory' in Tom Condit & Gabriel Cooney (eds), *Archaeology Ireland Heritage Guide no. 49* (Dublin, 2010).
Graves, James, 'Implements and ornaments', *TKAS* (later *JRSAI*), 1:1 (1850), 30–2.
Green, Barbara & Andrew Rogerson, *The Anglo-Saxon cemetery at Bergh Apton, Norfolk: Catalogue*, East Anglian Archaeology Report no. 7 (Norfolk, 1978).
Greene, Sharon A., 'Settlement, identity and change on the Atlantic islands of north-west Co. Mayo, c.AD 400–1100' (PhD, UCD, 2009).
Grogan, Eoin, 'Excavation of an Iron Age burial mound at Furness', *JKAS*, 16:4 (1983), 298–316.
— *The Rath of the Synods, Tara, Co. Meath: excavations by Seán P. Ó Ríordáin* (Dublin, 2008).
Grogan, Eoin & George Eogan, 'Lough Gur excavations by Seán P. Ó Ríordáin: further Neolithic and Beaker habitations on Knockadoon', *PRIA*, 87 C:7 (1987), 109–506.
Grogan, Eoin, Lorna O'Donnell & Penny Johnston (eds), '1181. Inchinclare' in *The Bronze Age landscapes of the pipeline to the West* (Dublin, 2007), pp 284–5.
Guido, Margaret, *The glass beads of the Prehistoric and Roman periods in Britain and Ireland* (London, 1978).
Hackett, Liam & John Twomey, 'N9–N10 Kilcullen to Waterford scheme: phase 3, Kilcullen to Carlow. Archaeological Services Contract No. 5 – Resolution, Kilcullen to Moone and Athy Link Road. Final report on archaeological investigations at Site E2973, in the townland of Mullamast, Co. Kildare' (2009: Headland Archaeology), Unpublished report prepared for Kildare County Council and the NRA.
— 'N9–N10 Kilcullen to Waterford scheme: phase 3, Kilcullen to Carlow. Archaeological Services Contract No. 5 – Resolution, Kilcullen to Moone and Athy Link Road. Final report on archaeological investigations at Site E2972, in the townland of Mullamast, Co. Kildare' (2010: Headland Archaeology), Unpublished report for Kildare County Council and the NRA.
Hamerow, Helena, 'Furnished female burial in seventh-century England: gender and sacral authority in the conversion period', *Early Medieval Europe*, 24:4 (2016), 423–47.
Hamlin, Ann & Chris Lynn (eds), *Pieces of the past: archaeological excavations by the Department of the Environment for Northern Ireland 1970–1986* (Belfast, 1988).
Hamlin, Ann Elizabeth, *The archaeology of Early Christianity in the North of Ireland*, BAR 460 (Oxford, 2008).
Harbison, Peter, 'Old Testament prefigurations of New Testament events on Irish high crosses', *PRIA*, 118C (2018), 123–40.

Harbison, Peter & Valerie Hall (eds), *A carnival of learning: essays to honour George Cunningham* (Roscrea, 2012).

Harding, Dennis William, *The Iron Age in Lowland Britain* (London, 1985).

Harrison, Stephen H. & Raghnall Ó Floinn, *Viking graves and grave goods in Ireland* (Dublin, 2014).

Hawkes, Christopher F.C., 'The wearing of the brooch: Early Iron Age dress among the Irish' in Brian G. Scott (ed.), *Studies on Early Ireland: essays in honour of M.V. Duignan* (Belfast, 1982), pp 251–73.

Hayden, Alan R., 'Early Medieval shrines in north-west Iveragh: new perspectives from Church Island, near Valentia, Co. Kerry', *PRIA*, 113C (2013), 67–138.

Hedges, Robert E.M., Rupert A. Housley, Christopher Bronk Ramsey & G.J. Van Klinken, 'Radiocarbon dates from the Oxford AMS system: archaeometry datelist 17', *Archaeometry*, 335:2 (1993), 305–26.

Heinrich-Tamaska, Orsolya, Niklot Krohn & Sebastian Ristow (eds), *Christianisierung Europas: Entstehung, Entwicklung und Konsolidierung im archäologischen Befund* (Regensburg, 2012).

Hemer, Katie A., Jane A. Evans, Carolyn A. Chenery & Angela L. Lamb, 'Evidence of Early Medieval trade and migration between Wales and the Mediterranean Sea region', *JAS*, 40 (2013), 2352–9.

— 'No Man is an island: evidence of pre-Viking Age migration to the Isle of Man', *JAS*, 52 (2014), 242–9.

Hennessey, W.M. (ed. and trans.), *The annals of Loch Cé* (London, 1871).

Henry, Françoise, 'Early Christian slabs and pillar stones in the West of Ireland', *JRSAI*, 67:2 (1937), 265–79.

— 'Remains of the Early Christian period on Inishkea North, Co. Mayo', *JRSAI*, 75:3 (1945), 127–55.

Herity, Michael, 'Irish decorated Neolithic pottery', *PRIA*, 82C (1982), 274–404.

Herbert, Máire, *Iona, Kells and Derry: the history and hagiography of the Monastic familia of Columba* (Dublin, 1996).

Hight, George A. & Peter Foote, *The saga of Grettir the Strong* (London, 1972).

Hill, Peter, *Whithorn and St Ninian: the excavation of a monastic town, 1984–91* (Stroud, Gloucestershire, 1997).

Hilts, Carley, 'Great Ryburgh: a remarkable Anglo-Saxon cemetery revealed', *Current Archaeology*, 322 (2017), 18–23.

Hines, John & Alex Bayliss (eds), *Anglo-Saxon graves and grave goods of the 6th and 7th centuries AD: a chronological framework*, Society for Medieval Archaeology Monographs 33 (Abingdon, 2017).

Hirst, Susan M., *An Anglo-Saxon inhumation cemetery at Sewerby, East Yorkshire*, York University Archaeological Publications 4 (York, 1985).

Howlett, David R., *The book of letters of Saint Patrick the Bishop* (Dublin, 1994).

Hull, Graham, 'N18 Ennis Bypass and N85 Western Relief Road. Site AR131, Claureen, Co. Clare' (2006: TVAS), unpublished final archaeological excavation report for Clare County Council.

Hurl, Declan P., Caroline Sandes & Laureen Buckley, 'The excavation of an Early Christian cemetery at Solar, County Antrim, 1993', *UJA*, 61 (2002), 37–82.

Ireland, Aideen, 'The Stonyford burial: fact or fiction (part I)', *JRSAI*, 142–3 (2012–13), 8–27.

— 'The Stonyford burial: fact or fiction (part II)', *JRSAI*, 144–5 (2014–15), 27–44.

Ireland, Colin, 'Aldfrith of Northumbria and the Irish Genealogies', *Celtica*, 22 (1991), 64–78.

James, Heather, 'Early Medieval cemeteries in Wales' in Edwards & Lane (eds), *The Early Church in Wales and the West* (1992), pp 90–103.

James, Simon & Valery Rigby, *Britain and the Celtic Iron Age* (London, 1997).

Jay, Mandy, Colin Haselgrove, Derek Hamilton, J.D. Hill & John Dent, 'Chariots and context: new radiocarbon dates from Wetwang and the chronology of Iron Age burials and brooches in East Yorkshire', *Oxford Journal of Archaeology*, 31:2 (2012), 161–89.

Jay, Mandy, Janet Montgomery, Olaf Nehlich, Jacqueline Towers & Jane Evans, 'British Iron Age chariot burials of the Arras culture: a multi-isotope approach to investigating mobility levels and subsistence practices', *World Archaeology*, 45:3 (2013), 473–91.

Johnson, Stephen, *Burgh Castle, excavations by Charles Green, 1958–61*, East Anglian Archaeology Report 20 (Norfolk, 1983).
Johnston, Elva, 'Ireland in Late Antiquity: a forgotten frontier?', *Studies in Late Antiquity*, 1:2 (2017), 107–23.
Jope, Edward Martyn & Basil C.S. Wilson, 'A burial group of the first century AD from "Loughey" near Donaghadee', *UJA*, 20 (1957), 73–95.
— 'The beads from the first Century AD burial at "Loughey" near Donaghadee – supplementary note', *UJA* (1960), 23–40.
Joynt, Maud, *Contributions to a dictionary of the Irish language (DIL)*, 'N–O–P' (Dublin, 1940).
— *Contributions to a dictionary of the Irish language (DIL)*, 'R'. (Dublin, 1944).
Kavanagh, Rhoda, 'The encrusted urn in Ireland', *PRIA*, 73C (1973), 507–617.
— 'Collared and cordon cinerary urns in Ireland', *PRIA*, 76C (1976), 293–403.
— 'Pygmy cups in Ireland', *JRSAI*, 107 (1977), 61–95.
Keating, Denise, 'An analysis of the human skeletal remains at Colp, Co. Meath, and their contribution to the Early Christian period in Ireland' (MSc, University of Bradford, 2001).
— 'Human skeletal remains' in Tobin & Sunderland, *Excavation and specialists reports, Enclosure and associated features; Corbally, Kilcullen, Co. Kildare* (2004), pp 24–43.
— 'An analysis of the human skeletal remains from Parknahown 5, Co. Laois' in Tara O'Neill, *Report on the archaeological excavation of Parknahown* (2009), vol. 3.
Keeley, V.J. Ltd, 'Archaeological excavation at Marlinstown, Co. Westmeath' and 'A ringfort at Marlinstown, County Westmeath', Unpublished articles submitted to the NRA in mid-1990s by VJK Ltd (obtained courtesy TII).
Keeley, Valerie J., 'Archaeological excavation of a burial ground, Greenhills Townland', *JKAS*, 17 (1987–91), 180–201.
— 'Marlinstown, Co. Westmeath – ringfort' in Isabel Bennett (ed.), *Excavations 1990* (Dublin, 1991), p. 55, no. 113.
— 'Marlinstown, Co. Westmeath' in Isabel Bennett (ed.), *Excavations 1991* (Dublin, 1992), no. 126.
— 'Preliminary report: archaeological excavations Ballydavis Td, Portlaoise By-Pass, Co. Laois' (1995), Unpublished report for NRA (obtained courtesy TII).
— 'Ballydavis. Early Iron Age complex' in Isabel Bennett (ed.), *Excavations 1995* (Dublin, 1996), pp 51–2, no. 173.
— 'Ballydavis, Co. Laois, 95E111' accessible at Section 9.1 www.heritagecouncil.ie/unpublished_excavations/section9.html, significant unpublished Irish archaeological excavations, 1930–97. The Heritage Council.
— 'Iron Age discoveries at Ballydavis' in Pádraig G. Lane & William Nolan (eds), *Laois history & society* (Dublin, 1999), pp 25–34.
Kehnel, Annette, 'Clonmacnois – the church and lands of St Ciarán: change and continuity in an Irish monastic foundation (6th to 16th century)', *Vita regularis: Ordnungen und Deutungen religiosen Lebens im Mittelalter* 8 (Münster & New Brunswick, NJ, 1997).
Kelly, Amanda, 'An African red slip shard from Kilree 3, Co. Kilkenny (AR093, E3643)' (2009), Unpublished report prepared for Irish Archaeological Consultancy.
— 'The discovery of Phocaean Red Slip Ware (PRSW) form 3 and Bii ware (LRI amphorae) on sites in Ireland – an analysis within a broader framework', *PRIA*, 110C (2010), 35–88.
Kelly, Bernice, Niall Roycroft & Michael Stanley (eds), *Encounters between people*, National Roads Authority Monograph Series 9 (Dublin, 2012).
— *Fragments of lives past: archaeological objects from Irish road schemes*, National Roads Authority Monograph Series 11 (Dublin, 2014).
Kelly, Eamonn, 'Ferganstown and Ballymacon' in Tom Delaney (ed.), *Excavations 1975–76* (1976), p. 35.
Kelly, Eamonn P., 'A burial at Farganstown and Ballymacon, Co. Meath', *Ríocht na Midhe*, 6 (1977), 65–7.
— 'Ringed pins of County Louth', *JCLAHS*, 21:2 (1986), 179–99.
— 'Betaghstown, 0159730, Iron Age cemetery', *JIA*, 4 (Excavations Bulletin 1977–79: summary account of archaeological excavations in Ireland) (1987–8), 75.

— 'The Iron Age' in Patrick F. Wallace & Raghnall Ó Floinn (eds), *Treasures of the National Museum of Ireland (Irish Antiquities)* (Dublin, 2002), [4:7], p. 137.
— *Kingship and sacrifice: Iron Age bog bodies and boundaries*, Heritage Guide No. 35 (Dublin, 2006).
— 'Re-evaluation of a supposed inland promontory fort at Knoxspark, Co. Sligo – Iron Age fortress or Viking stronghold' in Cooney et al. (eds), *Relics of old decency* (Dublin, 2009), pp 485–97.
Kelly, Fergus, *A guide to Early Irish law* (Dublin, 1988).
— *Early Irish farming* (Dublin, 1997).
Kelly, Fergus (ed. and trans.), *Marriage disputes: a fragmentary Old Irish law-text* (Dublin, 2014).
Kennett, David H., 'Pottery and other finds from the Anglo-Saxon cemetery at Sandy, Bedfordshire', *Med. Arch.*, 14 (1970), 17–33.
Kiely, Jacinta & Niamh O'Callaghan, 'Archaeological excavation report, 02005, Ballydowny, Killarney, Co. Kerry', *Eachtra Journal*, 7 (August 2010).
Kiely, Jacinta & John Tierney, 'Excavation of skeletons from Newtown Ringfort DU014-006001. Dublin Airport Logistics Park, Fingal, Co. Dublin' (2018, Eachtra Archaeological Projects), Unpublished report prepared for Rohan Holdings.
Kimber, Mike, 'RN105 A4/A5, Site 25, Halftown Road, Annaghilla' in Isabel Bennett (ed.), *Excavations 2007* (Dublin, 2010), p. 501, no. 1745.
King, Heather A., 'Clonmacnoise, high crosses' in Isabel Bennett (ed.), *Excavations 1993* (Dublin, 1994), no. 186.
— 'Clonmacnoise, high crosses' in Isabel Bennett (ed.), *Excavations 1994* (Dublin, 1995), pp 74–5, no. 196.
— 'St Columba's Monastery at Durrow: some additional discoveries' in Harbison & Hall (eds), *A carnival of learning: essays to honour George Cunningham* (2012), pp 125–32.
King, Heather A. (ed.), *Clonmacnoise studies. Volume 2. Seminar papers 1998* (Dublin, 2003).
Kjølby-Biddle, Birthe, 'Dispersal or concentration: the disposal of the Winchester dead over 2000 years' in Steven Bassett (ed.), *Death in towns: urban responses to the dying and the dead, 100–1600* (Leicester, 1995), pp 210–47.
Knox, H.T., 'The Turoe Stone and the Rath of Feerwore', *JGAHS*, 9 (1916), 190–3.
Koch, John T. & John Carey, *The Celtic Heroic Age: literary sources for Ancient Celtic Europe and Early Ireland and Wales* (MA, 1995: Celtic Studies Publications).
Lane, Pádraig G. & William Nolan (eds), *Laois history & society, interdisciplinary essays on the history of an Irish county* (Dublin, 1999).
Lanting, Jan N. & Anna L. Brindley, 'Dating cremated bone: the dawn of a new era', *JIA*, 9 (Dublin, 1998), 1–7.
Lapidge, Michael & Michael Herren (ed. & trans.), *Aldhelm: the prose works* (Cambridge, 1979).
Lash, Ryan, 'Pebbles and *Peregrinatio*: the taskscape of Medieval devotion on Inishark Island, Ireland', *Med. Arch.*, 62:1 (2018), 83–104.
Lawlor, Henry C., *The monastery of Saint Mochaoi of Nendrum* (Belfast, 1925).
Leech, Roger, 'The excavation of a Romano-British farmstead and cemetery on Bradley Hill, Somerton, Somerset', *Britannia*, 12 (1981), 177–252.
Lehane, John, 'Final report, N6 Galway to East Ballinasloe road scheme: archaeological resolution of human skeletal remains Ballygarraun West townland, Co. Galway' (2008: Valerie J. Keeley), Unpublished report for Galway County Council.
— 'Owenbristy— cashel and cemetery' in Delaney & Tierney (eds), *In the lowlands of South Galway* (2011), pp 71–84.
Lehane, John & Finn Delaney, 'Final archaeological excavation report, Owenbristy, Co. Galway. Cashel and burial ground' (2010: Eachtra Archaeological Projects), Unpublished report prepared for Galway County Council and NRA.
Lehane, John, Marta Muñiz Pérez, Jerry O'Sullivan & Brendon Wilkins, 'Three cemetery-settlement excavations in County Galway, at Carrowkeel, Treanbaun and Owenbristy' in Corlett & Potterton (eds), *Death and burial in Early Medieval Ireland* (2010), pp 139–56.
Lenihan, Orlaith & Emer Dennehy, 'Final report on archaeological investigations at Site E2982, in the townland of Moone, Co. Kildare. N9–N10 Kilcullen to Waterford Scheme: Phase 3,

Kilcullen to Carlow. Archaeological Services Contract No. 5 – Resolution, Kilcullen to Moone and Athy Link Road' (2010: Headland Archaeology), Unpublished report prepared for Kildare County Council and TII (NRA).

Leon, Barbara C., 'Mesolithic and Neolithic activity on Dalkey Island – a reassessment', *JIA*, 14 (2005), 1–21.

Lillehammer, Grete & Eileen Murphy (eds), *Across the generations: the old and the young in past societies*, Childhood in the Past Monograph Series 8 (Stavanger, 2018).

Longley, David, 'Early Medieval burial in Wales' in Edwards (ed.), *The archaeology of the Early Medieval Celtic churches* (2009), pp 105–32.

Lewis, Samuel, *A topographical dictionary of Ireland* (London, 1837).

Liversedge, G. David, 'Excavations at Dalkey Island, Co. Dublin, 1956–1959', *PRIA*, 66C (1968), 53–233.

Lucas, Anthony T., 'National Museum of Ireland, archaeological acquisitions in the year 1970', *JRSAI*, 103 (1973), 177–213.

Lynch, Linda G., *Osteo-archaeological report on human skeletal remains excavated at Corbally, Co. Kildare* (2005: Aegis Archaeology), Unpublished report prepared for Kilsaran Concrete.

Lynch, Linda G. & Eileen Reilly, 'Early Medieval human burials and insect remains from Kildimo, Co. Limerick', *JIA*, 20 (2011), 65–76.

Lynn, Christopher J., 'Excavations at 46–48 Scotch Street, Armagh, 1979–80', *UJA*, 51 (1988), 69–84.

Lynn, Christopher J. (ed.), *Excavations at Navan Fort, 1961–71. D.M. Waterman*, Northern Ireland Archaeological Monographs 3 (Belfast, 1997).

Macalister, Robert A.S., *The archaeology of Ireland* (London, 1928).

— 'On some antiquities discovered upon Lambay', *PRIA*, 38C (1929), 240–6.

MacCana, Proinsias, *Celtic mythology* (London, 1970).

— 'The *topos* of the single sandal in Irish tradition', *Celtica*, 10 (1973), 160–6.

Macdonald, Philip & Naomi Carver, 'Archaeological excavations at Ballyhanna graveyard – chronology, development and context' in McKenzie, Murphy & Donnelly (eds), *The science of a lost Medieval Gaelic graveyard* (2015), pp 47–84.

MacGregor, Morna, *Early Celtic art in North Britain: a study of decorative metalwork from the third century BC to the third century AD* (Leicester, 1976).

Maldonado, Adrián, 'Burial in Early Medieval Scotland: new questions', *Medieval Archaeology* (2013), 1–34.

— 'Materialising the Afterlife: the long cist in Early Medieval Scotland' in Pierce, Russell & Maldonado (eds), *Creating material worlds* (2016), pp 39–62.

Mallory, Jim P., 'The conundrum of Iron Age ceramics: the evidence of language' in Cooney, Becker, Coles, Ryan & Sievers (eds), *Relics of old decency* (2009), pp 181–92.

Malo, David, *Hawaiian antiquities*, trans. Nathaniel B. Emerson (2nd ed. Honolulu, 1951).

Manning, Conleth, 'Archaeological excavation of a succession of enclosures at Millockstown, Co. Louth', *PRIA*, 86C 4 (1986), 135–81.

— 'The base of the North Cross at Clonmacnoise', *Archaeology Ireland*, 6:2 (1992), 8–9.

McCarthy, Ciara, 'The Ballynakelly ringfort, Co. Dublin' in Corlett & Potterton (eds), *Settlement in Early Medieval Ireland* (2011), pp 239–50.

— 'An Iron Age ring-ditch at Ballynakelly, Co. Dublin' in Corlett & Potterton (eds), *Life and death in Iron Age Ireland* (2012), pp 157–59.

McConway, Cia., 'Successive Early Medieval enclosed settlements at Ninch, Co. Meath' in Corlett & Potterton (eds), *Death and burial in Early Medieval Ireland* (2010), pp 157–72.

McCormick, Finbar, 'A new light on burial practice', *Archaeology Ireland*, 8:3, Issue 29 (1994), 27–8.

— 'The Farta horse burial' (2013), Unpublished osteo-archaeological report prepared for the Mapping Death Project.

McCormick, Finbar, Gerry Cribbin, Michael E. Robinson & David W. Shimwell, 'A pagan Christian transitional burial at Kiltullagh', *Emania*, 13 (1995), 89–98.

McErlean, Thomas, 'Burials' in McErlean & Crothers, *Harnessing the tides* (2007), pp 345–50.

McErlean, Thomas & Norman Crothers, *Harnessing the tides: the Early Medieval tide mills at Nendrum Monastery, Strangford Lough*, Northern Ireland Archaeological Monographs 7 (Norwich, 2007).

McGarry, Tiernan, 'Irish Late Prehistoric burials' (PhD, UCD, 2008), available on-line.

— 'The Knowth Iron Age burials in an Irish and wider context' in Eogan et al., *The archaeology of Knowth in the first and second millennia AD* (2012), pp 689–94.

McHugh, Ronan & Brian G. Scott, 'The Prehistoric archaeology of County Fermanagh' in Claire Foley & Ronan McHugh, *An archaeological survey of County Fermanagh, Volume 1. Part 1: the Prehistoric period* (Belfast, 2014), pp 126–33.

McIlreavy, David, 'Post-excavation assessment report, Carroweighter 2, N60 Oran realignment road project' (2018: IAC), Unpublished final report prepared for Roscommon County Council.

McKenzie, Catriona J., Eileen Murphy & Colm J. Donnelly (eds), *The science of a lost Medieval Gaelic graveyard: the Ballyhanna Research Project*, TII Heritage 2 (Dublin, 2015).

McKeon, Jim & Jerrry O'Sullivan (eds), *The quiet landscape: archaeological investigations on the M6 Galway to Ballinasloe national road scheme*, NRA Scheme Monographs 15, with CD-ROM containing final reports (Dublin, 2014).

McKinley, Jacqueline I., 'Cremations: expectations, methodologies, and realities' in C.A. Roberts, F. Lee & L. Bintliff (eds), *Burial archaeology: current research, methods, and developments*, BAR 211 (Oxford, 1989).

— 'Bone fragment size and weights of bone from modern British cremations and the implications for the interpretation of archaeological cremations', *IJO*, 3 (1993), 283–7.

— 'A pyre and grave goods in British cremation burials; have we missed something?', *Antiquity*, 68 (1994), 132–4.

— 'Bronze Age "Barrows" and funerary rites and rituals of cremation', *PPS*, 63 (1997), 129–45.

— 'Ballymacaward, Co. Donegal, cremated bone report', Unpublished report no. 44864.1 (April 1998), Prepared for Julian Richards – BBC, *Meet the Ancestors* and Elizabeth O'Brien.

McLoughlin, Catherine, 'Excavation of an Iron Age ring-ditch and associated features at Kerlogue, Co. Wexford' in Corlett & Potterton (eds), *Life and death in Iron Age Ireland* (2012), pp 161–74.

McLoughlin, Catherine, 'Archaeological excavations at Xerox Technology Park, Haggardstown, Dundalk, County Louth', *JCLAHS*, 27:4 (2012), 503–35.

McLoughlin, Gill, 'Preliminary report of archaeological excavation at Station Road, Portmarnock, Co. Dublin. Phase 1B (Area 3) Excav. no. 16E0613' (2017: Courtney Deery Heritage Consultancy), Unpublished report for Sherman Oaks.

McManus, Damian, *A guide to ogam*, Maynooth Monographs 4 (Maynooth, 1991).

McNamara, Siobhan, 'N18 Gort to Crusheen road scheme. E3719 Ballyboy 1 Ringditch' (2010: IAC), Unpublished final report for Galway County Council. Downloaded from www.clarelibrary.ie.

— 'N18 Gort to Crusheen road scheme. E3718 Ballyboy 2' (2010: IAC), Unpublished final report for Galway County Council. Downloaded from www.clarelibrary.ie.

McNamara, Siobhan & Shane Delaney, 'Iron Age ring-ditches and cremation burials at Ballyboy' in Delaney, Baley, Lyne, McNamara, Nunan & Molloy (eds), *Borderlands* (2012), pp 123–37.

McNeill, John T. & Helena M., *Medieval handbooks of penance: a translation of the Principal Libri Poenitentiales* (New York, 1938; repr. 1990).

McQuade, Melanie, 'Final report on archaeological excavations at Premier Business Park on the site of Cappogue Castle, Cappogue, Dublin 11' (2009: M. Gowen), Unpublished report for Harcourt Developments.

McQuade, Melanie, Bernice Molloy & Colm Moriarty (eds), *In the shadow of the Galtees: archaeological excavations along the N8 Cashel to Mitchelstown road scheme* (Dublin, 2009).

McQuade, Melanie & Molloy, Bernice, 'Recent Iron Age discoveries in south County Tipperary and County Limerick' in Corlett & Potterton (eds), *Life and death in Iron Age Ireland* (2012), pp 175–87.

McSparron, Cormac, 'Dating the emergence of souterrain ware', *UJA*, 74 (2017–18), 86–73.

Meaney, Audrey, *A gazetteer of Early Anglo-Saxon burial sites* (London, 1964).

— *Anglo-Saxon archaeology: archaeology of ritual and magic*, BAR 96 (Oxford, 1981).
Mercer, Roger J., *Grimes, Graves, Norfolk. Excavations 1971–72*, vol. 1, Department of the Environment Archaeological Reports 11 (London, 1981).
Mikhailova, Natalie, 'The cult of the deer and "shamans" in deer hunting society', *Archaeologia Baltica*, 7 (2006), 187–98.
Moisl, Hermann, 'The Bernician royal dynasty and the Irish in the seventh century', *Peritia*, 2 (1983), 103–26.
Molloy, Bernice, 'Final report: N8 Cashel to Mitchelstown road improvement scheme, Knockcommane, Co. Limerick. Site 4700. 1a' (2007: Margaret Gowen), Unpublished report for South Tipperary County Council. Accessed December 2017, via TII at www.dri.ie.
Moloney, Colm, 'Final report on archaeological investigations at Site E2989, in the townland of Burtown Little, Co. Kildare; N9–N10 Kilcullen to Waterford scheme: phase 3, Kilcullen to Carlow; Archaeological Services Contract No. 5 – Resolution, Kilcullen to Moone and Athy Link Road' (2010: Headland Archaeology), Unpublished draft prepared for Kildare County Council. Obtained courtesy TII, August 2015.
Moloney, Colm, Louise Baker, Jonathan Millar & Damian Shiels, *Guide to the excavations at Ardreigh, County Kildare* (Dublin, 2016).
Montgomery, Janet, Jane Evans & Caroline Chenery, 'Report of the lead, strontium and oxygen isotope analysis of the Iron Age burial from Rath, Ireland' (2006), Unpublished report prepared for CRDS, Dublin.
Montgomery, Janet & Julie Milns, 'Report on the strontium isotope analysis of four prehistoric and Early Medieval burials from the Holdenstown and Kilree areas of the Nore Valley' (2010), Unpublished report prepared for Irish Archaeology Consultancy.
Montgomery, Janet & Vaughan Grimes, 'Appendix 21.1. Report on the isotope analysis of a burial from Ratoath, Co. Meath' in Corlett & Potterton (eds), *Death and burial in Early Medieval Ireland* (2010), pp 309–11.
Moore, Caitríona, *2014:026 – Tlachtga, the Hill of Ward, Meath* (2014), Report accessed at www.excavations.ie-report-2014–Meath-0023689–.
Morris, John (ed. and trans.), *Nennius: British history and the Welsh annals* (London, 1980).
Mount, Charles, 'Excavation and environmental analysis of a Neolithic mound and Iron Age barrow cemetery at Rathdooney Beg, Co. Sligo, Ireland', *PPS*, 65 (1999), 337–71.
— 'Excavation of an Early Medieval promontory fort and enclosed cemetery at Knoxspark, Co. Sligo' in Corlett & Potterton (eds), *Death and burial in Early Medieval Ireland* (2010), pp 187–216.
— 'Created and appropriated continuity at Rathdooney Beg, Co. Sligo' in Corlett & Potterton (eds), *Life and death in Iron Age Ireland* (2012), pp 189–98.
Muldoon, Ros (O'Maolduin), 'Ex. No. 03E00633, Site F West, Cappakeel Townland, Co. Laois, M7 Heath-Mayfield Motorway Scheme Co. Laois' (2011: VJK), Unpublished final report for NRA.
Mullins, Clare, 'Derryvilla' in Isabel Bennett (ed), *Excavations 1998* (Dublin, 2000), pp 175–6, no. 550.
Mullins, Gerry, 'Pagan or Christian? Excavation of a hilltop cemetery at Cross, Co. Galway' in O'Sullivan & Stanley (eds), *New routes to the past* (2007), pp 101–10.
— 'Cross, Co. Galway. N6 Galway to East Ballinasloe PPP Scheme. Archaeological Contract 3. Phase 2. Unpublished final report. Excavation E2069. Cross, Co. Galway, cemetery site: ring-barrows, cremations and extended' (2009: CRDS), Unpublished report for Galway County Council and NRA.
Mullins, Gerry & Nora Birmingham, 'Ring-ditches with cremations and inhumations at Cross' in McKeon & O'Sullivan (eds), *The quiet landscape* (2014), pp 100–5.
Murphy, Donald, 'Colp West: Prehistoric ritual site-Early Christian settlement site' in Isabel Bennett (ed.), *Excavations 2000* (2002), pp 253–4.
— 'Excavation of an Early monastic enclosure at Clonmacnoise' in Heather A. King (ed.), *Clonmacnoise studies. Volume 2. Seminar papers 1998* (2003), pp 1–33.
— 'Excavation of a multi-period settlement site at Colp West, Co. Meath' in Corlett & Potterton (eds), *Settlement in Early Medieval Ireland* (2011), pp 251–9.

Murphy, Eileen, Philip Macdonald, Colm Donnelly, Michael MacDonagh, Catriona McKenzie & Naoimi Carver, 'The "lost" medieval Gaelic church and graveyard at Ballyhanna, Co. Donegal: an overview of the excavated evidence' in Corlett & Potterton (eds), *Settlement in Early Medieval Ireland* (2011), pp 125–42.

Murphy, Eileen, & Colm Donnelly, 'Together in death: demography and funerary practices in contemporary multiple interments in Irish Medieval burial grounds' in Lillehammer & Murphy (eds), *Across the generations* (2018), pp 119–41.

Murphy, Eileen, & Barra O'Donnabhain, *The people of Prehistoric Ireland* (Dublin, forthcoming).

Newman, Conor, *Tara: an archaeology survey*, Discovery Programme Monographs 2 (Dublin, 1997), pp 156–7.

— 'The sword in the stone: previously unrecognised archaeological evidence of ceremonies of the later Iron Age and Early Medieval Ireland' in Cooney et al. (eds), *Relics of old decency* (2009), pp 425–36.

Newman, Conor, Michael O'Connell, Mary Dillon & Karen Molloy, Karen, 'Interpretation of charcoal and pollen data relating to a Late Iron Age ritual site in eastern Ireland: a holistic approach', *Vegetation History and Archaeobotany*, 16 (published on-line 26 April 2006), pp 349–65.

Newman, Conor, Mark Stansbury & Emment Marren (eds), 'The monastic remains at Cleenish, Co. Fermanagh: context, survey and excavation' in *Conference proceedings: Columbanus: Life and legacy*, vol. 3 (Forthcoming: Presses Universitaires de Rennes).

Ní Dhonnchadha, Máirín, 'The Guarantor List of *Cáin Adomnáin*, 697', *Peritia*, 1 (1982), 178–215.

— 'The Law of Adomnán: a translation' in Thomas O'Loughlin (ed.), *Adomnán at Birr, AD 697: essays in commemoration of the Law of the Innocents* (Dublin, 200), pp 53–68.

O'Brien, Billy, 'Toormore wedge tomb' in Isabel Bennett (ed.), *Excavations 1990* (Dublin, 1991), pp 20–1.

O'Brien, Elizabeth, 'Pre-Norman ecclesiastical sites of the half barony of Rathdown (South County Dublin)' (MA, UCD, 1980).

— 'Late Prehistoric-Early Historic Ireland: the burial evidence reviewed' (MPhil, UCD, 1984).

— 'Churches of south-east County Dublin, seventh to twelfth century' in Gearóid Mac Niocaill & Patrick F. Wallace (eds), *Keimelia: studies in Medieval archaeology and history in memory of Tom Delaney* (Galway, 1998), pp 504–24.

— 'Iron Age burial practices in Leinster: continuity and change', *Emania*, 7 (1990), 37–42.

— 'A re-assessment of the Great Sepulchral Mound containing a Viking burial at Donnybrook, Dublin', *Med. Arch.*, 36 (1992), 170–3.

— 'Pagan and Christian burial in Ireland during the first millennium AD: continuity and change' in Edwards & Lane (eds), *The Early Church in Wales and the West* (1992), pp 130–7.

— 'Contacts between Ireland and Anglo-Saxon England in the seventh century' in William Filmer-Sankey (ed.), *ASSAH* 6 (Oxford, 1993), pp 93–102.

— 'Post-Roman Britain to Anglo-Saxon England: the burial evidence reviewed' (DPhil, University of Oxford, 1996), available and searchable on-line at: http:—ora.ox.ac.uk-objects-uuid:e415687f-4964-4225-8bc3-23e4ab8e5e78.

— 'Past rites, future concerns' in John Blair & Carol Pyrah (eds), *Church archaeology: research directions for the future*, CBA Research Report 104 (London, 1996), pp 160–6.

— 'Burials at Derryvilla, Portarlington, Co. Offaly' (1997), Unpublished report prepared for National Monuments Service.

— 'Context and parallels for inhumation cemeteries on the Dublin–Dundalk Gas Pipeline' (1997), Unpublished report prepared for Margaret Gowen & Co.

— 'The location and context of Viking burials at Kilmainham and Islandbridge, Dublin' in Howard B. Clarke, Máire Ní Mhaonaigh & Raghnall Ó Floinn (eds), *Ireland and Scandinavia in the Early Viking Age* (Dublin, 1998), pp 203–21.

— 'A reconsideration of the location and context of Viking burials at Kilmainham–Islandbridge, Dublin' in Conleth Manning (ed.), *Dublin and beyond the Pale, studies in honour of Patrick Healy* (Dublin, 1998), pp 35–44.

— *Post-Roman Britain to Anglo-Saxon England: burial practices reviewed*, BAR 289 (Oxford, 1999).

— 'Excavation of a multi-period site at Ballymacaward, Ballyshannon, Co. Donegal', *Donegal Annual*, 51 (1999), 56–61.
— 'Burial practices in Ireland: first to seventh centuries AD' in Jane Downes & Anna Ritchie (eds), *Sea change: Orkney and Northern Europe in the Later Iron Age AD 300–800* (2003: Pinkfoot Press), pp 62–72.
— 'Report – Turoe Stone (Cloch an Túair Rúadh)' (2006), Unpublished report prepared for the Department of the Environment, Heritage and Local Government, Dublin.
— 'Report on burials located at excavation site in townland of Collierstown, Co. Meath. Excavation No. A008–015' March 2007: 'Further progress report' (2007: ACS), Unpublished.
— 'Literary insights into the basis of some burial practices in Ireland and Anglo-Saxon England in the seventh and eighth centuries' in Catherine Karkov & Helen Damico (eds), *Aedificia nova: studies in honor of Rosemary Cramp* (Michigan, 2008), pp 283–99.
— 'Early Medieval sentinel warrior burials', *Peritia*, 20 (2008), 323–30.
— 'Pagan or Christian? Burial in Ireland during the 5th to 8th centuries AD' in Edwards (ed.), *The archaeology of the Early Medieval Celtic churches* (2009), pp 134–54.
— 'A re-evaluation of the find-spot of, and a possible context for, the anthropoid hilted sword from Ballyshannon, Co. Donegal' in Cooney et al. (eds), *Relics of old decency* (2009), pp 193–8.
— 'Burnt magic' in Mary Davies, Una MacConville & Gabriel Cooney (eds), *A grand gallimaufry collected in honour of Nick Maxwell* (Dublin, 2010), pp 48–51.
— 'The context and content of the cemetery' in Delaney & Tierney (eds), *In the lowlands of South Galway* (2011), pp 94–8.
— 'Rediscovering Columba's monastery at Durrow, Co. Offaly' in Harbison & Hall (eds), *A carnival of learning* (2012), pp 111–24.
— 'Early Medieval burial on Tara – fact or fiction?' in O'Sullivan, Scarre & Doyle (eds), *Tara – from the past to the future* (2013), pp 240–6.
— 'Review: Christiaan Corlett & Michael Potterton (eds) *The Church in Early Medieval Ireland in the light of recent archaeological excavations*', *Peritia*, 26 (2015), 245–9.
— 'Into the west: a fifth–sixth-century lady and her horse join the ancestors' in Salvador Ryan (ed.), *Death and the Irish: a miscellany* (Dublin, 2016), pp 11–14.
— 'From burial among the ancestors to burial among the saints: an assessment of some burial rites in Ireland from the fifth to eighth centuries AD' in Edwards, Ní Mhaonaigh & Flechner (eds), *Transforming landscapes of belief in the Early Medieval insular world and beyond* (2017), pp 259–86.
— 'Impact beyond the Empire: pagan and Christian burial in Ireland 1st–8th centuries AD' in Sághy & Schoolman (eds), *Pagans and Christians in the Late Roman Empire* (2017), pp 341–55.
O'Brien, Elizabeth & Edel Bhreathnach, 'Irish boundary *ferta*, their physical manifestation and historical context' in Fiona Edmonds & Paul Russell (eds), *Tome: studies in Medieval Celtic history and law in honour of Thomas Charles-Edwards* (Woodbridge, Suffolk, 2011), pp 53–64.
O'Brien, Elizabeth & Blanche Weekes, 'Burials and enclosure of the seventh to ninth centuries AD' in Eogan et al., *The archaeology of Knowth in the first and second millennia AD* (2012), pp 45–71.
O'Brien, Elizabeth & Edel Bhreathnach, 'Burial in Early Medieval Ireland: politics and religion' in James Kelly & Mary Ann Lyons (eds), *Death and dying in Ireland, Britain and Europe: historical perspectives* (Sallins, Co. Kildare, 2013), pp 37–58.
O'Brien, William, *Sacred ground: megalithic tombs in coastal south-west Ireland* (Galway, 1999).
Ó Carragáin, Tomás, 'Cemetery settlements and local churches in Pre-Viking Ireland in light of comparisons with England and Wales' in James Graham-Campbell & Michael Ryan (eds), *Anglo-Saxon-Irish relations before the Vikings* (Oxford, 2009), pp 329–66.
— 'The saint and the sacred centre: the Early Medieval pilgrimage landscape of Inishmurray' in Edwards (ed.), *The archaeology of the Early Medieval Celtic churches* (2009), pp 207–26.
— 'Vernacular form, monastic practice in the early Middle Ages: evidence from Toureen Peakaun', *ASSAH*, 20 (2017), 67–79.
Ó Carragáin, Tomás & Sam Turner (eds), *Making Christian landscapes in Atlantic Europe* (Cork, 2016).

O'Connell, Aidan, 'Excavations at Church Road and the early monastic foundation at Lusk, Co. Dublin' in Baker (ed.), *Axes, warriors and windmills: recent archaeological discoveries in North Fingal* (2009), pp 51–63.
— 'The early church in Fingal; evidence from Church Road, Lusk, Co. Dublin' in Corlett & Potterton (eds), *The Church in Early Medieval Ireland* (2014), pp 173–86.
O'Connell, Aidan & Allister Clark, 'Final report on the archaeological excavation of Castlefarm 1, Co. Meath (M3 Clonee-North of Kells, Contract 1)' (2009: ACS), Unpublished report for National Roads Design Office, Meath County Council.
O'Connell, T.J., 'The dead amongst the living: keeping the ancestors close in Iron Age County Limerick', *NMAJ*, 50 (2010), 1–14.
Ó Corráin, Donnchadh, 'Creating the past: the Early Irish genealogical tradition', *Peritia*, 12 (1998), 177–208.
Ó Corráin, Donnchadh, Liam Breatnach & Aidan Breen, 'The Laws of the Irish', *Peritia* (1984), 382–438.
Ó Cróinín, Dáibhí, 'Rath Melsigi, Willibrord, and the earliest Echternach manuscripts', *Peritia*, 3 (1984), 17–49.
Ó Donnabháin, Barra, 'Appendix II. The human remains' in Manning, 'Archaeological excavation of a succession of enclosures at Millockstown, Co. Louth', *PRIA*, 86C 4 (1986), pp 171–9.
— 'Appendix 4: Human remains from Tara, Co. Meath' in *Discovery Programme Reports 6* (Dublin, 2002), pp 123–5.
O'Donovan, Edmond, 'Preliminary report: Archaeological excavation on the Wicklow Port Access Town Relief Road Licence Ref: 06E0091' (2007: M. Gowen), Unpublished report for Wicklow County Council.
O'Donovan, Edmond (with contributions by Ryan Allen, Niamh Curtin, Jonny Geber, Siobhán Scully and the 14CHRONO Centre, QUB), 'Archaeological excavations at the lost church of Drumkay, Glebe, Co. Wicklow' in Corlett & Potterton (eds), *The Church in Early Medieval Ireland* (2014), pp 187–224.
O'Donovan, Edmond & Jonny Geber, 'Archaeological excavations on Mount Gamble Hill: stories from the first Christians in Swords' in Baker (ed.), *Axes, warriors and windmills* (2009), pp 64–74.
— 'Excavations on Mount Gamble Hill, Swords, Co. Dublin' in Corlett & Potterton (eds), *Death and burial in Early Medieval Ireland* (2010), pp 227–38.
Ó Drisceoil, Cóilín, 'Life and death in the Iron Age at Carrickmines Great, Co. Dublin', *JRSAI*, 137 (2007), 5–28.
Ó Drisceoil, Cóilín & Emma Devine, 'Invisible people or invisible archaeology? Carrickmines Great, Co. Dublin, and the problem of Irish Iron Age settlement' in Corlett & Potterton (eds), *Life and death in Iron Age Ireland* (2012), pp 249–66.
Ó Floinn, Raghnall, 'Recent research into Irish bog bodies' and 'Gazetteer of bog bodies in Ireland' in Turner & Scaife (eds), *Bog bodies* (1995), pp 137–45; 221–34.
— 'Notes on some Iron Age finds from Ireland' in Cooney et al. (eds), *Relics of old decency* (2009), pp 199–210.
— 'Kildangan, Co. Kildare' in Cahill & Sikora (eds), *Breaking ground, finding graves*, vol. 2 (2011), pp 51–4.
— 'Lehinch, Co. Offaly' in Cahill & Sikora (eds), *Breaking ground, finding graves*, vol. 2 (2011), pp 139–66.
— 'Das Heilige in Bewegung: Reliquien, Reliquiare und Insignien in der frühen Kirche Irlands' in Heinrich-Tamaska, Krohn & Ristow (eds), *Christianisierung Europa* (2012), pp 202–13.
— 'Reliquair', Katalog No. 180, in Stiegemann, Kroker & Wolfgang (eds), *Credo* (2013), pp 2212–22.
Ó Floinn, Raghnall & Elizabeth O'Brien, 'Durrow Demesne, Co. Offaly' in Cahill & Sikora (eds), *Breaking ground, finding graves*, vol. 2 (2011), pp 120–39.
O'Hara, Rob, 'Final report: M3 Clonee-North of Kells; Dunshaughlin–Navan. Colliestown 1, Co. Meath' (2009: ACS), Unpublished report for Meath County Council.

— 'Collierstown 1: a Late Iron Age–Early Medieval enclosed cemetery' in Deevy & Murphy (eds), *Places along the way* (2009), pp 83–100.

Ó hEailidhe, Padraig, 'The Rathdown slabs', *JRSAI*, 87:1 (1957), 75–88.

— 'Early Christian grave slabs in the Dublin region', *JRSAI*, 103 (1973), 51–63.

Ó hEanaigh, Mícheál, 'Report on excavations at Collierstown, near Duleek, Co. Meath' (National Museum of Ireland, E31) (1934), Unpublished.

Okasha, Elizabeth, *Corpus of Early Christian inscribed stones of south-west Britain*, Studies in the Early History of Britain (Leicester, 1993).

O'Keeffe, Tadhg, 'Omey Island, Goreen and Sturakeen' in Isabel Bennett (ed.), *Excavations 1992* (Dublin, 1993), pp 30–1, no. 92.

— 'Omey Island – Goreen and Sturakeen' in Isabel Bennett (ed.), *Excavations 1993* (Dublin, 1994), p. 39, no. 111.

— 'Omey and the sands of time', *Archaeology Ireland*, 8:2 (1994), 14–17.

O'Kelly, Michael J., 'Church Island near Valentia, Co. Kerry', *PRIA*, 59C (1958), 57–136.

Olsson, Ingrid U. & Serap Kilicci, 'Uppsala natural radiocarbon measurements IV', *Radiocarbon*, 6 (1964), 291–307.

Ó Maoldúin, Ros, 'Cleenish, Fermanagh' in www.excavations.ie (2014), 310.

O'Neill Henken, Hugh, *Cahercommaun: a stone fort in County Clare*, An extra volume of the Royal Society of Antiquaries of Ireland for 1938.

O'Neill, Joseph, 'Cath Boinde' in Kuno Meyer & John Strachan, *Ériú*, 2 (1905), 173–85.

Ó Néill, John, 'The Cherrywood Science and Technology Park, Cherrywood' in Isabel Bennett (ed.), *Excavations 1999* (Dublin, 2000), p. 54, no. 169 (area A).

Ó Néill, John & Jennie Coughlan, 'An enclosed Early Medieval cemetery at Cherrywood, Co. Dublin' in Corlett & Potterton (eds), *Death and burial in Early Medieval Ireland* (2010), pp 239–50.

O'Neill, Tara, 'Report on the archaeological excavation of Parknahown 5, Co. Laois, 5 vols (M7 Portlaoise-Castletown–M8 Portlaoise–Cullahill Motorway Scheme)' (2009: ACS), Unpublished report for NRA and Laois County Council.

— 'The changing character of Early Medieval burial at Parknahown 5, Co. Laois, AD 400–1200' in Corlett & Potterton (eds), *Death and burial in Early Medieval Ireland* (2010), pp 251–60.

Opie, Hilary, 'Ballysadare, burial-ground' in Isabel Bennett (ed.), *Excavations 1995* (Dublin, 1996), p. 77, no. 244.

— 'Ardreigh, Medieval settlement and graveyard' in Isabel Bennett (ed.), *Excavations 2003* (Dublin, 2006), pp 228–9, no. 861.

Ó Ríain, Padraig, *Corpus genealogiarum sanctorum Hiberniae* (Dublin, 1985).

— *A dictionary of Irish saints* (Dublin, 2011).

Ó Ríordán, Breandán, 'Sonnagh Demesne, Co. Westmeath, E1179' in Cahill & Sikora (eds), *Breaking ground, finding graves*, vol. 2 (2011), pp 204–7.

Ó Ríordáin, A. Breandán & Etienne Rynne, 'A settlement in the Sandhills at Dooey, Co. Donegal', *JRSAI*, 91:1 (1961), 58–64.

Ó Ríordáin, Seán P., 'Excavations at Cush, Co. Limerick', *PRIA*, 45C (1939–40), 83–181.

— 'Excavation of some earthworks on The Curragh, Co. Kildare', *PRIA*, 53C:2 1950), 249–77.

O'Sullivan, Aidan, Finbar McCormick, Thomas R. Kerr & Lorcan Harney (eds), *Early Medieval Ireland, AD 400–1100: the evidence from archaeological excavations*, RIA Monographs (Dublin, 2013, 2014).

O'Sullivan, Jerry & Michael Stanley (eds), *New routes to the past*, Archaeology and the NRA Monograph 4 (Dublin, 2007).

O'Sullivan, Muiris, 'Haynestown, Co. Louth' in Isabel Bennett (ed.), *Excavations 1993* (Dublin, 1994), no. 167.

— 'Haynestown II, Dunleer, Co. Louth 93E0098' accessible at https://www.heritagecouncil.ie-unpublishedexcavations-section9.html *Significant Unpublished Irish Archaeological Excavations 1930–1997: Section 9: Iron Age Burial Practices* (Dublin: Heritage Council) pp 5–6.

— *Duma na nGiall: The Mound of the Hostages, Tara* (Dublin, 2005).

O'Sullivan, Muiris, Chris Scarre & Maureen Doyle (eds), *Tara from the past to the future* (Dublin, 2013).
Park, Victoria, 'Skeletal report; Ninch, Co. Meath, 02E017' (2008: Archaeological Development Services), Unpublished report for Woodgreen Builders.
Philpott, Robert, *Burial practices in Roman Britain: a survey of grave treatment and furnishing AD 43–410*, BAR (Oxford, 1991).
Pierce, Elizabeth, Anthony Russell, Adrián Maldonado & Louisa Campbell (eds), *Creating material worlds: the uses of identity in archaeology* (Oxford & Philadelphia, 2016).
Poirier, David A. & Nicholas F. Bellantoni (eds), *In remembrance: archaeology and death* (Westport, CT, 1997).
Powell, Caroline, 'Ninch stratigraphic report, Area N, 02E0017 ext' (2004: Archaeological Development Services), Unpublished report for Woodgreen Builders.
Power, Catryn, *The cremated bone from Cahermackirilla (02E1041)* (2003), Unpublished report prepared for Christine Grant, National Monuments Service.
Power, P., 'Ballygarran Cill, near Waterford', *JRSAI*, 71 (1941), 63–4.
Raftery, Barry, 'Iron Age burials in Ireland' in Donnchadh O'Corráin (ed.), *Irish antiquity* (Cork, 1981), pp 173–204.
— *La Tène in Ireland: problems of origin and chronology* (Marburg, 1984).
— *Pagan Celtic Ireland: the enigma of the Irish Iron Age* (London, 1994).
— 'The conundrum of Irish Iron Age pottery' in Barry Raftery, Vincent Megaw & Valery Rigby (eds), *Sites and sights of the Iron Age*, Oxbow Monograph 56 (Oxford, 1995), p. 152.
— 'Discussion of diagnostic finds' in Lynn (ed.), *Excavations at Navan Fort 1961–71*, pt 2 (1997), pp 90–5.
Raftery, Joseph, 'The Tumulus Cemetery of Carrowjames, Co. Mayo, part 2', *JGAHS*, 19:1–2 (1941), 16–88.
— 'Long-stone cists of the Early Iron Age', *PRIA*, C46 (1941), 299–315.
— 'The Turoe Stone and the Rath of Feerwore', *JRSAI*, 74:1 (1944), 23–60.
— 'A long stone cist in Co. Wicklow', *JRSAI*, 74:3 (1944), 166–9.
Raftery, Joseph & H.G. Tempest, 'A burial at Dromiskin, Co. Louth', *JCLAS*, 10:2 (1942), 133–7.
Raftery, Joseph & Allerton Moore, 'Two Prehistoric burials in Co. Mayo', *JRSAI*, 74:3 (1944), 71–176.
Rahtz, Philip, Sue Hirst & Susan M. Wright, *Cannington Cemetery*, Britannia Monograph Series 17 (London, 2000).
Rajic, Milica & Colum Hardy, 'Final archaeological report, E4239, Coolnahorna 3, Co. Wexford. M11 Gorey to Enniscorthy Scheme, Co. Wexford' (2013: TVAS), Unpublished report for Wexford County Council and TII.
Randolph-Quinney, Patrick, 'Osteological analysis of human skeletal remains from Ardsallagh Site 1 (A008–035), M3 Clonee to North of Kells Motorway' (2006: ODK Resources), Unpublished report for Archaeological Consultancy Services and NRA.
— 'Osteological analysis of human skeletal remains from Ballygarraun West (AR024–E2534), N6 Galway to East Ballinasloe road scheme' (2006: ODK Resources), Unpublished report for Valerie J. Keely and NRA.
— 'An unusual burial at Ballygarraun West', *Seanda, NRA Archaeology Magazine*, 2 (2007), 30–1.
Read, Christopher, 'Remembering where the bishop sat: exploring perceptions of the past at the Bishop's Seat, Kilteasheen, Co. Roscommon' in Thomas Finan (ed.), *Medieval Lough Cé: history, archaeology and landscape* (Dublin, 2010), 41–66.
Reade, George H, 'Description of the ancient interment lately discovered at Dromiskin, Co. Louth', *Journal of the Kilkenny and South-East of Ireland Archaeological Society*, n.s., 4:1 (1862), 199–206.
Redknap, Mark, 'Glitter in the dragon's lair: Irish and Anglo-Saxon metalwork from Pre-Viking Wales c.400–850' in Graham-Campbell & Ryan (eds), *Anglo-Saxon/Irish relations before the Vikings* (2009), pp 281–309.
Reimer, Paula et al., 'IntCal 13 and Marine 13 Radiocarbon Age calibration curves 0–50,000 years Cal BP', *Radiocarbon*, 55:4 (2013).

Reynolds, Andrew, 'Burials, boundaries and charters in Anglo-Saxon England: a reassessment' in Sam Lucy & Andrew Reynolds (eds), *Burial in Early Medieval England and Wales*, Society for Medieval Archaeology Monograph 17 (London, 2002).

— *Anglo-Saxon deviant burial customs* (Oxford, 2009).

Richards, Julian, 'The lady of the sands' in Julian Richards, *Meet the ancestors* (London, 1999), pp 170–91.

Richards, Melville, 'The Irish settlements in south-west Wales: a topographical approach', *JRSAI*, 90:2 (1960), 133–62.

Riddler, Ian & Nicola Trzaska-Nartowski, 'Worked antler and bone objects' in Robert O'Hara, *Final report, Collierstown 1, Co. Meath* (2009), appendix 13.

— 'Bone and antler finds report. 05–09 Parknahown 5' in Tara O'Neill, *Report on the archaeological excavation of Parknahown 5, Co. Laois*, vol. 2 (2009), appendix 10.

— 'Report on worked bone gaming piece from E3719 Ballyboy, 1' in Siobhán McNamara, 'Ballyboy 1, ring-ditch, final report on behalf of Galway County Council' (2010: Irish Archaeological Consultancy), pp xliii–xivii. Unpublished.

— 'Antler bone die' in Delaney et al. (eds), *Borderlands* (2012), p. 132.

Riley, F.T., 'Excavations in the townland of Pollacorragune, Tuam, Co. Galway', *JGAHS*, 17 (1936), 44–54.

Roche, Helen, 'Excavations at Ráith na Ríg, Tara, Co. Meath, 1997' in *Discovery Programme Reports* 6 (Dublin, 2002), pp 19–82.

Rolleston, George, 'Researches and excavations carried on in an ancient cemetery at Frilford, near Abingdon, Berks. In the years 1867–1868', *Archaeologia*, 42 (1870), 417–85.

Russell, Ian, 'Final report on the archaeological excavation at Claristown 2, Co. Meath' (2004: ACS), Unpublished report for Meath County Council and NRA. Accessed via TII Digital Heritage Collections at www.dri.ie.

Russell, Ian R., 'The excavation of an Iron Age site at Claristown, Co. Meath' in Corlett & Potterton (eds), *Life and death in Iron Age Ireland* (2012), pp 267–72.

Ryan, Frank, 'Findings from excavation of an Iron Age ring-ditch at Ferns, Co. Wexford' (2001), Unpublished report for Mary Henry Archaeological Services.

Ryan, Frank & Laureen Buckley, 'Excavation of a Late Iron Age ring-ditch at Ferns Lower, Co. Wexford' in Corlett & Potterton (eds), *Life and death in Iron Age Ireland* (2012), pp 273–89.

Ryan, John, 'The abbatial succession at Clonmacnoise' in John Ryan (ed.), *Féil-Sgríbhinn Éoin Mhic Néill* (Dublin, 1940; repr. Dublin, 1995), pp 490–507.

Ryan, Michael, 'Native pottery in Early Historic Ireland', *PRIA*, 73C (1973), 619–45.

Rynne, Etienne, 'La Tene and Roman finds from Lambay, Co. Dublin', *PRIA*, 76C (1976), 231–44.

Sághy, Marianne & Edward Schoolman (eds), *Pagans & Christians in the Late Roman Empire: new evidence, new approaches (4th–8th centuries)* (Budapest, 2017).

Scally, Georgina, 'The church and earlier structures at High Island, Co. Galway' in Corlett & Potterton (eds), *The Church in Early Medieval Ireland* (2014), pp 225–40.

Scally, Georgina and other contributors, *High Island (Ardoileán), Co. Galway: excavation of an Early Medieval monastery*, Archaeological Monograph Series: 10 (Dublin, 2014).

Schweitzer, Holger, 'Iron Age toe-rings from Rath, County Meath, on the N2 Finglas–Ashbourne road scheme' in Jerry O'Sullivan & Michael Stanley (eds), *Recent archaeological discoveries on national road schemes 2004*, National Roads Authority Monograph 2 (Dublin, 2005), pp 93–8.

Scott, George Digby, *The stones of Bray* (Dublin, 1913).

Seaver, Matthew (2010) 'Back to basics: contexts of human burial on Irish Early Medieval enclosed settlements' in Sheelagh Conran, Ed Danaher; & Michael Stanley, *Past times, changing fortunes*. NRA Monograph Series No. 8. 113–29. (Dublin, NRA).

— 'The earliest archaeological evidence for an ecclesiastical site at Trim, Co. Meath' in Corlett & Potterton (eds), *The Church in Early Medieval Ireland* (2014), pp 241–6.

— *Meitheal: the archaeology of lives, labours and beliefs at Raystown, Co. Meath*, TII Heritage 4 (Dublin, 2016).

Semple, Sarah, 'A fear of the past: The place of the prehistoric burial mound in the ideology of middle and later Anglo-Saxon England', *World Archaeology*, 30:1 (1998), 109–26.

Sharpe, Richard, 'Churches and communities in Early Medieval Ireland: towards a pastoral model' in Blair & Sharpe (eds), *Pastoral care before the parish* (1992), pp 81–109.

Shea, S., 'Report on the skeletons found in Pollacorragune', *JGAHS*, 17 (1936), 54–64.

Sheehan, John, 'A peacock's tale: excavations at Caherlehillan, Iveragh, Ireland' in Edwards (ed.), *The archaeology of the Early Medieval Celtic churches* (2009), pp 191–206.

— 'Caherlehillan, Co. Kerry: ritual, domestic and economic aspects of a Corcu Duibne ecclesiastical site' in Corlett & Potterton (eds), *The Church in Early Medieval Ireland* (2014), pp 247–58.

Smyth, Alfred P. (ed.), *Seanchas: Studies in Early and Medieval Irish archaeology, history and literature in honour of Francis J. Byrne* (Dublin, 2000).

Stanley, Michael, Rónán Swan & Aidan O'Sullivan (eds), *Stories of Ireland's past*, TII Heritage 5 (Dublin, 2017).

Stead, Ian M., *Iron Age cemeteries in East Yorkshire*, English Heritage Archaeological Report 22 (London, 1991).

Stenberger, Mårten, 'A ring-fort at Raheennamadra, Knocklong, Co. Limerick', *PRIA*, 65C (1965), 37–54.

Stevens, Paul, 'Burial and ritual in late prehistory in north Wexford, excavation of a ring-ditch cemetery in Ask townland' in O'Sullivan & Stanley (eds), *New routes to the past* (2007), pp 35–46.

— 'Final report, Excavation No. 03E0151, Site 1, Ballydavis Townland, Co. Laois' (2011: Valerie J. Keeley), Unpublished report for TII, M7 Heath–Mayfield Motorway Scheme.

— 'Burial and ritual in Early Medieval north Wexford: new evidence from Ask townland' in Kelly, Roycroft & Stanley (eds), *Encounters between peoples* (2012), pp 49–60.

Stiegemann, Christoph, Martin Kroker & Wolfgang Walter (eds), *Credo: Christianisierung Europas im Mittelaiter*, Band 2 Katalog (Petersberg, 2013).

Stout, Geraldine & Matthew Stout, *Excavation of an Early Medieval secular cemetery at Knowth Site M, County Meath* (Dublin, 2008).

Ström, Folke, *On the sacral origin of the Germanic death penalties* trans. Donald Burton (Stockholm, 1942).

Sweetman, David, 'Reconstruction and partial excavation of an Iron Age burial mound at Ninch, Co. Meath', *Ríocht na Mídhe*, 7 (1983) 58–68.

Swift, Catherine, 'Sculptors and their customers: a study of Clonmacnoise grave slabs' in King (ed.), *Clonmacnoise Studies*, vol. 2 (2003), pp 105–23.

— 'The early history of Knowth' in Byrne et al. (eds), *Historical Knowth and its hinterland: Knowth Excavations 4* (2008), pp 5–53.

Taylor, Kate, 'An Early Medieval enclosure and cemetery at Carrigatogher (Harding), Co. Tipperary' in Corlett & Potterton (eds), *Death and burial in Early Medieval Ireland* (2010), pp 281–93.

— 'N7 Nenagh to Limerick, High Quality Dual Carriageway, Archaeological Resolution Project E2483, Ballycuddy More Site 1, Co. Tipperary. Final archaeological excavation report for Limerick County Council' (2011: TVAS), Unpublished report for Limerick County Council, and TII.

Thomas, Charles, *Christianity in Roman Britain* (London, 1981).

— *And shall these mute stones speak?* (Cardiff, 1994).

Thompson, Edward A. (ed.), *Who was Saint Patrick?* (Woodbridge, Suffolk, 1999).

Thompson, Tok, 'Clocha Geala/Clocha Uaisle: white quartz in Irish tradition', *Béaloideas*, 73 (2005), 111–33.

Timoney, Martin, 'Excavation of a tumulus at Knocknashammer, Co. Sligo. E170' (1977), Unpublished summary report.

— 'No. 15: Knocknashammer' in Göran Burenhult & others, *The archaeology of Carrowmore: environmental archaeology and the megalithic tradition at Carrowmore, Co. Sligo, Ireland* (Stockholm, 1984), pp xx.

— 'Knocknashammer tumulus', *JIA*, 4:77 (1987/8), entry no. 66.

Tobin, Maeve, 'Osteological analysis of human remains from Kill of the Grange, Dublin' in Paul Duffy, 'Final report on excavation at Saint Fintan's Park, Kill of the Grange, Co. Dublin, Ministerial consent C000845; Reg. No. E004940' (2019, IAC), appendix 4.1, Unpublished report prepared on behalf of Elliot Group, for Dún Laoghaire Rathdown County Council.
— 'Osteological analysis of human skeletal remains from Carroweighter 2, Co. Roscommon (Reg. No. E004887)' (2019), Unpublished report prepared for IAC.
Tobin, Maeve & Faith Bailey, 'Burials and boundaries at Britonstown, Co. Wicklow', *JIA*, 23 (2014), 157–69.
Tobin, Red, 'Houses, enclosures and kilns – excavations at Corbally, Co. Kildare', *Archaeology Ireland*, 17:3 (2003), 32–7.
Tobin, Red & John Sunderland, 'Excavation and specialists reports, enclosure and associated features; Corbally, Kilcullen, Co. Kildare' (2004: M. Gowan & Co.), Unpublished report for Kilsaran Concrete Products.
Toner, Gregory, 'Identifying Ptolemy's Irish places and tribes' in D.M Parsons & Patrick Sims-Williams (eds), *Ptolemy: towards a linguistic atlas of the earliest Celtic place-names of Europe* (Aberystwyth, 2000), pp 73–82.
Tourunen, Auli & Albina Hulda Pálsdóttir, 'Appendix 9 – Final report on the faunal remains from Moone (E2982), Co. Kildare' in Lenihan & Dennehy, *Final report on archaeological investigations at Site E2982* (2010).
Toynbee, Jocelyn M.C., *Death and burial in the Roman world* (London, 1971).
Troy, Carmelita, Auli Tourunen & Albina Hulda Pálsdóttir, 'The osteological remains from Bruff, Co. Limerick (07E0558)' in Cosham & MacLeod, *Preliminary report on the archaeological excavation of a ring-barrow and other features in the townland of Bruff, Co. Limerick* (2009).
Troy, Carmelita & Susan Lalonde, 'Appendix 10 – The osteological remains from Moone F2982' in Lenihan & Dennehy, *Final report on archaeological investigations at Site E2982* (2010).
Troy, Carmelita, 'Appendix 11 — The osteological remains from Prumplestown Lower, Co. Kildare (E2967), in Lyndsey Clarke & Patricia Long, 'Final report on archaeological investigations at Site E2967, in the townland of Prumplestown Lower, Co. Kildare' (2010), Unpublished report prepared for NRA.
— 'Osteological report of human remains from Donacarney Great, Co. Meath' (2014: Rubicon Heritage), Unpublished.
Turner, Rick C. & Robert G. Scaife (eds), *Bog bodies: new discoveries and new perspectives* (London, 1995).
Vejby, Mara, 'New radiocarbon dates from Loughcrew Cairn H carved bone slips', *Past: Newsletter of the Prehistoric Society*, 75 (2013), 12–14.
Waddell, John, 'The Bronze Age burials of County Galway', *JGAHS*, 34 (1975) 5–20.
— 'Knocknagur, Turoe and local enquiry', *JGAHS*, 40 (1985–6), 130–3.
— *The Prehistoric archaeology of Ireland* (2nd ed., Dublin, 2000).
Wade, Keith, 'Ipswich, Buttermarket and St Stephens Lane' in Medieval Britain and Ireland in 1988', *Med. Arch.*, 33 (1989), 209.
Wait, Gerald A., *Ritual and religion in Iron Age Britain*, 2 vols, BAR 149 (Oxford, 1985).
Wallace, Angela, 'Excavation of an Early Medieval cemetery at Ratoath, Co. Meath' in Corlett & Potterton (eds), *Death and burial in Early Medieval Ireland* (2010), pp 295–316.
Walsh, Fintan, *N2 Carrickmacross–Aclint Road realignment, Co. Monaghan Site 109, Cloghvalley Upper 1* (2007: IAC), Draft final report for NRA.
— 'Seeking sanctuary at Kilmainham, Co. Meath', *Archaeology Ireland*, 25:2 (2011), 9–12.
Warner, Richard B., 'Some observations on the context and importation of exotic material in Ireland, from the first century BC to the second century AD', *PRIA*, 76C: 9 (1976), 267–92.
Waterman, Dudley M., 'The Early Christian churches and cemetery at Derry, Co. Down', *UJA*, 30 (1967), 53–69.
Weadick, Sharon, www.museum.ie/The-Collections/Documentation-Discoveries/June-2013/Late-Roman-Amphora-Shards-in-Co-Waterford (2013), Accessed 26 July 2018.
Wheeler, Robert E. Mortimer, *Maiden Castle, Dorset*, Report Research Comm. Society Antiquaries of London 12 (Oxford, 1943).

Whimster, Rowan, *Burial practices in Iron Age Britain c.700BC–AD43*, 2 vols, BAR 90 (Oxford, 1981).
White, R.B., 'Excavations at Arfryn, Bodedern, long cist cemeteries and the origins of Christianity in Britain', *Trans. Anglesey Antiq. Soc. & Field Club* (1972), 19–45.
White, Roger H., *Roman and Celtic objects from Anglo-Saxon graves*, BAR 191 (Oxford, 1988).
White Marshall, Jenny & Grellan D. Rourke, *High Island, an Irish monastery in the Atlantic* (Dublin, 2000).
White Marshall, Jenny & Claire Walsh, *Illaunloughan Island: an Early Medieval monastery in County Kerry* (Dublin, 2005).
Whitty, Yvonne & Maeve Tobin, 'Rites in transition: the story told by Holdenstown 1 and 2', *Seanda*, 4 (2009), 19–21.
Whitty, Yvonne & Jennie Coughlan, 'An Iron Age ring-ditch complex at Holdenstown 1, Co. Kilkenny' in Corlett & Potterton (eds), *Life and death in Iron Age Ireland* (2012), pp 313–26.
Wiggins, Ken & E. Kane, 'Report on the archaeological excavation of Killeany 1, Co. Laois, vol. 2. (M7 Portlaoise–Castletown–M8 Portlaoise–Cullahill Motorway Scheme)' (2009: ACS), Unpublished report for Laois County Council and the NRA.
Wiggins, Ken, 'An Early Medieval ditched enclosure with burials and cereal-drying kilns at Killeany, Co. Laois' in Corlett & Potterton (eds), *The Church in Early Medieval Ireland* (2014), pp 273–86.
Wilkins, Brendon & Susan Lalonde, 'Cemetery-settlement enclosure at Carrowkeel' in Jim McKeon & Jerry O'Sullivan (eds), *The quiet landscape: archaeological investigations on the M6 Galway to Ballinasloe national road scheme*. NRA Scheme Monographs 15 (Dublin, 2014), pp 75–81. Final report included under 'Archaeological excavation final reports' 2 vols, on accompanying CD-ROM, Carrowkeel, Co. Galway.
Williams, Howard, 'Monuments and the past in early Anglo-Saxon England', *World Archaeology*, 30:1 (1998), 90–108.
— *Death and memory in Early Medieval Britain* (Cambridge, 2006).
Williams, Margaret, 'Smiths, pits and burials: the role of the smith in funerary rites in Early Medieval Ireland' in Susan Curran & Karen Dempsey (eds), *Trowel*, 13 (2012), pp 39–55.
Wilmot, G.F., 'Three burial sites at Carbury, Co. Kildare', *JRSAI*, 68:1 (1938), 130–42.
Wilmot, G.F., C.D. Ovey & Stephen Shea, 'Two Bronze Age burials at Carrowbeg North, Belclare, Co. Galway', *JGAHS*, 18:3–4 (1939), 121–40.
Worley, Fay & Dale Serjeantson, 'Red deer antlers in Neolithic Britain and their use in the construction of monuments' in Karis Baker, Ruth Carden & Richard Madgwick (eds), *Deer and people* (Oxford, 2015), pp 119–31.

Index

Abhainn Bhriste (broken river) *see* Owenbristy, Co. Galway
aceramic 32
ACS Ltd 101
Additamenta 214
Adomnán (abbot of Iona) 55, 62, 110, 119, 122, 149, 169–70, 176, 197; *Cáin Adomnán* (also known as *Lex Innocentium* ('Law of the Innocents')) 4, 149–50, 169–70; Life of Columba 4, 173
Aegean, the 127
Aeschylus 136
afterlife 46, 74, 110, 121, 126
Agamemnon 136
Aghalahard, Co. Mayo 64, 112, 126, 230, 234, Map 5
Aidan (bishop of Lindisfarne) 173
Aided Dhiarmada ('The Death Tale of Diarmait') 140
Aldchú (of Dom Liacc) 201
Aldhelm (bishop) 173
Alexander III (pope) 210
alien burial rite 36, 69, 159, 172, 174, 182–3
Allen, Bog of 77
Allen, Hill of, Co. Kildare 77
Amlaib (son of Sitriuc) 75
Amlaib Cúarán (Olaf the Sandal) 109
Ammianus Marcellinus 4, 49
amputated/amputation 46, 137, 149, 236–40; *see also* decapitated/decapitation; dismemberment; mutilated/mutilation
amulet/s 117–19, 131, 233–5; stone 110, 131, 159; *see also* bead/s; evil eye; jewellery; locket/s
An Tulcha see Tolka (river)
ancestor/s 5–6, 12–15, 29, 32–7, 45, 64, 66, 69–71, 73, 76, 83, 88, 92, 96, 97–8, 100, 102, 116, 119, 130, 135, 164, 177, 182–3, 188–90, 195–200, 226; veneration of 5, 12, 32, 64, 226; *see also* ancestral burial place/cemetery; indigenous; pagan/s
ancestral burial place/cemetery 5, 10, 12, 48, 64–6, 68, 70–1, 75, 77, 81–6, 88, 92, 96–7, 100, 102, 114–16, 120, 126–7, 164, 169, 173, 178–9, 182, 185n11, 186–90, 192–3, 195–200, 226; *see also* ancestor/s *and* fert/ferta (ancient burial monuments)

Anchorage *see* Betaghstown, Co. Meath
ancillae (female slaves) 149
Andover, Hampshire, England 129
angels 62, 184, 197–8
Angles 171; *see also* Anglo-Saxon/s
Anglo-Norman 72n39; pre-Norman period 210, 213
Anglo-Saxon/s 5, 56, 74, 81, 85n99, 94, 103–5, 108, 111, 129, 135–6, 138, 159, 174, 180, 192, 215, 222–3; language 128; England 56, 64–5, 75, 110, 113, 128–9, 140, 168, 180
animal bone/remains 6, 16, 19, 20, 40, 51, 63, 84, 92, 123, 126, 131, 163, 192, 233–5; burnt 13, 169, 208; cattle 44n30, 124, 217–18; dog 142; jawbone/s 71, 123; pig/boar 41–2, 96, 126, 130, 151, 155, 190; sheep 218; *see also* bone object/s *and* horse/s
Annaghilla (Site 4), Co. Tyrone 15, 31–2, 50–1, 69, 102, 182, 232, Map 1, Map 4
annals 4–5, 81, 140, 154, 184; *see also* early Irish *and individual texts*
Annals of Loch Cé of 81
Annals of Ulster (AU) 4–5, 75
antler 42, 62–3, 120, 124–5, 131, 176, 233–5, 243; bead/s 120; in pelvic area 188–9; pick/s 18, 96–7, 113–17, 189, Figs 5.6, 5.7; stag; 117; tine/s 75–6, 115–17, 125, 152
apocryphal 56n11, 184, 204
Apostles, Acts of the 185
archangels *see* angels
Ardd Mache *see* Armagh, Co. Armagh
Ardfert, Co. Kerry 199
Ardnagross, Co. Westmeath 162
Ardreigh, Co. Kildare 58, 155, 211–12, Map 8
Ardsallagh, Co. Meath, 234; Ardsallagh 1 90–1, 107, 148–9, 167, 186, 230, 239, Fig. 5.2, Map 1, Maps 4–6; Ardsallagh 2 15, Map 1
Arfryn, Bodedern, Anglesey, Wales 61
Armagh, Co. Armagh 201, 214; 46–8 Scotch Street 61, 214–15, 228, Maps 4, 8; *Na Ferta* 140, 214, 236, 245, Map 6
Armit, Ian, Graeme T. Swindles & Katharina Becker: 10n6
armlet/s 27–8; *see also* bracelet/s
arrowhead/s 86
Asia 119

Ask, Co. Wexford 15, 27, 31, 227, Maps 1–2; enclosure E 31
assembly 41n18, 199
Atacotti (tribe) 49
athgabáil treise ('seizure or reprisal by force') 123
Athgoe Hill *see* Ballynakelly, Co. Dublin
Atlantic Trading Estate, Barry, Wales 61
Atlantic, the 47, 215, 217
attire *see* cloth/clothing/clothed burial
atypical burial/s *see* deviant burial/s
Augherskea, Co. Meath 126, 147, 151, 155, 234, 239, Fig. 6.2, Maps 5–6
auguries 26, 32, 48, Fig. 1.5; *see also* die/dice; divination; gaming piece/s; occult
Augustine (saint) 185

badger-sett 138
Baile-an-tobair, near Ballintubber Abbey, Co. Mayo 81, 81n85
Balcombe Pit, Glynde, Sussex, England 129
Balladoole, Isle of Man 174
Ballasadare (river) 147
Ballinchalla, Co. Mayo 81, 230, Map 4
Ballybannon 5, Co. Carlow 15, Map 1
Ballyboy, Co. Galway: Ballyboy 1 17–18, 20–2, 26, 182, 227, Fig. 1.5, Plate 2, Maps 1–2; Ballyboy 2 17–18, 20–2, 227, Plate 2, Maps 1–2
Ballybronoge South, Co. Limerick 10, 19, 26, 227, Fig. 1.5, Maps 1–2
Ballybrowney, Co. Cork Map 1
Ballycuddy More, Site 1, Co. Tipperary 19, Map 1
Ballydavis, Co. Laois Maps 1–2; Ballydavis 1 15, 17, 17n32, 76, 92, 100, 127, 160, 230, 234, 238, Maps 4–6; Ballydavis Townland 17n32, 20, 22–4, 26–8
Ballydowney, Co. Kerry 14, Map 1
Ballydribeen, Co. Kerry 227, Maps 1–2
Ballygarran, Co. Waterford 141, 208–9, 245, Map 8
Ballygarraun West, Athenry, Co. Galway 62–3, 116–17, 130, 176–7, 188, 228, 233, 241, 243, Fig. 5.8, Maps 5, 7
Ballyhanna, Co. Donegal 58, 121–2, 147, 199, 210–11, 223, 236, 245, Maps 6, 8
Ballykeel South, Co. Clare 63, 228
Ballykilmore, Co. Westmeath 147, 147–8n45, 162, 199, 210, 240, 244–5, Maps 6, 8; Ballykilmore 6 138, 155, 155n68, 193–4
Ballykilroe, Co. Westmeath 16n27
Ballymacaward, Co. Donegal 13, 29–30, 72–3, 127, 178–9, 182, 187, 228, 233, 241, 243, Fig. 4.2, Plates 10, 11, Maps 1, 4–5, 7

Ballynakelly, Co. Dublin 15, 228, 236, Map 6; Athgoe Hill 63, 140
Ballysadare, Co. Sligo 106, 235, Map 5
Ballyshannon, Co. Donegal 13n8, 187 *see also* sword
Ballysimon, Co. Limerick 138, 238, Map 6
Ballyvass, Co. Kildare, 227, Maps 1–2
Ballyvelly, Co. Kerry 28–9, Map 1
Bamburgh, Northumbria, England 140
ban echlach (female horse messenger) 75
Bangor, Co. Down 173
Banshenchas ('Lore of Women') 184
baptism 50, 62, 65, 119, 122; *see also* resurrection
Barrow (river) 8, 173n10
Barrow Hills, Radley, Oxfordshire, England 114
barrow/s 65n17, 81, 85n100; barrow-mound 14, 47; bowl barrow 10n5; pond-barrow 114; ring-barrow 10, 10n5, 13–14, 20–2, 51n3, 77, 85, 166n102; *see also* prehistory/prehistoric *and* ring-ditch/es
battle *see* conflict
Baysrath, Co. Kilkenny 76, 153, 155, 230, 237, Maps 4, 6
Bé Fáil (queen) 184
bead/s 117–19, 131, 233–5; amber 227, Plate 2; antler 120; blue glass 17, 17n36, 20, 22–3, 32, 38–9, 45, 48, 77, 118, 172, 227; blue-green glass 20, 22, 32; bone 81, 103n1, 163, 224, 227; brown glass 22; cable 22; class 1 Arras type (Guido) 22; class 6 Oldbury type (Guido) 22; decorated 227; Garrow Tor type 22; glass 13, 172, Plate 2; Meare variant type 'a' (Guido) 22; Meare-type, class 10 (Guido) 22; oculus 22; paternoster 103n1, 224; spiral 22; unburnt 17, 20, 23; white glass 22; yellow glass 13, 17, 20, 22, 32, 227; *see also* amulet/s
Beccán (saint) 222
Becker, Katharina, 12n7
Bede 173, 198, 217, 218n64; *Ecclesiastical history of the English people* 4–5, 198; *see also* Cuthbert (bishop)
Beginish Island, Co. Kerry 215
Begnat (saint) 222
Begu (nun) 198
beheading *see* decapitated/decapitation
bell/s 87, 87n105, 220; *see also* handbell/s
Belladooan, Co. Mayo 63–4, 230
belt/s 110–12, 205; belt buckle/s 92n139, 110–12, 159; strap-end 112; *see also* buckle/s *and* cloth/clothing/clothed burial

Index

Bend of the Boyne, Co. Meath 65; *see also* Dowth, Co. Meath; Knowth, Co. Meath; Newgrange, Co. Meath
Bendigeidfran 168
Benedict (abbot) 217
Beowulf 29
Berchán (saint) 211
Bergh Apton, Norfolk, England 103–5, 180, 192, Fig. 5.1
Betaghstown, Co. Meath 94, 159, 164, Map 3; Anchorage 39, 45–6, 80, 94–5, 137, 159–60, 172, 174, 183, 231, 239, 241–2, Fig. 2.6, 6.6, Maps 4, 6–7; Brookside 94–5, 110–11, 159–60, 174, 178–9, 193, 231, 234, 239, 242, 244, Fig. 5.4, Maps 5–7
Bettystown *see* Betaghstown, Co. Meath
Bhreathnach, Edel, 3, 113n25, 183n8,
bier/s 61, 108; *see also* transporting of body
Birr, Synod of 149
Bitel, Lisa 184
Black Death, the 130
Blacksod Bay, Co. Mayo 219
Blackwater (river) 100
Blair, John 129, 136n4
blow-fly (blue-bottle) 94; *see also* puparia
boat 197
Bóind (goddess of River Boyne) 79
bone object/s 123, 163; discs 103n1, 224; handle 16, 44, 112
Book of Armagh 214; *Additamenta* 214
Borsje, Jacqueline 44, 118
boundary/boundaries 2, 18n41, 42–4, 66, 73, 75–7, 79–80, 82, 179, 187, 206, 209–10, 225; markers 65, 68, 102, 199; cemetery boundary 222; church/monastic 179, 199, 202, 206–7, 220–2; field 43–4; natural 66; sacred 41; territorial 44, 65–6, 72–3, 75, 167, 186–9; *see also* fert/ferta *and* liminal/liminality
Bourke, Edward, Alan R. Hayden & Ann Lynch, 217n62
box (cylindrical) 26–8, 32, 227
box set (stone and wood) 6, 108, 131, 233–5, Fig. 5.3
box (wooden, with grain) 129
Boyle (river) 137
Boyne (river) 36, 64–5, 79, 83–4, 101, 109, 127, 189–90; *see also Bóind* (goddess of River Boyne)
bracelet/s 44; *see also* armlet/s
bracket/s 164, 164n98, Fig. 6.7
Bradley Hills, Somerset, England 61
Braga, Portugal 122
Bran Arddchenn (king) 184

Bray, Co. Wicklow 2, 45–6, 48, Map 3
Brayne, Jane 187n18
Brega 105, 184, 192; Northern 71, 144
Brehon law 123; *see also* early Irish: law
Bresal 184
Bretha Comaithchesa (Judgements of neighbourhood) 122
Brian Borumha 141
Bricketstown, Co. Wexford 18, Map 1
Brigid *see* Brigit (saint)
Brigit (saint) 56, 56n11, 63; *Bethu Brigte* 4–5, 63; Lives of 184; *Vita Prima Sanctae Brigitae* (Life of Brigit) 4–5, 56, 63, 184, 197; *see also* Cogitosus
Britain/British 5–8, 22, 24, 27–8, 36,38, 44, 47–50, 55, 57, 62, 70–1, 74–5, 94, 97–9, 105, 107–8, 111, 135, 140, 159, 164, 164n98, 168, 171–4, 176–8, 180–1, 183, 188–9, 193, 201, 207, 214–15, 219, 225–6, 241–2; British (language) 44; Devon and Cornwall 50; *see also* England/English
British Museum, the 7
Briton/s 50n1, 214
Britonstown, Co. Wicklow 120–1, 235, Map 5; extension 120
Brocidius 214
Broichan (foster-father of Brude) 119
Bronze Age 7–10, 12–15, 18, 22, 28–30, 34, 36, 42, 63, 68–9, 72–3, 75–7, 81, 84, 87, 88, 90, 94, 99, 101, 115, 129, 142, 155, 162–3, 176, 187, 189, 195, 212; early 15, 16n27; middle 68; late 34, 34n1, 47, 80–1; *see also* grave/s: cist/s
brooch/es 6, 233–5; Fowler Type B (penannular) 110, 110n18, 159; Nauheim (and derivative) type 24, 24n63, 26; Navan (and derivative) type 24, 24n63; omega type 110–11, 131, 159; penannular 103n3; *see also* fibula/e *and* pin/s
Brookside *see* Betaghstown, Co. Meath
Brude (Pictish king) 119
Bruff, Co. Limerick 10, 15–16, 227, Maps 1–2
buckle/s 6, 82, 110–12, 131, 233–5; *see also* belt/s *and* cloth/clothing/clothed burial
Buckley, Laureen 123n57
bullaun/s 210
Burgh Castle, Norfolk, England 108
Burghfield, Berkshire, England 129
burial in: bogs 1, 47, 136; ditch termini 6, 142, 164–7, 169, 236–40, Plate 9; enclosure entrance/s 6, 90, 142, 164–7, 169, 236–40, Plate 9; flood-plain/s 31, 50–1, 68–9, 100; sand/gravel ridge/s 62, 68, 75, 75n52, 82, 84, 88–9, 93–5, 102, 106, 112;

burial in *(continued)*
see also barrow/s; *fert/ferta*; imitative monument/s; ring-ditch/es
burial position/s: bound 59, 138–9, 157, 160; crouched 5–7, 26, 34–46, 48, 51, 71, 77, 80–1, 84, 94–5, 101, 105–6, 109–110, 118, 123, 137, 139, 142, 150, 154–67, 169–72, 174, 178–9, 181–3, 190, 193–5, 221, 224, 236–40; extended 5, 15, 31–2, 45–6, 48–51, 54, 57–8, 62–4, 68–9, 71–3, 75–9, 81–2, 84–8, 91, 94–6, 100, 102–3, 106–9, 111–12, 119–20, 123–6, 135–6, 139–40, 142, 148, 150–3, 160, 165n102, 168, 173–4, 178–80, 187, 189, 193, 201, 204–6, 208, 210, 214, 220, 222, Map 3; flexed 36, 40, 77, 84, 100, 126, 135, 137–8, 148, 153, 155–7, 161–6, 172, 189–90, 193 (*see also* crouched); foetal position 157–9; prone 6, 36, 38, 46, 48, 76, 76n60, 95–6, 126, 135–8, 143, 150, 153–5, 162, 167, 169–70, 172, 183, 193–5, 202–10, 224, 236–40, 243–4; sleeping position 157, 161, 163–7; splayed 38, 46, 135, 160, 172, 183, Plate 8; supine 49, 54, 56–61, 63–4, 68, 72, 84–6, 88–9, 91, 94–5, 100, 103, 106–8, 112, 125–6, 135–7, 139, 141–3, 148, 150–3, 160, 162, 166–9, 187, 190, 192, 194, 201, 205–6; trussed/bound for transport 106, 139, 158–64, 178, 194; *see also* disarticulated remains
burnt grain (in burials) 6, 62, 128–31, 233–5; *see also* hearth/s *and* kiln/s
Burren, the, Co. Clare 66, 80, 188
Burtown Little, Co. Kildare Map 1
Busherstown 5, Co. Carlow 15, Map 1
bustum (method of cremation) 28–9, 28n74
Buttermarket, Ipswich, Suffolk, England 56
Byrne, Paul 123n57
Byzantine/Byzantium 108

Cabinteely, Co. Dublin *see* Mount Offaly, Cabinteely, Co. Dublin
Cáelán *see* Mo-Choí
Caer, Bayvil, Wales 61
Cahercommaun, Co. Clare 141, 236, Map 6
Caherlehillan, Co. Kerry 207–8, 245, Map 8
Cahermackirilla, Co. Clare 13–14; Cairn D Map 1
Cahill Wilson, Jacqueline 72n41, 78n68, 69, 187n16,
Cahill, Mary & Maeve Sikora, 2, 84n95, 93
Caintigern (daughter of Conndach) 183
cairn/s 13, 31, 42, 62, 80, 83, 85, 141, 187–8; pseudo-cairn 13; *see also* prehistory/prehistoric

Camlin, Co. Tipperary 60, 99, 112, 118, 161, 166–7, 232, 235, 240, Maps 5, 6;
Canaan, land of 196
Cannington, Somerset, England 129
canon/s 1, 122, 128–9, 182, 196; *see also* penitential/s *and individual texts*
Capel Maelog, Powys, Wales 122
Cappakeel, Site F, Co. Laois 13, Map 1
Cappogue Castle, Co. Dublin 95, 151, 228, 236, Map 6
Cappydonnell Big, Co. Offaly 13, 22, 227, Map 1, Map 2
Carbury Hill, Co. Kildare 14; Site A 14, Fig. 4.7, Map 1; Site B 14, 24, 77–9, 112–13, 127, 178–9, 192–3, 227, 229, 233, 241, 243, Figs 4.7–4.8, Fig. 5.5, Maps 1–2, 4–5, 7; Site C 14, Fig. 4.7, Map 1
Carlow, Co. Carlow 173n10
Carnfanny, Co. Galway 84
Carrickmines Great, Co. Dublin 31, Map 1
Carrigatogher (Harding), Co. Tipperary 60–1
Carrowbeg North, Co. Galway 2, 81
Carroweighter 2, Co. Roscommon 46, 137
Carrowjames, Co. Mayo 14, 20–2, 24, 227, Maps 1–2;
Carrowkeel, Co. Galway 120–2, 125, 154, 160, 165, 233, 237, Plates 8, 9, Maps 5–6
Carrowmore, Co. Sligo 14, 71, 82, 189, Map 4; (Tomb 51) 71, 232
Carty, Niamh 19, 141n17,
Cashel, Rock of, Co. Tipperary 168
cashel/s 98, 98n166, 218, 220, Fig. 4.16
Castle Upton, Templepatrick, Co. Antrim 86
Castleblunden, Co. Kilkenny Map 1
Castledyke South, Barton-upon-Humber, Lincolnshire, England 56; St Peter's Church 56
Castlefarm, Co. Meath 99–100, 142, 166–7, 198, 231, 239, Fig. 6.8, Map 6; Plate 5
Cath Boinde 75
Cathal 184
Catstane, the, Kirkliston, Midlothian, Scotland 61
ceallúnach/ceallúnaigh (burial place for unbaptised children) 208–10, 208n9, 212–13, 217, 223, 225
Cedd (Chad's brother) 198
Cellach (daughter of Dúnchad) 184
Cellach (saint) 154; *Betha Cellaig* (Life of St Cellach) 154
'cemetery-settlement' *see* cemetery/cemeteries: settlement
cemetery/cemeteries: church 5–6, 141, 197–25, 201, 207–8, 223, 225; communal 5, 32, 62,

Index

96, 102, 115, 126, 138, 143–5, 147, 150–1, 158–9, 170, 173, 179–81, 186, 194–5, 198–201, 207, 216; community church 6, 202, 209–12; enclosed 71, 151,189; flat 10, 12, 15, 18–19, 29–30; island church 202, 215–22; organised 76, 95–6, 99,102, 115, 120, 151; secular 5–6, 39, 54–102, 108–9, 111–12, 115, 120, 126, 129–30, 138, 144–5, 147, 151, 155n68, 173, 179, 190, 198–201, 207, 210–12, 223–6; settlement 5, 15, 31–2, 51, 61–2, 81, 91, 96, 98n169, 98–103, 108–9, 111–12, 117–18, 120, 139, 141n18, 141–4, 147, 150, 152n61, 152–3, 155, 155n68, 161, 166, 176, 188–9, 192–4, 199, 211, 224, 228–32, Plate 5; unenclosed 39, 62, 76, 80, 89, 91, 93–6, 100, 102, 106, 112, 114, 129, 142, 145, 151, 159, 176, 191, 193, 228–32; unorganised 95–6

Cenél Cairprí (dynasty) 73; *see also* Uí Néill
Cenél Conaill (dynasty) 73; *see also* Uí Néill
Cenél Loarn (father of Erc)183
Cenn (deity) 44
central burial/s 84, 86, 91, 101, 106, 191; *see also* foundation burial/s
Ceolfrith (abbot) 217
ceramic utensils 7, 32, 101,123, 207, 225; *see also* feasts/feasting
cereal drying and milling *see* kiln/s
cere-cloth 54n9; *see also* linen; shroud/shroud wrapped; winding sheet/s
Chad (bishop) 198
changeling/s 137, 154; *see also* infant/s; child/children; burial position/s: prone burial; otherworld/otherworldly
Charles-Edwards, Thomas 4n4, 18n41, 31n80, 44n33, 50, 122n54
charnel 141, 213
Charon's obol 45–6
Cherrywood, Co. Dublin; Site 4, 13, 227, Maps 1–2; Site 18, 111, 151, 162, 233, 236, Maps 5–6
child/children 17, 38–9, 41, 48, 71, 73,78, 86, 88–9, 91–2, 95–6, 100–1, 117–18, 120–2, 127, 129, 137, 143, 149–50, 154, 161, 166, 169–72, 177, 186, 190–1, 194, 209–13, 215, 223–5, 228–42, 245; unbaptised children 154, 208n29, 225; *see also* ceallúnach/ceallúnaigh; infant/s; juvenile/s
Christ 54–7
Christ Church, Dublin, canons of 210
Christian/Christianity 5–6, 29–31, 49–50, 51, 54–7, 65n19, 71–2, 84, 88, 90, 99, 102, 108, 110, 119–23, 125, 128, 129, 130-1, 136, 139–4, 140n14, 153–4, 173, 187–8, 190, 196–201, 205–7, 210, 214–15, 224, 226; authorities/governance 6, 32,196; Christianised 130; church reforms 198; early Christian 117; martyrs 65, 65n19, 140, 140n14, 197, 214–15; pre-Christian 44, 51, 72, 128, 188 (*see also* pagan/s)
chronicle of Ireland, The 4–5, 140n15, 183n9
Church Island, Valencia Harbour, Co. Kerry 215–16, 223, 245, Map 8
church structures and monuments: antae 210, 213, 213n45; basilica 31; beehive structures 217–20; cross/es 202–6, 216–18, 220, 222; dry-stone structures 216–18, 220; holy well 210; mortared 217–18; organic 218; oratory/oratories 208, 215–18; ruined church 121–2, 141, 213, 222; stone 201–2, 210–13, 218–19, 222–3, 245; turf/turves 215–16, 225; wooden 201 209, 215–16, 223, 225
Ciarán (saint) 202
cilleen *see ceallúnach/ceallúnaigh*
cist/s *see* grave/s
Claristown 2, Co. Meath 41–2, 139, 148, 239, Map 3
Claureen, Co. Clare 17, 20, 23, 227, Plate 2, Maps 1–2
Cleenish, Upper Lough Erne, Co. Fermanagh 143, 170, 215, 220–1, 237, 245, Maps 6, 8
cleric/s 81, 149, 170, 173, 181, 185n12, 195, 202, 206; *see also* Christian/Christianity *and* priest/s
cloak 111, 123; fastener 123; *see also* cloth/clothing/clothed burial; dress; pin/s
clocha geala see quartz
Cloghvalley Upper, Co. Monaghan 112, 232, 235, Map 5
Clonbroney, Co. Longford 184
Clonenagh, Co. Laois 209
Clonfert, Co. Galway 199
Clonkeen, Co. Dublin 209
Clonmacnoise, Co. Offaly 123n57, 125, 140–1, 202–6, 225–6, 245, Map 8; cathedral Fig. 10.1; Interpretative Centre 123–4, 202–4, 245; North Cross 202–5, 204n8, Fig. 10.1; Nun's Church Fig. 10.1; round tower Fig. 10.1; South Cross 202–5, Fig. 10.1; Temple Ciarán Fig. 10.1; Temple Connor Fig. 10.1; Temple Dowling Fig. 10.1; Temple Finghin Fig. 10.1; Temple Hurpan Fig. 10.1; Temple Kelly Fig. 10.1; Temple Melaghlin Fig. 10.1; West Cross (Cross of the Scriptures) 54–5, 123–5, 202–6, Fig. 3.4, Figs 5.10, 10.1, Map 5

Clonmelsh (*Cluain Melsigi*), Co. Carlow 173
cloth/clothing/clothed burial 30, 38, 45, 48, 55–6, 59, 81, 94, 106–7, 110–13, 118, 131, 157n73, 159, 172, 174, 183, 193, 243–4; *see also* brooch/es; clothes-fastener/s; fibula/e; linen; pin/s; shroud/shroud wrapped; winding sheet/s
clothes-fastener/s 30; *see also* cloth/clothing/clothed burial
Cluain Aird *see* Toureen Peakaun, Co. Tipperary
Cluain Brónaig *see* Clonbroney, Co. Longford
Cluain Caoin *see* Kill of the Grange, Co. Dublin
Cluain Credail *see* Killeedy, Co. Cork
Cluana Eidneach *see* Clonenagh, Co. Laois
Cluain Melsigi see Clonmelsh, Co. Carlow
Cnobheresburg (Burgh Castle, Suffolk) 173
Coffey, George 73
coffin/s *see* grave/s
Cogitosus 184; *Life of Saint Brigit* 184; *see also* Brigit (saint)
Coibnes Uisci Thairidne (Kinship of conducted water) (Law Tract) 64–5
coin/s 45–6, 48, 222; *see also* Charon's obol
collar/s *see* neck ring/s
Collectanea *see* Tírechán: *Collectanea*
Collectio Canonum Hibernensis (*Hib*) 4–5, 31, 196–8, 202; 'A Roman Synod' (*Sinodus Romana*) 185, 185n12; Canon *Hib* XLIX *De martyribus* ('Concerning martyrs'), Cap. 10, 'Concerning the resurrection of translated relics' 140; XVIII, *De jure sepulturae* ('Concerning the law of burial') 185, 196; *see also* Cú Chuimne *and* Rubin
Collierstown, Co. Meath 130, 234, 244, Figs 4.2, 5.8, Map 5; Collierstown 1 60, 91, 96, 117, 127, 148, 179, 190, 231, 239, 242, Maps 4, 7; Collierstown 2 121–2, 141, 213, 245, Map 8
Colp West, Co. Meath 152–3, 164, 164n98, 239, Map 6; Colp West 1 91, 101, 127, 164, 231, 239, Fig. 6.7, Maps 4, 6
Columba (saint) 4, 55, 62, 94, 110, 119, 122, 173, 197, 206; Columban 199
Columbanus (saint) 173
comaithmet anma (commemoration of the soul) 122
'Conall Corc and the Corco Luigde' (text) 168
Condal (abbess) 183
cone beaker/s 127
conflict 132, 141–2, 145, 149, 170, 180; *see also* injury/injuries; trauma; violence, death by
congenital anomaly 154, 193

Conleth (archbishop) 184
Connacht (province) 154, 168
Conndach (mother of Caintigern) 183
Connor (church of) 140
Continent, the 173
continental Europe *see* Europe/European *and* Continent, the
convert/conversion 30, 119, 128; conversion period 5, 15, 49, 54, 119, 121, 128, 202, 214–15; Anglo-Saxon conversion 56, 110
Coolbeg, Co. Wicklow Map 1
Coolnahorna, Co. Wexford: Coolnahorna 2 227; Coolnahorna 3 15, 22, 24–6, 28, Maps 1–2
Cooney, Gabriel 44n32
Corbally, Co. Kildare 88, 93; Corbally 1, 153, 178–9, 191, 193, 229, 237, 241, 243, Fig. 4.14, Maps 4, 6–7; Corbally 2, 88–9, 138, 138n10, 150, 179, 191, 194, 194n49, 229, 237, 242–3, Fig. 4.14, Maps 4, 6–7; Corbally 3 89, 147–8, 237, Fig. 4.14, Fig. 6.3, Maps 4, 6–7
Corbally, Moycullen, Co. Galway 72–3n44, 188n20
Cork (county) 129–30
Corlett, Christiaan & Michael Potterton 2
Coroticus 50, 50n1; *see also* Patrick (saint)
Córus Bésgnai (Old Irish law tract) 4, 122, 196
Courtmacsherry, Co. Cork 64, 228
craft working 98, 100n172
Crídán (cleric) 206
Croagh Patrick, Co. Mayo 62n7
Croghan, Co. Offaly 210
Crom Crúaich see Cenn (deity)
cropmark/s 199, 207
Cross of the Scriptures, Clonmacnoise, Co. Offaly *see* Clonmacnoise, Co. Offaly: West Cross
Cross, Co. Galway 18–19, 80–1, 87–8, 88n113, 120–1, 190, 228, 233, 243, Fig. 4.13, Maps 1, 4–5
crozier 220
Cruacháin, Co. Roscommon 65, 65n17
crucifixion scene 220
Cú Chuimne (compiler of *Collectio Canonum Hibernensis*) 4n4
Cú Chulainn 145n37, 165
cú glas ('grey hound/wolf') 144, 173, 186; *see also* stranger
Cualu 184
Cudda (abbot) 56
Culbin Sands, Moray, Scotland 24
cumal 190
Cummean, Penitential of 145

Index

curad mir *see* dant mir
Curragh, the, Co. Kildare 95n100; Site 4 84–5, 132–6, 191–2, 229, 237, 243, Fig. 6.1, Maps 4, 6; Site 6 84–5, 141–2, 229, 237, Fig. 4.11, Maps 4, 6
Cush, Co. Limerick 14, 227, Fig. 1.5, Maps 1–2; Tumulus I 14; Tumulus II 14, 26, 28; Tumulus III 28
Cuthbert (bishop) 56, 198; *Bedae Vita Sancti Cuthberti* 4–5; letter on the death of Bede 198

dagger/s 27; *see also* sword/s
Daire *see* Derry (city) 54
Dair-Inis (Molana Abbey, near Youghal, Co. Cork) 4n4
Dál Messin Corb (sept) 211, 222
Dál Ríada (kingdom) 173, 183
Dalkey Island (*Delg Inis*, 'Thorn Island'), Co. Dublin 215, 221, 245, Fig. 10.2, Map 8; Martello tower 222
Dalkey, Co. Dublin 222
Daly, Niamh 88n113, 114, 135
Danesfort, Co. Kilkeny Map 1
dant mir (the hero's or warrior's portion) 72, 123–6, 131, 192, 205–6
Dar Ercae (also known as Mo Ninne) (saint) 184; Life of 184n10
daub 94
daughter/s 62, 65, 65n17, 73, 94, 149–50, 183–4, 186, 188, 190, 194, 198, 201; *see also* sibling/s *and* son/s
Davis, Stephen 41n17
decapitated/decapitated 6, 37, 46, 106–7, 136, 138, 140–5, 147–51, 155, 162–3, 165–7, 169–71, 176, 180, 194–5, 221, 223, 236–40; head as trophy/warning 145, 147, 167, 209; head cist 141, 209; head missing 75, 76, 84–5, 138–43, 147–8, 150, 152, 155, 161–3, 169, 194–5, 221, 236–40; head moved elsewhere 142–3, 145, 147, 166, 168, 209 (*see also* burial position/s: trussed/bound for transport); head only 6, 236–40; head replaced with stone 138, 155, 193; severed head in grave 140–1, 215; later removal of head 138; *see also* mutilated/mutilation *and* deviant burial/s: revenant/s
deer (*Cervidae*) 113; deer antler 18, 62, 74–6, 99, 113–7, 131, 152, 176–7, 180, 188, Fig. 5.7; deer cult 113; *see also* antler
Deerpark, Co. Galway Map 1
degenerative joint disease 135, 191–2
Déisi 49

demon/s 66, 197
Dent, John, 27
Derry (city) 54
Derry, Co. Down 213, 245, Map 8
Derryvilla, Portarlington, Co. Laois/Co.Offaly 95
desecration *see* mutilated/mutilation
desert *see* díseart (desert/hermitage places)
deviant burial/s 5–6, 46–7, 132–70, 224, 236–40; crime/criminals 147, 150, 154, 155n71; deformity/deformities 4, 74, 154, 178, 189, 195, 243–4; 'different' 84n99, 88–9, 154, 176, 186, 191, 193, 195; exclusion from cemetery 139, 150, 155, 170, 199, 207, 210, 221; live burial 6, 132–6, 169, 191–2, 195, 236–40, 243–4, Fig. 6.1 (*see also* sacrifice/s); outcast/s 147, 155n71, 210; revenant/s 39, 46, 48, 106, 153–4, 159, 163–4, 169–70, 193–5; suicide/s 155n71, 210, 224; *see also* burial position/s: splayed *and* punitive death and burial/s
Devinish, Co. Fermanagh 220
Devon and Cornwall *see* Britain/British
Di Dligiud Raith 7 Somaine ('On the law relating to the fief and profit of a lord') 122
Dictionary of the Irish Language (*DIL*) 75, 123
die/dice 26, 32, 37, 227; Fig. 1.5; *see also* divination; gaming piece/s; occult
Digital Repository of Ireland (DRI) 2
Din Techtugad ('The legal process of taking possession of land') (law tract) 65–6
Dinllaen, Wales 50
disability/disabilities 73, 187, 189, 193, 195; bilateral medial torsion 73, 189; *see also* deviant burial/s
disarticulated remains 6, 48, 75n53, 86, 91–2, 100, 127, 140, 143, 150, 153, 164–5, 169, 189, 213, 218–19; *see also* burial position/s
Discovery Programme Ltd, the 1–2
díseart (desert/hermitage places) 6, 197, 202, 215, 217, 222–3, 225
dismemberment 47, 147; *see also* amputated/amputation; decapitated/decapitation; mutilated/mutilation
Ditchfield, Peter 218, 218–9n69
divination 38n4, 171; *see also* occult
divorce 145, 185; *see also* marriage
DNA 177, 185, 226
Dom Liacc *see* Duleek, Co. Meath 201, 225

domestic *see* habitation
Domnall 184
Donacarney Great, Co. Meath 20–22, 227, Plate 2, Maps 1–2
Donaghmore, Co. Meath Map 1
Donnchad (king) 184
Dooey, Co. Donegal 112, 141, 233, 236, Maps 5–6
Dowth, Co. Meath 65
dragon/s 66
Drakelow, England 136
dress 110–11; dress ornament/s 110; *see also* cloth/clothing/clothed burial
Dromiskin, Co. Louth 108, 234, Fig. 5.3, Map 5
druid/s 30–1, 105–6
Drumanagh, Co. Dublin 8, 46–7
Drumkay, Glebe, Co. Wicklow 211, Map 8; *see also* Glebe, Co. Wicklow
Dublin, archbishop of 212
Dúchas 220; *see also* Office of Public Works (OPW)
dug grave/s *see* grave/s
Duleek (*Dom Liacc*), Co. Meath 201, 225
Dún Aonghasa, Inis Mór, Aran Islands, Co. Galway 47, 162, 167
Dúnchad 184
Dúngal (father of Flann) 184
Dúnlang 51; sons of 168; *see also* Uí Dúnlainge
Durrington Walls, Wiltshire, England 113
Durrow, Co. Offaly 141, 199, 206–7, 224–6, Plate 12; Durrow Demesne 207; high cross 55; Sheean Hill (also known as Relic Fort and Fairy Hill) 199, 206–7, 245, Plate 12, Map 8
Dyfed, Wales 49

Early Historic period 86
early Irish 7, 128, 182, 184, 195, 226; law 61, 65, 68, 102, 122, 145, 182, 185, 195, 199; *see also* annals; Brehon Law; Irish (language)
earring/s 6, 84, 109, 131, 190, 233–5
East Anglia, England 74, 173
Easter 65; *see also* resurrection
ecclesiastical site/s 58, 143, 145, 152n61, 155, 184, 197, 206–8, 210, 213, 218, 220, 222–4, 245; cemetery/cemeteries *see* cemetery/cemeteries: church enclosure 207, 223; *see also* Christian/Christianity *and* monastery/monastic
Ecgburh (Anglo-Saxon nun) 56
Egbert 198; Confessional of 128
Egypt 196

Eithne (queen) 184
elite 29, 176, 226; *see also* kingship *and* royal
Emhain Macha *see* Navan Fort, Co. Armagh
enamel 13, 26–7
England/English 26, 29, 103–5, 128–30, 173, 180, 192; *see also* Britain/British
Éogan Bél (king of Connacht) 154, 168
Eorcenbhert (Anglo-Saxon king) 198
Eorcengota (Anglo-Saxon princess) 198
Erc (daughter of Loarn) 183
érlam ('a founding saint') 207
Erne (river) 13n8, 72–3, 187, 210
erosion (coastal/soil) 29, 46, 212, 215,
Étgal (of Scelec) 218
Éuginis (queen) 184
Europe/European 27, 39, 44, 92, 95, 99, 117, 171–4, 181, 183, 193, 201, 207; central 92, 99, 160, 164, 176–7, 186; eastern 92, 99, 159–60, 164, 176–7, 186; northern 164
evil eye 117–19, 131; *see also* amulet/s *and* bead/s
execution 66, 136, 141–2, 147–8; *see also* punitive death and burial/s *and* torture
Ezechiel 140

Fáelán (king) 184
Faichnae Lurgan (king of Ulaid) 183
Fairy Hill *see* Durrow, Co. Offaly
familial cemetery/cemeteries *see* cemetery/cemeteries: communal
family group/s *see* kin group/s
Fanning, Tom 208
Farne Island, Northumbria, England 56
Farta, Loughrea, Co. Galway 2n2, 73–6, 73n46, 86, 115–16, 176, 180, 189, 199, 229, 233, 241, 243, Figs 4.6, 5.7, Maps 4–5, 7
Faughart, Lower, Co. Louth 118, 144, 148, 152, 154, 161, 163, 193, 198, 230, 234, 238, 244; Fig. 6.5; Map 5, 6
feasts/feasting 19, 44, 122–8, 131; feast of death-lying 122
Fedelmid (grandson of Loíguire) 214
Feerwore (Rath of), Co. Galway 86–7, 191, 229, 243, Map 4
Féichín (saint) 212, 218
Felix 56; *Life of Saint Guthlac* 5
Fer Diad 145n37
Ferganstown and Ballymacon, Co. Meath 64, 189, 231, 244
Ferns Lower, Co. Wexford 10, 16–23, 27, 227, Maps 1–2
fert/ferta (ancient burial monuments) 5, 62, 64–82, 96–8, 102, 115, 120, 142, 173, 177,

Index

179, 184, 187–9, 198–200, 214–5, 226, 245; *see also* ancestral burial place/cemetery *and* imitative monument/s
fertae martyrum 65, 214–15; *see also ferta/fertae*
Fertagh, Co. Cork 199
Fertagh, Co. Kilkenny 199
Fertagh, Co. Leitrim 199
Fertagh, Co. Meath 199
fertility 41, 44, 51, 113, 115, 117, 131; *see also* regeneration
Fíacc 65; *ferti virorum Feec* ('the burial place of the men of Fíacc') 65
fibula/e 7, 13, 24, 26, 28, 32, 44–5, 48, 227; Langton Down-type 44; Roman 44; rosette-type 44; Fig. 1.4; *see also* brooch/es *and* pin/s
fingal (kin slaying) 145, 149
Finglesham, Kent, England 85n99
Fintan (saint) 209
Fionán (saint) 218
FitzPatrick, Elizabeth 72–3n44
flabella/flabellum 207, 216, 220
Flann (queen) 184
flax: fibre 187; thread 187; *see also* cloth/clothing/clothed burial
flint 16, 63, 77, 86, 113–14, 161
focal burial/s *see* central burial/s *and* foundation burial/s
Fohrde, Germany 110n18
Foillán (abbot) 173
Foran, Richard 217n63
Fore, Co. Westmeath 7–8, 212, 227, Plate 1, Maps 1–2
fossam rotunda/m ('a circular ring-ditch') 65, 82; *see also* ring-ditches
foster/fostering 88, 119, 145, 169, 217
Foulds, Elizabeth 22n58
foundation burial/s 62, 91–2, 96–102, 115, 130, 142–3, 164n99, 173, 177, 179, 186, 189–91, 195, 204, 228–32, 243
Four Winds, Longniddrey, East Lothian, Scotland 61
France/French 7, 128, 168
Furness, Co. Kildare 31, Map 1
Fursa (monk) 173

Gabhra (river) 91n127, 179; Gabhra Valley 91n127
Gaelic ruling dynasties 199
Gallows Hill (Cnoc na Croiche), Co. Kilkenny 66n20
gaming piece/s 26, 32, 48, 118, 171; Fig. 1.5; *see also* die/dice; divination; occult

garment/s *see* cloth/clothing/clothed burial
Garton Station, Yorkshire, England 40
gatepost/s 45, 132, 135, 192
Gaul 96, 127, 207–8, 222, 225
Geake, Helen 56
Geat (race in Beowulf) 29
gentes ('heathens') *see* Viking/s 218
German/Germanic 129, 168
Gibbet Hill (Cnoc na Croiche), Co. Wexford 66n20
Gibbet Hill (Cnoc na Croiche), Middlethird, Co. Waterford 66n20
Glam (ghost) 136
Glass 8, 100n72, 123, 127, 222, 245; *see also* bead/s *and* vessel/s: glass
Glastonbury, Somerset, England, bowl from 7–8, Plate 1
Glebe South, Co. Dublin 15, 20, 24, 31, 69, 227–8, Maps 1–2, Map 4
Glebe, Co. Wicklow 211, 245
God (Christian) 30, 81, 185
god/ess 44, 66,79
Gogan, Liam 213
Góre (layman in Columba story) 110
Gormgal (saint) 218–19
Gormlaith (daughter of Donnchad) 184
Gotland, Sweden 136
Grannach, Co. Galway *see* Grannagh, Co. Galway
Grannagh, Co. Galway 1–2, 2n1, 20n52, 22, 24, 227, Fig. 1.4, Maps 1–2
grave goods 5–7, 16, 19–28, 32, 36, 42, 44, 56–7, 94, 96, 103–31, 147, 159, 171–2, 192, 205–6, 233–5; *see also* amulet/s; antler; armlet/s; arrowhead/s; bead/s; bell/s; belt/s; bone object/s; box/es; bracket/s; brooch/es; buckle/s; burnt grain; Charon's obol; clothes-fastener; coin/s; collar/s; cone beaker; dagger/s; dant mir (the hero's or warrior's portion); die/dice; earring/s; fibula/e; flint; gaming piece/s; glass; hair ornament; handbell/s; hearth residue; hone; hook with suspension ring 141; jewellery; knife/knives; lachrymatory (tear jar); line-sinker; locket/s; loom weight/s; mirror/s; nail/s; neck ring/s; pin/s; plaque/s; pottery; quartz; repoussé; ring/s; rivet/s; rock-crystal; sandstone disc; scabbard mount/s; scallop shell/s; sceptre/s; scramasax (large knife); shears; shield/s; spade-shoe/s; spear/s; spindle/s; sword/s; torc/s; tool/s; urn (cinerary); vessel/s

grave/s: brick-lined 136; box burial (disarticulated) 6, 164, 164n98, 169, 236–40, Fig. 6.7; cist/s 2, 58, 61, 63, 108,126, 138, 143, 160, 216–17, box-shaped 141, 213; Bronze Age 13, 81, 101, 142, 163; cist-like grave/s 58, 102 (*see also* lintel grave/s), head cist/s 141, 209, 213, long cist/s 2, 61n6, 63–4, 72, 80, 108, 112, 126, 138, 143, 187, miniature cist/s 216–17, slab-covered cist/s 64, slab-lined cist/s 58, 61, 64, 72, 80, 86, 92, 94, 102, 112, 160, 187–9, 209, 212–13, 219, Fig. 4.1; coffin/s 55–7, 102, 136, 165n10, 212, log coffin 61, 102, 140, 215; dug grave/s 42, 54, 55–9, 61–3, 68, 70–1, 76, 82, 84, 86, 88–92, 94–5, 98, 100, 103, 106, 107, 109, 112, 120, 124, 126, 132, 135, 138–9, 141–3, 147–8, 150–2, 154, 160, 163, 167, 169, 178, 189–92, 194, 204, 206, 208–11, 213, 215–16, 219, dug pit-grave 159, lined with wood 69, 84, 89, 102, 148, 189, 191; unprotected 42, 54, 59, 72, 82–4, 100, 102–3, 107, 142, 187, 212, Fig. 4.2; earmuffs 205; lintel grave/s 58, 61, 64, 102, 152, 206, 208, 211, 213 (*see also* cist-like grave/s); marker/s 17–18, 63, 78, 124, 140, 204, 214, 222 (*see also* grave/s: slab/s) ; oval 132–3, 160; oval pit 17, 91, 100, 132; shallow 70, 135, 143n30, 169, 221–2; slab-lined 54, 57, 58, 59, 61–2, 64, 70–2, 80–2, 84, 86, 92, 94–5, 98, 102, 111–12, 118, 143, 149–51, 159, 169, 177, 179–80, 187–9, 191, 194, 206, 209, 212–3, 215–16, 219, Fig. 4.1 (*see also* cist grave/s); slab-covered 64, 149, 169, 186, 194; slab/s 55, 125, 202, 206–8, 213, 213n46, 218–20 (*see also* grave/s: marker/s *and* Rathdown, Co. Dublin); stone-lined 51, 54, 57, 59–62, 75–7, 86–9, 91, 94–5, 97, 102, 119–20, 125, 142, 145, 152, 159, 174, 186, 206, 209, Fig. 4.1; wood-covered 59, 68, 77, 89, 96, 102, 125, 142, 150n51, 160, 169, 186, 190; wood-lined grave 54, 60–1, 69, 84, 89, 102, 148, 189, 191, Fig. 4.2

Great Chesterton, Essex, England 74
Great Ryburgh, Norfolk, England 61
Greek cross 209
Greek Synods, Canons of the 122
Greene, Sharon 219, 219n77
Greenhills, Co. Kildare 89–90, 93, 180, 191, 229, 242–3, Fig. 4.14, Maps 4, 7
Grettir the Strong, Saga of (Icelandic) 136
Grimes Graves, Norfolk, England 113–14
Grimswold, Connecticut, US 136; *see also* Walton family
guardian/s 12, 66, 73, 82, 91, 165, 167, 186, 189, 199; *see also* burial in: enclosure entrance/s
Guido's typology 22, 22n58; *see also* bead/s
Guthlac (saint) 5, 56, 81, 94; *see also* Felix

habitation 15–16, 44, 98n169, 98–9, 100n172, 102, 208, 213, 216, 219–20, 222
Hadrian (emperor) 45–6, 48
Haggardstown, Co. Louth 166, 239, Map 6
hair ornament/s *see* plaque/s
Hallowhill, St Andrews, Scotland 61
Hamlin, Ann 206n21
handbell/s 206, 212–13, 216, 245
hanging 138, 148; *see also* execution
Hawaii 157
Haynestown, Co. Louth 20, 227, Maps 1–2
hazelnuts 79; *see also* imbas (poetic or prophetic inspiration)
headstone/s *see* grave/s: marker/s *and* grave/s: slab/s
Heahfrith 173
hearth/s 6, 42, 98–100, 169; hearth residue in burials 62–3, 96, 117, 128–31, 177, 188, 190, 233–5; *see also* burnt grain (in burials) *and* kiln/s
heathen/s 65, 119, 218; *see also* pagan/s *and* Viking/s
heirloom/s 105, 109, 192; *see also* memento/s
Henry, Françoise 219
Heptad XXVIII 75
Heritage Council, the 12n7; INSTAR (Irish National Strategic Archaeological Research) scheme 2
hermitage *see* díseart (desert/hermitage) places
hide (animal) 54, 54n9; *see also* linen; shroud/shroud wrapped; winding sheet/s
high crosses 55, 202, 210
High Island (Ard Oileán), Co. Galway, 215, 218-9, 245, Map 8
Hild (abbess) 198
hláw (Anglo-Saxon name for burial mound) 64
Hohenferschesar, Germany 110n18
Holcombe, Dorset, England 27
Holdenstown, Co. Kilkenny 96–7n160, 177; Holdenstown 1; 18, 79–80, 96–7, 114–15, 120–1, 173, 177, 179–80, 230, 234, 242, Figs 4.9, 5.7, Maps 4–5, 7; Holdenstown 2; 79–80, 96–7, 97n161, 115, 177, 179–80, 230, 234, 242, Plate 11, Maps 5, 7
Holmes, Mark 61
homosexual/homosexuality 145

Index

hone 219
honour price 173, 186
horse/s 66, 73-5, 115, 117, 120, 124, 126, 152, 176, 189, 195; ban echlach (female horse messenger) 75; British-Welsh horses (*ech mBretnach*) 75; *gaillite tacair* (foreign mares) 75; horse meat 76, 117, 124-5, 152, 180; horse tooth 118, 120, 125 (*see also* bead/s); horse skull 19; human and horse burial 74, 176, 199; *see also* Farta, Loughrea, Co. Galway
hostage/s 106
Hull and East Riding Museum, Hull, Yorkshire, England 27n72
husband/s 117, 185, 197; *see also* marriage; spouse/s; wife/wives

Iceland/Icelandic 136
Íde (Íta) 184; Life of 184-5n10
Illaunloughan (Loughan's Island), Co. Kerry 215-16, 218n64, 223, 245, Map 8
imbas (poetic or prophetic inspiration) 79
imitative monument/s 5, 10, 12-14, 32, 47, 62, 65-6, 68, 82-92, 102, 189, 228-32
immain anmae ('hymns for the soul') 122
immairche or *immairge see* migrant/s
immigrant/s 27, 48, 71, 92, 108, 110, 159-60, 163-4, 171-4, 176-7, 179-81, 183, 189; *see also* migrant/s
Inber Colpdi (inlet of Boyne) 65; *see also* Colp West, Co. Meath
Inchinclare, Co. Limerick 31, Map 1
increduli see pagan/s 30-1
indigenous 5, 7, 28, 32, 34, 36-7, 44, 48, 57, 70, 75, 92, 97, 106-7, 111, 117, 129-30, 147n44, 159, 163-4, 171-2, 174, 179-81, 183, 192-3; *see also* ancestor/s
industrial activity 3, 87, 96, 98-101, 198, 210; *see also* craft working; iron working; metal working
infant/s 16, 40-5, 48, 51, 80, 83-4, 109, 118, 120-1, 137, 154, 162, 172, 180, 188, 190-1, 217, 223, Figs 2.7-2.8, 3.1-3.2; babies 117-18; foetus 121; neonate/s 42, 78, 85, 127; perinate 51, 92, 153; swaddled 120; *see also ceallúnach/ceallúnaigh*; child/children; juvenile/s
Inis Mo-Choí (Island Mahee) *see* Nendrum, Mahee Island, Strangford Lough, Co. Down
Inis Mór, Aran Islands, Co. Galway 47, 162, 167, 237, Map 6
Inishkea North, Co. Mayo 215, 219-20, 245, Map 8; Bailey Mór 219-20

Inishmurray, Co. Sligo 215, 220, 220n82, 245, Map 8; Relickoran (cemetery) 220
injury/injuries 4, 47, 106, 138-9, 147, 149-52, 194, 224-5; cut marks 138, 143-4, 150-1, 167; defensive 142, 144, 147, 151, 167; healed 76, 125, 150-2; *see also* trauma *and* violence, death by
inscription/s 50, 125, 178, 202, 206, 209-10, 213, 216, 220, 222, 245; *see also* stone slab/s (decorated): cross-inscribed slabs; Latin; ogam (ogham); rune/runic
insular 27-8, 31
Intcal 13; 3, *see also* Oxcal
intermediary (between living and dead) 135, 192
intruder/s 135, 147, 147n44, 167-8; warning to 167; *see also* decapitated/decapitated: head as trophy/warning *and* deviant burial/s
Inver, Co. Donegal 72n44, 188n20
Iógenán (priest) 176
Iona, Inner Hebrides, Scotland 4n4, 55, 149, 169-70, 173, 204, 206
Írgalach (king) 184
Irish (language): early Modern Irish 154; Middle Irish 44, 140, 182, 184; late Middle Irish 75; Old Irish 4, 64, 106, 122, Primitive Irish 44
'Irish Life of Colum Cille' 204
Irish Sea 39, 82, 91-2, 94, 159, 168n111, 201, 215, 221
iron working 40, 87, 102, 208-9, 213; iron smelting 42, 44, 100, 208; *see also* metal working
Isle of Man 174, 181
isolated burial/s 5, 34n1, 62-4, 102, 112, 117, 126, 130, 140-1, 176-7, 188-9, 192, 225n95, 228-32, 243-4; *see also* cemetery/cemeteries
isotope (stable) 218
isotope/isotopic analysis 1, 3, 5, 6, 36, 39-41, 44, 48-9, 62, 70-2, 74-6, 78-9, 83n93, 84, 88-9, 88n113, 92, 96, 99, 103, 105, 110, 135, 143-4, 150, 152-3, 159, 163-4, 171-4, 176, 180-7, 191, 219, 226, 241-2; *see also* laser ablation *and* tooth enamel
Iveragh peninsula, Co. Kerry 217

Jacob (Old Testament) 196
Jamestown, Co. Dublin Map 1
Jerome 185
Jesus *see* Christ
jewellery 30
John (evangelist) 119; letter to the church at Pergamum (Turkey) 119

Johnstown, Co. Meath 91, 100, 142–3, 154, 163, 189, 193, 198, 231, 239, 244, Fig. 6.4, Maps 4, 6
Joseph (Old Testament) 196
Judgement Day 51, 140, 142, 153
juvenile/s 14, 16, 38, 40–2, 44–5, 48, 77–8, 85, 88–91, 94, 101, 118, 120, 137, 144, 147–50, 154–5, 160, 162–3, 165–7, 169, 172, 174, 176, 180, 190–1, 199, 206, 213, 217–18, 218n64, 224, 233–42, 245; *see also* child/children *and* infant/s

Keeley, Valerie J. 26
keening 94; *see* laying out/laid out
Kells, Co. Meath: Market Cross 55
Kentish Chronicle *see* Nennius, *Historia Brittonum* 168
Kerlogue, Co. Wexford 15
Kerry coast/coastal region 178, 193
Keshcarrigan, Co. Leitrim 8
Kilcorney, the Burren, Co. Clare 80, 188, 228, 243, Map 4
Kildangan, Co. Kildare 84, 189, 229, 243, Map 4
Kildare, Co. Kildare 184
Kildimo, Co. Limerick 93–4, 230
Kill of the Grange, Co. Dublin 126, 155, 170, 209–10, 236, 245, Map 8; Church of Ireland churchyard 210; Roman or the Briton's well 210
Killaree, Co. Kilkenny 95, 112, 230, 234, Map 5
Killeany, Co. Laois 103n1, 150, 154, 160, 165–7, 194–5, 224, 238, 243, 244, Maps 6, 8;
Killeedy, Co. Cork 184
killeen *see* ceallúnach/ceallúnaigh
Killeenagh *see* Ballygarran, Co. Waterford
Killegar (Cell Adhgair?), Co. Wicklow 213, 245, Map 8
Killevy, Co. Armagh 184
Kilmahuddrick, Co. Dublin Map 1
Kilmainham, Co. Meath 225n95
kiln/s 63, 88, 96n159, 98–9, 101, 152–3, 170, 211, 224; burial in 6, 88, 101n179, 152–3, 169–70, 178–9, 193, 195, 236–40, 243–4; *see also* deviant burial/s; burnt grain (in burials); hearth/s
Kilree 3, Co. Kilkenny 126, 177, 192, 234, 242–3, Maps 5, 7; Kilree 4 Map 1
Kilshane, Co. Dublin 112, 129, 228, 233, Map 5
Kilteasheen, Knockvicar, Co. Roscommon 137, 240, Map 6
Kiltierney, Co. Fermanagh 13, 22, 24, 27, 39, 227, Fig. 1.4, Maps 1–2; Mound 13 Fig. 1.4

Kiltullagh Hill, Cos Mayo and Roscommon 77; Kiltullagh Hill 1, Co. Mayo, 230; Kiltullagh Hill 2, Co. Roscommon 232, Maps 1, 4
kin group/s 18n41, 48, 69, 73–4, 83, 88, 92, 96, 98, 105, 115, 126, 130, 159, 170–2, 177, 186, 188–9, 191–2, 195, 198, 207; *see also* cemetery/cemeteries: communal; fingal; *túath/túatha*
kin slaying *see* fingal
King Cormac's mound *see* Rossnaree, Co. Meath
King, Heather A. 123n57, 125, 204
King's River 8
kingship 40, 75, 109, 145; *see also* elite *and* royal
knife/knives 64, 82, 95, 110, 112, 126, 131, 233–5; blade 138–9, 152; sheath 110; tanged 112; wounds 34, 143, 145, 149-52, 194, 221
Knockanacuig, Co. Kerry 29
Knockcommane, Co. Limerick 17, 20, 182, 227, Plate 2, Maps 1–2
Knockgraffon, Co. Tipperary 18, 23, 227, Maps 1–2
Knockmark 1, Co. Meath Map 1
Knocknarea, Co. Sligo 154, 168
Knocknashammer, Co. Sligo 82–3, 82n89,189, 232, 244, Map 4
Knowth, Co. Meath 26, 36–40, 45–6, 45n34, 48, 65, 69–71, 135, 137, 144, 171–2, 176–7, 180, 182–3, 231, 239, 241–2; Figs 2.2–2.6, 4.4, Maps 3–4, 6–7;
Knowth, Site M, 71, 71n34
Knoxspark, Co. Sligo 107, 111, 128, 147, 147n44, 150, 162, 194, 194n51, 235, 240, 244, Maps 5–6

La Tène III 13n8
lachrymatory (tear jar) 8
Lagney on the Marne, France 173
Laigin *see* Leinstermen (Laigin)
laity 122, 196–200, 207; laymen 202; laywomen 202; *see also* Christian/Christianity; monachus; oblate/s
lake/s 72, 72–3n44, 98, 98n166, 187–8, 188n20, 218; *see also* turlough/s
Lakenheath, Suffolk 75
Lambay Island, Co. Dublin 44, 44n31, 45, 45n35, 46, 48, Map 3
Lamberton Moor Hoard, Berwickshire, Scotland 7–8, Plate 1
lamenting *see* keening

Index

laser ablation 180–1, 226; *see also* isotope/isotopic analysis
late antique period 50
Latin; language 4n4, 31, 50, 65n18, 128; geometric display capitals 206; script 178
laying out/laid out 10, 29, 45, 49, 54, 57, 64, 72, 76, 89, 94, 96, 123, 128, 154, 161, 168–9, 187, 189, 224–5; *see also* keening
leacht/leachta (stone-built platforms or altars) 212, 218–20, 223; *see also* shrine/s
Lehinch, Co. Offaly 74–6, 117, 125–6, 142, 152, 180, 232, 235, 240, 242, Fig. 5.8, Maps 4–7
Leinster (province) 51, 176, 211, 222; *see also* Leinstermen (Laigin)
Leinstermen (Laigin) 49–50, 184
Lerr (river) 68
Leth Cuinn 168
Levitstown, Co. Kildare 129
Lex Innocentium ('Law of the Innocents') *see* Adomnán: *Cáin Adomnán*
Liffey (river) 36, 168n111, 169; *see also* Liffey plain
Liffey plain 51, 51n7, 63, 168; *see also* Liffey (river) *and* Mullamast, Co. Kildare
liminal/liminality 41–2, 44, 79, 215
Limnos 44; *see also* Lambay Island, Co. Dublin
Lincoln, England 168
Lindisfarne (Holy Island), England 56, 140, 173
linen 54–7, 81; *see also* winding sheet *and* shroud/shroud wrapped
line-sinker (stone) 219
lintel grave/s *see* grave/s
Lisnacroghy or Gallowstown, Ballintober, Co. Roscommon 66n20
Listoghil *see* Carrowmore, Co. Sligo: Tomb 51
literature *see* early Irish *and individual texts*
Lithica (early Christian poem) 117
Lleyn, Wales 50
Llŷn peninsula, Wales 50
Loarn *see* Cenél Loarn
Lochrea *see* Loughrea, Co. Galway
locket/s 81; *see also* amulet/s
Loíguire (king, son of Níall) 51, 65, 94, 168, 186, 214
Lommán (saint) 214
Lommanus *see* Lommán (saint)
loom weight/s 208; *see also* spindle/s
Lough Cé, Co. Roscommon 137
Lough Gill 154
Lough Gur, Circle J, Co. Limerick 154, 238, Map 6

Lough Namanfin (*Loch na mBan Finn* (the lake of the fair/bright women)), near Ballymacaward, Co. Donegal 72, 187–8
Lough Namanfin, Bogagh, Co. Donegal 72–3n44; 188n20
Loughbown 1, Co. Galway 165, 237, Plate 9, Map 6
Loughcrew, Co. Meath 26
Loughey, near Donaghadee, Co. Down 20, 22–4, 227, Fig. 1.4, Maps 1–2
Loughrea, Co. Galway 2, 2n2
Luke (evangelist) 54, 57
Lusk, Co. Dublin 106, 145, 223, 236, Maps 6, 8
Lynch, Linda 94n144,
Lynn, Christopher J. 165n101

Mabinogi, Second Branch of the 168
Mac Cerbaill, Diarmait (king of Tara) 140
Mac Cuilinn (of Lusk) 223
mac Nad Froích, Óengus 168
Macalister, R.A.S., 1
Máel (name) 113
Mael Fothartaig 54
Mag Liphi *see* Liffey plain
Magheradunbar, Co. Fermanagh 120–1, 233, Map 5
Maistiu 51, 51n7, 168; *see also* Mullamast, Co. Kildare
Maltese cross 207, 216
manuport *see* quartz
Manusmore, Co. Clare Map 1
'Mapping death: people, boundaries and territories in Ireland, first to eighth centuries AD' (INSTAR project) 2; Mapping Death database 2; *see also* Heritage Council, the
Mark (evangelist) 54, 57
Marlhill, Co. Tipperary 17, 20, 227, Plate 2, Maps 1–2
Marlinstown, Co. Westmeath 101, 143, 150, 155, 161, 166, 194–5, 232, 240, 244, Map 6
marriage 185; alliances 181, 192–3; *see also* divorce; husband/s; *Marriage disputes: a fragmentary Old Irish law-text*; spouse/s; wife/wives
Marriage disputes: a fragmentary Old Irish law-text 4–5, 61, 122, 185
Marston St Lawrence, Northamptonshire, England 129
Martin (bishop of Braga, Portugal) 122
Mayo–Roscommon county boundary 77
McGarry, Tiernan 2n3
McKinley, Jacqueline I. 16n28
McLoughlin, Gill 63n11

medieval period; high 2, 68, 81; late 82, 122, 165n101
Mediterranean, the 94, 96, 127, 159, 174, 201, 207–8, 222, 225; *see also* pottery
'Meet the Ancestors' (BBC programme) 187n18
Mel (bishop) 63
Melchú (bishop) 63
memento/s 118; *see also* heirloom/s
Mesolithic 68, 113, 221
metal detecting 169
metal working 98, 101; *see also* iron working
Metrical Dindshenchas ('Topographical lore of Ireland') 44, 184
Michael (saint) 218
midden/s 212, 221–2
Middle Ages *see* medieval period
Mide (kingdom) 41n18, 184
migrant/s (*immairche* or *immairge*) 63, 117; *see also* immigrant/s
Migration Period 92, 171
Miliucc (Patrick's slave master) 30
Millockstown, Co. Louth 152, 239, Map 6
Mine Howe, Orkney, Scotland 40
mirror/s 8, 27, 32, 44, 227; mirror handle/s 13, 27
Mo Ninne *see* Dar Ercae
mobility (of peoples) 6, 23–4, 92, 99, 159, 171–81, 226; *see also* isotope/isotopic analysis
Mo-Choí (original name Cáelán) 206
MOLA (Museum of London Archaeology) 61
Molaise (saint) 220; bell and crozier 220
Moloney, Colm 211n40,41
monachus (lay tenant of church) 196, 207; *see also* Christian/Christianity *and* laity
Monaghan, Nigel 73n46
Monasterboice, Co. Louth, Muiredach's Cross 55
monastery/monasteries/monastic 173, 212, 216; cemeteries 2123, 125, 141, 197, 202–7, 217–8, 224; monastic enclosure 199, Plate 12; monk/s 125, 173, 196; *sanctum* 202; *see also* Christian/Christianity *and* ecclesiastical site/s
Monesan (British princess) 62
Mongán 183
Mons Aigli (near Croagh Patrick, Co. Mayo) 62
Moone, Co. Kildare 42–44, 51–3; *see also* Mullamast, Co. Kildare
Morett, Co. Laois 95–6, 155, Map 6; Site D 95–6, 186, 230; Morett 5 238; Morett 13 230

mother/s 149–50, 183–4, 189, 191, 194–5, 214; 'A list of the Mothers of the Saints' 184; *see also* daughter/s *and* son/s
Mound of the Hostages *see* Tara, Hill of, Co. Meath
Mount Gamble, Co. Dublin 145, 161, 236, Figs 6.2, 6.4, Map 6
Mount Offaly, Cabinteely, Co. Dublin 58, 61, 118, 127, 144, 155, 162, 198, 233, 236, Maps 5–6
Moyle Big, Co. Carlow Map 1
Muirchertach (king of Tara) 183
Muirchú 30, 54, 62, 65, 92, 214; *Vita Patricii* 4–5
Muireann (daughter of Cellach) 184
Muiredach 183
Muiresc Aigli *see* Murrisk, Co. Mayo
Muirgel (queen of the Leinstermen) 184
Mullacash Middle, Co. Kildare 138, 143, 237, Map 6
Mullamast, Co. Kildare 15, 19, 34n1, 42–4, 51, 51n7, 168, Maps 1, 3; Mullamast Hill (Moone townland) 42–3, 51, Figs 2.7–2.8, 3.1–3.2; Long Stone 51; Mullamast Stone 51, Fig. 3.3
Mullet peninsula, Co. Mayo 219
Munster (province) 168; plantations 129
Murchad (abbess) 183
Murchadh Ua Briain 141
Murphy, Eileen & Colm Donnelly, 145n38
Murrisk, Co. Mayo 62
mutilated/mutilation 6, 136–40, 143, 169, 236–40; genital 143; removal of heart 136, 138–9; *see also* decapitated/decapitation

nail/s 16, 27–8, 89, 120, 164, 164n98; nailed coffin 165n101
Nanny (river) 82
nasc 105–6; *nasc druad* ('a collar worn by a druid') 105–6; *nasc niad* ('a chain or collar worn by an approved champion') 105–6; *see also* neck ring
National History Museum 73n46
National Monuments Service 204
National Museum of Ireland 2, 64, 78n68, 82n87, 93, 108n9, 129, 209, 213; Topographical files 93
National Roads Authority (NRA, now Transport Infrastructure Ireland (TII)) 2, 12n7; Monograph series *SEANDA* 2
Navan Fort, Co. Armagh 24n63, 26, 165, Fig. 1.5; Site A 165n101
Neave, Richard 187n18
Nechtan (deity consort of *Bóind*) 79

neck ring/s, collars 6, 103, 103n1,3, 105-6, 110, 131, 160, 178, 180, 192, 233-5, 243-4, Plate 6; *see also* torc/s
Nenagh North, Co. Tipperary 141, 240, Map 6
Nendrum, Mahee Island, Strangford Lough, Co. Down 206, 206n20, 21, 215, 245, Map 8
Nennius, *Historia Brittonum* 49-50, 168; Kentish Chronicle 168
Neo-Babylonian period 40
Neolithic 7, 12-15, 19, 26, 36-9, 42, 65, 71, 77, 86, 88, 91, 99, 113, 115, 119
Ness (river) 119
New Downs, Co. Westmeath Map 1
New England, US 136
Newgrange, Co. Meath 65
Newtown Rath, Swords, Co. Dublin 61, 61n4, 81, 101, 198, 215n50, 228, Maps 4, 6
Níall 51, 168
Ninch, Co. Meath 164; Ninch 1; 54, 82, 231, Map 4; Ninch 2; 99, 154, 160, 173, 176, 231, 239, 242, Plate 5, Maps 4, 6-7; Ninch 3; 91-3, 99, 111, 160, 173, 176-7, 186, 190, 231, 235, 242, 244, Maps 5, 7
non-indigenous *see* immigrant/s *and* migrant/s
Nore (river) 8, 18, 177
Normandy, Counts of 222; silver coin 222
north Africa/north African 94, 159, 164, 174

O'Coinnegain, Brian Caech 81
Ó Corráin, Donnchadh, Liam Breatnach & Aidan Breen 51
Ó Maoldúin, Ros 34n1, 143n30
O'Sullivan, Aidan, Finbar McCormick, Thomas R. Kerr & Lorcan Harney 3
O'Sullivan, Jerry 220
oblate/s 217; *see also* Christian/Christianity *and* laity
occult 37n4, 171; *see also* divination
Odrán (Orán) 204
óenach 173; *see also* assembly
Office of Public Works (OPW) 208, 218
ogam (ogham) 50, 144, 178, 216
oil 187n19, 201, 208, 225; *see also* pottery *and* wine
Olaf the Sandal *see* Amlaíb Cúarán
Old Testament 185
Old Warden, Bedfordshire, England 27
Omey Island, Co. Galway 212, 215, 218, 245, Map 8
oral tradition 186
Oranbeg, Co. Galway 20, 20n52, 27-8, 227, Maps 1-2

Ordnance Survey map (1837) 211-12
organic material 3, 19, 30, 61, 92n138, 97, 108n10, 201; church/es 218; containers 7-9, 32; structure 202; *see also* vegetable/vegetative material
Origen 140
Osgyð (Anglo-Saxon female name) 222
Oswald (king) 140, 173
Oswiu 140
otherworld/otherworldly 37, 79, 109, 154; portal to 37; *see also* occult *and* supernatural
outsider/s 106, 135, 142, 144, 179, 183, 187, 224, 241; *see also* intruder/s *and* stranger/s
Owenbristy, Co. Galway 98, 98n166, 105-6, 143, 149-52, 160, 178, 180, 185-6, 191, 194, 224, 225n95, 229, 233, 237, 241, 243, Figs 4.16, Plates 6, 7, 13, Maps 5-8
OxCal 3, 7n1, 208n28; *see also* Intcal

pagan/s 6, 29-31, 54, 65, 71-2, 76, 80-1, 87-8, 99, 119-21, 128-9, 136, 139, 176, 196-200; non-Christian 30, 65, 102, 110, 119, 125, 153, 206, 215; pagan-Christian transition 128-9; *see also* ancestor/s; heathen/s; pre-Christian
Paget's disease 153, 178, 193, 195
paired burials 145, 145n38, 147-9, 169, 236-40
Parknabinnia, Co. Clare 34n1
Parknahown 5, Co. Laois 118-21, 137, 150-2, 154-5, 162-3, 193-4, 198, 234, 238, 243-4, Maps 5-6
passage tomb/s 13-14, 36, 65, 69-71, 144, 176; *see also* prehistory/prehistoric
paternal grave *see* ancestral burial place/cemetery
Patrick (saint) 4, 30, 50, 54, 56, 56n11, 62, 65, 94, 168, 196, 201, 214-15; *Confessio* 4; *Epistola ad Milites Corotici* (letter to Coroticus) 4, 50, 50n1; pre-Patrician 214
patron/s 55, 125, 202, 206
Paul (saint) 185
peacock 207
Pega (sister of Guthlac) 56, 94
Pelletstown, Co. Dublin 127-8; Pelletstown East 168-9, 236, Map 6
penance 128, 145, 149
'Penitential Canons from Regino's Ecclesiastical Discipline' 128
penitential/s 1, 125, 128-9, 145; *see also* canon/s *and individual texts*
peplos (garment) 110
Pergamum, Turkey 119

periostitis 137
Petrie, George 226, 226n1
petrous bone 83n93, 226
phallic 117, 188
phosphate analysis 208
Pict/Picti/Pictish 49, 119, 144–5, 149, 176, 183; Pictland 144
pilgrims/pilgrimage 173, 215–20, 220n82; 222–3, 225; *see also* Christian/Christianity
pin/s 14, 24, 27, 78, 108, 233–5; bone 71, 123, 163, 219; copper alloy 120; dress 108, 131; ringed 108, 108n9, 11, 111,118; shroud 54, 57; *see also* brooch/es *and* fibula/e
plague *see* Black Death, the
plaque/s: bone 14; bronze 44, 110
Platin Fort, Duleek, Co. Meath 42, Map 3
pleurisy 137
pneumonic plague 137
poisoning 148; *see also* execution
Pollacorragune, Co. Galway 84, 106, 126, 229, 233, Maps 4–5
pollen 12
porphyry 219
Portmagee Channel, Co. Kerry 216
Portmarnock, Co. Dublin 228; estuary 63
pottery 7, 16, 81, 123, 174, 208; African red slipware 126; B ware 101, 222; Bi amphora 127; Bii (Late Roman 1) ware 96, 127, 159, 201, 207–9, 225; Biii ware 208; D ware 127; E ware 96, 101, 127, 207–9, 216, 222, 225, 245; Leinster cooking ware 209; Mediterranean 96, 127, 174, 208, 222; Phocaean Red Slip Ware (PRSW) 96, 127, 159; souterrain ware 7, 213
Poundbury, Dorset, England 40, 61, 164n99
pre-Christian 44, 51, 72, 128, 188
prehistory/prehistoric 12, 16, 46, 51, 64, 80–1, 86, 225n95; burial places 10, 68, 71, 73, 80–1, 188 195; burials 80, 221; crouched burials 221–2; Late Prehistoric 2n3, 10n6, 12n7; *see also* ancestor/s *and ferta/fertae*
priest/s 145, 176, 214; *see also* Christian/Christianity *and* cleric/s
progenitor 98, 115, 173, 177; *see also* ancestor/s *and ferta/fertae*
progeny 73, 188; *see also* ancestor/s *and ferta/fertae*
promontory/promontories 7–8, 42, 46–7, 100, 141, 147, 221–2
Prumplestown Lower, Co. Kildare 31, 50–1, 68–9, 93, 119–21, 229, 233, Fig. 4.3, Maps 4–5

pseudo or imitation graves 218–19
Ptolemaeus, Claudius (Ptolemy) 44
punitive death and burial/s 46, 71, 76, 96, 132, 141–3, 147–8, 153, 155, 161, 163, 166–7, 169–70, 179, 183, 195, 215; *see also* deviant burial/s
puparia 94; *see also* blow-fly (blue-bottle)
purification ritual 17, 128
pyre/s 8–10, 16n28, 19, 23, 26, 28–30, 32; pyre-pits 28–9; *see also* bier

quarry/quarrying 42n23, 77, 86, 88, 93, 95, 112, 142n22, 173; sand quarrying 95, 112, 213
quartz 68, 119–22, 213, 220, 223, 233–5, 245; cobbled floor 219–20; pebbles 6, 68, 88, 118–22, 131, 202, 213, 216–20, 223

Raffin, Co. Meath 92–3
Raftery, Barry, 2
Raftery, Joseph, 2, 84n95
Raheennamadra, Co. Limerick 82
raiding 50
Ráith Becc (near Antrim) 140
Ranelagh, Co. Roscommon 108–9, 109n13, 117, 188, 232, 235, 244, Fig. 5.8, Map 5
ransom 75
Rath Melsigi *see* Clonmelsh (*Cluain Melsigi*), Co. Carlow
Rath of the Synods *see* Tara, Hill of, Co. Meath
Rath, Co. Meath 14, 39–40, 84, 109, 172, 183, 190, 241, Maps 1, 3
rath/s *see* ringfort/s
Rathdooney Beg, Co. Sligo 14, 28, 47, 227, Maps 1–2
Rathdown, Co. Dublin, slabs; 213, 213n46; *see also* grave/s: slab/s *and* stone slab/s (decorated)
Ratoath, Co. Meath 103–5, 112, 139, 150, 152, 161, 180, 192, 194, 235, 240, 242, 244, Fig. 5.1, Maps 1, 5–7
Raystown, Co. Meath 91, 100–1, 111–12, 118, 127, 144, 151, 153, 190, 198, 231, 235, 240, 244, Maps 4–6
Reask, Co. Kerry 118, 208, 233, 245, Maps 5, 8; pillar-stone 208
red deer (*Cervus elaphus*) 18, 75, 97, 113–16, 130, 188, Figs 5.6, 5.7; stag 113–14; *see also* antler *and* deer (*Cervidae*)
Reformation, the 207, 210, 212
regeneration 63, 113–14, 117, 119, 131, 188–9; *see also* fertility
Reilly, Eileen 94n144
relic (burial place/cemetery) 65; *see also fossam rotunda/m*

Index

Relic Fort *see* Durrow, Co. Offaly
relic/s (corporeal) 108, 140, 164, 214–15; reliquary boxes 108; *see also* shrine/s
replica/s 123, 204
repoussé 44
resurrection 119, 140, 140–1n15, 197, 209; *see also* Easter
rigor mortis 135, 157, 163
ring/s 14, 24, 38, 42, 44, 78, 172, 227; from sandal 40, 108–9, 172, 183; Roman type 84, 172, 190; silver ring with herring-bone decoration 84, 109, 172, 180, 183, 190, Fig. 4.10; toe ring/s 40, 84, 109, 172, 183, 190, 227, 233–5; *see also* earring/s, neck rings
ring-ditch/es 10, 10n5, 12–20, 22, 24–8, 30–2, 32n90, 39–40, 42, 46, 51, 65, 65n17, 68–9, 75–7, 79–82, 84–93, 95–6, 99–102, 107, 114–15, 119–21, 132, 135, 138, 138n10, 141, 144, 148, 150–1, 153, 155, 160, 164, 167, 172, 176–7, 179–80, 182, 186, 190–1, 192–5, 194n49, 243–4; annular 12–13, 15–17, 31–2, 51, 80–1, 87–9, 92, 102, 182; Bronze Age 10, 13–14, 22, 24, 30, 155; imitative 5, 84–92; penannular 12, 14–17, 24, 75–6, 84n99, 86, 88–92, 96, 100–2, 107, 120, 144, 151, 164, 176–7, 180,182, 186, 190–1, 209-10, 224
ringfort/s 63, 76, 76n63, 82, 98–9, 101, 165
rivets 26–7, 108, 118
rock-crystal 121
Rockfield, Co. Kerry 28
Roman Britain 8, 44, 46, 140; Romanised Britain 49, 201; Romano-British 45–6, 61, 165n101
Romanesque 222
Rome/Roman 40, 44–6, 49, 50, 57, 81, 84, 109, 171–2, 180, 183, 185n12, 190, 208, 210; Empire 50, 171; Late Roman 159, 164n98, 215; letterforms 50; post-Roman 92, 99, 129; Romanised 8,49, 57, 201
Rossnaree, Co. Meath 40, 83–4, 109, 180, 190, 231, 235, 242, 244, Fig. 4.10, Maps 4–5, Map 7; King Cormac's mound 190
royal 31, 125, 140, 165, 179, 202, 223; royal site/s 65n17, 72, 123, 179–80; *see also* elite *and* kingship
Rubin (compiler of *Collectio Canonum Hibernensis*) 4n4; *see also* Dair-Inis
rune/runic 206
Rynne, Etienne 1–2, 20n52, 22n59

sacrifice/s 41, 122, 135; of first born 44; *see also* feasts/feasting
sailor/s 47
saint/s 4, 154, 164, 184, 198–9, 202, 207, 209, 211, 214–15, 222–3, 226, 245; *see also* érlam *and individual saints*
Samhtann (saint) 184; Life of 184–5n10
sandstone disc 221
Sandy, Bedfordshire, England 129
sati 73
Saxons 171; *see also* Anglo-Saxon/s
scabbard mount/s 44; *see also* sword/s
scallop shell/s 217
Scandinavia/Scandinavian 70–1, 95, 144, 159, 174, 176, 193
Scelec *see* Skellig, Co. Kerry
sceptre/s 6, 90n125, 107, 110, 131, 233–5, Fig. 5.2
Scotland/Scottish 7, 24, 26, 39, 61, 61n6, 70, 144, 172–4, 176, 183
Scotti (tribe) 49
scramasax (large knife) 112; *see also* knife/knives
sealing (or closure) burial 89–90, 162, 167, 187, 191, 220
sealing deposit 75, 116, 189
secondary burial 68–9, 81, 142–3, 171; *see also* ancestor/s; ancestral burial place/cemetery; foundation burial/s; imitative monument/s
secular *see* habitation
Sedgeford, Norfolk, England 74, 176
Segais (well) 79; *see also* Carbury Hill, Co. Kildare
sentinel burial (possible) 167–9
Seskin, Co. Kilkenny 112–13n23
settlers 28, 33, 50, 129, 225; *see also* immigrant/s; migrant/s; trader/s
Sewerby, East Yorkshire, England 135–6
Shannon (river) 202
shears 6, 79, 112–13, 112–13n23, 131, 179, 233–5, Fig. 5.5
Sheastown, Co. Kilkenny 95, 112, 230, 234, Map 5
Sheean Hill, Co. Offaly *see* Durrow, Co. Offaly
shield/s 29, 84, 106, 131, 233–5; shield boss/es 44, 84, 106
shrine/s 164, 207–8, 211, 216–17, 220, 223, 245; corner-post 222; gable shrine/s 216; reliquary shrine/s 211, 216–17; *see also leacht/leachta* (stone-built platforms or altars)
shroud/shroud wrapped 54, 56, 88, 94, 99, 106–7, 110, 123, 125, 150, 166, 204–5, 221; *see also* linen; pin: shroud; winding sheet/s

siblings 145, 149–50, 185, 190–1, 194
Síd Nechtain see Carbury Hill, Co. Kildare
sidh (mythical dwelling places) 66; *see also ferta/fertae*
Silbury Hill, Wiltshire, England 113
Silos, Penitential of 128
sindon 56
Sinell (saint) 220
Sitruic (father of Amlaib) 75
Skane (river) 91n127
Skellig, Co. Kerry 215, 217–18, 223, 245, Map 8; lighthouse 217n63; monastery 217n62; South peak 217n62, 218; St Michael's church 217–18
Skye, Isle of, Scotland 62
slab-lined grave/s *see* grave/s
slag 16, 161, 209
Slane, Co. Meath 65, 71
slave/s 30, 50, 73, 119, 149; *see also ancillae* (female slaves)
Slíab Miss 30
Sligo coast 220
smothering 148; *see also* execution
Soderberg, John 123n57
Solar, Co. Antrim 118, 163, 212, 233, 236, 245, Maps 5–6, 8
son/s 51, 75, 168; *see also* daughter/s *and* sibling/s
Sonnagh Demesne, Co. Westmeath 142, 163, 240, Map 6
soul 122, 197–8; *see also comaithmet anma* (commemoration of the soul) *and immain anmae* ('hymns for the soul')
souterrain/s 82, 98, 101, 141, 166
spade-shoe/s (iron) 111
Spain 128, 174
spear/s 6, 106–7, 131, 154, 168, 233–5; spearhead 107, 145, 147; spear-shaft 110
Spetisbury Rings, Dorset, England 7–8, Plate 1
spindle/s 187; spindle whorl/s 207–8; *see also* loom weight/s
spine/spinal: curvature 187; degeneration 161; distortion 154; osteoporosis 72, 187
Spong Hill, Norfolk, England 129
spouse/s 153, 185–6, 189–91, 193; *see also* husband/s *and* wife/wives
St John's Point, Co. Down 121, 212–13, 233, 245, Maps 5, 8
St Peter's, Broadstairs, Kent, England 85n99
stable isotope analysis *see* isotope/isotopic analysis
standing stone/s 51, 66, 77, 93
Stapenhill, England 136
Star Carr, Yorkshire, England 113

stone slab/s (decorated) 207–8, 216, 220; cross-inscribed slabs 206, 210, 213, 216–18, 220, 245
Stonehenge, Wiltshire, England 113
stone-lined grave/s *see* grave/s
Stoneyford, Co. Kilkenny 8, 8n4, 27, 171, 227, Fig. 1.2, Maps 1–2
Stout, Geraldine & Mathew Stout, 98n167
stranger 186; *see also cú glas* ('grey hound/wolf')
strangulation 148; *see also* execution
Styx (river) 45–6
succession dispute 145; *see also* kingship
Suibne (queen) 184
Summed Probability Functions (SPF) 10n6
sundial/s 222
supernatural 1
Sutton Hoo, Suffolk, England 74–5
sword/s 27, 44, 136, 147; Iron age 13n8; hilt/s 96; hilt-guard/s 27; sword-sharpening 51; wound 147, 149, 152, 194; *see also* dagger

Táin 145n37; story of Cú Chulainn and Fer Diad 145n37
tapa (or *kapa*) (Hawaiian) 157, 157n73
Tara, Hill of, Co. Meath 14, 29–30, 41n18, 51, 51n7, 65, 65n17, 71–2, 91n127, 123, 140, 163, 168, 179, 183, 190; Mound of the Hostages 30; Ráith na Ríg (Enclosure of the Kings) 40–1, 172, 241, Map 3; Rath of the Synods 41, 45, 71–2, 123, 139, 163, 172, 178–80, 231, 235, 240–2, Maps 1, 3–7
Teathba 141
tellach ('legal entry') 18n41, 65–6
territory/territories 2, 44, 66, 71–3, 80, 83, 154, 167–8, 173, 181, 186, 188–9; *see also* boundary/boundaries
Thaithlaithe (queen) 184
Theodore, Penitential of 128–9
Thompson, Edward A. 50n1
thrall 136
Timoney, Martin 82n89
Tinnapark Demesne, Co. Wicklow 64, 232
Tírechán 30, 51, 54, 62, 65, 65n17, 82, 94, 168, 186, 201, 214; *Collectanea* 4–5, 30–1
Tlachtga, Hill of Ward, Co. Meath 41, 41n18
togher (trackway) 50–1, 68–9
token burial/s *see* bead/s
token cremation deposit/s 10, 13, 16–18, 31
Tolka (river) 168–9, 168n111
tool/s 113–15, 117; *see also* antler *and* bone object/s
Toormore, Mizen peninsula, Co. Cork 129–30
tooth enamel 3; *see also* isotope/isotopic analysis

torc/s 44, 105, 160; *see also* collars, neck ring/s
torture 138; *see also* punitive death and burial/s
Totmáel (Patrick's charioteer) 62
Toureen Peakaun, Co. Tipperary 222–3, 245, Map 8
trackway *see* togher
trader/s 44, 50, 159, 171, 174
Trajan (emperor) 45–6, 48
Transport Infrastructure Ireland (TII) *see* National Roads Authority (NRA)
transporting of body 61, 102, 106, 139, 143, 158–9, 161–3, 178; retrieved by followers or kin 170; translation of burials 140, 214–17; *see also* bier; *and* burial position/s: trussed/bound for transport; log coffin/s
trauma 6, 89, 101n179, 125–6, 138–9, 142–54, 169–70, 180, 194–5, 223–5, 236–40, 243-4; ante-mortem 139, 152; axe blow/s 149, 194 (*see also* sword/s); blade wound/s 138, 143–5, 147, 150–2, 194 (*see also* knife/knives *and* sword/s); peri-mortem 144, 147, 150–1, 180, Fig. 6.2; post-mortem 139, 151; stab wound/s 34n1, 139, 143, 145, 149–51, 194, 221; *see also* conflict; injury/injuries; knife/knives; sword/s; violence, death by
trephination (of skull) 141n16, 213
Trim, Co. Meath 214, 245, Map 8; Loman Street 214
túath/túatha 130, 149, 173; *see also* kin group cemetery/cemeteries: communal
tuberculosis (TB, 'the wasting disease') 136
Tullyallen 1, Co. Louth 14, Map 1
turlough/s 98n166; *see also* lake/s
Turoe Stone, Co. Galway 86–7, 191, Fig. 4.12
Tyrellspass, Co. Westmeath 210

Uamhain Bhriste (broken cave) *see* Owenbristy, Co. Galway
Uasal (queen) 184
UCD Mícheál Ó Cléirigh Institute 2
Uí Dúnlainge 51, 168
Uí Liatháin 49, 184
Uí Néill 51, 71, 73, 144, 154; Northern Uí Néill 154
Ulaid *see* Ulstermen (Ulaid)
Ulster (province) 7; *see also* Ulstermen (Ulaid)
Ulstermen (Ulaid) 49, 183
UNESCO World Heritage 217
unprotected dug grave/s *see* grave/s
Upper Lough Erne, Co. Fermanagh 143, 215, 220; *see also* Cleenish, Upper Lough Erne, Co. Fermanagh

urn (cinerary) 14, 27, 72, 129; Isings 67A type, 8
ustrina (method of cremation) 28–9, 28n74

Valencia, Co. Kerry 223
vampires 136
vegetable/vegetative material 18, 30, 110, 130; vegetation 54, 59, 96, 187, 190; *see also* organic material
Verca (abbess) 56
vessel/s: glass 222, 227; metal 227; *see also* pottery
Viking/s 1, 107, 147, 147n44, 174n11, 194n51, 218
violence, death by 45n34, 135, 138, 144–5, 147, 149–51, 155n71, 167, 169–70, 194–5, 210, 221, 243–4; *see also* injury/injuries *and* trauma
Vortigern (father or Vortimer) 168
Vortimer (son of Vortigern) 168
votive deposit 63, 208; *see also* grave goods

wake/waking the dead *see* laying out/laid out
Wales/Welsh 49–50, 61, 61n5, 75, 79, 103n2, 122, 159, 174, 178, 181
Walton family 136
War Cemetery, Maiden Castle, Dorset, England 40
warrior/s 74, 103, 106, 125, 145, 167–9, 192; *see also* dant mir (the hero's or warrior's portion)
Waterford, Co. Waterford 8
wattle 30, 94; *see also* daub
wedge tomb/s 34n1, 129; *see also* prehistory/prehistoric
Westreave, Co. Dublin 92, 111–12, 228, 233, Fig. 4.15, Maps 4–5
Wetwang, Yorkshire 26–7, Plate 3; Cart Burial No. 2 26–7; cylindrical box Plate 3
White Hill, London, England 168
white stones *see* quartz
Whithorn, Scotland 61
Wicklow (county) 213n46
wife/wives 117, 173, 183–5, 195; *see also* husband/s; marriage; spouse/s
Wihtfrith 173
winding sheet 54–5, 57, 59, 72, 94, 110, 187; *see also* linen *and* shroud/shroud wrapped
Windmill Hill, Wiltshire, England 113
wine 96, 123, 127, 201, 208–9, 225; *see also* pottery *and* oil
wood-lined grave/s *see* grave/s

Yorkshire, England 27, 39, 70, 172, 174, 183
Youghal, Co. Cork 4n4
Youngs, Susan 31n86